P9-BJG-339

55. IF HITLER ASKED YOU TO ELECTROCUTE A STRANGER, WOULD YOU?
AE p. 280

Under what conditions do people hurt other people? One hypothesis centers around obedience: people are willing to hurt others when ordered to do so by a credible authority. Perhaps such obedience explains the behavior of many officials of Hitler's Germany and American troops "under orders" at My Lai in Vietnam. The research conducted by social psychologist Stanley Milgram and reported in the article lends support to the obedience hypothesis.

Learning Objectives
After reading the article, you should be able to:
1. Define: the Shirer thesis; autonomy.
2. Contrast the moral and situation ethicist.
3. Describe Milgram's experimental technique.
4. Compare the Yale and the Bridgeport experimental settings.
5. Contrast the state of agency and the state of autonomy.

Essay Questions
1. According to Milgram, certain conditions encourage obedience to authority and others disobedience. What are examples of each? How does the average school classroom fit into this analysis?
2. When do you operate in a state of autonomy and when in a state of agency? Do particular people or situations cause you to shift modes?

56. PATHOLOGY OF IMPRISONMENT
AE p. 287

Are prisoners less than human? Do our prisons serve as breeding grounds of crime? What happens within prison walls that might cause a malfunction of our rehabilitation system? In this article, Stanford University psychologist Philip Zimbardo reports on his recent prison experiment. Using mature, emotionally stable college students as both prisoners and guards in a mock prison, Zimbardo obtained frightening results.

Learning Objectives
After reading the article, you should be able to:
1. Define: parole, contingency, self-image, recidivism.
2. Compare the behavior of Zimbardo's "prisoners" and "guards."
3. State three reasons why we underestimate the power of situational controls over behavior.
4. List four recommendations for prison reform.
5. State the recidivism rate.

Essay Questions
1. Based on the findings in his abbreviated study, Zimbardo suggests several possible penal system changes. What are some of them? How adequate do you feel they are in dealing with the implications of the study reported on?
2. Zimbardo discusses changes in the present penal system. Describe the type of penal system you would prefer in place of the present one. Justify your recommendations.

57. HOW GROUPS INTENSIFY OPINIONS
AE p. 290

Several studies show that we obtain social recognition and emotional support in primary associations with others who share our basic values and interests. Much small group interaction consistently polarizes the individual's attitudes. The author proposes that discussion and social comparison processes are the primary mechanisms of group polarization. In the absence of these mechanisms, the group is less likely to polarize the attitudes of the individual.

Learning Objectives
After reading the article, you should be able to:
1. Compare the impact of the mass media and informal groups on public opinion.
2. Explain why increasing numbers of problems are dealt with in small groups.
3. Describe how small group interaction polarizes the initial opinions of the individual participants.
4. Explain how religious fellowship is an example of group polarization.
5. Describe the two principal mechanisms that underlie group polarization.

Essay Questions
1. Why are increasing numbers of Americans trying to solve their problems through participation in small groups?
2. How do discussion and social comparison facilitate the process of group attitude polarization?

58. THE SOCIAL DISEASE CALLED SHYNESS
AE p. 294

Stanford University psychologist-researcher Philip Zimbardo and students Robert Norwood and Paul Pilkonis describe the pathology of withdrawal and loneliness. They suggest that therapy for shyness rests on an understanding of the cultural values creating these personal prisons.

Learning Objectives
After reading the article, you should be able to:
1. List four painful consequences of shyness and state the implications that they suggest for modern psychology.
2. Cite three characteristics of the typically shy individual.
3. State the crucial difference between the shy personality and the non-shy personality.
4. Describe three types of shyness and identify the personality traits that accompany each type.
5. Describe the impact of social factors on shyness in individuals from different cultural backgrounds.

Essay Questions
1. Describe your own experiences with shyness and relate them to cultural demands placed upon you in terms of competition, individual success and personal responsibility for failure.
2. Discuss changes in modern society that you feel might reduce shyness and nurture self-confidence in individuals.
3. Discuss how you, as a therapist, would help an individual overcome shyness.

59. THE AMERICAN WAY OF MATING
AE p. 297

Angus Campbell, winner of the American Psychological Association's Distinguished Science Contribution Award, reports the results of a recent national survey which indicates some special joys and special strains in marriage and child-rearing.

Learning Objectives
After reading the article, you should be able to:
1. List three categories of life-styles which contain people who diverge from the typical patterns.
2. Compare and contrast the relative effects of marriage on the happiness of young women and young men.
3. State three ways in which the arrival of a child places a strain upon a marriage.

Essay Questions
1. Discuss the changes in reported happiness and stress that occur from the time that a young couple first marries until the time that their youngest child marries. If possible, relate your discussion to your own family.
2. Compare and contrast the health, happiness and stresses experienced by unmarried men and women with those experienced by married couples.
3. Discuss some ways in which married couples might reduce the impact of stress produced by having children. How can the couple help each other? Can the children themselves help reduce the stress that the parents feel?

Learning Objectives

After reading the article, you should be able to:
1. Describe the methods and results of the Rosenhan study.
2. Describe several popular interpretations of the Rosenhan findings.
3. Distinguish between the legal and psychiatric definitions of sanity and insanity.
4. State the warranted and unwarranted conclusions drawn from Rosenhan's findings.
5. Evaluate the costs and benefits of the traditional categories of psychiatric diagnosis.

Essay Questions

1. Discuss the advantages and disadvantages of eliminating the traditional categories of psychiatric diagnosis.
2. How might Rosenhan reply to this reading?

49. MEDICAL TREATMENT OF MENTAL ILLNESS   AE p. 247

The advent of certain psychoactive drugs has enabled many patients to leave institutions and to lead more nearly normal lives than would otherwise have been the case. Yet these drugs are not a panacea. Their side effects can be irreversible, they don't benefit all patients, but they do relieve human suffering in many cases. The search for even more effective medications continues.

Learning Objectives

After reading the article, you should be able to:
1. Describe the predrug era.
2. Discuss the pros and cons of psychotherapeutic drugs.
3. State the specific drugs for schizophrenia, mania, and depression.

Essay Questions

1. Should physicians give drugs to patients who do not understand the nature or the treatment of their disease? Why or why not?
2. How has the advent of psychotherapeutic drugs affected the search for the cause of mental illnesses?

50. THE SECOND DEATH OF SIGMUND FREUD   AE p. 256

A straightforwardly antiFreudian article dissects the theory and practice of psychoanalysis, calling it unscientific and unworkable. Instead, the author sees greater promise of better results from current research findings in biochemistry.

Learning Objectives

After reading the article, you should be able to:
1. Describe the biochemical explanations for certain brain activities.
2. State the author's arguments against psychoanalysis.
3. State why the author compares psychoanalysis to a religion and a conspiracy.

Essay Questions

1. Is the author's dissection of psychoanalysis convincing? Why or why not?
2. Discuss our current state of knowledge of neurotransmitters.

51. NEW LIGHT ON SCHIZOPHRENIA   AE p. 260

For the first time, some medical researchers are optimistic about discovering the cause and reliable means of detection of schizophrenia. Painstaking research has shed new light on the nature-nurture controversy and its relationship to this crippling mental disorder that affects one in every hundred Canadians.

Learning Objectives

After reading the article, you should be able to:
1. Describe the genetic theories of schizophrenia.
2. Describe the environmental theories of schizophrenia.
3. Define endorphin, enkephalin, dopamine, schizophrenia.

Essay Questions

1. What are the relative contributions of genes and environment to schizophrenia?
2. What factors lead scientists to conclude that schizophrenia may have a biochemical origin?

52. A DARKNESS AT NOON   AE p. 264

Many people will at one time or another experience debilitating depression, and many will seek medical treatment for it. The article discusses origins, types, and treatments for this widespread disorder.

Learning Objectives

After reading the article, you should be able to:
1. Describe the various types of depression.
2. State the incidence of depression.
3. State the treatments for depression.

Essay Questions

1. Do you agree or disagree with the idea that depression is a product of a rootless and industrial age?
2. What are the benefits of the various types of treatment for depression, and what are the drawbacks?

53. THE AGE OF MELANCHOLY   AE p. 268

The nation's chief mental health officer reviews the evidence that depression is replacing anxiety as our country's most serious psychiatric problem. Depression is most frequently caused by the disruption of attachment bonds. The loss of emotional intimacy through death, divorce, and involuntary separation occurs ever more frequently in the United States and traditional structures of long-term attachment such as the church, family, and neighborhood have lost their bonding functions. However, the author states that depression may also be related to genetic factors, early life experiences, lowered self-esteem, and the individual's lack of adequate social skills.

Learning Objectives

After reading the article, you should be able to:
1. Explain why depression is replacing anxiety as America's most serious psychiatric problem.
2. Describe established sex differences in frequencies of depression.
3. Identify the community structures that protect the individual from depression.
4. Describe the extent of the individual's recovery from widowhood and bereavement.
5. Describe nonattachment factors that also contribute to depression.

Essay Questions

1. Why is depression replacing anxiety as the nation's principal psychiatric problem?
2. What are the principal causes of depression? Describe the extent to which individuals recover from disrupted attachment bonds.

54. SHOPPING FOR THE RIGHT THERAPY   AE p. 273

As modern society becomes more demanding, complex, and turbulent, the concepts of psychology must change with it. Although psychotherapy encompasses only four major schools of thought, more than 130 subschools have emerged. Thus, the consumer of psychological products, in the form of therapies and theories, is faced with an awesome challenge in seeking the services which best meet his/her needs. In this article, Morris B. Parloff, clinical psychologist and chief of the Psychotherapy and Behavioral Intervention Section, Clinical Research Branch, of the National Institute of Mental Health, attempts to guide the prospective consumer through a confusing maze of therapeutic possibilities.

Learning Objectives

After reading the article, you should be able to:
1. Define: transactional analysis, family therapy, radical therapy, and primal therapy.
2. Name the four major schools of therapy and give a brief description of each.
3. Identify and describe the three major forms of transpersonal therapy.
4. Describe the three major factors that make the problem of choosing a therapist complex.

Essay Questions

1. Explain how the role of the psychotherapist has changed during the last decade and describe the impact that these changes have for the average psychological consumer.
2. Discuss the most consistent trends in therapy that Morris B. Parloff observed in his review of psychotherapeutic techniques. Give special attention to the discussion of effectiveness, patient improvement, and the applications of behavior therapies.

43. SEXUALITY AND THE LIFE CYCLE: A BROAD CONCEPT OF SEXUALITY
AE p. 204

Lester Kirkendall and Isadore Rubin, prolific contributors to professional literature concerning sexual behavior, discuss the nature and role of sexuality throughout the life cycle. They suggest that the time has come to reassess the place of sex in the individual's life cycle and in society as a whole.

Learning Objectives
After reading the article, you should be able to:
1. List five criteria for classifying an individual as male or female.
2. State three theories of the definition of masculinity and femininity in individuals.
3. Describe the three primary conditions which are necessary to normal heterosexual development.
4. Identify three important ways in which the development of the gender role is aided.
5. List the three crucial factors used to explain the difference between male and female attitudes toward sexual expression.
6. State at least two patterns of role behavior that are a common source of confusion and conflict in women, and explain whether the patterns you listed are of biological or cultural origin.

Essay Questions
1. Discuss the various Freudian stages involved in the development of sexuality, particularly with respect to your sexual development.
2. Compare and contrast the roles of biological factors and environmental or cultural factors in the development of sexuality in humans. Which factors do you feel are the most important?
3. Discuss the role of the parents in the development of a child's sexual identity. What types of parental actions can lead to abnormal development of the child?

44. WHAT WE KNOW AND DON'T KNOW ABOUT SEX DIFFERENCES
AE p. 211

The ideas that people have about differences between the sexes are often so strongly held that reliable, unbiased observations are difficult to obtain. Researchers Maccoby and Jacklin survey the psychological literature on sex differences and come to the conclusion that there may be some truth to a few myths, but many of the myths are clearly wrong or are based upon insufficient and contradictory evidence.

Learning Objectives
After reading the article, you should be able to:
1. Describe the extent to which boys differ from girls on measures of sociability.
2. Explain the difference between auditory behavior and verbal behavior.
3. State the ages at which males and females show the greatest differences in aggressiveness, verbal abilities, spatial abilities, and mathematical abilities.
4. Explain why many of the questions about sex differences are unresolved.

Essay Questions
1. Why do you think that some sex differences are so easy to demonstrate and others so difficult? Do you think an inability to demonstrate sex differences actually reflects a lack of sex differences or does it reflect an inability to perform worthy experiments?
2. What does the demonstration of sex differences say about the causes of these sex differences? Is it possible to decide from the information given in the article if these differences might have a biological basis?

45. MENTAL PATTERNS OF DISEASE
AE p. 216

Medical researchers now point to links between certain personality types and the propensity to certain physical diseases or impairments. Heart attack, cancer, arthritis, asthma, and ulcers are all correlated with certain constellations of personality traits. Yet this approach is not without its critics.

Learning Objectives
After reading the article, you should be able to:
1. Define Type A and Type B personalities.
2. Relate the occurrence of diseases to certain personality types.
3. Explain the mechanism by which psychosomatic illnesses may occur.

Essay Questions
1. Do you believe or disbelieve that there is a connection between personality and disease? Why or why not?
2. If there exists a link between personality and disease, list at least six things that medical personnel should do to alleviate such a problem.

46. CANCER AND THE MIND: HOW ARE THEY CONNECTED?
AE p. 220

Various research studies have indicated a connection between certain personality profiles and the incidence of cancer. More recently, new information about the immune system suggests that there may be a correlation between specific emotions and certain biochemical events.

Learning Objectives
After reading the article, you should be able to:
1. State various studies about the effects of emotion on cancer.
2. Generalize about the psychological precursors of cancer.
3. State the personality traits associated with cancer-proneness.

Essay Questions
1. What factors are contributing to the interest in relating cancer and psychological factors?
2. Explain how psychological treatment might best help known cancer patients and their families.

47. ON BEING SANE IN INSANE PLACES
AE p. 226

Psychologists still debate the origins of mental illness: is it genetic, environmental, or both? Recently a few professionals including Thomas Szasz and R.D. Laing have suggested that mental illness is a myth. Szasz contends that there is a condition that we *label* "mental illness," but he claims it is not truly an illness, merely a deviation from socially-acceptable norms of behavior. This article, for the journal *Science*, reports on a California psychologist's study of psychiatric labeling that attracted national attention.

Learning Objectives
After reading the letters, you should be able to:
1. Define: pseudopatient; remission; pathology.
2. State the legal definition of insanity.
3. Compare type 1 and type 2 errors.
4. State five hospital practices that induce feelings of powerlessness in patients.
5. State five behaviors that induce feelings of depersonalization.
6. Describe Rosenhan's experimental method.

Essay Questions
1. What problems does Rosenhan see in the present mental health system?
2. What consequences would you foresee if the practice of psychiatric labeling were abolished? Would you be in favor of such action, and why?

48. MORE ON PSEUDOSCIENCE IN SCIENCE AND THE CASE FOR PSYCHIATRIC DIAGNOSIS
AE p. 235

In a devastating critique of Rosenhan's study of sanity in insane places, a distinguished psychiatrist contends that Rosenhan's findings are pointless and irrelevant to the real problems concerning the reliability and validity of psychiatric diagnosis. The author further claims that persistent misinterpretations of Rosenhan's findings imply unjustifiable criticisms of present psychiatric methods and that diagnostic categories play an indispensable role in the treatment of the mentally ill. Rosenhan's more recent proposal for the abolition of psychiatric categories is dismissed as unrealistic. The author argues that diagnosis is a legitimate clinical procedure regardless of the existence of effective treatment.

Learning Objectives

After reading the article, you should be able to:
1. Describe the results of previous research studies on the relationship between child-rearing variables and adult-outcome variables.
2. Describe the three measures of maturity used in the present investigation.
3. Identify the two principal child-rearing determinants of maturity uncovered in the present investigation.
4. Describe the relationship between measures of maturity and measures of moral behavior.
5. Describe the paradox of maturity.

Essay Questions
1. Why is it difficult to find significant relationships between specific child-rearing variables and specific adult-outcome variables?
2. What are the implications of the paradox of maturity for changing several widely used child-rearing practices?

38. MUST EVERYTHING BE A MIDLIFE CRISIS?   AE p. 150

A professor of human development critically evaluates stage theories of adult crisis. She finds that stage theories of adult development are oversimplified and that many normal status transitions of adulthood are not attended by emotional crises. Stage theories are also criticized for ignoring memory and individual differences. The author calls for greater recognition of human diversity at all age levels.

Learning Objectives

After reading the article, you should be able to:
1. Describe the basic premises of several popular stage theories of adult development.
2. State the most frequent criticisms of stage theories of adult development.
3. Explain why the idea of biological and social timeclocks invalidates stage theories of adult development.
4. Explain why only some adult status transitions are attended by emotional crises.
5. Explain why stage theories are inadequate to deal with individual differences within various age groups.

Essay Questions
1. Why have stage theories of adult development become so popular in the last decade?
2. How does a theory of adult status transition provide an alternative to stage theories of adult development?

39. "OLD" IS NOT A FOUR-LETTER WORD   AE p. 182

Advanced industrial societies have growing populations of older people who are consistently victimized by negative social stereotypes. The natural processes of aging are still poorly understood. The intellectual powers of the aged decline very unevenly, and the negative attitudes of younger people contribute decisively to the disengagement of the elderly from social and occupational activities. The aged are still subject to many myths about declining powers. The author describes the physical and health characteristics of the elderly and calls for reduced calorie intake and increased exercise as the most reliable methods for extending the longevity of all Americans.

Learning Objectives

After reading the article, you should be able to:
1. Describe the rapidly increasing numbers of the aged in the United States population.
2. Describe several negative social stereotypes about the aged.
3. Describe several basic health statistics about the aged.
4. Evaluate several of the myths surrounding the declining powers of the aged.
5. Describe several changes that may prolong the lifespans of more Americans.

Essay Questions
1. What are several recent social changes that have resulted from the political activity of the aged?
2. What can each individual do to increase his or her longevity?

40. SOME OF US MAY NEVER DIE   AE p. 188

As medical science progresses, or so the argument goes, it will be able to cure the ills that people now die from. Thus some believers are having themselves preserved cryonically until that time arrives. The article also reviews the various theories about what causes death and longevity and the consequences of extending the life span.

Learning Objectives

After reading the article, you should be able to:
1. Define: cryonic preservation, DECO, cloning, tachyon, free radical.
2. State various approaches to longevity.
3. State various theories of the causes of death and aging.
4. Describe the theory of a death clock.

Essay Questions
1. Explain what the author means when she states that "Data now are beginning to indicate that life-extension is inevitable."
2. Discuss some of the prevalent theories of aging.

41. ATTITUDES, INTERESTS, AND IQ   AE p. 194

Two educational psychologists review the evidence for the environmental and hereditary determination of intelligence and conclude that both are important. Their finding was confirmed in the authors' study of intelligence among adopted children. There is evidence that the verbal components of intelligence are the most heavily determined by environmental factors and additional research suggests that social attitudes and vocational interests are influenced by genetic factors. The article describes the political and social implications of recent controversies on the relative impact of heredity and environment on human behavior.

Learning Objectives

After reading the article, you should be able to:
1. Describe the extent to which the different components of intelligence are influenced by heredity and environment.
2. Explain how authoritarian attitudes and vocational interests are partly determined by genetics.
3. Describe the relationship between verbal intelligence and authoritarianism.
4. Describe the effects of genetic variability within reasonably good environments.
5. Describe the relationship between hereditarianism versus environmentalism and conservative versus liberal social policies.

Essay Questions
1. Why has environmentalism dominated the Western philosophy of child-rearing and social policy for many years?
2. On the basis of your reading, what are the specific individual differences most and least likely to be affected by environmental variables?

42. NEW LIGHT ON IQ   AE p. 201

Investigations into the correlations between ethnic groups and immigrants to this country reveal that IQ tends to rise—or not to rise—along with socioeconomic status. Many of the claims by Arthur Jensen on the peculiarities of IQ testing among blacks take on very different meaning when viewed in an historical context.

Learning Objectives

After reading the article, you should be able to:
1. Identify Arthur Jensen and some of his claims about blacks' IQs.
2. Refute many of Jensen's claims.
3. Trace the historical movement of IQ among population groups.
4. Identify the uses of intelligence tests.

Essay Questions
1. Why would the IQ scores of immigrant groups rise over time? Give several reasons to support your answer.
2. Discuss the claims of Arthur Jensen. Do you agree or disagree with the assessment of Jensen as a racist? Why?

32. RECONSIDERATION: JEAN PIAGET AE p. 142

Robert Coles, the sociologist, places Jean Piaget within the context of a long line of western thinkers from the 19th century to the present. In describing the contrasting traditions of western intellectual life, he tells us what Piaget is and what he is not. And in comparing him with Freud, William James, Kant, and others, he places Piaget within the highest intellectual company.

Learning Objectives
After reading the article, you should be able to:
1. Distinguish the historical patterns that Coles perceives.
2. Explain where Piaget belongs in the line of western psychological thinkers.
3. Explain the fundamentals of Piagetian thought.

Essay Questions
1. What are the two major lines of intellectual development that Coles traces and how do they differ?
2. Describe the Piagetian concepts of assimilation and accommodation.

33. ERIK ERIKSON'S EIGHT AGES OF MAN AE p. 145

Perhaps the most famous description of the major changes that occur in an individual during development is Freud's theory of psychosexual development (oral, anal, phallic, latency and genital stages). Erik Erikson, a modern proponent of Freudian theory, has added to and modified this theory. He expanded Freud's stages to the eight discussed in this article by psychologist David Elkind. Perhaps the most widely accepted of Erikson's stages is his description of the "identity crisis" which typically occurs during adolescence. Unlike many others, Erikson has not denied the basic Freudian framework but does emphasize social factors and the environment.

Learning Objectives
After reading the article, you should be able to:
1. Define: identity crisis, autonomy, industry, generativity, self-absorption, integrity.
2. Cite Erikson's three major contributions to Freudian theory.
3. State Douvan and Adelson's criticism of Erikson's identity theory.
4. List Erikson's eight stages in order and state the approximate age at which each begins.

Essay Questions
1. Compare and contrast the stages of development identified by Freud and Erikson.
2. Which of Erikson's stages do you believe you have gone through? Where do you believe you are now? Do you feel you have successfully resolved the conflicts of any of these stages?

34. TELEVISION AND THE YOUNG VIEWER AE p. 153

Following a review of "Sesame Street" as an example of beneficial children's programming, Professor Rubinstein presents evidence that televised violence facilitates aggressive behavior in some children. While children are also influenced by television advertising, very little is presently known about the specific effects of advertising for different products directed at different age groups. Children's learning of sex-role stereotypes is associated with heavy television viewing, but there is no evidence that children are directly influenced by depictions or verbal references to sexual behavior. The author concludes that present television studies do not provide adequate evidence for the development of policy and calls for the funding of more comprehensive and long-term research on the effects of television viewing.

Learning Objectives
After reading the article, you should be able to:
1. Describe the conditions that lead to beneficial television programming for children.
2. Compare the three basic hypotheses that link televised violence to individual behavior.
3. Describe the effects of television advertising on younger children.
4. Explain why the sexual content of television programming has increased as violence has decreased.
5. Describe the types of television research that will be most useful for the development of social policy.

Essay Questions
1. Why has there been more research on the effects of television violence than on the effects of television sex?
2. What kinds of television research studies are necessary for the development of social policy?

35. MORAL THINKING: CAN IT BE TAUGHT? AE p. 162

The Just Community is a cluster of 35 teenagers who are pursuing moral education through group action. According to Lawrence Kohlberg's theory, moral development progresses through six stages, but his theory and its supporting research have frequently been criticized as unreliable, invalid, elitist, sexist, and ideological. Field applications of Kohlberg's techniques among prisoners have met with mixed results, but the Cluster School seems to successfully advance adolescents one or two stages during their high school years. The article contends that the maintenance of democratic idealism depends on special combinations of people and resources and that United States society is presently shifting towards a new privatism as its dominant social ethic.

Learning Objectives
After reading the article, you should be able to:
1. Describe the demographic composition of Kohlberg's Just Community.
2. Describe each of the six stages of Kohlberg's theory of moral development.
3. Discuss the principal criticisms of the research stimulated by Kohlberg's theory.
4. Describe the application of Kohlberg's techniques in prisons and cluster schools.
5. Describe the relationship of the Just Community to other experiments in democratic idealism.

Essay Questions
1. Describe several of the reasons for the revival of interest in moral education.
2. Describe the problems that resulted when the Just Community experiment was tried in several state prisons.

36. THE FATHER OF THE CHILD AE p. 171

Recent findings suggest that fathers are becoming more involved in the care of their infants and many fathers now seem capable of assuming the primary care-giver role. Father-infant interaction is more physical and stimulating than mother-infant interaction, but both parents show increased involvement with infants of their own sex. Closely related findings show that different kinds of paternal and maternal care contribute to the infant's cognitive development. The author cites successful intervention techniques that increase paternal involvement. He urges increased social opportunities for fathers to become co-primary care-givers to their young children.

Learning Objectives
After reading the article, you should be able to:
1. Describe the specific aspects of newborn care fathers are most and least likely to be involved in.
2. Compare the basic characteristics of father-infant and mother-infant play.
3. Compare the behavior of fathers as secondary and primary care-givers.
4. Describe the characteristics of each parent's increased involvement with infants of the same sex.
5. Compare the specific contributions of fathers and mothers to the development of the infant's cognitive skills.

Essay Questions
1. Why are fathers more actively involved in some aspects of infant care than in others?
2. What are the determinants of stronger father-infant attachments?

37. MAKING IT TO MATURITY AE p. 174

Since the research literature shows that differences in child-rearing practices do not generally lead to predictable differences in adult personality, the authors report a massive study of the relationship between 35 child-rearing variables and 37 adult-outcome variables. The extent of maternal affection and overall parental permissiveness appear to be the two principal determinants of adult maturity, and there is some evidence that parental demands for moral conformity inhibit the child's growth to adulthood. The chief paradox of the findings is that the successful promotion of maturity leads first to a decrease in moral behavior, and it is proposed that the most effective parents have faith in their children in addition to using easygoing and loving child-rearing practices.

13. BRAIN DAMAGE: A WINDOW ON THE MIND   AE p. 61

Howard Gardner, researcher in brain damage and symbol-using behavior, describes a number of brain malfunctions in mental activity and explains what they tell us about normal mental functioning. He also suggests therapies for brain damage and learning disabilities. This article received honorable mention for magazine writing from the American Psychological Foundation.

Learning Objectives
After reading the article, you should be able to:
1. Define: aphasia, alexia, agraphia.
2. Describe the symptoms of Korsakoff's disease.
3. State two opposing views concerning the relationship between language and thought.
4. Describe some therapies for adults with brain damage and for children with learning disabilities.

Essay Questions
1. Do any of the disorders described here conflict with your personal experience with the relationships among mental activities?
2. In what ways have the therapies discussed in this article resulted from the research information?
3. How might the research information discussed in this article affect our educational systems?

14. HOPE FOR DAMAGED BRAINS   AE p. 65

Patrick Young, science writer for the *National Observer*, describes current animal research that may shed new light on the problem of treating brain-damaged humans. A related article of interest is "Brain Damage: A Window on the Mind" (AE p. 61).

Learning Objectives
After reading the article, you should be able to:
1. Describe the effects that an enriched environment produces in brain damaged rats.
2. List changes in the brain that occur during the learning process.

Essay Questions
1. Describe the procedures that have been used by investigators in an effort to explore the effects of the environment on the brain. What major conclusions have been drawn from this evidence?
2. How did changes in genetic chemicals affect the problem-solving ability of brain-damaged rats? As a result of their studies, Bennet and Rosenzweig say their findings raise what three questions that neurologists should consider in treating the human victims of brain damage?

15. OBSERVING THE BRAIN THROUGH   AE p. 67
A CAT'S EYES

Are we all born with the same predetermined ability to see? Does our environment have anything at all to do with this ability? In this article, Dr. Roger Lewin reviews current research on the neurological system of cats. The research suggests that although we may be born with the same visual apparatus, the ability to "see straight" does not develop automatically, but is strongly shaped by our early experiences.

Learning Objectives
After reading the article, you should be able to:
1. Define: orientation-selective; binocular cells; "sensitive period," plasticity.
2. Compare the two types of "feature detectors."
3. Contrast the physical differences between vertical and horizontal cats.
4. State the survival value of a cat's visual-sensitive period.
5. State what may produce an infant's intense curiosity.

Essay Questions
1. Experiments with cats' vision imply the importance of both environmental and genetic information to complete development. Describe the contributions of each and their interactions.
2. "Probably the most important skill that children learn is how to learn." List a dozen skills which you believe necessary for a child's development with specific proposals for *how* and *when* (in the child's life) you would implement them.

16. WOBBLY BIORHYTHMS   AE p. 70

Despite world wide interest in the charting of the individual's physical, emotional, and intellectual biorythms, there is suprisingly little scientific evidence that a person's good days and critical days can be known in advance. Only modest evidence has linked biorythms to academic performance and industrial accidents, and the author reports a detailed study of biorythms and psychiatric counseling that shows additional negative findings. Finally, a second experiment has shown that students respond to false biorythmic information as if it were true information. Thus biorythms appear to work largely through the power of suggestion.

Learning Objectives
After reading the article, you should be able to:
1. Describe the history of research on physical, emotional, and intellectual biorythms.
2. Evaluate the principal methodological problems that occur in much biorythm research.
3. Describe the generally positive findings that occasionally emerge from biorythm research.
4. Describe the effect of providing individuals with false biorythm information.
5. Describe the role of suggestion in accounting for the results of biorythm research.

Essay Questions
1. Why does popular interest in charting biorythms continue in the light of negative scientific evidence?
2. How does evidence that biorythms work through the power of suggestion affect the idea of good days and critical days?

17. THE HUMAN BODY AS A BIOLOGICAL CLOCK   AE p. 73

Although most units of time are defined culturally, many have their basis in nature. This article describes the natural rhythms we are subject to, including those with periodicities from the 90-minute sleep cycle to the annual rhythms of birth patterns. Not only are humans subject to these natural rhythms, but other animals are, too.

Learning Objectives
After reading the article, you should be able to:
1. Define *Zeitgeiber*, periodicity, circadian rhythm, ultradian, infradian.
2. Describe the various periodicities mentioned in the article.
3. Contrast the exogenous and endogenous views of biologic clocks.

Essay Questions
1. Describe the contrasting viewpoints on the biological clock as represented by the exogenous and endogenous schools. Which do you agree with, and why?
2. What are the implications for medicine in understanding the biological clock?

18. A SCIENTIFIC BASIS FOR ACUPUNCTURE?   AE p. 75

Two Cambridge investigators examined the marriage of traditional Chinese and modern Western medical knowledge with respect to acupuncture. The anesthetic benefits of acupuncture have now been established beyond question, and the authors believe that its scientific rationale involves increasing the individual's resistance to disease by stimulating the nervous system to produce beneficial antibodies. The scientific effects of acupuncture are viewed primarily in immunological terms, and it is suggested that restorations of the body's nervous and hormonal balances are the principal health-giving mechanisms of this ancient medical procedure.

Learning Objectives
After reading the article, you should be able to:
1. Compare the basic characteristics of traditional Chinese and modern Western medical knowledge.
2. Describe the use of acupuncture as a surgical anesthetic.
3. Evaluate the claim that acupuncture is a form of mass hypnosis.
4. Describe how acupuncture stimulates the immunological defenses of the body.
5. Identify the specific diseases for which Western physicians are most likely to recommend acupuncture.

Essay Questions
1. How does medical practice in contemporary China indicate a marriage of traditional and modern medical knowledge?
2. Explain how acupuncture is believed to increase the body's resistance to disease.

7. PSYCHOBABBLE

AE p. 29

Emerging from the political activism of the 1960s and the language of the human potential movement, psychobabble is the dialect of psychological pseudoinsight, inappropriate candor, and self-involvement that everybody, it seems, is talking these days. The glibness with which people discuss psychological mechanisms and turn them into cocktail party chatter is, says the author, demeaning and dehumanizing.

Learning Objectives

After reading the article, you should be able to:
1. Define psychobabble.
2. Describe the cultural factors that contribute to psychobabble.
3. Explain the historical roots of psychobabble.
4. List some of the terms used by psychobabblers.

Essay Questions
1. Describe why you agree or disagree with the author's condemnation of "Psychobabble."
2. List several steps we might take as a culture to get rid of "Psychobabble."

8. GENETIC ENGINEERS: NOW THAT THEY'VE GONE TOO FAR, CAN THEY STOP?

AE p. 36

As our knowledge of biological processes increases, we may find that we are unprepared to handle the knowledge intelligently. If our knowledge of genetics continues at its present rapid rate, we may soon find that we can predict most of the characteristics of a person before she/he is born and perhaps even control those characteristics.

Learning Objectives

After reading the article, you should be able to:
1. Define: DNA; RNA; *in vitro* fertilization; amniocentesis; PKU; sickle cell disease; gene transfer; legal theory of "wronged life."
2. State the major concerns about creating life outside of the womb.
3. List the kinds of defects which can be detected by use of amniocentesis.
4. Discuss how the knowledge of a person's genetic makeup could be harmful.
5. Explain what people mean when they refer to the danger of a "Doomsday Bug."

Essay Questions
1. What kinds of guidelines could you draw up which would allow genetic research to go on but which would minimize the chances of creating some of the dangers that are mentioned in the article?
2. What are some of the reasons that many people object to amniocentesis? Are there some instances in which the use of amniocentesis is more acceptable than in other instances?

9. SPECIAL ABILITIES OF THE SEXES: DO THEY BEGIN IN THE BRAIN?

AE p. 43

While established sex differences in aggression and verbal, spatial, and mathematical skills have traditionally been attributed to learning, recent evidence from neurological research suggests that many of these differences result from the increased lateralization of men's brains. Closely related findings indicate greater hemispheric specialization and increased electrical potentials in women's brains. Overall, these neurological and biochemical characteristics may account for sex differences in such abilities as daylight versus night vision, visual and auditory acuity, distractability, coordination, and tolerance of extreme temperatures and noises. On the basis of this evidence, several authorities recommend the development of separate teaching techniques for elementary school boys and girls.

Learning Objectives

After reading the article, you should be able to:
1. Describe Maccoby and Jacklin's findings on sex differences in behavior.
2. Compare the differences in brain lateralization between adult men and women.
3. Compare sex differences in the hemispheric arousals of men and women.
4. Compare the electrical potentials of men's and women's brains.
5. Describe McGuiness and Pribram's comparisons of the abilities of adult men and women.

Essay Questions
1. Explain why increased brain lateralization seems to be correlated with greater abilities for some skills and lower abilities for others.
2. Describe the results of Caplan's research on sex differences in children's play.

10. THE ORIGINS OF VIOLENCE

AE p. 50

Cross-cultural studies show that societies which provide infants with large amounts of physical affection and bodily contact also produce comparatively nonviolent adults. Research on monkeys and human infants confirms that movement and physical contact are required for normal development, and the author speculates that specific parts of the cerebellum comprise a pleasure system which is activated by physical affection. Child abusers and other violent people may suffer from deficient pleasure systems. Recently developed techniques of artificial cerebellar stimulation now raise the possibility of producing less violent adults and societies.

Learning Objectives

After reading the article, you should be able to:
1. Describe basic cross-cultural findings on the origins of violent societies.
2. Describe the implications of animal research for understanding individual differences in violence among human adults.
3. Explain why the cerebellum provides an explanatory model for the effects of social isolation.
4. Describe the results of Heath's research on electrical stimulation of the limbic system and cerebellum.
5. Describe the characteristics of adults with inadequately developed pleasure systems.

Essay Questions
1. To what extent is the Harlows' research on the social isolation of monkeys useful for understanding the development of normal humans?
2. Describe Prescott's techniques for providing artificial cerebellar stimulation.

11. THE SPLIT BRAIN LAB

AE p. 53

Laboratory research into the location of the "psyche" has uncovered the fact that the brain has two halves, each of which dominates a different kind of consciousness. The right half works intuitively, and the left operates rationally. Radical surgery in which the two hemispheres of the brain were disconnected has shown that two completely independent visual worlds exist within the same head, cut off from each other. Researchers have demonstrated the unsuspected connection between brain hemisphere and functions such as speech and vision, emotions and dreams.

Learning Objectives

After reading the article, you should be able to:
1. Define the functions of each brain hemisphere.
2. Discuss some results of Roger Sperry's research on split brains.
3. Discuss some far-reaching implications of Sperry's research.

Essay Questions
1. Discuss the ramifications of split brain results that may tip the scale in the heredity-environment debate.
2. Discuss the implications of Sperry's findings for the fields of psychology, medicine, and behavior.

12. SUPERBRAIN

AE p. 57

Scientific workers from a number of disciplines are engaging in peptide research to learn about how these substances stimulate brain cells to overcome deficiencies and to enhance already present qualities. The promise of this kind of research is enormous, extending from memory and learning functions to pain control and alleviation of mental illness.

Learning Objectives

After reading the article, you should be able to:
1. Describe the current areas of peptide research.
2. Identify peptide, TRH, LRH, scotophobin, ameletin, endorphin, enkephalin.

Essay Questions
1. How does the research described in this article promise to shed light on the process of acupuncture?
2. Detail the many areas in which peptide research promises to show positive results.

1. PSYCHOLOGY: THERE ARE OTHER THERAPISTS AT WORK   AE p. 4

Psychology is the largest of the social and behavioral sciences. Roughly one third of psychologists are clinical psychologists, or psychotherapists, and the next largest group are the social psychologists. There are more than 3,000 basic researchers, and most psychologists believe that behavior can be measured. Another large group studies human development. Among the important thinkers in the field, reports this article, are Jean Piaget on cognitive development, Lawrence Kohlberg on moral development, Jerome Kagan on nature-nuture issues, Arthur Jensen on testing, and others. Evaluation and psychotherapy are among the most important functions of psychologists today.

Learning Objectives
After reading the article, you should be able to:
1. Define: psychologist; psychiatrist.
2. Describe what clinical psychologists do.
3. Cite three highly influential thinkers in psychology, and describe their fields of concentration.

Essay Questions
1. According to "Psychology: There Are Other Therapists at Work," what are the largest subspecialties within psychology? Describe the practical applications of each.
2. Describe the two sides of the argument about including psychotherapy in National Health Insurance. Which side do you agree with, and why?

2. NEW PSYCHOLOGY: NEW IMAGE OF MAN   AE p. 6

Eleanor Hoover, human behavior writer for the *Los Angeles Times*, won the 1975 American Psychological Foundation Media Award for outstanding newspaper reporting for this article. Hoover presents a view of people that extends beyond psychology's traditional image which is limited by an insistence on scientific objectivity. The article includes a glossary of new terms and concepts.

Learning Objectives
After reading the article, you should be able to:
1. Describe at least five ways in which the "New Image of Man" differs from traditional views in psychology.
2. Define "peak experiences," and explain how they are achieved.
3. State how a humanistic orientation conflicts with a scientific orientation.
4. Explain how this conflict between different orientations might be resolved.

Essay Questions
1. Does the "new image" add anything to the study of psychology that could not be considered from the traditional points of view?
2. Have you ever had "peak experiences?" Would you recommend that people strive to achieve as many peak experiences as possible?
3. What are the advantages and disadvantages of studying subjective experiences?

3. WHY AREN'T WE USING SCIENCE TO CHANGE BEHAVIOR?   AE p. 13

B.F. Skinner, one of the founders of the behaviorist school of psychology, argues in this article that we are so devoted to our habit of interpreting our actions through emotions that we fail to take advantage of what social science can do to help solve problems. We are just as blind in this way, he argues, as the people we scorn for rejecting advanced agricultural technologies.

Learning Objectives
After reading the article, you should be able to:
1. Define reinforcement; values; survival value.
2. Describe Skinner's idea of how to use behavioral science.
3. List the Chinese inventions that advanced civilization.

Essay Questions
1. Discuss the central idea of "confidence" in this article.
2. To what end does Skinner use the extended comparison of our society to those more primitive that go without modern agricultural techniques?

4. SHAPING BEHAVIOR CONTEST FOR MINDS   AE p. 16

Behavior modification is an effective and highly controversial type of therapy for controlling behavior by manipulating reward and punishment. Its use among the sick is not so hotly disputed as its use among populations that are well. Behaviorists argue that, properly applied, behavior modification will produce happy, productive, and peaceful societies. Critics, many of them "humanists," react with fear, stating that behavior modification reduces the free will that we need to make intelligent decisions about ourselves and our environment. The debate has taken on large proportions as followers of each camp have argued their views and founded many and varied types of psychotherapy.

Learning Objectives
After reading the article, you should be able to:
1. Define and describe behavior modification.
2. Identify the critics and their arguments against behavior modification.
3. Name several important behaviorists.
4. List the ways that scientists can mold human behavior.

Essay Questions
1. Explain the pros and cons in the argument over behavior modification. Which side do you agree with, and why?
2. Under what circumstances is behavior modification very effective? What disorders is it most successful in treating? Under what circumstances might it be dangerous?

5. TESTING DR. FREUD   AE p. 20

Sigmund Freud's theories of personality development have profoundly affected the field of psychology. Yet Freud's theories have often been thought impervious to systematic testing. By combing the scientific literature, however, the authors have found that many studies of the validity and reliability of many of Freud's hypotheses have been conducted. This article describes the findings about such topics as psychoanalysis, homosexuality, oral and anal phases, etc.

Learning Objectives
After reading the article, you should be able to:
1. Define psychoanalysis, oral phase, anal phase, Oedipus complex.
2. Attest to the validity of Freud's statements about the topics covered in this article.
3. State the areas of Freud's strengths and weaknesses, as reported in this article.

Essay Questions
1. The article states that objections have been raised to Freud's theory of the Oedipus complex, and one of these is that it is *not* most intense at the ages Freud said it was. When is it most intense? When did Freud say it was?
2. Why have people despaired of subjecting Freudian theory to rigorous analysis? What problems have they faced?

6. TOWARD A PSYCHOLOGY OF NATURAL BEHAVIOR   AE p. 25

The author argues that psychology lags behind other fields in developing adequate field work methods. He also believes that psychology needs a better balance between field and laboratory. Many studies performed in laboratory situations do not have relevance to events in nature, and they may lack validity when psychologists try to generalize from laboratory results to "real life." We have "hedged on the issue of generalization," the author maintains, and we must now "look at how people actually behave in their homes, their schools and their work places."

Learning Objectives
After reading the article, you should be able to:
1. Contrast laboratory methods with field work methods.
2. Understand the relative advantages and disadvantages of laboratory research.
3. Know what skills the naturalist must possess.
4. Define "generalization" in the context of research results.

Essay Questions
1. What does the author mean by the statement, "Too often the means of our research have become the ends"?
2. Define and describe several differences in method and result between naturalistic and laboratory research.

Volumes in the Annual Editions Series

Abnormal Psychology
- Aging
- American Government
- American History Pre-Civil War
- American History Post-Civil War
- Anthropology
Astronomy
- Biology
- Business
Comparative Government
- Criminal Justice
Death and Dying
- Deviance
- Early Childhood Education
Earth Science
- Economics
- Educating Exceptional Children
- Education
Educational Psychology
Energy
- Environment
Ethnic Studies

Foreign Policy
Geography
Geology
- Health
- Human Development
- Human Sexuality
- Management
- Marketing
- Marriage and Family
- Personal Growth and Adjustment
Philosophy
Political Science
- Psychology
Religion
- Social Problems
- Sociology
- Urban Society
Western Civilization
Women's Studies
World History
- World Politics

● *Indicates currently available*

PSYCHOLOGY 80/81

A GUIDE TO THE STUDY AND ENJOYMENT OF ANNUAL EDITIONS: PSYCHOLOGY 80/81

This guide has been prepared to help the reader get the most from the 59 articles contained in *Psychology 80/81*. For each article the guide contains (1) a brief introduction which provides background on the topic of the article and the author(s) and occasionally shows the relationship of one article to another, (2) a Guide to Study which lists a number of learning objectives directing the reader to some of the important terms, concepts, and issues treated in the article, and (3) Questions for Thought and Discussion which hopefully will stimulate the reader to go beyond the article in thinking about the issue involved.

There are a number of ways this guide can be useful. One suggestion is that it be reviewed prior to reading the article, that the article then be read through for enjoyment, that the article then be reread to answer the study guide objectives and finally reviewed in the context of the thought questions.

We hope you find this guide useful. We would appreciate any comments you have on how it can be improved in next year's Annual Edition.

Prepared by John C. Touhey,
Florida Atlantic University

A GUIDE TO THE STUDY AND ENYOYMENT OF ANNUAL EDITIONS

PSYCHOLOGY 80/81

"Tenth Edition"

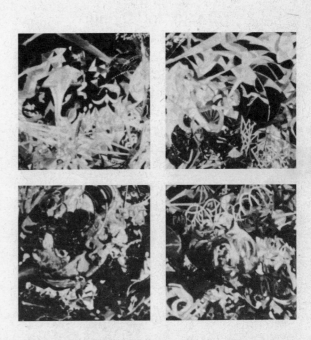

Cover Painting: "Battle of Lights, Coney Island" by Joseph Stella. Courtesy, Yale University Art Gallery. Gift of Collection Societe Anonyme.

ANNUAL EDITIONS

The Dushkin Publishing Group, Inc. Sluice Dock, Guilford, Ct. 06437

Volumes in the Annual Editions Series

Abnormal Psychology
- Aging
- American Government
- American History Pre-Civil War
- American History Post-Civil War
- Anthropology
Astronomy
- Biology
- Business
Comparative Government
- Criminal Justice
Death and Dying
- Deviance
- Early Childhood Education
Earth Science
- Economics
- Educating Exceptional Children
- Education
Educational Psychology
Energy
- Environment
Ethnic Studies

Foreign Policy
Geography
Geology
- Health
- Human Development
- Human Sexuality
- Management
- Marketing
- Marriage and Family
- Personal Growth and Adjustment
Philosophy
Political Science
- Psychology
Religion
- Social Problems
- Sociology
- Urban Society
Western Civilization
Women's Studies
World History
- World Politics

● *Indicates currently available*

© 1980 by the Dushkin Publishing Group, Inc. Annual Editions is a Trade Mark of the Dushkin Publishing Group, Inc.

Copyright © 1980 by the Dushkin Publishing Group, Inc., Guilford, Connecticut 06437

All rights reserved. No part of this book may be reproduced, stored, or transmitted by any means—mechanical, electronic or otherwise—without written permission from the publisher.

Tenth Edition

Manufactured by George Banta Company, Menasha, Wisconsin, 54952

Library of Congress Cataloging in Publication Data
Main entry under title: Annual editions: Psychology.
   1. Psychology—Addresses, essays, lectures—
Periodicals. I. Title: Psychology.
BF149.A58   150:5   79-180263
ISBN 0-87967-312-5

ADVISORY BOARD

Members of the Advisory Board are instrumental in the final selection of articles for each year's edition of *Annual Editions*. Their review of articles for content, level, and appropriateness provides critical direction to the editor and staff. We think you'll find their careful consideration well reflected in this volume.

Karen Duffy
State University of New York, Geneseo

Fran Yeager Fehlman
El Camino College

Bradley Glanville
California State University, Chico

Robert Howells
Purdue University

Curtis W. McIntyre
Southern Methodist University

Mary Reuder
Queens College of CUNY

Linda Shadburne
Mt. Hood Community College

Harry Strub
The University of Winnipeg

Jeffrey Topping
Mississippi State University

Roy Weinstock
Mary Washington College

AND STAFF

Rick Connelly, Publisher
Ian A. Nielsen, Program Manager
Celeste Borg, Editor
Addie Kawula, Acquisitions Editor
Brenda Filley, Production Manager
Cheryl Kinne, Permissions Coordinator
Charles Vitelli, Designer
Jeremy Brenner, Graphics Coordinator
Bertha Kinne, Typesetting Coordinator

CONTENTS

1
The Science
of Psychology

2
The Biological
Bases of
Behavior

3

Processes Underlying Behavior

4 Development

Individual Differences

Disorders and Therapy

7

Social Behavior

TOPIC GUIDE

This topic guide can be used to correlate each of the readings in *Psychology 80/81* with one or more of the topics usually covered in psychology books. Each article corresponds to a given topic area according to whether it deals with the subject in a primary or secondary fashion. These correlations are intended for use as a general study guide and do not necessarily define the total coverage of any given article.

TOPIC AREA	TREATED AS A PRIMARY ISSUE IN:	TREATED AS A SECONDARY ISSUE IN:
Aging & Death	39. "Old" Is Not a Four-Letter Word 40. Some of Us May Never Die	33. Eight Ages of Man 43. Sexuality and the Life Cycle
Behavior	3. Why Aren't We Using Science	2. New Psychology 4. Shaping Behavior Contest 20. Little Brother Is Changing You
Behavior Modification	4. Shaping Behavior Contest 20. Little Brother Is Changing You 21. Can't Remember?	35. Moral Thinking
Biology & Behavior	8. Genetic Engineers 11. The Split Brain Lab 12. Superbrain 13. Brain Damage 14. Hope for Damaged Brains 15. Observing the Brain 16. Wobbly Biorhythms 17. The Human Body as a Biological Clock 22. That Filing System Inside Your Head 44. What We Know and Don't Know About Sex Differences 45. Mental Patterns of Disease	23. Thought into Speech 40. Some of Us May Never Die 49. Medical Treatment of Mental Illness
Body Rhythms	16. Wobbly Biorhythms 17. The Human Body as Biological Clock	
Brain Chemistry	11. Split Brain Lab 12. Superbrain 13. Brain Damage 14. Hope for Damaged Brains 15. Observing the Brain 17. The Human Body as Biological Clock	25. Dream World 51. New Light on Schizophrenia
Brain Damage	13. Brain Damage 14. Hope for Damaged Brains	10. Origins of Violence
Cognition	29. Babies Can Communicate 30. Infant Thought 34. Television and the Young Viewer 35. Moral Thinking	
Development	32. Reconsideration: Jean Piaget 33. Eight Ages of Man 34. Television and the Young Viewer 35. Moral Thinking 41. Attitudes, Interests, and IQ 43. Sexuality and the Life Cycle	31. Learning the Mother Tongue 36. The Father of the Child 37. Making It to Maturity 38. Must Everything Be a Midlife Crisis?
Disease & Personality	45. Mental Patterns of Disease 46. Cancer and the Mind	51. New Light on Schizophrenia 53. The Age of Melancholy
Dreams	25. Dream World	
Drugs	19. What Marijuana Does 49. Medical Treatment of Mental Illness 52. A Darkness at Noon	

TOPIC AREA	TREATED AS A PRIMARY ISSUE IN:	TREATED AS A SECONDARY ISSUE IN:
Humanistic Psychology	2. New Psychology 7. Psychobabble 54. Shopping for the Right Therapy	4. Shaping Behavior Contest
Individual Differences	9. Special Abilities of the Sexes 41. Attitudes, Interests, and IQ 42. New Light on IQ 44. What We Know and Don't Know About Sex Differences	
Language	23. Thought Into Speech 24. Navigating the Slippery Stream of Speech 29. Babies Can Communicate	44. What We Know and Don't Know About Sex Differences
Mental Illness	51. New Light on Schizophrenia 52. A Darkness at Noon 53. The Age of Melancholy	5. Testing Dr. Freud 6. Toward a Psychology of Natural Behavior 47. On Being Sane in Insane Places 48. More on Pseudoscience in Science 49. Medical Treatment of Mental Illness
Parapsychology	27. The Case for Parapsychology 28. A Skeptic's View of Parapsychology	
Parenting	31. Learning the Mother Tongue 36. The Father of the Child 37. Making It to Maturity	
Perception & Memory	15. Observing the Brain 21. Can't Remember? 22. That Filing System Inside Your Head	19. What Marijuana Does 23. Thought into Speech
Psychotherapy	5. Testing Dr. Freud 50. Second Death of Sigmund Freud	2. New Psychology 25. Dream World
Sexuality	9. Special Abilities of the Sexes 43. Sexuality and the Life Cycle 44. What We Know and Don't Know About Sex Differences	5. Testing Dr. Freud 34. Television and the Young Viewer 53. The Age of Melancholy
Social Behavior	34. Television and the Young Viewer 55. If Hitler Asked You to Electrocute a Stranger 56. Pathology of Imprisonment 57. How Groups Intensify Opinions 58. The Social Disease Called Shyness 59. The American Way of Mating	3. Why Aren't We Using Science 9. Special Abilities of the Sexes
Stress	26. Stress 38. Must Everything Be a Mid-life Crisis?	45. Mental Patterns of Disease 46. Cancer and the Mind
Therapy	1. Psychology: There Are Other Therapists at Work 47. On Being Sane in Insane Places 48. More on Pseudoscience in Science 49. Medical Treatment of Mental Illness 50. Second Death of Sigmund Freud 54. Shopping for the Right Therapy	2. New Psychology 4. Shaping Behavior Contest for Minds

PREFACE

The emphasis of psychology is people: how we think, behave, develop, and perceive our world. While its roots are deeply entwined in the history of philosophy, the branches of psychology have extended to the scientific laboratory and beyond, to psychic phenomena. The field of psychology is filled with different schools of thought and methodologies which contribute new discoveries to our rapidly expanding body of knowledge about the human animal.

If these discoveries are not communicated, they are useless. Professional journals disseminate information to specialists in the field, but what of the nonspecialist? The popular media has taken up this challenge to provide the valuable communications link between psychologists and the public. Radio, television, newspapers, and magazines regularly carry reports of significant and intriguing psychological research. It is not surprising that this coverage frequently informs the professional as well as the layperson about the most recent developments in the field.

Unfortunately, tracking down and sorting through this wealth of material requires a great deal of time. *Annual Editions: Psychology 80/81* is designed to simplify this task. This tenth edition includes a broad cross-section of articles from a variety of sources. Many of these articles have earned awards for distinguished scientific writing from the American Psychological Foundation. Others are the work of experienced science writers who regularly scan the professional literature for reports to the lay public. Some of the articles are first-hand reports written by the scientific researchers themselves, providing rich detail for all of us who are interested in what is happening today in the laboratory and in field work.

Some of the selections are theoretical, some empirical—and others both. Some contain intriguing, even frightening, implications. Many are concerned with the ethical issues inherent in the science. This broad range of attitudes and outlooks reflect the field of psychology itself, as a profession and a science.

We think that *Annual Editions: Psychology 80/81* is one of the most useful and up-to-date books available. But we'd like to know what you think. Please take a minute to fill out the article rating form on the last page of this book, and let us know your opinion. Any anthology can be improved, and this one will be—annually.

Rick Connelly
Publisher

The Science of Psychology

1

Psychology may be defined as the science of the nature, function, and phenomena of humans and other animals. Philosophers have long been involved in this study, but the recognition of psychology as an empirical science is comparatively recent, usually marked by the opening in Germany in 1879 of the first psychological laboratory. Since that time several schools of thought have developed to influence and comprise the science of psychology, including, among others, structuralism, functionalism, psychoanalysis, behaviorism, and Gestalt theory.

This section includes articles that survey the major issues and areas of agreement/disagreement in the field of psychology today. "Psychology: There are Other Therapists at Work" distinguishes between psychologists and psychiatrists, and catalogues trends and areas of emphasis in psychological studies, citing the work and theories of some of the prominent people in the field.

Whether psychology should be a humanistic (subjective) or a scientific (objective) study is one of the most pervasive and argued questions in the field. Several articles collected here address this question. "New Psychology: New Image of Man," an APA award-winning article, discusses humanistic psychology as an alternative to and reaction against classic behaviorism and Freudian psychoanalysis, and offers a glossary that helps in the understanding of the "new psychology." B.F. Skinner's "Why Aren't We Using Science to Change Behavior" presents the eminent behaviorist's evaluation of the problems created by subjectivity and his imperative call to use behavioral

science to "help solve the problems of the world now." "Shaping Behavior Contest for Minds" catalogues the ways in which behavior modification has gained acceptance and cautions against the creation of "Skinner's engineered society."

In "Testing Dr. Freud" two psychologists review the myriad scientific evaluations of Freud's theories, including psychoanalysis, dreams, complexes, homosexuality, and personality. "Toward a Psychology of Natural Behavior" examines the role of empirical laboratory investigation in the field of psychology.

This section concludes with "Psychobabble," a broadside look at the often ludicrous effects of the proliferation of psychological cant and conceptual oversimplification.

A review of this section will show how professional psychologists attempt to reconcile our capability for controlling behavior with the requirements of personal freedom. Shifting trends in the field and the most recent perspectives are reported along with discussions of ways in which the study of psychology may contribute to human welfare.

Looking Ahead: Challenge Questions

Should students of psychology be more concerned with collecting and communicating data, or with interpreting it?

Need the study of behavior automatically translate into behavior control? In what ways is behavior control the legitimate concern of parents? of school administrators? of prison officials? of psychologists?

Is psychology a culture-bound science?

Psychology: There Are Other Therapists at Work

Ruth Mehrtens Galvin

Ruth Mehrtens Galvin is a senior correspondent for Time magazine, specializing in studies of behavior.

Psychology is the science that seeks to understand and predict behavior by relating external events and the internal processes of the individual to behavior. Far and away the largest of the behavioral and social sciences, it has 71,000 practitioners in the United States.

Because so many—roughly a third—are clinical psychologists who devote either all or part of their time to therapy, psychologists are often confused with psychiatrists, who must be physicians. The number of psychologists doing therapy passed the number of psychiatrists within the last two years, and the President of the American Psychological Association in 1977 was for the first time a private practitioner: Dr. Theodore Blau, of Tampa, Fla. Nevertheless, only 18 percent of psychologists practice therapy full time, and most do no therapy at all.

The largest single group of psychologists next to the psychotherapists is the 6,000 in social psychology, dealing with such subjects as crowding, helping, hostility and love. "Attribution theory," concerning how people find meaning in their world through the motivations they attribute to others, is currently the most popular topic among social psychologists.

Most psychologists are linked by the belief that behavior can be measured. There are more than 3,000 basic researchers in psychology, and the two most famous living American psychologists, Dr. B.F. Skinner of Harvard and Dr. Neal Miller of Rockefeller University, are laboratory men. Dr. Skinner's demonstration of the degree to which behavior is determined by its consequences has resulted in the use of reward systems to change the behavior of retarded children, mental patients and convicts, and has influenced much of the behavior therapy so popular today. Dr. Miller is the man most responsible for the great interest in biofeedback, a technique for the control of brain processes.

In the last 20 years, there has been a shift away from studying the learning of behavior patterns to the functions of the brain, particularly the processes of perception and memory. "Split-brain" research—the behavior of the left and right hemispheres of the brain—is growing, along with a budding controversy over whether male and female brains function differently.

The first psychologist to head the National Science Foundation, Dr. Richard C. Atkinson, whose appointment as director was confirmed in May, is one of the experimental psychologists and a mathematician whose theory about the basis of memory has inspired much of the current research in human memory. Dr. Atkinson has also designed a computer instruction program, now used to teach reading in schools, that can adjust to the individual student's knowledge at any moment in time.

Some 1,300 psychologists study human development from infancy to old age, and there has been growing recognition that important learning takes place not just in childhood but throughout the life span. There is also increasing interest in how language develops, including the intriguing possibility, indicated by work with chimpanzees, that language is not unique to the human animal.

In all, 34 different specialities are represented among the 45,000 members of the American Psychological Association, the profession's largest organization. As might be expected, better than half of them are employed in either schools or colleges. But over ten percent now work for either government or business (where psychologists test, measure and map strategies for more effective and contented workers). A new and growing group is in environmental psychology, helping design housing projects for the elderly, schools, landscaping, and, increasingly, addressing such public policy problems as the uses of energy.

American psychology began officially in the late 19th century. Borrowing many of its ideas from Europe, it spent its early years in a war of theories: introspectionist, Gestalt (for *Gestalten* or patterns of experience) and

From *The New York Times Magazine*, August 14, 1977. Copyright © 1977 by The New York Times Company. Reprinted by permission.

behaviorism, which puts its money on the observation of external behavior. Outside these three groups, still other psychologists, following in the wake of Sir Francis Galton of Britain and Alfred Binet of France, worked to develop new tests of learning. Learning theory has always held a particular fascination for American psychologists, partly, perhaps, because of the American tendency to believe in the infinite perfectibility of human nature—a notion fostered by American 19th-century moral philosophers.

In more recent years, the work of the Swiss researcher, Dr. Jean Piaget, has created a growing interest in innate stages of cognitive development, and inspired a new theory of moral development as well. Drawing on Piagetian evidence that cognitive development involves a series of stages that emerge as the child interacts with its environment, Dr. Lawrence Kohlberg of Harvard has demonstrated that similar stages of moral development emerge as the individual gains experience in making moral judgments. His theory is now being put to work in several schools and in a Connecticut prison.

An important debate going on in developmental psychology parallels Piagetian concern with innate processes.

Challenging the long-held belief in the indispensability of infant stimulation for ultimate congentive and emotional maturity, Prof. Jerome Kagan of Harvard has found remarkable recovery from retardation in children who were deprived of challenge during their first year but later lived in more stimulating surroundings.

"Nobody denies the importance of environment, but I now believe that inherited sequences of growth are more powerful than we had thought," says Professor Kagan, once an ardent "environmentalist."

Dr. Kagan and other psychologists are asking more complicated questions about both heredity and environment, and the challenge of the next 10 or 20 years will be to understand the interaction of the two.

The strength of psychology, say such leaders as Charles Kiesler, a social psychologist who is the executive officer of the American Psychological Association, is in its rigorous insistence on the testing of hypotheses and in psychologists' ability to evaluate whatever they do.

Evaluation has become one of psychology's most important specialties, whose star is Northwestern

1. Psychology: There Are Other Therapists at Work

University Prof. Donald Campbell, a past president of the association. Evaluation is now a built-in ingredient of federally funded programs, bringing psychology into the public arena as never before.

One concern has been to make clear to both the public and public officials the significance of psychological research. Dr. Campbell, for one, has been at pains to counteract Dr. Arthur Jensen's interpretation that I.Q. test scores indicate innate differences by race, emphasizing, instead, the evidence that society limits black children's opportunities to learn white middle class vocabulary and skills.

The ethics of psychological research, its interpretation, confidentiality and public uses have become important interests across psychology.

The burgeoning business in psychotherapy since World War II, with its melange of schools, methods and theories, inspired Dr. Nicholas Cummings, chief psychologist for the Kaiser-Permanente health plans in San Francisco, to find a way of setting professional standards for nonacademic psychology. In 1969, he founded the first of a number of professional schools of psychology. Nine other professional schools have followed, and there are 32 more on the drawing boards.

Impressed by such efforts, many insurance plans now reimburse psychologists for therapy, and they are now being considered for inclusion in National Health Insurance. A running battle is now going on between psychologists like Dr. Cummings, who offers evidence that brief psychotherapy such as that done by psychologists can save enormous expense by forestalling problems like hypertension, migraine and backaches, and those who, like Prof. George Albee of the University of Vermont, argue that neither psychiatry nor psychology should be covered under national health legislation.

"I am not against psychotherapy," Dr. Albee insists, "but we really ought to be spending our efforts in clinical psychology discovering the causes of the enormous amounts of distress in our society, and doing something about *them.*"

By many different methods, suggests Dr. Kiesler, psychologists are doing just that. "Both the experimentalists and the therapists are now approaching the same kinds of problems," he says. "That is both part of the conflict and the potential excitement for the future."

New Psychology: New Image of Man

BY ELEANOR HOOVER

John Brodie, the articulate former quarterback for the San Francisco 49ers, reports an ecstatic interlude when "time stood still" while he was dropping back to throw a pass . . .

A young man working his way through medical school by drumming in a jazz band reports many years later, that in all his drumming he had three peaks when he suddenly felt like a great drummer and his performance was perfect . . .

Experience—any experience—once was ignored in psychology as "unscientific." Particularly these, which the late psychologist Abraham Maslow called "peak experiences."

They are vivid moments when things fall into place, one's vision is clear and life is meaningful.

They happen, it was thought, only to artists, poets, mystics or saints. But Maslow found they also happen to the healthiest, most creative and happy people.

Now a new study indicates they are "widespread, almost commonplace in American society today." Nobody talks about them "because somehow they seem odd, illogical—inexplicable," says the Rev. Andrew M. Greeley, the sociologist who conducted the study for the National Research Opinion Center.

It seems that such moments are linked to feelings of self-fulfillment, creativity, achievement—or simple at-one-with-the-universe reverie. Apparently, they can happen to anyone. Interest in them is part of something loosely called the "new psychology."

"The core of the new psychology," says Hugh Redmond of Johnston College at the University of Redlands, "is based on a new image or vision of man—on what he is and what he can do."

If the new psychology needs a label, "humanistic" probably fits best.

What humanistic psychology has triggered is a growing interest in expanding man's awareness—to enhance creativity, health, learning, problem solving and to produce what one brain researcher calls "intrinsically rewarding ecstatic experiences."

Much of what is happening is still outside the ivied halls of the academy. But not for long.

The curriculum committee of Harvard University recently approved an undergraduate course in altered states of consciousness.

"Students," one professor says, "are coming into the colleges and demanding that these experiences be recognized."

Humanistic psychology grew out of opposition to the major expressions of traditional psychology—mainly Skinnerean behaviorism and Freudian psychoanalysis.

"For as long as I can remember—until now—if it didn't have pink eyes, a long tail and a twitchy nose and run in a maze, it wasn't psychology," an older psychologist says.

It has been called everything from a "post-Freudian revolution" to a "brain revolution" and "a revolution in consciousness."

If such terms seem to overstate the case for humanistic psychology (and they do to many), they are not strong enough for a few who, in the words of one observer, see it as nothing short of "a Reformation slouching to meet its Luther at a yet undiscovered cathedral door."

Taken as a whole, humanistic psychology consists of a loose but important network of approaches, disciplines, techniques, and areas of mind and brain research which see man from all sides—wholly different from the view we are used to.

Its main aspects, which tend to overlap, are these:

—Where once man was seen as merely a bundle of responses to stimuli, moldable in any direction, there is a focus on individuality, the person and the intrinsic complexity,. richness and power of mind and consciousness.

—Where once mind and body were split, there is a "coming together," a regard for wholeness and the way the mind affects the body and the body affects the mind. This "holistic" approach can be found today in education, medicine and sports as well as psychology.

—Where thought, logic and rationality were once dominant, there is more recognition of emotions as well as "spiritual" feelings. The goal is to be a whole person who is a harmonious blend of all his parts.

—Where once "objectivity" meant banishing subjective experience from science, it is now being allowed back in. The belief of humanistic psychologists is that there is no basic contradiction and that a new science can be built which also includes the observer's experience.

—Where once man was seen as blindly buffeted by instinctual forces such as the id. superego and ego, there is a new belief in man's built-in capacity for growth, self-transcendence or self-actualization.

From the *Los Angeles Times*, April 6, 1975. Copyright © 1975 *Los Angeles Times*. Reprinted by Permission.

—Where once, under the old Freudian "medical model," Man was seen as either "sick" or "well," he is now seen as having a natural ability to make changes in himself rather quickly, once he sees what needs to be done. "The basic idea is," says James Fadiman of Stanford, "that you are capable of being more than you are and you know how to do it."

—Where once Man was seen as a more or less static or "fixed" system, there is a new interest in "energy flow" and "energy fields"—in Eastern meditation and yoga, seen as a means of releasing energy. A new polarity therapy is based on this idea of energy and the "natural ability of the body to balance itself."

—Where once the idea of will and willpower was so loaded with guilt and repression that generations rebelled against it, there is a renewed interest in the will and in responsibility for self as a positive, natural and liberating force.

—Where once purpose or meaning were seen as "religious," each is finding its way back into psychology. This recognition of a "spiritual dimension" to man is a major change. Esalen's founder, Mike Murphy, calls this "the cutting edge—the psychology of the future."

Humanistic psychology began with the work of Abraham Maslow more than 20 years ago, grew and expanded in the Human Potential Movement for about 10 years, and became a full-fledged "psychology" only two years ago.

That was when humanistic psychology was accepted by the American Psychological Assn. as its newest and 32nd branch—along with experimental, physiological, clinical, educational, child and other such venerables, some of which go back almost 65 years.

To some unregenerate members of the Assn. for Humanistic Psychology—remembering its bitter turbulent history as a "third force" movement—recognition by the American Psychological Assn. may be "death by victory." They are proud, but they hope their "joyous movement" will not be diverted.

(That there were tensions between the two groups is understandable. The American Psychological Assn. is made up largely of psychologists with university affiliations. Many Assn. for Humanistic Psychology members work outside the academy—many as therapists—or in university departments other than psychology. Lacking university support, they developed much of the new psychology at "growth centers" around the country like Esalen at Big Sur.)

To understand humanistic psychology, there must be an understanding of classical behaviorism and Freudian psychoanalysis—the two traditional psychologies to which Maslow's work, humanistic psychology and the Human Potential Movement stand more or less opposed.

A main point at issue is the notion of an "inner man."

Behaviorism (which, since its founding, has evolved into Skinnerean behaviorism, from B. F. Skinner of Harvard, its most famous spokesman) takes the view that all we can know or scientifically study about an organism is what it does, how it behaves—hence the name behaviorism. Its tools are stimulus-response and reward-punishment, and its body of knowledge is called learning theory.

The experimental schema is simple. A hungry rat is put in a maze. Hunger is its stimulus. Reward is a food pellet at the end of the maze. To get the food, the rat must learn, for example, to overcome obstacles put in his way.

How the rat behaves—what it does and how it learns—is what is important to classical behaviorists. Nothing more. And nothing further is inferred. The rat model is, of course, an analogy to human behavior.

A therapy based on this system—behavior modification—is well thought-of by most psychologists. At least it isn't often challenged. It has had good success in reducing obesity, phobias, and in helping cases of autism—a disorder in which a child remains regressed at early stages of development.

Behavior modification assumes that disorders, habits, ills—whatever one wishes to call them—are learned, and can be changed by methods worked out in the labs. That is, undesired behavior can be stopped through punishment and desired behavior increased through reward.

Another name for this is operant conditioning, which, simply put by one therapist is, "people do what they are rewarded for doing." As Skinner told a Reed College symposium on "Behavior Control" two weeks ago, "inner man is an illusion."

The humanists deplore this view and all else in psychology that fragmentizes and reduces.

Freudianism is more concerned with what goes on inside the individual. In fact, it sees man as buffeted by internal unconscious urges and the battlefield of instinctual drives like the id. ego and superego, with "neurosis" (a term less used today) the almost inevitable result.

Psychoanalysis, of course, was the "sole" time-honored way of alleviating such complaints until the newer, freewheeling humanistic-oriented "therapies" came along.

But sexual repression was a pressing problem in Freud's day. It is less so now. And nowhere did Freud have much to say about what has become one of today's most pressing problems—a sense of meaninglessness in life.

Freud's was a pessimistic view. He once wrote to a friend, "I have always confined myself to the ground floor and basement of the edifice called Man." Aldous Huxley once said he should have said the basement-basement.

If Freud is the basement, the humanists see themselves as the attic or penthouse. Rollo May, a founder of the Assn. for Humanistic Psychology, sounded the clarion call at the beginning of the movement.

"We represent the New Underground in psychology," he said. "I see a crucially important value for the (association) if we are able to find and be the kind of psychology that speaks out of the being of man, rather than out of techniques."

May thinks psychology owes Freud a debt of gratitude for bringing "repressed hostilities, irrational urges" and other "dark" areas of the unconscious out into the open. But he feels Freud's system left out too much that is human.

He warns the behaviorists they run the risk of creating a totally mechanical society. The title of Skinner's latest book. "Beyond Freedom and Dignity," suggests just that to most humanists. The Skinnerian reply is that Man's "freedom" is illusory and leaves him abandoned to uncontrollable forces in his environment.

1. THE SCIENCE OF PSYCHOLOGY

This issue has political overtones. The battle continues.

Maslow was the first major American psychologist to postulate that man is an evolutionary creature whose higher nature is just as "instinctoid" (his word) as his lower nature . . . and to see problems, difficulties and "sickness" arising when this upward-evolution—this need for "self-actualization"—is blocked.

"This higher nature," Maslow said, "includes the need for meaningful work, for responsibility, for creativeness, for being fair and just, for doing what is worthwhile and for preferring to do it well."

Peak experiences are way stations along the path of this upward evolution—way stations that are both necessary and desirable. Maslow believed.

"Maslow's importance," explains British author-psychologist Wilson, "is that he places these experiences of transcendence at the core of his psychology. Peak experiences are moments of meaning which enhance our self-image and stimulate our will.

" . . . As the meaning pours in, you ask yourself, 'Why doesn't this happen all the time?' . . . . and the answer is obvious: 'Because I allow the will to become passive and the senses close up. If I want more meaning then I must force my senses wide open by an increased effort of the will . . . ' "

One of those with reservations about peak experience is Sam Keen of the Assn. for Humanistic Psychology. He favors a more "Zen, homogenized way of living . . . Some neurotics reach the point where they need peak experience all the time."

"We can't assume our own experiences are always correct either," says Stanford's Fadiman.

"By that I mean that my gut feelings may be no more accurate than my intellectual feelings. I've made as many mistakes being led by my gut or my gonads as by my mind. That's where a lot of encounter got stuck."

Humanistic psychology is already way ahead of any simple definitions. Its adherents—or, at least, its avantgarde—say that man, as we usually think of him, is far too narrow a concept.

The language of the humanists now takes on a "spiritual," almost mystical tone—something unheard and unheard-of in scientific circles before.

But then the humanists have been outrageous right along. Once after Maslow had delivered a paper at an American Psychological Assn. meeting, a famous psychologist rushed at him shouting, "Maslow—you are an evil man—you want to destroy psychology."

Ironically, Maslow went on to become the association's president a few years later.

What is different today is that humanistic ranks—although small—include so many well credentialed and influential scientists that they can no longer be dismissed as merely "misguided," "misled," "unscientific"—or, least of all, "kooky."

Nor can these new ideas be credited to the "squishy California atmosphere" or California's "tolerance for peculiar life-styles" as some writers do. They seem to be everywhere.

Anyone who remembers the flashy, flamboyant Human Potential Movement of a few years back may have trouble reconciling it with humanistic psychology's newfound respectability.

The Human Potential Movement (which was to blend with, and finally become indistinguishable from, the Assn. for Humanistic Psychology) was born out of the cultural upheaval of the 60s.

Affluence, the sexual revolution, the campus revolt, changing life styles, women's liberation, drugs, the flower children, television, more leisure and rising middle-class expectations all played a part. For whatever reason, thousands of people found their lives somehow flat and self-limiting.

Much earlier, after World War II, the GI Bill of Rights had brought thousands of ex-GIs onto the campuses where, with the newfound existential wisdom of war, many went into clinical psychology.

"Until then, the practice of psychotherapy had been limited almost exclusively to professionals having an MD degree—owing to the accidental historical fact that Freud just happened to be an MD himself. No other reason," says Dr. Tom Greening, a humanistic therapist.

With the flood of clinical psychologists into the market-place, psychotherapy ceased to be the monopoly of the MDs and the luxury solely of the rich. It unleashed a floodgate of self-exploration, self-examination and self-awareness.

Much of this had begun before Maslow and the humanists appeared on the scene. Astrology, I Ching, Tarot cards, esoteric religions and meditation were flourishing.

And encounter—that crucible of honest, bruising group plain talk, where people "can drop their masks and express true feelings"—was on everyone's lips if not in their living rooms.

"What happened," says Fadiman, the Stanford psychologist, "is we learned that being 'well-bred' meant dying slowly. 'Well-bred' in the sense of suppressing our real feelings. What has finally come across is that emotional honesty is necessary for mental health."

He adds, "And there were an awful lot of dead people walking around."

Encounter was big business. Corporations like TRW had major programs aimed at "sensitizing" employes, believing this resulted in more productive work. (Now some of them offer yoga classes at lunch.)

By the end of the 60s, National Training Laboratories could claim that more than half the presidents of the 500 largest U.S. corporations had exposed themselves to group experience. Encounter finally filtered down to churches, schools, police departments, the Army—and around the world.

At the same time, Esalen was deep in its far-out forays in self-exploration. Some called it "freaky audacity and a willingness to try anything that stretches the self."

Whatever it was, it met a a real need of the time (and still does: there are Esalen-like growth centers now in Scotland, London, Amsterdam, Munich, Paris, the Costa del Sol in Spain, and Japan.)

Esalen and humanistic psychology met officially when Murphy, Esalen's founder, had a first, "chance" meeting with Maslow who "just happened" to be lost in the hills above Big Sur one day in the early '60s—a story Murphy tells which is positively eerie in coincidence.

But nowhere else could one glimpse the real "cutting edge" of change as readily as at Assn. for Humanistic Psychology conventions.

Its members tended to greet each other with bear hugs, lie around on convention floors and create culture shock at famous hotels by skinny-dipping in the early hours of the morning.

They danced to bongo drums by the pool, held workshops on "play" where they romped and cavorted like children, and practiced what they preached—a celebration of life.

("The battle to maintain a balance between the theoretical and the experiential still rages," says one member today.)

This freewheelingness cost them some of their most eminent members some years ago. After an episode where students pitched a tent in the lobby of the elegant Fairmont Hotel in San Francisco to protest high room rates, Rollo May, Gardner Murphy and some others resigned.

But May rejoined two years later with a simple statement:

"Somewhere, there has got to be a psychology that includes poetry, art, a movement toward social justice and that will help me understand myself—and nowhere does it exist—even beginningly—outside the (association)."

Packed seminars and workshops introduced professionals, and the lay public who attended in large number, to the latest developments in techniques for self-discovery: aikido, gestalt, rolfing, autogenic training, bioenergetics, transactional analysis, sensory and body awareness, Zen meditation, Tibetan Buddhism, sensual massage, transpersonal workshops, biofeedback, psychosynthesis and much more.

Many seminal ideas and subjects got their first airing at Assn. for Humanistic Psychology forums, among them the now famous seminar on "Should a Professional Therapist Go to Bed with His Patient if Mutually Attracted?"

"It was an attempt," explains Eleanor Criswell, a California State College, Sonoma, psychology professor, "to bring certain things out in the open that are well known in the profession but seldom talked about. Actually, it was more or less engineered by a psychiatrist who had written a book on the subject which was being released that day.

"Many of our people—among them Albert Ellis, the famous sexologist, and onetime firebrand—argued against the practice, warning that it could interfere with people getting well, totally disrupt the therapeutic situation and easily be exploitive on the part of the therapist."

Members of the audience—some women—wanted to know if the therapist would, with equal impartiality, sleep with an old and homely female patient or say, a male patient "who needed it."

"The press went wild," continues Criswell. "It was in every magazine and newspaper . . . People were aghast. But the next year, at their meeting in Hawaii, the American Psychological Assn. held a seminar on the same subject and it wasn't mentioned anywhere in the media."

This point about the trend-setting capacities of the Assn. for Humanistic Psychology is well taken. For years, since its founding in 1962, it has always held its convention in the same city as the American Psychological Assn.—only a few days before or after, so that psychologists who wished to attend both meetings could do so conveniently.

It was always a study in contrasts. The button-down academicians would file in, university-style, with decorum, and listen to formal papers formally delivered at a lecture.

"But," said one observer, "it was clear that, with each successive year, more and more of their colleagues turned up bearded and braless, and some even enrolled in the 'touchie-feelie' seminars run by that 'wild bunch'—the Assn. for Humanistic Psychology."

Now the "movement" seems to be settling down, its youthful exuberance curbed, if not peaked. At last year's Assn. for Humanistic Psychology convention in New Orleans, observers noted fewer "thrill seekers," fewer crowds and a growing trend toward the transcendental—and a mystical language.

Humanistic psychology is working a change in the traditional academic fare long taught to psychology students in the universities.

Words like love, consciousness, values, meaning and purpose are creeping back into the textbooks. For a long time, the only chapter on love was to be found in a standard text by Harry Harlow—and that was on love between primates.

Now human love comes under scrutiny. So do trust, altruism, self-esteem. One of psychology's leading learning theorists, Ernest R. Hilgard, is studying hypnosis at Stanford.

While animal experimentation is not necessarily on the wane, Claremont College Graduate School phased out its rat laboratory—in deference to new priorities.

Courses in the new psychology, including parapsychology, are turning up on campuses in all parts of the country. Experimental Johnston College at the University of Redlands bases an entire four-year course around new transpersonal psychology—which combines the humanistic with the "spiritual." Students use encounter at the beginning of each semester to decide on their course of study.

At Northern Illinois University, psychologist-educator Thomas Roberts uses an imagery technique much used in the new psychology called "fantasy journey" to instruct electric shop teacher trainees. He asks students to relax and begins, softly:

"Now imagine you are an electron in a wire . . . you are hopping, swirling, leaping, brushing around with other electrons, all pushing and bumping against each other—rapidly, heatedly . . . now you are outside the wire, feel the force, the pull and intensity of the electronic field . . . now take a trip down an electric coil itself, feel yourself sliding, bumping, interwinning with other electrons in the rush of forces . . ."—and it goes on.

"Its been very successful," Roberts says, "because people learn better when they have the experience of something."

Symbolic visualization, twilight images and directed daydreams are being used in classrooms, mind-dynamic and creativity workshops, the newer "spiritual" disciplines (once called "therapies") like transpersonal psychology and psychosynthesis, and memory and hypnosis courses.

For centuries, of course, they have been part of many ancient systems of Eastern meditation, notably Tibetan Buddhism—all of which are attracting growing numbers of people in the West, particularly among students of the new psychology.

1. THE SCIENCE OF PSYCHOLOGY

Psychology has always had an identity crisis.

As an outgrowth of philosophy and wanting to earn its spurs as a "real" science, a young psychology needed the security of imitating medicine and physics.

From medicine, it took the sickness model and studied pathology.

From early physics, it took the mechanistic idea of studying the parts and not the whole.

It chopped behavior into segments like reaction time and worked with worms, rats, dogs and apes that could be managed and controlled.

The results were often criticized—in the profession and out.

Ten years ago, writer-critic Gerald Sykes called psychology "a raw ungainly science" and declared:

"We know less about ourselves than about any other portion of society, and our lack of self-knowledge is now our most acute social problem . . . I would like to know what the psychologists have done to help us."

Now, the debate between the "new" psychology and the "old" raises the same basic questions: What is science, what is psychology and what should it be studying? Most crucial—what is man?

Neuropsychologist Robert Ornstein, author of the bestselling "Psychology of Consciousness," threw out this battle cry to a UCLA audience last year:

"Somehow, academic psychology got diverted from the study of the most interesting areas and into the most trivial. It was a terrible mistake but this kind of meeting marks the end of that kind of diversion. We're here to turn the mainstream of psychology back to the time when methods and techniques were devoted to the study of real phenomena such as mind and how people experience the world to the fullest."

Donald Hebb, though, speaking at a recent American Psychological Assn. convention in Montreal on "What Psychology Is All About," assailed misguided people "who want us to deal directly with the mystery of existence now. Some of this is simply antiscience . . . which we needn't bother with here. When someone thinks a science can be run that way, there is much to be said. Subjective science? There isn't such a thing."

Can psychology, in fact, be humanistic and scientific at the same time? A growing number of professionals are saying yes.

But since, in the "new psychology," man is being redefined, it may require a redefinition of scientific method.

The scientific method has always demanded "objectivity" (that the experimenter see impartially what is there), verifiability (that the experiments can be repeated by others) and predictability.

At issue, of course, is "objectivity." Humanistic psychologists demand that this term be reexamined and that the subjective be let back in—where they believe it has always been anyway.

They say that overwhelming evidence shows that we "choose" what we see or perceive as surely as we choose our words or a new pair of shoes.

What the humanists call for is a new science of ordinary and extraordinary subjective experience.

And, they say, it isn't so extraordinary after all— hypnosis has been studied scientifically for a century and a half.

Charles Tart of Davis proposes a new method. He calls it "specific state science." In it, scientists do research by entering into the research area themselves.

Instead of remaining outside and "objective," they go into states like meditation, hypnosis, sensory deprivation and other altered states of consciousness.

Then their collected reports can be tested against one another to verify the validity of the knowledge obtained.

This, he says, is not really different from the way science now works with normal consciousness to achieve consensus on certain observable data.

Tart's point is that all knowledge is basically experiential.

This is the belief of John Lilly—the MD-biophysicist, neurophysiologist-psychoanalyst who did the famous work with dolphins. He sees it as the best tradition of an older science. He quotes British biologist J.B.S. Haldane's advice to his students: "You will not understand what is necessary in the way of scientific control unless you are the first subject in your experiment."

In what is surely the most remarkable and little known scientific meeting of its kind in the world, a diverse group of psychologists, medical doctors, holy men, physicists, philosophers and anthropologists from everywhere converge on Council Grove, Kan., once a year for a special conference.

It is cosponsored by the Assn. for Humanistic Psychology and the Menninger Foundation.

Its purpose? The study of experience involving an expansion or extension of consciousness beyond the usual ego boundaries and the limitation of time and space. It is by invitation only.

Some psychologists still feel that such areas as altered states of consciousness are off limits, off base and too far out.

But to Andrew Weil, MD, author of "The Natural Mind," the desire to alter consciousness periodically is an innate, normal drive comparable to hunger or the sex drive. He believes it is visible in 3- and 4-year-olds when they whirl themselves into dizziness or squeeze each other around the chest until they lost their breath.

Some evidence for this seems to come from research on a part of the brain called the limbic system. Sensations which range from mild pleasure to intense joy or euphoria come from electrical stimulation of the limbic.

James Olds has found that hungry rats will give up on getting food if they have to cross an electric grid containing 60 microamperes of electricity, but to obtain this brain stimulation, they will cross grids charged with 450 microamperes.

To the behaviorists, the humanists are fuzzy-minded, romantic and unscientific—and are leading us to disaster with the "carrot" of freedom and no controls. Some behaviorists say they are the true humanists.

To the humanists, behaviorists, by and large, are scripting a "Clockwork Orange" future for mankind. Some admire behavior modification therapy and would like to see it adapted to humanistic goals—but (and it is a big but) with the control coming from the person himself.

Fortunately, the humanists overall show a talent for the self-awareness they preach.

Psychologist Richard Farson, for example, cautions that "peak experiences" may only have meaning in terms of valleys. "The fact that we can't always sustain such moments shouldn't make them invalid. We must learn to appreciate them while they last. Art and education also make life better—but. by the same token, make it more complicated and difficult. But then, everything we value tends to make life more difficult."

In "Power and Innocence," Rollo May once wrote: "The Human Potential Movement has fallen heir to the form of innocence prevalent in America, namely that we grow toward greater and greater moral perfection." He means, he explains, that the darker side of Man must be faced too, and sensitivity developed to both.

"A sense of wonder . . . ," Maslow has said of happy, creative people, "like that of an unspoiled child . . ."

The children's story, "The Wizard of Oz," tells how the Tin Woodman, the Cowardly Lion and the Scarecrow already have what they traveled so far to ask from the wizard–brains, courage and a heart. All the wizard could do for them was to make them aware that they already owned what they wanted so badly.

The Terms and Concepts

Here is a glossary of terms and concepts associated with the "new psychology:"

Altered states of consciousness—Defined by Hugh Redmond of Johnston College as ". . . no more than any state or experience that we have which is significantly different from the 'normal' way we experience ourselves or reality—as in meditation or the hypnagogic state which is when we are between dreaming and waking."

Therapy—An unpopular term among many humanistic psychologists who seek to "demmystify" the process. They believe that the medical model—the usual "sick-well" dichotomy—is distorting: that most people are not "patients" in the traditional sense but are in need of the releasing of self-actualizing potentialities; that the therapist should be open, honest and self-disclosing rather than "removed" as in the classic psychoanalytic mode.

Esalen—The original "growth center" on the rocky, coastal hills of Big Sur, where in experiential seminars, workshops, classes and "happenings," the Human Potential Movement began. It cautions that some of its programs may be "risky" to some people and that "no one come whose interest is 'cure.' " It explores trends in education, religion, philosophy and the physical and behavioral sciences which emphasize potentialities and values of human existence.

Aikido—An ancient Japanese martial art involving *ki* or the universal flow of energy which is inhibited by tension, conflict or competition. The idea is to remain centered, balanced and "in harmony with the laws of nature" in the face of attack or any attempt to throw you off balance.

Rolfing—A rigorous deep massage and manipulation of the body aimed at realigning the body structure so as to release excessive, long built-up tensions. The assumption is that one's body mirrors one's emotional past and that rolfing is the way to greater physical and emotional freedom and balance. Ten individual sessions are usually required. Also known as structural integration.

Gestalt—An existential, nonanalytic form of therapy developed by Fritz and Laura Perls and perfected at Esalen. The focus is on what IS rather than might have been, was, should be, could be, etc. The endless "why-because" games are avoided and emphasis is on choice and growth. A favorite technique involves a person being in the "hot seat" while the leader and others in the group make you act out who you are.

Autogenic feedback training—A Western method for learning to control such body functions as heartbeat and temperature. Alyce and Elmer Green of Menninger Clinic have adapted a system first developed by German psychoanalyst Johannes Schultz, which uses words and phrases to quiet the mind and turn it inward. They combine it with biofeedback to enhance awareness.

Human Potential Movement—A spontaneous middle-class cultural movement begun in the early '60s largely in California, which shares with humanistic psychology the revolt against "dehumanizing" instituions and practices believed to lead to flat, narrow, self-limiting lives, both professionally and otherwise. Emphasis is on seeing man as a whole being—a blend of body, mind, emotions and even spirit—and on tapping inherent built-in capacities for growth and development through a wide variety of sensory-awareness, encounter and other techniques.

Encounter—The ground rules for this group process is that participants be open and honest, avoid theorizing and instead talk about their feelings. The object is to explore interpersonal relations. Derived from several sources, it was a mainstay of Esalen for many years where it now includes techniques and ideas from gestalt, sensory awareness, bioenergetics, massage and structural integration.

Bioenergetics—The theory is that when people are hung up in the head, they are emotionally musclebound as well. This is another technique, like rolfing, which attempts to break those blocks and allow repressed emotions to rise into consciousness, according to Alexander Lowen, its founder.

Sensory awareness—Yet another method developed at Esalen for climinating the tyranny of the head, it includes relaxation verbal and nonverbal communication, sensory encounter, meditation, massage plus some yoga and zen.

Yoga—An ancient method of tuning in to both body and mind at the same time, of achieving deep relaxation, of toning muscles and inner organs, and as a means to higher self-realization in "cosmic consciousness." It has many forms which emphasize different things—Hatha, raja, bhakti and juana.

Zen—A classic, meditative practice which emphasizes no-mind and is an ancient gateway to deep inner-consciousness. One suspends thoughts and concentrates on breathing. Usually involves zazen—meditative sitting in the lotus position. One sect uses koans—ancient riddles ("What is the sound of one hand clapping?") intended to "trick" the mind into new thoughts and perceptions.

Biofeedback—A process by which you are wired to machines which allow you to see and monitor the continual responses of your heart, skin, blood pressure or brain waves and thus learn to consciously control them. An important byproduct is relaxation.

Transpersonal psychology—The avant-grade of humanistic psychology. What used to be suggested by "spiritual" or "transcendental" but something new. A nonreligious focus on what Abraham Maslow called "the farthest reaches" of the person; a questing for meaning and purpose which transcends individual differences. Sometimes called the "fourth psychology (the other three being behavioristic, psychoanalytic and humanistic.)

Psychosynthesis—The "farthest reaches" of transpersonal which begins with a synthesis of body-mind-emotions. A rich, electic blend of esoteric disciplines, exercises, imagery, movement, self-identification, creativity, gestalt, meditation, training of the will, symbolic art work, journal-keeping, ideal models and development of intuition. Developed by the late Italian humanistic psychoanalyst, Roberto Assagioli, and growing fast.

Massage—Not thought of as a "service" to be performed but as a "caring" relationship between two people. First consideration is given to the feelings and sensory relationship between both partners and then to technique.

Tibetan Buddhism—After Chinese troops invaded their homeland a decade ago, 4,000 lamas fled mountainous Tibet taking their eclectic religion (it incorporates all forms of Buddhism) around the world. The Vajrayana the oldest and most sophisticated sect which has a center in Berkeley—believes that enlightenment comes from stripping away false values from the "perfection" which lies beneath—a very humanistic and transpersonal view.

Parapsychology—That branch of psychology dealing with those psychic effects and experiences that appear to fall outside the scope of physical law such as ESP, telepathy and psychokinesis. First explored in the '30s by J. B. Rhine of Duke University and recognized two years ago by the National Assn. for the Advancement of Science as a legitimate area of inquiry.

Why Aren't We Using Science to Change Behavior?

B. F. Skinner

B.F. Skinner is a professor emeritus of psychology at Harvard University and author of "Beyond Freedom and Dignity." This article is excerpted, with permission, from Human Nature magazine.

Things are happening today that seem completely senseless, irrational, insane. The population of many countries has been allowed to reach a point at which two or three bad harvests will mean death by starvation for tens or even hundreds of millions of people. The United States and Russia spend a staggering part of their incomes on military systems that everyone hopes will never be used and will therefore prove to be a total waste. Our supplies of energy and many critical materials are running out, but we have done little to curtail current or future use. The environment grows steadily less habitable.

With the technologies of physics and biology, the species has solved problems of fantastic difficulty. Yet with respect to its own behavior, something always seems to go wrong. It is easy to understand why people ask: "When shall we have the behavioral science and technology we need to solve our problems?"

I believe that that is the wrong question and that we should be asking: "Why do we not use the behavioral science we already have?"

Consider the position of an agricultural specialist visiting a developing country. He sees farmers planting varieties of grain that are not best suited to the soil, rainfall or climate or the most resistant to disease. He sees them using too little fertilizer, fertilizer of the wrong kind. They are cultivating and harvesting with primitive equipment and processing and storing food in wasteful ways. If they then ask him, "When shall we have the agricultural science we need to make better use of our land?" must he not reply, "Why are you not using the science which already exists?"

There could be many answers. Special seed, fertilizer, machinery and storage space are costly. If money is available, those who have it must be convinced that spending it will bring results. New methods often throw people out of work and take control out of the hands of those who have profited from the old.

But there is a special kind of explanation that is more important. We have all heard stories of Third World farmers who change to new methods while they are being demonstrated, only to change back as soon as the reformer leaves. The stories may be apocryphal but they are easy to believe, because people do persist in doing things as they have always done them. The entrenched ways often postpone or block any advance toward something better.

We have no reason to feel superior to those who reject improved methods of agriculture, for we are doing much the same thing with respect to behavioral science. The parallel with agriculture breaks down because I cannot point to any part of the world today in which a behavioral technology flourishes, but recent advances in a science of behavior have led to substantial achievements in the management of human behavior in such special fields as government, industry, schools and colleges, institutions for the care of psychotic and retarded people, and personal and family counseling. I shall not review this work, or try to indicate how extensive it is. I simply want to ask why it is not more widely accepted in the solution of our problems.

The main obstacle is the entrenchment of old practices—in this case, old ways of thinking about human behavior. It is not so much the complexity of human behavior that causes trouble as the traditional practice of looking for explanations inside the behaving person. People are said to act as they do because of their feelings, their states of mind, their intentions, purposes and plans. They act because they will to act.

Let us look at some examples in which this abiding concern for an inner explanation has diverted attention from environmental measures that might have brought us closer to solving our problems. A feeling or state of mind familiar to everyone is confidence. The term is useful in daily communication. As a behaviorist I do not blush to say that I am at this moment possessed of a number of different feelings of confidence, and I shall list a few in order of degree. I have complete confidence that this chair and desk will hold me as I write. I have a fair degree of confidence that the words I am writing will eventually reach readers. I have some confidence that a number of those who start reading will finish the paper, and just a touch of confidence that some of them will come to behave in a slightly different way because of what they read. I thus report certain conditions of my own body.

But I hasten to point out that the degree of my

confidence is related to the extent of my past successes and failures. Similar desks and chairs have always held me. Similar writing has usually been published. But I am writing because of the consequences, not because of the feelings. My feelings and my behavior are collateral products of my personal history.

The point is important when the word is used in discussing practical affairs. The Journal of the Royal Society of Arts in London recently reported the remarks of a speaker who had discussed the appearance of the British countryside. He had told his audience that "the key to the survival of our present landscape lay in the word 'confidence'—without which people would not plant trees." In the past year or two, he said, "confidence had been completely destroyed."

But the important fact was simply that people no longer planted trees. Why did they not do so? It is not difficult to point to relevant facts. People move about a great deal these days, and when they do so they never watch a tree they have planted grow to maturity. As new roads are built and land is broken up for housing developments, trees are likely to be wantonly destroyed. More people now live in cities where the government plants the trees. Changes of this sort make it less likely that people will plant trees, and are, therefore, the real key to the survival of a landscape. There is no reason to say that they first destroy confidence in tree-planting; "confidence" is not a key to anything.

Several years ago, in a weekly news magazine, David E. Lilienthal discussed "the prevailing American mood," which he said "has become negative and fearful." It is "a mood of self-doubt and fear which paralyzes the very will to act," and, he added, it is the will to act that alone can "remove the causes of fear and lack of confidence." What America needed was more confidence, and Lilienthal offered the Tennessee Valley Authority as an example.

In the early 1930s the soil in the valley of the Tennessee River had lost its fertility, the forests had been almost destroyed, the land was eroding and nothing much could be done. People were idle and poor.

After the TVA dams were built, electric power and fertilizer were available and the people turned to new methods of agriculture and restored the land. Their incomes rose and the valley became green. Lilienthal attributed this highly desirable change to "restored self-confidence." But surely it was the dams and their products that made the difference. People began to do things they could not do before, and being successful, they no doubt felt confident.

When we speak of a nation's confidence in itself, the behavior at issue is much more complex than planting trees, and we are therefore much more likely to give confidence a power of its own. But if we are content to say that all America needs today is a new spirit of confidence, we shall neglect the things that can be done to bring about the changes we desire.

Feelings play a different and possibly more destructive role when they are seen not as causes that precede behavior but as values that follow it. Nutritious food is essential to the survival of the individual; is it not therefore extremely important that it taste good? Sexual behavior is essential to the survival of the species; is it not extremely important that sexual contact feel good?

But the important thing for the individual and for the species is not how things taste or feel but whether they are reinforcing—that is, whether they strengthen the behavior upon which they are contingent. Susceptibilities to reinforcement have presumably evolved because of their survival value. When, through a mutation, an organism's behavior is more strongly reinforced by nutritious food or sexual contact, the organism is more likely to get the food that it needs and to have offspring. The increased susceptibility to reinforcement is then contributed to the species. The important thing is that the susceptibility should survive. The feelings involved are incidental.

The same thing is true of social reinforcers, which are more likely to be called values. People are said to treat each other in ways that express compassion and love and which inspire gratitude, but the important thing is the contribution of this treatment to the way the culture functions. The kind of behavior we describe as ethical makes a group function more effectively. The feelings or states of mind associated with such behavior are collateral products.

Happiness is a feeling often taken as a value. We often feel happy when we behave in ways that lead to the possession of goods, and we then mistakenly take the possession to be the cause of the feeling.

Whole philosophies of government have been based on the theory that if goods are distributed "to each according to his need," people will be happy. But happiness is the accompaniment of successful action, rather than of whatever goods the action brings. It is characteristic of getting, rather than of possessing. Possession leads to happiness only when it makes further action possible. Whether people are happy is of great political significance, but a subjective measure of the quality of life will do little more than tell us whether most people are in situations that allow them to act successfully.

And so, in general, we enjoy life and call the world beautiful and ourselves free and happy when our behavior leads to an abundance of good things. No structural account of the things themselves or any analysis of the feelings that arise when these things strengthen behavior will make life more enjoyable and ourselves freer and happier. Only discovering the contingent relations between specific behavior and its consequences will help us move toward those goals.

Such a program does not rob people of their feelings. It simply puts feelings in their proper place, and by doing so allows us to move more rapidly toward the kind of environment in which they can be enjoyed. In refusing to accept feelings and states of mind as causes, we do not make the behavior that is said to follow from them any less important; instead we make it possible to deal with behavior more successfully.

There must be some reason why we have failed to make the same kinds of technological advances in the management of human behavior that are so obvious in other fields; the reason could be our lingering commitment to the individual as an initiating agent. When it comes to human behavior, seemingly trivial causes have profound effects, and there is a historical example which illustrates the point. I am not a historian, nor do I usually trust arguments based upon history, but in this instance the evidence is, I think, persuasive.

From the Fifth Century BC to about 1400 AD, China was as advanced in physical technology as any culture in the world. The recent exhibition of early Chinese pottery and ceramic and bronze sculptures sent around the world by the Chinese government displays an art and a technology fully equal to those of the Greeks of the same period. The two cultures maintained a comparable position for nearly 2,000 years. Then three great Chinese inventions—the compass, gunpowder and moveable type—brought about extraordinary changes. But not in China. Gunpowder was of little practical use in China because military activities there were ceremonial and largely under the control of astrologers. Long sea voyages were forbidden and the compass did little to increase the efficiency of coastal shipping. The Chinese system of notation, with its thousands of characters, could not take advantage of moveable type.

But the West seized upon these three great Chinese inventions and exploited them with extraordinary results. With the compass the West explored the world, and with gunpowder conquered it. Moveabe type and the printing press brought the revival of learning and the spread of western thought. As William McNeill points out in "The Rise of the West," while Chinese inventions were changing western culture, China remained a medieval society. Certain inoffensive cultural practices had deprived it of the benefit of its own discoveries.

Something of that same sort may be happening again. This time western culture may suffer from essentially ceremonial, astrological and geomantic practices. China, fortunately untouched by the Greek "discovery of the mind," could take over the behavioral equivalents of compass, gunpowder and moveable type and dominate a new era. But perhaps it is not too late to profit from our discovery of behavioral science and use it to help solve the problems facing the world now.

Shaping Behavior Contest for Minds

Joel Greenberg

At the center of the conflict is the very nature of man.

It's 1984, or sometime thereafter, and you're getting ready for work. You smile into the bathroom mirror and soothing strains of Brahms' "Eternal Love" fill the air. When the smiling stops, so does the music.

You greet your fellow workers with a cheerful "good morning," and they respond with warm handshakes and grins. Any other greeting, and they would ignore you.

Those are the rules.

The rest of the day, and month, and year, are governed by similar "rewards" and "non-rewards." Your behavior becomes nearly automatic. You are "happy."

That this type of society—or worse—will become a reality in America is a growing fear among a significant number of psychologists.

They are concerned about "behavior modification"—a form of therapy that has been highly successful in the 1970s in treating certain emotional illnesses and mental retardation.

Particularly in cases of severe retardation, autism, learning disabilities and toilet training, few argue with the effectiveness of the technique.

Rather, it is the use of behavior modification to control "healthy" populations in schools, businesses, towns and perhaps entire societies that is spurring nightmarish predictions.

Behaviorists who advance such far-reaching uses of control say the fears are unfounded. Applied properly, they say, behavioral techniques will mold a happier, more productive culture free of war and major conflict.

They note that industry and education have already begun to use behavior modification, and with encouraging results.

Their critics—mainly of the "humanistic," individualized school of psychology—remain far from convinced. Some predict nothing less than a "Clockwork Orange" society of automatons with no free will to act as they please.

At the center of the conflict is nothing less than the very nature of human beings.

Free will is not a factor, some behaviorists say, because people have practically none to begin with. Like an animal's search for food and shelter, man's search for happiness is almost totally dictated by the outside environment and events over which he has no control, they say.

Humanists counter that free will is the major factor that separates man from lesser forms of life. Behavior control is dangerous, they say, because it works, and could effectively stamp out man's humanness by robbing him of his free will.

"Behavior control does not involve a change in attitude or motivation—it's not much different from the way we train dogs and horses," says one critic.

The debate has become so heated and widespread that the entire question of behavior control and personal freedom was the theme of the recent annual meeting of the *American Psychological Association* in Washington, D.C.

Behavior modification is basically a system where rewards are administered to a person who behaves in a desired way. Undesired behavior results in no reward or some form of punishment.

Rewards can range from candy to money to subtle actions, such as friendship and certain privileges. Punishments may be simply the withholding of those things or in some cases, the administration of "aversive" techniques, such as electric shock.

Though behaviorism was founded by John B. Watson in 1912, it was not until the early 1970's that it became widely popularized by Harvard University psychologist B.F. Skinner.

Skinner, a spry, skinny 72-year-old man, astounded the psychological community with his book, "Beyond Freedom and Dignity." He proposed boldly that man has no free will and would be infinitely better off in a controlled society governed by a complex system of rewards and punishments for almost all aspects of behavior.

Since then, the therapeutic use of behavior modification has spread rapidly throughout the country. Along with it—though not necessarily a product of behavior modification—has been a boom in the use of psychoactive (behavior changing) drugs; and a partial resurgence of psycho surgery, an updated form of lobotomy.

Behavior modification is threatening to traditional psychotherapists because it ignores such long-held

 From *The Miami Herald*, October 3, 1976. Reprinted by permission.

Freudian concepts as the subconscious and intellect. Instead, it focuses on comparatively mechanical means of changing a person's current actions to what the therapist thinks they should be.

Says Skinner, simply: "I don't believe feelings or states of mind are important."

Personally, Skinner—"Fred" to close acquaintances—projects an image far less threatening than the "Big Brother" portrait some have assigned him. He speaks softly, is quick to smile, and listens attentively to opposing arguments.

He talks soothingly of "designing a social environment in which people treat each other well, keep the population size within reasonable bounds, learn to work productively, preserve and enhance the beauty of the world and limit the use of energy and other resources."

Even Carl Rogers, Skinner's counterpart in the humanistic psychology movement, concedes that the two men "want the same things."

But their proposed means of achieving such long-sought human goals are so diametrically opposed that some humanists have called Skinner "the next Hitler."

Humanists believe that man has an infinite capacity to make choices and judgements on his own. Only by developing that capacity "within" the person—rather than by outside control—can man improve himself and create a better world, they say.

In contrast to behaviorism, humanism is practiced in relatively unstructured "encounter" sessions—sometimes painful meetings where people try to help uncover one another's inner feelings; or in various forms of introspection, where the individual confronts himself in isolation.

That philosophy has spawned a counter-behaviorism avalanche of "human potential" groups in this country over the past decade. Since the Esalen Institute in California kicked off the large-scale group encounter movement in the 1960s, hundreds of thousands of Americans have flocked to numerous personal growth programs in search of the road to nirvana.

There are now an estimated 8,000 ways to raise your consciousness in America. The methods have names like bioenergetics, est (Erhard Seminars Training), psychosynthesis, Silva Mind Control, Arica, and rolfing, along with meditation, yoga and many variations on the standard encounter technique.

All focus in one way or another on the individual's inner strength and power to develop it.

Rogers first began promoting personal growth methods in 1946 by organizing encounter groups where returning servicemen were encouraged to share their gut emotions.

"The human being is a trustworthy organism, and has vast abilities to improve himself if exposed to the right attitudinal climate," Rogers says. "The individual modifies his own behavior, rather than having someone else in control."

Therein lies the key to the controversy surrounding behavior modification: who will be chosen to manipulate the lives of others and decide what is "desirable" behavior, opponents ask. And what guarantee is there the controllers will not abuse such massive powers?

"I question whether an ordered, regulated life is the kind of life I want to live," says Carmi Harari, professor of psychology at Goddard College in Vermont and director of the Humanistic Psychology Center of New York. "No system of one person doing something to another leads to a very good end."

Skinner says that argument is academic, since we are already living in a highly controlled society, and one that is becoming more so every day.

Nearly everything we say and do, he suggests, results from a network of laws and controls imposed by government, businesses, school and social interaction with groups and individuals. Stopping at a red light, buying a certain brand of hot dogs, doing a homework assignment, showing up for work and even kissing your spouse or petting the dog are largely dictated by the conscious and unconscious rewards and punishments offered by each, according to Skinner. Such actions are not products of a person's free will, he says, because people are not free to choose.

National governments have historically chosen to direct societies through the use of legal punishments, or "aversive control," he says. Behaviorists should use their sophisticated techniques, Skinner says, to wrest such powers from the government and "return (to) the control of people by people."

Such a system would be based on positive rewards, rather than punishments such as imprisonment and monetary fines, he says. People would behave in order to gain something, rather than to avoid punishment for breaking a rule or law.

"I do not mean modification of behavior through the use of implanted electrodes or psychotropic drugs," assures Skinner. "I do not mean respondent conditioning with vomit-inducing drugs or electric shock."

Former APA President Kenneth B. Clark of the City University of New York created a national furor five years ago when he suggested using "peace pills" to control the destructive behavior of national leaders.

Clark, like Skinner, believes that the tools of power and control are much safer in the hands of behavioral scientists than in those of politicians.

"We must control the moral behavior and ethical perceptions of our national leaders," he said at this year's meeting, defending his previous stance.

"We need to control the human power drive, and we can control human abuses of power through science," Clark says. "The issue of behavior modification abuse is a danger we face now. The power and control of the human species is (already) in the hands of a very few people—for freedom to be meaningful, (that) species must survive."

How Psychology Can Shape the Behavior of People

Behavior modification is widely used in the treatment of emotionally disturbed, retarded or disruptive individuals. More recently, the technique has spread to "healthy" groups, such as industrial workers and school children, in an effort to increase productivity and learning.

The concept's roots were planted more than 70 years ago when Pavlov learned how to make dogs salivate on command. Several years later John B. Watson adopted the theory for human psychology.

Harvard psychologist B.F. Skinner created modern behaviorism when he learned that he could get almost any kind of behavior from a pigeon by rewarding and punishing properly.

Human application of behavior control has grown rapidly in the 1970s. Some of the ways that scientists mold human behavior include:

● Positive reinforcement—rewarding someone with kind actions or words or material goods if they act in the desired way. The technique is the basis for teaching retarded or chronically mentally ill persons to be more self-sufficient.

● Extinction—ignoring disruptive conduct, such as a student's annoying actions in class. At the same time, the teacher rewards another well-behaved student with a compliment.

● Contracting—negotiating an actual, written contract for behavior between husband and wife, employer and employe, patient and therapist or parent and child. Living up to the contract brings certain rewards, primarily an improved relationship between the parties concerned. Breaking the agreement may carry specific punishments.

● Token economy—reinforcing a person's desired behavior with tokens that entitle the person to certain privileges or monetary purchases. This is frequently used in mental hospital settings.

● Behavior rehearsal—enacting a scene of conflict between two people before it actually takes place. Rehearsing a "healthy" response can lead to a more healthy relationship, some scientists say.

● Desensitization—simulating a situation that may be frightening to an individual. This method is used primarily in treating persons suffering from fears and phobias, and may help them realize much of their distress is unfounded.

● Aversion therapy—punishing undesired behavior with electric shock, discomfort-inducing drugs or other means. The technique, severely criticized by many scientists, is used mainly in treating sex offenders, chronic drug addicts, and other persons with extreme personality problems.

Skinner says he too is against the method, but concedes there are some instances in which "nothing else works."

Along with the behavior modification boom has come the widespread use of psychoactive drugs to help people cope with the pressures of modern society; and, in some cases, the continued use of psychosurgery to alter the behavior of persons with "incurable" emotional handicaps.

Even those who might agree idealistically with Skinner and Clark say there is one fatal flaw in their vision of a utopian society: ultimately, some person or group must decide what is "desirable" for everyone else.

And that, they say, smacks of totalitarianism.

"The question is not what can we do, but what ought we do?" says Harari. "You either view people as innately good, or wild, antisocial beings that need control. The aim of control is to suppress the human spirit. Nazi Germany used the very techniques we are talking about."

He and others argue that no one, no matter how good his intentions, has the capacity or the right to decide what is best for other people.

Responds Skinner: "The implication is that a technology of behavior will naturally fall into the hands of despots. It will no doubt do so if no action is taken by those who are not despots. Behavioral scientists are no more likely to use their principles to control people than atomic scientists are to build and use atomic weapons."

The humanists advocate systems of far less control than exists now, where people have a wide range of choices based on what they want, not on a contrived reward.

In education, for example, Rogers advances a "person-centered approach" where students share more in deciding what is to be taught, and the teacher does "not hide behind the instructor's mask."

Harari agrees. "A kid who is ordered around all the time never makes intelligent choices."

Rogers says the experiments with this approach in the classroom and industry, as well as encounter groups, have yielded not only more humanistic relationships, but increased efficiency as well.

Behaviorists such as Nathan H. Azrin of Anna State Hospital in Illinois would disagree.

One of behavior modification's staunchest proponents, Azrin states flatly that the technique has "no competition" for effectiveness in areas such as classroom management, retardation, child discipline at home, obesity, fears and phobias and some marital problems.

Skinner is reluctant to talk about the exact mechanics of molding a happier society. But when pressed, he speculates like Rogers that at least initially the process could begin—and already has to an extent—in schools, offices and controlled communities such as he described in his book, "Walden II."

Some observers believe much of the behaviorism/humanism controversy is premature because neither side has found an effective technique to substantially alter the course of the human race.

"We're a long way from 1984, even though the years are getting pretty close," says Nicholas Hobbs, a Vanderbilt University psychology professor.

Hobbs, not opposed to behaviorism on ethical grounds, says he favors it, "everywhere it would work. But what upsets me are the extravagant statements that (behavior control) can engineer all kinds of happiness and social contentment."

Controlling the behavior of individuals is far more complex than many, including Skinner, would admit, Hobbs says. "In some cases, it's probably more effective to simply ask a youngster to do something than spend days trying to coax him with sugar cubes," he suggests.

He believes Skinner has admirable motives, but may be unrealistic when he talks of applying his techniques to 200 million people.

But even Hobbs says Skinner's visions of totally engineered societies "eventually may come to be possible."

And that possibility even now is frighteningly real to humanists and other critics of behavior control.

"Skinner has made a lot of contributions," says Harari. "And I'm not saying there is only one right way to do things—it simply doesn't exist. But if Skinner's engineered society ever came about, it would indeed be a Clockwork Orange situation. Make no mistake, we *can* train human beings to do almost anything. Behavior control can work, and with devastating effects.

TESTING DR. FREUD

ROGER P. GREENBERG
and
SEYMOUR FISHER

Believe it or not, thousands of scientific studies have been performed worldwide to check out the validity of Freud's ideas. Now two psychologists have reviewed the evidence and found that Freud holds up pretty well, after all.

Roger P. Greenberg is Professor of Psychology and Director of Psychology Internship Training at the Upstate Medical Center, State University of New York, Syracuse.

Seymour Fisher is Professor of Psychology at the same institution.

Sigmund Freud's pronouncements have permeated major aspects of our society. His human development theories have channeled the thoughts and actions of millions of parents concerned with such issues as toilet training, feeding practices and the imparting of sexual information to their children. In addition, his notions about how behavior is motivated and the nature of the unconscious have been imbedded in the core of work done by a multitude of social scientists, philosophers and mental health practitioners. Characters in countless plays and novels have been similarly built on Freud's views of people and their dreams. Perhaps most important of all, Freud's views have been widely adopted by many persons as a way of understanding how they function psychologically. Thus, they may make important decisions about themselves and others on the basis of Freud's model of personality.

Strange as it may seem, Freud's ideas initially swept the United States and other parts of the Western world with virtually no proof of validity. Further, psychoanalysis as a form of treatment for neurotic disturbances grew to be the accepted approach without an iota of objective evidence offered for its effectiveness. For years, the unexpected insights and scope of Freud's ideas armored them with an almost self-evident power of truth. It was as if a new psychological world had been discovered, and people were so fascinated with the novelty of the sights that few questioned their reality. Adding to the fascination was the fact that the theories provided vivid new perspectives for experiences, feelings and events that touch the lives of everyone. The family, dreams, sexuality and childhood are among the many areas that took on new meaning through the vistas opened up by Freud's writings.

Naturally, over time, Freud's ideas spawned a wide variety of critics, skeptics and revisionists. Yet, both the detractors and supporters of Freud relied more on authority and passionate belief than on empirical evidence to justify their positions. Personal convictions, "clinical experiences" and loud voices were all pressed into service to try to resolve the disputes engendered by Freud's theories. Without objective and systematic tests, there was no logical way for such disputes to be resolved, and the arguments droned on. The validity of Freud's formulations thus seemed to be forever relegated to a twilight zone just beyond the reach of empirical science.

About seven years ago, we decided to gather every piece of scientific data we could find bearing on Freud's work. Our chief goal was to fairly and comprehensively assess the validity of his work. The outcome of this search for evidence became our book—*The Sci-*entific Credibility of Freud's Theories and Therapy, published by Basic Books in 1977.

Obviously, we were aware of how prodigiously Freud had labored to present his theories as rationally convincing. Yet, as with all clinical observers, Freud was not in a good position to present scientifically convincing data. He could report his observations and conclusions, but there was no way of testing for bias and distortion. Nor was there any way of telling how much Freud had influenced patient reports. Such problems of reliability and validity have continually plagued psychoanalysts. Many scientists eventually threw up their hands, declaring that psychoanalytic theories were so subjective and illogical that they could see no way of ever deciding whether the ideas were right or wrong.

To the surprise of many people, we discovered that literally thousands of scientific studies performed by investigators all over the world had attempted to test various aspects of Freud's thinking. A wealth of information was also discovered in unpublished doctoral dissertations. By integrating this great mass of data, we were able to conclude that Freud was right in some areas, wrong in others and at times too vague to be put to the test.

In our quest for the evidence on Freud's thought, we discovered that it is possible to assess his proclamations objectively on the basis of a wide spectrum of empirical findings. Our search also makes clear that psychoanalysis is not an entity that must be totally rejected or accepted as a package. It is a complex structure consisting of many parts; some of which should be accepted, others rejected and the rest at least partially reshaped.

From *Human Behavior*, September 1978. Reprinted by permission of the authors.

TREATMENT OUTCOMES

What happened to the patients Freud treated? He placed relatively little stress on patient outcome in his writings and focused more on trying to explain the personality dynamics of the people he saw. Surprisingly, we found that he described in detail only four cases he had seen using psychoanalytic therapy. Of the four, only one showed any evidence of significant improvement. It is both striking and curious that Freud chose to demonstrate the utility of psychoanalytic therapy through the presentation of largely unsuccessful cases. Indeed, we were forced to conclude that he never presented any evidence, in case study or statistical form, demonstrating the beneficial effects of Freudian treatment for a significant number of his own patients.

We examined a wide array of studies in trying to come to some conclusions about the treatment effectiveness of current Freudian analysts. The literature reveals that chronic neurotic patients achieve better results with analysis than without treatment. However, granting certain limitations in the data, there is currently no evidence that a therapy labeled "psychoanalysis" is either usually better or worse than approaches given other labels including psychoanalytically oriented therapy. It would appear that there are overlapping active ingredients in a number of psychotherapy treatment approaches. Also, there is evidence that analysts vary, and the results of psychoanalytic treatment may be quite dependent upon who the treating analyst is.

Incidentally, our review of the data suggests that psychoanalysis may be underestimated as a potential treatment for physical disorders. Symptoms associated with such diseases as ulcers and colitis have been found to respond to this treatment approach. Surveys of patients with different diagnoses also hint that psychosomatic symptoms may be particularly responsive to this type of intervention. In addition, one fascinating study demonstrated that patients treated psychoanalytically were less likely than members of the general population to enter a hospital for any health reason during the five years following treatment. The finding is made more impressive by the fact that the treated patients had used hospitals to a significantly greater degree than the rest of the population during the five years before their psychoanalytic treatment.

On the basis of the evidence, a number of Freud's ideas about treatment are open to question. For example, Freud's admonition that analysts should remain "emotionally cold" and "opaque" is at variance with a number of studies indicating that therapists tend to achieve better therapeutic results when they show more warmth, empathy and involvement with their patients. We also feel that Freud underestimated the importance of therapist influence and suggestion, which were so evident in his own work with patients. There is a good deal of experimental literature now indicating that many types of symptoms—from phobias to sexual disorders—can be dealt with directly by straightforward therapist intervention.

Freud's early notion that personality change can be automatically achieved solely through insight does not seem to square with what we now know; even he eventually moved away from a direct link between insight and change. He developed the idea that the patient needed time with the analyst to "work through" resistances to newly acquired perceptions. The idea of a working-through process occurring before change takes place fits the research findings better than Freud's earlier implication of symptom abatement arising from a brilliant flash of insight.

Freud's concern that an analyst's blind spot could lead to harm for patients appears justified. As he predicted, maladjusted therapists, whose own needs predominate over those of their patients, have been found to be harmful to those they work with.

DREAMS

No discussion of Freud's ideas would be complete without considering his dream theory. He was particularly proud of it and saw it as a paradigm for many of his other models of how unconscious forces infiltrate behavior. In brief, he theorized that an individual's dream consists of both latent and manifest elements. The latent elements involve a secret unconscious wish that seeps out during sleep, when customary censoring controls are relaxed but that must be disguised so as not to alarm the dreamer. Incidentally, he thought that an important function of the disguising process was to preserve sleep. Presumably, if the forbidden wish were to gain open access to awareness, the dreamer would be jarred from sleep. This notion has not been substantiated by dream research that indicates that dreaming occurs in a regular cyclical fashion that is closer to a fixed biological rhythm than to a pattern indicating defensive adaptation to threatening material from moment to moment. In any case, Freud theorized that in the latent or disguised elements of the dream, the dreamer manages to vent a certain degree of tension built up in the unconscious.

The manifest elements represent the story or facade introduced into the dream structure to camouflage the unconscious wish. Freud stated that the dream could be understood only after the manifest content had been penetrated and the underlying unconscious wish decoded. His dream theory has been widely accepted and typically provides the context for dream interpretation.

When we examined the considerable research literature concerned with dreaming, we did find support for the proposition that the dream has a venting function. It does serve to discharge tensions. Those deprived of dream time develop signs of discomfort and even disturbance. Also, consistent with the tension-venting hypothesis, individuals who are diagnosed as neurotic or psychotic, along with those undergoing increased life stresses, show a heightened intensity in their dreams. However, there is no evidence that each dream contains a secret unconscious wish. No one has reliably demonstrated that the dream is simply built around a forbidden wish. On the contrary, multiple studies have shown that the manifest content of the dream is not mere camouflage. Rather, it contains important and easily observable information about the dreamer's feelings, preoccupations, conflicts and personality. The so-called manifest content is no less, and may be more, revealing than the elusive latent content.

Overall, the research literature suggests that a dream is another form of thinking that occurs during sleep.

HOMOSEXUALITY

Although it is not well-known, Freud ascribed considerable importance to constitutional factors in the development of homosexuality. He considered bisexual elements to be present biologically in all persons but theorized that some individuals are born with a particularly intense bisexual makeup. They are more likely to be drawn to homosexual relationships. Unfortunately, little is scientifically known at present about the importance of constitutional factors in shaping homosexual preferences.

However, information has accumulated that does bear on Freud's model of how early relationships influence homosexual behavior. He proposed that the boy who is likely to become homosexual has had special difficulty in resolving his oedipal conflicts. More specifically, such a child is typified by an unusually intense "erotic attachment" to mother, which was "favored by too much love from the mother herself" and furthered by the "retirement or absence of the father during the childhood period." The intense oedipal conflict presumably associated with this pattern arouses great castration anxiety and concern

As such, it may have multiple functions. It may be a means for reviewing events, solving problems, mulling over anxieties or reexperiencing a pleasurable experience. Freud was

about penis loss. This, says Freud, becomes the basic cause for the homosexual's inability to take a woman as a love object. Not only does the homosexual equate any female love object with his intense forbidden relationship with his mother, but the sight of a woman's genitals, lacking a penis, magnifies his castration anxieties to an intolerable level. Freud depicted the male homosexual who is beset by such anxieties as retreating to an identification with mother, choosing to love others as he assumes she would.

The scientific literature is amazingly in accord with what Freud declared about the male homosexual's father. In study after study, this father emerges as unfriendly, threatening or difficult to associate with. He does seem to be the kind of person who would be an intense oedipal competitor. Less clear is whether the male homosexual's mother has been especially close and seductive toward him. After a careful analysis of the data, we conclude that the supportive studies have an edge over the negative ones. It is important to note that there is some scientific support for Freud's idea that homosexuals have elevated

correct in detecting that dreams may serve as vehicles to release tensions, but incorrect in assuming that they are containers for wishes too alarming for the dreamer to confront.

castration anxiety. There is also evidence that, during childhood, homosexuals are highly concerned about getting hurt and preoccupied with their physical frailty.

Freud's concepts about female homosexuality were relatively unclear and therefore difficult to evaluate. He did feel that constitutional bisexuality was just as important a factor as it was in the case of the male homosexual. Investigations of female homosexuals have affirmed, as Freud suggested, that they experience their fathers as unusually frustrating and disturbing. With minor exceptions, scientific observation indicates that female homosexuals do perceive their fathers as particularly unfriendly, unpleasant persons who have little to offer by way of a relationship. However, the available literature does not indicate that they see their mothers any differently than do heterosexual women. But it is difficult to evaluate this fact in view of Freud's vagueness about the nature of the female homosexual's perceptions of her mother. At present we are not yet in a position to decide whether Freud's concept of female homosexuality is reasonable.

PSYCHOANALYSIS

Originally, Freud was motivated to develop psychoanalysis because of his desire to help patients overcome a variety of symptoms. The emphasis was on the potential for treatment. Over time, however, the emphasis shifted toward attaining knowledge concerning how symptoms originate and what underlies them. The shift from treatment to understanding personality was paralleled by changes in Freud's techniques.

Initially, Freud, following the lead of Josef Breuer, tried to help patients overcome a variety of physical symptoms with no apparent organic basis by having them hypnotically reexperience traumatic memories and forgotten feelings. Freud concluded from his early cases that these "hysterical symptoms" had an unknown symbolic meaning that, once uncovered, would end the symptoms. The central therapeutic task was to help

a patient become aware of the repressed painful memories that lay beneath the symptoms. The therapy had a dual focus—gaining insights and overcoming resistances to "making the unconscious conscious."

When Freud realized that merely recalling forgotten memories was not enough to produce a therapeutic effect, he tried to help patients discover how their histories led them to distort present perceptions and behaviors. But the basic idea of trying to understand one's deepest thoughts and motivations continued. Freud assumed, particularly in his early writings, that the more thoroughly patients understood the historical roots of present behavior, the more likely they were to experience lasting and positive changes. Depth of exploration and potential for cure were directly linked. In addition, he initially implied that change would come automatically as

a result of the insights attained; so the therapist need make no special efforts to help patients to change their behavior or to overcome symptoms.

Freud supported his theory of therapy through published accounts of cases. Yet, as we have indicated, such accounts have serious drawbacks as evidence. They are open to many types of potential distortion and uncontrolled influences. Further, when we looked specifically at the material Freud reported, we found much inconsistency in what was reported in the different cases, along with a tendency to pick out only material supportive of particular ideas. We were intrigued too by how few cases Freud reported in any detail and the clear biases that were built into the sample of patients he worked with. Thus, although we know he saw many patients, he wrote at length about only 12 major cases and briefly mentioned

133 minor cases. Generalizations are also limited by the fact that the majority of Freud's published cases were upper-class, relatively young (between ages 20 and 44) females. The question of diagnosis is of similar concern. Freud suggested that the original patients were neurotic. Yet many have concluded that significant numbers of Freud's patients would be diagnosed as psychotic today. Numerous people are described as quite disturbed with hallucinations, delusions, bizarre symptoms and instances of disorganized thinking.

OEDIPUS COMPLEX

The postulation of an "Oedipus complex" involving sexual attractions and jealous hostility toward one's parents is one of the central ideas in Freud's theory of personality development. The way in which the child coped with the guilt, anxieties and conflicts of the Oedipal dilemma was thought to strongly influence later adaptation and the ability to comfortably enter into heterosexual relationships.

Freud speculated that fear (castration anxiety) was the primary factor in the resolution of the oedipal struggle for boys. The boy fantasizes that father will attack him if he continues to compete with father for mother. Therefore, mother is given up as a sex object, and identification with father takes place. The groundwork for the boy's conscience was laid through the act of identifying with father and his values. In short, the oedipal sequence was used to explain the process of sexual identification, the development of conscience, the channeling of sexual drives and the adjustment to the intimate relationships of family life.

Freud's oedipal formulations concerning women are much less clear and are difficult to evaluate. However, the scientific evidence generally indicates, as Freud suggested, that children do have to cope with erotic feelings toward the parent of the opposite sex and hostile feelings toward the same-sex parent. It is impressive, too, that investigations show that castration anxiety (fear of bodily harm or attack) is a relatively common occurrence in men and intensifies when they are exposed to erotic heterosexual stimulation. This is exactly what Freud would have predicted. The research literature also upholds the idea, derived from the oedipal theory, that women are more motivated by fears about loss of love.

Not all of Freud's oedipal ideas have stood up so well when tested. For example, there is little proof that oedipal problems crest at the time he pinpointed (roughly ages four through five). Also, many of Freud's ideas concerning the psychology of women are incorrect. Women do not, as he assumed, have more difficulties in attaining sexual identification. Nor do they usually experience their bodies as inferior to those of men because they have a vagina instead of a penis. Further, Freud's controversial idea that the sexually mature woman prefers vaginal to clitoral stimulation is completely contradicted by the data. In fact, women who prefer vaginal to clitoral stimulation tend to be more anxious and experience their bodies as more depersonalized. They have an exaggerated need to mute the intensity of experiences. Finally, we should note that Freud was not correct in his assumption that children evolve a conscience primarily out of fear arising during the resolution of oedipal conflicts. Parent nurturance, warmth and friendliness have a good deal more to do with the acceptance of moral standards than does fear.

ORAL AND ANAL PHASES

Freud's theory of personality was built on the idea that each person passes through a series of developmental stages in which different zones of the body acquire particular prominence. Freud speculated that every infant and child must deal with a succession of early experiences that require mastery over impulses involving different body areas. In the first or oral phase, children focus on their mouths and must master problems relating to incorporation and the impulse to use the mouth for biting or expressing anger. The anal phase follows, during which children learn control of the anal sphincter and master the related problems of dealing with authority figures and the development of self-control. Next in sequence is the genital phase, where children must resolve the "oedipal" conflict caused by being sexually attracted to the parent of the opposite sex.

Individuals were thought to move smoothly through the oral, anal and genital phases unless they encountered some negative conditions in their environment. Such conditions could partially "fixate" a person at one of the earlier phases and place a recognizable stamp on the personality. Thus, oral characters were described as people who because of either early overindulgence or frustration of oral needs had not mastered oral problems. The result was individuals who have an unusual need to be close to others and to gain their support. In contrast, the anal character, due to experiences around the toilet-training period, presumably has unconscious wishes to soil and to vent aggressive impulses that are "bad" and "dirty." Fears of "losing control" and letting things spill out remain paramount.

Our review of the scientific literature uncovered a good deal of evidence for many of Freud's ideas concerning the oral and anal personality types. Researchers have shown, for example, utilizing a wide array of measures, that the oral personality traits—dependency, passivity and pessimism—do tend to cluster together in people as Freud predicted. Also, people unusually preoccupied with oral themes (as measured, for instance, by the number of food- or eating-related responses they produce on the *Rorschach Inkblot Test*) tend to crave approval and support from those they consider significant. Oral people use submission and passivity to maintain contact with potential supporters. Evidence suggests, for example, that such individuals will distort their own judgments to conform to the unreasonable judgments of others who are perceived as important. There are hints, too, that the orally oriented may cultivate skills that lead them to be sensitive to the motives of other people, presumably so they can maintain contacts and ties.

Particularly solid support has emerged for the idea that people who are especially sensitive to oral images and dependency themes are also prone toward overeating, smoking and consuming large amounts of alcohol. One study demonstrated that oral characters are particularly motivated when rewarded by food.

Freud's concept of an anal character has also received impressive support. Studies indicate that the three characteristics of the anally oriented—orderliness, parsimony and obstinacy —do tend to hang together as Freud suggested. In addition, one study found that the amount of anxiety expressed by people about anal matters predicted how carefully they arranged magazines that were in disarray. Anality thus predicted a concern for order. The same study showed that difficulty in coping with a fecallike substance related to resistance or obstinacy in shifting one's opinions.

In contrast to the findings for the oral character, anality has been related to a negative response to praise but a positive response to monetary rewards. Another indication of the link between anality and parsimony—or the desire to hoard and collect—is revealed in a study that found a relationship between being a stamp collector and selectively responding to words with anal connotations. Overall, a full reading of the evidence seems to impressively support Freud's model of oral and anal personality types.

We want your advice.

Any anthology can be improved. This one will be— annually. But we need your help.

Annual Editions revisions depend on two major opinion sources: one is the academic advisers who work with us in scanning the thousands of articles published in the public press each year; the other is you—the person actually using the book.

Please help us and the users of the next edition by completing the prepaid article rating form on the last page of this book and returning it to us. Thank you.

Toward a Psychology of Natural Behavior

Robert Sommer

Social psychologist Robert Sommer is professor of psychology and environmental studies at the University of California at Davis.

Psychology entered the laboratory almost a century ago and has not yet recovered from the experience. Since the centenial of the first psychological laboratory founded by Wilhelm Wundt in 1879 is rapidly approaching, this seems a fitting time to examine the role played by this important and ubiquitous institution in the development of psychological research.

It has been only recently that the effects of laboratory settings have been made the subject of social psychological investigation. Researchers had operated in much the same way as the experimental psychologists who tested rats, mice and monkeys without ever knowing the effects of the cage environment upon the animals. The trend to the laboratory peaked some time in the 1960s. Although things seem to have improved, traces of the preoccupation with control and contrived encounters still remain.

Too many researchers look upon field research as laboratory studies done outdoors. Rather than leave the laboratory, these psychologists have either snail-like carried their laboratories with them or tried to turn the world into an experimental chamber with separable dependent and independent variables. No doubt those researchers who are dark-adapted and sallow from years spent in dim closets gazing through one-way mirrors will benefit from the fresh air and exercise, but there is more to field work than this. What is omitted or neglected is sensitivity to the setting. The credo of the naturalist is to study nature while disturbing it as little as possible since any deviation from natural conditions will lower the validity and generalizability of the results.

The term field can be applied to any setting which has not been deliberately created by the psychologist. Appropriate research techniques include observation, archival research using trace measures, surveys and experiments. These differ in their degree of reactivity, i.e., in the extent to which they affect on-going behavior. There are frequently good reasons for introducing a variable into a field setting on a systematic basis. The crucial question is whether the changes and the means of introduction are appropriate to the setting. If they are, generalization to life will be easier. Instead of spending weeks on the street corner waiting for an event

to occur, such as a person stopping to ask for assistance, it is terribly tempting to stage it artificially. I will not deny the value of shortcuts when the terrain is well known. Common sense tells us that when an area is *terra incognita,* one should be wary of shortcuts. It is important to know not only people's reactions to someone asking for help, but how often this actually occurs, the sorts of people they approach and so on. Such information is indispensible in designing a field experiment and in generalizing from it. Ideally the sequence should *always* be non-reactive observation before interviews or experimentation.

If field research is not the same as doing laboratory studies outdoors, what is it? The answer can be seen in the work of those psychologists who have studied ongoing behavior in an environmental context, people such as Evelyn Hooker, who has been studying the gay community in Los Angeles for several decades; the Sherifs in their studies of teen-age gangs; and Stanley Milgram who has been doing research on sensory overload and alienation in the city. Milgram does not study overload in some abstract sense, but as it occurs in a particular neighborhood among a particular group of residents. When the process under study cannot be observed directly, questionnaires and interviews are indispensible.

Roger Barker and his associates have pioneered a strictly naturalistic approach to child psychology at their field station in Oskaloosa, Kansas. Barker's students subsequently applied his methods to churches, schools, public housing projects and most recently, Dew Line stations. When I reviewed a book of Barker's, I was struck by how few of his studies and those of his students had appeared in APA journals. This situation is not atypical of other field researchers. The ingenuity that is required for doing naturalistic research is also helpful in locating sympathetic outlets for publication.

Some years ago, I was interested in testing the social facilitation hypothesis that people in groups would drink faster and more than people alone. The method I used was straightforward and appropriate both to the hypothesis and the beer parlor. My students and I visited each of the pubs in a middle-sized city, ordered a beer, and then sat down and recorded on napkins or pieces of newspaper the consumption of lone and group

From *APA Monitor*, January 1977. Copyright 1977 by the American Psychological Association. Reprinted by permission.

drinkers. We found that group drinkers consumed more, not because they drank faster, but because they remained longer in the pub. The longer people remained, the more they drank.

It can be noted that time-in-the-setting is usually excluded from social facilitation studies done in the laboratory. People are tested alone and in groups for specified periods of time and their performance compared. The notion that people in groups would remain longer did not enter experiments on social facilitation because time-in-the-setting is not a typical laboratory variable. Under natural conditions, however, we vote with our feet in expressing our likes and our dislikes. The reviewer of my paper expressed concern that I had not controlled the two populations, and there might have been other differences (unspecified) between lone and group drinkers to influence these results.

Perhaps there were, I don't know. We sampled all 32 beer parlors in town and there were no obvious differences between the lone and group drinkers in age or dress. There was no way that we could control whether people who entered the premises sat alone or in groups. Maybe we could have undertaken random assignment in the basement of the psychology department if we had gotten everyone's permission and authority to do this from the state liquor commission and money to buy the beer, but I am not sure that the results would have been valid or generalizable to any other place. My colleague Rudy Kalin sponsored beer busts for fraternity students and found that their responses in their own living rooms were very different from those in the laboratory.

The important questions in assessing a naturalistic study are whether the researcher learns what went on and whether this knowledge is important to a psychological audience. The notion of control has little or no meaning in a naturalistic study. It can be imposed in some metaphorical sense while analyzing the data by breaking down observations into categories, but this bears so little resemblance to the behaviorist's use of control that it is better to dispense with the term.

One cannot learn how to do field research simply by reading about it. We must develop the means to provide supervised experiences in field observation and recording. This may involve the establishment of research stations in the community. If field stations can operate in Oskaloosa and the Gombe Reserve, why not in St. Louis and Cleveland?

Barker and his associates operated in a completely open relationship with the residents of Oskaloosa. They knew he was there to study them and they accepted it. In settings with transient populations, such as street corners or playgrounds, this may not be possible. Researchers must rely either on non-reactive observation such as sitting on a park bench and watching children play or participant observation where one has a role in the action. Psychologists may opt for participation observation since it provides the opportunity to be in a service capacity as well. It is a method ideally suited for the clinical student who must serve an internship at a mental health clinic. Field research will make much more sense to such students than the umpteenth correlation of the MMPI with the Rorschach.

At present, there are not many dissertation committees that would allow a purely observational study. Observation has been equated with anecdote, and is considered less rigorous and reliable than experimentation. This is partly true because psychologists receive no training and encouragement in observation and therefore most don't do it very well. In theory it shouldn't require training to become a naturalist, since it amounts to doing what comes naturally. However, following decades of formal schooling and discipline in classification and conceptual learning, a student's abilities to observe have largely atrophied. Students look at things and try to figure out what they are supposed to remember. Training in observation requires some bracketing of categorical thinking.

The ability to "read" environments is the basis of the naturalist's craft. One is able to examine a living room, classroom or street corner in terms of constraints this puts upon behavior, the kind of actions it facilitates, encourages, demands. There are lessons in the kind of furniture in a person's living room, how it is arranged, how it is cared for, the decorations, the location of the television set or stereo, and so on. One can also "read" a city park, prison or restaurant interior, in each case attending to somewhat different items. Experience in making observations and comparing different settings provides clues as to what is important. Frequently the omission of something (the absence of books in a living room, or the absence of wall decorations in a college classroom), is as significant as what is there.

Although one begins with seemingly mundane behaviors, rather quickly the questions become more complex and far reaching. Why aren't there green plants in a classroom? Should there be plants there? What is the role of decorations or amenities in motivation, interest or learning? Do people have a need at some level for plants? Is there likely to be vandalism and if so, how can it be minimized? How can living plants be maintained with a transient population?

It doesn't matter where one starts, the inquiring mind soon reaches questions of considerable relevance and depth. Not all of these may be regarded as psychological questions—some may be more adequately handled by sociologists, anthropologists, horticulturists or police. However, the relationship between people and living plants is of considerable ethological and psychological importance and it has hardly been touched as a research area. There are profound design implications in giving apartment dwellers, workers in high-rise office buildings or college students in dormitories, prisoners, and old people in convalescent homes access to garden plots or at least a window location for growing plants.

We will have to give students specific skills for handling the richness, complexity and flow of ongoing behavior—courses in content analysis, behavioral mapping, observational methods, archival measurement and photography. The camera is an indispensable tool for gathering naturalistic data and conveying it to others. The specialty within psychology that has had the most experience using photography is animal behavior which also has a strong field orientation. I have occasionally found it helpful to ask my students to sketch a place to sensitize them to what is going on. There are methods for using the camera or the sketch pad in a minimally reactive way without playing "super spy." Often the best approach is to be very open and obvious as a tourist might act.

Very few psychology departments offer courses in field work and indeed there are very few psychologists who are capable of teaching it. The situation is better in anthropology where studies *in situ* of both humans and non-humans are emphasized, and somewhat better in those sociology departments where the traditions of the Chicago school are still felt. Of all the behavioral sciences, psychology lags furthest behind in the development of field methods. Serendipity is the rule in field research and flexibility of mind and quick reflexes are necessary to capitalize upon it. Because there has been very little money available for naturalistic studies, field researchers are skilled at borrowing, improvising and scrounging. This is not a bad model for graduate students and researchers in an era of tight budgets. No-budget research often involves the use of local people as data collectors and analysts.

Too often the means of our research have become the ends. Animal behavior which was once seen as a way of learning about people became a subject of study in its own right. The same occurred with statistics, methodology and test construction. This is not necessarily undesirable since specialists in techniques are needed as well. However, we have to make sure that the original goals are not forgotten in the search for better tools and theories. We also should try to learn the extent to which this means-centeredness is produced by institutional and professional pressures. And we are going to have to be sure that at least some of our graduates have a problem-solving orientation because we can't go on indefinitely identifying group differences and computing correlation coefficients.

When it comes to making decisions on campus, issues such as enrollment predictions, curriculum planning, traffic flow, attitudes towards intramural sports, or the effectiveness of counseling services, psychology faculty operate as blindly as faculty from other departments.

Training in evaluation and generating useful data could be complementary to using the campus as a research station. For this to happen, we will have to change student and faculty conceptions about the nature of appropriate research. Somehow we have gotten to the point where studying monkeys in cages or rats in mazes is real psychology while studying undergraduates in dormitories or libraries is not.

I do not advocate abandoning the laboratory as a workplace or training tool. There are some topics for which it is the best approach available. But even here it should be supplemented by field methods. When the response is made that no analogues to the behavior exist in nature, then one must raise questions about the importance of the topic. Not exclude the research automatically on this basis, but at least face the question my grandmother raised—Why is a grown person like you spending your time doing something like this? A better balance between field and laboratory would benefit all areas of psychology.

The tremendous leap of faith needed to go from laboratory to life is particularly evident to the increasing number of psychologists who are being asked to testify before government committees, courts and administrative bodies. Whether the issue is abortion, busing, prison reform, visual pollution or occupational health, it is a good bet that there will be a psychologist testifying.

For those of us who have done this, the chasm between what is known and what information is needed is enormous. Reviewing the research literature as a potential witness on the effects of solitary confinement, I was appalled by the absence of relevant data. Although countless inmates have served time, sometimes years, in solitary confinement, there is little or no research documenting its effects. Judges are not terribly interested in stories about crowded rats or Sika deer. Nor is it clear that the predicament of inmates in smelly, filthy and noisy steel cages eating prison slop and facing occasional brutality resembles the antiseptic circumstances of the paid volunteer in the sensory isolation experiment.

For ethical reasons and for face validity, the only fully convincing data on solitary confinement or long-term imprisonment will have to come from studies of actual prisoners or long-term mental patients or others who have been subjected to involuntary confinement for long periods. I do not question the value of studying crowded rats. This work has been very important in shaping our thinking about crowding. But if we want to generalize from lab to life, we are going to have to learn more about life too.

We know that misperceptions of reality occur in the laboratory, but not how often and under what circumstances in the outside world. We know more about how students learn nonsense syllables than we do about how elementary pupils learn geography or college students cram for exams—and most do cram despite our exhortations that spaced practice is superior to massed practice. We also know much more about laboratory rats in mazes than about wild rats in their own habitats. The list could be continued indefinitely.

We have developed a science of psychology based largely on behavior in the laboratory and have hedged on the issue of generalization. Some say we are not ready yet to generalize. Give us 10 years, 20 years, 50 years, then we may be ready. If I had confidence that we would have answers on issues like solitary confinement or visual pollution in 20 years, I would be willing to wait. But what I have seen is a *decreasing* generalizability as the problems and methods chosen by experimenters become more esoteric and hermetic.

Researchers such as Montrose Wolf and Teodoro Ayllon who have applied behavior modification in schools and mental hospitals have found that their work is *dis*continuous with the previous animal studies. They had to develop new techniques, reinforcements and contracts appropriate to the setting. The plea for "more time" makes good sense if the researchers are actually working on problems important to society. It seems disingenuous if they are not.

We have come far down the road to developing a laboratory model of human behavior based on studies of people on our turf and our terms. Now it seems time to look at how people actually behave in their homes, their schools and their work places.

PSYCHOBABBLE

A monotonous psycho-
logical patter is tyran-
nizing conversations
everywhere—all in the
name of candor

R. D. Rosen

R.D. Rosen is a staff writer for the
Boston Phoenix.

While having drinks recently with a
young woman I had not seen for some
time, I asked how things were going and
received this reply: "I've really been
getting in touch with myself lately. I've
struck some really deep chords." I
recoiled slightly at the grandeur of her
remarks, but she proceeded undaunted,
to reel out a string of broad psychological
insights with an enthusiasm attributable
less to her Tequila Sunrises than to the
confessional spirit that is sweeping
America.

I could not help thinking that I
disappointed her with my inability to
summon more lyricism and intensity in
my own conversation. Now that reticence
has gone out of style, I sensed an
obligation to reciprocate her candor but
couldn't bring myself to use the popular
catch phrases of revelation. Would she
understand if I said that instead of
striking deep chords I had merely tickled
the ivories of my psychic piano? That
getting my head together was not exactly
the way in which I wanted to describe
what was going on above *my* neck? Surely
it wouldn't do any good if I resorted to
more precise, but pompously clinical,
language and admitted that I was well on
may way to resolving my attitude toward
my own maternal introject.

"Whenever I see you," she said
brightly, "it makes me feel very good
inside. It's a real high-energy experience."

So what was wrong with me that I
couldn't feel the full voltage of our
meeting. Unable to match her incan-
descence, I simply agreed. "Yes, it's good
to see you too," then fell silent.

Finally she said, her beatific smile
widening, "But I can really dig your
silence. If you're bummed out, that's
OK."

If anything characterizes the cultural life of the Seventies in America, it is
an insistence on preventing failures of
communication. Everything must now be
spoken. The Kinsey Report, Masters and
Johnson, *The Joy of Sex* and its derivatives; The *Playboy* Advisor, the *Penthouse* Forum, *Oui*'s Sex Tapes; con-
traception; Esalen and the human potential movement; the democratization of
psychotherapy—all these various oils
have helped lubricate the national
tongue. It's as if the full bladder of
civilization's squeamishness has finally
burst. The sexual revolution, this therapeutic age, has culminated in one pro-
fuse, steady stream of self-revelation,
confessed profligacy and publicized
domestic trauma.

It seems that almost everybody
belongs to the Cult of Candor these days,
and that everyone who does speaks the
same dialect. Are you relating? Good.
Are you getting in touch with yourself?
Fine. Gone through some heavy changes?
Doing your own thing? (Or are you, by
some mistake, doing someone else's?) Is
your head screwed on straight? Are you
going to get your act together, or just
your shit? Are you mind-fucked, or just
engaging in mental foreplay?

One hears it everywhere, like endless panels of a Feiffer cartoon. In
restaurants distraught lovers lament, "I
wish I could get into your head." A man
on a bus says to his companion, "I just got
back from the coast. What a different
headset!" The latest reports from a cor-
rupt Esalen provide us with new punch
lines: A group leader there intones that
"it's beautiful if you're unhappy. Go with
the feeling. . . . You gotta be you 'cause
you're you and you gotta be, and besides,
if you aren't gonna be you who else's gonna be you, honey. . . . This is the
Aquarian Age and the time to be oneself,
to love one's beauty, to go with one's process."

Are you sufficiently laid back to
read this article? Will it be a heavy experience, or merely the mock?

It's time we lend a name to this
monotonous patois, this psychological
patter, whose concern is to faithfully
catalog the ego's condition: Psychobabble. As Psychobabble begins to tyrannize
conversations everywhere, it is difficult
to avoid, and there is an embarrassment
involved in not using it in the presence of
other Psychobabblers that is akin to the
mild humiliation experienced by
American tourists in Paris who cannot
speak the native language. It is now
spoken by magazine editors, management
consultants, sandal makers, tool and die
workers and Ph.Ds in clinical psychology
alike. What the sociologist Philip Rieff in
the mid-Sixties called "Psychological
Man," that mid-20th century victim of his
own interminable introspection, has
become Psychobabbler, the victim of his
own inability to describe human behavior
with anything but platitudes.

Psychobabble seems to have
emerged toward the end of the Sixties,
distilled from the dying rad/lib dialects of
political activism and the newly thriving
language of the human potential movement with its Fritz Perls of wisdom. Activism was acquiring more and more of a
therapeutic cast, and the radical battles,
once fought exclusively in the real
political world, were now being enacted
in the individual psyche. T-groups, encounter groups, sensitivity training,
group gropes, drama and primal therapies
all helped shape the trend. Two years
ago, when Jerry Rubin proclaimed in
Psychology Today that he was going back
to his body, where the real wars of liberation were taking place, those who hadn't
already preceded him now clamored to
trade in their political critiques for
therapeutic ideals. The disaffected were
saying "Off the pigs" one day and "Man, I
really feel tense, don't mess with my
head" the next.

Of course, this is not the first time
in our history that psychological ideas
have dominated national conversation.
The old Psychobabble, however, was re-

From *New Times*, October 31, 1975. From PSYCHOBABBLE by R.D. Rosen. Copyright © 1975, 1976, 1977 by Richard D.
Rosen. Reprinted by permission of Atheneum Publishers.

ally just the wholesale use of Freudian terms, less banter than a sort of intellectual one-upmanship. In post-World War II America, Freudian terminology was embraced by liberal magazines, novelists and enough of the middle class so that the growing demand for psychoanalysis easily outdistanced the supply of doctors.

As one Boston psychoanalyst, who has practiced for over 30 years, says, "After the war, everyone was talking simplistically about the Oedipus complex. It was the rage. Everyone had the idea that knowledge itself would make you free." Now he has to listen to the new Psychobabble. A social worker patient in his 30s, himself a group leader, eagerly responded at the beginning of therapy to each interpretation his analyst made by saying, "I hear you, I hear you."

"I'm sorry," said the doctor, "I didn't know you were a little deaf."

"I'm not. I *hear* you. It means I comprehend."

"Well, *what* do you comprehend?"

The patient paused. "Jesus," he replied, "I don't know."

Psychobabble, the psychoanalyst says, "is just a way of using candor in order not to be candid." The dangers of the old Psychobabble were remarked upon as early as 1929 in an article by Joseph Jastrow in *The Century* entitled "The Freudian Temper and Its Menace to the Lay Mind." In it, Jastrow quotes a Boston analyst, Dr. Myerson of Beacon Street: "Everybody talks glibly of repression, complexes, sublimation, wish fulfillment and subconsciousness as if they really understood Freud and what he was talking about. Gentle reader, let me say this, that with the exception of a few professional philosophers, psychologists, psychiatrists and psychoanalysts, I have not met a dozen people who knew more than the terms of Freud."

The new Psychobabblers, however, don't even seem to know the terms—of Freud, Jung, Adler, or any body of psychological thought. Their language seems to free-float in some linguistic atmosphere, a set of repetitive verbal formalities that kills off the very spontaneity, candor and understanding it pretends to promote. It's an idiom that reduces psychological insight and therapeutic processes to a collection of standardized insights, that provides only a limited lexicon to deal with an infinite variety of problems. "Uptight" is a word now used to describe an individual who is experiencing anything from mild uneasi-

ness to a clinical depression. To ask someone why he or she refers to another as being "hung-up" produces a reply along the lines of: "*Why?* Man, he's just *hung-up.*" Oddly, those few psychiatric terms borrowed by Psychobabble are used recklessly. One is no longer fearful; one is *paranoid.* The adjective is applied to the populace with a generosity that must confuse real clinical paranoiacs. Increasingly, people describe their moody friends as *manic-depressives,* and almost anyone you don't like is psychotic, or at least *schizzed-out.*

The Cult of Candor, and particularly its language, Psychobabble, is a feature of contemporary decorum, a form of *politesse,* a signal to others that one is ready to talk a certain kind of turkey, to engage in *real dialogue.* And real dialogue, it turns out, is often no more than a monologue. When I asked a man to whom I had just been introduced at a party recently, "How do you do?" he responded by describing, with an utter disrespect for brevity, his relationship with his wife. Confession is the new handshake.

If Psychobabble were a question of language alone, the worst one could say about it is that it is just another example of the corrosion and unimaginativeness of spoken English. But the prevalence of Psychobabble reflects more than a mere "loss for words." It indicates that, in an era when the national gaze has turned inward, and in a country that needs therapy perhaps more than any other, Americans still have enormous difficulty in understanding the depth of their psychological problems, perhaps even in understanding that psychological problems *have* depth.

Even among the well-analyzed and congenitally content there is a tendency to believe in the new ethos of "being oneself" and in the promises of total liberation. This trend has been well-documented in some excellent books during the last ten years. In his recent *Social Amnesia: A Critique of Conformist Psychology from Adler to Laing,* leftist historian Russell Jacoby noted that the reasons for this current occupation with self and individuality go beyond the voluntary desire to be spiritualized: "The more the development of late capitalism renders obsolete or at least suspect the real possibilities of self, self-fulfillment and actualization, the more they are emphasized as if they could spring to life through an act of will alone." For in-

stance, here's an advertisement from *Publishers Weekly* for Martin Shepard's latest book, *The Do-It-Yourself Psychotherapy Book:* "This book will save you thousands of dollars and give you control of your own life and your best self. *No More* Paid Advisors, Sex Hangups, Feelings of Inferiority, Psychosomatic Illness, Guilt. *Enjoy* More Personal Power, Boundless Sensual Pleasure, New-Found Self Reliance, Your Birthright of Health, New Lifestyles."

This notion that psychological growth may be achieved through an act of sheer ego that takes into account neither history nor one's own unconscious leads to a kind of narcissism, perfectly embodied by our previously quoted Esalen group leader in this conversation reported in a *Village Voice* article:

"Leo," said Miriam, "you have to realize the important thing is living in the present moment. You have to be fully aware in the now, that's the trick."

"Beautiful," said Shirley, "beautiful. It's just like the Aquarian Age."

"Shirley," said Leo, "you've got to stop that Aquarian Age stuff. If this is the Aquarian Age, we're in trouble, we've been screwed by Nixon, we've been screwed by Ford, and we're letting Kissinger screw everyone he wants."

"I don't understand politics," said Shirley. "I don't know anything about politics, so I don't feel as if I'd been screwed. It's not part of my reality, so it's not true for me."

Psychobabble has insinuated itself into many American art forms, and in most cases this is no surprise. That we can now hear it on *The Bob Newhart Show,* in which Newhart plays a Chicago psychotherapist, seems only fitting for a medium that unerringly reflects mid-cult values. In rock music, the incidence of Psychobabble is high, which is only natural for an art form whose audience does not prize it above all for its ability to elucidate and whose requirements of rhyme and comprehensibility do not encourage the refinement of insights (ideas are normally at the mercy of "love/above," "out tonight/treat her right" couplets). But it is interesting to note that the English progressive rock group Gentle Giant has a song called "Knots," based on R.D. Laing's book, that the American group The Flock has a new cut titled "My O.K. Today," inspired by their reading of *I'm O.K! You're O.K!* and that lines like Todd Rundgren's "Get your trip together, be a real man" abound more than ever. But the most eloquent Psychobabbler in rock music today is John Denver, who, fresh from Erhard Seminars Training in California, now sounds like the Fritz Perls posters that adorned the walls of student cells in 1971. From his *Rolling Stone* interview of last May:

> How far out it is to be a bird and fly around the trees. I am what I've always wanted to be and that is the truth. And I think—in fact, it's not what I think, but I observe that if people were to really take a good look at themselves, they are exactly the way that they have always wanted to be. . . . My experience is that if I can tell you the truth, just lay it out there, then I have totally opened up a space for you to be who you are and that it really opens up all the room in the world for us to do whatever we want to do in regard to each other. If I don't like you, I'll tell you. And that's great.

As for contemporary films that deal in Psychobabble (*Alice Doesn't Live Here Anymore, Diary of a Mad Housewife, I Love You, Alice B. Toklas* and others), one is always tempted to praise highly those that capture the essence of Psychobabble dialogues, simply on the basis of verisimilitude. Because film and also rock music are to some extent engaged in *representing* the way people talk, and not in analyzing why, they are easy targets to attack for using Psychobabble. One has to look elsewhere to find a medium that has truly suffered at the hands of Psychobabble.

Such a victim is American publishing (although one might also say it victimizes itself). Psychobabble's influence on publishing in this country has been disastrous, and the number of Psychobabble books offered to the public with a solemnity reserved for great works is astounding. Seventeen years ago, Alfred Kazin derided the Myth of Universal Creativity engendered by the Freud craze, "the assumption," as he put it, "that every idle housewife was meant to be a painter and that every sexual deviant is really a poet." The time has never been more propitious than now for ordinary citizens to spill their beans in print. To an older and still mistaken belief that you only had to be

neurotic to create has been added the more recent societal sanction—that, according to the Cult of Candor, it is virtuous to reveal to as many people as possible the tragedies and erotic and emotional secrets of one's private life. It seems that all one needs today in order to become a bona fide author is a few months of therapy and an ability to compose grammatical sentences.

Books written in Psychobabble almost always seem "touchingly human," as the phrase goes, but in their simplification of human problems they engage in what Jacoby has called (referring to the neo-Freudians, to whom Psychobabblers are indebted) "the monotonous discovery of common sense." They present revelation uninformed by history, unmediated by ideology; like verbal home movies.

Now this tendency has flowered in the garden of rampant Psychobabble. In the newly released book *Intimate Feedback: A Lover's Guide to Getting in Touch With Each Other* by Barrie and Charlotte Hopson (Simon & Schuster), we are offered these startling insights, quintessentially Psychobabble:

> Who am I? This is a question which has always been central to man's awareness of himself.
>
> Human existence is exemplified by one person trying to communicate with others.
>
> When couples say that they have nothing new to learn about each other, this is due to stereotyped communication patterns, unless they really do not like one another and have no interest in their partner.

Last winter, Delacorte Press published an autobiographical account by Harry C. Lyon Jr. entitled *It's Me and I'm Here!* Even the title, all too reminiscent of Transactional Analysis' bible, *I'm O.K! You're O.K!*, suggested a giddy infatuation with self-actualization—and the contents did not disappoint. Lyon was raised bourgeois, attended West Point, bedded women by subtle coercion and then realized that he was living by a morality that directed emotional traffic without getting him anywhere. Off to Esalen, naturally. In the book's foreward, human potential psychologist Carl Rogers tells us that he "became thoroughly convinced that [Lyon] was 'for real.'" Lyon concurs in his own introduction:

> Look, my life has been excit-

ing. It has been strange and painful, and I don't know quite what to make of it myself. But I want you to touch it—touch me—because I so much want to reach you. I want you to feel that pain and joy I have felt. . . .

It's Me and I'm Here! is just another tale told by an ego tumescent with spiritual pride.

What Psychobabble encourages in the way of shoddy thinking, and this is easily observed in recent books written in Psychobabble, is the propensity to interpret psychological characteristics as conscious choices or determined purely by culture instead of functions also of the unconscious, instinctual life. In *Harper's* magazine's "Wraparound" section on "Masculinity" a couple of months ago, one woman wrote:

> I chose lesbianism because I'm a female chauvinist. The strongest reason for my female chauvinism is woman's innate respect for life, unshared by men, I believe, because men do not bear or nurture living things.

It is not uncommon these days to hear people speak about their homosexuality as a "preferred" form of sexual life or defend their three divorces because "marriage simply doesn't work anymore"—all as if what one is, what has become of one has been nothing more than a *moral* choice, a decision to participate in a prevailing and attractive ideology; as if the instinctual life of one's childhood and the concept of repression have nothing to do with it, outdated "Freudian" ideas designed to undermine one's will, one's ability to do and be exactly what one wants. Even the existence of the unconscious has fallen out of favor, now just some quaint notion that only complicates the breezy formulations of Psychobabble. Pop psych culture has seized on the Laingian assertion that there isn't even a difference of degree anymore between "sanity" and "insanity"; one can choose between them like a grocery shopper at the frozen food section. Note, for instance, the way that Psychobabble obscures the subtle, but existing distinctions between pathology and habit. Psychobabble describes anyone with a commitment or highly developed interest as a *freak*. A composer is a *music-freak*, a writer a *word-freak*, a cyberneticist a *computer-freak*—as though one's profession is in fact just one's chosen perversion or stimulant.

1. THE SCIENCE OF PSYCHOLOGY

We now have the ideals of "the totally liberated person" and "doing your own thing," concepts that dislodge the goals of human growth from the sources of the conflicts that impede it. Take Louise Diane Campanelli, whose recent book, *Sex and All You Can Eat* (Lyle Stuart), is a masterpiece of the banality of liberation. Repulsed by her husband's obesity, she went out and had, at last count, 62 lovers. Her psychiatrist, himself a Psychobabbler, has provided an introduction in which he tells us that the book's theme "concerns the poignant life story of a young woman of foreign parentage who is caught in a clash of cultures, as well as in an identity crisis." From his description, it sounds like Henry James. "As her psychiatrist," he concludes with all the solicitude of a child's piano teacher, "I can say with confidence that she has come a long way. She still has a long way to go."

Campanelli herself begins by reassuring her readers that:

> There is a tremendous amount of adultery going on in America today. Going on, indeed, at this very minute. Yes, while you read, thousands upon thousands of couples are coupling in hotel and motel rooms, in the rear seats of automobiles, and in "his" or "her" bedroom because the spouse is safely away.

By the book's end, she has refined her perceptions: "Adultery has changed my life. . . . One thing I've learned is that there are very few men and women in our society who are true to another person 24 hours a day, 365 days a year."

If women are testing their independence and making domestic jailbreaks, then many men are certainly suffering as a result. Male response has been in many quarters a sudden and useful self-scrutiny, culminating here and there in pedantic apologies. (In America, where movements spring up overnight like fast-food outlets, the New Femininity must be met with a New Masculinity; all God's children gotta have ideology.) In the case of the pseudonymous Albert Martin and his recent *One Man, Hurt* (Macmillan), though, there is only a bewildered lament. His wife of 20 years asked him for a divorce in 1972. He couldn't understand why she didn't love him, but readers of his 278-page account will no doubt get some idea. Martin, in reality a New York public relations ex-

ecutive by another name, has a very one-dimensional understanding of his failed marriage and yearns, in interminable paragraphs, for an uncluttered security in the face of this threat to his male's world-view, one he is not in the least capable of modifying to accommodate his wife's side of the story. His writing has all the flair of a personal letter dashed off at 3:00 in the morning. *One Man, Hurt* is self-justification dressed as compassion—and reading it only inspired respect for his ex-wife for not having felt similarly compelled to burden the reading public with her grievances.

When Martin tries to be reflective (which requires a great effort), he pawns his troubles off on external forces:

> I think there are bad times to be certain things in history. It was bad to be a witch in Salem in the 1700s, bad to be a Negro in America before May 1954 [and it's a joy being one now, Al?], bad to be a polio victim the year before they discovered the vaccine. And I know it is bad to be in marital trouble in America today because the times have never been worse for getting effective help.

The implied equation of his predicament with religious persecution, racial injustice and severe physical handicap is an indication of how little Martin is willing to understand the nature of marriage, and his in particular. *One Man, Hurt* is further proof that there is today a publishing house (and its promotion and advertising department) ready to hear anybody's complaint.

The publishing industry's enthusiasm for Psychobabble of the above variety as well as of the more explicitly therapeutic strain *(How To Be Your Own Best Friend, How To Be Awake & Alive, When I Say No, I Feel Guilty)*—a story in itself—was foreshadowed during the past five or six years by the success of confessional books. To name but a few, Gestalt Therapy "refounder" Fritz Perls' *In and Out the Garbage Pail* was a lesson in incontinent narcissism ("I am becoming a public figure," he announces on page 1); R.D. Laing's *Knots* made relationships seem irresistibly complex; Nancy Friday gave women's sexual fantasies a good name with *My Secret Garden* and *Forbidden Flowers*; Erica Jong aired her own fantasies in her too-touted *Fear of Flying*; and an equally overrated book, Nigel Nicolson's tribute to his famous

parents, Harold Nicolson and Vita Sackville-West, in *Portrait of a Marriage*, endowed the polymorphous perverse with historical dignity.

Now that the genre has been appropriated by every other divorcee, adulterer and successfully therapized individual, there may be no end in sight to the number of truisms published as striking revelation, to the prurience parading as sociology. The apparently insatiable American appetite for Psychobabble in print may be an indication of several things: That this society has become so atomized that the emotional strength once derived from communities and the extended family can now only be obtained from books; that the simple conviction in the noble savagery of freely playing emotions and the unqualified virtues of "liberation" has now displaced an understanding of the difficult, dialectical nature of psychological growth and change; that a country with a paltry sense of its own short national history (and therefore an imperialist disregard for the history of other, older nations) breeds citizens who cannot grasp the importance of their own private history and childhood and so act as if they were free to select any form of enlightenment that they find appealing.

The popularity of Psychobabble has eclipsed the public taste for literature, in which there are surely more compelling answers to human problems than there are to be found in the books I've mentioned and those like them. Novelists are slowly going out of business while small-town gurus appear on talk shows to exchange insights with Joey Bishop.

Please! No more books by unhappy housewives crying, "I've just got to be me!" No more 33-year-old ad agency executives telling me how they make men want to get into their pants at the singles bar! No more divorced men screaming for justice! No more daydreams of Great Danes with searching tongues! Enough!

This very week in the bookstores, one can find on the hard-cover nonfiction shelf *Your Inner Conflicts—How To Solve Them; How To Give and Receive Advice; How To Live With Another Person; Free To Love: Creating and Sustaining Intimacy in Marriage; Stand Up, Speak Out, Talk Back* and countless others. The field of self-help and confession is becoming so specialized that before long we might well have Psychobabble books written on the thinnest pretexts: *How To Grocery Shop Without Having an Anxiety Attack, How To Achieve Transference in Elevators, You CAN Marry Your Mother, The Promiscuous Coleus.*

Words themselves do not "cure" a person, and words themselves, even the most virulent Psychobabble, cannot make one "sick." However, in the absence of more profound understandings of what we feel and why we feel it, Psychobabble deludes many people into thinking they need not examine themselves with anything but its dull instruments. The danger of Psychobabble is that it anesthetizes curiosity, numbs the desire to know. And, in that state, emotional growth is eventually stunted, no matter how many times one repeats, "I've just got to go with my feelings." Knowledge itself may not free anyone, but the lack of it only reinforces the chains.

Language may, in the end, prove too inadequate to systematically describe wants, desires and emotional states in general. Even the borders delineated by clinical terminology blur badly in the face of actual human behavior. The best one can do now is challenge Psychobabble by declining courteously to accept its usage, as did a young man I know who grew up in a suburb with a group of peers who were "morbidly sensitive to each other's feelings, you know the kind. They'd get into these psychosensitive moods." He dated a girl from the group who one day asked him point-blank if he was getting his head together.

"Yes," he replied. "I can feel it congealing."

The Biological Bases of Behavior

Psychologists have long sought to define and describe the biological correlates of behavior. They have wanted to explore and comprehend the brain and nervous system, the basic cellular components, in order to treat illnesses and disorders and to program and reprogram behavior. Contributions from laboratory scientists have vastly improved our knowledge of the biological underpinnings of behavior. And as our knowledge increases, our ability to control that behavior raises profound ethical and social questions.

Some of these questions are discussed by Caryl Rivers in "Genetic Engineers: Now That They've Gone Too Far, Can They Stop?" When scientists unlocked the secrets of DNA and learned the techniques for recombining it in the laboratory, they also discovered the potential for creating new forms of life—monstrous, deadly, or benign. The philosophical and social implications of this ever-advancing scientific knowledge are staggering, and we have only begun to realize, let alone deal with, them.

Research into the relationship between brain processes and behavior is the subject of several articles. "Special Abilities of the Sexes: Do They Begin in the Brain?" studies the effects of social conditioning and physiology on sex differences. "The Origins of Violence" presents the psycho-biological theory of human violence, which traces defects in normal brain development, resulting in violent behavior, to inadequate early mothering experiences. The effects of brain processes on perception are studied in "The Split Brain Lab" and "Observing the Brain Through a Cat's Eyes."

The complex chemistry of the brain is examined in "Superbrain" and "Brain Damage: A Window on the Mind." It may be a long time before we can accurately map the functions of larger parts of the brain but we do know already that brains starved of certain necessary stimulation or nutrients during their formative periods will never fully recover, and the organism is forever doomed to diminished capacity. An important practical application of psychological research into brain damage is various forms of therapy for those who have suffered impairment.

Another therapeutic function of psychology involves the examination of chemical and other organic bases for mental diseases. Various claims to establish the influence of biological rhythms on mental and physical well-being are discussed in "Wobbly Biorhythms" and in "The Human Body as a Biological Clock," which also provides a bibliography for further reading on this subject.

Finally, two controversial areas of study are spotlighted in "A Scientific Basis for Acupuncture" and "What Marijuana Does (and Doesn't Do)."

A review of this section will provide some insight into the biological bases of behavior, and the likely relationships between personality and disease. It will suggest ways in which this knowledge may be used to alleviate human suffering.

Looking Ahead: Challenge Questions

What capabilities do we now have to improve human psychological welfare through application of existing knowledge about physiology?

What ethical questions arise regarding the physiological manipulation of behavior?

What are potential areas of disagreement between behaviorists and humanists regarding the issues discussed in this section?

GENETIC ENGINEERS
Now That They've Gone Too Far, Can They Stop?

Caryl Rivers

Caryl Rivers is an associate professor at the School of Public Communication at Boston University. She is the author of "Aphrodite at Midcentury" (Doubleday).

Human control of human life has always been a vision with a dark underbelly of nightmare. The classic image is Mary Shelley's "Frankenstein"—alive, but grotesque and misshapen. In Aldous Huxley's *Brave New World*, babies pop like olives out of bottles to confront a society in which human beings are manufactured, chemically adapted and conditioned to the functions they are expected to perform. There are grave taboos associated with the wellsprings of life. It is a territory, like that of the ancient Indian burial grounds, into which one does not trespass without arousing the ire of the gods.

Some may think it excessive to begin the consideration of such a serious scientific topic as The New Biology, with nightmares. But sometimes the prophets and the poets who probe the shadows see more clearly than the scientists. Some nightmares turn solid. Hiroshima ten seconds after zero made all those medieval murals depicting the terrors of hell seem pale by comparison. The human capacity to destroy can outrun even the human imagination.

There are, of course, other human capacities—to create and to cure. They are the compass points for those who want to chart a full ahead course for genetic technology.

Most of us remember encountering Gregor Mendel and his peas in high school biology, and learning that the tiny microscopic specks inside our cells were called genes and were the carriers of heredity. Alone, or in combination, those particles would determine the color of our eyes and the range of our abilities in math. The process was inevitable. We inherited our genes from our parents and we were stuck with what we got.

But the past three decades have seen an explosion of knowledge in the biological sciences. "Genetic engineering" is in its infancy, but the infant shows signs of maturing at an alarming rate.

The cells inside our bodies house as much activity as a steel mill going full blast, and are densely populated. The genes are composed of hundreds of subunits linked together in a spiral shape. Hundreds of genes linked together form the long, threadlike strands of genetic material called DNA (deoxyribonucleic acid) that is the main substance of the chromo-somes. DNA is the basic genetic material, the "governor," so to speak, of the mechanisms of cell reproduction.

In the early 1950s two young scientists, Francis Crick and James Watson, working in Cambridge, England, developed a model of the DNA molecule. It was found that DNA transmits its messages in a four "letter" code, each letter being a specific chemical compound. The messages are carried by RNA, another chemical compound. The achievement won the Nobel prize for Crick and Watson, and the science of molecular biology took off like an express train.*

The New Biology raises the most immediate and perhaps the most far-reaching questions in the field of human reproduction. There are two types of cells in the human body: body cells, which contain a full set of chromosomes, and sex cells (sperm or egg), which each contain only half the required number. It takes a merger of sperm with egg for human reproduction to begin. The

---

*A recent book, Anne Sayre's *Rosalind Franklin and DNA* (Norton), argues that Franklin, a scientist who worked with Watson and Crick, has not been given due credit for solving the riddle of DNA. Sayre says that without the work done by Franklin—the refined use of X-ray crystallography to gather data on DNA—the achievement of Watson and Crick would not have been possible. (Franklin died of cancer in 1950 at age 37.)

From *Ms.*, June 1976. Copyright *Ms.* Magazine Corp. 1976. Reprinted with permission.

merger occurs inside a woman's body, but what if it were to happen outside, in a test tube? Would the cells continue to grow and divide? In 1959 an Italian scientist, Dr. Daniele Petrucci, announced he had achieved test-tube fertilization. His work was condemned by the Pope, and the scientist destroyed the results. The Papal frown did not dissuade all scientists, however, and the most advanced work with what is called *in vitro* fertilization is now going on in England.

In vitro means, literally, "in glass," and a husband-and-wife team in the physiology department of Cambridge University have devised a way to obtain healthy human eggs for their experiments. Dr. R.G. Edwards and Dr. Ruth Fowler work with volunteer subjects, usually women who are unable to conceive because of blocked Fallopian tubes. (Sperm must travel up the tubes to merge with an egg before conception can occur naturally.) The women are given fertility drugs, which cause the production of a number of eggs. These are removed from their uteruses by minor abdominal surgery. Edwards and Fowler bring the eggs together with sperm in culture dishes, and they have been able to produce human embryos in very rudimentary stages.

Both doctors see their work as being in the best traditions of medical science, since its aim is to enable women with blocked or damaged tubes to conceive. An egg is removed from a woman, fertilized with her husband's sperm, then reimplanted in her uterus. So far, the embryos have not attached themselves to the lining of the uterus so that pregnancies would result.

But embryo transplants have been done in animals, cattle in particular, with success. In fact, in the 1960s sheep embryos were implanted into the uterus of a rabbit—flown from England to South Africa in their temporary "incubator"—and then removed from the rabbit and implanted into other female sheep, who later gave birth to ewes.

No one knows what effect the handling of human embryos would have on their development. Would the result be a high proportion of damaged babies? Paul Ramsey, the Yale theologian who has written extensively on the ethics of genetic control, says that *in vitro* fertilization is unethical experimentation subject to absolute moral prohibition. Another objection to work with human embryos is that too little research so far has been done with primates, the animals closest to humans in complexity.

Some scientists, while arguing for caution, feel that the fear of gross abnormalities may be overstated. Mouse embryos have developed to normal birth even after extreme manipulation. They question whether *in vitro* fertilization is any riskier than what is going on right now. For example, physicians give women fertility drugs that often result in multiple births despite the dangers to the embryos of prematurity, stunted growth, and respiratory disorders. Often, one or more of the fetuses does not survive.

Edwards and Fowler feel that an additional benefit of their work is that they will be able to bypass sex-linked diseases. This might work in the case of hemophilia where male children are afflicted and female children are not. Edwards and Fowler say, "Placing female embryos in the mother would avoid the birth of affected males, though half of the female children would be carriers of the gene."

In vitro fertilization also raises a welter of legal and social questions. If a damaged child resulted from an embryo transplant, could the parents sue the doctor for malpractice? Could the child sue the parents? That sounds bizarre, but there is a legal theory called "wrongful life," which holds parents responsible for willful damage done to a child before its birth. The doctrine is not established and perhaps never will be, but there have been cases argued, including one involving a

blind child born to a syphilitic mother.

Does a childless woman have a *right* to have children? Is infertility a sickness, to be "cured" by any process, no matter how risky?

Perhaps even more disturbing questions for society are raised by bolder applications of embryo-transplant technology. If a cow embryo can be transplanted from one womb to another, why not a human embryo? A woman with a heart condition who could not undergo the rigors of childbirth could still be the mother of her own natural child. A "test tube" embryo could be implanted into the uterus of another woman, who, out of friendship or for payment, would carry and deliver the child.

It is possible that this technology would mean still another way that women's bodies would be used—as temporary havens for other people's children. One could imagine a flourishing "rent-a-uterus" business. One British doctor has even suggested a "reasonable" price for such a service—2,000 pounds (or about $4,000). It wouldn't be the first time that poor women found that their bodies are their one salable commodity.

How far should we go in manipulating embryos? There has been speculation that in the future we may be able to change the sex, the hair color—even the intelligence of embryos. The most outrageous fantasy is that of "designing" people—a legless astronaut for a life in space or a human being with gills to live in the oceans.

It is not the fantasies that are disturbing. Asexual reproduction, or cloning may be possible in the next 10 years, or sooner. Have we, as a society, thought much about where we will draw a line?

James Watson, whose work 20 years ago helped create The New Biology, has been outspoken in calling for serious concern: "If we do not think about (the matter) now, the possibility of a . . . free choice will one day suddenly be gone."

2. THE BIOLOGICAL BASES OF BEHAVIOR

Dr. Sissela Bok, who has written extensively on medical ethics, and who now lectures at Harvard and at Simmons College, shares that concern. "In some ways," she says, "our society is so brittle that it cannot take much more strain in regard to questions of living, dying, and being born." We must be very conservative in our attitudes toward the new technology, she believes. It is not right for one doctor to forge ahead.

But there is at least one who is going to try. One unnamed American scientist told science writer Albert Rosenfeld, "If I can carry a baby all the way through to birth *in vitro*, I certainly plan to do it—although obviously, I'm not going to succeed on the first attempt—or even the twentieth."

Whether or not we tamper with it, the very fact that we are coming to know more and more about the machinery of heredity will bring us to difficult—sometimes agonizing—choices. Already much can be learned about an embryo through an increasingly common procedure known as amniocentesis. (In amniocentesis, a hypodermic needle, inserted through the mother's abdomen into the amniotic sac, is used to withdraw amniotic fluid which contains fetal cells.) Examination of the cells can reveal some 60 genetic disorders. The woman who finds that the embryo she is carrying has a serious genetic defect can choose to abort. Amniocentesis can also detect the sex of the fetus from the chromosomal structure of the cells.

Despite the fact that amniocentesis is no longer an exotic procedure and is an essential diagnostic tool, some women who seek it find resistance from physicians similar to the opposition that they find doctors have toward abortion. In a survey of 25 couples, Dr. John Fletcher of the Interfaith Metropolitan Theological Education, Inc., in Washington, D.C., found that five of the couples had encountered opposition from

doctors. One 40-year-old mother of three was told that her mental health needed attention because she sought amniocentesis. Another woman, a carrier of the gene for a rare and usually fatal disease, Lesch-Nyhan syndrome, said that one doctor "as much as called me a murderer when I said I wanted the test."

As fetal detection becomes more sophisticated, choices will get tougher. One case, presented in a scientific journal as a question of "bio-ethics" is a good example. A woman in her forties with three children sought amniocentesis to test for Down's syndrome (mongolism). The test showed the fetus was a male, with no evidence of Down's syndrome. But the fetus did have an extra "Y" (male) chromosome, an abnormality whose effect is not known. There has been some evidence presented that "extra Y" males are prone to aggression and antisocial behavior, but that evidence has been vigorously disputed. Was the woman's physician obliged to give her the full report, or just to tell her there was no sign of Down's syndrome?

The fact that amniocentesis can detect the sex of the fetus presents another moral quandary. A Utah doctor wrote an outraged letter to the *Journal of the American Medical Association* in 1972, citing what he called a "possible abuse of prenatal chromosome evaluation of the fetus." A 38-year-old patient, mother of one boy and two girls, asked for amniocentesis to rule out Down's syndrome. The embryo was diagnosed as a normal female. The woman decided to abort, since she and her husband wanted another son, not a daughter.

Is it morally right for parents who want a child to abort a normal fetus simply because it is the "wrong" sex? This raises questions even for strong supporters of the idea that a woman should have control over her own body. Is abortion a proper method of sex selection? Studies of preferences for sons or daughters

done in the United States have consistently favored male children, so one suspects that the majority of the aborted fetuses would be female.

Selective abortion is not the only method of choosing the sex of a child. It is probable that in the next few years the technology will be available to preselect the sex of a child before conception. (If a sperm bearing an X chromosome fertilizes an egg, the child will be a female; if a Y chromosome, a male.) There have been numerous articles and books about possible methods of sex selection based on the fact that male sperm swim faster than female sperm. But such methods are usually based on the timing of intercourse and are rather hit-and-miss, since it's hard for a woman to tell precisely when ovulation occurs. More effective techniques will probably be available in the near future based on the differences in sperm. Male and female sperm differ not only in speed but in weight (female sperm are heavier). This makes it possible to separate them.

Reports in the British journal *Nature* in 1973 said that strong antibodies directed against substances in male sperm of mice reduced the likelihood of their fertilizing an egg. The male sperm were in effect "hobbled," leaving the race to the X-bearing sperm. It is also possible to collect Y-bearing sperm in a condition that would allow them to be used in artificial insemination, ensuring a male child. A sperm separating technique which results in a high percentage of male offspring is being used in some American fertility clinics. One clinic is also accepting applications from couples who want male children. One argument for the use of such techniques is that if parents could choose the sex of their children, it would tend to lower population levels.

But what effect would sex selection have on the ratio of males to females in society? At first, a rash of boy babies could be expected. Some demographers believe the balance would right itself. Marc Lappe, Associate for the Biological Sciences at the Hastings Center (an institute set up to examine the ethical and social questions proposed by science and technology) suspects the opposite. By artificially selecting one sperm type over another, "we may be selecting for sperm that would produce offspring whose own gametes (be they sperm or egg) would again have a predilection for the same sex." We might not be selecting just a male child, but a dynasty of male children. He feels that, given the sexual inequality in society, we are not ready to assume the responsibility of sex selection.

Still another thorny question may arise from our increasing knowledge about genetic makeup. Today, people who seek genetic testing do so voluntarily. At what point will society step in and say we *must* be tested?

Mass genetic screening may be on the horizon. In some states, testing of newborns for PKU (phenylketonuria)—a genetic disorder that causes retardation and can be treated by special diet early in life—is mandatory. In some areas, testing for sickle-cell disease, a disorder that mainly affects blacks—is mandatory for schoolchildren or for persons about to marry. The National Research Council of the National Academy of Sciences has called mass screening a progressive health concept. But there is confusion about *victims* of sickle-cell disease and carriers of the *trait*. The latter are not sick, but have sometimes been refused insurance, or fired from jobs because of the confusion. The various states have a confusing welter of laws regarding testing for PKU, sickle-cell, and other genetic disorders.

According to Tabitha Powledge, research associate for genetics at the Hastings Center, the increasing knowledge society will have about each of us may cause our options to become narrower and narrower. She uses as an example the research

on certain chemical substances in the human body called antigens. Some antigens seem to be statistically associated with the presence of certain diseases. If, at some future time, we could screen for those antigens to identify people with a predisposition toward a certain disease, we might, for example, be ruled out of a job because of a disease we don't have but might get, or we could be denied insurance, or rejected by potential spouses.

A bitter battle over screening for another genetic disorder—the "extra Y" chromosome—erupted in Boston in 1974. Since 1968, all the baby boys born at the Boston Hospital for Women had been screened for chromosomal abnormalities, including the extra Y. Psychiatrist Stanley Walzer of Harvard Medical School followed the development of 40 of these boys. A citizens' health-advocacy group called Science for the People (which included some of Dr. Walzer's peers at Harvard and the Massachusetts Institute of Technology) attacked the study. They charged that the children would be unfairly stigmatized by being labeled as "extra Y" males.

In the past few years there have been widespread reports in the press about the extra Y chromosome as the "criminal" chromosome. Dr. Walzer said publicly that the "criminal-chromosome" theory was nonsense, but that there were indications that some extra-Y males may have behavorial problems and learning disabilities.

It was an example of a head-on clash between two well-intentioned groups. Dr. Walzer and his colleagues doing the study believed that the information would be helpful to the children and the parents. As a parent, I would certainly want to know if my child had any abnormality that could lead to problems. I hope I would have the wisdom to deal with the information wisely. On the other

hand, as Science for the People argued, children who are expected to be "problems" usually live up to those expectations. What would happen when a boy got into normal kid's mischief in school if his medical records showed an extra Y? Would a teacher or principal mark this as the beginning of a pattern of "antisocial" behavior? The study was finally halted after a heated public debate. In the next few years we will see more of these battles over genetic screening.

It is not only in the area of human reproduction that The New Biology raises controversial issues. The invasion of the cellular mechanism has been relentless in the past five years. For example, in 1970 Dr. H. Gobind Khorana headed a team at the University of Wisconsin that achieved the first synthesis of a gene in a test tube. The methods for chemical synthesis had been established—theoretically now any gene could be made in the test tube. In 1975 a team of biochemists at Harvard artificially reproduced a mammalian gene—a much more complex structure than the one produced five years previously.

Scientists have not only duplicated genes, but they have changed cell construction. In 1971 a team of scientists at Oxford University corrected a defect in a cell. They worked with mouse cells that were not able to produce a necessary enzyme. The deficient mouse cell was injected with some healthy pieces of chick chromosome using an inactivated mouse virus as a carrier. The same enzyme deficiency in humans produces the rare and fatal Lesch-Nyhan syndrome. The new genetic material enabled the mouse cells to produce the enzyme, and the new genes not only remained part of the permanent cell machinery, but were duplicated as new, healthy cells grew and divided. The journal *Nature* said the achievement meant that it was now possible in principle to remove defective cells from a human patient, to introduce new genes, and to return the cured cells to the patient.

However, the genetic mechanisms of the human body are very complex and the day of genetic medicine—the curing of genetic disease by the transfer of material into cells—is probably a long way off. Which is not to say that science hasn't taken the first tentative steps in that direction. The first known attempt at gene therapy came in 1970, and it caused an international controversy which is still going on. Two sisters, then seven years and two years, were brought into a hospital in Cologne, Germany; they were suffering from a rare, hereditary enzyme deficiency which caused high levels in their blood and spinal fluid of a substance called arginine. The girls suffered from palsy, epileptic seizures, and retardation.

An American virologist, Dr. Stanfield Rogers at Oak Ridge National Laboratory, worked with German doctors to attempt gene therapy. They injected the girls with a virus, which had caused a lower concentration of arginine in the blood of laboratory workers exposed to that virus than to a control group who was not. Could the virus eliminate the lethal substance in the children's blood? Possibly, but there was also a known risk. The virus, when tested on rabbits, produced cancerous skin lesions.

The therapy was tried, and in 1975 Dr. Rogers announced that it had failed, possibly because the virus used was not full-strength. It had deteriorated in storage. He said they would try again, although this time there was no possibility that the girls could be helped. Their symptoms were then irreversible. But could the knowledge gained help others in the future? Or would the second injection of the cancer-causing virus possibly doom them to even more suffering? Scientists on both sides of the Atlantic were bitterly divided over the case. The questions in this debate will be raised again and

again as society grapples with the risks and benefits of genetic medicine.

Possibly the most significant development in genetic research has been the success of "gene transfer" techniques. For the first time scientists can take a gene out of its environment and get a closer look at its machinery—why it shuts off and on, how it transmits messages. By understanding the behavior of a gene, scientists may be able to probe the causes of the uncontrolled cell growth of cancer. Scientists have been able to use enzymes like a surgeon's knife, to lift pieces of DNA out of complex cells and put them into laboratory bacteria, where they can multiply. The "transferred" genes are usually housed in bacteria known as *E. coli*, a common inhabitant of the human colon. The new techniques enable researchers to combine genetic material in a way never before possible, to concoct a "genetic stew." A Swedish team, for example, has crossed genes of different species to produce live hybrid cells. The team combined human cells with those of rats, mice, and even insects.

What if a bit of this stew were to escape from the lab, in a tiny piece of the *E. coli*. The bacteria might travel to its natural habitat in the human gut, depositing there pieces of genetic material unknown to nature.

Since one of the substances used for gene transfer—a genetic material called a plasmid—can confer resistance to antibiotics, the specter has arisen of mass infections for which there is no known cure. Could gene-transfer procedure create the "Doomsday Bug"? The incidence of laboratory-acquired infections—5,000 cases in the past 30 years—suggests it could.

In 1974 a group of American scientists were so alarmed by the possible hazards of gene transfers that they called for an international moratorium. At the "Asilomar"

conference held in Pacific Grove, California, in 1975, an international group of scientists met and hammered out safety guidelines for work with hybrid cells. It was, probably, the first time in the history of science that scientists gathered together to discipline themselves before—not after—the dangers had materialized.

However, in the face of such potential hazards, are voluntary safeguards enough? And are they being discussed in the right places by the right people? The places where decisions about research are made—congressional and corporate offices, government agencies, university science departments—are conspicuous for the absence of certain people. Women and minorities are not often included in high-level decisions. In our society, the mechanisms for bringing disenfranchised groups into decision-making are few. In some scientific quarters, there is a suspicion of the public process. In 1971 during a Senate hearing on a bill to set up a commission to look at issues in the biological sciences, Senator Walter Mondale (D.-Mont.) expressed surprise at the resistance to what he called a "measly little study commission." He said, "I sense an almost psychopathic objection to the public process, a fear that if the public gets involved, it's going to be antiscience."

In fact, it was the emotionally charged issue of research on aborted fetuses that prompted Congressional action. Senator Edward Kennedy (D.-Mass.) introduced a bill that led to the National Commission for the Protection of Human Subjects, which had a majority of nonscientists as members. The commission is an advisory body to the Department of Health, Education, and Welfare. Its first job was to draw up a set of guidelines for fetal research, which it did in 1975. The commission is now looking into the question of research involving

Cloning:

A Generation Made to Order

Human reproduction begins with the merger of the sex cells, sperm and egg. Since each contains only half a set of chromosomes, the joining of sperm with the egg is the first step in the creation of a new and unique individual, with traits inherited from both parents. But this is not the only possible way for life to begin.

The other type of cells in the human body already has a full set of chromosomes. All the genetic information necessary for an organism to reproduce itself is contained in the nucleus of every cell in that organism. If body cells could be made to divide, the result would be asexual reproduction—the production of offspring with only one parent. Such a process is already being used with other species—it is called cloning. It has been tried successfully with plants, fruit flies—and more significantly, with frogs.

In 1968, J.B. Gurdon at Oxford University produced a clonal frog. He took an unfertilized egg cell from an African clawed frog and destroyed its nucleus by ultraviolet radiation. He replaced it with the nucleus of an intestinal cell of another frog of the same species. The egg, suddenly finding itself with a full set of chromosomes, began to reproduce. It was "tricked" into starting the reproductive process. The result was a tadpole that was a genetic twin of the frog that donated the cell. The "mother" frog contributed nothing to the genetic identity of the tadpole, since her potential to pass on her traits was destroyed when the nucleus of her egg was obliterated.

How would it work with human beings? Roughly the same way. A healthy egg could be removed from a woman's body, in the same way that Edwards and Fowler obtain eggs

for their work. But instead of fertilizing the egg with sperm, scientists could destroy the nucleus of the human egg and replace it with a cell taken from the arm or anywhere of a donor we'll call John X. The egg would be reimplanted in the uterus of a woman. Although its identity would be wiped out with the destruction of its nucleus, it could nonetheless start to divide, because it had received the proper signal—the presence of a full set of chromosomes. The baby that would be the result of that process would have only one parent—John X. It would, in fact, be a carbon copy of John X—his twin, a generation removed. (Or her twin, if the cell donor were female.)

In March of this year scientists announced major progress on the hunt for the substance that "switches on" the reproductive mechanisms of the cell. Gurdon's first experiments with the frog proved that such a mechanism exists and that all cells—not just sex cells—could be made to reproduce. Now, work done by Gurdon at Cambridge and by Ann Janice Brothers at the University of Indiana is moving science closer to discovering the identity of the "master switch."

Gurdon inserted the nuclei of human cancer cells into immature frogs eggs, and the human cell nuclei responded in dramatic fashion, swelling in size to as much as a hundredfold.

Brothers, working with amphibians, axolotls, has observed that a molecule identified as the O+ factor appears to be the substance that signals the reproductive process to carry on. Eggs produced by axolotls that did not contain the O+ factor did not develop past very rudimentary stages until they were injected with O+ substance. Brothers and her colleagues at

Indiana report that O+ appears to be a large protein molecule that is somewhat acidic. The scientists are working to isolate and define that molecule. The identification of the "master switch" would be a giant step toward understanding cancer and would bring the day of human cloning closer.

The consequences of human cloning are almost impossible to imagine. Widespread human cloning would alter human society beyond recognition. The family would no longer exist, sexuality would have no connection with reproduction. The idea of parenthood would be completely changed. The diversity of human beings provided by sexual reproduction would vanish. One could imagine entire communities of people who looked exactly the same, whose range of potential was identical. Some scientists have suggested that "clones and clonishness" could replace our present patterns of nation and race.

The misuses of cloning are not hard to predict. Would an aging dictator try to insure the continuance of his regime by an heir apparent who was his genetic double? Would women and men project their egos into the future by producing their own "carbon copies"? Would society choose to clone our most valued citizens? Artists? Generals? Members of elite groups? The capacity of our species to change and adapt may be rooted in the diversity of the gene pool. By tampering with that process we could be limiting our own ability to survive.

There are some who believe that current work in test-tube fertilization to extract eggs is a first step in the direction of cloning. There have been some estimates that human cloning will be a reality within the decade. Who will say where we draw the line?

2. THE BIOLOGICAL BASES OF BEHAVIOR

prisoners and minorities, but it will be phased out of existence after its final report, sometime in 1977.

The Pandora's box of genetic technology may be opened and its inhabitants long gone before the public process catches up. The revolution in molecular biology will affect the destinies of women in a profound way, but few women will be asked to be involved in policy decisions that will chart its direction. Do we want proxy mothers or clones or handy methods for choosing the sex of our children or mass genetic screening? Do we as a species have the wisdom to direct our own evolution by tinkering with our genes? Dr. Leon Kass of the Kennedy Institute Center for Bioethics at Georgetown University says, "We trimph over nature's unpredictabilities only to subject ourselves to the still greater unpredictability of our capricious will and our fickle opinions. Thus, engineering the engineer as well as the engine, we race our train we know not where."

And if women remain mute, we will simply go along on the ride.

SPECIAL ABILITIES OF THE SEXES: DO THEY BEGIN IN THE BRAIN?

Researchers are finding evidence that
some differences between the sexes—chiefly in spatial
and verbal talents—start with differences
in the way male and female brains are organized.
Other experts challenge the data and warn
that they could provide a scientific justification for sexism.
At the moment, there is no hotter issue in psychology.

Daniel Goleman

Daniel Goleman is an associate editor of *Psychology Today*. He holds his Ph.D. in psychology from Harvard.

One of the most common findings in psychological research is that there is a difference in performance between men and women. It is also one of the most politically loaded issues in the field today. The facts are that women excel at certain tasks, men at others. Many personality dimensions are skewed in one direction for women, another for men. Women show one perceptual pattern, men a contrasting one. With the wave of feminism sweeping through psychology, these differences have come overwhelmingly to be interpreted as reflecting dissimilarities in the way the sexes are raised and treated. Boys and girls are brought up in divergent ways, taught different skills, rewarded for diverse acts. Sex differences, many psychologists have assured us, are due to learning and not biology.

Now a new breed of researchers—many of them women—are taking a second look at the biological substrates of behavior and reaching some different conclusions. While acknowledging that a vast range of sex differences reflects social influences, they also assert that the neurological constitutions of men and women lead them to think and behave in different ways.

Their conclusions are based largely on evidence that women's brains are organized differently from men's for certain tasks and functions. There are no agreed-on, observable differences in the physical size, structure, and biochemical components of the brains of the two sexes. However, scientists infer from the performance of the sexes on varied tests that their brains control certain processes in different locations and in different ways. Some researchers set forth evidence that these organizational differences are inherited. Diane McGuinness and Karl Pribram of Stanford University believe they are influenced by different sex hormones. Monte Buchsbaum of the National Institute of Mental Health has found that the electrical activity in men's and women's brains varies significantly in response to stimuli; as a result, he says women are more sensitive to visual stimuli, sound, and touch, but may be less able to handle heavy stress.

While much of the work has been done by reputable scientists, almost every study has its vehement critics as well as its defenders. There are widespread fears that some of the data will be misinterpreted. "The real danger in this line of research," says Marcel Kinsbourne, a neurologist at the Hospital for Sick Children in Toronto," is that the findings could be misinterpreted and used as a scientific justification for sexism, just as ambiguous genetic findings were often cited to provide a scientific basis for racism."

It is also important to remember that psychological differences between large groups, such as men and women, are not absolute, but a matter of proportion and degree. If women in general are superior in fine coordination and the ability to make rapid choices, they may, for example be faster typists than men. But this means only that proportionately more women than men score higher on typing tests. Many men will still be among the faster typists. And, finally, the social environment also shapes the way skills are employed, so that more women might also make superior neurosurgeons if given sufficient opportunity to pursue such a career.

With these various caveats in mind, let us review the most significant recent findings, while appraising the strengths and weaknesses of the evidence.

The Evidence— Past and Present

Eleanor Maccoby and Carol Jacklin's* 1974 book, *The Psychology of Sex Differences,* is the most thorough review of past research. The authors picked apart the methods and results of hundreds of studies to discover which common beliefs about sex differences are myths, which are supported by evidence, and which are untested. Most studies, they concluded, were either unfounded, inadequately tested, or ambiguous. The only well-established differences Maccoby and Jacklin found were that girls have greater verbal ability than boys and that boys excel in visual-spatial and mathematical skills, and are more aggressive than girls.

A/E Editor's note: See article # 44, page 211 for further discussion.

The meager yield of verifiable sex differences reflected the paucity of tests available that weren't biased by differences in how boys and girls are raised. The way a parent views the role of a daughter or a son will have a great impact on the child's behavior, less impact on his or her psychophysiology, and virtually no effect on the child's neurochemistry and neurophysiology. But researchers in these latter two fields have not been interested in psychological sex differences until recently, so only now have they found divergences that they believe are unlikely to be the product of a sex-biased society.

Maccoby and Jacklin scarcely mention the brain as a source of sex differences, largely because the major findings on sex disparities in the brain have come since they wrote their book. Many differences, in fact, have yet to be reported in scientific journals. Two of the sex differences Maccoby and Jacklin did list—women's better verbal ability and men's better spatial ability—have been the focus of much recent brain research. Verbal ability in girls matures more rapidly in infancy; it drops to near equality with boys from preschool to about the age of 11; but, from that point on, female verbal superiority increases. Females do particularly well on a wide range of verbal tasks that involve hearing, from tests of fluency and comprehension to the ability to sing in tune. Boys' spatial skills don't seem much better than girls' in childhood, but the male advantage increases from adolescence on. Their spatial skills show up in tasks that involve seeing: perception of depth in space mazes, picture completion, map reading, and the ability to mentally rotate an object in space.

Neurologists have had evidence for some time that in right-handed adults, damage to the left hemisphere of the brain disrupts language, while damage to the right side harms nonverbal, spatial abilities. Only very recently, though, did they realize that this neurological observation, which reflects variations in brain organization, might help to explain sex differences.

Some of the earliest evidence that various mental skills were controlled in different parts of male and female brains came from studies of epileptics who had part of their temporal lobe removed to ease their seizures. In the early 1960s, Herbert Lansdell, a psychologist at the National Institutes of Health, gave some of these patients the Graves Design Judgment Test, which asked them to express a preference among a series of abstract designs. Since neurologists believed that the visual center was located in the right hemisphere, Lansdell expected that patients who had part of their right hemisphere removed would do poorly in the test. Instead, he found no major difference—until he separated the patients according to sex. The men who had surgery in the right half of the brain did poorly in the design test, but the women who had the same surgery did not.

Lansdell wrote a letter to the British journal *Nature*, suggesting that the sexes might differ in brain organization. It was almost a decade, however, before others showed that his hunch was right.

Some of the evidence was provided by Jeannette McGlone at University Hospital in Ontario, who examined 85 right-handed adults admitted to a neurology ward for damage in one or the other side of the brain. McGlone gave each patient a battery of psychological tests, including some that tested verbal skills and some that assessed nonverbal, spatial abilities. If a mental function is localized in a particular half of the brain, she theorized, it should be impaired when that hemisphere is damaged. This turned out to be much truer for men than women. Only men showed specifically verbal deficits after left-hemisphere damage or nonverbal spatial deficits after right-side damage. The women showed less severe losses in both verbal and spatial ability, whether the damage was in the right or left hemispheres. McGlone's work supported the idea that a woman's verbal and spatial abilities are more likely duplicated on both sides of the brain, while a right-handed man is more likely to have his speech center on the left, spatial skills on the right.

Lansdell and McGlone had studied people with brain damage; psychol-ogist Sandra Witelson at McMaster University in Hamilton, Ontario, was among the first to study the relative contributions of the two hemispheres in a normal group. She gave children two objects of irregular and unfamiliar shape, making sure they couldn't see them. Each child handled the two objects simultaneously—one in the right hand, one in the left—after which each tried to pick them out from a display of similar objects. Since information from the right hand goes predominantly to the left hemisphere of the brain, and vice versa, the children's answers enabled her to compare the accuracy of each hand and determine which hemisphere was better in form perception.

After testing 200 right-handed boys and girls between the ages of six and 14, Witelson found that both sexes did equally well in terms of total accuracy. But when she examined performance scores for each hand, the boys did significantly better with their left hands than with their right—a sign of greater right-hemisphere involvement in this task. The girls did equally well with both.

Brain Specialties

During tests in which people perform a given skill, scientists sometimes find that one hemisphere of the brain is more activated (that is, shows more electrical activity) than the other. They call this phenomenon "hemisphere specialization" or "brain lateralization." From the ratio of activation between the two hemispheres, they can tell whether one half is more involved in a certain skill than the other. The precise relationship between degree of hemispheric specialization and performance of particular skills is an open question. Marcel Kinsbourne, the Toronto neurologist, says, "There is an assumption of a one-to-one correspondence between hemispheric specialization on the one hand, and performance or electrical asymmetry on the other. But there is as yet no acceptable evidence for this claim. For instance, how hard a person tries, how good he is at the task, and the way he goes about it, all could affect the right-left ratio. Only if you hold all these factors constant can you compare the hemispheric specialization of individuals or of samples of males and females. No one has yet done that."

Sandra Witelson agrees that the relationship is complex: "For example, men are superior on tests of spatial skills and tend to show greater lateralization of spatial function to the right hemisphere. Here greater lateralization seems to be correlated with greater ability. However, in the case of language, women, in general, are superior to men, who show greater lateralization of language skills to the left hemisphere. Thus, with language, greater lateralization may be correlated with less ability."

This difference between the sexes in the degree of brain lateralization, Witelson proposes, may have implications for activities that combine linguistic and spatial skills. Because women's hemispheres may be less specialized for spatial and linguistic functions, it may be easier for them to perform tasks which combine the two in a single activity, such as reading or understanding a person's behavior from his or her facial expression, body language, and words. Men's brains, Witelson conjectures, may make it easier for them to keep separate cognitively different activities done simultaneously, such as running a drill press while talking.

The sex differences revealed in various tests seem to become more distinct as the child matures. This could mean that the ways boys and girls are treated explain why they develop distinct patterns of brain organization. Not so—at least for verbal and spatial skills—says University of Chicago psychologist Jerre Levy. She worked with Marylou Reid of the University of Massachusetts, who used simple tests of neurological performance to determine verbal and spatial abilities in boys and girls five and eight years old. Reid found that right-handed boys develop their right hemisphere—and their spatial skills—more rapidly than their left, while right-handed girls develop their left hemisphere more quickly than their right, and so race ahead in verbal skills. By itself, the result wouldn't prove an inborn brain difference—

perhaps boys and girls simply spend more time practicing the skills they are expected to have, and therefore develop those skills and the associated hemisphere more quickly.

In fact, Reid then studied another group of children for whom this explanation didn't work: left-handed children who hold their pencil straight up like right-handers when they write (other lefties hold their pencils in a hooked position) had

---

WHY BOYS BUILD TOWERS

Freud's dictum that "biology is destiny" has long infuriated feminists. The main charge against it is that such biological determinism ignores the role socialization plays in producing sex differences. Now, psychoanalyst Erik Erikson's long-cherished notion that the shape of a man's genitalia leads to an orientation toward "outer space," while a woman's orients her toward "inner space," has been attacked by new research.

Erikson argued that while boys and girls can think and act alike, they do not experience their bodies—and thus the world—alike. The shape of the genitals in each sex is somehow translated into a profound difference in the sexes' sense of space. The ground plan of the human body leads to a particular kinesthetic experience, which in turn gives form to a sensory reality.

For a woman, that reality is defined by "a productive inner-bodily space, set in the center of female form and carriage." This "inner space" is a prime factor in the formation of a woman's identity, involving her biological role of bearing and raising children. "In female experience," wrote Erikson, "an 'inner space' is at the center of despair even as it is the very center of potential fulfillment."

The basis for Erikson's theorizing was an experiment in which 140 boys and girls between 11 and 13 built an imaginary scene out of a selection of toys. Erikson found in the configurations an expression of biological sex differences: "For it is clear that the spatial tendencies governing these constructions closely parallel the morphology of the sex organs: in the male, *external* organs, *erectable* and *intrusive* in character, serving highly mobile sperm cells; *internal* organs in the

female, with vestibular access, leading to statically *expectant* ova." In the popular mind, Erikson's finding translated to: "Boys build towers; girls build enclosures."

In the 20 years since Erikson published his study, it has never been rigorously replicated; instead, his interpretation became part of the collective wisdom of psychology, even though Erikson himself cautions against crediting all sex differences in play to biology.

Now, Paula Caplan, a psychologist at the Toronto Family Court Clinic, has redone Erikson's study and found his conclusions don't hold. She presented her results at the American Psychological Association meeting in Toronto in August. Seeking to minimize the effects of sex-stereotyping in play, Caplan used children two to four years old rather than the preadolescents Erikson tested. Like Erikson, she gave the children a wide selection of blocks and other toys, and asked them to make an exciting scene. To control the influence of the objects themselves, Caplan first gave the child blocks only, then all the toys other than blocks, and, finally, the blocks and toys together.

Caplan found no differences between boys and girls in their constructions. The number of towers and their height, the number of enclosures, and every other aspect of the scenes were virtually identical for both sexes. Erikson's results, Caplan conjectures, may have been an artifact of the toys he used. Preadolescent boys and girls might be more likely to choose toys appropriate to sex-stereotyping: dolls and furniture for girls, cars and blocks for boys. The reason boys would build more towers, then, is simple: blocks stack better than doll furniture does.

—**D. G.**

brains whose organization was the mirror-image reverse of other people's. While right-handers almost always have their primary speech center in the left hemisphere and their spatial center in the right, these lefties have their primary speech centers on the right side and their spatial center on the left. In this group, Reid found, girls did better on spatial tasks, while boys showed greater verbal abilities—the exact opposite of the usual sex pattern.

Nevertheless, Reid's left-handers showed the same hemispheric maturation pattern as other children: the right half developed more rapidly among boys and the left more rapidly among girls. Levy feels this finding rules out socialization as the determining factor in the different brain organization of men and women. The brain matures by its own preprogrammed laws, and learning and experience cannot change that progression. "Although a culture might selectively reward verbal skills in girls and spatial skills in boys, and so promote more rapid maturation of that hemisphere's abilities," Levy says, "there is no way a parent could reward the more rapidly maturing hemisphere independent of the skills for which it is specialized."

Turning on the Hemispheres

While the two hemispheres of women's brains seem to be less specialized than men's on verbal and spatial skills, the distribution of most other mental functions is about the same for both sexes. Psychologist Richard Davidson and his coworkers at Harvard have found another hemispheric sex difference, however; one that involves hemispheric arousal as well as specialization. They studied the degree of electrical activity in each half of the brain during a series of mental tasks quite unlike the perceptual tests other researchers—including Lansdell, Witelson, and Reid—have used. The Harvard group had their subjects *generate* a response rather than simply perceive something. For example, they asked them to whistle the melody of a song, then speak the lyrics, and, finally, sing it. They also asked the subjects to relive the feelings of an angry scene and then a relaxing one from the past, to imagine

writing a letter about the experience, and to picture the events.

Sex differences did not appear on every task, but when they did, they invariably showed that females' brains became selectively more activated than did males'. That is, when a task required verbal skills, the left hemisphere was relatively more activated; when it required nonverbal skills, the right was more active. Women seemed better able to activate only those zones that were needed for the task at hand. The difference between the sexes in what happens where in the brain depends in part on what mental skill being is exercised.

The patterns of activation in men and women, says Davidson, can help us understand their different cognitive skills. Women are better at perceiving emotion in a face—which Davidson sees as a right-hemisphere talent that could be hampered by simultaneous activation of the left hemisphere's verbal centers. Women also excel at verbal tasks, a left-hemisphere skill that would likewise be hindered by right-hemisphere activity. Both these skills may require unilateral activation of the hemispheres; one half turns on while the other quiets down.

Thus, Witelson's theory that women don't do as well when they are required to perform two cognitively different tasks at the same time has a corollary: the possibility that women may be better cognitive specialists. As Davidson discovered, women seem better able to focus attention on one particular task—whether it is driving a strange route or carrying on a conversation—and do it more efficiently. Men, as we have seen, seem to be better at tasks that require two different cognitive approaches at the same time.

Blueprint for the Brain

Witelson points out that if environmental factors were the major cause of sex differences in cognition, those differences should increase with age. Such is not the case: what data there are tell us that, although most females are superior to males in some verbal abilities, this sex difference declines over the lifespan; the male superiority in spatial ability is quite

marked, but it remains fairly constant throughout the lifespan, according to Witelson. "That the behavioral differences between the sexes do not increase from childhood to maturity," she concludes, "suggests biological rather than environmental factors as the cause."

Another finding that buttresses the biological view is that spatial ability seems to be inherited. Psychologists R. Darrell Bock and Donald Kolakowski tested family members for spatial ability and found that a correlation of scores between family members fit the pattern that would be expected if this skill were transmitted by a recessive gene on the X chromosome.

Some researchers, such as Marjorie LeMay of Harvard Medical School, have found in fetuses and newborns the same types of disproportions in the size of various parts of the brain as were discovered for adults in 1968 by Norman Geschwind, also of Harvard Medical School. Autopsies on right-handed people, for example, reveal that their left temporal lobe is larger than their right; left-handers also exhibit anatomical asymmetry, but it can be on either side of the brain. Unlike electrical activity in the brain, however, there is no difference between the sexes on these size differences. Although investigators believe that they underlie the functional specialization of the halves of the brain, this has not yet been proven.

The presence of these structural asymmetries from birth suggests that there is a genetic blueprint for them, but it is still unclear whether functional specialization is present at birth or develops as the child matures. Jerre Levy is one who thinks that brain specialization does not develop as a child matures, but exists from birth. She believes that the tests are inadequate to detect them; in most young children, she says, neither hemisphere has cognitive skills adequate to the challenge of most tests for brain function. Levy emphasizes, however, that while the site of a particular skill may be fixed from birth, learning determines how much that skill develops. "A brain is meant to experience," she says, "and the rate of brain maturation depends on how much the growing child experiences." Even if sex differences are wired in from birth, treating little girls and little boys differently will affect drastically how each develops; being aware of sexism in socialization is still vital.

We have anthropological evidence that sex differences in an ability can be large, small, or even disappear, depending on how children are raised. In cultures where women aren't allowed to roam freely, their visual-spatial skills are very poor relative to those of men; but where both sexes are given independence early in life, as among the Eskimo, they are much closer in this ability. Any skill improves with practice, and how well a person's genetic potential for a given ability is realized depends on practice.

Electrical Potentials

Monte Buchsbaum's new line of research has uncovered biochemical differences in the brain that affect perception—differences that may have far-reaching consequences for the ways men and women react to stress and sensory overload. Buchsbaum, who is chief of the section on clinical psychophysiology at the National Institute of Mental Health, used electroencephalographs and computers to analyze the evoked potential (EP), a measure of the brain's electrical response to stimuli such as light and sound. An EP will have a different wave form and size, depending on such factors as the stimuli's intensity and how much interest they arouse in the individual. The more attention a person pays, or the louder the stimulus, the larger the EP.

Women, Buchsbaum found, usually have larger EPs than men do, whether the stimulus is a flashing light, a repeated tone, or an electric shock on the forearm. Across the board—in every sense tested, and especially at higher levels of intensity—women's brains react more. This sensitivity to stimulus marks proportionately more women as "augmenters," people who increase the intensity of their reaction to a stimulus in their brain response (see "The Sensoristat in the Brain," *Psychology Today*, May 1978).

Researchers have found that augmenting is most pronounced among individuals who have very small amounts of monoamine oxidase

(MAO) in their bodies. MAO is an enzyme important in the metabolism of the brain's chemical neurotransmitters, which carry messages between the synapses. There is evidence, Buchsbaum notes, that high levels of the female sex hormone estrogen suppress MAO. Perhaps estrogen interacts with low MAO to enhance augmentation in certain women, he theorizes. Whatever the reason, more women than men show the augmenting EP pattern.

Buchsbaum ties this greater brain response in women to a range of behavioral differences between the sexes. He believes it may explain why women rate life changes, such as moving, marriage, loss of a job, as more stressful than do men. Augmenters exaggerate the impact of such stressors.

Hard psychophysiological measures such as the evoked potential, says Buchsbaum, might be a more fruitful method of studying sex differences than the verbal tests normally used. Such tests are influenced strongly by socialization and learning; to pinpoint a difference due to biology, those social effects must be pared away. The higher ratings for stress that women give for life changes, for example, could just as well be due to the ways they are raised or their openness to answering certain questions as to their augmenting pattern. Much more research is needed before we would be justified to conclude that women react more poorly to stress than do men because of biological differences. Studying processes less vulnerable to social biases—such as brain waves, chromosomal abnormalities, and hormones—can reduce various social biases, Buchsbaum maintains.

A Vote for Sex Hormones

Diane McGuinness and Karl Pribram are among those who hold that differing ratios of sex hormones acting on particular brain structures underlie sex differences. They favor the view that males function better at tasks in which the two hemispheres are not in competition, while females are better able to shift flexibly from one to another—a conclusion in keeping with the findings of Davidson and his group at Harvard, among others.

McGuinness and Pribram find the

key to sex differences in the brain's sensorimotor processes. They speculate that male and female hormones start the process by acting on different parts of the brain, which produces different behavior. The varied behaviors, in turn, would lead to development of certain parts of the brain (which become more complex as connections are made between cells) and not others. For example, boys' gross movements, such as rough-and-tumble play, would require the eye and brain to learn to help the body adjust to sudden major shifts in the visual environment. In women, fine movements in touching or speaking would lead to development of brain areas controlling dexterity and auditory sensitivity.

HOW BRAINS DIFFER IN ELECTRICAL POTENTIAL

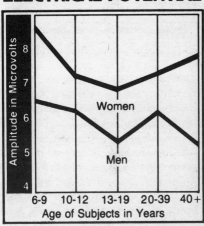

The activity of male and female brains in response to a burst of light, as measured on an electroencephalograph by Monte Buchsbaum. Shown here are average responses for 79 males and 87 females of various ages. Buchsbaum has found a strong sex difference in reactions to all such stimuli.

We have seen that there are several competing views on what differences exist in brain function between men and women, and several theories of *why* they exist. To reach one's own conclusions, it is necessary to wade through a mass of studies and reject some views while emphasizing others. McGuinness and Pribram have done just that. They admit quite a different range of findings as pertinent evidence, after examining the senses and attention as well as cognitive skills. The profiles they sketch for sex competencies are unique in the field (see box below).

Summarizing these sex-specific abilities, McGuinness and Pribram characterize man as a "manipulative animal" who tends to express himself in actions, while woman is a "communicative animal," who prefers to receive, remember, and transmit signs and symbols to others. These differences are only in degree, of course—both sexes manipulate and communicate, but each has its preferred mode. McGuinness and Pribram say these modes fit observations of primate behavior, where cultural influences are not a factor:

"In all primate societies the division of labor by gender creates a highly stable social system, the dominant males controlling territorial boundaries and maintaining order among lesser males by containing and preventing their aggression, the females tending the young and form-

ing alliances with other females. Human primates follow this same pattern so remarkably that it is not difficult to argue for biological bases for the type of social order that channels aggression to guard the territory which in turn maintains an equable environment for the young."

Different patterns of brain organization seem to be a legacy of our evolutionary past. Brains of apes show anatomical asymmetries similar to those in the human brain. More significantly, the fossil remains of skulls of early man also show that the halves of the brain are similarly mismatched. Levy interprets this fact in terms of the evolutionary advantage flexibility in brain localization might bring to an evolving species. Human social groups would benefit greatly from a brain flexibility that provided a range of people with varied mental talents who could fill specialized roles. Levy theorizes that the present

pattern of sex differences in brain localization may have developed during the several hundred years that humans were hunter-gatherers. Women's superior verbal fluency, facial recognition, and ability to read emotions, for example, are well-suited to the traditional mother's role; male facility in mental mapping and greater aggression would suit them to roam in search of food. Since society changes more rapidly than do genetic blueprints, many of the various sex differences in brain organization that were highly functional during that early stage of human development linger on.

People presumably select jobs requiring skills they have in good measure. The fact that women are underrepresented in certain professions could be due to differences in brain functions as well as sex bias in hiring. There may be fewer female architects, engineers, and artists, Witelson sug-

MALE-FEMALE CONTRASTS: THE McGUINNESS-PRIBRAM VIEW

With a fair amount of courage, Diane McGuinness and Karl Pribram have tried to summarize what the growing psychological literature tells us about the various brain-based competencies of men and women. Both are respected neuropsychologists at Stanford. While critics have attacked the exercise, claiming they were too generous in accepting some data as valid, their conclusions* are, nonetheless, interesting:

Men, say McGuinness and Pribram, have better daylight vision than women. They are, in general, less sensitive to extreme heat and more sensitive to extreme cold. Men have faster reaction times from mid-childhood on; even as infants, they tend to be more interested in objects than in people, and are more skilled at gross motor movements. Boys engage in rough-and-tumble play more than girls; as infants, they spend more time playing with objects other than toys, and invent novel uses for them. Men excel in a

*To be published in *Cognitive Growth and Development—Essays in Honor of Herbert G. Birch*, Morton Bortner, ed., Brunner/Mazel.

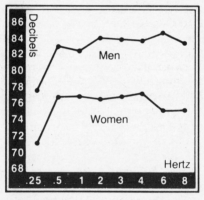

Males generally tolerate higher volumes than females, according to work by Stanford's Diane McGuinness. The chart shows average responses of 25 male and 25 female college students asked to note the point at which a sound became uncomfortably loud. (Hertz numbers represent thousands of cycles per second.)

wide range of skills involving the perception of depth in space, an ability that gives them an edge in mechanical tasks. Boys' greater ability in math could also be a spatial skill, since it shows up strongest when geometry and trigonometry are included. Finally, the fact that boys are more easily distracted by novel objects, combined with their greater exploratory behavior, sug-

gests a kind of curiosity that leads to success in problem-solving tasks that require manipulation.

Women, by contrast, have more sensitive taste, are more sensitive to touch in all parts of the body, have better hearing (particularly in the higher ranges), are less tolerant of loud volumes (at 85 decibels and above, any sound seems twice as loud to them as it does to males), are less tolerant of repetitive sounds, and have better night vision. From infancy on, women excel in many verbal skills, are better in manual dexterity and fine coordination, and process information faster, particularly in tasks (like neurosurgery) that require rapid choices. Women are more interested in people, as infants are more attentive to sounds and their emotional meaning, and are more socially responsive and empathic. They are less distracted by sights while listening, more accurately perceive "subliminal" messages, and are better at remembering the names and faces of old high-school classmates. Women's greater interest in people also shows up in better empathy.
                                    —D. G.

gests, "because such professions require the kind of thinking that may depend on spatial skills. Similar factors may account for the smaller number of female . . . musical composers. In contrast, women performers (vocalists, instrumentalists) and writers are less rare. This may be because the skills involved in these talents may depend on functions women do well—linguistic and fine motor coordination. Different neural organization may underlie contrasting profiles of ability, and thus, the different representation of the sexes in various professions may have a biological basis." Witelson goes on to note that these *average differences shouldn't shut women out of any profession*: "Females may differ from males in the *number* of individuals with excellent skills in certain spheres of activity, not the *level* of skill possible in the highly skilled individual."

Should boys and girls be taught differently because of sex differences? Girls progress faster in reading than do boys, Witelson admits, but this needn't be the case. Learning to read is not purely a linguistic skill—learning to recognize letters, for example, is a spatial process. Since the brains of boys and girls seem to be organized differently for verbal and spatial skills, reading may draw on different parts of the brain in the two sexes. If so, boys may respond better to one teaching approach, girls to another.

The "phonics" method, for example, stresses sound recognition, mainly a left-hemisphere function, while the "look-say" method calls for recognizing words on sight, an approach that involves both hemispheres. Since girls are more likely to

have spatial skills on both sides of the brain, they can probably learn about as well either way. But because most boys have greater separation of verbal and spatial skills in their brains, the integration of these skills may be more difficult. "What they might need," Witelson speculates, "is an approach that combines phonics and 'look-say,' thus helping them to integrate verbal and spatial skills. This might even suggest that separate groups or classes for the sexes would be beneficial for teaching reading, as is the case for physical education."

Such a proposal may be disturbing for some people, as indicated by a recent response to Witelson's suggestion in the British journal *New Scientist:* "Witelson puts her head in a potential noose of controversy by suggesting that . . . different techniques should be used to teach boys and girls to read. The social and organizational disadvantages of doing that would almost certainly far outweigh the small educational advantage it might conceivably prove to have."

If differences in brain organization mean men and women have differing intellectual strengths and weaknesses, should we always cater to their strengths, as Witelson proposes for teaching reading? Psychologist Robert Glaser, reviewing past attempts to teach people more effectively by concentrating on their preferred mode of perception, finds many have failed. On the other hand, he argues that there may be good reason to focus teaching efforts on a student's weakness. Schools already do this for verbal skills with remedial-reading classes and clinics, in which boys are

considerably overrepresented. But there are no comparable remedial programs for those weak in spatial skills, where presumably girls would be in the majority.

Our knowledge of the specifics of sex differences in the brain is still in its infancy. The views of Witelson and Glaser are among many speculations, each equally viable at this point. Since the social and personal implications of any one viewpoint can vary drastically, we must be careful about jumping to conclusions.

Even when we are more sure of the true nature of sex differences in the brain, how much should we let them affect our lives? In *A Room of One's Own*, Virginia Woolf wrote, "The nerves that feed the brain would seem to differ in men and women, and if you are going to make them work their best and hardest, you must find out what treatment suits them." Well aware of how biological determinism can be used as a "scientific" justification for sexist bias, McGuinness and Pribram make a plea that echoes Virginia Woolf's sentiments: "Men and women are *different*. What needs to be made equal is the value placed upon these differences."

For further information, read:
Maccoby, Eleanor E. and Carol N. Jacklin. *The Psychology of Sex Differences*, Stanford University Press, 1974, $18.95.
McGuinness, Diane and Karl Pribram. "The Origins of Sensory Bias in the Development of Gender Differences in Perception and Cognition," in *Cognitive Growth and Development—Essays in Honor of Herbert G. Birch*, Morton Bortner, ed., Brunner/Mazel, in press.
Parsons, Jacquelynne E., ed. *Biopsychological Factors Influencing Sex-role Related Behaviors*, Hemisphere Publishing Corporation, in press.
Witelson, Sandra F. "Sex and the Single Hemisphere: Specialization of the Right Hemisphere for Spatial Processing," *Science*, Vol. 193, No. 4251, 1976.
Wittig, Michele A. and Anne C. Petersen, eds. *Sex Related Differences in Cognitive Functioning: Developmental Bases*, Academic Press, in press.

The Origins of VIOLENCE

Richard Restak

IN RECENT YEARS psychobiologists have started assembling the pieces in a vast jigsaw puzzle whose solution may finally result in an understanding and reduction of violence in different cultures. Anthropologists are fond of pointing out that not every culture is violent. Some, in fact, are nonviolent. The key question is, of course, What accounts for the differences?

One intriguing association that emerges from cross-cultural studies relates early infant-care practices to the later development of violence. With few exceptions, societies which provide infants with a great deal of physical affection and bodily contact produce relatively nonviolent adults. In societies where infants are touched, held, and carried, the incidence of violence is much less than in societies where infant care is restricted to merely feeding and changing. Left at this, such findings tell us little about the mechanisms involved. A superficial interpretation might be that touching and carrying are two aspects of good mothering. Or put differently, infant stimulation and interaction with a mothering (or fathering) figure are important for normal development.

In the late 1950s and early '60s, Harry and Margaret Kuenne Harlow, at the Primate Laboratory of the University of Wisconsin, began a series of experimental observations on rhesus monkeys that provided the first experimental evidence to suggest that abnormal early brain development, brought on by poor mothering, might be the key to understanding some forms of violence. Rhesus monkeys make excellent experimental subjects for investigating such a relationship. Along with humans, rhesus monkeys undergo a long period of physical and emotional development which is heavily dependent on early physical contact and attachment between infant monkeys and their mothers. The Harlows first studied the effects of isolating the infant rhesus monkeys soon after birth. Alone in a cage, the isolated monkeys were able to view other monkeys in similar cages across the laboratory, but weren't able to make physical contact with them.

When later studied as adults, the isolated monkeys were withdrawn, often sitting for long periods of time staring blankly into space. In addition, they exhibited self-mutilating behavior, often pinching a patch of skin between their fingers hundreds of times a day. On occasion, the animals bit parts of their own bodies, often in response to the approach of their human caretakers. At still a later point, self-aggression changed into aggression toward others, a "cringing fearfulness" merging into "prominent displays of hostility."

But the most intriguing observation of the isolated monkeys concerns their later behavior toward their young. Isolated females become brutal, indifferent mothers who, as a group, show less warmth and affection and, on occasion, kill their offspring. This was the first indication that the mother-infant interaction was a reciprocal one. Isolated, unstimulated monkeys grew up to become unstable, brutal parents. Deprivation of some aspect of the physical closeness usually bestowed on an infant resulted in a later inability to be a good parent. But what aspect of the mother-infant interaction is most important?

In an attempt to understand the mothering process, the Harlows placed a group of newborn monkeys in cages with two types of surrogate mothers—one made of cloth, the other made entirely of wires. In almost all instances the infant monkeys spent more time clinging to their cloth-covered mothers than to their wire mothers, even when the monkeys obtained milk from a bottle attached to the wire mothers! The Harlows interpreted these findings as showing the overwhelming importance of bodily contact and the immediate comfort it supplies in forming the infant's attachment for its mother.

If the wire surrogate was replaced with a cloth mother, one capable of rocking, the monkeys, in most cases, preferred the rocking to the motionless cloth mother. When the two groups were later compared, their behavior contrasted dramatically. Those monkeys raised with motionless cloth mothers now showed repetitive rocking motions, while the monkeys provided earlier with moving cloth surrogates failed to show abnormal movement patterns. From here, psychobiologists speculate that sensory stimulation might be an absolute requirement for normal brain development. If this is true, however, what kinds of stimulation are most important?

Infants and children immobilized in bed for the treatment of bone fractures often develop emotional disturbances marked by hyperactivity and outbursts of rage and violence. Since only movement, and not sight or hearing, is restricted, a relationship is suggested between early diminished movement and later abnormal, often violent, behavior.

A similar correlation can be demonstrated in adults. When a group of adult faculty members at a university took part in an experiment testing the effects of immobilizing their heads in a halter, 85 percent reported the experience as "stressful." Vision and hearing were not interfered with and the subjects were free to converse with each other and engage in any activity they wished as long as their heads remained in the halter. Restriction of movement alone resulted in "intellectual inefficiency, bizarre thoughts, exaggerated emotional reactions, and unusual bodily sensations." In adults, as well as infants, immobility alone, despite intact vision or hearing, can result in abnormal mental experiences, disturbed behavior and, in many cases, violence.

Observations of mother-infant interactions in the laboratory yield similar results. Physical holding and carrying of the infant turns out to be the most important factor responsible for the infant's normal mental and social development. Dr. Frank Pedersen, chief of the Section on Parent-Child Interaction of the National Institute of Child Health and Human Development, compared the effects of visual, auditory, and movement stimulation on the infant's mental and psychomotor development. Out of six variables ranging from social re-

From *Saturday Review*, May 12, 1979. From THE BRAIN: THE LAST FRONTIER by Richard Restak. Copyright © 1979 by Richard M. Restak. Reprinted by permission of Doubleday & Company, Inc.

sponsiveness to object permanence, movement correlated positively with all six areas, whereas vision and hearing were important in only one.

So far, the results I've been describing are a matter of hard scientific fact. From here we move into issues that are more speculative. Not all psychobiologists are in agreement here, but the general trend is toward a revolution in our concept of the role of the environment in normal brain development and the subsequent tendency toward violence.

Any type of body movement, even something as passive as being held or rocked, results in a train of impulses directed toward a specific part of the brain, the cerebellum. Tradi-

---

Without physical closeness, the infant's pleasure system is stunted. His difficulty in feeling pleasure may later tip him toward violence.

---

tionally, the cerebellum, a small three-lobed structure behind the occipital lobe at the posterior part of the brain, is considered an important coordinator for movement. When you reach for a cup of coffee, for instance, the cerebellum is responsible for the smooth coordination necessary to bring the liquid to your lips. Patients with diseases of the cerebellum cannot lift a cup of coffee without spilling it. They also frequently sway when walking and, in some cases, cannot even sit without tilting to one side or the other. In a phrase, the cerebellum is responsible for smoothly coordinated muscular efforts. A ballet dancer represents perfect cerebellar functioning in which thousands of muscles are controlled with exquisite precision.

When an infant is rocked or cuddled, impulses are directed to the cerebellum that stimulate its development, a process that goes on until at least age two. In fact, the cerebellum is unique, since it is the only part of the brain where brain-cell multiplication continues long after birth.

"The cerebellum provides an explanatory model for the effects of social isolation," says Dr. James Prescott, a developmental neuropsychologist at the National Institute of Child Health and Human Development. "The rocking behavior of isolation-reared monkeys and institutionalized children may result from insufficient body contact and movement. Consequently, both touch and movement receptors and their projections to other brain structures don't receive sufficient sensory stimulation for normal development and function."

Prescott's unorthodox theory emphasized the role of a brain structure, the cerebellum, which, according to traditional psychobiological thinking, has nothing to do with behavior. Not surprisingly, it was originally greeted with a good deal of disbelief and skepticism. For one thing, how could such a radical proposal be proven? What data exist to prove that emotional reactions, such as violence, are related to activities in the cerebellum?

"The first requirement was to demonstrate that the cerebellum is connected with the emotional control centers of the limbic system," says Prescott. "There was really no reason to think that there were such connections other than the observation that lack of cerebellar stimulation, such as with isolation-reared monkeys or institutionalized children, leads to emotional disorders. The obvious place to look, it seemed, was in the brains of Harlow's isolation-reared monkeys."

In 1975, Prescott sent five isolation-reared monkeys from Harlow's laboratory to Robert G. Heath at Tulane University in New Orleans. Heath, a 64-year-old neuropsychiatrist, is a fiercely controversial figure who, over the past 25 years, has implanted stimulating and recording electrodes deep within the brains of a wide variety of people. In the process Heath, a flamboyant but indefatigable researcher, has created for himself an international reputation for work which has ranged from studies measuring the brain's electrical changes accom-

panying normal orgasm to the detection, by electron microscope, of the subtle alteration in the brains of monkeys trained to smoke marijuana. Heath's principal research interest, however, has always remained the psychobiology of psychosis and violence.

Psychosis, particularly schizophrenia, is marked by dramatic alterations in the patient's ability to experience pleasure. Anhedonia—literally the loss of the pleasure sense—is often accompanied by excessively painful emotional behaviors such as fear or rage. Although seemingly incapable of deriving pleasure, schizophrenics have heightened appreciations of pain, anguish, and loneliness. In 1954, Heath began a lifetime study looking for the brain mechanisms responsible for this pleasure-displeasure disturbance.

What emerged from Heath's rather unorthodox experiments (one patient retained an electric stimulator in his head for over three years) was a "map" of the brain's pleasure and displeasure centers. Patients implanted with electrodes in their septum, for instance, would selectively self-stimulate repeatedly. At other times during pleasure, such as an orgasm, activation could be detected in the septal region. With more intense sexual orgasm, faster-frequency activity occurred which appeared similar to the brain waves seen during some forms of epileptic seizures. In some cases, even talking about sexual matters was enough to elicit similar septal activations.

Heath's experimental findings on pleasure-displeasure complemented Prescott's observations on the important role of early movement stimulation and violence. Certainly, according to traditional ideas about the cerebellum and the limbic system, there seemed to be no way to correlate them.

At the base of Prescott's hunch that emotion and movement are interrelated were some common observations. Children like to be picked up, rocked, and taken on merry-go-rounds and roller coasters, as well as being whirled through the air. Most of us enjoy warm baths and soothing massages as calmers of tension and anxiety. Physical exertion such as sports or hard physical work can be exhilarating, even on occasion providing a "natural high." In all these instances, body movement seems to induce pleasurable emotions.

If these behavioral correlations exist, then, Prescott reasoned, there *must* be connections between the brain areas responsible for emotion (the limbic system) and those controlling movement (cerebellum). To look for these connections, Dr. Heath employed the method of evoked potentials. After implanting electrodes into several brain sites, a brief electrical stimulus was delivered to one of them while simultaneous recordings were made from the other sites. If activity could be detected, it provided an indication that the two sites were interconnected.

Heath's initial results with the Harlow monkeys showed, not surprisingly, that the limbic areas responsible for emotion (hippocampus, amygdala, and septal areas) were directly linked. What was more surprising, however, was the discovery of connections between these emotional centers and the cerebellum. In addition, two-way communication could be shown between the centers in the cerebellum and the emotional areas of the brain for pleasure and displeasure.

These results, Prescott believes, provide a preliminary basis for a psychobiological theory of the origin of human violence, which may result from a permanent defect in the pleasure centers secondary to inadequate early mothering experiences. The infant who is deprived of movement and physical closeness will fail to develop the brain pathways that mediate pleasure. In essence, such people may be suffering at the neuronal level from stunted growth of their pleasure system.

In this model the expression of pleasure cannot be transmitted through the appropriate parts of the brain, because there are fewer cell connections. Since the infant is deprived of movement and touch stimuli, fewer impulses are relayed to the immature cerebellum; as a result, it develops abnormally.

2. THE BIOLOGICAL BASES OF BEHAVIOR

Fewer connections are then made between the cerebellum and the pleasure centers. Later, the person may have problems experiencing pleasure and, as a result, develop an insatiable need for it. In the absence of pleasure, the balance tips toward dysfunctional states such as violence.

"Think of these people as similar to diabetics," suggests Prescott. "As long as the diabetic gets his regular supply of insulin, everything is fine. Deprive him of insulin, and all kinds of physical and emotional disturbances may result. In a similar way, a child deprived of physical closeness will develop an extraordinary need for affection later in life which is unlikely to be fulfilled in the real adult world. This person often lapses into periodic violence."

Obviously, the relationship of environmental stimulation, brain development, and subsequent violence is complex. So far, the theory that early physical contact and movement may play a later role in a tendency toward violence remains an intriguing but unproven possibility which can only be settled by further psychobiological research. In the meantime, however, increasing violence on our streets and in our homes underscores the importance of carrying out whatever research will enable us to decide one way or another.

Child abuse is one promising area worthy of further research. Pediatricians have known for years that violent parents are often themselves the victims of child abuse. Psychiatric interviews with child abusers reveal a pattern of reduced pleasure in daily living. In addition, they typically report little enjoyment of sexuality, with only a few of the mothers reporting that they have ever experienced orgasm. Most appear so involved in catering to their own insatiable emotional needs that they have little time to respond to the basic needs of their children.

Open discussion with such parents often reveals an isolated, alienated person with a quick temper, low frustration tolerance, and a sense of personal deprivation. Since they cannot receive pleasure, they are also poor providers of pleasure to their infants. Child-abusing mothers rarely report having "fun" with their babies, and in a physician's office demonstrate little positive interaction, often spending the examination time concentrating on how to satisfy their own emotional needs. The abusive parent's behavior is, in essence, reminiscent of the mothering patterns of Harlow's isolated monkeys, who, in many cases, had to be physically restrained from abusing their infants. The most pernicious aspect of the child-abuse syndrome, of course, is its tendency to repeat itself from generation to generation.

Thanks to a greater awareness of child abuse on the part of

physicians and the general public, child abusers are now coming to public attention sooner. In addition, major hospitals are setting up child-abuse clinics with established protocols designed to improve the quality of interaction between parent and child. Increased infant-care instruction, a lengthened period of maternal "lying in" arrangements, instructions on feeding patterns which emphasize physical closeness—these are only a few of the newer methods being tried, all of which tend to increase cerebellar stimulation through early and sustained physical contact between parent and child.

Child abuse, along with other forms of violence in our society, is a multifaceted problem. To explain violence as entirely the result of a brain dysfunction is unrealistic and socially disastrous. Still, I consider the current attempts to relate pleasure-displeasure states, mental illness, and the early patterns of parenting as exciting and promising. If the technique of cerebellar stimulation works as well as early reports are suggesting, psychobiologists may soon be able to improve the lives of thousands of "hopeless" patients. Despite the success of medication in the control of mental illness, there remains a small core of untreated, frequently violent patients who are doomed to spend the rest of their lives in institutions. It is with these patients that the cerebellar-stimulation techniques seem to work best.

Along with basic brain research, however, we need parallel studies on the social aspects of violence and child abuse. Warm, demonstrative parents...should...be less likely than their cold, aloof counterparts to produce violently disturbed children. Is this true? At this point, no one can be certain. In fact, research couldn't begin to investigate the question until the recent suggestion that movement might be important for healthy brain and behavioral development. The acceptance of such a view, however, requires a paradigm change in our attitude toward the effects of the environment on brain development. It isn't intuitively obvious that the cerebellum, a regulator of movement, might also be involved in the modulation of pleasure or the later propensity to violence. Although we are still not sure a new and exciting approach is now available which may reward the collaboration of psychobiologists and social scientists. Who would have even imagined 10 years ago that studies on early brain development and infant stimulation might someday suggest a provisional theory about the origin and treatment of human violence?

Richard Restak is a neurologist and author of Premeditated Man: Bioethics and the Control of Future Human Life.

THE SPLIT BRAIN LAB

WAYNE SAGE

While some researchers study human behavior for the meaning of consciousness and a dual mind, neurobiologist Roger Sperry continues his careful scientific scrutiny of the physiology of the human brain.

Wagne Sage is a contributing editor of HUMAN BEHAVIOR.

The suspicion that we each have not just one mind, but two, has been around for a long time. The mind with which we communicate with the outside world as we reason our way along fails all too often to convincingly explain our behavior. If, as Freud insisted, a second consciousness influences what we do and say in ways our conscious minds can only try to rationalize, those who tried to probe that subliminal second psyche generally ended up beguiled by the vagaries of human nature. Psychology, determined to be a science, turned to mindless behaviorism.

But a new mentalism may be upon us. This time the theories of dual consciousness are not borne of conjecture and inference, but of laboratory experiments that seem to make the conclusions logically inescapable.

For more than 20 years, neurobiologist Roger W. Sperry, Ph.D., of the California Institute of Technology in Pasadena and his colleagues, most notably J. E. Bogen, now at Ross-Loos Medical Group in Los Angeles, and Michael Gazzaniga at the University of California, Santa Barbara, have sought the psyche not in their subjects' ramblings, but in the physiology of their brains. They seem to have discovered in each subject two distinctly different consciousnesses, worlds of perception and thought that are more than the neurological circuits through which they channel. Says Dr. Sperry: "The term 'mental forces' would seem to be appropriate."

The grand guru of the theories themselves is psychologist Robert Ornstein, whose book *The Psychology of Consciousness* split not only the mind, but the cultures of the world in his double-barreled view of mentality. The left hemisphere of the brain, concludes Ornstein on the basis of Sperry's findings, operates rationally; it dominates the mental way of the Western world. The right hemisphere works intuitively and is the consciousness of the East. From such groundwork, Ornstein points to everything from peyote to yoga to the symbolism of Walt Disney cartoons as manifestations of such divergent mentalities.

The objective evidence from which Ornstein expounds is Sperry's demonstration that the two hemispheres of the cerebrum are basically different in the way they think and relate to the world outside the human skull. As the left brain to Ornstein's right brain, Sperry was intrigued by the fact that each of the hemispheres of the cerebrum—the centers of higher intellect that sprout like two giant cauliflowers from the more primitive areas of the brain—have always seemed oblivious to each other's existence. Patients could lose virtually the entire right hemisphere through injury or surgery, it was found, and be unaware that it was gone until it was demonstrated for them through laboratory tests that parts of their visual field were missing. Also, experiments with animals, in which the nerves connecting the two hemispheres were split, showed that each side of the brain learned independently and had a separate memory. A task or response taught to the left hemisphere, which normally controls the right hand or paw, had to be retaught to the right hemisphere, which performed the same task with the left hand or paw. Even more intriguingly, one side of the brain could be put to work on one task while the other side of the brain was being trained simultaneously to do something else.

The full significance of such separation became evident only within the last 12 years, when the opportunity arose to study the hemispheres separately in humans. That opportunity was made possible by Los Angeles Drs. Phillip J. Vogel, chief of neurosurgery at the White Memorial Medical Center, and Bogen at Ross-Loos Medical Group, who surgically severed all nerves connecting the left and right hemispheres of the cerebrums of 16 patients. Those patients provided the only chance to study separately the two lobes of the human brain.

All the patients were intractable epileptics. The surgeons were trying to isolate seizures so they would not transfer from one side of the brain to the other. While a seizure was going on in one side of the brain, they hoped the other side would take over control of the body. It worked, and the patients continued their lives with no apparent repercussions from the surgery.

How such radical surgery could leave patients apparently unaffected became known through Sperry's experiments with them. Investigating the apparent indifference of the two hemispheres to the fact that all communication had been cut off between them, Sperry colleagues Jerre Levy and Colwyn Treverthen constructed a set of "chimeric stimuli." They gathered a set of photographs of different faces—a beautiful young female fashion model, a pudgy-cheeked boy, an old codger and so on—and cut each photo down the middle of the face. The halves of two different faces were pasted together, and the reconstructed photos were then covered and mounted precisely at the midpoint of the subject's visual field so that the left side of the photo would be visible only to that part of the retina relaying information to the right hemisphere of the brain. The right half of the picture (which was half a photo from a different face) would appear in the visual field of the brain's left hemisphere. With the subject's head held still, the image was then flashed before his or her eyes at one-tenth of a second—too fast for the eyes to jerk to examine the opposite visual fields.

The result was the discovery of two

From *Human Behavior*, June 1976. Copyright © 1976 *Human Behavior* Magazine. Reprinted by permission.

completely separate visual worlds within the same head. When the subjects were asked what they had seen, the response was the name of the old man in the right half of the photograph when half old man and half young man was shown. But when asked to point with their left hand to the complete photo of the person they had seen, the left hand pointed to the photo of the young boy. With the subjects saying they had seen one photo but with their left hand pointing to another photo, the experimenters asked the subjects if they had noticed anything unusual about the picture that had been flashed before them. They said no, nothing at all. Clearly, each side of the brain had seen half a face, filled it in (as experiments in perception have shown the mind is wont to do), and neither side was aware of what the other had seen.

Further experiments were conducted with other types of images. In one such trial, the phrase *key ring* was shown to the subjects, again set at the midpoint of the visual field so that the first word, *key*, went into the right hemisphere while the latter, *ring*, was relayed to the left hemisphere. When asked to read the word they had seen, the subjects said "ring." When asked to retrieve the object with their left hand from a group of objects on the table, the subjects picked up the key—without realizing any contradiction in what they were doing.

"Each hemisphere has its own inner visual world, each cut off from the conscious awareness of the other," wrote Sperry following the investigations. But the full significance of that finding was just dawning. Later, after further experiments, he would add: "Each of the separated hemispheres appears to have its own private sensations, perceptions, thoughts, feelings and memories. Everything we have seen so far indicates that the surgery has left each of these people with two separate minds, that is, with two separate spheres of consciousness."

With the subjects straddled across their visual fields, each arm extended behind a partition and their eyes fixed forward, all visual input was channeled separately to the left and right hemispheres. Each side of the brain was presented with a puzzle of geometric forms. The experimenters stood back and watched in amazement as each hand went about trying to figure out the puzzle on its own, each approaching the problem in its own way, the left hand literally not knowing what the right hand was doing.

The left hemisphere, using the right hand, seemed to approach the task in a logical manner, examining edges, murmuring to itself about similarities and differences and how the forms might fit together. The right hemisphere, using the left hand, seemed to take a totally intuitive approach, trying various spatial arrangements and, interestingly, generally solving the puzzles much more quickly than did the reasoning left hemisphere.

This difference in the way the two hemispheres of the brain think would revolutionize the psychology of consciousness. As the experiments progressed, the left brain, as the left hemisphere of the cerebrum came to be called, was found consistently to be our rational lobe. It takes in information bit by bit, processes it in linear, logical fashion and carries on verbal and mathematical reasoning. It is verbal and uses language to communicate with the outside world. The right hemisphere never speaks. It perceives images holistically in gestalts. It thinks abstractly, processes information in a spatial and intuitive way and seems to be the locus of our creative and artistic capabilities and our appreciation of forms and music.

The question as to why such doubling in visual perception should take place also seemed to make sense at last. All visual input was being seen separately by each side of the brain because each hemisphere was making quite different use of it.

How two completely separate consciousnesses could coexist may seem almost incomprehensible, at least to the left hemisphere reading this article. But such oblivion is maintained throughout our lives. Each lobe of the brain sees the world through the same eyes, hears through the same ears and, generally by virtue of living in the same body, has the same experiences as they develop. The left brain talks, rationalizes and reasons its way through life; the right rides along silently absorbed in its own mental world, contemplating it in its own nonverbal way.

"The brain is oblivious to what it lacks," explains Sperry. "Neither hemisphere knows about the experiences of the other; one hemisphere remains oblivious to the existence of the other. It's what you lose when you have a deep sleep without dreams," he adds, explaining the lack of awareness of brain-damaged patients who lose their right hemisphere and do not know it's gone.

One expert in dream research has suggested that the hemispheres may dream separately as well. This may explain the prevalence of strangers in our dreams. Over 40 percent of the characters in dreams are people who subjects say they have never seen before, research has shown. They may be people the right hemisphere has seen, but whom the left hemisphere does not remember because they have no verbal label. Research under Sperry has shown that the right hemisphere easily associates names with faces, but the left hemisphere has difficulty doing this. Also, researchers probing the REM (dream) stages of sleep often dredge up verbal content that does not correspond to the images. This may happen when the left hemisphere goes off dreaming verbally on its own, paying no attention to the images dreamed up in the brain's right lobe.

Unlike the brains of Sperry's subjects after surgery, the hemispheres of our brains do normally engage in a sort of cross talk. But just how they communicate and cooperate and in what terms is only dimly understood. Although either hemisphere can take control of the motor system, the left hemisphere—that consciousness we usually see in action and communicate with in others—is the more aggressive, executive (and some have said "masculine") hemisphere in running the body. Traditionally, it was called the "major hemisphere." Some experts were reluctant to believe the "minor hemisphere" on the right was even conscious, because they could not communicate with it.

"The reasoning seemed to be that the conscious self by nature has to be single and unified, as if the gates of heaven shall be opened only to one psyche per cranium," says Sperry. "The mute minor hemisphere seems to be carried along much as a passive, silent passenger who leaves the driving of behavior mainly to the left hemisphere . . . lacking language like the animal brain and unable to communicate what it is thinking or experiencing. It is much less accessible to investigation, and accordingly the nature and quality of its inner mental life . . . have remained relatively obscure."

Sperry's experiments seemed to demonstrate that the right hemisphere is not only conscious but, indeed, may be vastly underestimated in its capability and influence. "It is our interpretation, based on a large number and variety of nonverbal tests, that the 'minor hemisphere' is indeed a conscious system in its own right, perceiving, thinking, remembering, reasoning, willing and emoting, all at a characteristically human level," says Sperry.

Indeed, when the "minor hemisphere" of the lowest-scoring patient on the test of spatial forms was allowed to work without interference from the left hemisphere, it scored better than 31 percent of the college sophomores with whom the test was standardized. When the subject was presented the same test with free vision and unrestricted hand use, he scored lower than 99 percent of the same group, apparently due to the left hemisphere's interference and suppression of the right hemisphere's efforts. In laboratory tests in which the two hemispheres are in equal and free competition, it was found that either hemisphere was capable of capturing and controlling the motor system.

Perhaps more importantly, the silent right hemisphere may influence what we do and say on subtle and primitive levels, and in ways the left hemisphere does not always comprehend. In one experiment, Sperry and his colleagues flashed a series of photographs before the visual field of the right hemisphere. Among the usual dull laboratory photos were planted arousal photos, such as a picture of a nude body. The instant such a photo flashed by, a female subject became disturbed. She blushed. While the left hemisphere's words denied that anything had happened, her tone of voice made it obvious that this was not the case.

"Emotion is a pretty primitive basic system that has a lot of organization throughout the brain system," explains Sperry. When an emotion is triggered in one hemisphere, the other hemisphere very quickly realizes something is wrong in the body; but in this case, the left hemisphere had not seen the photo and could not explain why it was feeling so disturbed and aroused.

Even with the direct lines of communication cut, extreme care must be taken to keep the two hemispheres from finding other ways to communicate with each other, often in the most subtle ways. For example, the right hemisphere was able to perform well in tasks involving the construction of three-dimensional forms from two-dimensional drawings. When the left hemisphere attempted the task, it fumbled about with the right hand trying to reason its way through and finally gave

up. The right hemisphere, as if unable to restrain itself in the face of incompetence, reached over with the left hand and tried to take over.

In another instance, the left hemisphere was asked to try to figure out which light in a system of colored lights had just flashed. Since the lights were set to come on solely within the visual field of the right hemisphere, only the right hemisphere had seen the flash and knew the answer. Yet gradually, the left hemisphere was able to start coming up with the correct response. Since the right side cannot speak, when it heard the left hemisphere make a wrong guess, it would shake the person's head to let the left hemisphere know it had made the wrong choice. On the next guess, the left hemisphere would give the correct answer, unaware that it had been helped out by the right hemisphere. The researchers thus discovered that the right hemisphere was listening in.

Considerable confusion can also occur. If one hemisphere sees or hears the other give an answer it considers erroneous, it may make the person grimace or frown; or if it is the verbal hemisphere, it may make remarks such as, "What made me do that?" Sperry says, "We purposely do not dwell on these conflicts and pass along to the next trial.

"When one hemisphere takes command of the motor system of the brain stem or cord, it tends to prevent the other hemisphere from getting into that system. We sometimes deliberately put the right hand to a task, like doing a tic-tac-toe or sketching or rolling balls, just to keep it out of the picture so we can get to the right hemisphere."

The most important recent development in efforts to establish and maintain communication with only one hemisphere at a time is the "Z lens," invented by Dr. Eran Zaidel, a young biologist working with Sperry at Cal Tech. The equipment consists of a series of lenses, a prism, a mirror and a screen arranged in an ingenious optical system that focuses light only on that part of the retina that relays information to the left or right hemisphere. The apparatus includes a special contact lens that moves with the eye. With the Z lens, experiments are no longer limited to work with information flashed to one hemisphere during a tenth-of-a-second interval. The system can be set up so that the right hemisphere, for example, can scan a picture or printed page, examine objects before it and otherwise look out at the world on its own for as

long as it pleases. The lens has made possible a series of tests carried out by Zaidel and Sperry that have even further elucidated the nature of the mysterious and silent right hemisphere.

The prevalent theory on the matter holds that the two hemispheres of the brain develop at an equal rate albeit along separate paths and are equipotential in all functions until around age five, when the hemispheres lose their ability to act interchangeably, each moving into its own specialty, apparently in response to genetic programming due to evolutionary advantage.

Indeed, that seems to be the case, but the theory may seriously underestimate the right hemisphere's ability to figure out such things when called upon to do so. Using the Z lens, Zaidel and Sperry were able to administer standard language tests three times to each subject—once to each hemisphere and then again to both hemispheres together. Despite the fact that the persons tested were considerably different in intelligence, when their right hemisphere was given tests of syntax, in each case it performed at the level of a five-year-old, apparently using what abilities it had developed in such areas before it turned to other matters. Yet its vocabulary was found to be much greater than expected, roughly that of a 14-year-old. It could read single words and very simple sentences and could even read a simple instruction and respond to it in writing.

For example, at one point, a subject was asked in writing to write his name and address.

"Do what it says," Zaidel told him.

The right-handed subject picked up a pencil with his left hand and laboriously wrote his name. When verbally asked what he had done, he replied (that is, his verbal left hemisphere replied), "I have no idea." Yet when the subject was shown four pictures, one of which showed someone writing, he could immediately point it out in response to the question. "Although in a verbal sense he was not aware of what he had done, in some nonverbal sense, he was," explains Zaidel.

Now that they are better able to communicate with one hemisphere at a time, the researchers are developing nonverbal tests (since the right hemisphere is completely speechless despite its ability to comprehend words and to read and write somewhat). They also hope to test for personality differences between the two sides of the brain. So far, judging from its reactions to pictures of the subject's self, acquain-

2. THE BIOLOGICAL BASES OF BEHAVIOR

tances, belongings, pets and public figures, the right hemisphere seems to have a characteristic social, political, personal and self-awareness roughly comparable to that of the left brain.

The implications of Sperry's findings reach into practically every arena of psychology and beyond. In the field of therapy, it offers hope for those who have suffered severe brain damage if we can learn ways to train one hemisphere to take over the job of the other in it absence. It challenges the priorities of our educational system, which is almost totally geared to the development of the left hemisphere, missing what may be tremendous untapped potentials of the right hemisphere. "Our educational system and modern society

generally discriminate against one whole half of the brain," says Sperry.

There may be critical periods for the development of different talents, some experts believe. Music and foreign languages can be learned very readily at an early age, but later these subjects become more difficult. If there are critical periods for the development of the right hemisphere's mechanical ingenuity, for instance, it may be necessary to train it at that age or lose forever the possibility of realizing its full potential. "It could be that females in general, if exposed to mechanical toys, would be more adept as adults at this kind of mental activity," suggests Sperry.

Such experiments also tip the scale in the age-old heredity-versus-en-

vironment argument back in the direction of the importance of heredity after many years' swing in the opposite direction. Minds are not infinitely malleable in response to their experience, it seems to show. Certain brain circuits appear to be genetically preprogrammed to develop in certain ways.

Perhaps most far-reaching is the fact that the psyche seems inextricably embedded in the physiology of the brain. If consciousness is the crucial element in reestablishing some of the dignity and freedom psychology has denied us of late, the work of Sperry and his colleagues seems to show not only that consciousness exists, but that it is dual in nature and is a vital force in the workings of the human mind.

SUPERBRAIN

Some smart scientists are beginning to learn what goes on inside the human head.

During the historic descent of the Apollo II astronauts to the moon, a momentary crisis occurred when the astronauts' computer announced that it could no longer compute. The worried ground controllers considered aborting the mission. Fortunately they made a courageous and memorable decision; they closed off the computer and let the astronauts manage the final stages of the moon landing on their own.

Despite its limitations, the computer is the most important technological invention of our century, and it can do many extraordinary things, which no brain can duplicate. A million or more times faster than the most facile human mind, a computer can count the stars, or the blood corpuscles in the bloodstream, or the particles in an atomic explosion, and deliver in seconds the answer that the slower human brain would take years to complete. A modern computer, moreover, will not make an error in a billion billion calculations, while the best human brain, it is esti-

mated, will commit at least one error in every 200 calculations.

On the other hand, the computer is no match for the brain in flexibility. No matter how sophisticated, a computer cannot look at a Picasso and tell you whether it is real or fake; it cannot emulate the physician's art and diagnose a sick gall bladder by its feel; it cannot search through its memory to "read" a lunar landscape unknown to it. All this the human brain can do. What's more, it can spin its miracles through a compact, relatively tiny, three-and-a-half-pound container of neuronal tissue. At present, the fastest, smallest computer with a large memory bank is many times heavier, and takes perhaps 300 watts of operating power.

New discoveries about the brain and its chemistry, as the following article shows, may open a new era of cerebral potential. Among the possible payouts may be its ability to also create a new and superior generation of computers.

Lee Edson

Lee Edson is the author of five books and numerous articles on science and medicine. His book, How We Learn, *won the First Prize in All Media of the American Psychological Association. This article is an expanded version of one that appeared in* THINK *Magazine, published by IBM copyright 1978 by International Business Machines Corporation.*

In a classic science fiction tale of the Thirties called "Vision of the Hydra," a professor named Alanson Willenborg dedicates his life to tapping the latent power of his brain. Through heavy concentration, the professor forces his laggard brain cells to work on three complex subjects at once. With his right and left hands he writes different treatises, while at the same time discussing a technical subject with a colleague.

Eventually, Prof. Willenborg adds two other tasks—reading and chess playing—to his simultaneous mental repertoire. But he remains unsatisfied. He wants all 10 billion neurons of his mind to be so productive he can focus them all like an intense laser beam on a single great problem of the cosmos.

Finally, he achieves his ambition and notifies his

colleague, who excitedly arrives at the professor's home to see the hydra mind in action and describes the scene: "I looked in and saw Alanson seated at his horseshoe desk . . . writing rapidly on sheets of paper with both hands. What was happening? Then I leaned over and understood . . . The pads of paper were scribbled with a senseless jumble of words. And a vapid face turned up to me grinningly . . ."

The moral of this horror tale, of course, is that it is dangerous to tamper with the work of Mother Nature—especially with something as intricate as the brain. Real-life stories of psychologists who have tried to raise their children to become mental giants have as often as not ended in disaster. But now, thanks to recent discoveries about the human brain, we may have found a way to enhance the power of this three-and-a-half-pound organ—even create a superbrain—without exacting a penalty.

The major find is that the brain can make its own drugs—a family of proteins known as peptides—that can act directly on the organ to change aspects of mental activity hitherto thought to be unchangeable by chemistry. Do you want a fresh burst of creativity? There is a peptide from the brain that may provide it. How about a boost of intelligence? Believe it or not, scientists have recently found that the brain manufactures a protein substance that seems to help the mentally retarded and may provide a few extra I.Q. points for the rest of us. What about imagination, good memory, and all the other desirable traits of the mind? They, too, are attainable to some degree, thanks to the new chemical discoveries that are sweeping our understanding of the mechanics of the brain. "In the future," speculates one psychologist, "we may all go to a psychopharmacy to pick up brain pills that give us whatever mental or emotional traits we may want at a given time."

This is not as farfetched as it may seem. In a recent experiment, Dr. Abba Kastin, head of endocrinology at the Veterans Administration Hospital in New Orleans, gave a brain substance known as melanocyte stimulating hormone (MSH) to one group of volunteers and a neutral sugar pill (placebo) to another. The brain substance was known to create a change in the nervous system of animals that made the animals learn faster. When both groups of human subjects were tested on a variety of tasks, Dr. Kastin found a significant difference in the group injected with the brain extract over those given the placebo. The former group showed increased attention and learning ability, while the second group remained virtually the same. In another experiment, Dr. David de Wied of the Netherlands gave the same substance to a group of mentally retarded subjects and found that it enhanced memory as well as learning ability.

The existence of built-in chemical patterns and their influences on the brain that underly behavior has fascinated scientists for years. Sigmund Freud, in fact, once said that behind every mental event lies a chemical event. And a professor from the University of California at Irvine went him one better when he added that behind every twisted mind is a twisted molecule. Until recently, however, only a few chemicals were ever obtained from the brain and linked to behavior; these became known as neurotransmitters because they carried messages from neuron to neuron across a minuscule gap—the synapse— between the neurons.

In the last few years scientists have been able to penetrate deeper into this chemical makeup of the mind and to pinpoint the actual substances that are related to mood, memory and other mental events, and to track these substances and their paths in a fairly precise way through the brain. It has now been found that there is an unexpectedly large range of neurotransmitters—some 25 have been turned up so far—and that each is secreted by its own neuron and has its own path. This knowledge has given scientists a new perspective of the brain and opened up a way to determine how pain is perceived and transmitted to the brain, how eating and drinking, mood, even sex, are regulated deep within the cortical structure.

The three key figures in this breakthrough are Ph.D.s Roger Guillemin, a physiologist at the Salk Institute in La Jolla, Calif. (and a former French Resistance fighter

in World War II); his colleague, biochemist Andrew Schally of the University of Texas; and Rosalyn Yalow, a physicist at the Veterans Administration Hospital in the Bronx, N.Y. In the 1950s Dr. Guillemin—an intense, scholarly man—became interested in the cherry-sized pituitary gland, because of its role in controlling the thyroid, pancreas, sex and other endocrine glands. Textbooks described it as the master gland of the body.

Dr. Guillemin thought, however—as did Dr. Schally and others—that the pituitary might take its orders directly from the hypothalamus, a cluster of cells in the middle of the brain long known as a kind of relay point for messages that tell the body when to eat and drink. Hints of the supervisory role of the hypothalamus had come from several experimenters who extirpated the tissue from animals and found that the pituitary failed to secrete its normal load of hormones. Dr. Guillemin felt that a triggering chemical was somehow involved in this reaction. He knew that if such a chemical existed, it had to be in tiny traces or it would not have escaped the chemists' notice over the years.

Fortunately, in the Bronx, Dr. Yalow had developed a sophisticated radioactive technique that enabled scientists to tag and measure exceedingly tiny amounts of trace chemicals as they moved through the bloodstream. With the help of this technique, Dr. Guillemin and his associates begin a long search—somewhat similar to that of Madame Curie's hunt for a speck of radium in tons of pitchblende. Dr. Guillemin's hunt was for a trace of hormone in the pulverized brains of nearly two million sheep, arduously collected from slaughterhouses. At the same time, Dr. Schally started looking for the elusive chemical in an equal tonnage of pigs' brains. In the 1960s the race between the two scientists was on in earnest.

After years of grinding, straining, filtering, and tracking their prey, Drs. Guillemin and Schally almost simultaneously found what they were after—a fragment of hormone made in the brain that released another hormone from the pituitary to control the thyroid gland. They named the trigger chemical TRH, for thyrotropin releasing hormone. It proved to be so potent that a milligram could affect hormonal output throughout the human body; this fragment could stimulate the flow of milk in all mammals and boost the mental power of cretins. What's more, although the substance was short-lived, its effects lasted for hours—something not accomplished by other chemical substances extracted from the brain and glands.

The discovery of TRH was only the beginning of a veritable spate of useful hormones found in the brain, many of them subsequently isolated and purified by Dr. Guillemin. One of them, LRH (luteinizing releasing hormone), controls reproduction—useful in resolving infertility problems. This hormone also appears to have an aphrodisiac effect on the brain, causing impotent males to become virile. Still another hormone plays a role in stopping involuntary muscle tremors. It has been used with an oral dose of L-dopa (the famous drug now in use against Parkinson's disease) in treating tardive dyskinesia, an uncontrollable movement of head and tongue. These hormonal fragments proved to be part of a newly discovered body message system that provides a rapid-fire linkage between the great but slow acting endocrine system and the faster acting nervous system. One scientist describes it as the Mailgram of the body.

In 1977 the Nobel Prize in Medicine was awarded to Drs. Guillemin, Schally and Yalow for their work in shedding light on the connection between the nervous and endocrine systems and for putting the pituitary in its proper place. The pituitary, explains Floyd Bloom, an associate of Dr. Guillemin's, "used to be the conductor of the endocrine symphony. Now it is only the concertmaster."

Today the role of neuropeptides in human behavior continues to open up new vistas in medicine and research. At the University of Basel in Switzerland, Marcel Monnier and Guido Schoenenberger discovered that injecting blood from sleeping rabbits into awake rabbits put the latter to sleep. The scientists isolated a chemical, which proved to be a peptide, and synthesized a chemical of the same structure. This is now being clinically tested for severe cases of insomnia. The advantage of the peptides over some conventional sleeping pills is that they allow dreaming to occur during sleep. Dreaming is an important mechanism for relieving the individual of psychic tensions and is also related to creativity. It is thought that a peptide taken from a dreaming stage and given to a sleeping individual might actually induce "creative dreams" and thus help solve the sleeper's problems through forced image-making.

If peptides can bring on dreaming, can they also be used to transmit memories? Georges Ungar, a Hungarian-born biochemist, has gone on record as saying, Yes. In 1970 he caused a stir in scientific circles when he announced that he had taught a rat to fear the dark and then transferred this fear to another animal by merely injecting it with a peptide known as scotophobin from the brain of the first animal. Scientists were skeptical, and writers had a field day with the concept. The plot of *Hauser's Memory,* for instance, a novel made into a TV movie, is based on giving the memories of a dying German scientist to a young American scientist. The American not only remembers everything the older man experienced but also the German's enemies, and spends his life trying to exterminate them in revenge.

Just before his death last year, Ungar announced that he had been able to extract other memory peptides from the brains of rats. One such peptide, called ameletin, was obtained from the brains of animals trained to ignore a certain repeated sound. When the chemical was injected into other animals, they, too, responded by ignoring the same sound.

Perhaps the most intriguing peptide usage is in the understanding and control of pain. A few years ago Avram Goldstein of Stanford University stirred more scientific curiosity by announcing that the brain had natural receptors for opiates. Why would nature provide such a thing? One possibility was that the brain made its own opiates, and the search was on to find them and extract them from the brain.

In 1975 two scientists, Dr. Lars Terenius of the University of Uppsala in Sweden and Dr. John Hughes of the University of Aberdeen in Scotland, independently found an opiate-like substance in the brain. It was labeled endorphin, for endogenous morphine (the morphine within). Goldstein also found the opiate in the pituitary gland. Smaller peptide molecules found earlier are called enkephalin (Greek for "in the head"). Interestingly, they are concentrated in the brain's limbic system, the so-called seat of emotion.

What is the function of the brain's own morphine? To find out, Goldstein placed a number of normal people into stressful situations and then gave them naloxone, a drug that antagonizes morphine and prevents its action, while others were given a placebo. Those receiving the placebo relaxed when the stress was removed; those on naloxone remained keyed up, indicating that the morphine within is needed to keep us on an even keel. "Maybe we all carry our own dope within our heads," says Goldstein, "so we don't get uptight—or at least to help us overcome our being uptight." Dr. Lewis Thomas of Memorial Sloan-Kettering in New York suggests that Nature in its wisdom may have provided these substances in the brain to make death more peaceful.

Peptides may also be the key to the chemistry of mental illness. Dr. Guillemin, for instance, found an endorphin called somatostatin that turned a rat stiff as a board for three hours. Nothing could make the animal move a muscle. Some scientists became interested because the immobile state suggested that endorphins may be the key to catatonic schizophrenia, a form of the disease in which the patient remains rigid and silent. It is too early to tell what it means, but Dr. Terenius and his colleagues have found that this endorphin does appear in unusual amounts in the urine of schizophrenics.

Dr. Frank Ervin at the University of California at Los Angeles tracked down another endorphin, called leu-(for leucine) endorphin, in the dialysis fluid of schizophrenics treated for kidney disease. These patients all lost their hallucinatory symptoms after dialysis.

In still another study, Dr. Nathan Kline, director of the Rockland Research Institute of Orangeburg, N.Y., gave endorphins to several schizophrenic and depressed patients and found positive effects in all of them. The depressives had a mood lift, and the schizophrenics felt a sense of euphoria that lasted for hours.

Is the endorphin the elusive, long-sought key to man's most recalcitrant mental disorder? Nobody yet knows, but the research is moving rapidly ahead. These brain substances may clear up the mystery of acupuncture, the ancient Chinese system of sticking needles into the body at precise places to produce anesthesia. According to some scientists, the needles work because they are placed in areas where they trigger large amounts of enkephalin, which then work on the nervous system to produce their pain-killing properties. This is still theory, of course, but has been backed up by preliminary experiments at the University of Toronto and elsewhere.

Only a few years old, peptide research is already drawing scientific workers from many disciplines from all over the world. Peptides have shown an extraordinary capacity to stimulate brain cells to overcome deficiencies and to enhance qualities of memory and learning already there. They hold the secret to mood and emotion and to pain perception. If their promise continues to be borne out by subsequent research, the peptides may indeed create through chemistry the era of the superbrain.

Brain Damage: A Window on the Mind

by Howard Gardner

Over the past decades our understanding of brain chemistry, of neural circuitry, of sensory and motor processes, has so increased as to render obsolete the medical textbooks of an earlier generation. But how much have these lines of neurological investigation—usually conducted with "lower" animals and dependent upon microscopic preparations—revealed about the functioning of the human mind? Can we draw from studies at the cellular level insights about those intellectual, emotional, and social capacities of pivotal importance within human society? In truth, it must be said: the gap between most work in the brain

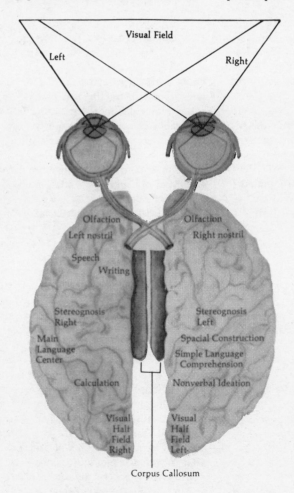

Corpus Callosum

Visual and speech pathways—They can be disrupted in curiously selective ways by brain damage.

sciences and the elucidation of our own "higher functions" remains enormous.

Accumulating over the past century, however, has been an unexpected but highly revealing set of insights, one that illuminates precisely those functions central in human intellectual activity. From the careful study of normal individuals whose brains have been injured, we receive penetrating insights into the nature of such cerebral activities as reading, writing, speaking, drawing, doing mathematics, and making music. We can uncover the links—and the distances—between such activities. And we can gain fertile clues about those enigmas that have long intrigued both philosophers and laymen. What is the nature of memory? Can one think without language? Are all art forms cut from a single cloth?

An uncomfortably large number of circumstances can injure the adult brain, but by far the most common and—as it happens—the most revealing, is the cerebral vascular accident, or stroke. Each year, in this country alone, approximately 300,000 individuals suffer a stroke when blood vessels leading to their brains are occluded by deposits of fat, a clot lodges in an artery, or an artery bursts. These events threaten the loss of the two elements upon which the brain is crucially dependent: oxygen and glucose. Deprived of these precious substances for more than a few minutes and having no reservoirs upon which to draw, brain tissue is damaged or destroyed. And, once de-

stroyed, it cannot be regenerated. Instead, one may await an unpalatable set of failures in those functions controlled by the brain cells: loss of motor and sensory capacities, failure of "high cognitive functions," and, perhaps, coma and death.

In the most fortunate cases, injury to the brain caused by a stroke may be so slight that it remains undetected; on other occasions, death or total disability occurs. But a sizable number of strokes each year prove to be of intermediate severity—insufficient to kill, yet virulent enough to affect permanently the individual's mental functioning. By what they can (and cannot) do, these unfortunate victims yield invaluable information to the neurologists, psychologists, and other scientists involved in the study of the brain.

Were the destruction wrought by a stroke, tumor, or head trauma completely general, so that all mental abilities were reduced by an equivalent proportion, little knowledge could be gained about the nature and organization of intellectual skills. (The victim would simply be a "dulled" normal individual; any insights gained from studying him might as readily be procured from the investigation of other normal individuals.) In fact, however, brain damage is highly selective. The victim may lose some abilities completely, while others remain wholly or virtually unaffected. An individual with a lesion in his left hemisphere may be completely unable to speak while remaining able to draw or hum with skill. An individual with a lesion in his right hemisphere may be unable to dress himself properly and may lose his way in the hospital while he can read and speak just as before.

As a result of these somewhat surprising circumstances, the brain-damaged patient constitutes a unique experiment in nature. What could never be done experimentally occurs daily as a result of inexorable fate.

As a neuropsychological researcher at the Aphasia Research Center of the Boston Veterans Administration Hospi-

"Brain Damage: Window on the Mind," Howard Gardner, *Saturday Review*, August 9, 1975. Copyright © 1975 Saturday Review, Inc.

tal, I have come to know several hundred victims of brain damage. Most of our patients are aphasic: their language abilities have been disrupted as a result of damage to the brain, such injury implicating their left cerebral cortex in nearly all cases. About one third of our patients suffer from other kinds of brain injury in other sites which, while sparing their language functions, vitiate other abilities. And so I have had the instructive opportunity of comparing the functioning of two kinds of patients—those whose language is impaired but who have retained other abilities and those who, while losing other capacities, retain the abilities to express themselves verbally and to understand spoken language. In what follows, then, I shall sketch some of the insights that other researchers and I have obtained from studying various brain injuries that may befall the normal adult.

One of the first lessons gleaned from work with brain-damaged patients is that common-sense notions of the relationships among abilities may be invalid. Take, for example, the set of symptoms encountered in a bizarre but not infrequent condition called *pure alexia without agraphia*. Patients afflicted with this disorder are unable to read text (they are alexic) yet remain able to write (they are not agraphic). One's immediate thought is that they must be in some sense blind; but in fact the patients can copy or trace out the very letters and words that they fail to read. To complicate the matter even further, the same patients are often able to read numbers. They may even read "DIX" as "509," while proving incapable of reading it as "diks." They are able to name objects but are frequently unable to name samples of colors shown to them.

On its own this syndrome confounds a raft of intuitions about how the mind works. Reading can be separated from writing; verbal symbols differ from numerical symbols; objects are named in a way different from colors. No one completely understands pure alexia, but the major facts of the syndrome described above have been repeatedly described and are widely accepted. Some researchers hold that the individual's visual powers and his verbal-language capacities are reasonably intact but that the connections between them have been disrupted. As a result purely visual configurations—like letters or colors—cannot be named (or read). But those visual configura-

tions that arouse sensory or tactile associations (like objects or numbers) can be satisfactorily processed. Evidently, such findings not only undermine common sense; they also challenge the researcher to devise a model of mind that can account for this bizarre blend of abilities and disabilities. And they

provide intriguing clues about why some normal individuals can master arithmetic before they can read or why others can more easily remember the names of rare objects than rare colors.

Pure alexia demonstrates that symbols which might have been thought similar (numbers and words) are processed in different ways by the brain. In a condition that accompanies injury to the parietal and occipital lobes of the left hemisphere, patients can understand single words and declarative sentences but fail to decode utterances that employ prepositional phrases like "on top of" or "next to," possessive constructions ("my brother's wife"), or the passive voice ("the lion was killed by the tiger"). Other syndromes demonstrate precisely the reverse situation; skills usually thought independent of one another in fact turn out to be closely related. Further investigations with these patients reveal difficulties in carrying out mathematical operations and in analyzing a spatial array. These disabilities co-occur with sufficient regularity to suggest that the same underlying "mental operations" may be drawn upon in understanding certain linguistic structures, in performing arithmetic, and in comprehending a spatial layout. And so, in this instance, the modeler of mental processes is challenged to unite skills that, on intuitive grounds, may appear quite unrelated. By the same token, the schoolteacher receives an impetus to use linguistic examples to aid mathematical understanding or to draw upon mathematical exercises in explicating the principles of grammar.

In most cases the deficits exhibited by brain-damaged patients are only too apparent, to the victim as well as to those who know him. Sometimes, however, a victim may be completely unaware of his deficits, and they may even escape

the casual observer as well. An instructive example of this is Korsakoff's disease, a syndrome that results from damage to the mid-brain and is often the pathetic climax of many years of alcoholism.

The Korsakoff patient exhibits no evident physical disabilities. He may per-

---

"The brain-damaged patient constitutes a unique experiment in nature. What could never be done experimentally occurs daily as a result of inexorable fate."

---

form at an average or above average level on an intelligence test. He can solve a variety of problems posed to him; he can converse in an intelligent manner for hours. And yet, once his deficit has been revealed, it becomes painfully obvious. For a victim of Korsakoff's disease cannot remember anything that is told to him or anything that has happened to him since the onset of his disease.

FEW MEDICAL DEMONSTRATIONS are as powerful (and memorable) as that of Korsakoff's disease: one tells an apparently normal patient one's name, engages him in distracting conversation for a few moments, and then hears the patient not only claim ignorance of one's name but also deny that it has ever been told to him. Yet, if all memory were of a single piece, the mechanisms underlying this process would not be illuminated by Korsakoff's disease.

In fact, however, the Korsakoff patient *is* able to learn things providing only that one does not accept his testimony concerning what he knows. For instance, one can teach such a patient to play a new piece on the piano; the next day he will deny ever having learned the piece, but, once given the opening bars, he (or his fingers) will play the piece perfectly. One can teach a Korsakoff patient a complex new motor skill—say, solving a maze or copying an intricate pattern; once again, despite his sincere protestations of ignorance, the patient (or his hands) will reveal mastery of this new skill. And, most surprisingly of all, one can even teach such a patient a new line of verse, a nonsense slogan, or a series of answers to questions.

Such findings document at least two forms of memory. Given sufficient drill the brain of the Korsakoff patient can learn new patterns—motor, musical, even verbal—and can spew these patterns back under appropriate circumstances. But the Korsakoff patient has largely lost the ability to learn something new—particularly if it is verbal. And he is completely incapable of knowing what he has learned or of drawing upon such new skills in the voluntary way available to normal individuals.

The Korsakoff patient, finally, illuminates some of the quirks of our own mnemonic capacities: we can now better understand why we may be able to repeat a game, a motor activity, or a prayer that apparently had been forgotten; why a line of verse is more effortlessly retrieved when its meaning is ignored and its syllabic sequence is allowed to unfold without interruption; why a forgotten town becomes instantly familiar once we return to its environs; or why we can sometimes parrot back a recently heard phrase whose meaning has totally eluded us.

STUDY of the brain-damaged individual not only can illuminate the ordinary processes of ordinary individuals; it can also help to unravel highly developed skills possessed by talented individuals. Among the individuals who have proved extremely difficult to study under ordinary conditions are artists; such creative persons are few, are often unsympathetic to empirical investigators, and usually possess skills of such fluency that they defy dissection and analysis. Here, again, the accidents of brain damage offer a unique investigative opportunity.

Only on rare occasions has an artistically knowledgeable neurologist encountered an accomplished artist whose brain has been damaged. But from such rare happenings considerable insight has been gained into the operation of the artistic mind. Typically, painters can continue to create significant works after their language powers have been seriously disturbed; indeed, more than one researcher has claimed that visual artistry actually improves as a result of aphasia. But, interestingly enough, painters with right-hemisphere disease—whose language has remained unaffected—often exhibit bizarre patterns in the paintings: they may neglect the left side of the canvas, they may distort the external form of objects, or they may portray emotionally bizarre or even repulsive subject matter. Apparently, painting and linguistic capacities can exist independently of one another.

On the other hand, the relationship between linguistic and musical skills seems more complex. Some aphasic musicians prove able to compose or perform; some (among them the composer Maurice Ravel) have lost the ability to create musically even though their critical powers seem to be intact; still other musicians have been completely disabled by aphasia.

The striking individual differences found among brain-damaged musicians suggest that musical capacities may be organized in idiosyncratic ways across individuals. Perhaps most individuals learn in rather similar ways to speak and to draw, but the organization of music in the brain may differ dramatically depending on whether one has learned an instrument, what instrument one favors, whether one plays by ear, the extent to which one sings, and so on. No wonder that the preparation of musical exercises suitable for all students poses enormous challenges to even the most gifted and enterprising musical teacher!

Of the diverse conundrums that populate the area of human neuropsychology, none is more persistent and more endlessly fascinating than the relationship between language and thought. Opinions on this issue vary enormously. Some investigators (for example, those influenced by the American linguist Benjamin Lee Whorf) view all thought processes as shaped by language and consider aphasia the death of cognition. Other researchers (for instance, those influenced by the Swiss psychologist Jean Piaget) see language and thought as separate streams; they believe that thought can proceed in a virtually unimpaired manner despite a pronounced aphasia.

Dozens of studies inspired by this vexing question reveal quite clearly the inadequacy of both extreme positions. Unquestionably, certain cognitive and intellectual abilities depend quite heavily on linguistic intactness: the ability to reason about abstract issues, the capacity to solve scientific problems, and, in most cases, skill at mathematics. (Just try to think about a comparison between socialism and communism without resorting to words.) However, an equally impressive list details reasoning powers that may be well preserved despite a severe aphasia: the ability to solve spatial problems, sensitivity to fine differences in patterns or configurations, and alertness to the emotional contours of a situation. (Just try to describe a spiral staircase using only words.) And, though this area has not been much studied, it seems probable that an individual's sense of himself is not noticeably affected by linguistic impairment—even as "the self" can be decimated while linguistic powers remain completely unaffected.

WITH EVERY PASSING YEAR new neuropsychological laboratories are opened; virtually every issue of the leading journals documents fascinating new cases or pivotal experimental discoveries. Our knowledge of the skills detailed above, as well as many others not alluded to here, is certain to increase and to change. And yet it is already possible, on the basis of well-documented findings, to posit reasonably convincing models of human mental processes, particularly in the area of language. Moreover, it should be possible within the next decade to begin integrating what is known about relatively discrete cognitive functions—such as reading, memory, or visual recognition—with insights concerning such subtle and elusive areas as the individual's emotional life, his preferences and fears, his relations with other people, and, most intriguing of all, his consciousness of his own experiences and of the world about him.

Understanding the brain-damaged individual, and extrapolating to the normal person, is a worthwhile scientific endeavor in its own right. I do not at all wish to detract from it. However, work with the victims of brain damage provides both an opportunity and a challenge to aid these often hapless individuals. It is therefore encouraging to report that in the area of aphasia the increased understanding obtained from neuropsychological investigation has suggested some promising avenues of rehabilitation.

Once it had been established that skills in musical and visual tasks could be at least partially dissociated from linguistic skills, the possibility arose that such spared capacities might be marshalled to aid individuals in communicating with other persons. At our own unit novel forms of aphasia therapy have been desired for use with patients who have not benefited from traditional language therapy. The most successful of these new therapies, one devised by Martin Albert, Nancy Helm, and Robert Sparks, involves the use of singing (or melodic intonation) in order to aid the patient who is unable to express himself orally. A still-experimental therapy, developed in association with Edgar Zurif and several other investigators, involves the ordering of visual symbols drawn on index cards. Patients learn to associate these symbols with objects and actions in the world and then communicate their wishes and thoughts by manipulating the cards. Still other therapies, designed with the aphasic patient's strengths and limitations in mind, draw on sign language and on manipulation of an artificial speech synthesizer. It is still too early to pass final judgment on the efficacy of these therapies, but they at least offer hope that those areas of the brain that have been spared may to some extent be placed in the service of apparently destroyed functions.

BECAUSE THE PATIENT ordinarily studied by neuropsychologists was once normal, those parts of his brain that still function are presumed to reflect the way in which mental capacities are typically organized in the intact individual. In this respect he differs from the young child whose brain is much less differentiated into specific zones and, at the same time, is much more flexible. The adult with even a relatively small lesion may suffer permanent damage of major skills; the toddler can lose as much as half of his brain (via the removal of a hemisphere) and yet remain able to function quite effectively in intellectual matters, presumably because spared areas "take over" function.

Despite these telling differences in brain organization and potential, knowledge about children's learning abilities and disabilities can be obtained from a study of the brain-damaged adult. In my view, the kinds of brain injury that befall adults often seem to reveal conditions found, perhaps in somewhat less clearcut form, in schoolchildren with learning disabilities. For instance, individuals with acquired alexias (or reading disorders) often resemble children with dyslexia (otherwise-competent children exhibiting special difficulties in reading). Similarly, adult patients with selective disorders in calculation often resemble children who experience special difficulties in learning arithmetic. (Selective sparing may also prove illuminating: patients who can decode written symbols or who can repeat language without understanding resemble certain hyperlexic, autistic, or retarded youngsters.)

These clinical findings suggest that some children may be born with neurological abnormalities that yield the behavioral pattern found in certain normal adults whose brains have been injured. The rehabilitative clue here arises from the fact that the brain-damaged adult could once perform the now-disrupted function. Should one succeed in devising a way to "reactivate" this skill, using a channel that is as yet unimpaired, one might accomplish two goals. Even while aiding the adult in recovering an ability of importance, one has developed methods that may facilitate the acquisition of these same skills by the learning-disabled child. For one has developed an alternative-training régime that, while unnecessary for the completely normal child, may prove highly serviceable for the child with a slightly atypical brain.

RETURNING TO our original example of pure alexia without agraphia, one finds further applications of this procedure. Studies have documented that, if given three-dimensional letters to touch, alexic patients can read with greater skill. And, most intriguingly, studies of alexic patients in the Orient have revealed that they may be able to read ideographic characters while they fail to read phonetic characters. Just these insights have recently been drawn upon in the education of American children with selective disabilities in reading. Thus Paul Rozin and his colleagues at the University of Pennsylvania have developed an ideographic system effective with inner-city dyslexic children. And Jay Isgur, working with learning-disabled youngsters in Pensacola, Fla., has reported marked success in a program that builds upon the use of three-dimensional, "object-like" letters.

Whether such rehabilitative measures prove to be potent prosthetics, or of only marginal assistance, remains to be determined. Once destroyed, brain tissue is forever beyond repair, and the loss of this precious substance almost invariably involves serious cost. Yet, given that some brain damage is inevitable, and that transplants of neural protoplasm will not soon be with us, efforts to assist the injured child or adult must certainly be encouraged. And, indeed, such efforts constitute one of the most rewarding portions of research on brain damage. Even as insights into our own minds, and into mental processes generally, have been coming forth rapidly, it has proved possible to apply what has been learned to those individuals who, willingly if inadvertently, have contributed to our understanding.

Howard Gardner conducts research on the symbol-using skills of normal children and brain-damaged adults. He is author of The Shattered Mind: The Person After Brain Damage *(Knopf, 1975).*

HOPE FOR DAMAGED BRAINS

Research on rats may hold clues to human rehabilitation.

Patrick Young

A gray rat pokes its twitching nose out of a compartment and scurries busily through a maze toward food at the other end. Kenneth Chin, an animal technician here at the University of California, notes the animal's time on a chart and repeats the exercise seven times. Then he begins again with another rat.

Such activity seems far removed from the neurological ward of a major hospital. Yet recent work here may have major implications for the rehabilitation of people whose brains have been injured by strokes, tumors, accidents, gunshot wounds, and blows to the head.

Researchers have found that brain-injured rats, whether young or old, recover the ability to solve problems better if they are kept in "enriched" cages, filled with a variety of games and ladders that provide the animals mental stimulation.

Extrapolating the findings of rat research to the human condition is a risky venture. Nonetheless, a research team here says its work adds new support to the notion that the brain has a remarkable ability to recover from injury throughout life. And thus, they argue, their rat research is worth notice from human-brain specialists.

"Neurologists are divided on how to handle a variety of people with brain damage," says psychologist Mark R. Rosenzweig. "There are those who say let the patient alone in a normal environment and nature will take care of itself. Others say: 'No, we need therapy to help the patient regain what's been lost.' And there are a few that say they need to protect the patient and will even sedate the patient.

"Some clinicians say you can tell fairly rapidly how a patient is going to do in therapy; others argue that recovery will take place over years. It seems to us that animal experiments like this, perhaps, will be a basis for better therapeutic efforts in humans."

Rosenzweig and neurochemist Edward L. Bennett have been working together since 1954, aided at various times by other colleagues. They pioneered experiments in the late 1950s and early 1960s that showed that normal rats raised in enriched living conditions had changes in their brain chemistry and grew larger brains than rats kept in "impoverished" cages.

"Our main interest is in the fundamental mechanism of learning and memory," says Rosenzweig. "This [brain-injury work] is part of a general study on how memories are stored and how learning affects the brain."

Working with Bruno E. Will—a French psychophysiologist now returned home—Rosenzweig and Bennett set out to replicate and expand a 1964 study. That experiment involved rats whose brains had been damaged the day after birth; the results showed that those raised in an enriched environment demonstrated a greater ability to solve problems.

"The environment seemed to be acting as a sort of therapy, making up for the deleterious effect of the brain damage," says Rosenzweig. "As far as we knew, no one had followed up on it and we considered it an important experiment."

Half Undergo Operations

The researchers conducted a number of experiments. In each, half the rats underwent operations in which a small amount of the cerebral cortex, the brain's outer bark, was removed; the other half had sham operations in which their skulls were opened but no brain damage was inflicted.

Then half from each group—brain-damaged and sham operation—were placed in roomy, enriched cages that contained blocks, tiny jungle gyms, ladders, tubes, and rotating wheels. The remaining rats were placed in small cages with only food and water. After certain lengths of time the rats were tested in mazes to determine their problem-solving abilities.

The animals were coded so that the technicians testing them would not know which rats came from which group. The brain-damaged rats suffered no disabilities that could be detected visually. "The fact they were so normal is the reason we could conduct this experiment," says Rosenzweig. "Only after all the testing was done did we break the code."

Not surprisingly, the noninjured rats from enriched cages scored highest and the brain-damaged rats from the impoverished cages scored lowest. But when the researchers compared the brain-injured animals raised in enriched cages with the noninjured rats living in impoverished cages, both scored about the same.

Changes in Genetic Chemicals

Moreover, the researchers found that the enriched environment greatly improved the problem-solving ability of brain-damaged rats, whether they had

From *The National Observer*, May 1, 1976. Reprinted with permission from The National Observer, copyright Dow Jones & Company Inc. 1976.

been operated on a day or two after birth, at 30-days old, or at 120 days— young adulthood for rats. And rats exposed to the therapy of an enriched cage for only two hours daily scored almost as well as rats living in those special cages 24 hours a day.

"We can't say the beneficial effects are the same in the older rats as in the younger, but the effects are there and they show up very thoroughly," says Rosenzweig. "There are clear effects at all ages."

When the researchers killed the rats and examined those with brain injuries, they found several significant differences. Although the brain-damaged rats all weighed about the same, those raised in enriched cages had longer and heavier brains. Those from the enriched environment also showed tiny changes in the ratio of the genetic chemicals RNA and DNA in their brains.

"The ratio of RNA to DNA is greater, which is indicative of larger cells and more active cells," says Bennett. "We think it indicates a more active metabolism. Cells that have more functions to carry out probably take more RNA."

Previous studies indicate that in the learning process the animal brain does not grow new cells but rather an increase occurs in the number of nerve-cell branches that make contact with other cells. "When one speaks of repair of the brain, it doesn't mean new growth of brain cells, but that the existing cells take over in some way," says Rosenzweig.

Bennett and Rosenzweig say their findings raise questions that neurologists should consider in treating the human victims of brain damage:

● Is the human brain, even in the aged, far more capable of repairing itself than previously thought?

● Should brain-injured patients be placed in therapy quickly, rather than left in isolation?

● Should therapy continue for long periods, even though the patient shows no signs of progress?

"We hope some clinicians will become interested in this and set up some proper experiments," says Bennett.

Observing the Brain Through a Cat's Eyes

Pioneer vision research on cats leads to new ways of learning how we learn.

by Roger Lewin

Dr. Roger Lewin is life-science editor of the British-based magazine New Scientist.

A kitten raised to see only horizontal planes is blind to vertical objects.

W hat does a baby see when it gazes out on the world around itself? Does it pretty much see what its parents see? Or does each baby see a "mud-luscious, puddle-wonderful" world quite different from the one its parents—and for that matter, all other babies—are looking at?

Scientists and philosophers have argued this question of vision since Aristotle's day. But now researchers experimenting on cats have made revolutionary discoveries about the way we see—discoveries that apply not only to cats but also to the people who feed them.

The main revelation is that the ability to "see straight" does not develop in children automatically, that is, quite apart from any outside influences. Instead, the researchers have found, our visual machinery is strongly shaped by our early experiences—experiences that drastically affect the way we see the world in later life and that may even determine how gifted we will be musically and linguistically. It may be that areas of great potential in child development are being wasted simply because we don't teach the right things at the right time, the time when children's brains are most receptive.

The pioneers of the vision research on cats are two Harvard biologists, David Hubel and Torsten Wiesel. When they began their study, in the early Sixties, they expected to find that a cat's early environment has some small shaping influence on the way its vision develops.

But like all the other biologists now interested in the work, Hubel and Wiesel have been absolutely amazed by the remarkable flexibility and plasticity displayed by the cat's visual system as it slowly develops. It now appears possible to persuade nerve cells in the cat's brain to do jobs for which they were never designed. Even if the rest of the brain is capable of only a fraction of the plasticity evident in the workings of the visual cortex, there is still a great deal of scope for external influences affecting the way the brain develops.

In the beginning Hubel and Wiesel looked at the activity of nerve cells in the so-called primary area of the visual cortex. These cells turned out to be "feature detectors"—that is, they respond to specific shapes seen by the eye. Generally, there are two types of feature detectors: the ones that are found in many animal species and others that are specific to

a particular species. These latter usually enable the animal to flourish in its behavioral environment. For instance, the frog has visual cells that are almost lightheartedly called "bug detectors"; these react when an object the size of a fly enters the animal's field of vision. One can argue that these specific feature detectors are programmed genetically, but it is also tempting to think that they may be at least partly shaped by early environmental influence.

The feature detectors, which Hubel and Wiesel located by means of minute electrodes pushed into the adult cat's brain, turned out to be orientation-selective; that is, they respond to—or, in scientific terms, are "specific to"—any line or edge moving across the animal's visual field along a particular orientation or angle. Any one cell is specific to a particular orientation, but all angles through the entire range of 360 degrees

"Observing the Brain Through a Cat's Eyes," Roger Lewin, *Saturday Review World,* October 5, 1974. Copyright © 1974 *Saturday Review World.*

"Our visual machinery is strongly shaped by our early experiences—experiences that . . . may even determine how gifted we will be musically and linguistically."

are "covered" by the population of nerve cells in this area of the brain. The Harvard team also discovered that most of the cells here are binocular, or wired up to both eyes.

In contrast to the adult cat, the visually naive kitten has practically no mature feature detectors. The cells are certainly present in the brain, but they have not yet been recruited to their job. The binocular connections in the kitten are just like the adult's. In one of Hubel and Wiesel's early experiments to try to discover the forces (genetic or environmental) that convert an infant eye to an adult one, they kept a growing kitten in total darkness and then examined its brain. They discovered that the binocular wiring had remained intact, but that the feature detectors had suffered terribly, remaining very immature. Here was a strong indication of environmental input determining brain development.

Next Hubel and Wiesel tried covering just one of an animal's eyes to see what that does to the brain. This time the feature detectors worked fine, but the binocular connections were thrown awry; they had all gone to the one seeing eye. Hubel and Wiesel found that the visual brain was plastic only during a "sensitive period" of the animal's life: from three weeks to three months. Again, this fits in with the notion that early experience is important in brain development.

The obvious implications of this work for an understanding of human development soon drew other research teams in to probe the problems, and the results have been astounding. For instance, Colin Blakemore and his colleagues in Cambridge, England, have found that in a visually inexperienced kitten they can induce the switch from inbuilt binocularity to monocularity after just *six* hours' vision through one eye. The change isn't made immediately; a period of consolidation is required following the programming exposure. Blakemore likens this response to learning and memory: in learning, an experience is slotted into a temporary store (short-term memory), and then a more permanent record is made (long-term memory).

The binocular/monocular switch is even more remarkable because it can

be repeated again and again. If first one eye is covered, and then the other, and so on, the brain connections with the eyes will switch each time to the seeing eye, but once again this elaborate neural dance is possible only during the sensitive period.

The most remarkable results come from the plasticity of the feature detectors. Following up the early Harvard experiments, Colin Blakemore and Graham Cooper at Cambridge and Nico Spinelli and Helmut Hirsch at Stanford hit on the same idea: to put visually naive kittens into artificial environments to see if the feature detectors can be manipulated. It turns out that they can.

For instance, the Cambridge kittens were reared in visual environments consisting only of vertical stripes *or* horizontal stripes, not both. When the animals emerged from their striped worlds into the real visual world, they behaved in a most extraordinary way. "Horizontal" cats were perfectly capable of jumping onto a chair to settle down for a sleep; but when walking on the floor, they kept bumping into the chair legs, just as if the legs were invisible. In contrast, "vertical" animals had no difficulty in negotiating the chair-leg hazards, but they never tried to jump onto a chair; it was as if the seat were not there.

When the Blakemore team looked inside the kittens' heads, the animals' curious behavior was explained at once. The vertical cats had no horizontal-feature detectors; so they literally could not see anything that was composed of horizontal lines, like the seat of a chair. And the horizontal animals had only horizontal detectors, which made it impossible for them to see the vertical chair legs. These animals really were blind to things in their environment that were perfectly visible to you and me and to any self-respecting cat, all because of their unusual early experience.

This curious saga gets more curious still. Very recently Blakemore and his team, and California researchers Jack Pettigrew and Horace Barlow, managed to pervert all of the orientation detectors in cats: the researchers made the detectors respond to spots, not lines—something that the cells were never "designed"

to do. The trick was simply to bring up the animals in a spotty environment rather than a stripy one. Electrodes probed into the animals' brains revealed that it was spots displayed in the visual field that excited the cells in the visual cortex, not lines as in normal animals. Because the animals have to create a picture of their external world by synthesizing the responses of these nerve cells, it is anyone's guess what the unfortunate felines actually "saw" when they emerged—probably a fuzzy, hazy picture, somewhat like fog.

Blakemore and Don Mitchell, a colleague from Dalhousie University, Canada, decided to measure the speed at which the character of the feature detectors is specified. The researchers were more than astounded at the result, for they discovered that, with as little as one hour's visual experience, the way an animal's feature detectors function can be pretty well changed. The analogy with learning again enters one's mind.

Most people now agree that the cat's "visual-sensitive" period falls within the three-week-to-three-month span that Hubel and Wiesel noticed, with the most sensitive time occurring at about five weeks. This makes good developmental sense, because it is at this time that the animal's eyes have just about swung round to their correct positions in the sockets and the fluid within the eyes has become clear. But what about humans? Is there the same plasticity? If so, is there a sensitive period? If so, when is it?

Inevitably, the evidence for humans has to be rather more indirect than it has been for cats, but the indications are that there is not much difference between us and our feline cousins. For instance, infants with uncorrected squint or severe astigmatism finish up with permanent defects; spectacles cannot help them because it is the brain that appears to be at fault, not the eyes. In contrast, astigmatism that develops in adulthood can be corrected optically. This indicates that, like the brain of the cat, the immature human brain *is* plastic, while the adult brain is not. Blakemore says that the human visual-sensitive period probably spans the years from two to four. Visual defects really should be corrected before then.

Possibly the most intriguing discovery in this whole tale has come just recently from Canadian researchers Robert Annis and Barrie Frost. They examined the visual abilities of city-dwellers and

"Probably the most important skill that children learn is <u>how</u> to learn. . . . Too often we give children answers to remember rather than problems to solve. This is a mistake."

compared them with those of Cree Indians living in tepees on the east coast of James Bay. In the past researchers had found that "normal" people have better visual acuity (can see most sharply) in the horizontal and vertical axes. But what Annis and Frost found throws into question this concept of normality. They discovered that the Cree Indians have no particular axis of high visual acuity and are not especially attuned to horizontal and vertical lines. These people had, of course, been brought up in the country and away from the city, which is dominated by rectangular shapes. It may well be that the normal horizontal and vertical visual-acuity preferences are imposed on us simply because we live in a rectangular world. If houses were spherical instead of boxlike, things might be different. Despite the Cree Indians' lack of particular acuity in vertical and horizontal axes, they'd be able to get around New York City just as well as the rest of us. The crucial point is that human vision does appear to display the same kind of plasticity found in the experimental cats. And what is true of vision probably applies to our other senses as well.

Pediatricians have long recognized that infants should not be closeted in drab, visually unstimulating nurseries; the work with cats now gives that intuitive realization some scientific backing. But can we go further than this? Will a child become a musical genius if he is bombarded with Beethoven, Bach, and Berlioz from the day he is born? Will talking to a child in a spectrum of languages enhance his linguistic talent? And will one be the parent of a great mathematician if one teaches his infant the elements of logic at a tender age? The answer to all of these is, probably, "up to a point."

Almost certainly, the learning capacity of the human brain has not been exploited to the full by current educational approaches. The essential point is the possible existence of sensitive periods, not just for visual development, but for music, language, logic, and artistic talents. For instance, everyone acquires the elements of his language between the age of two and four. So why wait another six years before teaching a child a second and third language? The brain is clearly attuned to language acquisition in the early years, and there is a lot of evidence about the ease with which youngsters pick up a foreign language to which they are exposed. It would probably be a mistake to try to teach children two languages at once when they are only two years old, because there would be retroactive interference between the languages. But a child of four could start on a new language.

Musical talent very often runs in families. It may be "in the genes," of course, but there is undoubtedly a large environ-mental element, too. Children exposed to a lot of music when young are almost always more musically talented than average; how much this development is due to encouragement and opportunity is difficult to tell. But evidence that the musical brain becomes keyed in to its early experiences comes from the observation that people who develop perfect pitch while exposed to a slightly out-of-tune instrument always match their pitch to the instrument's. Although playing Beethoven to one's infant will probably not cause an environmentally generated reincarnation of the grand master, it may well produce a more-than-usually musically talented child.

Probably the most important skill that children learn is *how* to learn. The mark of intelligence is the facility for solving problems. Too often we give children answers to remember rather than problems to solve. This is a mistake. Unless children develop the art of problem-solving—whether by analytical logic or by non-sequential intuition—their brains will remain underexploited. Everyone knows that infants go through a period of being intensely curious. This curiosity is probably a behavioral expression of the brain's most sensitive period for acquiring knowledge and learning techniques.

Researchers will now turn their minds to discovering more about specific sensitive periods in the development of the brain, whether it be for language acquisition, enhancing musical talent, or simply learning how to learn. Unless these periods are exploited to the full at the right time, their potential may be lost forever.

WOBBLY BIORHYTHMS

PHILIP DEMUTH

Nearly 90 years ago, Sigmund Freud had a new idea about human behavior: body cycles . . . biological rhythms determined at birth. We all have them—three of them, in fact, according to a theory held by many scientists. An emotional cycle . . . an intellectual cycle . . . and a physical cycle. The little Biomate computer shown here will chart your life cycles for you— and tell you a lot about yourself.

Or, as another advertisement for a biorhythm computer assures us, "It's not hocus pocus. It's a behavioral science."

Why not? The biorhythm method has drawn considerable publicity over the last several years (see HB April 1973). In Switzerland, it is standard practice for surgeons to consult their patients' biorhythm charts in order to determine the best day for surgery. In Japan, the Ohmi Railway Company inaugurated a biorhythm safety program for its employees, cutting its accident rate 50 percent in one year alone. United Air Lines achieved even better results over a 12-month period with a biorhythm safety program for its ground crew at National Airport in Washington, D.C. It is well-known, too, that many coaches and trainers find biorhythms helpful in predicting the performance of their players. No wonder millions of people currently use biorhythms in plotting out their daily lives. As Bertram Brown of the National Institutes of Mental Health has said, "These biorhythms seem to have a lot of validity."

By now many people are familiar with the fundamental biorhythm curves. The theory states that three cycles begin at the time of every person's birth. These cycles remain constantly and invariably in motion throughout our lives. During the positive phase of our 23-day cycle of physical stamina and endurance, we are strongest; we can work harder, longer and with better coordination. Also, our resistance to disease is increased. During the negative phase, however, the body is recuperating. We are weaker and tire more easily. Critical days are likely to occur at the beginning and middle of each cycle, when the phase shifts from positive to negative or vice versa. On these days, we are said to be in a state of transition, or flux, and, as one would expect on such days of stressful readjustment, more accidentprone.

The second cycle is the 28-day rhythm of emotional sensitivity. During its positive phase, creativity, mood, cooperation and feelings are all enhanced; but in its negative course, we tend to be more sullen and withdrawn. The critical days similarly occur at the switch points between the phases, and at these times we more easily become emotionally upset. The third biorhythm is the 33-day intellectual rhythm. When it is above the median line, thinking is reported to be clearer, crisper and more decisive; while in the negative phase, the reverse holds true. The critical days again fall at the beginning and middle of the cycle, and on these days we are liable to make errors in judgment.

Advocates of the system claim that by knowing our personal biorhythm cycles in advance, we can compensate for our low periods, exercise extra caution on our critical days and take full advantage of our periods of peak performance. The theory has even been extended to cover such areas as marriage compatibility and predicting the sex of unborn infants. Indeed, if the theory were true, its potential applications in personal relationships, business, government, athletics and medicine would be numerous. But is the theory true? Have biorhythms really been discovered, or have they only been invented?

Biorhythms were first discussed by Wilhelm Fliess, who was a close friend of Sigmund Freud early in Freud's career. The popular biorhythm books portray him as an erratic, unsung genius of Freud's stature. As a Berlin nose-and-throat specialist at the turn of the century, Fliess began to notice some periodicity at work in his patients' illnesses. After making some calculations, he came upon the 23- and 28-day periods, which he labeled the male and female rhythms, respectively. This finding started him on a far-reaching flight of ideas. His major work, *Der Ablauf des Lebens* (1906), held that the interaction of these two cycles predicted the date of an infant's conception, the infant's date of birth and sex, the appearance of each of the baby's teeth, the date of its beginning to walk, the date of a girl's onset of menstruation, the dates of all illnesses during life, the date of death, the date of Gauss's discovery of the law of induction, the life course of plants and animals and the dates of the composition of all of Schubert's *Lieder*, among other things.

The problem was that, as a mathematician, Fliess made a great nose and throat specialist. He would juggle the numbers 23 and 28 with such reckless abandon that he could relate *any* critical date to them. As had Procrustes, he fitted all phenomena to his formula whether they fit or not. Hermann Swaboda, Fliess's successor, made the same mistake. Having been leaked Fliess's discovery by Freud, Swaboda went on to beat Fliess to publication. It is for this reason that many of the biorhythm books erroneously credit Swaboda and Fliess with being "codiscoverers" of biorhythm, despite the fact that Swaboda expressly acknowledged the idea to be Fliess's discovery in his book *Studien zur Grundlegung der Psychologie*. Although all of Fliess and Swaboda's data were lost during World War II,

From *Human Behavior*, April 1979. Copyright © 1979 *Human Behavior* Magazine. Reprinted by permission.

it really was no loss at all, because their findings all contained the same fundamental mathematical error.

The third biorhythm was revealed during the 1920s by Alfred Teltscher, a high school engineering teacher in Innsbruck, Austria. Teltscher found that his students' academic performance varied over time; and when he plotted this out, he observed that it obeyed a regular 33-day fluctuation. But as his method was entirely exploratory, and his findings were never verified or even committed to publication, it is impossible to say whether the cycle was genuine or essentially an artifact of randomly distributed data points. Nor do we know if the figure of 33 days was fixed and exact, or only an average for all his students. Most surprisingly of all, there is no evidence that he ever related the 33-day intellectual cycle to his students' birth times, as the current biorhythm theory assumes.

This illustrates a major problem endemic to most biorhythm research. What looks at first glance to be supportive evidence for the theory proves, on closer examination, to have little bearing on the question. A perfect example of this is found in the most widely cited instance of biorhythm in action, the case of the Ohmi Railway Company in Japan, mentioned earlier. Ohmi operates a fleet of taxis and buses. Of their 331 accidents between 1963 and 1968, 59 percent had occurred on a driver's critical day, or the day before or after. Therefore, in 1969 Ohmi's perspicacious management decided to implement a biorhythm safety program by issuing a special warning to its drivers on their biorhythm critical days. As noted, in the first year Ohmi's accident rate decreased 50 percent, and it continued to decline in each year following. The seemingly inevitable conclusion is that biorhythm rescued the company from its desperate condition. But notice that, at the outset, the company's accidents were occurring on biorhythm critical days with no greater than chance frequency. As any given day has about a 21 percent probability of being a biorhythm critical day by chance alone, their figure of 59 percent for the three-day period surrounding the accident is actually slightly less than chance would predict (63 percent). Next, there was no control group. This makes it impossible to relate the improvement in the accident record to the biorhythm intervention per se. Yet even if it was, it could have worked for reasons having nothing whatever to do with biological cycles. It could have been due to the placebo effect: since drivers were shown special attention and consideration by their company on certain days and provided with a scientific-sounding rationale for being so treated, the extra attention is itself sufficient to account for their improved driving record. Also, a basic principle of behavior modification is that intermittent reinforcement works better than a continuous reinforcing. Since "critical" days—and the extra attention they bring—come around periodically rather than being a constant presence, we can predict that biorhythm scheduling would provide an effective behavior modification safe driving program. No wonder, then, that it has often been successful when tried. But this success in no way proves the existence of the three biological cycles, since it is totally explainable from other grounds.

Another study often cited as providing evidence for the existence of biorhythms was done by Rexford Hersey, PhD, of the University of Pennsylvania between 1928 and 1932. Hersey conducted intensive interviews with factory workers over a period of months, observing them many times daily. He concluded that there was a definite pattern to the flow of the workers' moods. But unlike

biorhythms, these cycles were highly individualistic, ranging from four days to five weeks in length depending on the worker, and irregular rather than fixed in their periods. The biorhythm proponents frequently point to the other cycles existing in nature—in everything from sunspots to soil erosion, meteorites to body metabolism—in order to make the existence of the biorhythm cycles more plausible. Some of the popular books devote as much as one-half their text to discussing cycles other than biorhythms. The paralogism goes this way: because there are cycles in nature, and because biorhythms are cycles, it therefore follows that biorhythms are actual cycles existing in nature. But the existence of other cycles does nothing to establish the existence of biorhythms, despite the fact that they both equivocally share the same name. In fact, no known human or animal cycles operate with the precision and total invulnerability to variation that biorhythm professes. This error is again traceable to Fliess, who used the language of biology to justify his findings. But his use of biological terms was really metaphysical. For example, he spoke of the "genital cells" existing in the nose. While this would go a long way toward explaining why Eskimos rub noses, such talk leaves most biologists cold.

Biorhythm has also been used to forecast athletic events. A recent biorhythm book, containing the birth times of numerous sports figures, carries the sham warning across its cover: "Caution—not for use by professional gamblers." "Jimmy the Greek" Snyder, the Las Vegas oddsmaker, uses biorhythm to help him make book of major baseball and football games. However, in the only reliable study ever conducted on biorhythm and sports performance, following 85 major league baseball players throughout the 1975 season, James Fix, MD concluded that biorhythm had no effect on the players' batting averages on any type of day.

Automobile accidents form another frequently cited index of biorhythm critical days. Students under the direction of Harold Willis, a psychologist at Missouri Southern State College, studied 100 fatal single-car accidents in Missouri. They found that 46 percent of them occurred on the drivers' critical days, as opposed to the 21 percent expected if chance alone were operating. But a closer look at their data shows that they took the critical "day" to be 48 hours in length, and hence their findings are really only at the chance level. More recently, Shaffer et al reported in the Archives of General Psychiatry that in 205 carefully examined highway crashes, the results provided no evidence for a relationship between purported biorhythm cycles and accident likelihood. As for biorhythms and aircraft accidents, Wolcott and associates scrutinized a total of 8,625 pilot-involved accidents and ruled out biorhythm as a causal factor in aircraft crashes. A hard look at biorhythm and on-the-job accidents came from Frazier Damron and Dan Leetz at the University of Wisconsin. Studying 379 accident reports compiled by the Wisconsin Worker's Compensation Division, they found "no evidence that biorhythms had any influence on accident occurrence."

While other studies pro and con could be cited, most are plagued with serious methodological flaws that invalidate them. Some genuine positive findings have been reported by Douglas Neil, PhD, of the Naval Postgraduate School in Monterey, California. In one experiment, Neil followed four graduate students' academic performance over a 14-month period. He found that above-average test scores consistently appeared during the positive phase of their biorhythm cycles, although poor performance did not consistently occur during their negative biorhythm phases. In another study, Neil analyzed 127 accidents from an airline maintenance shop. He found that the accidents were significantly more likely to have occurred during the negative phase of the biorhythm cycles, although this did not hold true for the 28-day emotional sensitivity rhythm. Additionally, the accidents happened on the workers' critical biorhythm days significantly more often than if chance alone were operating. However, given the small scale of these research probes in relation to the large claims made by biorhythm proponents, Neil remains duly cautious in interpreting or generalizing his findings.

In my own research, I was interested in whether people were more likely to experience psychological distress on their critical days. I selected a group of 100 students who came in to a university counseling center for "drop-in" appointments (that is, students whose problems were so pressing that they said they could not wait to see a counselor by appointment). I assumed that, on the average, this was more likely than others to be a critical day. Next I went to a Community Mental Health outpatient clinc and pulled the charts of 50 patients who, like the students, had come in demanding immediate attention. The third group was composed of 50 people who came in to a hospital emergency room having made some suicidal gesture; while the fourth group, gathered from the records at the County Coronor's Office, consisted of 50 people who had committed suicide. I presupposed that the day when a person kills him- or herself or attempts to do so is a critical day for that person.

Gathering the birthdates of all these individuals, I computed their biorhythms to determine whether the day of the critical event was also a biorhythm critical day. I also collected information on the subjects' sex and age and looked at the three biorhythm cycles individually and in combinations, and at the fringe area surrounding the subjects' critical-event days. This was to determine whether a biorhythm critical day characteristically occurred, for example, on the day before a suicide attempt. I was also interested in observing whether the critical-event days clustered in the negative phase of the biorhythm cycles.

The results were underwhelming. In no case, along any of the above measures, was a biorhythm effect uncovered. The data were distributed in an array remarkable only for its randomness, with biorhythm conspicuous only by its absence. As an overall measure, consider that while 53 critical event days also were found to be biorhythm critical days, 54.7 days would be expected to be biorhythm critical days by chance alone. At this juncture, I decided to try another approach.

Visiting a college classroom of 44 students, I gave the class a brief explanation of biorhythms and distributed a calendar for the coming two weeks. I had taken the birthdates for one-half of the class, computed their biorhythm critical days and entered this information on their calendars. For the other half of the students, I wrote no biorhythm information on their calendars. Both groups were instructed to mark on their calendar any day that they felt would be critical for them over the coming two weeks. If people did not experience their critical days as being critical, it would be difficult to maintain that the biorhythm theory was accurate.

What I failed to tell the students at the time was that the biorhythm information I had given them for their critical days was completely false. I had obtained the dates not by calculating the students' biorhythms, as alleged, but rather from a table of random numbers.

The results, as anticipated, showed that students given no biorhythm information only hit on their biorhythm critical days at the chance level. However, the students supplied with misinformation were statistically significantly more likely to designate their false biorhythm critical days as critical. In other words, my study demonstrated that biorhythm can work by the power of suggestion. If a person is told that he or she may experience a certain day as being critical, this can increase the likelihood of that person having difficulty on that day.

Biorhythm appeals to our hunger for order, our desire to know and plan the future. But considering its dubious historical origins, and the lack of data substantiating biorhythms on empirical grounds, these cycles have failed to prove their existence. In our quest for self-knowledge, biorhythm answers with a mechanistic and deterministic formula, when what is really involved is the more complex and subtle interrelation between the physical, emotional and intellectual parts of ourselves.

THE HUMAN BODY AS A BIOLOGICAL CLOCK

JOHN J. NATALINI

JOHN NATALINI, PH.D., is an instructor of anatomy and physiology at Blessing Hospital School of Nursing and assistant professor of biology at Quincy College, Quincy, Ill. He has also been a teaching fellow and has been conducting research in circadian rhythms for the past eight years.

In our society, we give time a dominant and integral place in our activities. We gear at least some part of our lives to units of time: seconds, hours, days, weeks, months, or years, and to less defined time periods such as "coffee breaks," "cocktail hours," rest periods, and meal times. Our very existence is based upon periodic, structured, recurring processes.

Most units of time are defined by man, but they have a basis in nature. Each successive rising and setting of the sun determines the length of a day, and as the earth revolves around the sun, the seasons occur. These environmental parameters impose on man a periodicity which now is recognized a crucial part of life.

Periodic phenomena have been recorded for many years. Androsthenes, a foot soldier of Alexander the Great, observed while marching that the leaves of trees and plants drooped during the evening and elevated during the day. Eventually these activities became known as the "sleep movements" of plants. In 1729, Jean Jacques d'Ortous de Mairan, a French astronomer, discovered that these periodic movements continued for weeks, even though the plant was maintained in constant environmental conditions of light, temperature, and humidity(1).

Repeated reports of such biological rhythms have led to the concept of the biological or living clock. Animals and plants carry out periodically recurring activities, even under laboratory-controlled conditions. Somehow a "living clock" signals the time for physiological activities. A rhythm consists of recurring events, which are termed cycles. The period is the length of time of a single cycle. Many biological rhythms studied have a period of about 24 hours, which are called circadian (*circa,* about; *diem,* day) rhythms. Periods much less than a day are called ultra-dian, like those in the 90-minute sleep cycle, and rhythms that are greater than a day are called infradian. Other cycles can range from a month to a year and are considered circamonthly or circannual rhythms. The frequency is the reciprocal of the period; for example the body temperature peaks once every 24 hours, so the frequency is 1:24.

The phase is a specific point on a cycle and is commonly used to compare one cycle with another. For example, two rhythms may be in phase or may have a time displacement so that they are out of phase with each other. This displacement is called a phase shift. A phase shift can occur in either direction, leading or lagging the control rhythm. If the rhythm has the same period as some externally applied driving force, it is said to be entrained. The driving force behind a rhythm is called a *Zeitgeber* or synchronizer.

The most common *Zeitgeber* is the day-night cycle. Under the monitored conditions of a scientific laboratory it is called a light-dark cycle. In the absence of external *Zeitgebers,* the rhythm will exhibit a spontaneous period called the free-running period(2).

In addition to the many human circadian rhythms, there also are inconspicuous changes in our metabolism concurrent with the changing of the seasons. As yet we know little about these extended human rhythms. The Greeks noted annual trends in various diseases, for they believed that one's health was in harmony with nature. It is quite obvious that there are strong correlations between various symptomatic conditions and the day-night cycle, atmospheric pressure, electro-magnetic fields, and other weather factors.

Annual rhythms of live births demonstrate that the months of August and September are the peak periods, whereas most prenatal pathological conditions occur during January and February(3). Most suicides occur around May, accidental deaths around July, and ulcers around June(4).

Some people have the uncanny ability to wake at a predetermined time each morning or to take a nap exactly 15 minutes long. Others know exactly when to begin to walk toward the door of an elevator immediately before they arrive at the desired floor. This capability for estimating the passage of time has been called the "head clock." Studies show that one's ability to estimate a 60-second interval varies cyclically during the day(5). Even the behavior of man is cyclic, thus indicating that one is not the same person from one part of the day to another. We all know someone who is a "morning" or an "evening" person. And many circadian rhythms persist no matter what perturbation is provided. For instance, tissues removed from the body and maintained in tissue cultures may keep phase with their counterparts in the body.

Emotions, learning ability, and memory are periodic too. A stressful situation may affect a person quite differently depending upon the phase of his cyclic behavior. Failure to realize our natural periodicities can lead to unnecessary trauma, whereas understanding them may lead to the elimination of useless worry and dependency on prescribed medicines.

One scientist plotted his changes in mood based upon a 10-point scale for five years and discovered a weekly pattern with a low on Sunday and high on Wednesday(6). Another study of 200 volunteers indicated a Friday high point and a Tuesday low point. In this study, anticipation of a work-free weekend, interestingly, had no effect on mood(4).

There seems to be a phase relationship between learning, emotions, and the adrenal hormone levels. A stress or learning experience at one time of the day could cause a different impression if it occurred at another time of the day. A death in the family could leave a periodic impression such that the anxiety returns at the same time each day for several days after the incident. Also, periodicity in psychoses has been extensively observed(7).

Other illnesses are known to be periodic. One case reports that a patient had a manic-depressive type psychosis which consisted of 24 hours of elated, talkative behavior followed by 24 hours of depression and lethargy. His salivary secretions, urinary volume, and many other physiological parameters also indicated a 48-hour periodicity. This condition lasted for eleven years(8).

Every woman experiences monthly hormonal rhythms. Just before menses many women undergo what is commonly called premenstrual tension, including depression, headache, irritability, insomnia, vertigo, arthritis, gastrointestinal complaints, and altered appetite Viral infections increase premenstrually also. In addition, there are psychological changes, and during this time women might be admitted to psychiatric wards, attempt suicide, have accidents, and even suffer a decline in intelligence and in the quality of schoolwork(9).

If, in the harmony of human life, each rhythm is in synchrony with another, what happens when the rhythms become desynchronized? Experiments have been conducted in which human subjects lived under constant conditions, usually a homogenous environment in an underground bunker, with all the comforts of home except a clock. The various physiological rhythms indicated desynchronization with individual free-running periods. The experimental subjects had a statistically significant greater tendency to complain of physical ailments and to show neurotic behavior than the control subjects who were living in a normal periodic environment(10,11).

The "jet-lag syndrome," that "ill" feeling one acquires when traveling great distances either east or west but not north or south, is caused by desynchronization of biological rhythms. While at home, a person's physiological and psychological rhythms reach their peaks and valleys in phase with the physical environment. While traveling east or west in a jet plane, he either races or follows the sun; therefore, upon landing he must reestablish his rhythms to a new day-night cycle.

Sudden and frequent changes in one's work schedule can also cause internal desynchronization and the "shift syndrome." Rhythms fall out of phase and efficiency decreases so that frequent shifting is detrimental to performance. One becomes susceptible to noise, easily fatigued, vision is impaired, and depression is frequent(12,13). One of the grievances against the King of England during the American Revolution, as noted in the Declaration of Independence, reads:

"He has called together Legislative Bodies at Places unusual, uncomfortable, and distant . . . for the sole purpose of fatiguing them. . . ."

It appears that homeostasis is a cyclic phenomenon; thus, the very basic well-being of the body is cyclic. Everyone has observed that his moods change like the ebb and flow of the tides. Certain days one is elated; other days one is depressed. It should be emphasized that rhythms are easily entrained by various *Zeitgebers*, but the rhythms most experimentalists are interested in are those which continue in the absence of various time cues. One might distinguish two basic schools of thought concerning the biologic clock: the endogenous and the exogenous views. The endogenous school of thought basically believes that the clock is some internal mechanism, that is, a biochemical pathway, enzymatic feedback, hormone release, DNA-RNA-protein synthesis, and so forth. The latest theory suggests that the biological membrane cyclically controls substances entering or leaving the cell(14,15).

The exogenous school of thought hypothesizes that the basic timing mechanism (clock) is found outside the organism, that is, within the environment. It denies the possibility of "constant conditions." It states that no matter where one is located the body is unremittingly being bombarded with periodic, subtle, geophysical forces. Studies indicate that among these parameters are the geomagnetic fields of the earth. And, somehow, the living organism is responding to these *Zeitgebers* (14,15).

What does the future hold for circadian rhythms and the nurse? Obviously, there are more questions than answers, for each patient is unique with his own physiological and psychological rhythms.

Chronopharmacology, the study of the relationship between time and pharmaceuticals, implies that in the testing of certain drugs, the circadian rhythms of the test individual be taken into account. Without this criterion, a critical analysis of the data may be meaningless(16).

If the proper data were available, would it not be possible to vary the dosage depending upon the application time? Circadian treatment could diminish bad side effects or perhaps even overdoses(17).

Would it be possible for treatment to include bringing the patient's physiological and psychological rhythms back into harmony with each other? Will one see the addition of chronobiology and chronopharmacology education into present-day education programs?

References

1. WARD, R. R. *Living Clocks*. New York, Alfred A. Knopf, 1971, pp. 41-69.
2. ASCHOFF, JURGEN, AND OTHERS. Circadian vocabulary. In *Circadian Clocks*, proceedings of Feldafing Summer School, ed. by Jurgen Aschoff. Amsterdam, North-Holland Publishing Co., 1965, pp. x-xix.
3. JANERICH, D.T., AND GARFINKEL, JOSEPH. Season of birth and birth order in relation to prenatal pathology. *Am.J.Epidemiol.* 92:351-356, Dec. 1970.
4. LUCE, G. G. *Body Time, Physiological Rhythms and Social Stress*. New York, Pantheon Books, 1971, pp. 253-275, pp. 194-228.
5. PALMER, J. D. The many clocks of man. *Cycles* 22:36-41, 1971.
6. BRINKER, N. B. A 7-day cycle in human moods. *Cycles* 24:102-103, 1973.
7. CURTIS, G. C. Psychosomatics and chronobiology: possible implications of neuroendocrine rhythms. *Psychosom.Med.* 34:235-256, May-June 1972.
8. JENNER, F. A., AND OTHERS. A manic depressive psychotic with a persistent forty-eight hour cycle. *Br.J.Psychiatr.* 113:895-910, Aug. 1967.
9. U.S. NATIONAL INSTITUTE OF MENTAL HEALTH. Biological Rhythms in Psychiatry and Medicine, by G. G. Luce (USPHS Pub. No. 2088) Washington, D.C., U.S. Government Printing Office, 1970, pp. 109-110.
10. LUND, REIMER. Personality factors and desynchronization of circadian rhythms. *Psychosom.Med.* 36:224-228, May-June 1974.
11. CURTIS, G. C., AND FOGEL, M. L. Random living schedule: psychological effects in man. *J.Psychiatr.Res.* 9:315-323, 1972.
12. TAUB, J. M., AND BERGER, R. J. Acute shifts in the sleep-wakefulness cycle: effects on performance and mood. *Psychosom.Med.* 36:164-173, Mar.-Apr. 1974.
13. ABSTRACTS. *Int.J.Chronobiol.* 3(1):1-17, 1975.
14. RUSAK, BENJAMIN, AND ZUCKER, IRVING. Biological rhythms and animal behavior. *Annu.Rev.Physiol.* 26:137-171, 1975.
15. BROWN, F. A., JR., AND OTHERS. *The Biological Clock: Two Views*. New York, Academic Press, 1970.
16. REINBERG, ALAIN.Chronopharmacology. In *Biological Aspects of Circadian Rhythms*, ed. by J. N. Mills. New York, Plenum Press, 1973, pp. 121-15 .
17. REINDL, KARL, AND OTHERS. Circadian acrophase in peak expiratory flow rate and urinary electrolyte excretion of asthmatic children: phase shifting of rhythms by prednisone given in different circadian systems phases. *Rassegna di Neurologia Vegetativa* 23:5-26, 1969.

Additional readings on biorhythms are available upon request from the author at Quincy College, Quincy, Ill. 62301.

A Scientific Basis for Acupuncture?

Lu Gwei-Djen and Joseph Needham

Lu Gwei-Djen is an Emeritus Fellow of Lucy Cavendish College at Cambridge University. Joseph Needham, FRS, chief editor and author of SCIENCE AND CIVILISATION IN CHINA , an encyclopedic set of volumes published by Cambridge University Press, recently retired as Master of Gonville and Caius College, Cambridge.

This ancient Chinese medical practice may be based on physiological mechanisms

The system of acupuncture is among the most ancient components of Chinese medical art, and constitutes perhaps its most complicated feature. It is a system of therapy—and the relief of pain—which has been in constant use throughout the Chinese culture-area for some two and a half thousand years; and the labors of thousands of devoted practitioners through the centuries have given it a highly developed doctrine and practice.

Nevertheless its study presents great difficulties, partly because the books on acupuncture written in different dynasties have been elements in a long and gradual development, not always self-consistent and not free from loop-line elaborations now more or less abandoned; but even more because the physiology and pathology of the system are themselves so ancient that the clear-cut definitions and conceptions of modern science cannot be expected.

As the centuries passed, different masters emphasized somewhat different aspects and procedures as a result of their own deep study and practical expertise; and they handed on their understanding as clearly as they could to their particular disciples, or in the schools of medicine, by means of personal instruction and demonstration. Some wrote down specific guidance in the form of mnemonic rhymes which the student could learn by heart.

Since the revolution of 1949, however, a new phase has appeared in that the instruction given in the schools of traditional Chinese medicine is now being systematically set forth. Moreover, as is well known, China has developed a system in recent decades by which some physicians fully trained in modern-Western medicine continue their studies in colleges of traditional-Chinese medicine, while conversely others beginning with traditional medicine, including acupuncture, go on to qualify in modern medicine afterwards.

Marriage of Traditional and Modern Medicine

At the present time the traditional medical people in China are working side by side with the modern-Western-trained physicians in full cooperation. This is a very remarkable fact, which we ourselves have seen during four extended stays in China since the revolution. It has been brought about by the reevaluation of all national traditions in the country's mid-century renaissance, the convictions of its political leaders, the social needs and conditions, especially rural, and the relative paucity of physicians trained in modern scientific medicine.

The two types of physicians have joint consultations and joint clinical examinations, and there is the possibility for patients to choose whether they will have their treatment in the traditional way, including acupuncture, or the modern way; in other cases the physicians themselves decide which is best and proceed to apply it. There is, moreover, a steadily growing tendency to take all that is best from both traditions and combine them. Such fusion is destined, we believe, to occur more and more, giving rise to a medical science which will be truly modern and ecumenical, not qualifiedly modern-Western. And an example, outstandingly relevant here, is the successful application of acupuncture in recent years to induce analgesia in major surgery, constituting a remarkable marriage between traditional-Chinese and modern-Western medicine.

What Is Acupuncture?

Acupuncture is a method of therapy (including sedation and analgesia) developed first during the Chou period (before the first millennium B.C.), which involves the implantation of very thin needles (much thinner than the familiar hypodermic needles) into the body in different places at precisely specified points, according to a charted scheme

Copyright © 1979 Lu Gwei-Djen and Joseph Needham. This material first appeared in the May/June issue of *The Sciences,* excerpted from CELESTIAL LANCETS: A HISTORY OF RATIONALE AND ACUPUNCTURE AND MOXA, to be published in 1980 by Cambridge University Press.

based on ancient and medieval yet intelligible physiological ideas. Indeed the theory and the practice were, one finds, already well systematized before the second century B.C., though much development was to follow.

We ourselves have many times seen the way in which the implantation of the needles is done, attending acupuncture clinics in several Chinese cities (and in Japan also); and one can say that the technique remains in universal use in China at the present day. It also permeated centuries ago all the neighboring countries of the culture-area, and for three hundred years past has awakened interest, together with a certain amount of practice, throughout the Western world.

That acupuncture is a system of cardinal importance in the history of Chinese medicine is not disputed by anyone, but its actual value in objective terms remained until recently, and to some extent still remains, the subject of great differences of opinion. It is possible to find in East Asia modern-trained physicians, both Chinese and Occidental, who are wholly skeptical about its value, but it is notable that in China they are very few, and that the vast majority of physicians there, both modern-trained and traditional, do believe in its capacity to cure, or at least to alleviate, many pathological conditions.

Presumably no one will ever really know the effectiveness of acupuncture (or the other special Chinese treatments) until an adequate number of case-histories has been analyzed according to the methods of modern medical statistics—but the accomplishments of this may well take half a century, so great are the difficulties of keeping medical records in a country of eight-hundred million people, where the ratio of highly qualified physicians to the general population is relatively low, and the need for medical and surgical treatment of all kinds is so great and urgent.

We cannot wait that long in our work, and are therefore obliged to embark upon our historiography with a mild preference in one direction or the other. What that is will be stated in a moment, but first there are two points to be made. On the matter of published statistics it would not be fair to say that the Chinese medical literature contains no quantitative figures. But secondly the whole subject has taken a rather dramatic turn during the past fifteen years on account of the remarkable successes which have been achieved in China in the application of acupuncture for analgesia in major surgery. Here there is no long and tortuous medical history to be followed up, no periods of remission or acute relapse, no chronic conditions with uncertain responses, no psychosomatic guesswork. Either patients feel intolerable pain from the surgical intervention, or they do not, and the effectiveness can be known within the hour, or even quicker. More than

any other development, this acupuncture analgesia (or "anesthesia," as it is usually called, with undeniable but infelicitous logic) has had the effect of obliging physicians and neurophysiologists in other parts of the world to take Chinese medicine seriously, almost for the first time.

Now for our preference, it derives, one might say, from a kind of natural skepticism. But skepticism can work in more ways than one. What we find hard to believe is that a body of theory and practice such as acupuncture could have been the sheet-anchor of so many millions of sick people for so many centuries if it had not had some objective value; and it strains our credibility as physiologists and biochemists by training to believe that the effects

Made in Japan about 1880, papier-mâché anatomical doll maps 660 acupuncture points.

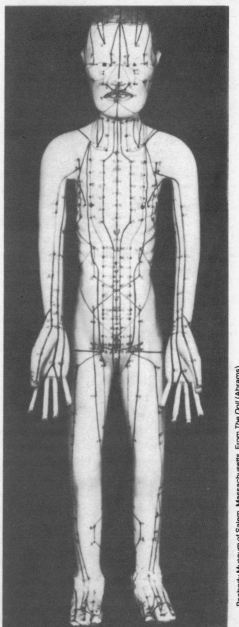

Peabody Museum of Salem, Massachusetts. From *The Doll* (Abrams).

were wholly subjective and psychological. One might almost think in terms of a calculus of credibility, pending that time which to us seems likely to be far ahead when all the mysteries of psychosomatic causation will have been resolved. It seems to us more difficult to suppose that a treatment practiced among so great a number of human beings for so long had no basis in physiology and pathology, than that it has been of purely psychological value.

Of course it is true that the practices of phlebotomy (blood-letting) and urinoscopy in the West had exceedingly little physiological and pathological basis on which to sustain their extraordinary and long-enduring popularity, but none of these had anything like the subtlety of the acupuncture system. Possibly blood-letting had some value in hypertension and hyperviscosity, and extremely abnormal urines could tell their story, but neither contributed much to modern practice.

Mass Hypnosis?

A view commonly expressed (mostly by Westerners) is that acupuncture has acted primarily by suggestion, like many other things in what they often call "fringe" medicine; and some do not hesitate to equate surgical acupuncture analgesia with hypno-anesthesia, in spite of many differences. To extend the term "hypnosis" to cover a general belief held by hundreds of millions of rational people for two millennia, and hence by prospective surgical patients today, would surely be a gross misuse of a term.

Of course we are far from wishing to deny the importance of a certain measure of suggestion and suggestibility, such as is known to be inevitable in all therapies which human beings have ever developed. But animal experiments, where the psychological factor is largely ruled out, support our view that physiological and physico-chemical things are happening in the nervous system under acupuncture, and animal experiments are increasingly being performed in laboratories investigating the technique. And not only this, but acupuncture has been a constituent part of veterinary medicine in China at least since the great treatises of the Yuan period, and continues to this day in widespread use for animal diseases. Theories of suggestion are here comparatively at a loss.

Is there a Scientific Basis?

Our belief is, then, that the scientific rationale of acupuncture will in due course be established. It is quite clear that in terms of neurophysiology the needles stimulate various receptors at different depths which send their afferent impulses up the spinal cord and into the brain. Perhaps they trigger events in the hypothalamus which activate the pituitary gland and lead to an increase of cortisone production by the suprarenal cortex. Perhaps they stimu-

late the autonomic nervous system in such a way as to lead to an increased output of antibodies from the reticulo-endothelial system. Both these effects could be of great importance from the therapeutic point of view, and others also could easily be visualized. Perhaps in another situation they monopolize afferent input junctions in thalamus, medulla or cord, in such a way as to prevent all pain impulses getting through to the cortex regions of the brain, and so successfully inducing analgesia. There are many other neurophysiological phenomena which deserve consideration in the context of acupuncture; for example, the "head zones" of the skin in mammals, which relate superficial regions to the viscera, and the multifarious effects of referred pain. So, too, some of the sensations experienced by patients undergoing acupuncture may have had no small effect on the formulations of the classical theory.

Still something more remains to be said about the theoretical setting of acupuncture—and indeed also other traditional Chinese methods, such as the medical gymnastics, for example, which originated very early in that culture. We have in mind the relative value placed in Chinese and Western medicine respectively on aid to the healing and protective power of the body, as against direct attacks on invading influences. A physiological mind might think of this as strengthening the response *versus* diminishing the stimulus.

Now in Western and in Chinese medicine both these conceptions are to be found. On the one hand, in the West, besides the seemingly dominant idea of direct attack on the pathogen, we have also the idea of the *vis medicatrix naturae*, a theme of resistance and the strengthening of resistance to disease which is strongly embedded in Western medicine from the time of Hippocrates and Galen onwards.

On the other hand, one can equally affirm that in China, where the holistic approach might be thought to have dominated, there was also the idea of combating external disease agents, whether these were malign or sinister *pneumata*, the *hsieh chhi* from outside, of unknown nature, or distinct venoms or toxins left behind, for example, when insects had been crawling over food (this is a very old conception in China); so the attack on external agents was certainly present in Chinese medical thought too. This may be called the *chhu hsieh* aspect (or, in pharmacological terms, *chieh tu*); and the other, the *vis medicatrix naturae*, was largely what the Taoists meant in China by *yang shêng*, the nourishment of life and the strengthening of it against disease.

Western vs. Eastern Approach

It should by now be clear that whatever the acupuncture procedure does, it must be along the lines of strengthening the patient's resistance (by increasing antibody or cortisone production), and not directly fighting the invading *pneumata* or organisms,

Acupuncture in the West

In approaching acupuncture through the works of representatives of the present-day practitioners in the Western world, some reserve should be exercised. Even when these works are based on translations of Chinese handbooks for professional acupuncturists, they all alike tend to approach Western readers with the assumption that all they need is a set of charts, a list of illnesses and a case of needles with instructions as to where to stick them in, then hope for the best. The Western enthusiast, unlike the "barefoot doctor," does not have a deeply skilled specialist at the base hospital to whom reference can be made. In the hands of real experts, acupuncture can, in our belief, be very effective, both for therapy and analgesia, but when performed by amateurs, cranks or under-educated practitioners, it can have ill effects. Indeed, acupuncture has been prohibited at times, both in China and Japan, for just such reasons.

—LU GWEI-DJEN AND JOSEPH NEEDHAM

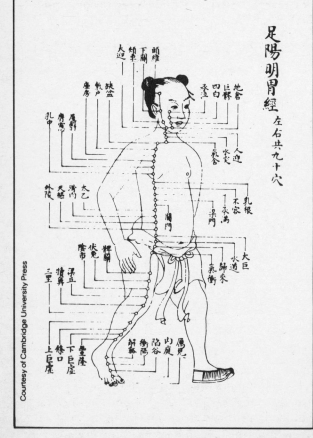

Courtesy of Cambridge University Press

venoms or toxins—not the characteristic "antiseptic" attack which has naturally dominated in the West since the time of origin of modern bacteriology. This is shown by the significant fact that while Westerners are often prepared to grant value to acupuncture in affections such as sciatica or lumbago (for which modern-Western medicine can do very little anyway), Chinese physicians have never been prepared to limit either acupuncture or the related moxa (mild or severe cautery and heat-treatment) to such fields; on the contrary they have recommended it and practiced it in many diseases for which we all now believe we know clearly the causative organisms—typhoid, cholera and appendicitis—and they have claimed at least remissions if not radical cure. The effect is thus in principle cortisone-like or immunological. It is assuredly very interesting that both these conceptions (the exhibition of hostile drugs, and the strengthening of the body's resistance) have developed in both civilizations, in the medicine of both cultures; and one of the things which any really adequate comparative history of world medicine would have to do would be to elucidate the extent to which these two contrasting ideas dominated in the thought of East and West at different times.

In addition there was of course always a third conception, that springing from the idea of balance or *krasis*, just as Chinese as it was Greek, in accordance with which disease was essentially a malfunction or imbalance, one or other component entity in the body having unnaturally gained the lead over the others. Since the development of modern endocrinology, this conception has indeed taken a new lease of life, but it was present from the beginning in both civilizations. European blood-letting and purging was a direct, if crude, result of it, since the thought was that "peccant humors" had to be got rid of; but in China a defective balance between Yin and Yang, or deviant relationships between the "five elements," was generally diagnosed and altered in a more subtle way, and it is very much to the point that acupuncture was the first court of appeal in this matter as well.

No one can miss the overwhelming importance of the Yin and Yang in the governance of the system which acupuncture undertook to affect, and we have little doubt that many interventions of this kind did return the living human body with its nerves and hormones to a more even keel, although exactly how the medieval physicians visualized the interplay of the two great forces remains, as always, hard for us to understand fully because of their philosophical nature. Neither Yin and Yang nor the "five elements" were readily capable of giving rise to a quantified science. Never mind, the results were what mattered, and once again acupuncture could accomplish something health-giving.

WHAT MARIJUANA DOES (And Doesn't Do)

ROBERT CARR

Grass has become a part of our lifestyle, like it or not, so it behooves us to find out what hazards, if any, it poses to our health and well-being. Here's what we know up to this point.

Robert Carr is an independent consultant with the Drug Abuse Council. Portions of this article are taken from an unpublished report prepared for the Council.

Marijuana has been accused of causing innumerable evils and debilities—from promiscuity and violence to impotency and passivity. Even the specter of permanent brain damage for users has been headlined in the past few years. Unfortunately, many isolated research reports alleging serious harm have received national publicity before their scientific validity was determined and before attempts to replicate their findings were made by other independent researchers. Although these scattered negative claims about marijuana have captured considerable media attention, the evidence that is now in suggests that marijuana poses far less threat to the user than do alcohol and tobacco.

Despite the fact that more is known about marijuana than any other single drug, there is still abundant controversy about the effects of pot. Research has focused on 11 major areas: alteration of motivation; progression to other drugs; chromosome breakage; crime; psychomotor skills; brain damage; immune response; lung damage; sexual dysfunction; therapeutic potential; and tolerance and dependence.

The Hippie Leap

Not surprisingly, considering the early use of marijuana in this country by minority populations and lower economic groups and later by the rebellious youth of the '60s, the link between marijuana and a rejection of societal values was inevitably inferred by the majority nonusing public. But the evidence to support a causal relationship between heavy cannabis use and a loss of traditional motivation has been and continues to be based on isolated observations and anecdotal accounts. Longitudinal studies of college students and studies of working-class populations in other countries have failed to confirm that marijuana leads to amotivation among users.

UCLA investigators Joel S. Hochman and Norman Q. Brill studied the drug habits of 1,400 UCLA undergraduates and found no statistically significant differences in the academic performance, in either high school or college, of users and nonusers of marijuana, even among the daily smokers. Among the students surveyed, "frequency or duration of marijuana use, up to daily frequency, did not appear to affect the ability or desire to obtain high grades." Chronic users, while they had more difficulty in deciding on career goals and more frequently dropped out of school one or more times, performed as well as their peers after their return. Results similar to the UCLA findings have been reported from a study conducted at the University of California in Berkeley from 1970-1973. The researchers were unable to isolate marijuana use as an independent factor in producing amotivational symptoms.

The evidence on how less gifted individuals fare when using marijuana regularly comes from studies of working-class populations in other countries. Under contract with the National Institute on Drug Abuse, anthropologists William E. Carter and Paul L. Doughty of the University of Florida sought to determine the social and cultural aspects of cannabis use in Costa Rica, where heavy marijuana use by the working class goes back a century. The average Costa Rican user in the survey had smoked 9.6 marijuana cigarettes daily for 16.9 years, with some persons smoking up to 80 cigarettes daily on occasion. Carter and Doughty report a clear inverse relationship between stability of work and level of cannabis use. "The heaviest users," say the researchers in a report presented to the New York Academy of Sciences, "have the highest incomes, the least unemployment and the most stable job histories of the entire user group. They also more frequently report that their preferred activity while intoxicated is to work." The anthropologists observed that the heaviest user averages 40 marijuana cigarettes per day and yet manages a very successful business with eight employees. "These facts," they suggest, "question the applicability of the amotivational syndrome among marijuana-using working-class Costa Ricans."

Another study, of Jamaican working-class smokers, also found them to be indistinguishable from nonsmokers on all of the socioeconomic profiles, such as ownership and control of property or income.

It would appear from studies of college students in this country and from investigations of working-class populations in Costa Rica and Jamaica that the use of marijuana, including chronic and long-term, does not produce the cluster of symptoms referred to as the amotivational syndrome. And the perceived threat to society of a generation of dropouts, smoking dope on street corners, rejecting societal values, has faded with the use of marijuana becoming a cultural norm for younger adult and teenage groupings regardless of status or ambition.

From *Human Behavior*, January 1978. Copyright 1978 Human Behavior Magazine. Reprinted by permission.

Path to Hard Drugs?

The issue is not whether marijuana users tend to use a wider variety of other drugs, which they do, but rather whether it is the heavy marijuana use that leads to or causes the use of those other drugs.

All drug-use surveys reveal that the use of *any* drug is statistically associated with the use of all other drugs. Marijuana sits as the pivotal illicit drug in time sequence in using a variety of drugs; alcohol is the pivotal licit drug in the sequence. A 1975 nationwide survey of nonmedical drugs used in the United States among a representative group of 2,510 men, ages 20 to 30, measured the nature and extent of drug use, including tobacco and alcohol. The highlights of the survey, supported by the National Institute on Drug Abuse (NIDA), defy simplistic causal links among multiple drug use:

- Ninety-nine percent of those who have used tobacco report having used alcohol.
- Fifty-nine percent of the tobacco users have used marijuana, in comparison with 27 percent of those who have never used tobacco.
- Ninety-seven percent have used alcohol, and the use of alcohol is associated with the use of the other drugs. Nonusers of alcohol rarely used any other drug, except tobacco.
- Forty percent of those who have used marijuana have also used psychedelics. On the other hand, virtually none of the nonusers report psychedelic use.
- Heroin users are at the pinnacle of drug use. They are likely to have at least used almost every other drug:

tobacco, alcohol, marijuana, psychedelics, stimulants, sedatives, opiates and cocaine. Two-thirds of those who have ever used heroin have also used *every single one* of the other drugs studied.

Alcohol was almost always the first drug used by multiple drug users, but the use of marijuana was antecedent to the use of stimulants, sedatives and opiates for 73, 84 and 77 percent, respectively. Ninety-six percent of those who have used cocaine and marijuana used marijuana first, and 90 percent of those who have used both heroin and marijuana used marijuana first. "While these data do not show that use of marijuana leads to use of heroin or cocaine," says the study, "it is clear that one behavior usually precedes the other in time."

The Hochman and Brill study of the drug habits of UCLA undergraduates, as reported in the *American Journal of Psychiatry*, concluded that "marijuana use does not cause the use of other drugs but does accompany it.... Other drug use represents experimentation, which becomes infrequent for the majority of drug users. At least for college students, acquiring an addiction to or regular use of a drug other than marijuana is so rare as to be remarkable, i.e., about 0.1 percent of marijuana users."

Nor is the relationship between heavy marijuana use and the inevitable escalation to harder drugs borne out in other societies. Cannabis in Jamaica, legally referred to as *ganja*, is used by an estimated 50 percent of all males over the age of 15, and the plant is used, even among nonsmok-

ers, for *ganja* teas and tonics for medicinal purposes. Perhaps the most thorough study on the social and health consequences of chronic cannabis use was conducted in Jamaica by Vera Rubin and Lambros Comitas of the Research Institute for the Study of Man in New York with a grant from the National Institute of Mental Health. Jamaican working-class users do not even experiment with other drugs, according to Rubin and Comitas; heroin and other hard drugs are virtually unknown. "The few cases of heroin toxicity that had come to the attention of physicians all involved tourists," they continue. "The concern that cannabis is the 'halfway house to heroin' is simply not borne out by the Jamaican data."

The decision to use an illicit drug in this country would no doubt lead to marijuana first because it is readily available and widely consumed. However, the predisposition to experiment with drugs, licit and illicit, relates to personality and situational factors beyond the control of society. Once the choice has been made to use one illegal substance, it should come as no surprise that some individuals may choose to use others as well. If marijuana were to magically vanish from this country, then some other illicit drug would likely assume its pivotal position. The use of heroin and other drugs would not be eliminated nor even be minimized if marijuana were to disappear tomorrow. Heroin users would simply start with another drug, maybe cocaine, judging by the recent upsurge in popularity it has undergone.

If marijuana were to magically vanish tomorrow, then some other illicit drug would be right there to take its place.

Link to Children

The National Institute on Drug Abuse convened two conferences in 1973 and 1974 to evaluate the published and unpublished data in the critical area of chromosome breakage. Overall, the conferees concluded, "it is still doubtful whether cannabis is a danger to human genetic and reproductive processes, under the conditions and in the doses commonly used by marijuana smokers."

The relationship between chromosome breaks and genetic defects is

not known. Many other substances are known to cause such breaks, including caffeine, aspirin and Valium.

Considering the millions of Americans and individuals from other parts of the world of childbearing age who have used and continue to use marijuana, one would expect if chromosome damage does occur from cannabis use that such harm would have surfaced and the world would now be saddled with countless numbers of deformed and mutated children. Such

is not the case here or elsewhere. Whatever chromosome damage may have been detected in test tubes and experimental animals is not evident in the children of marijuana users.

However, THC, the major psychoactive ingredient of pot, does cross the placental barrier in the first trimester of pregnancy. The *potential* seriousness of such effects on the offspring of users makes the use of marijuana during pregnancy an unnecessary risk.

The Healing Touch

Cannabis shows promise in reducing intraocular pressure in patients suffering from glaucoma; in relieving the pain of cancer patients and reducing or eliminating loss of appetite, nausea and vomiting following chemotherapy; in relieving asthmatic distress by temporarily dilating the bronchial passages; and in facilitating sleep as a sedative-hypnotic. There are endless possible therapeutic applications of marijuana if it should prove, as investigators now seem to be finding, to be useful as a general antivomiting drug and an analgesic. Investigations are underway to determine its efficacy in the treatment of alcoholism and narcotic addition; Jamaicans already view pot as a "benevolent alternative" to alcohol, and alcoholism is fractional compared to Caribbean islands without the cannabis tradition.

In many ailments where cannabis has been found to have therapeutic value, the side effects of the drug have mitigated against its acceptance by physicians and, of course, it remains illegal for pharmaceutical prescription. Synthetic THC has been developed that does not appear to have the disadvantages of natural THC such as undesired psychic effect, instability and insolubility. For glaucoma sufferers, eye drop preparations containing THC are being tested on laboratory animals with initial results showing great promise.

The further study of marijuana for various therapeutic applications has been given the blessing of the federal government, and several NIDA-sponsored studies are now underway. But whether or not marijuana or its chemically related synthetics will reach the pharmacists' shelf in the next few years awaits further investigations and careful evaluation of the findings. Chances are that it will be therapeutically accepted—at least in a limited way. Many currently marketed drugs have the inherent capacity for more harm than has been demonstrated for cannabis. The margin of safety in dosage is enormous. Overdose deaths are unknown in Western countries, and the few reports from other parts of the world are poorly documented. "The hemp plant and its derivative chemicals turn out to be neither the best nor the worst of substances," concludes the 1975 HEW report. "Like everything else, it should be used for its beneficial effects and avoided for its noxious aspects."

There is no scientific or common-sensical reason for our nation to continue hiding behind the curtain of medical research on the pretext that marijuana's severe health hazard eventually will be proven, so justifying a criminal response to recreational users. One of every three Americans already lives in a jurisdiction no longer treating those who use grass as criminals; decriminalization has been adopted in 10 states. And marijuana has become a permanent part of the lifestyle for millions of Americans. There is no reason to disagree with the latest HEW report when it observes: "Persistent use for nearly a decade by large numbers, despite significant attempts to discourage marijuana use, suggests that cannabis use is more than a fad and may well prove to be an enduring cultural pattern in the United States."

Many currently marketed drugs have the inherent capacity for more harm than has been shown for cannabis.

The Addict Nonproblem

Addiction to marijuana is virtually unknown in this country. The few scattered reports of such dependence in nations where cannabis consumption is extraordinarily large, rely upon definitions of addiction quite different from those most commonly applied in the medical literature.

Addiction implies a physiological change causing the individual to crave the habituated substance. If deprived, a user suffers such withdrawal symptoms as chills, pains, restlessness, perspiration, twitching of muscles, nausea and diarrhea. The withdrawal effects subside with time, but some symptoms may persist for up to six months. Tolerance is said to develop when the response to the same dose of a drug decreases with repeated use and increased dosages are necessary to achieve the desired high.

Withdrawal symptoms have been reported in animal experiments involving extremely high doses of THC for long periods of time. Mild and short-lived withdrawal symptoms have been reportedly induced in human subjects who used marijuana from 21 to 42 days in a clinical experiment at an orally ingested rate equaling 50 to 100 cigarettes per day. But withdrawal symptoms did not appear even with the heaviest Jamaican users after lengthy abstention.

Tolerance to marijuana at the dose levels of recreational users is rarely reported either anecdotally or experimentally. In fact, novice users very often have to use more of the drug to achieve a high than do experienced users who can identify and are more sensitive to the desired effects. A behavioral tolerance has been observed that allows the individual to compensate for his or her intoxication and to perform certain physical and mental functions that less experienced users would find difficult or impossible. The tolerances noted do not seem to present a problem since there are no reports of individuals escalating their dosages of marijuana solely to achieve an elusive high, although there are instances aplenty of indiscriminate use.

There is no question that marijuana can create a psychological dependence for some heavy users. Numerous surveys of marijuana users, however, demonstrate beyond doubt that for the overwhelming number of users consumption is controlled and intermittent. Even most regular users report that cannabis is relatively easy to give up for extended periods of time. For the few where psychic dependency may be a problem, the reason is probably found elsewhere than in the chemistry of cannabis.

Fighting Disease

In early 1974, a report by a quartet of researchers at Columbia University claimed a marked reduction in the immune response as measured in white blood cell cultures of marijuana smokers compared with nonsmokers. This reduction was said to be comparable to that of patients with known T-cell immunity impairment, such as cancer and uremia, and was interpreted to mean that marijuana smokers lack an essential means of defense against infection. The validity of the claim that marijuana may reduce the body's immune response, based on these *in vitro* (observable in a test tube only) findings, remains in doubt.

Attempts to replicate the Columbia findings and to explore their implications by testing for immune response depression by other means have resulted in contradictory reports. It was found, for example, that marijuana smokers off the street showed a reduction in immune response; this reduction, however, did not persist in users smoking quality-controlled marijuana. Thus, the reduction in immune response observed in some chronic drug users may be the result of some common factor of their lifestyle other than marijuana use.

Researchers at the Veterans Administration Hospital in Washington, D.C., attempting to replicate the findings of the Columbia investigators, reported that long-term marijuana smoking had no significant effect on the functional status of T-cells. UCLA investigators Melvin J. Silverstein and Phyllis J. Lessing evaluated the immune system response of 51 regular marijuana users by skin test reactions; this approach is contrasted with the Columbia procedure by testing the human body itself rather than in a test tube. The findings revealed no statistical difference between the reactions of the marijuana smokers and a control group, and no similarity to the immune reactions of 60 cancer patients. Also, the Jamaican study of long-term chronic *ganja* smokers found no deleterious effects on immune response attributable to cannabis.

Considering the extensive use of marijuana during the past 10 years in this country, especially among younger populations, one would have expected a major public health crisis to emerge in the high schools and colleges if cannabis consumption significantly impaired the immune response. No increase in infections has been reported by the public health services despite heavy pot use by the student groups.

Although the issue of possible impaired immune response may remain unresolved to some, the fact is that there is, as yet, according to the latest HEW report, "no evidence that users of marijuana are more susceptible to such diseases as viral infections and cancer that are known to be associated with lowered production of T-cells."

Lung Damage

There is growing evidence that smoked marijuana may have adverse effects on pulmonary function. THC and the other properties of marijuana smoke likely have some of the same kinds of effects on the lungs as tobacco and other kinds of smoke. The only major statistically significant medical difference between pot smokers and nonsmokers in the Jamaica study is that smokers had reductions in lung capacities. Rubin and Comitas concluded that chronic, heavy smokers (more than 20 tobacco cigarettes per day, plus chronic marijuana smoking) are at greater risk of having an oxygen deficiency in the body tissues.

However, the Jamaican research team did not isolate marijuana as the culprit in the pulmonary deficiencies because all users also used tobacco. Tobacco probably has more severe effects on the lungs than marijuana because of its much heavier consumption and because it does not dilate the bronchial passage as does THC. Nonetheless, the potential consequences of combining heavy marijuana use with heavy tobacco consumption is serious enough that David Smith, clinical director of Haight-Ashbury Free Clinic in San Francisco, is reported to have suggested that such users switch from marijuana smoking to other forms of consumption—such as drinking marijuana tea—to protect the lungs from smoke.

Sexual Debate

A research team headed by Robert Kolodny at the Reproductive Biology Research Foundation in St. Louis reported in 1974 that heavy marijuana use—at least four days a week for six months—by 20 healthy men significantly decreased their testosterone levels. Two subjects reported actual difficulty with sexual functioning. Testosterone levels for all the men, although lower than nonusers, were within what is considered to be normal levels, even for the heavy marijuana smokers (who have 10 or more cigarettes a week).

A study by the same St. Louis group the following year found that 13 marijuana smokers isolated in a hospital ward showed a decline in testosterone levels after the fifth week of smoking a predetermined amount of marijuana. But a major study by Jack H. Mendelson and his associates at Harvard failed to replicate Kolodny's findings. Twenty-seven men between the ages of 21 and 26 were the subjects of this study. Under controlled conditions, the researchers report, "high dosage marijuana intake was not associated with suppression of testosterone levels when multiple plasma samples were obtained before, during and after a 21-day smoking period."

How to explain the variance of findings between Kolodny and Mendelson, two widely respected researchers? Perhaps, more importantly, what is the effect on human sexual behavior of the reduced testosterone levels reported by Kolodny? Several commentators have noted that testosterone levels vary considerably from day to day and even from hour to hour. "It takes a very large decline to affect sexual performance much; even castration has very variable effects on sexual activity in monkeys," observe Harvard psychiatrist Grinspoon and James Bakalar, a law lecturer at Harvard Medical School. The 1975 HEW report to the U.S. Congress, after reviewing the Kolodny study, notes that the decreases in testosterone that have been found have still been within normal limits.

The debate over whether or not marijuana adversely affects testosterone levels has temporarily obscured the positive sexual effects claimed by many users of the drug. While no controlled studies of the sexual effects of marijuana use have been reported, the anecdotal accounts of many users indicate that cannabis can elevate sexual pleasure by altering a person's mood, distorting time and enhancing tactile sensation. The intoxicant properties of marijuana, like alcohol, reduce inhibition. Of course, too high a dose of marijuana, like alcohol, may dampen the sexual function temporarily, but with normal use and the proper setting, marijuana is likely to improve perceived sexual enjoyment.

Crime

There has never been a shred of empirical evidence to support the claim that marijuana is causally linked with crimes. A review of available evidence on the link between marijuana use and criminal and aggressive behavior by the National Commission on Marijuana and Drug Abuse concluded in 1972: "There is no systematic empirical evidence, at least that drawn from the American experience, to support the thesis that the use of marijuana either inevitably or generally causes, leads to or precipitates criminal, violent, aggressive or delinquent behavior of a sexual or nonsexual nature." Marijuana users are, in fact, underrepresented in crimes of sexual assault and in other violent criminal activity.

Further, it is clear that marijuana is not addictive in the same sense as heroin. And even if it was, enough to yield 30 to 40 cigarettes per week would cost no more thin $35—surely not enough to force the user into criminal activity and probably about the equivalent cost of supporting the heavy use of alcohol.

Body Impact

According to a 1975 HEW report on marijuana and health, "Present evidence, whether derived from driver test course performance, from actual traffic conditions or from the experimental study of components of the driving task, all indicates that driving under the influence of marijuana is hazardous. The increasing simultaneous use of both alcohol and marijuana by drivers poses a threat that may well exceed that of either substance alone. While the parameters of risk connected with the use of marijuana alone or in combination with alcohol prior to driving are not yet known, discouragement of such use appears justified."

There is a proven risk in mixing cannabis use with activities requiring exact time and spatial judgments, precise mental and muscular coordination or constant alertness—pursuits such as driving a vehicle, flying a plane or operating complicated machinery.

However, it is generally conceded that marijuana use results in less impairment of driving and other skills than does alcohol, not only because fewer individuals drive under the influence of marijuana but because the effects of marijuana appear to be more subtle and variable. Some marijuana users, for example, compensate by driving slowly and more cautiously, while alcohol users tend to be more aggressive and make more errors of judgment. And a few marijuana users, particularly at lower dose levels, have actually improved their driving performance under simulated conditions.

Nonetheless, limited surveys show that from 60 to 80 percent of marijuana users sometimes drive while intoxicated. The use of marijuana with alcohol before and during driving also seems quite common. And marijuana smokers were overrepresented in a study of drivers involved in fatal accidents in the Boston area.

Research is underway to measure marijuana intoxication through analysis for its presence in blood, saliva, urine and breath. Such detection methods will be particularly important to identify drivers under the influence of cannabis and to set limits for use like those for alcohol.

Brain Damage

There is undisputed evidence that cannabis produces reversible and dose-related changes in brainwaves. These changes are not markedly different from those caused by other psychoactive drugs and, in part, are the scientific analogs of what marijuana users would call being "high" or "stoned." While there is agreement that cannabis does produce such symptoms as short-term memory loss and time distortion, such symptoms disappear as the effects of the drug wear off, usually within a few hours.

The more serious allegations concern *irreversible* organic brain damage that is alleged to have certain permanent behavioral effects, such as the amotivational syndrome and other aberrant behavior. The only direct evidence to support permanent structural damage to the human brain from chronic use of marijuana was reported by A. M. C. Campbell and associates in 1971. Writing in the *Lancet*, a British medical journal, the authors claimed evidence of cerebral atrophy in 10 patients with self-reported histories of consistent cannabis use over a period of three to 11 years. They utilized a risky technique of injecting gas into certain portions of the brain to outline them for X-ray scans. The study is the cornerstone of the evidence supporting the relationship between marijuana and brain damage, and it is still cited as prime evidence by opponents in the marijuana debate.

Simply on the basis of the subjects' own anecdotal reporting of abnormally high levels of drug use other than marijuana, the designation of cannabis as the causative factor in whatever brain atrophy that might have been observed lacks scientific validity. All 10 subjects had used LSD, ranging from a few times to 30 or more. Eight subjects had extensive experience with amphetamines. Other intermittent drug use included mescaline, morphine and cocaine. Furthermore, as Lester Grinspoon, an associate professor of psychiatry at Harvard, has noted, at least one of the patients was a grand mal epileptic; another may have suffered from petit mal epilepsy; several had suffered head injuries from accidents; another was mentally retarded; at least one, and possibly as many as five, were schizophrenic; and there were a number of severe character disorders. All the patients were brought to the attention of Campbell and his associates for psychiatric difficulties. "These patients," Grinspoon noted wryly in *Contemporary Drug Problems*, "are not ideal candidates for this kind of brain research."

In short, the research techniques employed by Campbell and colleagues and the presentation of those results were seriously flawed to the point of rendering the study all but meaningless. Unfortunately, this type of report is typical of much of the research done in the marijuana field. Yet, such a claim cannot be ignored since the possible peril is so high.

The Jamaican and Costa Rican studies of long-term heavy marijuana users revealed no brain pathology inherent in extended use of the drug.

Similarly, two studies reported in *The Journal of the American Medical Association* (1977) found no evidence that heavy marijuana smoking changes the structure of the brain or central nervous system. The new studies, carried out independently by teams of researchers at Harvard Medical School and the Washington University School of Medicine in St. Louis, involved a recently developed X-ray technique to scan sections of the brain. Both research teams found no evidence of cerebral atrophy among a combined 31 young men with histories of extensive marijuana use.

On the basis of the evidence available, brain damage from chronic pot smoking is not demonstrated.

Processes Underlying Behavior

Behavior engineering involves the systematic use of reward to encourage some behaviors and discourage others. "Little Brother Is Changing You" describes a project that trained "incorrigible" junior high school students to use the techniques of behavior engineering on their teachers. The results were gratifyingly two sided: not only did the students discourage negative teacher behaviors, but they also derived from their training a sense of power that enhanced their own self-confidence and self-esteem. The principle of behavior engineering was then applied to parent and peer relationships, again with positive results. The authors point out that behavioral conditioning goes on all the time—why not train people to use it positively rather than negatively?

"Can't Remember? Put Popcorn in Your Bed" explores the mysteries of human memory—how it works, and how it can be trained to work better. Various memory-enhancing devices and strategies are outlined, including synesthesia, loci, the peg-word system, and narrative chaining. Further, "That Filing System Inside Your Head" catalogues some of the myriad factors affecting memory: age, stress, context, physiology, foods, and chemicals. The key to a good memory may be . . . exercise!

Memory also plays a role in language, especially in the production and understanding of speech. "Thought into Speech" considers studies regarding the way we put ideas into words, and the grammatical compromises that we make along the way to facilitate the hearer's understanding of what we say. "Navigating the Slippery Stream of Speech" describes the recent research in psycholinguistics that contributes to our understanding of how we hear and understand everyday speech. An important tool in this research is the spectrograph, which graphically records the stream of sound. Practical applications of information gleaned from the spectrograph may include helping deaf people to speak more clearly, and facilitating foreign language instruction.

Human life as well as that of many animals is played out within a cycle of rest and activity, biological ebb and flow. Sleep embraces one of the most interesting phenomena in psychology: dreaming. "Dream World" discusses the forms, theory, and folklore of sleep, as well as important research being conducted in this area.

Stress is part of the activity cycle, although it may be manifested in our rest behavior as well. Modern life contains many stress-producing factors, and the individual's inability to cope with any of these factors may produce one or more of the symptoms outlined in "Stress."

Parapsychology is the field of psychology that studies psychic phenomena, like extra-sensory perception. But is it a legitimate science? In "The Case for Parapsychology," D. Scott Rogo answers in the affirmative, citing scientific methodology and independently verified laboratory results. Martin Gardner rebuts Rogo's argument in "A Skeptic's View of Parapsychology."

A review of this section will provide a view of the general state of knowledge about some of the basic processes of behavior, including memory, language, dreaming, and stress responses. Behavior is discussed from several angles, from behavior engineering to parapsychology.

Looking Ahead: Challenge Questions

What are some of the ethical considerations of behavior control?

How might a psychotechnology be developed that emphasizes how we think rather than what we do?

Do dreams and psychic exploration offer a valid enrichment of self-knowledge?

What are some alternatives to live-animal laboratory research?

LITTLE BROTHER IS CHANGING YOU

Farnum Gray with Paul S. Graubard
and Harry Rosenberg

JESS'S EIGHTH-GRADE TEACHERS at Visalia, California, found him frightening. Only 14 years old, he already weighed a powerful 185 pounds. He was easily the school's best athlete, but he loved fighting even more than he loved sports. His viciousness equaled his strength: he had knocked other students cold with beer bottles and chairs. Jess's catalog of infamy also included a 40-day suspension for hitting a principal with a stick, and an arrest and a two-and-a-half-year probation for assault.

Inevitably, Jess's teachers agreed that he was an incorrigible, and placed him in a class for those with behavioral problems. Had they known that he had begun secret preparations to change *their* behavior, they would have been shocked.

The New Jess. His math teacher was one of the first to encounter his new technique. Jess asked for help with a problem, and when she had finished her explanation, he looked her in the eye and said, "You really help me learn when you're nice to me." The startled teacher groped for words, and then said, "You caught on quickly." Jess smiled, "It makes me feel good when you praise me." Suddenly Jess was consistently making such statements to all of his teachers. And he would come to class early or stay late to chat with them.

Some teachers gave credit for Jess's dramatic turnaround to a special teacher and his rather mysterious class. They naturally assumed that he had done something to change Jess and his "incorrigible" classmates.

Rather than change them, the teacher

had trained the students to become behavior engineers. Their parents, teachers and peers in the farm country of Visalia, California, had become their clients.

A Reward System. Behavior engineering involves the systematic use of consequences to strengthen some behaviors and to weaken others. Jess, for example, rewarded teachers with smiles and comments when they behaved as he wanted; when they were harsh, he turned away.

People often call reward systems immoral because they impose the engineer's values upon those he conditions. But the Visalia Project turns things around, according to Harry Rosenberg, head of the project and Director of Special Education for the school district. "The revolutionary thing here is that we are putting behavior-modification techniques in the hands of the learner. In the past, behavior modification has been controlled more-or-less by the Establishment. It has been demanded that the children must change to meet the goodness-of-fit of the dominant culture. We almost reverse this, putting the kid in control of those around him. It's kind of a Rogerian use of behavior modification."

Rosenberg was born and reared in Visalia and has been teacher and principal in a number of schools in that area. He began using behavior modification nine years ago, and he has kept experimentation going in the district with modest grants, mostly Federal. His proposals have emphasized that Visalia is an isolated district that, to avoid provincialism, needs contact with innovative educators from around the country. The grants have paid a variety of consultants to work with Vis-

alia schools over the years.

Reinforcing Opponents. The idea of training kids as behavior engineers arose from a single incident with a junior-high-school student. He was in a behavior-modification program for the emotionally disturbed. His teacher told Rosenberg that although the boy was responding fairly well to the class, he was getting into fights on the playground every day. As they discussed ways of helping the boy, the teacher suggested that they identify the kids with whom he was fighting and teach him to reinforce those kids for the behaviors that he wanted. The process worked.

Rosenberg mentioned the incident to Paul Graubard of Yeshiva University who was a consultant to the district. The incident intrigued him and he thought that training students as behavior engineers could have widespread implications in education, answering some philosophical objections to the use of behavior modification in schools.

Rosenberg had long believed that many students who were segregated in special-education classes should be reintegrated into regular classes. Graubard agreed. He designed an experiment to help children diagnosed as retardates, or as having learning or behavior problems, change their teachers' perceptions of them. This, predicted Graubard, would enable the child to be reintegrated into regular classes.

Special Classes: Incorrigibles and Deviants. For the pilot project, Rosenberg selected a local junior high school with an unfortunate but accurate reputation. It was the most resistant in the district to the integration of special-education students;

From *Psychology Today*, March 1974. Copyright © 1974 Ziff-Davis Publishing Company. Reprinted by permission of *Psychology Today* Magazine.

it had a higher percentage of students assigned to special classes than any other in the district. Classes for those labeled incorrigible held 10 percent of the school's 450 students; Rosenberg saw this as a disturbing tendency to give up on pupils too easily. He also found that minority children were more likely to be labeled incorrigible or tagged with some other form of deviancy. Directives from the principal and supervisors to treat all children alike regardless of race or ability had failed. To make matters worse, the school also had the highest suspension and expulsion rates in the district.

Graubard and Rosenberg selected seven children, ages 12 to 15, from a class for children considered incorrigible, to be the first behavior engineers. Jess and one other child were black, two were white, and three were Chicanos. A special-education teacher gave the seven students instruction and practice in behavior modification for one 43-minute class period a day. He then moved them into regular classes for two periods each day. The teachers of these classes became their clients. The teachers ranged in age from 26 to 63, and had from two to 27 years of teaching experience.

Shaping Teachers' Behavior. Stressing the idea that the program was a scientific experiment, the special teacher required each student to keep accurate records. During the experiment, they were to record daily the number of both positive and negative contacts with their clients. The students would not try to change the teachers' behavior during the first period; instead, they would keep records only to determine the norm. For the next phase, the students were to work at shaping the teachers' behaviors and to continue to keep records. For the last phase the students were not to use any of the shaping techniques.

Rosenberg had estimated that record-keeping could begin after two weeks of training students to recognize and to record teachers' positive and negative behavior. But this preliminary training took twice as long as he expected. While the students quickly learned to score negative behavior, they were seldom able to recognize positive behavior in their teacher-clients. Without the knowledge of the teachers or of the student-engineers, trained adult aides also kept records of teacher behavior in classes. Rosenberg compared their records to those of the students to determine accuracy; he found that the aides recorded substantially more instances of positive teacher behavior

than did the students. For example, an aide reported that a teacher had praised a child, but the child reported that the teacher had chewed him out. Rosenberg determined through closer monitoring that the aides were more accurate. He speculated that students were unable to recognize positive teacher behavior because they were accustomed to failure and negative treatment.

The students learned to identify positive teacher behavior accurately by role playing and by studying videotapes. This eventually brought about a high correlation between their records and those kept by adult teacher aides.

Building a New Smile. Rosenberg and Graubard taught the students various reinforcements to use in shaping their teachers' behavior. Rewards included smiling, making eye contact, and sitting up straight. They also practiced ways of praising a teacher, for example, saying, "I like to work in a room where the teacher is nice to the kids." And they learned to discourage negative teacher behavior with statements like, "It's hard for me to do good work when you're cross with me."

Each student studied techniques for making himself personally more attractive. One of the hardest tasks for Jess, for example, was learning to smile. Through use of a videotape, he learned that instead of smiling at people, he leered at them menacingly. Although he thought the process was hilarious, he practiced before the camera, and eventually developed a charming smile.

Learning to praise teachers with sincerity was difficult for the children. They were awkward and embarrassed at first, but they soon became skillful. Rosenberg said that the teachers' responses were

amazing, and added that "the nonverbal cues make the difference between being a wise guy and being believable. They had to *sincerely* mean it so it would be accepted by the teacher as an honest statement of a kid's feelings, not as smarting off." Besides learning to praise and to discourage teachers, they also learned to make small talk with them. This was a new skill for these students and, after considerable training, they excelled at it.

Ah Hah! The students enjoyed using a device that Fritz Redl, a child psychologist, has called "the Ah-Hah reaction." When a pupil was sure that he already understood a teacher's explanation, he would say that he did not understand. When the teacher was halfway through a second explanation, the pupil would exclaim, "Ah hah! Now I understand! I could never get that before." Unlike some of the other reinforcements used, this one does not directly help the teacher improve his teaching, and it is less than honest. But it does encourage the teacher to like the student who gave him a feeling of accomplishment, and it is hoped, will lead to a better relationship between them.

Rosenberg recorded the results of the project on a graph. It showed that during each of the five weeks of shaping, the number of positive comments from teachers increased while the number of negative comments decreased. The seven students in Jess's group felt that they had succeeded in engineering their teachers' behavior more to their liking. The "extinction" period proved to be a good indicator of the effects of this engineering. During those two weeks, there was a sharp drop in positive comments, but a marked rise in negative comments. The engineering had indeed caused the changes in

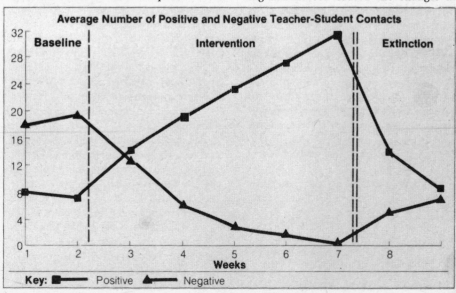

Average Number of Positive and Negative Teacher-Student Contacts

Key: ■ — Positive ▲ Negative

teacher behavior. As the extinction period showed, the teachers were like other people. Most were backsliders and they needed persistent reinforcement to maintain their new behavior.

When the project was over, the students resumed conditioning of the teachers, but they no longer kept formal records. Positive behavior increased once again, they reported; and in many cases, the negative comments ceased entirely. Rosenberg stressed the importance of requiring the children to keep data while teaching them reinforcement techniques. Projects that do not require data have failed. A student's success with a full, formal project, on the other hand, increases his ability to continue informal use of the behavior-engineering techniques that he has learned.

Who Really Changed? The teacher-clients were enthusiastic about the project, and Rosenberg reported that so far, none had expressed hostility or displeasure. Some teachers did question the right of aides to observe and to record their teaching methods. But Rosenberg pointed out that it was "justified by the necessity for scientific validation of the procedure." He assured them that the district did not use data from the project for evaluation of their abilities, and so, it would not affect their careers. When he explained the project to teachers afterwards, two or three said that it did change them. They admitted that they had become more positive toward their engineers. It is interesting to note, however, that most teachers tended to think of the projects as having changed the *children* rather than themselves.

Children, especially those in special-education classes, often suffer feelings of impotence when they encounter the school environment. The crucial goal of the project was to instill within the student a feeling of power, the ability to control the controllers, i.e., his teachers and the school. As a result of their training in behavior engineering, the students reported feeling more power in their relationships with their teachers and the school than ever before. And with that feeling of power came a new feeling of self-confidence.

Parents As Clients. When children shape the behaviors of their parents, procedures are much the same as they are in the teacher-training projects. One difference, however, is that Rosenberg first asks the parents to let him work with the child. He does not tell them, though, that their children will be shaping them.

After the parents grant permission, the student decides what he wants to change in their behavior. Then, Rosenberg or a special teacher will help him to design a project to bring about that change. After the child completes his project, Rosenberg talks with the parents in their home, and tells them what the child has been trying to accomplish. For example, one girl's mother seldom had meals on time, nor did she wash or iron the girl's clothes. Through systematic use of praise and other conditioning techniques, the girl made her mother into a much better homemaker. After more than a year, the mother had maintained her improvement and gained new self-respect.

Rosenberg cited other examples of adolescents who have shaped their parents to be less restrictive. But the critical result of each of these parent-shaping projects was the parents' increased awareness of their child's needs as a person. One father said that the project had really helped them with their child; for the first time the child talked to them about the different ways that they could help him.

Switch, Don't Fight. Since children have problems with each other as well as with adults, the students at Visalia have used the same conditioning techniques on their classmates.

"We can teach kids systematically how to make friends, how to get along with other students," Rosenberg said. "If they're being teased, we can teach them how to extinguish that permanently. If they're getting in fights, we can teach them to use basic learning principles to get the same thing they were trying to get by fighting."

He cited the example of Peggy, an attractive, intelligent girl who nevertheless encountered extreme problems in school. Her sixth-grade teachers sent her to the office frequently, and she was unable to make friends with the other students, whose hostility towards her made her miserable. She was gifted academically, but apparently because of her unhappiness in school, she had never achieved even an average report card.

The special teacher helped her to design and to carry out a project to change her classmates' attitudes towards her. She was spectacularly successful. She spoke of the experience later: "They told me it was a scientific experiment, but I really didn't know what that meant. At first I was confused, and I really didn't think it would help me. But then I thought I might as well try it. At least I would get out of the classroom for part of the time."

The teacher asked Peggy to name three people whom she would like to have as friends. She named Arthur, Elwyn and Doris, all of whom frequently insulted her. For two weeks, she and her teacher recorded both positive and negative contacts with them. Then they discussed how they could increase the number of nice things that those students said to her. She began to apply the behavior-modification theory and techniques that her teacher had taught her. "I ignored Doris if she said anything bad to me. But when she said anything nice to me, I'd help her with her work, or compliment her, or sit down and ask her to do something with me. She's been increasing saying the nice things about me and now we can ride on the bus together, and she'll sit by me in the class. I'll tell you that really helps me a lot."

She engineered Elwyn's behavior in much the same manner; she would turn her back on him whenever he said something bad to her. But the first time he walked past her without saying something bad, she gave him a big smile and said, "Hi, Elwyn, how are you today?" After he recovered from his initial shock at Peggy's overtures, he eventually became her friend.

Arthur proved to be a much tougher subject than the other two. As Peggy stated, "He calls *everybody* names. I don't think anybody likes Arthur." She attempted to ignore him whenever he called her names, but with Arthur, this tactic was unsuccessful. If the other children laughed, it just gave Arthur more encouragement. As she discussed her shaping of Arthur, Peggy showed her grasp of behavioral learning theory. She realized that the reward of the other children's laughter far outweighed her attempts to extinguish Arthur's teasing by ignoring it. They, not she, were reinforcing Arthur. She came up with a clever solution. "If Arthur was standing around with some kids, I tried to stay away from him. I'd wait until Arthur was by himself, and then I'd walk up to him, say "Hi" and smile. He just didn't know what to do! The first time, though, he still called me a name, because he thought I was being mean to him...I'd never said anything nice to Arthur...hardly anybody ever does. I guess the only way [he] ever gets anybody's attention is by calling people names...being mean, and fighting."

Arthur was a small sixth-grader and apparently, his stature caused him a great deal of self-consciousness. Peggy continued her positive reinforcement of Arthur, who is now friendly and no longer calls her names.

Peggy's social difficulties disappeared with dramatic speed as she made use of behavior-modification techniques. The teachers who once reported her attitude as disagreeable, now found her charming and delightful. Her grade average rose to B, and the following year, she was elected president of the seventh grade.

Gifted Students. Rosenberg also instructed a class of gifted children in the use of behavior engineering; each child chose as a client a classmate, an adult, or a sibling. The children met frequently to discuss ways of handling problems and to report on the progress of their projects.

One student related how he had modified the disruptive behavior of a fellow math student. "I compliment him when he's not disruptive, and when he is, I say things to him like, 'You know, you could be a real bright student, and I like you a lot more when you don't disrupt the class.' He doesn't do it so much now, and he makes good grades."

One student was near despair over her efforts to change a teacher who, the other students agreed, was a difficult person. This teacher seemed impervious to any type of conditioning technique. "His latest thing is to send everybody out to sit under a table," she reported. "The first minute you open your mouth, he sends you out, and he doesn't really give you a chance." She had tried unsuccessfully to tell him that she was not learning math while sitting under the table, or she would apologize for saying something she should not have. But his response was usually, "You're not sorry, you're *ignorant!*" or "You're a knothead!"

The special-education teacher asked the girl to name the behavior she most wanted to change. "Sending me out without a chance," the girl replied. "That's what bothers me most. I'm out in the *first 10 minutes* of the class!"

The special teacher then suggested that she say to the problem teacher, "I'd really appreciate it if you'd give me a warning be-

fore sending me out of the room, because I have trouble about talking anyway." It was necessary for her to repeat this several times, but it wasn't long before the teacher stopped sending kids out of the room.

Dignity & Worth. In *Beyond Freedom and Dignity*, B.F. Skinner points out that "Any evidence that a person's behavior may be attributed to external circumstances seems to threaten his dignity or worth. We are not inclined to give a person credit for achievements over which he has no control."

The people at Visalia are very concerned with maintaining the dignity of their clients. They believe that dignity is lost if the reinforcements given in behavior engineering are insincere. The individual must feel that he has earned rewards by his own actions, not because the engineer is using a technique. Otherwise the gesture lacks dignity and worth.

A junior-high-school boy drew agreement from his fellow students when he said, "If the person knows you're doing it, it won't work. At least not very well. He'll figure, 'Oh, he's trying to do it on me. He's not going to change the way I am!' " The boy cited his little brother as an example. He was trying to condition him not to curse, but the child found out about the conditioning techniques, and said, "Oh, you dumb little psychologist!"

Sincerity is also an integral part of instruction in behavior engineering. Rosenberg recalled with amusement that the teachers working with him on the experiment have at times doubted each other's sincerity. "One person compliments another, who says, 'You're just reinforcing me!' And the response is, 'Oh, the hell if I am! I really mean it.' With the kids, and with our own staff," Rosenberg said, "we've had to continually stress being sincere. You should really want the other person to change."

Many of the teachers felt that the engineering by the students created a more positive working environment; it eliminated the ever-present cutting and sarcasm. It also eliminated the meanness that

is so often characteristic of junior-high-school students, according to a humanities teacher. He found that children of that age often conform by being meaner than they would really like to be. "I feel these projects are very effective in giving kids an *excuse* to be positive. At this age, that seems very helpful to them."

The Visalia project revived the issue of whether it is *moral* for people to condition each other. Certainly, behavior engineering could appear to be a harbinger of *A Clockwork Orange*, or *Brave New World*. But Rosenberg, Graubard, and other behaviorists believe that people are always conditioning each other, and that often, in their ignorance, they strengthen behaviors that no one wants. Proponents believe that to make really *constructive* changes in behavior, people should be conscious of what they are doing.

Future Projects. Rosenberg envisions another three or four years of research on this project before its techniques are disseminated in the school district. The current research is to provide information for the effective matching of the student with the technique for behavioral conditioning. In the future, this "prescription" will aid the counselor in helping the student.

Additional experiments planned will compare the teacher-training effectiveness of a single child to that of two or three children working as a team. And in some projects, teachers will know that the students are trying to change them. In this instance, Rosenberg wants to find out if that will make a difference in the effectiveness of the conditioning.

Having students train teachers is inexpensive and effective. Since the students spend more time with their teachers than does any professional supervisor, they have more opportunity to change them. Students also have the most to gain or to lose from the quality of teaching. Rosenberg estimates that the students are doing about as well in exercising control over human behavior as professionals who charge 50 dollars an hour.

CAN'T REMEMBER?
PUT POPCORN IN YOUR BED

Earl Lane

In the mid-1920s, a man came to the laboratory of Alexander Luria, a noted Russian psychologist, and asked to have his memory tested. The man, a newspaper reporter, turned out to have truly remarkable recall.

When presented with a sequence of words or numbers or letters, the man was able to repeat them back without error. Luria increased the number of items in the sequence from 30 to 50 and then to 70. Still, the man had no problems repeating them in correct order. In another test, the man was able to learn columns and rows of digits, 50 in all, after just 3 minutes of study. He could recall them perfectly, in any order, as though he were reading them from a book.

The man, whom Luria dubbed S., was able to remember the material weeks, months and even years after it was first presented to him. He had a similar ability to remember events and scenes, and could easily memorize items as diverse as scientific formulas and poems in languages he did not know.

S. was one of the greatest practitioners of the art of mnemonics, the use of devices and strategies to aid memory. His case was described by Luria in a classic psychological study, "The Mind of a Mnemonist."

Today, memory training is largely a sideshow curiosity, although there have been efforts by mnemonists such as Harry Lorayne and Jerry Lucas, the former professional basketball player, to give memory training a widespread appeal.

Many mnemonic devices are relatively simple and easy to learn. Some we are all familiar with ("i before e, except after c . . . Thirty days hath September, April, June and November . . .). Other devices are complex and require a good deal of effort and concentration to master. They have been developed and described by professional mnemonists such as Lorayne, whose livelihoods depend on memorizing stupefying amounts of material. The major mnemonic devices also have been described in a variety of research studies.

Some psychologists, notably Gordon Bower at Stanford University, have studied mnemonics for the light the devices may shed on the structure and processes of normal memory. In related research, there also have been efforts to study the memory of chess masters. Like skilled mnemonists, chess experts appear to have very special abilities to store and rapidly recall information.

Aside from Luria's work and that of several other psychologists, there have been relatively few systematic studies of mnemonists and how they manage their remarkable feats. Stanford's Bower once visited a convention of mnemonists. He was understandably impressed by what he saw. One 96-year-old man memorized 50 three-digit numbers shouted out to him by the audience. Another could quickly scan a deck of cards and then recite them in order. Still another could take four six-letter words called out by the audience and write them in a complex alphabet soup, all the while reciting "The Shooting of Dan McGrew."

Yet when Bower asked the man what went on in his mind when he did the trick, he answered, "I practiced it so long that my hand just automatically knows what to do as my eye looks at successive letters of the key words." In other words, don't ask me how I can do it. I just can.

While there are very real difficulties in probing the mental processes of a skilled mnemonist, there have been fairly rigorous attempts to test such persons. Among them was Alexander Luria's pioneering work with S. Two other psychologists also tested a mnemonist they dubbed VP. By the time he was 5, VP had memorized the street map of a city of half a million. At the age of 10, he memorized 150 poems as part of a contest.

Both S. and VP were raised in Latvia. Their homes were, in fact, only 35 miles apart. VP, who was born in 1935, was much younger than S., however. The two men did not share the same experiences, although Roberta Klatsky, a psychologist who has written about memory, notes that both mnemonists were schooled in systems which emphasized rote learning. "In such a situation, it behooves the student to improve his rote-memorization ability," Klatsky says. "It is extremely speculative, to be sure, but it is tempting to conclude that this early training may have provided VP [and perhaps S. as well] with the impetus to hone his mnemonic skills."

When Luria studied S., he found that man's ability to remember was aided by a process scientists call synesthesia—the ability of one of the senses to evoke another. For example, sounds can evoke visual images. A high-pitched sound may bring to mind bright, bouncy colors while low-pitched sounds may be associated with darker colors.

In S., this interplay among the senses involved striking details. When Luria presented the man a loud tone with an intensity of 113 decibels and a pitch of 2,000 cycles per second, S. said, "It looks something like fireworks tinged

From *Newsday*, April 12, 1978. Reprinted by permission.

with a pink-red hue, and it has an ugly taste—rather like that of a briny pickle." On another occasion, he told a psychologist, "What a crumbly yellow voice you have."

S. used his skill with visual images to spur his memory. In his mind, for example, he could visualize dozens of items to be remembered by placing them along a familiar street in Moscow. When he was asked to recall the items, he would mentally walk along the street, noting the items as he passed. When he made errors, S. blamed it on a misperception rather than a mistake in memory. He once forgot the word "egg" because he had imagined it against a white wall. It blended into the background, and he did not "notice" it when he tried to recall the scene.

The art of distributing items in a mental location was not new with S. Probably the oldest mnemonic trick in the book, it is called the method of loci and is credited to the Greek poet Simonides around the year 500 BC. He had recited a poem at a banquet given by a nobleman, then was called outside for a moment. During Simonides' absence, the roof of the banquet hall collapsed, killing the nobleman and all his guests. The corpses were so mangled that relatives were unable to identify them. But Simonides remembered the places at which they had been sitting at the table and was able to tell the mourners which were their dead. Using the tragic experience at the banquet hall, Simonides realized that orderly arrangement is essential for good memory. He is credited with inventing the art of memory.

At a time when there were no printed books to carry around, the accurate recall of events and information was vital. Like many of the other arts invented by the Greeks, memory training was passed on to the Romans and subsequently into the European tradition. (The development of mnemonics, from classical times until the Renaissance, is described in "The Art of Memory," a book by a British historian, Frances Yates.)

The trick of Simonides is one of the more commonly described mnemonic devices. It and several others can be applied to such practical tasks as remembering a grocery list or important dates for a history exam. Here are some examples:

The method of loci—The method developed by Simonides. Imagine each item in a previously learned sequence of locations—a street, rooms in a house, parts of the body. The key is to develop vivid images. If you have to recall such items as milk, bread, popcorn, tuna fish and yogurt, for example, you might mentally place dozens of packages of yogurt on a table in the living room, stack bread in the bathtub, put popcorn in your bed and a huge tuna fish on the sun porch. Then go through the sequence of rooms, recalling which item you have "stored" in each place.

The peg-word system—Quite similar to the previous method, this one involves the use of specific concrete objects as pegs on which to hang the items to be memorized. It has been used by Bower in his research (which he described recently in the magazine Human Nature). The system is well-suited for learning lists up to 10 items, and can be expanded to include more. First learn the peg words:

One is a bun	Six is sticks
Two is a shoe	Seven is heaven
Three is a tree	Eight is a gate
Four is a door	Nine is wine
Five is a hive	Ten is a hen

Once you have learned the rhyme, think of the first item to be memorized. Make up a scene in which the item interacts with the first peg word. For example, if you are trying to recall cigarettes, think of a bun smoking a cigarette. Move on to the next peg word, and "hang" the second item of the list on it. Say the item is loaf of bread. Imagine a shoe kicking a loaf of bread. And so forth.

Narrative chaining—Try to link together diverse items using weird but vivid story. As Bower puts it, "to learn the list beginning milk, matches, apples and bread, I might imagine I am a milkman delivering milk to a kitchen where a small child is playing with matches. I try to distract the child by giving him an apple to play with. His mother rushes in, misunderstands my intentions, screams and hits me over the head with a long stick of French bread."

Bower and his colleagues tested the narrative-chaining method on Stanford undergraduates. Students who were told how to use the method and then given a list of items to memorize were able to recall about 93 per cent of the items. Others who were left to their own devices, usually rote memorization, recalled only about 14 per cent of the items.

Digit-letter systems—Various schemes have been developed to help in the memorization of digit sequences. The systems were made popular a century ago by an English clergyman and schoolmaster named Brayshaw, who published a book, "Metrical Mnemonics," which contained a collection of rhymes embodying over 2,000 dates and numerical facts from history, geography, physics and other sciences.

The aim of such systems is to break up numbers—dates, telephone numbers, statistics—and convert them into words. Break up the long numbers into series of two- or three-digit numbers. Then use a code to convert each number into a consonant. A silent vowel or letter may then be inserted to make the consonants form a word. Bower gives as one suggested code:

0 = Z or s	5 = L
1 = T or D	6 = J, CH or SH
2 = N	7 = K or C
3 = M	8 = F or V
4 = R	9 = P or B

"Thus 32, a friend's apartment, becomes MN," writes Bower, "and can be sounded out as MAN or MOON, so I remember that my friend lives on the moon; a colleague's phone extension, 8751, translates as VCRD and can become VICE RAID." It takes practice, Bower notes, but the time spent in learning the code can repay the student who needs to remember many numbers.

3. PROCESSES UNDERLYING BEHAVIOR

There is limited value to mnemonics. The devices are of little use in helping to integrate knowledge from diverse sources and make critical judgments. But studies of mnemonists and expert chess players have helped psychologists to better understand how the brain can encode, store and retrieve "chunks" of data. The research dovetails with other explorations of memory. Bower and his colleagues at Stanford, for example, are now interested in how people understand and remember brief stories.

Alan D. Baddeley, a British psychologist, writes that "mnemonic systems reflect the same basic processes that underlie normal unaided memory. They reflect some of these processes particularly clearly (as in the case of visual imagery), and if we ignore them our view of human memory is likely to be impoverished and distorted."

But he adds that mnemonic systems are not particularly helpful in remembering the sort of information we require in everyday life. "They are, of course, excellent for learning the strings of unrelated words which are so close to the hearts of experimental psychologists, but I must confess that if I need to remember a shopping list, I do not imagine strings of sausages festooned from my chandeliers and bunches of bananas sprouting from my wardrobe. I simply write it down."

Most of us have used coined words, phrases or rhymes to help us remember a group of items. Some people, such as medical students, appear particularly adept at making up mnemonic devices. The particular devices may be a help over the short term, but they can sometimes prove to be as difficult to remember as the material to be memorized. Or a student may recall a rhyme long after forgetting the trick for using it correctly.

Nevertheless, here are a few mnemonics that have been devised over the years to help you remember more than you probably care to:

How I want a drink, alcoholic, of course, after the eight chapters involving quadric mechanics—Pi to 14 decimal places, 3.14159265358979; count the number of letters in each word.

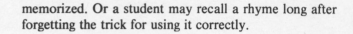

On old Olympus' towering top, a fat-armed German vaults and hops.—The order of the 12 cranial nerves: olfactory, optic, oculomotor, trochlear, trigeminal, abducents, facial, acoustic, glossopharyngeal, vagus, spinal accessory, hypoglossal.

Roy G. Biv—colors of the visible spectrum: red, orange, yellow, green, blue, indigo, violet.

Never lower Tillie's pants, mama might come home.—Bones of the wrist: navicular, lunate, triangular, pisiform, multangular (greater); multangular (lesser), capitate, hamate.

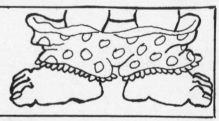

My very earnest mother just served us nine pickles—The order of the planets from the sun: Mercury, Venus, Earth, Mars, Jupiter, Saturn, Uranus, Neptune and Pluto.

Washington and Jefferson made many a joke,
Van Buren had to put the frying pan back,
Lincoln just gasped, "Heaven guard America,"
Cleveland had coats made ready to wear home,
Coolidge hurried right to every kitchen jar nook.—The Presidents of the United States (through Nixon); The first letter of every word is the first letter of the last name of the Presidents.

The mites go up, the tights go down—In a cave, the stalagmites rise upward from the floor; the stalactites descend from the ceiling.

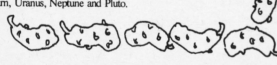

Neither leisured foreigner seized the weird heights—An obscure device listing the nonchemical exceptions to the rule, i before e, except after c, or sounded as a as in neighbor and weigh.

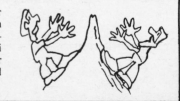

THAT FILING SYSTEM INSIDE YOUR HEAD

Memory remains a mysterious function. But one thing is known for sure: there are things you can do to improve it.

ROY ROWAN

Within milliseconds his facile brain can summon forth the whole summer production schedule, review unit costs under the new union contract, and match this information against the seasonally adjusted fall sales projections. This same steel-trap mind can put first and last names on a thousand faces over at the plant, or revive with uncanny clarity a directors meeting that took place ten years ago—right down to the timbre of the voices, the comptroller's cryptic comments, even the fragrant cigar aroma that permeated the pile-carpeted boardroom after it was all over. "J.B.'s like an elephant. He never forgets a thing," his awed subordinates say. "We don't know how he does it."

Fading at the peak

Most chief executives credit highly developed analytical powers, rather than a sharply honed memory, for their climb to the top. Nevertheless, many of them recognize memory as a great business asset, synonymous with efficiency. Sometimes, to their horror, they detect telltale signs that it's beginning to fade, often as they reach the peak of their career. Yet they do not always realize that, just as with a weak forehand in tennis or a stunted backswing in golf, memory can be trained to perform more effectively. A few corporations have even rung in pros to iron out the problems, not that the pros themselves fully understand how memory works.

And for that matter, neither do the scientists who have spent a lifetime studying man's information-retrieval process. They still don't know whether human memory is chemical or electrical, highly structured or random, and whether it has unlimited

Research Associate: Lisa Churchville

storage space or, like the file cabinets in an office, must be continuously culled to make room for new information. In fact, they don't know exactly where in the brain memories are filed.

This is not to say that the scientists have been sitting idle. To be sure, they have constructed elaborate computer models to simulate both "episodic memory" (used to recall a single event such as a name, face, or date), and "semantic memory" (used to recall entire information systems such as language, mathematics, or how to drive a car). They have also diagrammed the theoretical distinctions between "short-term" and "long-term" memory, made microscopic comparisons between new prenatal and old senile brains, even ground up the brain tissue of trained mice and injected the particles into their untrained brothers, to determine if memory is transferable from one living creature to another. (In mice it appears to be.) While nothing definitive has come from all these experiments, a number of new insights have been gleaned that should prove encouraging to business executives.

■ Biologically there is much less memory loss accompanying advancing age than was previously suspected. However, as more knowledge is acquired, there occurs what psychologists call "proactive interference" between competing new and old memories. (Ever reach for the emergency brake where it was in your previous car?) Also, you tend not to remember how much you used to forget. (Just ask your children.)

■ Memory impotence, like male sexual impotence, feeds on the fear of failure. Don't panic. Frequently a less direct attack on the elusive name or number will produce the answer.

■ A certain amount of stress can actually improve memory by forcing the body to produce chemical brain stimulants. Individuals usually have their own optimum levels of stress. Too much stress—"George, this $10-million contract hangs on your presentation"—may produce "final-exam syndrome," a disruption of the cognitive process resulting from high anxiety.

■ What is assumed to be a memory loss may simply be the effect of an environmental change. Psychologists refer to "summer" and "winter" memories, which become confused when triggered out of season. This same out-of-context bewilderment can cause you not to recognize your own secretary when you unexpectedly run into her at the airport. Similarly, transferred executives sometimes complain about memory slippage, when the problem is that they are in new surroundings.

From Plato's bed of wax

Ever since the Golden Age of Greece, man has been trying to solve the mystery of memory. The problem always was, he had only vague notions of what he was looking for. Plato, in *Thaetetus*, described memory as a "bed of modeling wax," receiving the impressions of thoughts and sensations as if they had been imprinted by a signet. Descartes pictured memories as "traces and vestiges that are just like the creases in a piece of paper that make it easier to fold again."

Today, most scientists subscribe to one form or another of the so-called "switchboard theory" of memory. They believe ten billion neurons composing man's brain arrange themselves into interconnected electrochemical circuits called engrams. According to this view, the engram is memory's pathway. Like the light bulbs in those moving signs that spell out late-news headlines across the front of a building, each neuron may be turning on and off in an infinite number of engrams. The problem is, nobody has ever seen an engram.

Reprinted from the August 28, 1978 issue of *FORTUNE Magazine* by special permission; © 1978 Time, Inc.

"THE EXECUTIVE WHO TELLS ME HE CAN'T REMEMBER NUMBERS TELLS ME THAT HE IS OPERATING ON QUICKSAND."

Scattered through American executive suites are men whose high-powered memories are held in awe by their colleagues. None of those *Fortune* tracked down claim to have any special system for remembering—but all have found a good memory useful in business.

Robert J. Buckley, fifty-four, chairman and president of Allegheny Ludlum Industries, says: "My memory is my hobby. For me, remembering is like collecting stamps. It's fun. I like to be able to quote poetry and books." Buckley can read over a speech once and then deliver it almost verbatim without notes. "That's a great ego trip," he says. "People think you're speaking extemporaneously." He considers it part of his job to know several thousand employees by name. Or to be able to pick up a conversation with one of them where it left off a year earlier. Buckley's main problem, however, is an overactive memory. "I'll see somebody walking through the railroad station, then I'll see him again sometime later and think he's my friend."

Lee Iacocca, fifty-three, the recently fired president of Ford Motor Co., believes that memory depends mainly on interest: "If you care, you remember." Every morning, Iacocca makes a mental list of the things he wants to accomplish that day. "The list helps me to remember my priorities. Of course, it helps to have a good secretary," he adds.

Jerome Hardy, sixty, president of the Dreyfus Corp., says, "I have a blackboard memory. I can remember what I need and erase what I don't." Hardy is on the board of seven Dreyfus funds, six outside corporations, and two public-service organizations,

and he finds that keeping the key figures in his head helps tremendously. "It so happens that I can also remember every golf hole that I ever played."

Robert O. Anderson, sixty-one, chairman of Atlantic Richfield, has such a phenomenal memory that "I don't carry a briefcase." He is currently writing a book on the oil industry totally from recall. "Experience is memory," he claims. "Remembering what not to do."

Russell Reynolds, forty-six, president of the executive-recruitment firm bearing his name, believes "memory feeds on itself." Though his office keeps complete files on employment candidates, Reynolds feels that his best head-hunting resource is his own head. "The most memorable people," he claims, "are probably the best suited for the jobs we have to fill."

William Agee, forty, chairman and president of Bendix Corp., says, "Memory is concentration. People who don't have good memories take longer to do their jobs."

Thomas Dittmer, thirty-six, president of Ray E. Friedman & Co., a trading firm on the Chicago Mercantile Exchange, finds that "it's on the slow days that you forget. When you're really busy you remember every trade—up to a thousand a day. You have to do it. Buy, sell, it's like a heartbeat. There's a rhythm to it that helps you remember."

James Grosfeld, forty-one, chairman of Pulte Homes Corp., a large Detroit construction company, regards his good memory as an invaluable asset, particularly in negotiations. "People are flattered if you remember them," he believes. "And clients have more confidence in you if your memory is sharp. They know you've done your homework."

Charles Housen, forty-five, president of Erving Paper Mills in Erving, Massachusetts, has taken courses in remembering names and numbers. "Memory is discipline," he says. A whiz at recalling such details as birthdays, anniversaries, who drinks what, and favorite brands of perfume, Housen believes that memory serves not only the arithmetic of business, but its politics, too.

Denis Robinson, seventy, chairman of High Voltage Engineering Corp. of Burlington, Massachusetts, says: "I always was a quick study." In college, the British-born engineer could memorize a Shakespearean role overnight. "One can improve memory," he says, "by working at it."

Alan Kiepper, fifty, general manager of Metropolitan Atlanta Rapid Transit Authority, which is responsible for building a subway system in the Georgia capital, feels that he must keep the budgetary and operating details in his head, though he admits to being poor at remembering names. "I concentrate on facts and review them for memory retention. It is not a natural gift."

Benton Love, fifty-three, senior chairman of the Texas Commerce Bancshares, believes "the sweetest words in any language are a person's name." Love, who thinks that the bigger a corporation gets the colder it is, adds: "One way to warm it up is to remember people's names." But he regards memory as being important in many other ways in business. "The executive who tells me he can't remember numbers tells me that he can't remember the significant part of his business and is operating on quicksand."

A radically different view of memory is offered by Dr. E. Roy John, director of the brain-research laboratories at New York University Medical Center. Dr. John does not envision memory as interconnected circuitry, but as "coherent temporal patterns" of resonating neurons. According to his theory, the neurons act in "ensembles," not as individual units. "The brain is a big democracy," he says. "It doesn't listen to a single voice." As for his frustrated fellow scientists searching for an engram, he thinks they're looking for the wrong thing. "Instead of a groove, they should be looking for a wave. The engram is like a radio signal. You can't see it. But you can pick it up on your receiver."

Although nobody's seen an engram, the brain's myriad neurons have been seen and studied for years. Each neuron consists of a nucleus, an axon that serves as the cell's transmitter, and a number of receiving antennae called dendrites. The gaps between the neurons are known as synapses. And it is the molecular action at the synapse, when one neuron fires and its chemical signal is picked up by neighboring neurons on the other side of the gap, that intrigues scientists. They see this action at the synapse gap as holding the secret to memory storage and transmission.

A memorable chat

Dr. James McGaugh, a noted psychobiologist and the executive vice chancellor of the University of California at Irvine, has experimented extensively with memory-enhancement drugs (caffeine is one) that amplify the signals between one neuron and another, presumably strengthening the synaptic connections. He offers laboratory confirmation of something everybody already suspects: fright or extreme elation can produce the same stimulus —provided, just as with the drugs, they immediately follow the experience. As an example, he cites a man called into the boss's office for a chat. "Nothing memorable about that," says McGaugh.

"I'm delighted to have this opportunity to talk to you," says the boss, still not making the encounter memorable. Then he adds: "Because YOU'RE FIRED."

"Wham!" says McGaugh. "Those two words, 'you're fired'—or they just as well could have been, 'you're promoted'—suddenly modify the encounter." According to McGaugh's hypothesis (developed in collaboration with Dr. Paul Gold, currently at the University of Virginia), escalating the emotional level of an experience can trigger the release of certain hormones that strengthen the synaptic connections, thus etching a sharp and lasting memory. McGaugh has found that rats will remember a mild electrical shock as a severe shock if they are immediately given an amphetamine injection, which serves as a memory stimulant. But the memory process can also be reversed. Scopolamine, a drug that blocks signal reception at the synapse, is frequently given to women to make them forget the pain of childbirth.

At M.I.T., Dr. Richard Wurtman is similarly studying nerve action at the synapse, but his experiments are with diet as a means of enhancing memory. Choline, found in such foods as eggs, soybeans, and liver, he discovered, is absorbed directly from the bloodstream by the brain, where it is converted into acetylcholine, a chemical transmitter that carries nerve impulses across the synapse. Dr. Wurtman is not ready to recommend that anybody who wants to sharpen his memory should begin each day with a hefty four-egg omelette. Yet he is optimistic that diet will someday play an important role in memory improvement.

A new brain every month

The idea that there may indeed be food for thought is new, but it has long been known that chronic and heavy drinking obliterates memory. Alcoholics are subject to Korsakoff's syndrome, a permanent impairment that causes them to create memories from fantasy, but prevents them from recognizing people they have daily contact with. Even social drinking weakens memory, probably because the brain tends to shrink under the influence of alcohol. Alcohol is known to interfere with the brain's ability to make proteins, the building blocks of the neurons, and possibly the real storehouse of memory. Although the neurons cannot reproduce themselves (a loss of brain tissue through illness or injury is permanent), their protein content is constantly forming and disappearing so that man in effect grows a new brain every month, but with the same neurons and engrams—just as the remake of an LP record has the same grooves and squiggles and plays the same old song.

While brain researchers are wrestling with the mysteries of the memory mechanism, and striving to improve its efficiency with drugs or diet, another group, the behaviorists, are looking for new ways to maximize its use. They, too, have their own picturesque analogies. "Memory is like a muscle," they maintain. "It must be exercised to retain its tone. Overreliance on a superefficient assistant or secretary can cause the mechanism to atrophy.

"Memory is like a library," they also say. "But there is no use in having books if you can't find them." However, they point out that memories can in effect be xeroxed and cross-filed in the mind under different headings for easier retrieval.

Some behaviorists, however, view memory as a more haphazard process, resembling the action of a pinball machine. We players, they indicate, can usually shoot the memory ball in the right direction, and nudge it along the desired path, though it may bounce out of control, lighting up unexpected names and numbers. They have an expression, "TOT (tip-of-the-tongue) syndrome," for this problem of being able to retrieve only memory fragments, but not the whole thing.

Behaviorists break down the memory process into three phases: registration, consolidation, and retrieval. In phase No. 1, paying attention is obviously essential for acquiring new information. "But usually you have to do more than just experience an event to remember it," says Thomas Landauer, a psychologist in the Human Information Processing Department at Bell Laboratories in Murray Hill, New Jersey. "You have to do some kind of work on it." But rapidly repeating the same fact over and over immediately upon its receipt, he believes, is futile, except for short periods; repetition will help one to remember a telephone number long enough to dial it, but that's about it.

For permanent retention, Landauer recommends what he calls "spacing of practice" (allowing an interval between rehearsals). With each practice, he claims, you are in fact creating a new memory, which may be stored in a different place. It has also been established that when memories are updated, as happens in periodic encounters with people over their lifetimes, your memory of them after they die tends to strike an average between a youthful and an older image.

Forming an "integrated image" with all the information concisely placed in a single mental picture also helps to preserve a memory. So does the use of verbal structure or cadence such as is found in poetry ("Thirty days hath September ..."). Categorizing, or "chunking," in the lexicon of the behaviorists, helps in the recall of lists (housewives out shopping should think of vegetables, meats, and dairy products separately). Landauer disdains reliance on the subconscious to abet memory. As an extreme example, he cites the use of under-the-pillow tape players by students to learn a foreign language while they sleep. "The amount they remember," he says, "is determined by how poorly they sleep."

"Relax to remember"

Other theorists do put reliance on the subconscious. Jerome Wahlman, a New York hypnotherapist and the only expert who advertises "Memory Improvement Training" in the Manhattan Yellow Pages, predicates his teaching on the belief that all memories are stored in the subconscious mind. "I try to make the subconscious perform in a predictable and controlled manner," he says.

Wahlman urges his students to switch into a relaxed "alpha state" (characterized by the slow alpha waves preceding sleep) when they are receiving new information. The alpha state is induced by what he calls "sense-imagery exercises," involving the recall of pleasurable experiences. "Learn passively," he advises. "Also, relax to remember, or your mind will set up a block." Dr. Arthur Hastings, director of the Holistic Medicine Project at the Institute of Noetic Sciences in San Francisco, gives scientific backing to this approach. He recommends meditation (a deep alpha state) to make stored ideas and facts become more accessible.

Memory systems such as Wahlman's are as old as civilization. Early Roman orators used *loci* (places)—e.g., the floor plan of their own homes—to help them recall long speeches. The opening thought would be associated with the front door, the next thought with the vestibule. In recent years numerous new memory systems have been devised that, depending on the jargon of their inventors, provide "hooks," "pegs," "chains," "links," or "locks" to help forgetful individuals dredge up the names, numbers, phrases, and faces that lie buried in their brains.

The yellow-pimpled moose

All of these systems rely on association—linking the thing you are trying to remember to something you already know. (The reason children can always draw a map of Italy.) Harry Lorayne, who frequently proves on the Johnny Carson and Merv Griffin shows that he can master the name of everybody in the audience within twenty minutes, is the most celebrated salesman of memory association.

Lorayne has been called in to lecture executives of I.B.M., G.E., Borg-Warner, Westinghouse, and U.S. Steel on memory improvement. He was flown to England to do the same thing for F.W. Woolworth's British suppliers. And Bear Stearns Co. in New York hired him to teach a hundred brokers how to memorize the name, face, and telephone number of every customer. "Businessmen think they have bad memories," he claims, "but they have fantastic memories. I become their motivator."

In Harry Lorayne's case this involves teaching them to make absurd associations. "It is essential to convert the verbal into the visual," he explains. "But it's weird pictures that you remember." If you want to remember the French word for grapefruit, *pamplemousse*, he suggests thinking of a moose covered with grapefruit-sized yellow pimples. Minnesota is easily remembered as a mini-soda, Nebraska as a new brass car. "Using the imagination this way," he adds, "further assists memory."

Lorayne also advocates "original awareness," which simply means making the initial encounter meaningful. Businessmen at conventions, he insists, spend too much time studying name tags instead of faces. Pick the most pronounced facial feature (pug nose, mole, cleft chin), he advises, and then merge it with a ridiculous word picture of the person's name. If you're introduced to someone with bushy eyebrows, named Miesterman, visualize yourself stirring the man's eyebrows (Me stir man's eyebrows) with a spoon.

Lorayne has written ten books, the last one a best-seller (*The Memory Book*, Ballantine, 1975), in collaboration with former Knick basketball star Jerry Lucas. Lucas, whose own mind-boggling memory system involves putting the letters of a name in alphabetical order the instant he hears it (Jerry Lucas becomes Ejrry Aclsu), once memorized 500 columns of the Manhattan phone book as a stunt.

For those who fear loss of memory almost more than death, researchers are coming up with some good news. Gerontology specialists are discovering that the human brain remains quite plastic and capable of learning until relatively late in life—into the seventies, and even the eighties and nineties—provided the person remains sufficiently challenged. This discovery, of course, had already been signaled by such late bloomers as Thomas Edison, Henry Ford, Pablo Casals, and Grandma Moses. But now the biological evidence has been gathered, too.

Dr. Arnold Scheibel of the Brain Research Institute of U.C.L.A. has spent five years performing microscopic studies of the brains of aged people within a few hours following their deaths. He can indeed pinpoint the deterioration of those synaptic connections, believed to be so crucial for memory transmission and storage. However, only in cases of severe senility (Alzheimer's disease) did he find the deterioration to be acute.

At the same time, experimenting with rats, he has discovered that those living in what he calls an "enriched environment" with wheels to run on and toys to play with, suffer noticeably less synaptic deterioration than rats who live in boredom. These two concurrent studies have led Dr. Scheibel, who is also a practicing psychiatrist, to make some observations about the memory of the aging executive.

"High-powered executives," he says, "suffer a narcissistic insult when their perks and responsibilities are taken away. After all, they have been nursed to the top by their companies in an enriched environment. Then suddenly they must adapt themselves to big losses." Scheibel is convinced that learning new skills, such as a foreign language or a musical instrument, or accepting new community responsibilities, will slow the retired executive's memory deterioration. "We sabotage ourselves," he says. "One has to be trained to age meaningfully. To retire *to* something, not *from* something."

Programmed obsolescence

Drs. Lissy Jarvik and Aseneth LaRue, a noted team of research psychologists at the Brentwood Veterans Hospital in Los Angeles, confirm Dr. Scheibel's findings. Their studies of people between sixty and ninety lead them to believe that depression and the lack of vocational and intellectual stimulation accounts for more memory erosion than does age.

According to Dr. Robert Butler, director of the National Institute on Aging in Bethesda, Maryland, only 4 to 6 percent of the population suffers from acute senility. And about a third of these individuals are actually suffering from such curable ailments as depression or nutritional deficiencies. Butler believes that most executives who complain of memory loss are in fact victims of "programmed obsolescence." "Businessmen get bored to death doing the same thing day after day," he says. "There are relatively few who wouldn't like to change careers after twenty-five years." Portable pensions, transferable from one company to another, he thinks, would keep executives from feeling locked in and would stave off memory deterioration.

But then, forgetting may help ease the pain of growing old in a youth-oriented society. Or it may simply keep the human memory bank from getting overloaded. Nobody knows. In any case, even the sharpest-etched memories can prove to be mercurial. Sometimes they just vanish into thin air.

Thought into Speech

Linguistic rules and psychological limitations in processing information determine how we put our ideas into words

James Deese

James Deese is Commonwealth Professor of Psychology at the University of Virginia, where he has been since 1972. From 1948 to 1972 he taught at the Johns Hopkins University. He is a fellow of the American Psychological Association, in which he has held numerous offices, a member of the Linguistic Society of America, and a member of the Society of Experimental Psychologists, and has authored or coauthored 7 books and approximately 100 scientific papers. Currently in press is his eighth book (with Lorand B. Szalay), Subjective Meaning and Subjective Culture. *The present article is by way of a progress report on a project that has occupied him for the past four years; currently the project is supported by NSF Grant BN577-02084. Address: Department of Psychology, University of Virginia, Charlottesville, VA 22901*

The great advances in linguistics of the past twenty years have been primarily theoretical. Inspired by, but by no means confined to, the work of Noam Chomsky, theory in every branch of linguistics has become vastly more sophisticated and capable of dealing with ever deeper and more general problems. As sometimes happens in the headlong rush of the development of theory, empirical investigation lags. It is not so much that there has not been empirical work as that what there is has been determined by, and largely limited to, theoretical problems rather than matters of general interest.

Furthermore, the experimental psycholinguist and the theoretical linguist have not always agreed about the nature of linguistic evidence. The experimentalist prefers to study the ability of people to react to, remember, paraphrase, or otherwise process samples of sentences or discourses that are designed to embody some linguistic principle. The theoretical linguist, on the other hand, prefers to use what he calls "linguistic intuition" in examining sequences of words and phrases that might or might not

plausibly be a part of a language. But in both approaches, the materials—the sentences and discourses—are artificial, concocted for the purpose of testing one or more theoretical points. Whether or not these sentences are in any sense representative of any real language is another matter.

Sociolinguists and those who study what might be called patholinguistics—disorders of language and speech—are far more likely to make use of realistic samples of language than are others interested in language. The concerns of the sociolinguist, however, center upon questions of dialect and the social determinants of dialect rather than upon cognitive–linguistic relations, while, of course, students of pathologies work almost exclusively with deviant language.

Recently, there has been some move away from the classical problems in sociolinguistics toward the more general problems of psycholinguistics. The work of Labov and Fanshel (1977) most clearly points in this direction. Certain developmental psycholinguists, such as Catherine Garvey and Susan Ervin-Tripp, have begun to use conversational samples from children in charting the growth of the relation between cognition and language. Nevertheless, it is true that naturalistic samples of language have been underutilized in the study of the basic psychological problem in language—how thought is transformed into speech.

My own interest in this problem originally came from a concern for the role of memory in language. While this concern has largely been swallowed by more general problems, it provides a good point of departure. Both linguists and psychologists have recognized that limitations of memory must be important in the pro-

duction and comprehension of speech. In his earliest published work, Chomsky (1957) pointed out that certain kinds of sentences are never produced by speakers of English, not because they are excluded by the grammatical structure of the language but because they place too great a burden upon memory. Ever since the seminal experiment by Jacqueline Sachs (1967), most investigators of memory and language have assumed, for most purposes, that we remember the grammatical structure of a sentence only long enough to disentangle the grammatical relations within the sentence. We store, for future reference, what Fillenbaum (1973) calls the "gist" of the sentence.

There are, of course, considerations other than memory that determine the particular way in which an idea will be embedded in a sentence. Every language provides its speakers with a seemingly endless variety of ways of saying the same thing. I find in my morning paper the following sentence: "When Cecil D. Andrus was governor of Idaho, few men were more popular in the West." Why didn't the reporter say instead: "Few men in the West were more popular than Cecil D. Andrus, when he was governor of Idaho"?

The reasons for such stylistic variations are, of course, many. One important way of putting the matter is to say that they enable us simultaneously to state some idea and to comment upon it. We can combine what linguists call "base phrase markers" into a single sentence; these correspond to the kind of information contained in basic propositions or ideas. In general, stylistic variations allow us to tell what kinds of relations we believe exist among ideas—what is dependent upon what in our minds, what idea is most important, and

From *American Scientist* 66, May 1978. Reprinted by permission of *American Scientist,* journal of Sigma Xi, The Scientific Research Society.

97

what we think our hearers already know.

In theory, there is no limit to the number of propositions or base phrase markers that may be combined into a single sentence. Yet sentences, even in the writings of William Faulkner, do not go on endlessly. Instead, we use certain supra-sentential structures to signal some very general relations (consider paragraphs, for example). Recent "text" grammars (e.g. Van Dijk 1972) tell us that there are intricate relations spanning entire discourses. It is often argued that certain very general relations are excluded from sentences because of the limitations of memory. For example, a newspaper story doesn't remind us of the headline in every other sentence, even though strict logic might require that the relation of those sentences to the headline be pointed out. Yet, such a notion finds the use of pronominalization difficult to explain. We use pronouns profusely, and we make them have antecedents many sentences back (rhetoricians tell us not to, but we do nevertheless). Certain grammatical features may be carried in memory across the boundaries of many sentences.

Thus, while students of memory in the laboratory find a distinction between short- and long-term memory to be convenient or even necessary, it is a difficult distinction to apply to the production of language in practice. Certain investigators have tried to identify the limits of short-term memory with the phrase boundary (e.g. the boundaries of the relative clause of a sentence) (Jarvella 1971), but the durations and characteristics of real sentences and real phrases make this identification difficult. The data we have gathered suggest that certain grammatical features (e.g. pronominalization) are carried over very long stretches of language, while most features must be retained for only a few seconds in order to complete a grammatical pattern. A more appealing picture of memory in the production of language is of an ever-changing set of features, some of which may be retained for only part of a phrase and others for entire sentences and beyond. We must re-member the topic of a story to be able to relate it to all relevant sentences, but we need not remember, say, how the subject of the first sentence in the story relates to the object in the last sentence.

This whole question of the nature and role of memory in language as well as the problem of stylistic variations are part of a fundamental concern, which is more easily seen in the production or generation of language than in the comprehension of it. Since most laboratory studies concern comprehension rather than production, this matter has been comparatively neglected. It is the matter of planning.

In order to produce a coherent discourse, we must have some plan encompassing all the ideas we wish to relate within and between sentences. Otherwise, our speech would be like that of schizophrenics, or it would be a sequence of free associations. In some way, the plan we have at the start of saying something must determine not only the first but also the last sentence in our message. Furthermore, as we execute the details of our plans in speech, we must keep track of what we have already said and what remains to be said, if we are not to be prosy and repetitious on the one hand, or mysterious and cryptic on the other. Such plans in action are apparent in spontaneous linguistic productions.

Although the investigation of naturally occurring language cannot be expected to shed light on all the vexing and interesting problems associated with planning, it will provide us with a fresh approach to the problems. Spontaneous language is clearly different from the kind of language studied in the laboratory, where the plans stem not from the need to communicate but from some instruction or set provided by the investigator. For this reason alone spontaneous language should help us gain some new understanding of how we translate our thoughts into speech.

Capturing spontaneous speech

Of course, in studying naturally oc-curring language, we do not simply go out and sample language. We sample a particular language, some specialized group of speakers of that language, and certain particular conditions under which they speak. Since my purpose was to observe the edge between the production of language and the intellectual processes behind it, I wanted samples in which this relation was as fully engaged as possible. Idle chitchat, ritualized social exchanges, or well-rehearsed productions would not do. I wanted to study people thinking on their feet. This had to be done without intervention, if I was to avoid the odor of the laboratory. Despite having to accept samples as they came, I believe we met our goals.

We have recorded graduate seminars, city council meetings, legislative committees at work, academic committees, business meetings—anything we could find and were able to use in which people were engaged in trying to inform one another, persuade one another, and formulate ideas. By now we have close to 100 hours of such speech on tape, only a portion of which has thus far been transcribed.

We have tried to limit our participants to mature, native, educated speakers of the standard American dialect. Thus far, we have only one person with less than a college education (though, to judge from the transcripts, he has an excellent grasp of the standard educated dialect), and the overwhelming majority of our participants have had four years or more of college. We have also tried to restrict our age sampling. We have not recorded the speech of persons less than 21 years of age because there is reason to suspect that the full adult dialect may not be completely formed until the early twenties. And, in the interests of minimizing unknown neurological problems, we have not used material from individuals more than 60 years of age.

I shall not describe our method of transcribing from the tapes. Suffice it to say that it is technical and complex—it requires as many as 100 passes through a given segment of tape. It uses a system for coding all

Table 1. Some sample sentences

Deviant sentences

1. In this case letters are produced that can often write letters. (3 sec)
2. Part of that was the impetus for going to the field was to build in a cushion. (6 sec)
3. They were monaural tasks are very difficult to do. (4 sec)
4. But one of them is assigned as a station duty is to handle the telephone. (3 sec)
5. How do the costs of the out—off grounds programs can students relate to the cost of on grounds programs? (6 sec)
6. You are all married to men whose husbands are in professions. (5 sec)

Run-on deviant sentence

1. But I think when you put it together with the animal literature the fact that you can train one side of an animal's brain and not get transfer effects to the other and so on very clearly beyond any doubt in a wide variety of species having a wide variety of relations between the two cortices that there the (the) notion and then put that together with the clinical literature on human beings. (23 sec)

Long sentence that parses

1. I think that the (that the) recognition latency data, if he reported it as a primary finding, would have at least borne up the conclusion that if you look at processing strategies—in other words the idea here is that experienced listeners are attempting to decompose the (the) melodic sequence while naive listeners are not—(that if you look at processing strategies) then you can generalize some form of analytic function to the left and some form of holistic function to the right. (Main sentence 21 sec; parenthetical sentence 12 sec.)

---

vocal information, including filled pauses and false starts, and it uses occasional spectrographic analyses at critical points. From the basic transcripts we make all tabulations, including recording the grammatical structure of sentences, false starts, internal corrections, deviant sentences, sentence transitions, and any other feature that strikes us as being relevant to some problem concerning the translation of thought into speech.

What sentences are like

The sentences surprised us as being, for the most part, very short. One would expect conversational sentences to be short, but we had supposed that arguments before committees, scientific presentations, and the like would require long and involved sentences. In one sample, taken from more than 20 hours of recording of a graduate seminar, some 20% of the sentences lasted for one second or less. In a sample of approximately 5 hours of Charlottesville City Council hearings, 17% of the sentences lasted one second or less. In the graduate seminar 50% of the sentences lasted three seconds or less, while in the City Council 50% were four seconds or less in duration.

These are our extremes thus far; samples from four other sources fall in between.

Measured in duration, these sentences would not appear to put much burden upon short-term memory, at least insofar as the speaker has to remember how he began a sentence when he finishes it. More than 90% of the approximately 20,000 sentences we have tabulated thus far last less than ten seconds. However, viewed from the other side, a very few sentences place an extraordinary burden upon short-term memory. The longest sentence we have found lasted 59 seconds, and several lasted more than 45 seconds.

Another surprise was that sentences which seem completely to fall apart grammatically are rare. My subjective impression is that I am liable, when under the pressure of communicating some difficult idea orally, to produce a high rate of garbled sentences. That isn't so (I was one of the participants in one of the most extensive samples). Run-on clauses are rare in all of our speakers, and only slightly more frequent are sentences that appear to be ungrammatical blends of two or more constructions. Although internal corrections, as we note below, are

common, genuinely faulty constructions account for, at the most, about 2% of our total sample of sentences.

Because we thought that deficiencies in memory would be the major cause of faulty sentences, we were surprised to find more short faulty sentences than long ones. It is true that the proportion of long sentences that do not work grammatically is higher than the proportion of similar short sentences, but in absolute numbers, sentences of five seconds or less in duration account for the majority of our deviant sentences.

Table 1 exhibits some characteristic faulty sentences, together with one example of a very long sentence that seems to parse. The well-formed sentence we chose for this table is interesting because the main clause is interrupted by a parenthetical remark—itself well formed—which took the speaker twelve seconds to say. When the speaker had finished his parenthetical remark, not only was he able to pick up the main clause where he left off but, apparently for the benefit of his listeners, he repeated word for word the last seven words of the main clause. Clearly, if memory span in the traditional sense is a limiting factor in sentence production, occasionally it must be stretched to extraordinary limits.

Faulty, or deviant, sentences have a pattern to them, as we shall see shortly. Contrary to our initial guess, they are not at all like the kinds of deviant sentences produced by brain-damaged persons—aphasics. There are occasional sentences reminiscent of those spoken by aphasics (we have found a total of three thus far), but whole categories of aphasic errors go unrepresented in the speech of normal persons, and by far the largest number of syntactic errors found in normal speech do not appear to be qualitatively like those found in aphasics.

Deviant sentences result from a failure of monitoring. One of the chief linguistic functions of consciousness is to enable us to monitor our own speech. We listen to ourselves and we can tell, most of the time, when we have made a mistake, and we correct it. When we are in some dissociated states (as when under the influence of a powerful drug) we cannot monitor carefully, and our speech becomes bizarre and disconnected. For reasons which will be pointed out later, we occasionally make mistakes even in a normal state when our awareness of what we are saying momentarily lapses. The result is an uncorrected error.

Much less frequent are the faulty pronunciations and semantic mistakes that are ordinarily called slips of the tongue. These are, with very rare exceptions, detected by the speaker and corrected. Some characteristic examples from our data can be seen in Table 2. These kinds of errors have been thoroughly studied by Fromkin (1971) and Garrett (1971). Our main contribution is to show that, in the kind of fully engaged discourse we examine, they occur at a rate of no more than one per hundred sentences. Strangely enough, we have found no true spoonerisms—perhaps they are very rare. However, the errors we do find, like spoonerisms, are contextually appropriate. For example, the person who said "mellabolic" for "metabolic" was talking about the ability to perceive melodies. "Stries" occurred where either "try" or "strives" would have been appropriate (the speaker eventually corrected it to "strives"). Perhaps these errors are qualitatively like the mistakes in production made by aphasics, as Fromkin has argued. However, with only one possible exception (noted below), semantic and pronunciation errors in our data were corrected by the speaker without prompting. This is something aphasics are rarely able to do, even though they may be aware, in a general way, that their speech is faulty.

For the moment, let us return to deviant sentences. There are two kinds. The more frequent variety are short and appear to be blends of two or more grammatical constructions. They are the result of the troublesome fact that the speaker's plans for producing coherent discourse are dynamic and not static. Our data show at every level that speakers are forever tinkering with the basic plans they have for their discourses. Be-

Table 2. Some examples of slips of the tongue; all were corrected by speakers without prompting

defects *for* deficit
mellabolic *for* metabolic
vergal (*hard g*) *for* verbal
convering *for* confirming
violation *for* volition
trime *for* time
collex *for* complex
reduce *for* reduction
indexing inget *for* indexing digit
perse *for* present
calculation *for* criterion
permit *for* prepared

cause the new plans do not always mesh easily with the old ones, there results a certain degree of incoherence. The examples in Table 1 occur at the level of the sentence or the phrase and are therefore revealed by syntactic mismatch. More often, as we shall see, the incoherence occurs between sentences over larger segments of discourse.

Less frequent are long, run-on sentences. It is possible that some of the problems with these reflect a simple failure of memory, but it is my belief that they, more often than not, also reflect a change in plans and failure of monitoring. I think that plans for sentences make use of just those syntactic features needed to complete the grammatical relations. It is only when plans are changed in mid-sentence or (as must surely sometimes be the case) before the speaker actually begins to put the sentence into speech that syntactic mismatch occurs. We shall need more and perhaps different kinds of data to demonstrate the correctness of this view, but it is consistent with everything we know thus far.

An even more obvious result of the dynamic character of plans behind speech is to be found in false starts and corrections within sentences. These are very common, though unlike fully deviant sentences false starts and internal corrections occur at a rate which varies with the conditions of speech. Depending upon the situation, they will occur in anywhere from just about zero percent to 50 percent of the sentences, and they seem to vary with the individual. We

have some speakers whose speech is almost free of them. However, they occur for most people, and for all persons they happen most often where speech is most spontaneous.

Of necessity, a certain amount of the speech we have recorded was planned ahead of time (we discarded all material that was read or clearly memorized). In speech that people have thought about ahead of time, disfluencies are comparatively infrequent. When people are pressed by unexpected questions or the need to rethink something, fragments, internal corrections, and false starts increase dramatically.

Table 3 gives some examples of fragments, false starts, and internal corrections. Note that the corrections are not semantic. In fact, semantic errors, corrected or uncorrected, are very rare. One of the faulty sentences in Table 1 may or may not involve an uncorrected semantic error: "You are all married to men whose husbands are in professions." To the extent that this sentence results from a confusion between "husband" and "wife" (an ambiguous context suggests that it may), it is typical of what semantic errors do occur. Pairs such as "buy" and "sell," "husband" and "wife," "east" and "west," and "left" and "right" are the kinds of things that result in semantic errors, as determined from the corrections that follow. However, since we have found only six clear cases of semantic errors (excluding the "husband" and "wife" sentence) in nearly 20,000 sentences, a pattern is difficult to perceive.

Once again, these rare errors are reminiscent of aphasic speech in a qualitative way (though, of course, they are vastly less frequent than the errors in speech associated with persons having known brain damage). Once again, we should remember that these errors are corrected by normal speakers, something aphasics find it very difficult to do. There are also occasional neologisms, but these appear to be merely idiosyncratic creations of the speaker. One of our speakers, for example, consistently uses "assumedly" in a context in which most persons would use "presumably."

Table 3. Sentences beginning with false starts or containing corrections

1. And so there's been a real . . . a lot of attention given by both X and myself and our staff.
2. Most of the . . . What we've done to expand our staff to meet this need is we have expanded our staff.
3. Well, don't you think . . . Does it ever occur to you that they might need a full time wife to support them, be there at home being a wife?
4. But I . . . I'm for a lot of massive courses in cook . . . cooking craft for males.
5. I think there . . . This is taken care of by good communities.
6. At least you have to, you . . . you may think you have to know this.
7. And of course the types of emergency seem to be provided [*fragment that followed* Operating procedures, cost distribution and recovery are matters for decision especially among political jurisdictions.]
8. In so doing originally we had anticipated putting in the two way . . . the capability for two way service.

One kind of semantic disfluency is not directly represented in our data simply by virtue of the nature of the data themselves, though we are certain that it must have occurred in the mental processes of our speakers. It is something we have all experienced—the inability to think of a word, usually a proper name. We suspect that such a difficulty may account for a very large proportion of the hesitations in speech, and context suggests that many changes in plans are occasioned by such an amnesia.

The most ubiquitous kinds of disfluencies, of course, are the filled and unfilled hesitation pauses. They occur in everyone's speech under all circumstances, though they are very much more frequent on some occasions than others and in some participants rather than others. They have been extensively investigated by Father Daniel O'Connell, of St. Louis University, as well as by others, and will receive only the briefest mention here.

Unfilled pauses, of course, are not always disfluencies. We use pauses to mark sentence boundaries and other segments of discourse. The usual practice is to treat very long pauses—more than one-quarter of a second—as disfluencies, but this leads to problems. Skilled actors and orators will often pause two or more seconds between and within phrases to emphasize a point. The truth of the matter is that some pauses represent failures of fluency and others do not. It is impossible to tell which is which without the full meaningful context of the discourse, and even then there are doubtful cases. Pauses belong with linguistic features of stress, intonation, and speech rate, which sometimes are influenced by such things as anxiety, uncertainty, or eagerness. They are governed by both linguistic and psychological considerations.

As with all disfluencies, pauses are very much under the control of the completeness of plans. In well-planned speech, they are relatively infrequent and nearly always easily attributable to some intent. In speech under the stress of forming a discourse from scratch, "ums" and "uhs" blossom forth in profusion. A small minority of speakers—four or five out of the nearly fifty speakers we have listened to thus far—show no filled pauses at all. These persons pause, often for very long times, but they do not, like the rest of us, "um" and "uh." They simply stop for a while and plan ahead.

When we put all these things together, it is difficult to find a single sentence in truly spontaneous speech that does not contain some kind of disfluency, though the vast majority of actual errors are corrected by our conscious monitoring of our own speech.

Grammatical features of sentences

A brief word about the kinds of sentences people produce before we turn to the nature of planning. It needs to be said that there are no "sentence types" or "sentence frames." In the nearly 20,000 sentences we have transcribed thus far, it is fair to say that almost every one represents some unique grammatical pattern. This will be no surprise to generative theorists (who are hard to impress with data anyway), but it is nice to know. The old structural view of grammar simply will not hold up to the bewildering variety of actual sentences.

What we do have are recurring grammatical features. We are now in the process of making a detailed tabulation of these features and their co-occurrences. Some of the results of this tabulation are surprising and bear on the general problem of planning in speech, and therefore I will say a word about them.

Two things must be said ahead of time. First, it is difficult to avoid talking as if there were sentence types. Talking that way, however, is just a convenience of expression. It is easier to say, "Simple sentences are in a minority," than to use the more accurate but clumsy locution, "The feature of simplicity occurs in a minority of sentences." The reader will know we mean to imply only the existence of features, not the realistic possibility of classification by features.

Second, we deviate somewhat from the kinds of grammar found in most school texts. For example, we describe as complex many sentences that some school grammars would describe as simple. All nominalizations (noun phrases with verbs or gerunds at the head), for instance, we counted as embedded in a main clause and hence complex. We did the same thing for infinitive complements (e.g. "I know that to do it would be difficult") and the like. Thus, "the pardoning of Mr. Nixon was responsible for Mr. Ford's defeat" would be treated somewhat as follows: It contains a main clause, "(the pardon) was responsible for Mr. Ford's defeat," which contains embedded in the subject phrase (the nominalization) the clause, "(somebody) pardoned Mr. Nixon."

We treated most compound sentences as two or more separate sentences. The overwhelming majority of independent clauses headed by a conjunction are connected to the previous sentence by "and." Adults are not quite so bad as children, who often connect all sentences in a narrative by "and," but adults, more often than not, simply use "and" to signal the end of one sentence and the beginning of another. Our idea was to restrict simple sentences to those with minimal grammatical ties to other sentences.

Overall, about one-third of all sentences consist of a single independent clause. Simple sentences become slightly more numerous in conversational exchanges, but it is impossible to find any extended sample in which they are in a majority. Of those sentences we describe as complex, the largest number contain complements. In fact, in one sample, fully 55% of the complex sentences contained one or more complements. The most common are object complements of the sort, "I think that there is some question as to how far Rivanna can go in terms of its legal authority." This example gives away the secret, of course. Complements provide a way of avoiding flat-out statements. "I think," "we feel" are the common examples. The speaker usually appears to be protecting himself from the full force of what he is saying. Occasionally, the complement will be used for the opposite purpose—to make a statement more emphatic: "I know that those figures are wrong."

The density of object complements in our speech samples is vastly greater than we could find in any kind of written samples (including dialogs in novels and plays). It is one of the grammatical features most characteristic of the oral dialect. It may occur as commonly in English as it does because English has no way of marking verbs for the gnomic status (the speaker saying how much he knows) of the utterance. As the late B. L. Whorf was fond of pointing out, many languages, by placing particles on the verb, enable the speaker to say whether he is reporting something he knows to be true (because he saw it himself) or is merely reporting hearsay. The complement as a construction serves something like this purpose, though it does make for a certain heaviness of style.

Relative clauses are the next most common feature, followed by the miscellaneous features of conjoining. Sentences containing relative clauses in which the relative pronoun is the subject of the relative clause are about twice as common as clauses in which the relative pronoun is the object. This is interesting because object relatives are more complex transformationally than subject relatives (Fodor, Bever, and Garrett 1974). For artificial samples of language, they are more difficult to understand (Hakes, Evans, and Brannon 1976), but we have reason to suppose that this would not be the case for relative clauses in real sentences. Our speakers compensate for the greater transformational complexity of object relatives by making other features of the clauses simpler.

Parenthetical constructions also occur with high frequency (more often than nominalizations, for example). These are constructions simply embedded in main clauses without any grammatical markers (there is an example in Table 1). They are very much more common in oral discourse than in written discourse on similar topics, and they clearly reflect the difficulties speakers have in executing their plans in an orderly way. They are mainly things that the speaker forgot to say earlier—and should have said earlier to make the discourse orderly.

Planning discourse

This brings us to the matter of discourse, because it is the case that most of the interrelations within and between sentences are determined by the context of some particular discourse. For example, dependent clauses do not always contain information semantically less important or more "dependent" than that in the main clause. This is obviously the case with object complements, but it is even true with many relative clauses. In context, the sentence, "He was talking about data which shows [sic] recovery even in older people," has its most important information in the relative clause. The main clause, when seen in its full context, is empty rhetoric. But this choice of a way to

say something was determined by the overall plan of discourse. It served to relate the essential new information to what had gone before.

What about the forms of discourse chosen by our speakers? There is currently a great interest in the analysis of discourse, and there are a variety of specialized grammars (Fredricksen 1975; Kintsch 1974; Van Dijk 1972) designed to describe the structure of text in terms of such fundamental relations as cause, existence, etc. These are mainly designed for narrative text and are not very useful for the kind of discourse we have recorded. However, whatever the grammar used to describe the relations within discourse, I believe that there is a very simple plan that describes the idealized structure of all coherent discourse. It is based upon the assumption that all discourse tends toward a strong hierarchy.

A strong hierarchy is a classification system in which a given entry never appears in more than one place. In discourse, it is a kind of outline for the information presented by the propositions in the discourse.

Figure 1 shows the hierarchical structure for the information presented in the *Columbia Viking Desk Encyclopedia* (Viking Press 1953) entry for the German poet Stephan George. It is, we should note, the way the information is presented, not the information itself, that makes the hierarchy. The information in the figure might have had a very different organization if it had been part of, say, an entry on German poets. Such a hierarchy has nothing to do with the way the world is organized, only with the way a speaker organizes the information he wishes to present at a given time. Propositions at lower nodes in the hierarchy explain, modify, or simply assume the existence of information at higher nodes.

Discourse occurs within discourse, and plans are embedded within plans. Conventional devices, such as paragraphs and chapters, are chiefly ways of marking off a longer work into self-contained segments—though, it should be admitted, we do not always segment carefully. Discourses may

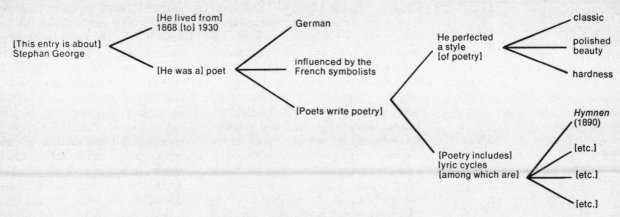

Figure 1. This entry, about the German poet Stephan George, from the *Columbia Viking Desk Encyclopedia*, is an example of hierarchical structure in written discourse. The representation makes many compromises in the interests of intelligibility. Missing phrases and propositions are in parentheses. One ambiguity concerns "classic." I read the entry as saying that the style was classic and of polished beauty, but if "classic" modifies "polished beauty," those two nodes should be combined.

even span separate works. Literary critics point out that the entire output of some writers forms a unified whole.

I believe that all coherent discourse tends toward a strong hierarchy for one simple, functional reason. It places the minimum burden on the memory of both the speaker and the hearer. If discourse were to form a more complex structure   a weak hierarchy or a generalized network— the dependency relations, or what the speaker was trying to relate, would be too complicated and confusing for both the speaker and the hearer.

Not all discourse is coherent, of course. Samples of schizophrenic speech suggest something like a generalized network. We have all had occasion to listen to people who are difficult to follow. They seem to jump from one topic to another, and such people may often appear to be "schizy" in their discourse. Furthermore, under the best of circumstances, spontaneous discourse only approximates a strong hierarchy because plans are forever changing. Also, nearly all human discourse is incomplete. We assume that our hearers can infer certain information from what we have told them, and we do not bother to point the inference out to them.

In fact, in such forms as parables, the essential "message" may never be stated at all. One of the short discourses we used in some early inves-

tigations was taken from a textbook on psychology. The point of the discourse, which formed a short paragraph, was that behavior is consistent or predictable, but this fact was never stated. The point was made by presenting the parable of the two businessmen, one who always pays his bills on time, etc., and the other who does not. Incidentally, students to whom we presented this discourse all got the point, and some who were asked to remember the paragraph organized their recall of it with the statement, "behavior is predictable," as the main proposition in their discourse structures.

Because of the dynamic character of planning and because of the fact that in speech only limited, local editing (to make corrections within sentences) is possible, discourse is much less well organized in speech than in writing. Something of that can be seen in Table 4, which compares some characteristics of ten samples of written discourses with sixteen samples of oral discourses. The written discourses were taken from a variety of sources—newspaper stories, advertising copy, etc.—while the oral discourses were taken from our graduate seminar sample. They differ in certain important ways. For example, oral discourses require implicit propositions (propositions the recipient must infer) at twice the rate of written discourses. Ambiguously placed propositions (propositions that might modify one or another of two higher nodes) occur in oral dis-

course at ten times the rate of written discourse.

False starts and corrections within sentences do not occur at all, of course, in written discourse. Not only do they happen in speech but the fragments which result contain information essential to the interpretation of the discourse. Even though the speaker corrects his start, he assumes that his hearer has assimilated the information in the false start.

The net result is that nearly a quarter of all the propositions in oral discourse either have something wrong with them or are missing. Only about 7 percent of the propositions in written discourse are so flawed, and in all but a tiny minority, these are merely missing propositions—propositions to be inferred by the reader.

Even this comparison fails to convey the full difference between the coherence of written and spoken discourse. Someone, of course, has to provide the outline, or tree, that reveals the structure of a discourse. For written discourse that is very easy. With little practice, almost anyone can outline short discourses, such as entries in desk encyclopedias, with ease. Trying to discover the structure of even short oral discourses is a difficult and frustrating matter. For the sixteen discourses in Table 4, we had three people work, first independently and then combining their opinions as to the structure. Even so, in some instances we had no real

Table 4. A comparison of a sample of 10 written discourses and 16 discourses taken from an oral sample (aphasia seminar)

	Written sources	Oral sources
Number of discourses	10	16
Total number of propositions	338	510
Mean no. propositions per discourse	33.8	31.9
Total implicit propositions	24	75
Mean no. implicit propositions	2.4	5.0
Mean no. ambiguously placed propositions	0.1	1.0
Percent ambiguously placed propositions	0.3	3.1
Total false starts containing information	—	12.0
Mean number of false starts		0.75
Total ill-formed or absent propositions	25	113
Percent ill-formed or absent propositions	7.4	22.2

confidence that we had captured the intent of the speaker.

Putting hierarchies into discourse

There is no necessary connection between the order of propositions in discourse and the hierarchical tree of propositions (in fact, because hierarchies form only what students of such matters call a partial ordering, complete correspondence is impossible). Textbooks of rhetoric tell us to place our "topical sentences" first in paragraphs. People often do so, both in writing and in speaking. It is hard to tell, because we have not yet analyzed a sufficiently large sample of oral discourses, but it would seem, paradoxically, that oral discourses have a more stereotyped organization than written discourses. In oral discourse, the topical sentence *is* more likely to come first. Furthermore, most speakers produce the structure from top to bottom (topical sentence first, etc.), and speakers are much more likely than writers to say the structure from left to right as well. Perhaps an example will help show why.

Someone spies a record jacket near the turntable and asks me, "Who is Charles Martin Loeffler?" I answer by saying, "He's an American composer of the first quarter of the twentieth century." At this point, rather than go on to explain what kind of music he writes, I may remember that he was not American born, and so, rather than hold that information for later, I will amplify "American" by saying: "He's not a native American. He was born in Alsace, but he spent most of his adult life playing with the Boston Symphony." Thus, "American" is explained before "composer" (the fact that he wrote impressionist music, etc.).

The example is an artificial one, but it is characteristic of oral discourse. The main rules, followed with many exceptions, are (1) produce from top to bottom, and (2) produce from left to right. The latter rule is mainly a matter of consistency. If you state propositions at the same level in the hierarchy in the order B, C, A, then you explain in the order B, C, A. Much less frequently, a speaker will go all the way down the same branch before going on to the next branch on the level at which he started. This result may be limited, however, to the kinds of shorter discourses we have studied in detail thus far.

It would be a mistake to assume that all this planning is done consciously. In fact, it is one of the cornerstones of modern cognitive theory that the most important executive functions are not carried out in consciousness. We use our consciousness to focus attention on one and then another part of the incoming information, and we use it to monitor our own output. Every so often we will say to ourselves, "I must remember to say X." More often than not, when the time comes, we forget to do so. Such a conscious decision is not part of the basic plan of execution of the discourse; it is only an addendum.

Speaker's limitations help listener

In this brief survey of our investigations into the natural production of language, we have emphasized the functional compromises the speaker makes in order to plan and produce speech simultaneously. The speaker appears to want to make the task as easy as possible for himself. We have had little to say about the listener, partly because investigations of comprehension are much less rare than investigations of production. We have, however, begun some investigations into comprehension that complement our studies of production. Just a word about the direction these studies are taking will demonstrate the functional adaptiveness of speech.

The late G. K. Zipf, in his analysis of the speaker-hearer relation (1949), portrayed the speaker and hearer as being at war with one another. Zipf believed that what was easy for the hearer to understand was difficult to produce and that what was easy to produce was hard to understand. In actual conversation, Zipf argued, there was a kind of least-effort compromise. There might well be a kind of least-effort compromise in speech, but nothing could be further from the truth than to suppose that it occurs between speaker and hearer. What is easy for the speaker to produce is easy for the hearer to understand.

Furthermore, the efforts of the speaker to produce coherence, given the multiple demands of production, are in the interests of making the mental burden easier not only for himself but for his listener as well. There is good reason to believe that the speaker's sacrifice of local coherence, at the level of the sentence or the phrase, in the interests of planning discourse as well as possible, given the dynamic nature of planning, is helpful to the listener as well as to the speaker. Unless disfluencies are extraordinary in frequency (and accompanied by irregularities in rate and other features of speaking), they are largely ignored. We did one careful comparison between sentences as originally spoken by our participants, sentences that were full of corrections and other disfluencies, and those same sentences re-recorded by a fluent speaker. There was a tiny difference in comprehensibility that, for 100 sentences, did not achieve statistical significance.

But if the lack of coherence is at the level of discourse, the hearer cannot grasp what the speaker is trying to say. There are individual differences in fluency, but even our least fluent speakers tend to sacrifice local coherence for discourse coherence, and this is helpful to their listeners. In short, transforming thought into speech is a functional process in which the compromises the speaker makes in his own self-interest help the hearer understand what is being said.

References

Chomsky, Noam. 1957. *Syntactic Structures*. The Hague: Mouton.

Fillenbaum, Samuel. 1973. *Syntactic Factors in Memory?* The Hague: Mouton.

Fodor, J. A., T. G. Bever, and M. F. Garrett. 1974. *The Psychology of Language: An Introduction to Psycholinguistics and Generative Grammar*. McGraw-Hill.

Fredricksen, C. F. 1975. Representing logical and semantic structure of knowledge acquired from discourse. *Cognitive Psych.* 7: 371–458.

Fromkin, Victoria. 1971. The non-anomalous nature of anomalous utterances. In *Speech Errors as Linguistic Evidence*, ed. V. Fromkin. The Hague: Mouton.

Garrett, M. F. 1971. The analysis of sentence production. In *The Psychology of Learning and Motivation*, ed. G. H. Bower. Academic Press.

Hakes, D. T., J. S. Evans, and L. L. Brannon. 1976. Understanding sentences with relative clauses. *Memory and Cognition* 4:282–90.

Jarvella, R. J. 1971. Syntactic processing of connected speech. *J. Verb. Learn. and Verb. Behav.* 10:409–16.

Kintsch, Walter. 1974. *The Representation of Meaning in Memory*. Erlebaum.

Labov, William, and David Fanshel. 1977. *Therapeutic Discourse: Psychotherapy as Conversation*. Academic Press.

Sachs, J. S. 1967. Recognition memory for syntactic and semantic aspects of connected discourse. *Perception and Psychophysics* 2:437–42.

Van Dijk, T. A. 1972. *Some Aspects of Text Grammars: A Study in Theoretical Linguistics and Poetics*. The Hague: Mouton.

Zipf, G. K. 1949. *Human Behavior and the Principle of Least Effort*. Addison-Wesley.

NAVIGATING THE SLIPPERY STREAM OF SPEECH

Ream ember, us poke in cent tense all Moe stall ways con tains words knot in ten did. If you read those words aloud, you'll discover one of the things psycholinguists have learned about spoken language: it "almost always contains words not intended." Not only that, the stream of speech also spawns some of our juiciest puns and riddles.

Ronald A. Cole

Ronald A. Cole received his Ph.D. in experimental psychology from the University of California, Riverside, and is associate professor of psychology at Carnegie-Mellon University. He has published more than 30 articles on speech perception, and coauthored with Jola Jakimik, a chapter on understanding speech in *Strategies of Information Processing*. He is editor of *Perception and Production of Fluent Speech*, to be published by Lawrence Erlbaum Associates this fall.

All spoken language is a rapidly changing stream of sound, instantly decipherable only by those on intimate terms with its complex laws. Because speech is continuous, the possibility of confusion from slurred words and phrases is virtually unlimited, as in *half fast/half assed, more rice/more ice, some more/some ore*. B. F. Skinner created one of the most intriguing examples: *Anna Mary candy lights since imp pulp lay things*. Each word in the sentence can be understood, but the whole is nonsense. Read aloud quickly, however, the whole becomes a comprehensible sentence: *An American delights in simple playthings*.

Researchers in psycholinguistics have made some important strides in recent years in learning how people understand everyday speech. With the aid of new experimental techniques and sophisticated electronic equipment such as the spectrograph (shown on the following page), we can record the variations in energy expended in speech as a person talks. By picturing the stream of sound, the spectrograph enables us to identify and measure the basic components of sound and analyze its patterns over time—a process that may yield knowledge helpful to deaf people trying to improve their speech, or to anyone learning a foreign language.

How do we hear and make sense of ordinary conversation? Most people have the mistaken impression that the words they "hear" are distinct, separate combinations of sound. The spectrograph demonstrates that words usually run together in more ambiguous sound patterns. Indeed, a word often cannot be heard correctly if it is taken out of context.

That fact was first shown experimentally more than 15 years ago at the University of Michigan by speech scientists Irving Pollack and James Pickett. From recorded conversations, Pollack and Pickett spliced out individual words, played them back to a group of people, and asked them to identify the words. Strangely, the listeners could understand only about half the words, on the average, although the same words were perfectly intelligible in the original conversation. The experiment has been replicated several times since with the same result: the particular sound pattern of a word, by itself, is often not enough to identify it.

Think of the difference between normal speech and the words on this page. Printed words are separated by space. They are the same wherever they occur. That isn't true of speech. There are no physical clues in the sound stream that consistently indicate where one word ends and the next begins, and the acoustic structure (pronunciation) of a word can be quite different from one moment to the next. The result is that speech can often be interpreted in different ways, as illustrated by many jokes, riddles, and puns. Take the old favorite:

I scream, you scream.
We all scream for ice cream.

Or this riddle:

Q: If you have 26 sheep and one dies, how many are left?
A: 19 sick sheep.

The explanation is that *26 sheep* and *20 sick sheep* sound virtually the same. The riddle works because nearly everyone hears the former.

The same slurring and ambiguity make it possible to create perfectly rational sentences that are incomprehensible at first hearing. Try these on a friend: *In mud eels are, in clay none are* and *In pine tar is, in oak none is*. If you say either sentence without allowing for pauses, your friend will be unable to repeat either, although each word is real, and the sentence makes sense.

Separating out words from the stream of speech—segmentation is the technical term—is only part of the problem. Word recognition is also complicated by the fact that a word's acoustic structure can change with the context. Consider the pronunciations of *what* in: *What do you want?, Watcha want?, Whaddaya want?*

From *Psychology Today*, April 1979. Copyright Ziff-Davis Publishing Company. Reprinted by permission of *Psychology Today* Magazine.

SPECTROGRAMS: VISUALIZING SPEECH

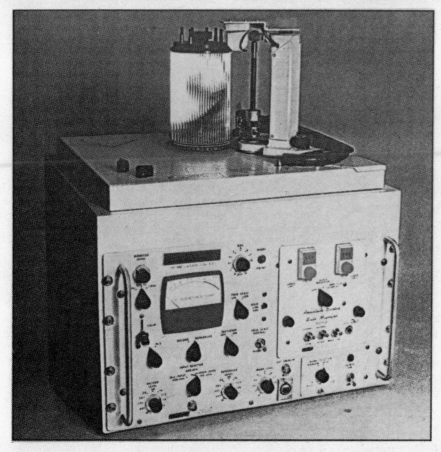

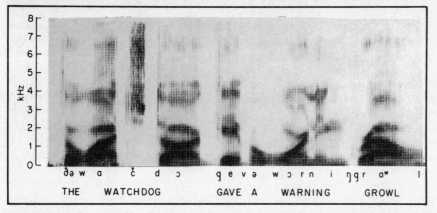

| | ð ə w | a | č d ɔ | g e v ə | w ɔ r n i ŋ g r | aʷ | l |

THE   WATCHDOG   GAVE A   WARNING   GROWL

A spectrograph—the most useful tool psycholinguists have for representing speech sounds—is shown above, along with a spectrogram. The drum at the top of the console is wrapped in heat-sensitive paper. Resting on the paper is a needle connected to a sound filter with a bandwidth of 300 cycles per second. The filter responds to sound by converting it to electric energy, which heats the needle. As the drum rotates, the needle moves up the heat-sensitive paper in response to the varying frequency of the sound. The marks on the lower part of the paper represent low-frequency energy produced by vowels and nasal sounds such as *m* and *n*; markings at the top of the paper are made by the high-frequency energy that accompanies sounds such as *ch* and *s*. The result is a spectrogram, a visual recording of speech energy that shows frequency along the vertical axis, time along the horizontal axis, and amplitude (loudness) by the darkness of the markings (loud sounds make the needle hotter).

The phonemes marked under the spectrogram, and the translation into words, are not part of the original spectrogram, but were added in order to show the sounds and words represented. It was once considered impossible to "read" spectrograms directly—that is, to pick out individual phonemes from the blurred continuum of a spectrogram. But, a few people now have this skill—the most fluent being Victor Zue, a phonetician at MIT.

People are as likely to say *Haya doin!* as *How are you doing*, or *Jeat jet!* as *Did you eat yet!*

Despite those problems, we usually understand one another. Indeed, we take our understanding of speech for granted. When people speak, we expect to know precisely what they are saying. Yet every time that happens, we have unknowingly made a series of complex decisions and, in the process, overcome numerous problems.

Sound and Syntax

Language is an intricately structured system. The grouping of the letters and words on this page, for example, depends on fixed rules of English syntax (the order of words), semantics (the meaning of words), and phonology (the structure of sound). Many sequences of phonemes—the consonant and vowel segments that are the basic sound components of speech—cannot occur in English words, and native English speakers are subconsciously aware of those restrictions. Playing Scrabble, we might bluff with *blit*, *shrats*, or *fren*, but we'd never try *dlit*, *srats*, or *vren*. We know, as our opponent knows, that English words cannot begin with *dl*, *sr*, or *vr*. That knowledge helps us group sounds into words.

Listening to someone talk, we can misconstrue *this lip* as *this slip* because *sl* at the beginning of a word is a permissible sound sequence. But we won't mishear *this rip* as *this srip*, because the *sr* sound cannot begin an English word.

Knowledge of these phonemic constraints—called phonotactics—is especially helpful in identifying words at the beginning of sentences, where they are most unpredictable. A sentence that begins *I'm a*, for example, can also be perceived as *I may*, or the start of *I'm making*. But a sentence beginning *I'm g . . .* can only be heard as *I'm* plus the start of a new word, since an *mg* sound can't begin a word in English.

The importance of syntactic and semantic knowledge in speech perception was demonstrated by psycholinguists George Miller and Stephen Isard at Harvard University in 1963. Miller and Isard began with normal sentences:

Gadgets simplify work around the house.

Accidents kill motorists on the highways.

Trains carry passengers across the country.

Bears steal honey from the hive.

Hunters shoot elephants between the eyes.

They constructed grammatical but meaningless sentences by combining the first word of one sentence with the second word of another sentence, the third word of still another, and so on: *Gadgets kill passengers from the eyes; Accidents carry honey between the house.* The researchers then produced ungrammatical strings of words by rearranging the same words haphazardly: *Around accidents country honey the shoot; Across bears eyes work the kill.*

After recording 50 sentences of each type, with noise in the background to simulate normal speech conditions, Miller and Isard asked their subjects to repeat each sentence. Under listening conditions in which subjects repeated normal sentences accurately 89 percent of the time, they repeated grammatical but meaningless sentences 79 percent of the time, and the random words 56 percent of the time. Obviously, the subjects used their knowledge of syntax and semantic structure to reconstruct what they had heard. When those clues were missing, they had trouble remembering the sentences.

One of the most dramatic illustrations of how context affects speech perception is the "phonemic restoration" experiment done by psychologist Richard Warren of the University of Wisconsin-Milwaukee. Warren replaced a phoneme—the first *s* in *legislatures*—with a coughing sound in the sentence *The state governors met with their respective legislatures convening in the capital city.* He then asked his subjects to tell him where in the sentence the cough had occurred. They couldn't tell, because they had unconsciously "restored" the *s* sound. People heard the *s* as if it were still intact; they perceived the cough as background noise. Under the right circumstances, then, listeners can use contextual information to generate sounds they have not actually heard because of noise or other distractions.

Psychologists John Long and John Morton, working in England, were the first to show that a word is recognized faster when it is predicted by previous words. Using a "phoneme-monitoring" technique invented by psychologist Donald Foss at the University of Texas, Long and Morton read sentences like the following to subjects, and asked them to push a signal button as soon as they heard a word beginning with *b*:

The sparrow sat on the branch singing a few shrill notes to welcome the dawn.

The sparrow sat on the bed singing a few shrill notes to welcome the dawn.

Morton and Long found that people responded more quickly to the *b* sound in predictable words, like *branch*, than they did in the unpredictable ones, like *bed*. They apparently combined what they heard (*The sparrow sat...*) with their knowledge of the world (*sparrows sit on branches*), to prime themselves for the rest of the sentence.

Extending that work, psychologist William Marslen-Wilson investigated how quickly and how accurately people can "shadow" speech (repeat it verbatim) while they listen to it. He found seven subjects who could speak intelligibly while shadowing a little more than a syllable behind what they were hearing. The subjects were able to say the beginnings of most words before they heard the finish. In addition, the errors they made were always syntactically and semantically appropriate. For example, in the sentence *It was beginning to be light enough so I could see,* two subjects inserted *that* following *so.* In the phrase *he heard at the brigade...,* five subjects replaced *heard at* with *heard that.* Marslen-Wilson concluded that our understanding depends strongly on preceding context, which includes the word immediately before the word we recognize.

Predictability and Patterns

In the past several years, my colleague Jola Jakimik and I have been investigating the role of knowledge in word perception by using a "listening-for-mispronunciations" task. Subjects listen to recorded sentences or stories and push a response key as soon as they detect a mispronounced word. We produce the mispronunciations by changing a single consonant to create an English nonsense word (for instance, *boy* to *poy, maybe* to *naybe*). The nonsense word is pronounced naturally, as if it were a real one. The listening-for-mispronunciations task has proved to be an extremely sensitive technique for examining the kinds of knowledge that listeners use automatically in understanding everyday speech.

We have found that the time it takes for a listener to detect a mispronunciation depends on what he has learned from the words preceding the mispronounced word. In one experiment, we constructed pairs of sentences, identical except for the word immediately preceding the mispronunciation. For example:

She wanted a mink poat (coat) to go with her Rolls Royce.
She wanted a pink poat (coat) to go with her Rolls Royce.

He wore a gold ling (ring) on his little finger.
He wore an old ling (ring) on his little finger.

People detected mispronunciations one syllable sooner when the word (*mink* or *gold*) preceding the word that was mispronounced primed them to expect a certain word (*coat* or *ring*). When the preceding word did not prime them, they needed to hear more of the words following to detect the mispronunciation.

The time it takes to recognize a word does not depend solely on its predictability; the sound pattern of the word itself is also important. If a word begins with a common first syllable, like *complain, contact, perform* or *provide,* there are many word possibilities we must consider (especially if the word is unpredictable). On the other hand, if the word begins with an unusual first syllable, like *sham*poo, *whis*per, *vam*pire, or *cran*berry, we have fewer candidates to consider. We should therefore expect the reaction time to second-syllable mispronunciations to be faster in words with unusual first syllables like *shampoo (shamboo)* than in words with common first syllables like *complain (comblain),* since in the first case, there are fewer possibilities to be considered. And, in fact, Jakimik confirmed that prediction as part of her doctoral dissertation.

To summarize, research shows that we make extremely rapid use of both sound and knowledge to recognize words, usually before a person has finished saying them. We rely both on the sounds that begin a word and on the information provided by the preceding words.

An Idiot-Savant Computer

Not even the most sophisticated of computers can match man's ability to use sound and knowledge to understand spoken language, despite numerous attempts to do exactly that. In 1971, the Advanced Research Projects Agency (ARPA) of the Department of Defense started a five-year, multimillion dollar project aimed at developing computer systems that can understand human speech. Only one system—HARPY, developed at Carnegie-Mellon University—met all of the project's performance goals. HARPY can recognize coherent speech in a quiet room if the speaker articulates carefully and uses a vocabulary limited to 1,011 words. Since HARPY is programmed to perform a specific task—document retrieval—it is especially good at recognizing questions like *Are there any articles on speech understanding by [Raj] Reddy?*

Though HARPY is the most successful speech-understanding system developed to date, it cannot even match the linguistic ability of a four-year-old child. HARPY is a kind of idiot savant, amazingly capable in a restricted area under ideal conditions. It works by storing all possible pronunciations of sentences that can be spoken in asking for documents, and then finds the best possible match to what it hears. For that reason, the computer system cannot recognize a novel sentence—something that four-year-olds do every day.

In its current form, it takes HARPY 10 times as long as it takes a human being to recognize speech. Thus, if a question takes two seconds to ask, HARPY will take 20 seconds to understand it. A college graduate has a vocabulary of about 20,000 words—20 times as large as HARPY's. In addition, a human being recognizes

speech under noisy conditions and understands many different accents. HARPY needs speakers who articulate carefully in a quiet room—and a Brooklyn accent can cause HARPY to draw a blank.

One of the computer's biggest problems occurs in recognizing phonemes. HARPY postulates several phonemes for each sound segment it identifies; it is correct on its first choice less than half the time. The computer's problem arises in comprehension because, in normal speech, the sound of a phoneme is sometimes changed by the neighboring phonemes: the g sounds different, for example, in the words *geese* and *goose*.

Reading a Spectrogram

Because of the complex relationship between sounds and phonemes, many psychologists and linguists believe that phonemes do not really exist as such in normal speech. Sounds are slurred and intermingled so completely, those scientists say, that they are indecipherable even when viewed on a spectrogram.

That argument presents a serious problem, however. If there are no independent sounds that correspond to phonemes (the building blocks of words), how do we understand one another? Psycholinguists who believe that phonemes do not exist in normal speech postulate a special "decoder," located in the left hemisphere of the brain, that takes speech as input and produces a sequence of intelligible phonemes as output. This decoder, the theory goes, is part of the brain's auditory system, inaccessible to the visual system. Therefore, according to those who take that position, no human being is capable of "reading" a spectrogram fluently: that is, capable of rapidly identifying individual phonemes on the tracings that represent speech energy.

The fact is, someone can. In 1971, Victor Zue of the Speech Communication Group at MIT decided to learn more about the relationship between sound and its representation on a spectrogram. Since then, working on his own, Zue has spent about an hour a day—more than 2,000 hours in all—studying spectrograms. He can now read them quickly and accurately. My colleague Alex Rudnicky of Carnegie-Mellon University and I

tested Zue's ability twice last year, and videotaped each session. We showed Zue spectrograms of normal English sentences, of semantically anomalous sentences (*Bears shoot work on the highway*), of random sequences of words, and of sequences of regular words mixed with nonsense words. His task was to identify all of the phonemes from the spectrograms. He first indicated the location of each phoneme, placing small vertical lines directly under it on the spectrogram, and then identified what the phoneme was.

We compared Zue's phoneme labels with those produced by experienced phoneticians who listened to tape recordings of the original sentences from which the spectrograms were made. The phoneticians identified 499 phonetic segments in the 23 sentences we used. Zue located 485 of them. He gave the phoneme the same label as the phoneticians on 85 percent of all segments—a level of agreement nearly as high as the average agreement (90 percent) among the phoneticians themselves.

Analyzing the videotapes, we discovered Zue's method. He identifies phonemes by recognizing characteristic visual patterns. He does not use his knowledge of the syntactic and semantic structure of English to interpret spectrograms—that is, he doesn't try to recognize words or otherwise make sense of the spectrograms he reads. After he labels a spectrogram, he often has no idea which words it contains. That fact was supported by our data, which showed he was as accurate in identifying phonemes in sequences of nonsense words as he was in identifying those in English sentences (about 85 percent in each). Although Zue doesn't usually "read" spectrograms in the normal sense—as words and sentences—I have seen him do so, and very quickly. When he reads words, he uses the context—the sense of the sentence—to group sounds into words just as we all do in normal conversation. I am optimistic that, given sufficient practice, Zue and others will one day be able to read spectrograms in "real time"—as the words are actually spoken.

More than thirty years ago, Bell Laboratories had some success with real-time speech reading, using equipment much less helpful than the spectrograms we now have. Participants in the Bell study—one of them a deaf engineer—attempted to recognize visual patterns for words on a "Direct Translator" (a device that produced a spectrographic display of speech as it was spoken). Although the display produced by the Direct Translator was not nearly so detailed as a modern spectrogram, the results were impressive. Most participants learned to identify about four words for every hour of study, and the deaf engineer learned to identify about 800 words in all. By the end of the project, after 90 hours of training, the participants were able to carry on conversations on the Direct Translator (without hearing one another), as long as participants spoke clearly and distinctly, with a common vocabulary, whenever they were using the device.

Victor Zue's accomplishment demonstrates a direct, learnable relationship between specific sounds and the visual patterns they produce on a speech spectrogram. That fact has important implications in teaching speech to the deaf or those with impaired hearing. The major problem the deaf have in learning to produce intelligible speech is that they can't hear what they say. Without that feedback, precise articulatory differences are almost impossible to learn or to retain. In fact, people who lose their hearing soon have trouble with their speech.

The problem may be solved by allowing deaf people to see the results of speech as soon as they have produced it. A real-time speech spectrogram now available commercially displays speech on a videoscreen as it is spoken. Using a split screen, the correct visual pattern of a sound can be shown on one half of the screen, and the results of each attempt to produce the sound can be reproduced on the other half of the split screen. Comparing the two patterns of sounds gives the speaker immediate feedback, helping him or her learn to say the words correctly—without ever having heard them.

The same procedure can be useful in learning the unfamiliar phonemic system of a foreign language. Think of the difficulty the Japanese have in pronouncing *l* and *r* in English. Since Japanese does not have an *l* phoneme, native Japanese speakers have never learned to hear the difference between the two sounds, and thus have great difficulty in articulating them in English. On a spectrogram *l* and *r* each look dramatically different. By trying to produce the correct *visual* pattern, with immediate feedback showing success or failure, a Japanese speaker can eventually learn to associate the correct sound with the articulatory movements that produce it.

Grasping the phonemic structure of a language is critical to understanding it. But that is only part of the knowledge we need to understand everyday speech. Even if we can identify all the phonemes in a sentence, additional knowledge is necessary if we are to recognize only the words the speaker intends us to hear. Remember, a spoken sentence almost always contains words not intended. Consider the sentence you have just read. Spoken, it contains the words *ream ember us poke in cent tense all Moe stall ways con tains words knot in ten did*. You might argue that only the intended words make sense. But that is just the point. To recognize the words we are meant to hear, we must make immediate sense of the sounds and hear only the intended combinations of those sounds.

To do that, we must use a knowledge of syntax and semantics—the same knowledge the speaker used to create the sound combinations in the first place. In a sense, we recognize words by recreating the other person's train of thought; the speaker and listener share in the process of putting the speaker's thoughts into words.

For further information, read:

Cole, R. A. *Perception and Production of Fluent Speech*, Lawrence Erlbaum Associates, in press.

Cole, R. A., J. Jakimik. "Understanding Speech: How Words Are Heard," in *Strategies of Information Processing*, G. Underwood, ed., Academic Press, 1978, $41.40.

Cole, R. A. "Listening for Mispronunciations: A Measure of What We Hear During Speech," *Perception and Psychophysics*, Vol. 13, No. 1A, 1973.

Marslen-Wilson, W. D., A. Welsh. "Processing Interactions and Lexical Access During Word Recognition in Continuous Speech," *Cognitive Psychology*, Vol. 10, No. 2, 1978.

Morton, J., J. Long. "Effect of Word Transitional Probability on Phoneme Identification," *Journal of Verbal Learning and Verbal Behavior*, Vol. 15., No. 1, 1976.

Warren, R. M., C. J. Obusek. "Speech Perception and Phonemic Restorations," *Perception and Psychophysics*, Vol. 9, No. 3B, 1971.

DREAM WORLD

EDWIN KIESTER, JR.

As the Old Testament and James Joyce attest, interest in dreams is scarcely new. But lately traffic down Freud's "royal road to the unconscious" has become a virtual stampede. It all began in 1952 when Nathan Kleitman and Eugene Aserinsky of the University of Chicago discovered the two types of mammalian sleep and identified one—rapid eye movement or REM sleep—as coincident with dreaming. Result: researchers were enabled to pinpoint the precise moment the midnight minidramas began. Ever since, they have been relentlessly and remorselessly arousing sleeping subjects to pry into their night lives. The Association for the Psychophysiological Study of Sleep now numbers about 500 members in at least 20 campus- and hospital-based "sleep laboratories"; by one estimate, 100 significant pieces of research have been added to the literature in the past 10 years.

Yet dreams remain elusive, fragile, mystifying. Squeeze one too tightly and it will disintegrate before your eyes as will a crystal goblet shattered by a high C. For all the intense research effort, the inner secrets of dreaming continue to escape us, racing tantalizingly ahead of our outstretched fingertips like Gatsby's green light. We know more facts about dreams than Freud, Jung or Shakespeare, but some of the old mysteries are as intransigent as ever.

First, the facts. Two decades of research have established beyond doubt who dreams and who doesn't. Everyone dreams—and that means everyone. Put those persons who vow up and down that they never dream into a sleep lab, jolt them awake when the REM period starts, and—what do you know—they've been dreaming. Under other conditions, the dream has just flitted away on awakening, and they have been too inattentive to notice.

We also know that the amount of dreaming is remarkably regular from night to night, and from person to person. Freud and Adler went along with folklore in maintaining that dreams increased when the mind was troubled [hence, "dreamless sleep" was idealized], but findings from the labs show dreaming is routine—and evidently necessary—for everyone, including children, who presumably have fewer troubles.

The curtain goes up on our first dream about 90 minutes after we fall asleep. The opening act lasts about 10 minutes. REM and non-REM periods alternate at 80- to 90-minute intervals through the night, with the REM periods gradually lengthening. The final period of dreaming lasts about 50 minutes. We usually have about five or six dreams totaling about 90 minutes—the length of a feature movie. In all, about 20 to 25 percent of sleeping is given over to dreams.

There is an old belief that dreams are instantaneous—a skein of rapid fantasies woven around a single external stimulus—but that, too, is now challenged. According to William C. Dement of Stanford University, perhaps the most prestigious of sleep and dream researchers, the idea probably originated with a famous dream recounted by the French writer Andre Maury in 1861. Maury dreamed that he was alive during the Reign of Terror. He was denounced as a monarchist and taken before Robespierre and condemned to death. A tumbrel hauled him to the guillotine at the head of a jeering mob. Up to the scaffold he went, and as the blade struck his neck, Maury awoke—to find that the headboard had fallen and struck him in the identical spot. Maury concluded that the dream had been initiated by the falling bedstead and the elaborate drama around it had been compressed into the few seconds between the accident and the time he woke up.

By some laborious research in his laboratory, however, Dement has shown that dreams consume about the same time that similar actions would in waking life. Dement has collected the dreams of subjects, counted the words and timed the activities they describe. Reconstructing the events show that about the same time elapses as if they were watched with open eyes.

Meanwhile, Rosalind Dymond Cartwright of the University of Illinois, Chicago, has shown that the night's dreams follow a ritualized sequence, as with a sonnet or symphony. The first dream states the theme—usually a quick review of a problem related to the day's events. The next two "scenes" recall earlier similar episodes. The fourth scene is set in the future and dramatizes a wish fulfillment: "Suppose I did not have this problem?" Act V ties all the elements into one bizarre present-tense extravaganza. Unfortunate-

From *Human Behavior*, December 1975. Copyright © 1975 *Human Behavior* Magazine. Reprinted by permission.

ly, Dr. Cartwright says, since most of us recall only portions of the final dream, we do not understand its meaning just as we would be baffled by the closing act of a play if we missed the earlier acts.

We can also now draw a profile of a "typical" dream. It usually contains two characters in addition to the dreamer; occurs indoors, is more passive than active, more hostile than friendly and more likely to be unpleasant than pleasant. Dreams contain more strange males than strange females, and most of the hostility centers on these male strangers.

Too, men and women dream differently. Men's dreams are more active and more friendly—but are also more likely to involve fighting. Men also dream more often of appearing naked in public places. Men are the most common characters in the dreams of both men and women— but in men's dream, they are more likely to be antagonists. In recalling their dreams, men are more likely to use the words *vehicle, travel, automobile* and *hit;* women use words of emotion. Women are more often pursued or endangered; men are more likely to find money.

Finally, it has been established that *no* time of night is free from some sort of mental activity. Even in stage-one sleep, the most dead-to-the-world form of non-REM (NREM) sleeping, the mind is working. Rouse a stage-four sleeper and he or she will indeed report thoughts flitting through the mind. Non-REM mentation, however, is more true to life, more quiescent and lacks the vivid fantasy of REM sleep. "I was thinking about what I had to do at the office tomorrow," is a common non-REM recollection.

The major mysteries about dreaming that still baffle and intrigue researchers are three, and they interlock:

(1) How can dreams be influenced, either in content or process, and, conversely, how do they influence the waking state?

(2) What is the significance of the dream content?

(3) Do dreams serve a function, or are they merely a form of free entertainment?

Everyone agrees—and common sense tells us—that dreams do not exist in a cocoon, that both internal and external stimuli, plus presleep activity and suggestion, affect them. Most of us have had dreams in which an outside noise smoothly in-

sinuated itself into the dream fabric. What we dreamed of as melodious cathedral chimes dissolved on awakening into the strident jangle of the alarm clock. Indeed, in Freud's day, dreams were considered "guardians of sleep," designed to protect the sleeper by disguising distractions that otherwise would keep the person awake all night. This guardian role is itself a minor mystery, since it does not operate in every instance. Dement once harried a group of subjects first with a stream of cold water, then a bright light, then a pure tone. Only 42 percent reported a dream involving water; 23 percent reacted to the light; and 9 percent to the tone.

A number of studies have shown that between 25 and 50 percent of dreaming time concerns itself with topics considered during the day. More deliberate attempts at programming dreams have had mixed results. In one intriguing study, in which first names were whispered into the ear of the dreaming subject, a "better than chance" correlation was reported that the stimulus was incorporated into the dream. Sometimes it was a "clang association—a sound similar to the name; other dreams incorporated the name itself; a third group had an emotional reaction based on personal connotations of the name. In other studies, a travelogue shown before sleep has been incorporated into a modest percentage of dreams, while impending surgery turned up in a high proportion. Still other studies have concluded that dreams sometimes compensate for what is lacking during the day. Subjects kept in social isolation, for instance, dream of being surrounded by people.

The problem is to assess objectively whether the stimulus actually triggered the dream. "Everyone has his own language," is the way Rosalind Cartwright puts it. "If you deprive a group of subjects of water, some may dream of the ocean; some may dream of the desert; some may dream of drinking; some may have dreams with an emotional quality whose association to thirst neither they nor we can understand; and some may have dreams that seem not related at all. We need a much more refined measure of dream content before we can judge how successful we are in manipulation."

Still, Charles T. Tart of the University of California at Davis, editor of *Altered States of Consciousness,* cites "incontrovertible" evidence that some

persons can deliberately cue their reactions while asleep. The classic case, he says, is the mentally disciplined individuals who can preset an internal alarm clock to wake themselves at an appointed hour. If we can learn that technique, Tart says, we can teach ourselves other responses.

In 1954, Australian anthropologist Kilton Stewart stumbled across a remote Malaysian tribe called the Senoi and launched the popular craze for dream control as a means of personal betterment. The Senoi, according to Stewart, made dreams the heart of their culture. The tribesmen assembled each morning for a dream breakfast to exchange dreams and try to divine their meaning. Children were taught from an early age to remember and discuss their dreams and to actually shape them.

Not unlike modern therapists, the Senoi believed that nightmares represented dark parts of the soul coming forward in disguised form. For the mental health of the sleeper, they had to be faced down and conquered. Senoi children were taught to will themselves not to run, but to fight, when a "dream enemy" appeared. They must consciously decide during the dream to brave out the threat. They were also told that when they dreamed of a friend, they should immediately tell that person, lest there be a continuing grudge between them.

The Stewart paper also focused interest on "lucid dreaming," the high point of the Senoi art and a form of dreaming familiar to Westerners. (It is also part of certain sacred American Indian rituals and is described by Carlos Castaneda in *The Teachings of Don Juan.*) Lucid dreaming is what we all do when we suddenly realize in the midst of a dream that we are asleep. With practice, the dream-control instructors say, you can learn to induce that moment of recognition, prolong it and actually control the flow of the dream thereafter. Thus you can bring the creative energies of the dream to bear on a subject of your choice.

What significance has the selection of characters, settings and activities in the dream? Most of us know that however fantastic our dreams, they are rooted in persons and places we know and events that have concerned us during the day. To Freud, dreams of matters close at hand were the "day residue," which had to be cleared out of the way so that the mind could get down to the "dream work" of dealing with the repressed infantile and sexual wishes bubbling up in symbolic form from the unconscious.

Adler, however, stressed the continuity of sleeping and waking and declared that the "day residues" were important in themselves, not mere screens for unconscious wishes. Most dream investigators now agree that dreams must be seen within the context of already ongoing mental activity. The real "dream work" is condensation, displacement and symbolization of the daily experiences. Dreams provide an outlet for suppressed feelings, using symbols so that they are not so blatant that the sleeper's inhibitions are offended.

Another departure from classic Freud dream theory is in interpretation. Instead of reciting their dreams to a therapist to have their symbolism explained, sleepers are now encouraged into do-it-yourself dream reflection. The objective is not only to understand the symbols and gain a different perspective on one's problems but to gain insight into the creative forces as the mind flits from thought to thought. Stanley Krippner of the Maimonides Dream Laboratory in Brooklyn, New York, puts it this way: "It is more important to appreciate your inner life than to become an amateur psychoanalyst." Krippner tells students in his dream workshops to immediately write down their dreams upon awakening and to lie quietly for 30 minutes or so reflecting on their possible meaning. He urges students to discuss their dreams with their friends and particularly to look for hidden puns and jokes such as might be created by an imagination freed from daytime restraints. A "dream journal" kept for several months will reveal recurrent images and themes that represent matters of concern to the sleeper, Krippner says.

One key point about content is that not all dreams may be significant. "Our mind in sleep has as many different facets as when we are awake," says one student of dreams and dreaming. Thus, it may spend only a small portion of time symbolically worrying over emotional problems, as we are not always thinking hard during the day. A certain amount of dreaming may be simple examination of the day's happenings, with modest emotional input. And some dreaming may be just plain woolgathering, with

the mind idly wandering and making jokes with itself.

After listening to literally thousands of dreams at the rate of five or six per subject per night, Cartwright of the University of Illinois has concluded that most dream symbolism is simple, easily understood and funny. "I wonder that people don't wake themselves up laughing," she says. She recalls one newlywed coed who was torn between continuing school and becoming a full-time housewife. "She dreamed that she was standing in the kitchen reading an anthropology text and it suddenly turned into a pot holder," Cartwright recalls. "But when she looked at the pot holder there was a hole in the middle, and she thought, 'What good is a pot holder like that?' When I began to laugh, she looked puzzled. Even when I suggested that perhaps the dream 'meant' she would be ineffective as a housewife, I had to explain it several times before she got the point."

In therapy, dreams are still important but the precise significance is a point of disagreement. A series of experiments have shown that the dreams of schizophrenics are quite different from those of "normals," and that "normals" with schizoid tendencies are still in a third group. Schizophrenic dreams have a far lower fantasy content and are much less vivid and rich; Stanford's Dement has described them as "sterile." The differences in dream content appear to be similar to the differences in waking fantasy, as shown when "normals" and schizophrenics are given the *Thematic Apperception Test*. Evidence seems to be convincing that those who cannot disentangle reality and fantasy during the day have less need for a fantasy outlet at night. (Another view maintains that the sterility of schizophrenic dream merely reflects the sterility with which they view the world.) A few theorists hold that a high fantasy quotient itself is evidence of illness. Only when dreams approach reality—"when your mother appears as your mother, and not as a gorilla," as one puts it—can the dreamer be considered sane.

What of the function of dreams? Do they indeed serve a purpose, or are they merely a sideshow? It has now been proven virtually beyond doubt that REM sleep is essential to the human body, for reasons unknown. If a person is deprived of REM sleep on a given night, the sleeper will make up the deficit on subsequent nights. If the deprivation continues, it becomes in-

creasingly difficult to prevent him or her from going into the REM stage of sleep. Even the clockwork cycles of REM and non-REM sleep appear critical. After a REM episode has been completed, it becomes impossible to induce another until at least 30 minutes have passed. The assumption is that some as yet unidentified neurophysiological process is going on during REM periods, and that it is as necessary as breathing.

Whether dreams are essential to the process or are simply a by-product is another of those elusive mysteries, but theories abound. Freud's was classic: he said that dreams are the necessary release mechanism for the repressed impulses in the unconscious; sleep arose out of the need to dream, not vice versa. He compared a dream to fireworks, taking hours to prepare and exploding in minutes. A more popular theory today is that dreams are a necessary interlude to assimilate the day's happenings, fitting them together with memories and previous experiences. All of one's emotional, conceptual and perceptual skills can be brought to bear on them before they are filed away for the future.

Another view is that of Milton Kramer of the University of Cincinnati, another eminent dream researcher. Kramer says that dreams are a mood regulator; using pre- and post-dream tests, he has shown distinct mood changes that are regular and predictable. Dr. Cartwright avers that dreams have an integrity of their own, apart from REM sleep. She points out that when a subject is deprived of dreams, the amount of fantasy-type thought increases in the waking state; in other words, dreams begin to invade non-REM sleep.

Probably the most intriguing of all theories is the "psychosynthesis" advanced by Ernest Lawrence Rossi of UCLA and others. Rossi holds that dreams are a biological process in which new protein molecules are actually being constructed as the brain "synthesizes" the events of the day. Rossi bases his hypothesis on the controversial discovery that flatworms and other primitive animals actually grow new cells as they "learn." Dreams represent actual physical changes within the brain, Rossi says —another tantalizing element of mystery in a subject that continues to generate interest as it has since the dreams of Eve.

How to Catch a Dream

In order for dreams to benefit waking life, one must quickly capture as many details as possible and record and reflect on their meaning. Patricia Garfield, Ph.D., of the University of California has been keeping a dream journal since she was 14 and has trained herself to wake up and write in the dark. For most of us, says Garfield, a more practical method of dream "recovery" is to:

(1) Place a pencil and paper where they can be reached without changing your position.

(2) Awaken gradually, if possible, without using an alarm; if you must use an alarm, choose one that wakes you to music instead of a jarring bell.

(3) Without arising, begin to make notes on the dream. Try to recall as many details of characters, setting, conversations, as possible. Don't edit or attempt to analyze—simply get down as much as you can remember. Be sure to record your feelings as well as details of the "story."

(4) Review the dream again, if possible from the point of view of the characters, to seek out more key details.

(5) Still in bed, look for hidden meanings and tie-ins to matters that presently concern you. Remember the dreaming mind may spend no more time in serious problem solving than the waking mind. Also look for jokes, puns and other evidence of "the mind at play."

(6) Discuss the dream with family and friends and ask for their interpretation of it.

(7) Enter each day's dream in a "dream diary" and review the entries every few months, looking for recurrent ideas and themes that might give greater insight into your "inner life."

A Short Course in Dream Control

Most people think dreams are the same as Disneyland: you can watch the spectacle and enjoy the rides, but controlling the show is out of your hands. Dr. Patricia Garfield is one of those who says you can learn to pull the switches, too. Her University of California extension course in "Creative Dreaming" (and her book by the same name) teaches you to choose the subject of your dream, shape the plot and rehearse your behavior for the events of the morrow or to enrich your creative life.

As an exponent of Senoi dream control, Garfield says that the first step for Westerners is to believe that it can be done. You must convince yourself that self-programmed dreams are possible, the psychologist says, pointing out that most of us inadvertently influence our dreams but aren't aware of it. Once you have become a believer, the next step is to plant in your mind what you will dream about. You must repeat through the day, in a positive and forceful way, your proposed agenda. "Tonight I fly in my dreams. Tonight I fly," is a Garfield example of the emphatic way the plan must be stated. Then you must lie down in a relaxed and peaceful state, much as the ancients reclining in a sacred place and focusing on the qualities of the gods to bring on visions, and your chosen dream will materialize.

The next step is the heart of the Garfield-Senoi technique. She calls it the "confront and conquer" gambit. Instead of passively watching events or recoiling in terror from nightmare threats, you must step forward and dominate them.

One example: Garfield had a recurring nightmare in which she was chased by rapists. Finally, employing dream-control techniques, she decided to end the pursuit. The next time the dream began, she steeled herself, stopped running and turned, terror-stricken but game, to face down her pursuers. As she did so, a can of chemical spray appeared in her hand. She vaporized the pursuers into an oblivion from which they never returned. Furthermore, she says, the successful confrontation bolstered her courage to face difficult problems in real life.

Another example involved a Garfield student, a timid sort, who dreamed that she was in an old-fashioned drugstore where the clerk refused to wait on her. Other customers were served, but he continued to ignore her. Suddenly, she began to scream the most obscene and scatological names she could think of, until he was compelled to attend to her. The feeling of mastery the dream provided carried over to the following day, when she felt brave enough to face her boyfriend with a problem that had been bothering her for months.

The Garfield method eventually leads to instruction in lucid dreaming so that one can program the dream, become conscious during it and work through whatever current problem is of concern. Dr. Garfield says she "lucid dreams" her speeches and even wrote a children's book that way. But lucid dreaming need not be all work and no play. Garfield says you can conjure up a dream lover and "go all the way through to orgasm in the lucid state." We may be on the threshold of X-rated dreaming.

REM and NREM Sleep

Anyone who's ever watched a sleeping dog's involuntary barks and twitches ("Oh, look at Rover! He's dreaming!") has witnessed the REM state. All mammals (and only mammals) have REM sleep, although the amount varies from species to species.

Like dogs, human beings twitch and breathe irregularly during REM sleep. Facial muscles and the fingertips move convulsively; breathing is fast, then slow. The bulges of the eyes can be seen to dart back and forth beneath closed lids, as if actually looking at something. Less visibly, the inner ear contracts, as with variations in sound intensity and pitch.

In the sleep lab, REM also produces distinct changes in the electroencephalograph (EEG), electrooccularograph and electromyograph, which measure brain waves, eye movement and muscle electrical impulses respectively. The EEG produces distinct spiky sawtooth patterns. All this activity closely parallels waking, yet the large muscles are as if paralyzed; the sleeper cannot move. One theory holds that REM is not a sleep state at all, but one in which the body is paralyzed but hallucinating.

NREM is the state most of us associate with "a good night's sleep." It is often graded into four stages, the essential difference among them being in the amount of smooth, quiescent delta waves that appear in the EEG. We slide rapidly from stage one into dead-to-the-world stage four, with the onset of sleep; then we slide back up to the beginning of the first REM period. As the night wears on, we spend increasing amounts of time in stage two. Although our senses are effectively shut off during this time, some form of mentation continues. With most, it is akin to a kind of desultory thinking; but about 10 to 15 percent of subjects report vivid dreaming during NREM. Whether they are actually different, or just more imaginative or sensitive than the rest of us, is not known.

One suspicion about REM is that it is somehow related to the development of the central nervous system (and perhaps in adult mammals, to its maintenance). The newborn spends about 50 percent of its sleeping time—eight or nine hours a day—in REM sleep; and premature infants, whose nervous systems have not even achieved the maturation of a newborn, have even more—up to 75 percent. During childhood, the amount of REM gradually diminishes, until a five-year-old, whose central nervous system has fully developed, is in REM only 25 percent of the time. Interestingly, newborn kittens and puppies have REM sleep only, while newborn guinea pigs, whose systems are mature, have no REM sleep at all.

Your Mood and Your Dream Characters

Most people know that they may wake up sad, happy or angry, depending on their dreams—even though they recall them. Milton Kramer, Ph.D., of the University of Cincinnati has found that these mood changes and the characters who trigger them are an integral part of everyone's dreams. Recording the dreams of eight men for 20 nights in the sleep lab, he found moods changed according to whom they had dreamed about.

As a group, Kramer said, the subjects were less unhappy, less friendly and less aggressive when they awoke in the morning than when they retired at night—as determined by a 48-item mood scale administered before retiring and on arising. Probing further, he found that the greatest correlation was between the happiness scale and the number of characters in a dream. The greater the number of characters, the happier the subject appeared on awakening. Kramer also found that particular people seemed to affect the subjects' morning moods. When the proper people appeared, the subjects awoke feeling fine; when they did not, or when others took their place, they awoke depressed or angry. Often the mood-elevating characters weren't even identifiable except as types of people. One man always felt better after dreaming about older women.

Whether mood determines characters or characters determine the mood is still an open question, but Kramer says that people can learn to influence who will appear in their dreams and, thus, can determine their own wakening mood. "You have to work at it, but it can be done with practice," he says. And he has also shown that schizophrenics and depressives have dreams decidedly related to their mood changes. Schizophrenics usually dream about strangers, depressives about family members. Characteristically, he says, depressives are in their blackest mood on awakening, and their outlook brightens as the day goes on.

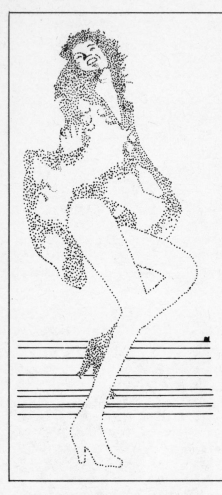

Dreams and the Dance

The young woman stood up, raised her arms above her head and began to glide across the room. As the others watched, she sinuously undulated around them, her face masklike, in the best interpretive-dance technique. The performance continued, silently, for about four minutes. Finally, she resumed her place in the group. Its leader, Joseph Hart, turned to the others. "Does anyone have any comment on Linda's dream?"

The Center for Feeling Therapy in Los Angeles places dreams at the heart of its "integrative psychology." Clients report their dreams in complete detail, acting them out and, as did Linda, dancing them. (Dance gets closer to feelings than words.) Hart, an early experimenter in Senoi dream-control methods, charts clients' progress through dream recall and believes dreams change dramatically when a person is "cured."

Hart and two colleagues founded the Center in 1972, as a spinoff from Arthur Janov's "primal scream" therapy. Its central philosophy is that people with unacknowledged feelings are, per se, insane—a philosophy spelled out in their new book, *Going Sane*. Dreams are one way we mask our feelings and impulses, because we cannot accept them directly. The integrated (sane) person no longer needs the dream's symbolism.

Hart says patients become gradually more direct and realistic, both in dreams and while awake. The milestone is what Hart calls "the transformative dream" in which problems are met head-on. "The parent now appears as a parent, not as some kind of monster," he says.

Even before therapy, Hart says, the dreams and waking lives of clients are virtually indistinguishable. One exercise at the Center is to ask for a "life-segment report," with the same details of dialogue, action, setting and feeling as in dream report. Invariably, Hart says, the same passivity and unawareness appear in the "life dream" as in the "sleeping dream."

The idea of dream transformation has its parallels in treatment of battle traumas, Hart says, in which drug therapy or hypnotherapy helped the dreamer experience and express feelings previously blocked. And they also occur in other abreactive therapies, such as primal scream. What he learned from the Senoi, Hart says, is the need for a supportive group so that when the transformation comes in both dreams and life the client can be helped to understand and benefit from it.

Do Dreams Have ESP?

Undoubtedly the most elaborate "experiment" ever carried out in dream research occurred in early 1971 and involved Drs. Stanley Krippner and Montague Ullman of the Maimonides Dream Laboratory in Brooklyn, the "psychics" Malcolm Bessent and Felicia Parise, the Grateful Dead rock group and an audience of 2,000 young people. The experiment went on for six nights and was intended to demonstrate that messages could be sent by ESP to a dreaming subject.

As Krippner recalls it, the lab had succeeded nine times out of 13 in sending messages from one individual to a sleeping subject over short distances. The "sender" viewed a randomly selected slide of a painting, then tried to "transmit" it to the subject sleeping in the lab. In the morning, the dreamer recalled the dream. Impartial judges then rated the slide and the report on a scale of 1 to 100 for correspondence.

Tying into the Grateful Dead concert held in Port Chester, New York, 45 miles from the lab, was an attempt to see if 2,000 senders would make the signal stronger. At precisely 11:30 each night, the audience was asked to send a picture to Bessent, a much-publicized "psychic," who was sleeping at the lab in Brooklyn. Parise, the control, was sleeping at home in Manhattan. The randomly selected slide was projected on a screen behind the stage, along with Bessent's name. Parise was not mentioned. The slide remained on the screen for 15 minutes, while the Grateful Dead continued to perform. In the morning, Bessent and Parise provided dream reports for judging.

According to Krippner, Bessent had four "direct hits" out of six nights; Parise had only one, on the final night. Bessent's best rating was for the second night, when *The Seven Spinal Chakras* was the slide chosen. The painting depicts a man in the lotus position, practicing yoga meditation. Vivid colors spurt from the seven "energy centers" along the spine (chakras) and a brilliant yellow halo surrounds his head. Bessent described his dream the next day:

"I was very interested in using natural energy . . . I was talking to this guy who said he'd invented a way of using solar energy and he showed me this box . . . to catch the light from the sun which was all we needed to generate and store the energy . . . I was discussing with the other guy a number of other areas of communication and we were exchanging ideas on the whole thing. . . . He was suspended in midair or something. . . . I was thinking about rocket ships. . . . I'm remembering a dream I had . . . about an energy box . . . and a spinal column."

The judges gave Bessent a score of 83.

Later, Maimonides received a grant from the National Institute of Mental Health to further explore the correlation between ESP and dreaming but could not produce significant results. However, according to Krippner, they have had greater success in transmitting telepathic messages to subjects in a state of sensory isolation, achieving a significant correlation in such cases.

Drugs and Dreams

Drug use is often associated with dreaming, but the pattern is more of a checkerboard than that. Alcohol, for instance, is thought to produce nightmares, but, in fact, the more horrifying nightmares come with withdrawal of alcohol—the dreams of the DTs —when REM sleep markedly increases. While the alcohol is in the system, REM and dreams are cut by half. Barbiturates have somewhat the same effect, both in terms of dream reduction during use and nightmares afterwards. They are also believed to change the quality of the dreams, making them more thought-like and less fantastic. Amphetamines also cut down dreaming time; certain tranquilizers both reduce time and change the dream content, usually in the direction of more hostility.

Partly because of drug laws, not too much has been proven in the laboratory about the effects of LSD, marijuana, cocaine and other illegal substances. Moderate use of marijuana seems to slightly decrease dreaming, and heavy use interferes with sleep. Dreaming time appears to remain about the same in chronic users. The effects of LSD seem to be governed by the amount of the dose and when administered. One study has shown that small doses administered just before sleep or an hour after sleep has begun markedly lengthened the second dreaming period. Other studies, however, have indicated that LSD-induced dreaming does not match REM sleep and therefore should be classified as hallucinations of a different sort.

Oh, yes. Coffee drinkers—when they are able to get to sleep— seem to dream in normal amounts. Reformed cigarette smokers, when they quit temporarily, enjoy more—and more intensive— dreams. Whether the dreams are about cigarettes is unknown.

Dreams and Moby Dick

The royal road to the unconscious may also be the sea lane to the Great White Whale. At Evergreen State College in Olympia, Washington, Dr. Richard Jones, a psychologist, teaches a multidisciplinary course that combines psychology and literature and employs the students' dream reflection to illuminate both.

At Evergreen, undergraduates concentrate on a single course each quarter, examining it from a number of perspectives. Jones and three other faculty members have 52 students who are assigned a reading list that includes Melville, Hawthorne, Freud, Jung, Erikson, Chaucer, Shakespeare, Anaïs Nin, Henry Miller and Joseph Heller. Monday and Tuesday, the class discusses the week's readings. On Wednesday morning, one student presents the rest with a written summary of the previous night's dream. They reflect on it together, trying to identify the symbols and tie them to the dreamer's life and to the assigned readings. Wednesday afternoon, all the students write their own papers, drawing on the dream discussion and their dreams to describe their insights into the literature.

Jones teaches his students that there is a "dream poet," the reverse side of the "dream censor," who approaches the day's events in a creative and imaginative way, instead of trying to suppress or disguise them. Dreams represent the mind at play, Jones says, mischievously tossing around ideas that are crowded out of the more structured day. Fanciful and artistic visions and puns and jokes are common. Recently, the class concluded that one student's dream was a long and humorous tone poem, in which the actors, locations and the events were selected because of the rhyming quality of ther names.

Not surprisingly, the peregrinations of Ahab and Ishmael provide some of the most insightful dreams, Jones says. The week Moby Dick was assigned, he himself described for the class an elaborate dream centered on Father Mapple's prow-shaped pulpit in the chapter entitled "The Sermon." Jones found himself surrounded by dried-out rice, old newspapers and worn-out shoes; up on the pulpit his two young children pranced. On reflection, he realized that he had been thinking about, and had even underscored in the book, a passage from the sermon: ". . . for what is man that he should live out the lifetime of his God?" Jones had wondered why Melville had used "live out" instead of "outlive"; now he saw that the meaning would have been directly opposite. His own symbols of "lived out (not outlived) usefulness" had appeared in his dream and had helped him recognize the difference.

By traditional standards, Jones says, perhaps half the students don't do as well as under conventional teaching. That is, they don't cover as much material, nor gain as much information. The other half flourish and produce the most brilliant and insightful papers he has ever read, Jones says—"and I'll settle for that." He sees no reason why dream reflection couldn't be applied to other subject matter, since tapping all the mind's creative forces could be equally beneficial in the social sciences and history. He had even persuaded a colleague to attempt mathematics instruction by the dream reflection method, the psychologist says, "but he got cold feet at the last minute."

Stress

*Sometimes harmful, sometimes helpful, it plays
a crucial role in life. Mastery of its demands, says this
expert, is a major key to improving the quality of life.*

Hans Selye, M.D.

*Director of the Institute of Experimental Medicine and Surgery at
Canada's University of Montreal, Dr. Selye holds doctoral degrees in
philosophy and science as well as in medicine. He is the author of
"The Stress of Life" (1956) and "Stress Without Distress" (1974).*

A WOMAN giving birth and her baby being born—both are under considerable stress. A child on that first terrifying day at school and a student cramming for a very important exam—both experience a great deal of stress. A trapeze artist concentrating on a death-defying jump and a painter producing his best work in a moment of brilliant inspiration are under stress.

A businessman worrying continually about office problems while he is at home, or about home problems while he is at the office, is also under stress. A doctor treating patients all day and answering sick calls at night undergoes stress. His patients fighting to regain their health are also under severe stress.

Nobody can escape stress because to eliminate it completely would mean to destroy life itself! We are confronted by stressful stimuli (stressors) innumerable times a day. The technical definition of stress implies the body's response to *any* demand. Stress is essential in our day-to-day living. It is the spice of life. It is a driving force in every man, woman, and child, urging them on to creativity in the arts, sports, science, business, and virtually every other field of human endeavor. An artistic accomplishment, a triumphant athletic victory, a successful business transaction, winning a lottery: these are all extremely pleasant and stimulating stresses, also known as *eustress*. But stress can also be extremely unpleasant and harmful. A large business loss, physical overexertion, death of a family member, or even fear can be most distressing, because they make the body work in an unusual way. *Distress*, of course, is the opposite of eustress.

Stress is a state in which a chain of glandular and hormonal reactions takes place to help our body adapt itself to changing circumstances and conditions in its physical and emotional environment. These reactions are not necessarily destructive. They prepare our body to withstand extreme weather changes, key us up to accomplish difficult and sometimes apparently impossible tasks, help us resist physical and emotional shock, and heal our wounds.

The human species has used these deeply rooted reactions since prehistoric times. Primitive man had to survive in a natural and brutal world, so he depended upon instant, automatic physical responses generated by the complex biochemical mechanisms of his brain.

Imagine a caveman who suddenly sensed a lurking saber-toothed tiger. That instant realization of danger sent a screaming message to his brain, and it in turn mobilized his body with a tremendous surge of reactions traveling along the various biochemical circuits to several glands. Adrenaline poured into his blood, giving him instant, much-needed energy through the use of sugar and other stored energy supplies. His blood pressure rose sharply with his increased respiration and quickened pulse rate. Certain functions prepared him for "fight or flight." (For example, his blood coagulation mechanism went on alert, accelerating his blood clotting time, in case he should suffer injury.) At the same time, other functions stopped instantaneously to allow his system to make an undivided demand on his vital "adaptation energy" so that he could meet this crucial moment of survival. When he realized that his chances were slim if he stayed to fight, he sped away to the safety of his den.

He slowly came down from his hormonal crisis, his body unwinding from the tension. He felt tired. He had drawn deeply on his vital adaptation energy, and rest was the best way to heal the tiny scars inflicted by the "wear and tear" of those crucial moments.

But the 20th century is a world quite different from the one inhabited by our prehistoric ancestors. The crises of our lives are different too. Our adaptive mechanisms keep up their defensive maneuvers with that same sheer intensity, but all this is elicited by more subtle, invisible stressors that have quietly invaded contemporary life.

Modern life—particularly urban life—exposes us to the everyday stressors of complex interpersonal relationships, job responsibility, richness of diet, and many associated mental or emotional stimuli. We try to cope as best we can, and usually we do so quite well. But not always. We often overreact. Many financial worries can weigh us down by constantly demanding our adaptation energy to defend us against this kind of stress. Bad news from the tax collector, the stock exchange, or commodities market has driven thousands of people to physical and mental rack and ruin.

A three-piece suit is no protection against the stress of life in the business world. Some executives unknowingly become stressed by a curt memo from a superior, by a change in company policy, by a failure to be promoted, or by a smaller than expected raise. The list of stressors in business and professional life is long.

In a 1973 article in The Business Quarterly, John H. Howard, a leading specialist in management stress, wrote: ". . . The stressful aspects of *responsibility* and *decision making* are perhaps best portrayed in the 'executive monkey' experiments. These experiments used four pairs of rhesus monkeys in a 'behavioral-stress' situation. In each pair of monkeys, one animal was designated the experimental animal and the other the control animal. In the experiment both monkeys in each pair were exposed to an electric shock, but only the experimental animal could learn to avoid the shock by pressing a lever at specific intervals. The lever was not available to the control animal. If the lever was pressed in time no shock was administered to either the experimental animal or the control animal. Thus, both animals were shocked an equal number of times, but only the experimental animal could determine whether or not the shock would occur.

"After a few weeks the experimental animal in all four pairs died because of gastrointestinal ulcerations. The control animals that received the same amount of electric shock but were not faced with the decision of controlling it all lived, were examined, and no ulcers were found.

"This experiment tends to convey the possibility for extreme stress when there is responsibility for making decisions on important issues. In real life the experimental situation is often compounded by assigning the responsibility while at the same time limiting the power needed to fulfill the obligation."

These experiments and the conclusions drawn from them are not unanimously accepted by all scientists and, besides, they cannot give us entry into the individual world of each and every business executive. We cannot fully share and feel everything that a businessman experiences, his job priorities, his relationships with his employees, family demands on his invariably limited time, and the many other exacting situations common to his daily schedule.

Picture an executive who receives a memo from his president or director, expressing harsh criticism over his decision in an important business transaction. The businessman's brain registers the censure, eliciting guilt, then perhaps outrage and repressed anger. His pulse rate accelerates, his blood pressure rises, hormones pour into his blood. His "system" mobilizes for instantaneous action but none is forthcoming. Unlike the caveman, our executive cannot run to his cave. Nor can he fight.

Anger turns inward, his own emotions become the target, and minute wounds are inflicted as a result of yet another hormonal crisis. If this type of stressful situation becomes chronic, irreparable damage is caused to his adaptive mechanisms through overwork. The executive is setting himself up as a prime candidate for a heart attack, mental breakdown, hypertension, a peptic ulcer, migraine headaches, or even cancer. These attacks on the physical chemistry of his body, in turn, join the vicious circle of stress, if the stressful situation continues unabated.

Fortunately, most stress-producing situations in everyday life are transient. But each episode of stress always causes chemical scars, which accumulate. Recurring exposure to intense stress, such as that experienced by air traffic controllers, depletes the body's finite resource of adaptation.

In 1936, I was working in the biochemistry department of McGill University in Montreal, trying to find a new ovarian hormone in extracts of cattle ovaries. All the extracts, no matter how prepared, produced the same syndrome, characterized by enlargement of the adrenal cortex, gastrointestinal ulcers, and involution of the thymus. It became evident from these and subsequent animal experiments that the same set of organ changes caused by my toxic, damaging, impure glandular extracts were also produced by cold, heat, infection, trauma, hemorrhage, nervous irritation, and many other stressors.

This reaction became known as the first phase in what I described as the "general adaptation syndrome" (G.A.S.) or the biological stress syndrome. The three phases of the G.A.S. are: the alarm reaction, the phase of resistance, and the phase of exhaustion.

Because of its great practical importance, it should be pointed out that the triphasic nature of the G.A.S. gave us the first indication that the body's adaptability to stress is finite.

Animal experiments have demonstrated without doubt that exposure to any type of stress can be withstood just so long. After the initial alarm reaction to physical as well as mental stress, the body becomes adapted and begins to resist, the length of the resistance period depending upon the person's innate adaptability and the intensity of the stressor. Yet, eventually, exhaustion sets in.

In everyday language we could say that stress is the rate of wear and tear in the human machinery that accompanies any vital activity and, in a sense, parallels the intensity of life. It is increased during nervous tension, physical injury, infections, muscular work, or any other strenuous activity, and it is connected with a nonspecific defense mechanism which increases resistance to stressful or "stressor" agents.

An important part of this defense mechanism is the increased secretion by the pituitary gland of ACTH (adrenocorticotrophic hormone) which in turn stimulates the adrenal cortex to produce other hormones. Various derangements in the secretion of these hormones can lead to maladies which I call "diseases of adaptation" because they are not directly due to any particular pathogen (disease producer), but to a faulty adaptive response to the stress induced by some pathogen.

An example from daily life will illustrate in principle how diseases can be produced indirectly by our own inappropriate or excessive adaptive reactions. If you meet a drunk on your way home from work and he showers you with insults, nothing will happen if you go past and ignore him. However, if you fight or even only prepare to fight him, the result may be tragic. You will discharge adrenaline-type hormones, which increase blood pressure and pulse rate while your whole nervous system will become alarmed and tense in preparation for a "fight."

If you happen to be a coronary candidate (because of age, arteriosclerosis, a high blood cholesterol level, obesity), the result may be a fatal brain hemorrhage or heart attack. Who killed you? You committed biologic suicide by choosing the wrong reaction.

Quite a few misunderstandings about the nature of stress arise from the fact that everybody does not react in the same way while under stress. This should not be surprising, however, since there are no two identical individuals. Each of us is conditioned by *endogenous* and *exogenous* factors.

By endogenous factors, we refer to internal, inherited traits, such as familial diseases, proneness to certain maladies, or weaknesses of specific organs. Exogenous factors encompass various external conditions in the environment, including social, intellectual, and psychological elements as well as climatic and physical surroundings prevailing at the time of stressful experiences. These endogenous and exogenous factors combine to make each individual different from the next.

Think, for instance, of a chain placed under physical tension—that is, stress. No matter what pulls on the chain and no matter in which direction, the result is the same—the chain is faced with a demand for resistance. Just as in the chain the weakest link (or in a machine, the least resistant part) is most likely to break down, so in the human body there is always one organ or system which, owing to heredity or external influences, is the weakest and most likely to break down under the condition of general biologic stress. In some people the heart, in others the nervous system or the gastrointestinal tract, may represent this weakest link. That is why people develop different types of disease under the influence of the same kind of stressors.

Let's extend my earlier definition of stress to "the *nonspecific* response of the body to *any* demand." It can result from tensions within a family, at work, or from the restraining influence of social taboos or traditions. In fact, any situation in life that makes demands upon our adaptive mechanism creates stress. From a psychological point of view, the most stressful experiences are frustration, failure, and humiliation—in other words, distressing events. On the other hand, we derive a great deal of energy and stimulation, considerable force and pleasure, from victories and success. These give us ambition for work, a feeling of youth and of great vitality. As the saying goes, nothing generates success like success, or failure more than failure. We are encouraged and invigorated by our victories, whereas constant defeat eventually deprives us even of the motivation to try.

Although these obvious differences exist between the effects of pleasant and unpleasant experiences, in biologic terms both have a common effect—they cause stress. Even such happy sensations as great joy or ecstasy cause stress, for we must adapt to *any* demands made upon us, whether favorable or unfavorable. *Distress* is much more likely to cause disease than *eustress*, although there is evidence that, in excess, both can be harmful under certain circumstances. There is still no compelling scientific proof of this, but perhaps eustress (for instance, ecstasy) is less likely to be harmful because it rarely equals the intensity and duration of suffering. Besides, it is merely a matter of conditioning that determines whether we perceive a particular experience as pleasant or unpleasant. The event itself is always a stressor causing the same stress. Conditioning can only modify our perception of the event as being either pleasing or displeasing. A thermostat can produce either cold or heat, using the same amount of energy.

There can be no doubt that both eustress and distress have certain measurable biochemical and nervous elements in common. The following example will explain this apparently paradoxical fact: a mother receives a telegram announcing that her only son has been killed at war, and one year later he steps into her living room in perfect health because the news was false. The first experience is extremely painful, the second fills her with joy. Her tremendous grief is significantly different from her great pleasure. If you ask this mother if both experiences were the same, she will obviously answer, "No! Quite the contrary!"

Nevertheless, from the viewpoint of nonspecificity, the demands made upon her body have been essentially the same: a need to adjust to a great change in her life. From a medical and biochemical point of view, the concept of stress implies only an adaptive reaction to change, whether change is for the better or worse.

There are various mechanical instruments—known as "stress meters" or "stress polygraphs"—which measure such physical characteristics as cannot be directly appraised by the layman; however they can register only a few indicators which are usually, but not always, characteristic of stress. Of course, the more signs and symptoms are measured, the more reliable the general picture becomes; yet even the best of these procedures miss the crucial difference between eustress and distress. Moreover, beyond this distinction there lies a still more significant fact: it is our ability to cope with the demands made by the events in our lives, not the quality or intensity of the events, that counts.

What matters is not so much what happens to us but the way we take it.

That is why I recommend that, in everyday normal life, you should judge your own stress level, by easily recognizable signs which tell how you are taking the stress of your life at any particular moment [for some of those signs, see below].

Each of us must learn to recognize *overstress* (hyperstress), when we have exceeded the limits of our adaptability; or *understress* (hypostress), when we suffer from lack of self-realization (physical immobility, boredom, sensory deprivation). Being overwrought is just as bad as being frustrated by the inability to express ourselves and find free outlets for our innate muscular or mental energy.

It is sad to see that many of us today have either lost or abandoned our role as guardians of our own health. We are our own best physician, but we have instead entirely entrusted this responsibility to health-care professionals, hoping that their wonder drugs and sophisticated surgical interventions will save our lives in time of crisis. We must realize that many of our troubles arise only because of neglect and self-abuse. Some diseases, even those caused by stress, are beyond our control, but generally we victimize ourselves through our own bad habits, unhealthy lifestyles, and high-risk working conditions.

Business-oriented careers generally tend to have their own particular type of stressors. Challenges and changes are inherently embedded in every business-oriented career. But they are also great sources of stress. Every businessman has to constantly adapt to changing finan-

Distress signals

A NUMBER of manifestations of stress, particularly of the more dangerous *distress*, are not immediately evident, not constant symptoms that we should monitor throughout life. Depending upon our conditioning and genetic makeup, we all respond differently to general demands. But on the whole, each of us tends to respond with one set of symptoms caused by the malfunction of whatever happens to be the most vulnerable part in our machinery. Learn to heed these signs:

● General irritability, hyperexcitation, or depression associated with unusual aggressiveness or passive indolence, depending upon our constitution.

● Pounding of the heart, an indicator of excess production of adrenaline, often due to stress.

● Dryness of the throat and mouth.

● Impulsive behavior, emotional instability.

● Inability to concentrate, flight of thoughts, and general disorientation.

● Accident proneness. Under great stress (eustress or distress) we are more likely to have accidents. This is one reason why pilots and air traffic controllers must be carefully checked for their stress level.

● Predisposition to fatigue and loss of *joie de vivre*.

● Decrease in sex urge or even impotence.

● "Floating anxiety"—we are afraid, although we do not know exactly what we are afraid of.

● Stuttering and other speech difficulties which are frequently stress-induced.

● Insomnia, which is usually a consequence of being "keyed up."

● Excessive sweating.

● Frequent need to urinate.

● Migraine headaches.

● Loss of or excessive appetite. This shows itself soon in alterations of body weight, namely excessive leanness or obesity. Some people lose their appetite during stress because of gastrointestinal malfunction, whereas others eat excessively, as a kind of diversion, to deviate their attention from the stressor situation.

● Premenstrual tension or missed menstrual cycles. Both are frequently indicators of severe stress in women.

● Pain in the neck or lower back. Pain in the neck or back is usually due to increases in muscular tension that can be objectively measured by physicians with the electromyogram (EMG).

● Trembling, nervous ticks.

● Increased smoking.

● Increased use of prescribed drugs, such as tranquilizers or amphetamines; or increased use of alcohol.

—HANS SELYE, M. D.

cial or economic situations. The bigger the change, the greater is the stress factor.

The many technologic innovations and the social changes in family structure, in the respective rights and duties of men and women, and in the type of work now in demand because of urbanization, present society with unprecedented requirements for constant adaptation. The task of balancing our biologic and psychologic forces is becoming a heavy burden.

That is one reason why my colleagues and I at the University of Montreal are trying to develop accurate stress tests and stress-reducing programs drawn up on the basis of our 40-odd years of research. We hope that our recently created International Institute of Stress will be a center for documentation, research, and dissemination of information about all problems related to stress, which touches virtually every aspect of modern society.

I think that with the information now available through our own work, and that of innumerable scientists throughout the world who have become interested in this topic, the stress concept has been sufficiently clarified to reach the "critical mass" necessary for its continued growth.

My decades of research into the causes and effects of stress have afforded me an opportunity to observe the wide spectrum of this phenomenon. Through my studies I have also developed my own philosophy about stress and the nature of life itself. By way of an admittedly unscientific conclusion, let me share some of these thoughts with you, the Rotarians of the world.

The idea of the *vis medicatrix naturae* (the "healing power of nature") is extremely old. Man has long known that there is a built-in mechanism in all living beings designed to help them right themselves, to restore their integrity when they become wounded or damaged in any way. The principle of the stability of the *milieu intérieur* has been known for centuries, and along with it stress has long been considered as some kind of tension, fatigue, or suffering. But it took many carefully conducted and often tedious experiments to obtain objective, measurable data,

which led to observations—all of which had to be critically evaluated—before we could arrive at the stress concept in its present form, including its implications upon human behavior.

Some of the results of the stress encountered in daily life can be treated with standard medicines, others cannot. In order to meet the social stresses of our time, suggestions have been made for better laws or more severe law enforcement, arms limitations, and so on. To counteract the effects of mental distress, people try out various techniques which they claim eradicate the ill effects or at least help us to cope with them. This is why so many people turn to psychotherapy, meditation techniques, tranquilizers, *ginseng*—the number of stress pills and psychological antistress techniques grows every day. When nothing seems to work, some find an outlet for their energy only in violence, drugs, or alcohol, thus creating still more problems for society. To my mind, the root of the problem lies in the lack of a proper code of motivation that gives our lives a purpose which we can respect.

Viewed from the pinnacle of the eternal general laws governing nature, we are all surprisingly alike. Nature is the fountainhead of all our problems and solutions; the closer we keep to it the better we realize that, despite the apparently enormous divergencies in interpretation and explanation, natural laws have always prevailed and can never become obsolete. The realization of this truth is most likely to convince us that, in a sense, all living beings are closely related. To avoid the stress of conflict, frustration, and hate, to achieve peace and happiness, we should devote more attention to a better understanding of the natural basis of motivation and behavior.

Wouldn't it be better if we could find a way to prevent the stress of life, rather than simply means to help us fight a hostile world? I believe that this should be our highest priority in formulating the policies of governments to meet the stresses of modern civilization, and in devising our personal philosophies of life.

THE CASE FOR PARAPSYCHOLOGY

D. Scott Rogo

D. Scott Rogo is the author of
Parapsychology: A Century of
Inquiry, *and many other books.*
He has been a visiting research
consultant for the Psychical Re-
search Foundation and a visiting
researcher at the Maimonides
Medical Center's division of
parapsychology and psycho-
physics.

I think everyone will agree that parapsychology is rapidly gaining scientific recognition. For example, within recent years symposia on parapsychology have been arranged at the annual meetings of the American Association for the Advancement of Science and the American Psychological Association. Even in 1975, Dr. J. B. Rhine, the father of modern parapsychology and then director of the Foundation for Research on the Nature of Man, was invited to give a keynote address to the APA. Likewise, papers on parapsychology are finding their way into such normally reserved publications as *Nature, Omega: The Journal of Death and Dying,* the *Journal of Communications,* and other voice boxes of more conventional science.

Parapsychology, however, has always had its critics. Just as parapsychology has been given more and more attention by the news media, so have the voices of the debunkers. These critics, after one hundred years of attacking parapsychology, are still complaining that the field has not proved itself a valid study, is a slipshod hybrid science at best (and a pseudo-science at worst), and is engaged in a fruitless quest to prove the existence of fictitious faculties in man. Publications such as *New Scientist* and *The Humanist,* as well as such columnists as Martin Gardner of *Scientific American,* have on several recent occasions voiced strong scientific objections to parapsychology.

Just what are these objections? I think it is quite interesting that, although the study of psychic phenomena is rapidly developing as a science, the basic criticisms that have been leveled against parapsychology over the years have *not* changed. For instance, in 1971 Champe Ransom, a research associate working in the division of parapsychology at the University of Virginia, made an up-to-date survey of the main contemporary criticisms against parapsychology. Writing in the July issue of the *Journal of the American Society for Psychical Research,* Ransom pointed out that these criticisms could be grouped into nine major objections: that the results procured by parapsychologists are not repeatable; that the possibility of fraud contaminates many allegedly conclusive experiments; that parapsychologists use improper mathematical methods when analyzing their data; that ESP and PK are a priori impossible; that parapsychologists misinterpret their evidence; that the existence of ESP has no relevance to organized science; and that parapsychologists use inadequate experimental designs; disagree on the quality of the evidence; and are biased in favor of the existence of psi.

It is interesting that in 1955 the Ciba Foundation held a symposium on parapsychology during which one of the field's most eminent scholors, J. Fraser Nicol, presented a similar paper on the nature of criticism against parapsychology. His list, although more general than Ransom's, covered virtually the same points.

So, it is fair to state that, while parapsychology has become increasingly sophisticated over the past two decades, its critics have not! Anyone with any scientific objectivity can see that many of these objections are not logical criticisms, but emotional charges or value judgments. In this category I would place the criticisms that parapsychologists are biased in favor of the existence of psi, that psi is irrelevant to science, and that psi is a priori impossible. Other often-heard criticisms of parapsychology have been adequately answered time and time again over the past years. It is always a wonder why these same criticisms are raised by the more enlightened skeptics of today. In this class I would place the argument that parapsychologists rely on improper methods of mathematical analysis. As far back as 1937, the American Institute of Mathematical Statistics certified that the statistics used in parapsychology were totally valid. Finally, one might point out that the methodology and types of analysis used in parapsychology were not invented by parapsychologists, as some critics seem to think. They were, instead, borrowed from experimental psychology. Any critic who believes that parapsychologists use faulty methods of experimentation and analysis of their data is thereby indicting all of experimental psychology as well. If parapsychology falls on these counts,

This article first appeared in *THE HUMANIST* November/December 1977 and is reprinted by permission.

all experimental science falls with it.

In the final run, there are only two really valid criticisms that can be leveled at parapsychology—either that fraud can account for the results parapsychologists are achieving in their laboratories or that they are misinterpreting what their data are telling them.

Frankly, neither of these criticisms can account for the type of successes being reported from several parapsychology laboratories across the country today. The establishment of sophisticated parapsychology laboratories, such as at Maimonides Medical Center in Brooklyn and at the American Society for Psychical Research in New York, have given research workers both the technology and the personnel to guard against faulty experimental procedures and fraud. Although experimenter fraud has been uncovered from time to time in parapsychology, the incidence rate in this field is no greater than what is found in any other science.

With all this in mind, let's take a look at what I call a "good" ESP experiment. To me a good experiment is one that is designed to safeguard against fraud and experimental error and uses a clear-cut method of analysis to see whether or not ESP actually occurred during the tests. The experiment that I am about to describe was run at the Maimonides Medical Center's division of parapsychology and psychophysics in 1973 by Charles Honorton, director of the lab, with his assistant, Sharon Harper. Thirty subjects were used, and the experiment was designed to see whether a certain sensory-isolation setting, called the "Ganzfeld," helps subjects gain access to ESP impressions. Note closely how the experimenter took several precautions to keep the subjects and themselves from cheating or normally learning anything about the ESP targets used for the trials.

Each subject was first placed in a soundproof sensory-isolation booth. Halved Ping-Pong balls were placed over his eyes and he was directed to stare into a red light set in front of him. In this position, all the subject could see was a diffused red field no matter where he turned his eyes. (This is the "Ganzfeld" setting, which literally means "homogeneous field.") Next, earphones were placed over his ears so that he could hear nothing but the monotonous sounds of ocean waves. The subject was instructed to describe orally over an intercom all the thoughts and mental images he experienced during the duration of the test, which lasted thirty-five minutes. While told that sometime during the test an ESP message would be sent to him, the subject was instructed not to anticipate the message but merely to give himself a mental suggestion that the message would appear in his mind at the proper time.

After the subject was secured in the booth, the ESP agent (or sender, if you prefer) was placed in another room down the hall and was instructed to close the door and then randomly select a packet of four thematically different View-Master reels. (There were several packets from which the selection was made.) This agent was allowed no contact with the experimenter who was actually monitoring the test and writing down what the subject was reporting from the booth. The agent merely took the top reel from the selected packet and, at a randomly determined time, looked at it while trying to "send" the pictures to the subject locked in the booth. After five minutes of "sending," the agent stopped and then blindly shuffled the reel back into the packet with the other three. At the end of the test, the agent was allowed only to hand the

target packet to the experimenter without speaking to him, and he then left the experimental area completely for the remainder of the session. This transaction took place before the subject was released from the booth. At this point, the experimenter entered the booth and reviewed the transcript of the session with the subject to remind him of what he had reported over the last thirty-five minutes. He was then let out of the booth and was directed to look at all four of the packet reels and to choose which one he felt was "sent" to him during the test and which best matched what he "saw" while in the Ganzfeld. Only after the subject had made and recorded his choice was the agent summoned and asked to reveal which reel had, in fact, been the target.

This experiment has built-in controls. First of all, a statistical appraisal can be made of the results. If ESP does not exist then obviously, of the thirty subjects tested, only 25 percent of them should correctly guess what reel was actually sent. This statistical appraisal of the experimental results will appeal to those skeptics who demand mathematical proof of ESP. However, this experiment can also appeal to the critic who argues that numbers and statistics mean nothing and who demands more striking evidence of ESP. To appease these skeptics, one can look over the target pictures and compare them to what the subjects reported during the test. If ESP exists, then we should expect some striking descriptions of the targets in the subjects' reports. Note, too, that if fraud were committed during the judging procedure, this still could not explain the ability of the subject to describe the target while securely locked in the booth.

This particular experiment, which Honorton and Harper reported in the April, 1974 issue of the *Journal of the American Society for Psychical Research,* was successful on both counts. Instead of the 25 percent first choices expected by chance, 43.3 percent of the subjects correctly identified which of the four reels was the target for the test. This result is statistically significant ($P = .017$, one tailed). On the other side of the coin, several of the subjects did give remarkable

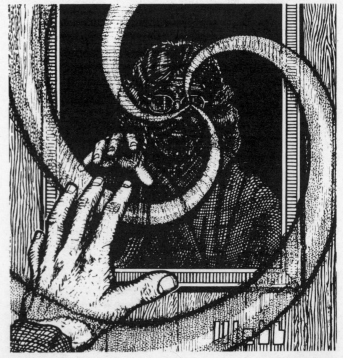

Drawing by Greg Webb

ESP-mediated descriptions of the target pictures during the actual sessions. One subject, whose target was entitled "Birds of the World," reported, "Sense a large hawk's head in front of me, a profile. The sense of sleek feathers. Now it turns its head and flies away." Another subject, whose target was "U.S. Air Force Academy," saw "an airplane flying over the clouds . . . planes passing overhead . . . Six stripes on an army uniform." Several other examples could be cited as well.

I have described this experiment in depth, not because it is a "perfect," foolproof, or conclusive experiment, but because it illustrates the care with which many parapsychology experiments are designed, conducted, and evaluated. I doubt if very many psychology experiments are run so cautiously. Experiments such as these certainly counter the silly notion that parapsychologists are a bunch of fanatics running slipshod guessing games with no regard for correct controls and experimental precautions. This experiment also counters the myth that no tightly controlled ESP test has ever been successful. Anyone who makes such a claim just hasn't kept up with parapsychology over the last twenty years.

Also, one might ask, "If ESP doesn't exist, why is it that the Ganzfeld has been successfully replicated by several other parapsychologists working independently and in different laboratories?" To date, several teams of researchers have replicated Honorton's and Harper's procedures and have procured remarkably similar results. The most notable of these have been the husband-wife parapsychology team of Drs. William and Lendell Braud, of Texas, who have had considerable success in using the Ganzfeld to help subjects gain access to ESP impressions. (See their report, "Free-Response GESP Performance During an Experimental Hypnagogic State Induced by Visual and Acoustic Ganzfeld Techniques: A Replication and Extension," which appeared in the April 1975 issues of the *Journal of the American Society for Psychical Research*.)

While I am on the subject of replication, I might as well correct another myth about parapsychology; namely, that the findings of specific ESP and PK experiments are rarely replicated. This is hardly the case. A critical study of this very problem was made by Charles Honorton in 1975. Speaking at the 1975 convention of the Parapsychological Association, which was held on the campus of the University of California at Santa Barbara, he pointed out that 43 percent of the reports being presented at that conference were successful replications of earlier experiments. In contrast, Honorton pointed out that surveys made of the experimental reports issued in the publications of the American Psychological Association have revealed that fewer than one percent were replication attempts. In other words, while parapsychologists diligently try to verify their own findings, and are seemingly rather successful at it, experimental psychologists don't even bother!

However, as a parapsychologist myself, there is one aspect of ESP and PK research that I find even more convincing than the evidence that has been obtained from so-called conclusive experiments. This is the fact that many researchers, working totally independently and in different laboratories, and even different countries, have often discovered the same trends and patterns in their data. In other words, several independent parapsychologists have, now and then, made the exact same discoveries about ESP. For example, when J. B. Rhine began his ESP testing at Duke University in the 1930s, he discovered that his gifted subjects uniformly tended to score better at the beginning of the test than toward the end. He called this pattern the "decline effect." However, Rhine was not the first to discover this effect. Back in 1925-26, Dr. George Estabrooks of Harvard University had made the same discovery while testing college students for ESP; and at about the same time, Ina Jephson discovered "decline effects" in her ESP tests in England.

Of course, critics of parapsychology have a ready-made explanation for these decline effects. They usually claim that the experimenters may have elicited some initial but spurious high scoring on their ESP card tests that they mistook to be genuine ESP, but then merely discontinued the tests when their subjects' scores evened out and fell down to chance. However, these decline effects have appeared in both ESP *and* PK tests in which the number of trials was determined *in advance* of the actual experiments.

How does the ESP critic explain away the fact that several independent workers have consistently found that certain personality factors correlate significantly with ESP? If ESP doesn't exist, it is hard to figure out why certain personality types always seem to do well on ESP tests. Take what is called the "sheep-goat effect," for instance. In 1958, Dr. Gertrude Schmeidler, a psychologist at the City College of the City University of New York, published a startling book (coauthored with R. A. McConnell) entitled *ESP and Personality Patterns*. In this report, Dr. Schmeidler recounted the results of ESP tests that she had carried out with hundreds of subjects whom she had classified as either believers in ESP (sheep) or disbelievers (goats). Schmeidler had tested her subjects with standard ESP cards and had run several series of subjects. In almost every case, she found that the sheep, as a group, scored slightly above chance, while the goats scored slightly below. (That is, the goats apparently used ESP unconsciously to block out knowledge of the target and consistently guessed incorrectly and below mean chance expectation.) The difference between the two subject populations was often statistically significant. Schmeidler was able to replicate her findings several times. But that isn't the end of the story by any means.

Let us suppose that ESP does not exist. How then can we account for this difference between the ESP scores of the sheep and the goats? Since all the subjects were tested with the same procedure, the results could not be an artifact arising from the way the test was administered. So, either the results were just a fluke, or some one fiddled with the statistics. The only way to answer these possibilities would be through replication. If ESP does not exist, one would hardly expect that independent researchers would also find their sheep subjects consistently outscoring the goats to a statistically significant degree. You would, instead, expect a random assortment of outcomes. For example, again assuming that ESP does not exist or that belief has nothing to do with the ability of a person to use it, what would happen if ten researchers ran ten sheep-goat tests? The answer is obvious. Three or so of them might find their sheep outscoring the goats (but probably not to a significant degree); another three or four would probably find their goats outscoring the sheep; and the results of the other tests would probably be completely ambiguous. Right? (This argument is addressed to those critics who believe that the statistically significant results procured in so many ESP tests are the result of chance, fluke scoring. If statistically significant ESP scores are only a result of such flukes, one would not expect a particular correlation between ESP and some variable to be widely replicated.)

Well, this just isn't what we find at all. In 1971, Dr. John Palmer, then a research associate at the division of parapsychology at the University of Virginia, made a critical examination of all published sheep-goat experiments. This survey, which was published in the October 1971 issue of the *Journal of the American Society for Psychical Research*, included a critical analysis of seventeen series of tests carried out by twelve different experimenters (or experimenter teams) between 1958 and 1968. Of these tests, six series significantly upheld the sheep-goat effect. However, although in several experiments the sheep did not outscore the goats to a statistically significant degree, *in no experiment published to date have goats ever outscored sheep to a significant degree*. In other words, there has never been a significant reversal of the sheep-goat effect, while there have been several successful replications of it. If ESP does not exist, one certainly would not expect this outcome. One would expect the goats to outscore the sheep just as often as the sheep beat the goats. Therefore, I would ask the skeptic, why do believers so consistently outscore nonbelievers on ESP tests?

There are many other findings about the nature of ESP that have also been broadly replicated by several independent researchers. For instance, over the years many ESP researchers have found that extroverts consistently score more positively on ESP tests than introverts, and that well-adjusted subjects score more positively than neurotic subjects, and so on. One could diagram quite a list of such consistent findings.

Frankly, when so many independent researchers in so many different cities, states, and even countries come up with identical findings about ESP and PK, it demonstrates to me that we really are studying a genuine, albeit capricious, human faculty. One can certainly pick holes in any one parapsychology experiment. But one can just as easily do the same to any psychology, biology, or chemistry experiment. However, one cannot so easily explain why independent researchers seem to be making the same discoveries about ESP while working totally independently of each other.

With results such as these at hand, how should the psychologist respond to the critic? I think the answer to this question will surprise many skeptics.

The notion that parapsychologists are deaf to the voices of their critics is another unfounded myth. In fact, parapsychologists have learned many valuable lessons by listening closely to the charges of the debunkers. Over the years, parapsychologists have continually sought to tighten their methodology in order to strengthen the evidence for ESP and PK. No one, I assure you, is more aware of the controversial and disputable nature of ESP and PK than the parapsychologist himself. And over the years, too, some of the more enterprising of them have devised ingenious ways of testing for psi by using methods and apparatus that make the possibility of fraud, malobservation, and recording error virtually fail-safe. Some researchers, knowing human error all too well, are now conducting totally automated ESP and PK tests. By having machines choose the ESP or PK target, record the subject's guess, and score the results, human error has been reduced to a minimum in some of the newer research coming out of parapsychology laboratories across the country. Some recent experiments of Dr. Helmut Schmidt typify this supercautious and highly ingenious approach to parapsychology.

Drawing by Greg Webb

Dr. Schmidt, formerly a physicist at the Boeing Research Laboratories in Seattle, was one of the first parapsychologists to appreciate the importance of automated ESP and PK experiments. For one of his tests, Schmidt used a specially constructed apparatus: a random generator run by a piece of strontium-90. As is well known, the decay of a radioactive particle is a totally random process. No one can predict when an electron will shoot off from the nucleus of a particular atom. Schmidt's machine also contains a high-speed oscillator that switches rapidly to any one of four possible positions. When the machine is activated, it will stop in any one of the positions as soon as the next electron is emitted by the strontium-90 and is registered by a Geiger-Muller tube in the apparatus. The subject for the ESP (in this case precognition) test sits before a panel of four lights that correspond to the four positions. He is instructed to guess which light will be illuminated by the next decaying electron. He makes his choice by pushing a button, and the machine stops oscillating as soon as the *next* electron is registered by the Geiger-Muller tube. The subject's guess and the actual target are automatically recorded. Also, the subject receives immediate feedback about the correctness of his guess by watching which light, in fact, turns on. Obviously, by chance, a subject should guess correctly only 25 percent of the time.

In his first tests, Schmidt ran across a few subjects who were able to score far above the chance expectation. This would indicate that these subjects were actually precognizing either the rate of the radioactive decay or which light would illuminate next. One of his subjects made 7600 trials on the machine and made 165 more hits than would be expected by chance. The odds of this happening by chance are about 100,000 to 1. Schmidt then worked with three additional gifted subjects. Their combined scores were so high that their results would only occur once in 500,000,000 experiments. After the experiment, Schmidt ran a control series on the machine by pushing the guess buttons at random. The results were only at chance level, so we can reasonably assume that the machine was not malfunctioning during the experiment.

Later, Schmidt adapted his generator for PK testing. In these experiments, the subject would try to *make* the apparatus stop in a certain position or positions. These experiments were successful as well. (For further information, the reader might wish to consult Schmidt's original report, "Precognition of a Quantum Process," which was published in the *Journal of Parapsychology* in 1969.)

Actually, parapsychologists have a certain attraction for precognition experiments, since by their very nature they obviate certain methodological pitfalls that can ruin a telepathy or clairvoyance experiment. For instance, there is no possibility in a precognition experiment that the experimenter might willfully or inadvertently cue the subject about the ESP target, since this target is not chosen until after the test is over.

One interesting approach to precognition, which illustrates the rigorous standards of testing and control parapsychologists employ in their work, was undertaken at the Maimonides dream laboratory (now the Division of Parapsychology and Psychophysics) in 1970 with a single subject. This subject, Malcolm Bessent, was a young British psychic who had chalked up quite a history of apparently making successful predictions. Here is how the test was run.

Bessent slept in the dream lab for sixteen nights. On every other night he was instructed to dream about an experience he would have the next day. Bessent's sleep was EEG monitored, and he was awakened by a lab technician when his brain waves and rapid eye-movement indicated that he was dreaming. At that time, he would describe his dream to the technician who made a record of it. This technician, by the way, was not a Maimonides staff member, but a helper who was especially brought into the lab for the purpose of the test and was deliberately kept in the dark as to the nature of the experiment. Twelve hours after Bessent's dream had been recorded and deposited with a person who transcribed it, an experimenter, totally unaware of what Bessent had reported about his night's dreams—randomly selected a target from a pool of ten packets. These packets contained slides on such themes as "police," "birds," "saints," and so on. They also contained tapes of appropriate accompanying musical selections. Looking at the slides while listening to the music was the "experience" Bessent was supposed to precognize.

Just as with the Ganzfeld test, this experiment can be evaluated two ways. First, one can look for obvious correspondences between Bessent's dreams and the themes of the target slides chosen for that particular night. Second, one can also evaluate the results of the test statistically.

If one is impressed by strong qualitative evidence for ESP, the results of this experiment, which were published in the July 1972 issue of the *Journal of the American Society for Psychical Research*, should fill the bill. For example, the target packet for one test was entitled "police." The night before this packet was chosen, Bessent dreamed; "It's like getting the armed guard or something, because if they arrive half an hour later and contribute nothing except silence and a kind of menacing silence . . . I forget what you call them in the States, kind of young policemen, but a particular kind to do with campus disorders . . . I wish I could remember the name—National Guard, perhaps . . . " Bessent also dreamed about people in uniform, confrontations between students and armed guards, a police state, and so on.

For another test, "birds" was the chosen target theme. The night before, Bessent dreamed about a parapsychologist well known for his psychological research on birds. Bessent told the experimenters of his dream: "I remember seeing various different kinds of doves. Ringtailed doves, ordinary doves, Canadian geese. There were many, many different kinds of varieties." Bessent himself on this occasion even realized that the target, when chosen the next day, would deal with birds.

The transcripts of all the sessions, along with the target packets, were also given to three independent and blind judges. They took each target and matched it against all of the transcripts, rating each on a 100-point scale of similarity. Naturally, if ESP took place during this experiment, one would expect the judges to give a transcript a high score when matching it with the night for which it was meant, and a low score when matching it against the other nights. And this is exactly what the judges did do to a statistically significant degree.

Unfortunately, I do not have the space to describe more examples of the many types of sophisticated and well-thought-out experiments that are reported yearly by parapsychologists in the United States, England, Germany, and virtually every other country in the civilized world. However, the Ganzfeld tests, Schmidt's experiments, and the Bessent dream studies all illustrate the care and planning that go into a typical parapsychology experiment. While using very different methodologies, all these experiments were run in such a way as to safeguard against everything from fraud to recording error. As I said earlier, parapsychologists have learned well from their critics.

I hope that I have made it clear in this presentation that parapsychologists do not spend their time listening to Jeane Dixon's questionable prophecies, gawking at Uri Geller as he bends keys, or casting horoscopes. Parapsychology is a descriptive science in that it collects, analyzes, and seeks to verify the psychic experiences of people like you and me by using standards of evidence that would apply in a court of law. And parapsychology is an experimental science in that it seeks to test assumptions and theories about ESP and PK in the laboratory. To do so, as I said before, it has adopted procedures borrowed basically from experimental psychology. As a science, parapsychology has nothing to apologize for. In fact it represents the Western scientific ethic at its best.

Dr. D. J. West, a British psychiatrist who left parapsychology some years ago in order to engage in more mainline behavioral research, summed up the situation very well in 1970 when he addressed an international parapsychology conference in St. Paul de Vence, France, sponsored by the Parapsychology Foundation. He stated: "Having had my first taste of research in the field of parapsychology, and then gone on to work in other branches of behavioral research, I am continually struck by the contrast in standards. Research workers in conventional fields of social and psychological inquiry are content with much lower standards. They are prepared to base conclusions upon observations known to be subject to a certain amount of bias and inaccuracy, and they are prepared to accept statistical evidence that falls short of certainty. If they tried to emulate the perfectionism advocated by some parapsychologists, the quality of their investigations might be improved."

I hope every reader of this magazine will ponder these words deeply.

A SKEPTIC'S VIEW OF PARAPSYCHOLOGY

Martin Gardner

Martin Gardner writes regularly for the Scientific American *and is the author of a new book,* The Incredible Dr. Natrix *(Scribner's). He is a member of the executive council of the Committee for the Scientific Investigation of Claims of the Paranormal.*

D. Scott Rogo, struggling to depict parapsychology as a science rapidly gaining respectability, has adopted a familiar tactic. He says nothing at all about the wild, preposterous claims now being made by leading workers in the field. Instead, he describes a few conservative experiments conducted by Charles Honorton and Helmut Schmidt. "I hope I have made it clear," he concludes, "that parapsychologists do not spend their time . . . gawking at Uri Geller."

There is no way a skeptic can comment meaningfully on the Honorton and Schmidt experiments, because there is no way, now that the tests are completed, to know exactly what controls were actually in force. An accurate evaluation, by a skeptical psychologist, would require months of intensive study, analyzing the raw data still available, interviewing all the participants, and so on. No top psychologist has time for such a task unless he is substantially funded; even then, he might not consider it worthwhile. In the few cases where this has been done—C. E. M. Hansel's investigation of the classic Pearce-Pratt tests, for instance—large loopholes in controls have come to light. Instead of acknowledging the loopholes, parapsychologists have reacted with enormous indignation.

A more promising approach is to try to replicate major experiments. Unfortunately, whenever skeptics do this and get negative results, parapsychologists invoke their favorite Catch 22, which is that skepticism inhibits psi. You will look in vain through the writings of psi journalists like Rogo for references to these replication failures. There have been, for example, several important failures to repeat the Maimonides dream experiments (see Adrian Parker's book, *States of Mind*). In some cases, negative results were obtained by the original researchers when they collaborated with skeptical outsiders.

R eaders of *The Humanist* may be interested in a few facts about Honorton and Schmidt that Rogo does not mention because they conflict with his thesis that modern parapsychology is uncontaminated by Geller-gawking. A few years ago, Honorton announced that he had discovered a young lady, Felicia Parise, who was capable of sliding a plastic pill-bottle across a kitchen counter by psychokinesis. This great event was witnessed only by Honorton and an amateur photographer, Norman Moses, who caught the event on film.

The first thing that occurred to the magician James Randi, when he saw the film, was that a superfine nylon thread was stretched, horizontally, a few inches above the formica counter. A small and empty pill-bottle was standing upright. As Felicia's long-nailed fingers, on either side of the bottle, crept forward, it would have been a simple matter for her to push against the thread. Fine nylon thread is absolutely invisible, even at close range, but it is easily broken and tends to be elastic. When Randi duplicated the test, he found that the nylon thread stretched when it pressed against the bottle, causing the bottle to move forward in a jerky manner, exactly as seen on the film made by Moses. Last year, for a BBC television show in London, Randi replicated the feat, using a stronger thread and a heavy wineglass.

It does not follow, of course, that because Felicia *could* have used nylon thread that she did, in fact, use it. It does follow that, because Honorton was not sufficiently informed about magic to evaluate what happened, his report of the event cannot be taken seriously. Nevertheless, he stands resolutely by his belief that he witnessed a paranormal feat. "I examined the counter," he told a *National Enquirer* reporter (see the December 30, 1975, issue, with its front-page headline: "First American to Move Objects with Her Mind"). "I virtually took it apart to ensure there was no mechanical aid she could have used to move the bottle. But I found none. I even checked the countertop to see if it sloped. I found there was a slight slope—but the bottle had actually moved uphill!"

Honorton was also present during tests of Felicia at Rhine's laboratory in 1972, when she moved a compass needle by PK. (See Honorton's "Apparent Psychokinesis on Static Objects by a 'Gifted' Subject," in *Research in Parapsychology, 1973*, edited by W. G. Roll and others.) It is amusing that Honorton, who is highly skeptical of Uri Geller's PK ability, has spent considerable time Felicia-gawking, and defending her powers in lectures and articles. Ms. Parise, by the way, stopped demonstrating her psi abilities several years ago and is no longer available for research. This is another fait accompli that no parapsychologist can replicate when a knowledgeable magician is present.

This article first appeared in *THE HUMANIST* November/December 1977 and is reprinted by permission.

Let's take a quick look at Schmidt. You will never learn from Rogo that Schmidt has long been a Geller-gawker. "Another source of particularly strong PK effects may be available in a few highly selected subjects . . ." Schmidt wrote in Edgar Mitchell's *Psychic Exploration*. "One such person is Uri Geller. . . . Geller can well match the feats of the spectacular performers studied by earlier workers in the field. Critical researchers . . . have seen Geller bend heavy metal objects 'mentally,' just by touching them slightly or even without any touch."

In 1970, Schmidt reported one of the great breakthroughs in modern parapsychology. Cockroaches, he announced, probably have the PK ability to cause a randomizer to turn on a device and give themselves electric shocks more often than chance allows. However, since Schmidt personally dislikes cockroaches, he admits that his experiment was inconclusive. It could have been his *own mind* that influenced the randomizer.

Walter J. Levy, former director of J. B. Rhine's famed laboratory, found that live fertilized chicken-eggs (in contrast to hardboiled eggs) also could influence a randomizer. In this case the randomizer controlled a heat source. "Psi-hitter" eggs kept the heat on longer than chance dictated, while "psi-loser" eggs influenced the randomizer the other way. When the two kinds of eggs were put together in the same box, their PK powers canceled out, and Levy got chance results. Since Levy resigned his post after being caught faking his records, parapsychologists have stopped citing his egg papers as major references. Cockroaches, however, are still suspected of being psychic.

Rogo's claim that parapsychologists do not waste time on Geller is simply not true. Harold Puthoff and Russell Targ spent vast amounts of time Geller-gawking, and finally declared Geller to be a genuine clairvoyant. Thelma Moss is another Gellerite who continually praises Uri. Gertrude Schmeidler is on record with similar remarks, not to mention her well-known tests of the PK powers of Uri's chief rival, Ingo Swann.

We all know about Andrija Puharich's Geller-gawking—he wrote an entire book about it. His next book will report on his research with a group of what he calls "Geller children." One of them, Puharich declared last May at a "Towards a Physics of Consciousness" symposium, held at the Harvard Science Center, succeeded in materializing a tree. Six of the Geller children, he said, were teleported to his home in Ossining, New York, from as far away as Switzerland. Puharich was followed by E. Harris Walker, a physicist who explains Geller's PK powers by a theory of his own involving quantum mechanics. John Taylor, the British paraphysicist, thinks the "Geller effect" is electromagnetic. Puharich attributes it to tachyons, conjectured particles that go faster than light. But the most popular theory at the moment is Walker's quantum theoretical explanation.

Rhine's associate, William Cox, is one of the loudest of all Geller-gawker squawkers. He has written about the "rigidly controlled" conditions under which Uri caused Cox's watch to start running after Cox had stopped the balance wheel with a tinfoil wedge and about how Uri made his key curl "like a burning match." I exchanged several long letters with Cox about the watch bit. Only Cox was present, and he allowed Uri to handle the watch briefly before it started running. Could Uri, under cover of that misdirection for which he is so famous, have opened the case with a thumbnail and pushed the tinfoil? No way, says Cox. Although I freely confessed that

Uri "might" have accomplished this miracle by psi power (though I gave it a low probability), I was never able to extract from Cox the comparable admission that Uri, to *any* degree of probability, could have fooled him with a trick.

Does Rogo, I wonder, consider Edgar Mitchell a "parapsychologist"? Mitchell has often described how Uri materialized part of a long-lost tiepin in a mouthful of ice cream. Indeed, one is hard put to think of many parapsychologists who have *not* been Geller-gawkers. I must add that in recent months their silence about Uri has become deafening as it becomes obvious that Uri has no more psi ability than such performers as Charles Hoy, Kreskin, Dean Kraft, Nina Kulagina, and Matthew Manning.

Rogo ends his article by comparing the reputed iron controls of modern parapsychology with the weaker controls of other sciences. Here he missed an all-essential point. Extraordinary controls are not demanded in experiments that demonstrate ordinary results. If, for example, a psychologist seeks to determine whether gerbils can roll Ping-Pong balls with their noses, unusual controls are not required. Gerbils don't cheat. But if someone says he or she can move a plastic pill-bottle with PK power, that is an extraordinary claim that calls for extraordinary precautions. In view of the long, hilarious history of fraud and gullibility in psi research, it demands at the very least the participation of the only expert on this kind of deception—a knowledgeable magician.

It is Rogo's inability to distinguish between these two kinds of investigations, with their different demands for controls, that has made him such a naive and unreliable reporter of the psi scene. Although he shares Honorton's low opinion of Geller, he has spent many years gawking at haunted houses. In his book *An Experience of Phantoms* (1974), Rogo argues that every person has an etheric double that not only survives death but can project itself as a phantom while the person is still of this world. "Apparitions, as no other phenomenon," he writes, "bring to the fore that man is a spiritual being."

In a 1970 article in *Psychic*, "Photography by the Mind," Rogo praises the laboratory controls of Jule Eisenbud, the psychoanalyst who demonstrated Ted Serios's ability to project thought-pictures onto Polaroid film. "Ted Serios," writes Rogo, "does represent the first case of psychic photography to confront parapsychologists in several years." Rogo regrets that Serios's ability "appears to have deteriorated," but he carefully avoids any mention of the famous *Popular Photography* exposé (October 1967) on how easily Ted could have cheated with a small optical device that he palmed in and out of his "gismo." Almost everybody now (except Rogo and Dr. Eisenbud) believes that Ted stopped doing thought-pictures only because a group of three magicians caught on to the simple method he was using, and poor Ted has been unable since to think of any better method.

In a more recent article in *New Realities* (the new name of *Psychic* magazine), Rogo discusses reports of Madonna statues that bleed in their palms or weep human tears. Does Rogo have any doubt about the reality of this paranormal phenomena? No. His only problem is deciding whether the blood and tears are Christian miracles or a form of poltergeist.

And in the latest issue of *Fate*—but I must spare the reader further disclosures about Rogo's adolescent enthusiasms. His phantom-gawking is, I submit, closer to the preoccupations of today's leading parapsychologists than the few sanitized, unspectacular, and highly dubious experiments that he cites in his article.

Development

Human development proceeds through a remarkable set of transformations that contour and color each inividual's personality. One goes from newborn, to infant, to toddler; from adolescent to adult; from one stage of cognitive and psychosexual development to another. The articles in this section deal with the dynamics of personal development.

One of the most intriguing subjects in developmental psychology involves the effect of the complex and subtle interplay of genetic and environmental factors on the developing organism. "Babies Can Communicate at Birth" discusses the view that babies are born with a considerable degree of intellectual ability, including that of rudimentary speech. "Learning the Mother Tongue" examines closely the process of language acquisition, and the critical role played by the mother in that process.

There are many obvious environmental pressures and influences that act on us throughout our lives. "Television and the Young Viewer" explores a subject that concerns parents as well as child development professionals. The author reports on research into the effects of TV violence, sex, and advertising on the young child's cognitive and social development.

Schools and prisons play a considerable role in shaping the behavior of large portions of our society. "Moral Thinking: Can It Be Taught" describes efforts under the leadership of Lawrence Kohlberg to use these institutions to effectively develop the conscious processes of moral reasoning.

Probably the most important environmental factor in early personal development is the home—or, more specifically, the care one receives there. More attention has been paid to the mother's role, but "The Father of the Child" spotlights the expanding role of fathers in the care and development of their young children. Research indicates that both caretakers provide important early experiences for their children, each in different ways. "Making It to Maturity" adds another dimension to this subject, citing a long-term study to determine the effects of various methods of parenting on the later development of social and moral maturity.

Making it to adulthood does not signal the end of personal development. In fact, the popular media have joined with some psychologists to outline crisis stages of adulthood much as child development theorists have demarcated childhood. Questioning this theory of life crises, "Must Everything Be a Midlife Crisis?" suggests that coping with the various problems and challenges of adulthood actually has little to do with one's chronological age.

Further, in "Old Is Not a Four-Letter Word," Alan Anderson cites evidence that chronological age indeed has little to do with aging—or at least less than is popularly supposed. This article examines and rejects many commonly held myths about the process and effects of aging.

The science of gerontology includes not only the study of aging, but also of prolonging healthy life. The latter concern has spawned some controversial movements, such as cryobiology, transplantation, regeneration, and others, that seek to dramatically prolong life. "Some of Us May Never Die" discusses the biology and philosophy involved in these processes.

A review of this section will acquaint you with the ongoing research into the roles of genetic and environmental factors in shaping individual development from conception to death. Some of these articles also provide an overview of the more controversial theories about human development that have only begun to be examined.

Looking Ahead: Challenge Questions

What are some of the qualities of effective parenting?

What impact would a national daycare system have on our society?

What aspects of development hold true for every age group?

What are some of the social and economic implications of scientific attempts to prolong life indefinitely?

'Babies Can Communicate at Birth'

Patrick Young

If they still burned heretics, Colwyn Trevarthen might find himself put to the torch by some irate psychologists. Trevarthen, you see, argues that babies are born far smarter than psychologists have given them credit for—that infants come into the world with a good deal of innate intelligence, including an embryonic form of speech.

"The ability of babies to communicate, using speech and gestures, is present at birth," he says. "There is a compulsion at birth to communicate." And that idea runs counter to the long-cherished notion that infants require months of tutoring before they can communicate at all with adults.

Trevarthen, a New Zealand-born biologist with an intense interest in the infant brain, grounds his theory on experiments he began at Harvard University in 1967 and resumed more recently at the University of Edinburgh in Scotland. His technique is simple; his results are intriguing; his extrapolations from his research are controversial. For example:

"I think culture and technology are innate in origin. There is no doubt man's mastery of the world is in his ability to co-operate and share knowledge. And this is not a discovery of man; it's part of his nature."

'It Didn't Make Sense'

Trevarthen began his studies confronted by two somewhat conflicting views of the brain, the biological and the psychological. The brain is an elaborate, if incomplete, structure at birth, containing all the nerve cells it will have throughout life. Over decades these cells mature and make interconnections in ways still not fathomed.

For decades psychologists emphasized the role of experience in intellectual development. They tended to view the brain as plastic and impressionable, and the development of language and communication as shaped almost exclusively by the baby's environment and experiences.

Granting the brain is far from fully developed at birth, Trevarthen was puzzled by the general view of psychologists in 1967 that a newborn's brain was almost totally incapable of perceiving and understanding the world around it and that any communication between baby and adults required months to develop.

"It didn't make sense from a biological point of view," he explained during a visit at the California Institute of Technology here. "Darwin's notion of human intelligence was that the fundamental features were innate and the human mind already endowed with complex processes."

'Talk' at 2 Months

Trevarthen favored a view—now winning larger acceptance—that much human behavior is innate and exists in embryonic form at birth. He set out to test his idea, to see if early signs of communication could be detected in infants. The result: "Newborn human beings show, in rudimentary form, many of the remarkable behaviors of adult intelligence, including a form of speech as a means of communication."

Trevarthen's procedure is to take hours and hours of movies of a baby and its mother. The child sits in an infant seat with its arms and legs free to move. The mother sits nearby so she can touch and talk to her baby. She is given no instructions except to chat with the child, a very natural thing for her to do. A mirror allows the camera to record the facial expressions of both.

Later the film is analyzed, often frame by frame, to see how the baby reacted. Trevarthen's aim is not to see how well an infant solves various problems at various ages—a standard test among psychologists—but rather to see how a child behaves and develops on its own.

"The films tell us what the baby chooses to do," Trevarthen says. He and his colleagues have now studied more than 200 children, many of them at weekly sessions throughout the first year of the child's life.

At Harvard, Trevarthen, Martin Richards, and Berry Brazelton quickly found that at 2 months infants know the difference between people and objects and that they make deliberate attempts to converse with their mothers and other adults. "This was a big discovery," Trevarthen says, noting that such behavior wasn't thought to occur until months later. "It meant that 2-month-old babies treated people as worth talking to. We found a 2-month-old is already equipped with the outline of speech and gestures."

Patterns of 'Prespeech'

Trevarthen has greatly expanded his studies of infant speech and gestures since joining the Edinburgh faculty in 1971. "Our studies show complex, conversationlike exchanges between mothers and infants when the latter are only a few weeks old," he says.

All the gooing, cooing, and mouthing movements infants offer adults apparently underlie language development. At 2 months, Trevarthen detects in infants what he calls "prespeech," a distinct pattern of elaborate lip and mouth movements that resemble the movements of adult speech. The baby may or may not make sounds in prespeech, but a specific breathing pattern is seen.

Prespeech is observed during "conversations" between mother and child. Mothers of 2-month-old infants, apparently unconsciously, adjust the pace of their talk to allow the baby to join in. The mother speaks, pauses, listens to her baby, and speaks again after letting the infant have his say. There is the rhythm of adult conversation,

 Reprinted with permission from *The National Observer*, copyright © Dow Jones & Company, Inc. 1976.

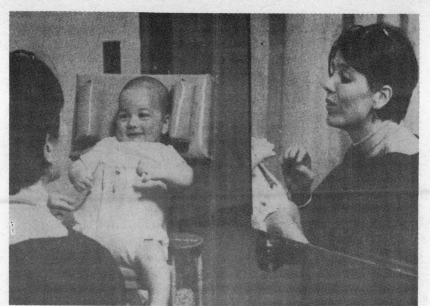

This arrangement allows Trevarthen to record the expressions of mother and child simultaneously.

if not the substance.

"The mother is drawing the child out," Trevarthen says. "She asks questions and shows quite clearly on her face that she's expecting an answer. Her eyebrows shoot up and her eyes go wide. The mother acts in a stimulating way, and the baby gets excited and responds."

Trevarthen also finds early signs of pre-speech, though far less developed, in new-borns and in premature babies within a week after their birth. He regards this as evidence that infants are born with a natural drive toward speaking and that man's language ability is present in innate form at birth. But language development, he agrees, definitely depends on each child's life experiences. "Environment has a tremendous voice," Trevarthen says.

Stimulus for Growth

He finds no evidence to support the fears voiced by some psychologists that talking "baby talk" to infants retards their linguistic growth or their development as persons. "Absolutely nothing that enters into communicating with the child can be bad for the child, unless it is carried to the point of dominating or smothering the child," Trevarthen says.

Infants use more than prespeech in attempting to communicate with adults. They also use a variety of hand movements. These parallel the animated gesturings of many adults during conversation. The beginnings of hand communication can be detected in the first month of life. "The shape of a hand greeting—a wave—exists at 3 weeks and is fully distinct at 8 weeks," Trevarthen says.

Week-old babies will try to grasp tiny objects. At a month, Trevarthen finds, efforts to handle objects are accompanied by mouth and tongue movements and facial expressions similar to those adults use. He even finds these infants sometimes make a grimace when they drop something, as if to say "Oops."

"It may be a sign that even this early in life infants are ready to pass comment on their acts to other people," Trevarthen says.

A sharing of embryonic communications with the mother provides the baby with stimulus for intellectual growth, Trevarthen suggests. "I think this paves the way for language development and intellectual reasoning. Though the acts are hard to measure, they are perceived by the mother and she reacts to them subconsciously. The fact she does react means her behavior turns into a kind of support for what the baby is doing. She provides the support, and then the baby discovers a lot of things it cannot discover on its own."

Trevarthen's team finds that prespeech occurs in both boys and girls to the same extent, but its expression varies by sex. Boys are more aggressive in communication, often using vigorous body movements and more frequently taking the initiative. Girls tend to be more co-operative and steady in conversation and to use gentle hand motions.

"In the balance between people and objects, we find female babies are more interested in personal communication and male babies show more active interest in objects," says Trevarthen. "It looks like the tendency of women to be concerned more with personal relationships has a strong biological basis, and that men depend on this.

"The way things occur, we don't very much think the differences are due to the attitudes of the mother to the baby. We don't think they're caused by the mother or the fact that she is female. I'm saying nothing about the relative quantity of intelligence at all. I'm talking about possible biological adaptations that make males and females different."

Trevarthen, a bit to his surprise, found that infants under 6 months rarely imitate their mothers. "It's a mistake to assume that because the mother helps the baby, the baby is imitating her," he says. "Frequently the mother is imitating the baby." This imitation apparently plays a vital part in encouraging the baby to increase its conversational activity. "You're showing you can do what he can do," says Trevarthen.

Baby Teaches Mother

A distinct change in infant-mother communication begins toward the end of the baby's third month of life. Trevarthen finds it recorded in film after film: The baby becomes rude to its mother.

When the mother begins speaking, the baby turns away, often looking at some toy or object, and refuses to answer. At first the mother increases her conversation, then lapses into silence. Finally she picks up a toy, usually the one the baby is looking at, and tries to interest the child in it. Then the baby responds. "It's a complicated process," Trevarthen says. "It seems to take two to three months of progressive steps to develop."

Trevarthen hazards an explanation of what this observation might mean—an explanation guaranteed to raise eyebrows. "What we believe happens is the baby introduces the mother to the idea their communication can involve objects," he says. "The baby says, 'We've got to stop this chat and find something to chat about.'"

"The mother is being trained by the baby. Having established a relationship, the baby transforms it and teaches the mother to be a teacher. And we take that as a general prototype for all education. I think children invented school."

Trevarthen's research has provided major new insights into the linguistic and behavioral abilities of infants. His work has helped change the old view that the brains of infants are like soft plastic, ready to be molded solely by their experiences. But he acknowledges that his interpretations of some of his findings have yet to win total acceptance. "The psychologists," he says, "are still skeptical."

Infant Thought

Jerome Kagan

Jerome Kagan is a professor of human development at Harvard. Recently he has revised his own earlier position about the long-range effects of early experience; he now believes that a particular quality in a young child is not likely to persist unless the environment continues to support it.

Experts are still wrangling over the old problem of nature versus nurture: Is it genetic endowment or upbringing that sets the limits of a child's achievement? Most psychologists today would agree that neither force holds total sway; a child's personality and his intellectual capacities are affected at each stage of growth by the interplay of heredity and environment. Debate has shifted to center on two related issues: *which* years and *what* influences have the greatest impact on a child's development?

Many psychologists believe that a child's future abilities are determined largely by what he experiences before the age of three. Others feel that the child's chances for emotional health are decided even earlier, by the kind of mother care received in infancy. In recent years a few dissenters have become increasingly vocal in their support of a "second chance" view: they cite cases of children who have suffered considerable deprivation early in life and yet seem to recover adequately once their circumstances have improved. The wisdom of a proverb from the journal *Presbyterian Life* is perhaps as good a guide as any: "Heredity is what a man believes in until his son begins to behave like a delinquent."

—M.W.

Neither imitation nor play nor drawing nor image nor language nor even memory . . . can develop or be organized without the constant help of the structuration characteristic of intelligence.

—Jean Piaget (1966)

A quarter of a century ago, most psychologists thought that a child's development followed two fairly discrete paths. He mastered new motor skills as his organism matured, but his intellectual growth was primarily governed by experience. Modern research suggests that the physiological maturing process also plays a major role in cognitive growth, which unfolds in the same well-ordered sequences in most environments.

To illustrate this point, let us look at a special set of new reactions that seems to emerge quite suddenly at eight to twelve months of age. Certain events that bored the child a couple of months earlier appear to take on a new interest; others that he responded to with equanimity then make him inhibited or even fearful now. He becomes wary if presented with a jack-in-the-box or a moving mechanical toy, and hesitates before reaching for an unfamiliar object that he would once have grabbed gleefully. At four months he probably smiled at strange adults; now he may cry if one approaches. Soon after his first birthday, he will also stop what he is doing if a strange child comes near. Most important, his behavior now suggests that he can remember events that happened moments before and can make use of that information.

A classic experiment devised by the Swiss psychologist Jean Piaget demonstrates this improvement in memory. An adult hides an attractive toy under a small cloth while the infant watches. A child under seven months typically does not reach for the cloth, as though he has forgotten about the toy once it is removed from view. After eight months, most children confidently reach for the hidden toy. With each succeeding month, the child becomes capable of tolerating a longer delay between the hiding of the toy and the moment when he is allowed to reach for it. What he has achieved is the ability to hold past knowledge on the memory stage and to juxtapose it with information currently being absorbed. This process of evaluation and comparison is one of the fundamental components of thought.

The enhanced ability to remember and evaluate is one reason the eight-month-old appears more purposeful in his activity. It may also explain why he soon begins to show a fear of separation. A one-year-old who sees his mother leave the room, or prepare to leave, generally becomes uncertain; if he is temperamentally prone, he may cry. This is probably because he is now mature enough to puzzle over unusual or unexpected events. He remembers that his mother was with him a few minutes earlier and can ask himself questions about her departure and how he will cope with it. Where is she? Will she come back? What should I do? If he cannot solve the puzzle, he becomes afraid. When he becomes old enough to answer such questions—some time between two-and-a-half and three years of age—his fears will vanish.

The probability that a child will protest, cry, or stop his playing when he sees his mother or principal caretaker leave emerges at about the same time in all cultures. My colleagues and I have observed children in lower-class mestizo families in the city of Antigua, Guatemala; in Indian families in an isolated village by Lake Atitlan, in

 Copyright © 1978 by *Harper's Magazine*. All rights reserved. Reprinted from the April 1978 issue by special permission.

My sole consolation when I went upstairs for the night was that Mamma would come in and kiss me after I was in bed. But this good night lasted for so short a time: she went down again so soon that the moment in which I heard her climb the stairs, and then caught the sound of her garden dress of blue muslin, from which hung little tassels of plaited straw, rustling along the double-doored corridor, was for me a moment of the keenest sorrow.

—Marcel Proust, *Swann's Way*

northwest Guatemala; in Israeli kibbutzim (where groups of infants spend most of the day with professional caretakers, rather than with their own parents); and in nomadic families of the !Kung San tribe in the Kalahari Desert. We have also studied American children who attended a research day-care center five days a week from three-and-a-half to twenty-nine months of age. Each child in the day-care group was paired with a control child of the same sex, social class, and ethnic origin who was being raised at home. The children's reactions to being left by their mothers in a strange room were observed at eight different points during the study. With both day-care and home-reared children, *and* with the children in all the other cultural groups, a similar pattern emerged. Crying when left by the mother in an unfamiliar stituation did not occur reliably until nine to twelve months of age. It grew more frequent and intense during the second year (generally reaching a peak between twelve and fifteen months), after which it declined.

Separation distress and its related phenomena can be delayed for several months in children being reared under extremely depriving conditions—environments that contain far less variety, less challenge, and less opportunity to practice new skills. But even in these instances the *pattern* of emergence remains essentially the same.

It seems reasonable to suggest that these diverse behavioral advances appearing suddenly and rather uniformly toward the end of the first year depend at least in part on correlated changes in the brain. Between nine months and one year of age there must be structural and/or biochemical changes in the central nervous system that permit more complex cognitive abilities to emerge. Sigmund Freud was apparently approaching a similar insight toward the end of his career. In a prophetic paragraph from *The Outline of Psychoanalysis* he questioned the formative power he had once assigned to the infant's individual experience with its caretaker and suggested that the process of physiological maturation would produce an essentially similar developmental profile in all children. He wrote:

> The phylogenetic foundation has so much the upper hand over personal accidental experience that it makes no difference whether a child has really sucked at the breast or has been brought up on the bottle and never enjoyed the tenderness of a mother's care. In both cases, the child's development takes the same path.

LEARNING THE MOTHER TONGUE

Acquiring language appears to be either inexplicable or miraculous, but close observation indicates that baby and mother work together and the role of the mother is crucial.

JEROME S. BRUNER

Jerome S. Bruner *is Watts Professor of Psychology at Oxford University and an advisory editor to* Human Nature. *He is also chairman of the Scientific Advisory Committee at the Max Planck Institute of Psycholinguistics in Nijmegen, Holland. Bruner, whose Ph.D. in psychology is from Harvard University, taught at Harvard from 1945 until 1971.*

While he was there, he helped found the Center for Cognitive Studies and was its director until he resigned to go to Oxford. Among his books are The Relevance of Education, Beyond the Information Given, The Process of Education, *and* On Knowing: Essays for the Left Hand. *With Michael Cole and Barbara Lloyd, he is editing* The Developing Child, *a series of books published by Harvard University Press that present research in child development to a general audience.*

Learning a native language is an accomplishment within the grasp of any toddler, yet discovering how children do it has eluded generations of philosophers. St. Augustine believed it was simple. Recollecting his own childhood, he said, "When they named any thing, and as they spoke turned towards it, I saw and remembered that they called what they would point out by the name they uttered. . . . And thus by constantly hearing words, as they occurred in various sentences, I collected gradually for what they stood; and having broken in my mouth to these signs, I thereby gave utterance to my will." But a look at children as they actually acquire language shows that St. Augustine was wrong and that other attempts to explain the feat err as badly in the opposite direction. What is more, as we try to understand how children learn their own language, we get an inkling of why it is so difficult for adults to learn a second language.

Thirty years ago, psychologies of learning held sway; language acquisition was explained using principles and methods that had little to do with language. Most started with nonsense syllables or random materials that were as far as researchers could get from the structure of language that permits the generation of rich and limitless statements, speculations, and poetry. Like G. K. Chesterton's drunk, they looked for the lost coin where the light was. And in the light of early learning theories, children appeared to acquire language by associating words with agents and objects and actions, by imitating their elders, and by a mysterious force called reinforcement. It was the old and tired Augustinian story dressed up in the language of behaviorism.

Learning theory led to a readiness, even a recklessness, to be rid of an inadequate account, one that could explain the growth of vocabulary but not how a four-year-old abstracts basic language rules and effortlessly combines old words to make an infinite string of new sentences. The stage was set for linguist Noam Chomsky's theory of LAD, the Language Acquisition Device, and for the Chomskyan revolution.

According to this view, language was not learned; it was recognized by virtue of an innate recognition routine through which children, when exposed to their local language, could abstract or extract its universal grammatical principles. Whatever the input of that local language, however degenerate, the output of LAD was the grammar of the language, a competence to generate all possible grammatical sentences and none (or very few) that were not. It was an extreme view, so extreme that it did not even consider meaning. In a stroke it freed a generation of psycholinguists from the dogma of association, imitation, and reinforcement and turned their attention to the problem of rule learning.

By declaring learning theory dead, it opened the way for a new account. George Miller of The Rockefeller University put it well: We had two theories of language learning—one of them, empiricist associationism, is impossible; the other, nativism, is miraculous. The void between the impossible and the miraculous remained to be filled.

Both explanations begin too late— when children say their first words. Long before children acquire language, they know something about their world. Before they can make verbal distinctions in speech, they have sorted the conceptual universe into useful categories and classes and can make distinctions about actions and agents and objects. As Roger Brown of Harvard University has written, "The concept . . . is there beforehand, waiting for the word to come along that names it." But the mystery of how children penetrate the communication system and learn to represent in language what they already know about the real world has not been solved. Although there is a well-packaged semantic content waiting, what children learn about language is not the same as what they know about the world. Yet the void begins to fill as soon as we recognize that children are not flying blind, that semantically speaking they have some target toward which language-learning efforts are directed: saying something or understanding something about events in a world that is already known.

If a child is in fact communicating, he has some end in mind—requesting something or indicating something or establishing some sort of personal relationship. The function of a communication has to be considered. As philosopher John Austin argued, an ut-

 From *Human Nature*, September 1978. Copyright © 1978 by Human Nature, Inc. Reprinted by permission of the publisher.

terance cannot be analyzed out of its context of use, and its use must include the intention of the speaker and its interpretation in the light of conventional standards by the person addressed. A speaker may make a request in several ways: by using the conventional question form, by making a declarative statement, or by issuing a command.

Roger Brown observed young Adam from age two until he was four and found that his middle-class mother made requests using a question form: "Why don't you play with your ball now?" Once Adam came to appreciate what I shall call genuine *why* questions (i.e., "Why are you playing with your ball?"), he typically answered these—and these only—with the well-known "Because." There is no instance, either before or after he began to comprehend the genuine causal question, of his ever confusing a sham and a real *why* question.

Not only does conceptual knowledge precede true language, but so too does function. Children know, albeit in limited form, what they are trying to accomplish by communicating before they begin to use language to implement their efforts. Their initial gestures and vocalizations become increasingly stylized and conventional.

It has become plain in the last several years that Chomsky's original bold claim that any sample of language encountered by an infant was enough for the LAD to dig down to the grammatical rules simply is false. Language is not encountered willy-nilly by the child; it is instead encountered in a highly orderly interaction with the mother, who takes a crucial role in arranging the linguistic encounters of the child. What has emerged is a theory of mother-infant interaction in language acquisition—called the fine-tuning theory—that sees language mastery as involving the mother as much as it does the child. According to this theory, if the LAD exists, it hovers somewhere in the air between mother and child.

So today we have a new perspective that begins to grant a place to knowledge of the world, to knowledge of the function of communication, and to the hearer's interpretation of the speaker's intent. The new picture of language learning recognizes that the process depends on highly constrained and one-sided transactions between the child and the adult teacher. Language acquisition requires joint problem solving by mother and infant, and her response to her child's language is close tuned in a way that can be specified.

The child's entry into language is an entry into dialogue, and the dialogue is at first necessarily nonverbal and requires both members of the pair to interpret the communication and its intent. Their relationship is in the form of roles, and each "speech" is determined by a move of either partner. Initial control of the dialogue depends on the mother's interpretation, which is guided by a continually updated understanding of her child's competence.

Consider an infant learning to label objects. Anat Ninio and I observed Richard in his home every two weeks from his eighth month until he was two years old, video-taping his actions so that we could study them later. In this instance he and his mother are "reading" the pictures in a book. Before this kind of learning begins, certain things already have been established. Richard has learned about pointing as a pure indicating act, marking unusual or unexpected objects rather than things wanted immediately. He has also learned to understand that sounds refer in some singular way to objects or events. Richard and his mother, moreover, have long since established well-regulated turn-taking routines, which probably were developing as early as his third or fourth month. And finally, Richard has learned that books are to be looked at, not eaten or torn; that objects depicted are to be responded to in a particular way and with sounds in a pattern of dialogue.

For the mother's part, she (like all mothers we have observed) drastically limits her speech and maintains a steady regularity. In her dialogues with Richard she uses four types of speech in a strikingly fixed order. First, to get his attention, she says "Look." Second, with a distinctly rising inflection, she asks "What's that?" Third, she gives the picture a label, "It's an X." And finally, in response to his actions, she says "That's right."

In each case, a single verbal token accounts for from nearly half to more than 90 percent of the instances. The way Richard's mother uses the four speech constituents is closely linked to what her son says or does. When she varies her response, it is with good reason. If Richard responds, his mother replies, and if he initiates a cycle by pointing and vocalizing, then she responds even more often.

Her fine tuning is fine indeed. For example, if after her query Richard labels the picture, she will virtually always skip the label and jump to the response, "Yes." Like the other mothers we have studied, she is following ordinary polite rules for adult dialogue.

As Roger Brown has described the baby talk of adults, it appears to be an imitative version of how babies talk. Brown says, "Babies already talk like babies, so what is the earthly use of parents doing the same? Surely it is a parent's job to teach the adult language." He resolves the dilemma by noting, "What I think adults are chiefly trying to do, when they use [baby talk] with children, is to communicate, to understand and to be understood, to keep two minds focussed on the same topic." Although I agree with Brown, I would like to point out that the content and intonation of the talk is baby talk, but the dialogue pattern is adult.

To ensure that two minds are indeed focused on a common topic, the mother develops a technique for showing her baby what feature a label refers to by making 90 percent of her labels refer to whole objects. Since half of the remainder of her speech is made up of proper names that also stand for the whole, she seems to create few difficulties, supposing that the child also responds to whole objects and not to their features.

The mother's (often quite unconscious) approach is exquisitely tuned. When the child responds to her "Look!" by looking, she follows immediately with a query. When the child responds to the query with a gesture or a smile, she supplies a label. But as soon as the child shows the ability to vocalize in a way that might indicate a label, she raises the ante.

She withholds the label and repeats the query until the child vocalizes, then she gives the label.

Later, when the child has learned to respond with shorter vocalizations that correspond to words, she no longer accepts an indifferent vocalization. When the child begins producing a recognizable, constant label for an object, she holds out for it. Finally, the child produces appropriate words at the appropriate place in the dialogue. Even then the mother remains tuned to the developing pattern, helping her child recognize labels and make them increasingly accurate. For example, she develops two ways of asking "What's that?" One, with a falling intonation, inquires about those words for which she believes her child already knows the label; the other, with a rising intonation, marks words that are new.

Even in the simple labeling game, mother and child are well into making the distinction between the given and the new. It is of more than passing interest that the old or established labels are the ones around which the mother will shortly be elaborating comments and questions for new information:

Mother (with falling intonation): What's that?

Child: Fishy.

Mother: Yes, and see him swimming?

After the mother assumes her child has acquired a particular label, she generally drops the attention-getting "Look!" when they turn to the routine. In these petty particulars of language, the mother gives useful cues about the structure of their native tongue. She provides cues based not simply on her knowledge of the language but also on her continually changing knowledge of the child's ability to grasp particular distinctions, forms, or rules. The child is sensitized to certain constraints in the structure of their dialogue and does not seem to be directly imitating her. I say this because there is not much difference in the likelihood of a child's repeating a label after hearing it, whether the mother has imitated the child's label, simply said "Yes," or only laughed approvingly. In each case the child repeats the label about half the time, about the same rate as with *no* reply from the mother. Moreover, the child is eight times more likely to produce a label in response to "What's that?" than to the mother's uttering the label.

I do not mean to claim that children cannot or do not use imitation in acquiring language. Language must be partly based on imitation, but though the child may be imitating another, language learning involves solving problems by communicating in a dialogue. The child seems to be trying to get through to the mother just as hard as she is trying to reach her child.

Dialogue occurs in a context. When children first learn to communicate, it is always in highly concrete situations, as when mother or child calls attention to an object, asking for the aid or participation of the other. Formally conceived, the format of communication involves an intention, a set of procedures, and a goal. It presupposes shared knowledge of the world and a shared script by which mother and child can carry out reciprocal activity in that world. Formats obviously have utility for the child. They provide a simple, predictable bit of the world in which and about which to communicate. But they also have an important function for the mother in the mutual task of speech acquisition.

When a mother uses baby talk, her intonation broadens, her speech slows, and her grammar becomes less complex. In addition, baby talk virtually always starts with the here and now, with the format in which the two are operating. It permits the mother to tune her talk to the child's capabilities. She need not infer the child's general competence for language, but instead judges the child's performance on a specific task at a specific time.

A second major function of speech is requesting something of another person. Carolyn Roy and I have been studying its development during the first two years of life. Requesting requires an indication that you want *something* and *what* it is you want. In the earliest procedures used by children it is difficult to separate the two. First the child vocalizes with a characteristic intonation pattern while reaching eagerly for the desired nearby object—which is most often held by the mother. As in virtually all early exchanges, it is the mother's task to in-terpret, and she works at it in a surprisingly subtle way. During our analyses of Richard when he was from 10 to 24 months old and Jonathan when he was 11 to 18 months old, we noticed that their mothers frequently seemed to be teasing them or withholding obviously desired objects. Closer inspection indicated that it was not teasing at all. They were trying to establish whether the infants really wanted what they were reaching for, urging them to make their intentions clearer.

When the two children requested nearby objects, the mothers were more likely to ask "Do you really want it?" than "Do you want the X?" The mother's first step is pragmatic, to establish the sincerity of the child's request.

Children make three types of requests, reflecting increasing sophistication in matters that have nothing to do with language. The first kind that emerges is directed at obtaining nearby, visible objects; this later expands to include distant or absent objects where the contextual understanding of words like "you, me," "this, that," and "here, there" is crucial. The second kind of request is directed at obtaining support for an action that is already in progress, and the third kind is used to persuade the mother to share some activity or experience.

When children first begin to request objects, they typically direct their attention and their reach, opening and closing their fists, accompanied by a characteristic intonation pattern. As this request expands, between 10 and 15 months, an observer immediately notes two changes. In reaching for distant objects, a child no longer looks solely at the desired object, but shifts his glance back and forth between the object and his mother. His call pattern also changes. It becomes more prolonged, or its rise and fall is repeated, and it is more insistent. Almost all of Richard's and Jonathan's requests for absent objects were for food, drink, or a book to be read, each having its habitual place. Each request involved the child's gesturing toward the place.

When consistent word forms appeared, they were initially idiosyncratic labels for objects, gradually becoming standard nouns that indicated the desired objects. The children also began initiating and ending their requests with smiles. The development of this pattern is paced by the child's knowledge, which is shared with the mother, of where things are located and of her willingness to fetch them if properly asked. Once the child begins requesting distant and absent objects, the mother has an opportunity to require that the desired object be specified. Sincerity ceases to be at issue, though two other conditions are imposed: control of agency (who is actually to obtain the requested object, with emphasis on the child's increasing independence) and control of "share" (whether the child has had enough).

Requests for joint activity contrast with object requests. I think they can be called precursors to invitation. They amount to the child asking the adult to share in an activity or an experience—to look out of the window into the garden together, to play Ride-a-cockhorse, to read together. They are the most playlike form of request, and in consequence they generate a considerable amount of language of considerable complexity. It is in this format that the issues of agency and share (or turn) emerge and produce important linguistic changes.

Joint activity requires what I call joint role enactment, and it takes three forms: one in which the adult is agent and the child recipient or experiencer (as in early book reading); another in which there is turn taking with the possibility of exchanging roles (as in peekaboo); and a third in which roles run parallel (as in looking around the garden together). Most of what falls into these categories is quite ritualized and predictable. There tend to be rounds and turns, and no specific outcome is required. The activity itself is rewarding. In this setting the child first deals with share and turn by adopting such forms of linguistic marking as *more* and *again*. These appear during joint role enactment and migrate rapidly into formats involving requests for distant objects.

It is also in joint role enactment that the baby's first consistent words appear and, beginning at 18 months, word combinations begin to explode. *More X* (with a noun) appears, and also combinations like *down slide, brrm brrm boo knee, Mummy ride*, and *Mummy read*. Indeed it is in these settings that full-blown ingratiatives appear in appropriate posi-

Mothers' questions when children request nearby objects

Type of question	Age in months		
	10-12	13-14	More than 15
About intention ("Do you want it?")	93%	90%	42%
About referent ("Do you want the x?")	7%	10%	58%
Number of questions	**27**	**29**	**12**

Forms of early requests

Request for:	Age in months				
	10-12	13-14	15-16	17-18	20-24
Near and visible object	100%	74%	43%	22%	11%
Distant or invisible object	0	16%	24%	8%	24%
Shared activity	0	10%	14%	23%	36%
Supportive action	0	0	19%	47%	29%
Minutes of recording	**150**	**120**	**120**	**120**	**150**
Number of requests/10 minutes	**1.5**	**1.6**	**1.8**	**4.3**	**2.3**

Adult responses to children's requests

Type of response	Age in months				
	10-12	13-14	15-16	17-18	20-24
Pronominal question					
Open question (who, what, which)	78%	55%	36%	8%	1%
Closed question (yes, no)	3%	10%	18%	30%	22%
Comment/Question (yes, no)	6%	27%	36%	25%	36%
Comment/Question on agency	8%	2%	0	20%	28%
"Language lesson"	6%	6%	9%	14%	4%
Request for reason	0	0	0	3%	5%
Other	0	0	1%	0	4%
Number of utterances	**36**	**51**	**22**	**116**	**100**

As children's requests change with increasing sophistication (center), their mothers switch from establishing the sincerity of a request to identifying the object wanted (top). The sharp increase in replies having to do with who will get or control an action ("agency") reflects a demand for sharing and a difference in wishes (bottom).

tions, such as prefacing a request with *nice Mummy*.

Characteristically, less than 5 percent of the mother's responses to a child's requests before he is 17 months old have to do with agency (or who is going to do, get, or control something). After 17 months, that figure rises to over 25 percent. At that juncture the mothers we studied began to demand that their children adhere more strictly to turn taking and role respecting. The demand can be made most easily when they are doing something together, for that is where the conditions for sharing are most clearly defined and least likely, since playful, to overstrain the child's capacity to wait for a turn. But the sharp increase in agency as a topic in their dialogue reflects as well the emergence of a difference in their wishes.

The mother may want the child to execute the act requested of her, and the child may have views contrary to his mother's about agency. In some instances this leads to little battles of will. In addition, the child's requests for support more often lead to negotiation between the pair than is the case when the clarity of the roles in their joint activity makes acceptance and refusal easier. A recurrent trend in development during the child's first year is the shifting of agency in all manner of exchanges from mother to infant. Even at nine to 12 months, Richard gradually began taking the lead in give-and-take games.

The same pattern holds in book reading, where Richard's transition was again quite rapid. Role shifting is very much part of the child's sense of script, and I believe it is typical of the kind of "real world" experience that makes it so astonishingly easy for children to master soon afterwards the deictic shifts, those contextual changes in the meaning of words that are essential to understanding the language. At about this time the child learns that I am *I* when I speak, but *you* when referred to by another, and so too with *you;* and eventually the child comes to understand the associated spatial words, *here* and *there, this* and *that, come* and *go.*

The prelinguistic communicative framework established in their dialogue by mother and child provides the setting for the child's acquisition of this language function. His problem solving in acquiring the deictic function is a *social* task: to find the procedure that will produce results, just as his prelinguistic communicative effort produced results, and the results needed can be interpreted in relation to role interactions.

For a number of years an emphasis on egocentrism in the young child has tended to blunt our awareness of the sensitivity of children to roles, of their capacity to manage role shift and role transformation. Although there is little doubt that it is more difficult for a young child to take the view of others than it will be for him later, this aspect of development has been greatly exaggerated. In familiar and sufficiently simple situations the child is quite capable of taking another's view. In 1975 Michael Scaife and I discovered that babies in their first year shifted their glance to follow an adult's line of regard, and in 1976 Andrew Meltzoff found in our laboratory that babies only a few weeks old appeared to have a built-in mechanism for mimicking an adult's expression, since they obviously could not see their own faces. More recently, Marilyn Shatz has shown that quite young children are

indeed able to "take another's position" when giving instructions, provided the task is simple enough.

According to Katherine Nelson and Janice Gruendel at Yale University, what seems to be egocentrism is often a matter of the child not being able to coordinate his own scripts with those of the questioner, although he is scrupulously following turn taking (which is definitely not egocentric). They found that when "egocentric" four-year-olds do manage to find a joint script, they produce dialogues like the following. Two children are sitting next to each other talking into toy telephones:

Gay: Hi.
Dan: Hi.
Gay: How are you?
Dan: Fine.
Gay: Who am I speaking to?
Dan: Daniel. This is your Daddy. I need to speak to you.
Gay: All right.
Dan: When I come home tonight we're gonna have . . . peanut butter and jelly sandwich . . . uh . . . at dinner time.
Gay: Uhmmm. Where're we going at dinner time?
Dan: Nowhere, but we're just gonna have dinner at 11 o'clock.
Gay: Well, I made a plan of going out tonight.
Dan: Well, that's what we're gonna do.
Gay: We're going out.
Dan: The plan, it's gonna be, that's

gonna be, we're going to McDonald's.
Gay: Yeah, we're going to McDonald's. And ah, ah, ah, what they have for dinner tonight is hamburger.
Dan: Hamburger is coming. O.K., well, goodbye.
Gay: Bye.

The child takes into account his or her partner's point of view, phrases his turns properly, and says things that are relevant to the script they are working on jointly. That is surely not egocentrism. But even managing the deictic function of language provides evidence that children realize there are viewpoints other than their own.

The last type of request, the request for supportive action, has a very special property. It is tightly bound to the nature of the action in which the child is involved. To ask others for help in support of their own actions, children need at least two forms of knowledge. One of them represents the course of action and involves a goal and a set of means for getting to it. The second requirement is some grasp of what has been called the

Toward the end of the first year the child gradually begins taking the lead in give-and-take games. Through such joint activity a child learns about sharing and taking turns.

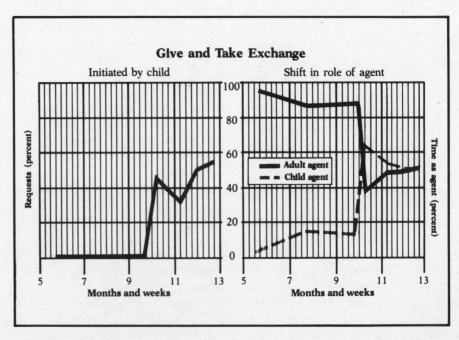

arguments of action: who does it, with what instrument, at what place, to whom, on what object, etc. Once children have mastered these, they have a rudimentary understanding of the concepts that will later be encountered in case grammar.

The degree to which a child comes to understand the structure of tasks is the degree to which his requests for support in carrying them out become more differentiated. These requests do not appear with any marked frequency until he is 17 or 18 months old and consist of bringing the "work" or the "action" or the entire task to an adult: A music box needs rewinding, or two objects have to be put together. In time a child is able to do better than that. He may bring a tool to an adult or direct the adult's hand or pat the goal (the chair on which he wants up). He is selecting and highlighting relevant features of the action, though not in a fashion that depends on what the adult is doing. Finally, at about the age of two, with the development of adequate words to refer to particular aspects of the action, the child enters a new phase: He requests action by guiding it successively. The pacemaker of the verbal output is progress in the task itself.

Let me give an instance of this successive guidance system. Richard, it transpires, wishes to persuade his mother to get a toy telephone from the cupboard; she is seated (and very pregnant). Successively, he voices the following requests:

Mummy, Mummy; Mummy come. . . . Up, up. . . . Cupboard. . . . Up cupboard, up cupboard; up cupboard. . . . Get up, get up. . . . Cupboard, cupboard. . . . Cupboard-up; cupboard-up, cupboard-up. . . . Telephone. . . . Mummy. . . . Mummy get out telephone.

His mother objects and asks him what it is he wants after each of the first two requests. She is trying to get him to set forth his request in some "readable" order before she starts to respond—to give a reason in terms of the goal of the action. Richard, meanwhile, achieves something approaching a request in sentence form by organizing his successive utterances in a fashion that seems to be guided by his conception of the needed steps in the action. The initial grammar of the long string of task-related requests is, then, a kind of temporal grammar based on an understanding not only of the actions required, but also of the order in which these actions must be executed. This bit of child language is an interpersonal script based on a young child's knowledge of what is needed to reach the goal in the real world; it is the matrix in which language develops.

In looking closely at two of the four major communicative functions (indicating and requesting), we discovered a great deal of negotiating by the mother about pragmatic aspects of communication: not about truth-falsity and not about well-formedness, but about whether requests were sincere, whose turn it was, whether it should be done independently or not, whether reasons were clear or justified.

There is, of course, more to communication than indicating and requesting. Another major function of speech is affiliation, the forming of a basis for social exchange. This involves matters as diverse as learning to acknowledge presence, to take turns, and to enter what has been called the "cooperative principle" underlying all speech acts.

The final function is the use of communication for generating possible worlds, and it has little to do with asking for help or indicating things in the real world or, indeed, with maintaining social connection. The early utterances of the children we have studied show one clear-cut characteristic: Most of the talking by mother and by child is *not* about hard-nosed reality. It is about games, about imaginary things, about seemingly useless make-believe. What is involved in the generation of possible worlds is quite useful for both conceptual and communicative development—role playing, referring to nonpresent events, combining elements to exploit their variability, etc.

Had we gone on to look at the other two functions, affiliative activity during which mother and child learn the rules for interacting and the sort of play in which possible worlds are created, the case for mother-infant interaction would have been as strong. There is an enormous amount of teaching involved in transmitting the language, though very little of it has to do with language lessons proper. It has to do with making intentions clear, as speaker and as actor, and with overcoming difficulties in getting done in the real world what we want done by the mediation of communicating. And this is why learning a second language is so difficult. The moment we teach language as an explicit set of rules for generating well-formed strings out of context, the enterprise seems to go badly wrong. The rule in natural language learning is that language is learned in order to interact with someone about something the two of you share.

Where does that leave the problem of language acquisition? Well, to my way of thinking it brings it back into the sphere of problem solving—the problem being how to make our intentions known to others, how to communicate what we have in consciousness, what we want done in our behalf, how we wish to relate to others, and what in this or other worlds is possible.

Children still have to learn to use their native lexicons and to do so grammatically. They learn this in use, in order to get things done with words, and not as if they were ferreting out the disembodied rules of grammar. I think we have learned to look at language acquisition not as a solo flight by the child in search of rules, but as a transaction involving an active language learner and an equally active language teacher. That new insight will go a long way toward filling the gap between the impossible and the miraculous.

For further information:

Clark, Herbert, and Eve Clark. *Psychology and Language: An Introduction to Psycholinguistics.* Harcourt Brace Jovanovich, 1977.

De Villiers, Jill G., and Peter A. de Villiers. *Language Acquisition.* Harvard University Press, 1978.

Miller, George A. *Spontaneous Apprentices: Children and Language.* The Seabury Press, 1977.

Snow, Catherine E., and Charles A. Ferguson, eds. *Talking to Children.* Cambridge University Press, 1977.

Reconsideration: Jean Piaget

Robert Coles

Until this century psychology was predominantly a province of philosophy and theology. Locke understood the workings of the unconscious, concerned himself with emphatic do's and don'ts of child rearing. Hobbes based a political philosophy on a particular notion of the human mind. Were Kierkegaard suddenly to be "called back" to us on this earth, he would have precious little to learn from textbooks of "psychodynamic psychiatry." Schopenhauer and Nietzsche were stunningly in touch with mental life, their own and everyone else's—so much so, Freud carefully avoided reading them, lest he find himself discovering what they had already discovered. He knew that a long line of writers (Sophocles, Shakespeare, Dostoevsky) had already charted the essentials of his theory of the mind's life. But a playwright or novelist is one thing: intuition given estimable, civilized leeway. The treatises of a philosopher are uncomfortably similar to the presentation and elaboration of psychiatric theory.

Both Schopenhauer and Nietzsche, surely the giants of late-19th century German philosophy, had in fact shown themselves all too interested in a kind of metaphysical speculation that, when compared, say, to Kant's reasoning could be considered "unscientific". In contrast, Freud was a brilliant theorist, but very much a clinician; and he was a clear headed essayist, anxious to win an audience for himself. He was no innocent about the world outside his office. He knew that each age requires its own symbols, metaphors. His "mythological theory of instincts," as he once candidly referred to his ideas (in an exchange with Einstein) had to be tethered to biology, medicine, the hospital and clinic—in sum, the god of science—if they were to be widely regarded, and more, believed. The man who flirted with the magic of hypnosis and cocaine, who handed rings to his close associates, who paused long and hard before taking a trip to Rome, knew in his bones how to ask the contemporary question of faith:

who among the secular bourgeoisie believes what—and for how long?

There is, however, quite another kind of psychology than that of the unconscious—less dramatic, less personal, less preoccupied with strife and symptoms, less appealing, perhaps, to many of us: the line goes from Kant to William James to Piaget. It is a psychology of knowledge, of intellect, of will; a psychology willing to settle for the quiet, discreet turmoil that accompanies the acquisition of ideas and values—as contrasted to the continuing, eruptive frenzy of emotional conflict. Kant was preoccupied during his long lifetime with matters which we today consider the property of "science". He studied Newton's work closely, and was enough of a natural scientist to be leery of a rationalism that set up arbitrary categories or definitions as a means of approaching psychological experience. He struggled against the temptations of speculative metaphysics, modestly acknowledged not only his own limits, but those that ought to bind others: pure thought can only penetrate so many of life's mysteries. Reason is a somewhat wayward, discursive entity; if it is to be utilized effectively, it needs to be fed "material" from the outside world —the so-called "data of the senses." A somewhat isolated, provincial man (he never left Königsberg, even to tour other parts of Prussia), he seems to have worried much that his wide-ranging, hungry mind would become all too imperiously self-satisfied—and confuse its "internal" operations with the workings, in all of us, of intelligence. One of his grandfathers was from Scotland, and may have served to remind him of the virtues of empiricism. William James needed no such reminders. His mind was at ease with biology and physiological psychology as well as moral and religious thought. He shunned ideas—scientific, philosophical, psychological—that were not, in some fashion, connected to concrete experience. Psychological statements or appraisals that could not be tied to the specifics of human behavior were, for him, self indulgent, if not self deluding.

Like Kant, James gave the intellect limited but great significance. The domain of religion constantly impressed itself on both men: there is always before us the duality Flannery O'Connor characterized so briefly, wondrously—"mystery and manners." The former eludes us; the latter demands not self-displaying generalizations, but descriptive scrupulosity. We ought to try to know exactly what we are describing, but we ought be careful about turning our observations into unqualified laws. And if anyone hands down the laws, with no evidence, no observations that tell how, when, where, in what way, degree, proportion or measure, then at the very least the gates of the metaphysical have been entered. James detested dogma handed down in the name of philosophy or psychology. In the textures of human experience he hoped to find whatever "truth" was allowed him as a "mortal being." But such tentativeness and humility were not meant to undercut the authority of the intellect. James rather quickly (in the first decade of this century) saw the high value of Freud's work, but never forgot that, after all, it was Freud's observing, interpreting intellect, his restless and bold "will"— the depth and resourcefulness of the Ego which Anna Freud described in *The Ego and the Mechanisms of Defense* (1936)— that had wrested the discoveries of *Die Traumdeutung*.

Jean Piaget, this year 82, a giant still with us, has given a lifetime to a pursuit of Kant's "reason", James's "will". A recently published thick "reference and guide" (*The Essential Piaget*, edited by two of his students, Howard Gruber and J. Jacques Voneche [Basic Books; $25]) reminds us how much we owe the Swiss psychologist who insists on being known as a philosopher (epistemology). He was, it seems, from childhood the careful observer—not inclined to boast or rush to announce a "finding". In 1907, at the age of 11, he described a sparrow which showed "all the visible signs of an albino." He watched intently, was sorry the bird abruptly flew away. Two years later he had no such problem with a mollusk he carefully described. He would become as a youth an attentive biologist, quick to connect the visible to the historical: "The mollusks in question in the present work have to struggle against all sorts of biological difficulties. It is only by the force of circumstances independent of their will that they have been recently precipitated to the depths." He describes what happened geologically, then salutes his subjects of inquiry: "They have exhibited such suppleness in their remarkable evolution that today these races withstand their exile very well and sometimes survive being brought back to the surface."

He would gradually move from biology to a kind of inquiry which others all over the world regard as "child psychology." For him, the work he does is "manageable" observation, which helps us comprehend how we become distinctively human. As a dreamy, idealistic young man he wondered why human beings are so murderous and greedy. Why not come up with answers, with ontological assertions? But he wanted to approach human "reality" as he once did the sparrow or the mollusk—with a mixture of objective regard and subjective enthusiasm. Moreover, he is a practical, earthy man, for all the dense thicket of prose he puts between himself and his readers. He will let others ask the "existential" questions; his studies are meant to give us clues about how we get to be the somewhat knowing, thoughtful people we are (some of us, some of the time). Put differently, he is a genetic epistemologist, ever anxious to learn how it is we obtain our knowledge of the world—an acquisition that begins during the first days of life.

Piaget is known by many for the "stages" he has postulated—the step-by-step manner in which children learn to comprehend the world. But he is the last one to hand out dicta and expect compliant faith. He is the direct observer almost to a fault. In *The Origins of Intelligence in Children* he provides us with pages of detailed description of babies—learning to come to terms with the strange, welcoming, confusing, frustrating world around them. As they do so, he points out, they engage in one or another stratagem. They "assimilate" what they have met up with, seen and heard and felt; that is, make it all part of themselves—to be used with per-

sistence, and sometimes, originality. They also "accommodate" their own initiatives to the resistance the world may offer.

Piaget spent years watching his own three children and others as well. He watched them as they used their eyes and ears and hands and legs in the first months of life. The infant is an active, responsive, increasingly knowing explorer. In time, he or she, as a result of the various experiences enjoyed or suffered, develops a sense of things—or rather, a series of notions about what happens under x, y, or z conditions. "Assimilation" is an abstract word Piaget uses to describe a continuing cycle, that starts early in life, of activity followed by, yes, contemplation: I cry, I reach, I get, I push, I see something move, and simultaneously, I hear noise. The child takes stock constantly of sequences, consequences, this or that chain of events; and remembers what has been experienced, uses in various actions what has been remembered. The child also notes what will *not* happen—what won't be pushed, what yields to no pressure, what has its own demands, momentum, authority, persistence. A wooden wall is not a wooden toy on wheels, and so on. There are mistakes, moments and longer of perplexity, reflection and an effort to compromise: what I cannot change or turn to my very own purposes, I will learn to respect—and even so, manage to use or gain from, though only by acknowledging certain limitations.

For Piaget the child is a master-builder, a constant activist, a person who has never felt it necessary to distinguish between doing and learning. Children show themselves able to exert astonishingly complex mental operations, but not *because* they have become a given number of months or years old. The "stages" Piaget has in mind are not static, categorical inheritances of sorts, thrust by fate (nature and its plans) upon the waiting young. Each child is an explorer, an adventurer, and makes for himself or herself the discoveries that a man named Piaget has seen fit to record, describe, classify. Boys and girls try to deal with ideas about the world—the same complex ideas that philosophers and scientists also ponder to this day. What is time? What are numbers? How to deal conceptually with notions of territory, distance, space? What is the beginning and ending—of objects, of a particular

experience, of life itself? How permanent are things—this, or that, or something else? And size, and density, and gravity—how does one come to fathom them, penetrate their secrets, gain some working acquaintance with them? Children of six, eight, ten are not usually given lessons in physics, in positivist or empirical philosophy, yet they acquire through their own exertions and speculations an exceedingly, intricate and subtle education. It is Piaget's belief that much of what children learn about space, time, distance, and so on, is a universal (trans-cultural) consequence of active exploration—when done at the "right age"; that is, at a moment in which enough prior experience and biological growth enable the mind to profit from what it goes through. The development of intelligence, then, is our biological adaptation to the environment—something achieved day after day, with varying degrees of success.

Still, there are mysteries to acknowledge as well as manners to be recorded: "Intelligence constitutes an organizing activity whose functioning extends that of the biological organization, while surpassing it due to the elaboration of structures." Here the philosopher's "dialectic" edges toward transcendance—as in the still to be "explained" moment when a child's noises turn into a person's words. The action of a "language center"? The expression of some reflexic, biological momentum? A moment of grace? The child of one or two "does it", starts talking; meanwhile, our most learned observers still marvel at the common-place, indeed the universal "event"—and using many more words than a baby can dream of, they try to circumscribe what has happened: the domains of psychology, neuroanatomy, neurophysiology, and ultimately, one day far off, biochemistry.

Piaget uses the word "structures" often, is a "structuralist". Lévi-Strauss has told us that "structuralism is the search for unsuspected harmonies," and Piaget has been searching for them a long time, with considerable success. He has taught us that the random cries and groans, thrusts and probes, of children amount to, finally, elements in a "search" no less honorable or difficult than the one Levi-Strauss mentions. The words and sentences of children, their ideas and judgments, are investigative, re-

4. DEVELOPMENT

flective moments—a pursuit of order, coherence, meaning. Piaget does not ask, at least publicly, *why* it is that we are destined to go through such cycles, sequences, stages—such a "search". He has spent many decades documenting the tactics and strategy of it all, the continual work, the disappointments, the achievements. His has been, like Kant's, a "critique" of reason; they share a reluctance to take things for granted, a wish to spell out precisely what the mind *does*—as opposed to what it *has*, or *is*.

Nothing in Piaget's work need be turned into a refutation of the psychoanalytic viewpoint. William James did not abandon his "will" to the demanding turmoil of Freud's early concept of the Id. The Yankee psychologist and philosopher was willing to add a room, an entire wing to the mental house he knew would always be, anyway, in the process of being built, rather than *there, finished*. If Freud has taught us how hard and even fierce a struggle each child must wage for

sanity, emotional stability, self-respect, Piaget has given us a glimpse of the work that goes into the gradually obtained victory we all too readily tend to think of as a flat given: intelligence—meaning competence, judgment and perceptiveness with respect to the things of this world. It is, of course, the ideologues who take a Freud, a Piaget, any interesting or persuasive observer and thinker, and go running off exclusively with him, her—it: words become The Word.

Erik Erikson's Eight Ages Of Man
One man in his time plays many psychosocial parts

David Elkind

DAVID ELKIND *is professor of psychology and psychiatry at the University of Rochester.*

At a recent faculty reception I happened to join a small group in which a young mother was talking about her "identity crisis." She and her husband, she said, had decided not to have any more children and she was depressed at the thought of being past the child-bearing stage. It was as if, she continued, she had been robbed of some part of herself and now needed to find a new function to replace the old one.

When I remarked that her story sounded like a case history from a book by Erik Erikson, she replied, "Who's Erikson?" It is a reflection on the intellectual modesty and literary decorum of Erik H. Erikson, psychoanalyst and professor of developmental psychology at Harvard, that so few of the many people who today talk about the "identity crisis" know anthing of the man who pointed out its pervasiveness as a problem in contemporary society two decades ago.

Erikson has, however, contributed more to social science than his delineation of identity problems in modern man. His descriptions of the stages of the life cycle, for example, have advanced psychoanalytic theory to the point where it can now describe the development of the healthy personality on its own terms and not merely as the opposite of a sick one. Likewise, Erikson's emphasis upon the problems unique to adolescents and adults living in today's society has helped to rectify the one-sided emphasis on childhood as the beginning and end of personality development.

Finally, in his biographical studies, such as "Young Man Luther" and "Gandhi's Truth" (which has just won a National Book Award in philosophy and religion), Erikson emphasizes the inherent strengths of the human personality by showing how individuals can use their neurotic symptoms and conflicts for creative and constructive social purposes while healing themselves in the process.

It is important to emphasize that Erikson's contributions are genuine advances in psychoanalysis in the sense that Erikson accepts and builds upon many of the basic tenets of Freudian theory. In this regard, Erikson differs from Freud's early co-workers such as Jung and Adler who, when they broke with Freud, rejected his theories and substituted their own.

Likewise, Erikson also differs from the so-called neo-Freudians such as Horney, Kardiner and Sullivan who (mistakenly, as it turned out) assumed that Freudian theory had nothing to say about man's relation to reality and to his culture. While it is true that Freud emphasized, even mythologized, sexuality, he did so to counteract the rigid sexual taboos of his time, which, at that point in history, were frequently the cause of neuroses. In his later writings, however, Freud began to concern himself with the executive agency of the personality, namely the ego, which is also the repository of the individual's attitudes and concepts about himself and his world.

It is with the psychosocial development of the ego that Erikson's observations and theoretical constructions are primarily concerned. Erikson has thus been able to introduce innovations into psychoanalytic theory without either rejecting or ignoring Freud's monumental contribution.

The man who has accomplished this notable feat is a handsome Dane, whose white hair, mustache, resonant accent and gentle manner are reminiscent of actors like Jean Hersholt and Paul Muni. Although he is warm and outgoing with friends, Erikson is a rather shy man who is uncomfortable in the spotlight of public recognition. This trait, together with his ethical reservations about making public even disguised case material, may help to account for Erikson's reluctance to publish his observations and conceptions (his first book appeared in 1950, when he was 48).

In recent years this reluctance to publish has diminished and he has been appearing in print at an increasing pace. Since 1960 he has published three books, "Insight and Responsibility," "Identity: Youth and Crisis" and "Gandhi's Truth," as well as editing a fourth, "Youth: Change ·and Challenge." Despite the accolades and recognition these books have won for him, both in America and abroad, Erikson is still surprised at the popular interest they have generated and is a little troubled about the possibility of being misunderstood and misinterpreted. While he would prefer that his books spoke for themselves and that he was left out of the picture, he has had to accede to popular demand for more information about himself and his work.

The course of Erikson's professional career has been as diverse as it has been unconventional. He was born in Frankfurt, Germany, in 1902 of Danish parents. Not long after his birth his father died, and his mother later married the pediatrician who had cured her son of a childhood illness. Erikson's stepfather urged him to become a physician, but the boy declined and became an artist instead—an artist who did portraits of children. Erikson says of his post-adolescent years, "I was an artist then, which in Europe is a euphemism for a young man with some talent and nowhere to go." During this period he settled in Vienna and worked as a tutor in a family friendly with Freud's. He met Freud on informal occasions when the families went on outings together.

These encounters may have been the impetus to accept a teaching appointment at an American school in Vienna

From *The New York Times Magazine*, April 5, 1970. © 1970 by The New York Times Company. Reprinted by permission.

founded by Dorothy Burlingham and directed by Peter Blos (both now well known on the American psychiatric scene). During these years (the late nineteen-twenties) he also undertook and completed psychoanalytic training with Anna Freud and August Aichhorn. Even at the outset of his career, Erikson gave evidence of the breadth of his interests and activities by being trained and certified as a Montessori teacher. Not surprisingly, in view of that training, Erikson's first articles dealt with psychoanalysis and education.

It was while in Vienna that Erikson met and married Joan Mowat Serson, an American artist of Canadian descent. They came to America in 1933, when Erikson was invited to practice and teach in Boston. Erikson was, in fact, one of the first if not the first child-analyst in the Boston area. During the next two decades he held clinical and academic appointments at Harvard, Yale and Berkeley. In 1951 he joined a group of psychiatrists and psychologists who moved to Stockbridge, Mass., to start a new program at the Austen Riggs Center, a private residential treatment center for disturbed young people. Erikson remained at Riggs until 1961, when he was appointed professor of human development and lecturer on psychiatry at Harvard. Throughout his career he has always held two or three appointments simultaneously and has traveled extensively.

Perhaps because he had been an artist first, Erikson has never been a conventional psychoanalyst. When he was treating children, for example, he always insisted on visiting his young patients' homes and on having dinner with the families. Likewise in the nineteen-thirties, when anthropological investigation was described to him by his friends Scudder McKeel, Alfred Kroeber and Margaret Mead, he decided to do field work on an Indian reservation. "When I realized that Sioux is the name which we [in Europe] pronounced "See us" and which for us was *the* American Indian, I could not resist." Erikson thus antedated the anthropologists who swept over the Indian reservations in the post-Depression years. (So numerous were the field workers at that time that the stock joke was that an Indian family could be defined as a mother, a father, children and an anthropologist.)

Erikson did field work not only with the Oglala Sioux of Pine Ridge, S. D. (the tribe that slew Custer and was in turn slaughtered at the Battle of Wounded Knee), but also with the salmon-fishing Yurok of Northern California. His reports on these experiences revealed his special gift for sensing and entering into the world views and modes of thinking of cultures other than his own.

It was while he was working with the Indians that Erikson began to note syndromes which he could not explain within the confines of traditional psychoanalytic theory. Central to many an adult Indian's emotional problems seemed to be his sense of uprootedness and lack of continuity between his present life-style and that portrayed in tribal history. Not only did the Indian sense a break with the past, but he could not identify with a future requiring assimilation of the white culture's values. The problems faced by such men, Erikson recognized, had to do with the ego and with culture and only incidentally with sexual drives.

The impressions Erikson gained on the reservations were reinforced during World War II when he worked at a veterans' rehabilitation center at Mount Zion Hospital in San Francisco. Many of the soldiers he and his colleagues saw seemed not to fit the traditional "shell shock" or "malingerer" cases of World War I. Rather, it seemed to Erikson that many of these men had lost the sense of who and what they were. They were having trouble reconciling their activities, attitudes and feelings as soldiers with the activities, attitudes and feelings they had known before the war. Accordingly, while these men may well have had difficulties with repressed or conflicted drives, their main problem seemed to be, as Erikson came to speak of it at the time, "identity confusion."

It was almost a decade before Erikson set forth the implications of his clinical observations in "Childhood and Society." In that book, the summation and integration of 15 years of research, he made three major contributions to the study of the human ego. He posited (1) that, side by side with the stages of psychosexual development described by Freud (the oral, anal, phallic, genital, Oedipal and pubertal), were psychosocial stages of ego development, in which the individual had to establish new basic orientations to himself and his social world; (2) that personality development continued throughout the whole life cycle; and (3) that each stage had a positive *as well* as a negative component.

Much about these contributions—and about Erikson's way of thinking—can be understood by looking at his scheme of life stages. Erikson identifies eight stages in the human life cycle, in each of which a new dimension of "social interaction" becomes possible—that is, a new dimension in a person's interaction with himself, and with his social environment.

TRUST vs. MISTRUST

The first stage corresponds to the oral stage in classical psychoanalytic theory and usually extends through the first year of life. In Erikson's view, the new dimension of social interaction that emerges during this period involves basic *trust* at the one extreme, and *mistrust* at the other. The degree to which the child comes to trust the world, other people and himself depends to a considerable extent upon the quality of the care that he receives. The infant whose needs are met when they arise, whose discomforts are quickly removed, who is cuddled, fondled, played with and talked to, develops a sense of the world as a safe place to be and of people as helpful and dependable. When, however, the care is inconsistent, inadequate and rejecting, it fosters a basic mistrust, an attitude of fear and suspicion on the part of the infant toward the world in general and people in particular that will carry through to later stages of development.

It should be said at this point that the problem of basic trust-versus-mistrust (as is true for all the later dimensions) is not resolved once and for all during the first year of life; it arises again at each successive stage of development. There is both hope and danger in this. The child who enters school with a sense of mistrust may come to trust a particular teacher who has taken the trouble to make herself trustworthy; with this second chance, he overcomes his early mistrust. On the other hand, the child who comes through infancy with a vital sense of trust can still have his sense of mistrust activated at a later stage if, say, his parents are divorced and separated under acrimonious circumstances.

This point was brought home to me in a very direct way by a 4-year-old patient I saw in a court clinic. He was being seen at the court clinic because his adoptive parents, who had had him for six months, now wanted to give him back to the agency. They claimed that he was cold and unloving, took things and could not be trusted. He was indeed a cold and apathetic boy, but with good reason. About a year after his illegitimate birth, he was taken away from his mother, who had a drinking problem, and was shunted back and forth among several foster homes. Initially he had tried to relate to the persons in the foster homes, but the relationships never had a chance to develop becuase he was moved at just the wrong times. In the end he gave up trying to reach out to others, because the inevitable separations hurt too much.

Like the burned child who dreads the flame, this emotionally burned child shunned the pain of emotional involvement. He had trusted his mother, but now he trusted no one. Only years of devoted care and patience could now undo the damage that had been done to this child's sense of trust.

AUTONOMY vs. DOUBT

Stage Two spans the second and third years of life, the period which Freudian theory calls the anal stage. Erikson sees here the emergence of *autonomy*. This autonomy dimension builds upon the child's new motor and mental abilities. At this stage the child can not only walk but also climb, open and close, drop, push and pull, hold and let go. The child takes pride in these new accomplishments and wants to do everything himself, whether it be pulling the wrapper off a piece of candy, selecting the vitamin out of the bottle or flushing the toilet. If parents recognize the young child's need to do what he is capable of doing at his own pace and in his own time, then he develops a sense that he is able to control his muscles, his impulses, himself and, not insignificantly, his environment—the sense of autonomy.

When, however, his caretakers are impatient and do for him what he is capable of doing himself, they reinforce a sense of shame and doubt. To be sure, every parent has rushed a child at times and children are hardy enough to endure such lapses. It is only when caretaking is consistently overprotective and criticism of "accidents" (whether these be wetting, soiling, spilling or breaking things) is harsh and unthinking that the child develops an excessive sense of shame with respect to other people and an excessive sense of doubt about own abilities to control his world and himself.

If the child leaves this stage with less autonomy than shame or doubt, he will be handicapped in his attempts to achieve autonomy in adolescence and adulthood. Contrariwise, the child who moves through this stage with his sense of autonomy buoyantly outbalancing his feelings of shame and doubt is well prepared to be autonomous at later phases in the life cycle. Again, however, the balance of autonomy to shame and doubt

set up during this period can be changed in either positive or negative directions by later events.

It might be well to note, in addition, that too much autonomy can be as harmful as too little. I have in mind a patient of 7 who had a heart condition. He had learned very quickly how terrified his parents were of any signs in him of cardiac difficulty. With the psychological acuity given to children, he soon ruled the household. The family could not go shopping, or for a drive, or on a holiday if he did not approve. On those rare occasions when the parents had had enough and defied him, he would get angry and his purple hue and gagging would frighten them into submission.

Actually, this boy was frightened of this power (as all children would be) and was really eager to give it up. When the parents and the boy came to realize this, and to recognize that a little shame and doubt were a healthy counterpoise to an inflated sense of autonomy, the three of them could once again assume their normal roles.

INITIATIVE vs. GUILT

In this stage (the genital stage of classical psychoanalysis) the child, age 4 to 5, is pretty much master of his body and can ride a tricycle, run, cut and hit. He can thus initiate motor activities of various sorts on his own and no longer merely responds to or imitates the actions of other children. The same holds true for his language and fantasy activities. Accordingly, Erikson argues that the social dimension that appears at this stage has *initiative* at one of its poles and *guilt* at the other.

Whether the child will leave this stage with his sense of initiative far outbalancing his sense of guilt depends to a considerable extent upon how parents respond to his self-initiated activities. Children who are given much freedom and opportunity to initiate motor play such as running, bike riding, sliding, skating, tussling and wrestling have their sense of initiative reinforced. Initiative is also reinforced when parents answer their children's questions (intellectual initiative) and do not deride or inhibit fantasy or play activity. On the other hand, if the child is made to feel that his motor activity is bad, that his questions are a nuisance and that his play is silly and stupid, then he may develop a sense of guilt over self-initiated activities in general that will persist through later life stages.

INDUSTRY vs. INFERIORITY

Stage Four is the age period from 6 to 11, the elementary school years (described by classical psychoanalysis as the *latency phase*). It is a time during which the child's love for the parent of the opposite sex and rivalry with the same sexed parent (elements in the so-called family romance) are quiescent. It is also a period during which the child becomes capable of deductive reasoning, and of playing and learning by rules. It is not until this period, for example, that children can really play marbles, checkers and other "take turn" games that require obedience to rules. Erikson argues that the psychosocial dimension that emerges during this period has a sense of *industry* at one extreme and a sense of *inferiority* at the other.

The term industry nicely captures a dominant theme of this period during which the concern with how things are made, how they work and what they do predominates. It is the Robinson Crusoe age in the sense that the enthusiasm and minute detail with which Crusoe describes his activities appeals to the child's own budding sense of industry. When children are encouraged in their efforts to make, do, or build practical things (whether it be to construct creepy crawlers, tree houses, or airplane models—or to cook, bake or sew), are allowed to finish their products, and are praised and rewarded for the results, then the sense of industry is enhanced. But parents who see their children's efforts at making and doing as "mischief," and as simply "making a mess," help to encourage in children a sense of inferiority.

During these elementary-school years, however, the child's world includes more than the home. Now social institutions other than the family come to play a central role in the developmental crisis of the individual. (Here Erikson introduced still another advance in psychoanalytic theory, which heretofore concerned itself only with the effects of the parents' behavior upon the child's development.)

A child's school experiences affect his industry-inferiority balance. The child, for example, with an I.Q. of 80 to 90 has a particularly traumatic school experience, even when his sense of industry is rewarded and encouraged at home. He is "too bright" to be in special classes, but "too slow" to compete with children of average ability. Consequently he experiences constant failures in his academic efforts that reinforces a sense of inferiority.

On the other hand, the child who had his sense of industry derogated at home can have it revitalized at school through the offices of a sensitive and committed teacher. Whether the child develops a sense of industry or inferiority, therefore, no longer depends solely on the caretaking efforts of the parents but on the actions and offices of other adults as well.

IDENTITY vs. ROLE CONFUSION

When the child moves into adolescence (Stage Five— roughly the ages 12-18), he encounters, according to traditional psychoanalytic theory, a reawakening of the family-romance problem of early childhood. His means of resolving the problem is to seek and find a romantic partner of his own generation. While Erikson does not deny this aspect of adolescence, he points out that there are other problems as well. The adolescent matures mentally as well as physiologically and, in addition to the new feelings, sensations and desires he experiences as a result of changes in his body, he develops a multitude of new ways of looking at and thinking about the world. Among other things, those in adolescence can now think about other people's thinking and wonder about what other people think of them. They can also conceive of ideal families, religions and societies which they then compare with the imperfect families, religions and societies of their own experience. Finally, adolescents become capable of constructing theories and philosophies designed to bring all the varied and conflicting aspects of society into a working, harmonious and peaceful whole. The adolescent, in a word, is an impatient idealist who believes that it is as easy to realize an ideal as it is to imagine it.

Erikson believes that the new interpersonal dimension which emerges during this period has to do with a sense of *ego identity* at the positive end and a sense of *role confusion* at the negative end. That is to say, given the adolescent's newfound integrative abilities, his task is to bring together all of the things he has learned about himself as a son, student, athlete, friend, Scout, newspaper boy, and so on, and integrate these different images of himself into a whole that makes sense and that shows continuity with the past while preparing for the future. To the extent that the young person succeeds in this endeavor, he arrives at a sense of psychosocial identity, a sense of who he is, where he has been and where he is going.

In contrast to the earlier stages, where parents play a more or less direct role in the determination of the result of the developmental crises, the influence of parents during this stage is much more indirect. If the young person reaches adolescence with, thanks to his parents, a vital sense of trust, autonomy, initiative and industry, then his chances of arriving at a meaningful sense of ego identity are much enhanced. The reverse, of course, holds true for the young person who enters adolescence with considerable mistrust, shame, doubt, guilt and inferiority. Preparation for a successful adolescence, and the attainment of an integrated psychosocial identity must, therefore, begin in the cradle.

Over and above what the individual brings with him from his childhood, the attainment of a sense of personal identity depends upon the social milieu in which he or she grows up. For example, in a society where women are to some extent second-class citizens, it may be harder for females to arrive at a sense of psychosocial identity. Likewise at times, such as the present, when rapid social and technological change breaks down many traditional values, it may be more difficult for young people to find continuity between what they learned and experienced as children and what they learn and experience as adolescents. At such times young people often seek causes that give their lives meaning and direction. The activism of the current generation of young people may well stem, in part at least, from this search.

When the young person cannot attain a sense of personal identity, either because of an unfortunate childhood or difficult social circumstances, he shows a certain amount of *role confusion*—a sense of not knowing what he is, where he belongs or whom he belongs to. Such confusion is a frequent symptom in delinquent young people. Promiscuous adolescent girls, for example, often seem to have a fragmented sense of ego identity. Some young people seek a "negative identity," an identity opposite to the one prescribed for them by their family and friends. Having an identity as a "delinquent," or as a "hippie," or even as an "acid head," may sometimes be preferable to having no identity at all.

In some cases young people do not seek a negative identity so much as they have it thrust upon them. I remember another court case in which the defendant was an attractive 16-year-old girl who had been found "tricking it" in a trailer located just outside the grounds of an Air Force base. From about the age of 12, her mother had encouraged her to dress seductively and to go out with boys. When she returned from dates, her sexually frustrated mother demanded a kiss-by-kiss, caress-by-caress description of the evening's activities. After the mother had vicariously satisfied her sexual needs, she proceeded to call her daughter a "whore" and a "dirty tramp."

As the girl told me, "Hell, I have the name, so I might as well play the role."

Failure to establish a clear sense of personal identity at adolescence does not guarantee perpetual failure. And the person who attains a working sense of ego identity in adolescence will of necessity encounter challenges and threats to that identity as he moves through life. Erikson, perhaps more than any other personality theorist, has emphasized that life is constant change and that confronting problems at one stage in life is not a guarantee against the reappearance of these problems at later stages, or against the finding of new solutions to them.

INTIMACY vs. ISOLATION

Stage Six in the life cycle is young adulthood; roughly the period of courtship and early family life that extends from late adolescence till early middle age. For this stage, and the stages described hereafter, classical psychoanalysis has nothing new or major to say. For Erikson, however, the previous attainment of a sense of personal identity and the engagement in productive work that marks this period gives rise to a new interpersonal dimension of *intimacy* at the one extreme and *isolation* at the other.

When Erikson speaks of intimacy he means much more than love-making alone; he means the ability to share with and care about another person without fear of losing oneself in the process. In the case of intimacy, as in the case of identity, success or failure no longer depends directly upon the parents but only indirectly as they have contributed to the individual's success or failure at the earlier stages. Here, too, as in the case of identity, social conditions may help or hinder the establishment of a sense of intimacy. Likewise, intimacy need not involve sexuality; it includes the relationship between friends. Soldiers who have served together under the most dangerous circumstances often develop a sense of commitment to one another that exemplifies intimacy in its broadest sense. If a sense of intimacy is not established with friends or a marriage partner, the result, in Erikson's view, is a sense of isolation—of being alone without anyone to share with or care for.

GENERATIVITY vs. SELF-ABSORPTION

This stage—middle age—brings with it what Erikson speaks of as either *generativity or self-absorption,* and stagnation. What Erikson means by generativity is that the person begins to be concerned with others beyond his immediate family, with future generations and the nature of the society and world in which those generations will live. Generativity does not reside only in parents; it can be found in any individual who actively concerns himself with the welfare of young people and with making the world a better place for them to live and to work.

Those who fail to establish a sense of generativity fall into a state of self-absorption in which their personal needs and comforts are of predominant concern. A fictional case of self-absorption is Dickens's Scrooge in "A Christmas Carol." In his one-sided concern with money and in his disregard for the interests and welfare of his young employee, Bob Cratchit, Scrooge exemplifies the self-absorbed, embittered (the two often go together) old man. Dickens also illustrated, however, what Erikson points out: namely, that unhappy solutions to life's crises are not irreversible. Scrooge, at the end of the tale, manifested both a sense of generativity and of intimacy which he had not experienced before.

INTEGRITY vs. DESPAIR

Stage Eight in the Eriksonian scheme corresponds roughly to the period when the individual's major efforts are nearing completion and when there is time for reflection—and for the enjoyment of grandchildren, if any. The psychosocial dimension that comes into prominence now has *integrity* on one hand and *despair* on the other.

The sense of integrity arises from the individual's ability to look back on his life with satisfaction. At the other extreme is the individual who looks back upon his life as a series of missed opportunities and missed directions; now in the twilight years he realizes that it is too late to start again. For such a person the inevitable result is a sense of despair at what might have been.

These, then, are the major stages in the life cycle as described by Erikson. Their presentation, for one thing, frees the clinician to treat adult emotional problems as failures (in part at least) to solve genuinely adult personality crises and not, as heretofore, as mere residuals of infantile frustrations and conflicts. This view of personality growth, moreover, takes some of the onus off parents and takes account of the role which society and the person himself play in the formation of an individual personality. Finally, Erikson has offered hope for us all by demonstrating that each phase of growth has its strengths as well as its weaknesses and that failures at one stage of development can be rectified by successes at later stages.

The reason that these ideas, which sound so agreeable to "common sense," are in fact so revolutionary has a lot to do with the state of psychoanalysis in America. As formulated by Freud, psychoanalysis encompassed a theory of personality development, a method of studying the human mind and, finally, procedures for treating troubled and unhappy people. Freud viewed this system as a scientific one, open to revision as new facts and observations accumulated.

The system was, however, so vehemently attacked that Freud's followers were constantly in the position of having to defend Freud's views. Perhaps because of this situation, Freud's system became, in the hands of some of his followers and defenders, a dogma upon which all theoretical innovation, clinical observation and therapeutic practice had to be grounded. That this attitude persists is evidenced in the recent remark by a psychoanalyst that he believed psychotic patients could not be treated by psychoanalysis because "Freud said so." Such attitudes, in which Freud's authority rather than observation and data is the basis of deciding what is true and what is false, has contributed to the disrepute in which psychoanalysis is widely held today.

Erik Erikson has broken out of this scholasticism and has had the courage to say that Freud's discoveries and practices were the start and not the end of the study and treatment of

4. DEVELOPMENT

the human personality. In addition to advocating the modifications of psychoanalytic theory outlined above, Erikson has also suggested modifications in therapeutic practice, particularly in the treatment of young patients. "Young people in severe trouble are not fit for the couch," he writes. "They want to face you, and they want you to face them, not a facsimile of a parent, or wearing the mask of a professional helper, but as a kind of over-all individual a young person can live with or despair of."

Erikson has had the boldness to remark on some of the negative effects that distorted notions of psychoanalysis have had on society at large. Psychoanalysis, he says, has contributed to a widespread fatalism—"even as we were trying to devise, with scientific determinism, a therapy for the few, we were led to promote an ethical disease among the many."

Perhaps Erikson's innovations in psychoanalytic theory are best exemplified in his psycho-historical writings, in which he combines psychoanalytic insight with a true historical imagination. After the publication of "Childhood and Society," Erikson undertook the application of his scheme of the human life cycle to the study of historical persons. He wrote a series of brilliant essays on men as varied as Maxim Gorky, George Bernard Shaw and Freud himself. These studies were not narrow case histories but rather reflected Erikson's remarkable grasp of Europe's social and political history, as well as of its literature. (His mastery of American folklore, history and literature is equally remarkable.)

While Erikson's major biographical studies were yet to come, these early essays already revealed his unique psycho-history method. For one thing, Erikson always chose men whose lives fascinated him in one way or another, perhaps because of some conscious or unconscious affinity with them. Erikson thus had a sense of community with his subjects which he adroitly used (he calls it *disciplined subjectivity*) to take his subject's point of view and to experience the world as that person might.

Secondly, Erikson chose to elaborate a particular crisis or episode in the individual's life which seemed to crystallize a life-theme that united the activities of his past and gave direction to his activities for the future. Then, much as an artist might, Erikson proceeded to fill in the background of the episode and add social and historical perspective. In a very real sense Erikson's biographical sketches are like paintings which direct the viewer's gaze from a focal point of attention to background and back again, so that one's appreciation of the focal area is enriched by having pursued the picture in its entirety.

This method was given its first major test in Erikson's study of "Young Man Luther." Originally, Erikson planned only a brief study of Luther, but "Luther proved too bulky a man to be merely a chapter in a book." Erikson's involvement with Luther dated from his youth, when, as a wandering artist, he happened to hear the Lord's Prayer in Luther's German. "Never knowingly having heard it, I had the experience, as seldom before or after, of a wholeness captured in a few simple words, of poetry fusing the esthetic and the moral; those who have suddenly 'heard' the Gettysburg Address will know what I mean."

Erikson's interest in Luther may have had other roots as well. In some ways, Luther's unhappiness with the papal intermediaries of Christianity resembled on a grand scale Erikson's own dissatisfaction with the intermediaries of Freud's system. In both cases some of the intermediaries had so distorted the original teachings that what was being preached in the name of the master came close to being the opposite of what he had himself proclaimed. While it is not possible to describe Erikson's treatment of Luther here, one can get some feeling for Erikson's brand of historical analysis from his sketch of Luther:

"Luther was a very troubled and a very gifted young man who had to create his own cause on which to focus his fidelity in the Roman Catholic world as it was then. . . . He first became a monk and tried to solve his scruples by being an exceptionally good monk. But even his superiors thought that he tried much too hard. He felt himself to be such a sinner that he began to lose faith in the charity of God and his superiors told him, 'Look, God doesn't hate you, you hate God or else you would trust Him to accept your prayers.' But I would like to make it clear that someone like Luther becomes a historical person only because he also has an acute understanding of historical actuality and knows how to 'speak to the condition' of his times. Only then do inner struggles become representative of those of a large number of vigorous and sincere young people—and begin to interest some troublemakers and hangers-on."

After Erikson's study of "Young Man Luther" (1958), he turned his attention to "middle-aged" Gandhi. As did Luther, Gandhi evoked for Erikson childhood memories. Gandhi led his first nonviolent protest in India in 1918 on behalf of some mill workers, and Erikson, then a young man of 16, had read glowing accounts of the event. Almost a half a century later Erikson was invited to Ahmedabad, an industrial city in western India, to give a seminar on the human life cycle. Erikson discovered that Ahmedabad was the city in which Gandhi had led the demonstration about which Erikson had read as a youth. Indeed, Erikson's host was none other than Ambalal Sarabahai, the benevolent industrialist who had been Gandhi's host—as well as antagonist—in the 1918 wage dispute. Throughout his stay in Ahmedabad, Erikson continued to encounter people and places that were related to Gandhi's initial experiments with nonviolent techniques.

The more Erikson learned about the event at Ahmedabad, the more intrigued he became with its pivotal importance in Gandhi's career. It seemed to be the historical moment upon which all the earlier events of Gandhi's life converged and from which diverged all of his later endeavors. So captured was Erikson by the event at Ahmedabad, that he returned the following year to research a book on Gandhi in which the event would serve as a fulcrum.

At least part of Erikson's interest in Gandhi may have stemmed from certain parallels in their lives. The 1918 event marked Gandhi's emergence as a national political leader. He was 48 at the time, and had become involved reluctantly, not so much out of a need for power or fame as out of a genuine conviction that something had to be done about the disintegration of Indian culture. Coincidentally, Erikson's book "Childhood and Society," appeared in 1950 when Erikson was 48, and it is that book which brought him national prominence in the mental health field. Like Gandhi, too, Erikson reluctantly did what he felt he had to do (namely, publish his observations and conclusions) for the benefit of his

Erikson in a seminar at his Stockbridge, Mass., home.

"Young analysts are today proclaiming a 'new freedom' to see Freud in historical perspective, which reflects the Eriksonian view that one can recognize Freud's greatness without bowing to conceptual precedent."

ailing profession and for the patients treated by its practitioners. So while Erikson's affinity with Luther seemed to derive from comparable professional identity crises, his affinity for Gandhi appears to derive from a parallel crisis of generativity. A passage from "Gandhi's Truth" (from a chapter wherein Erikson addresses himself directly to his subject) helps to convey Erikson's feeling for his subject.

"So far, I have followed you through the loneliness of your childhood and through the experiments and the scruples of your youth. I have affirmed my belief in your ceaseless endeavor to perfect yourself as a man who came to feel that he was the only one available to reverse India's fate. You experimented with what to you were debilitating temptations and you did gain vigor and agility from your victories over yourself. Your identity could be no less than that of universal man, although you had to become an Indian—and one close to the masses—first."

The following passage speaks to Erikson's belief in the general significance of Gandhi's efforts:

"We have seen in Gandhi's development the strong attraction of one of those more inclusive identities: that of an enlightened citizen of the British Empire. In proving himself willing neither to abandon vital ties to his native tradition nor to sacrifice lightly a Western education which eventually contributed to his ability to help defeat British hegemony—in

all of these seeming contradictions Gandhi showed himself on intimate terms with the actualities of his era. For in all parts of the world, the struggle now is for *the anticipatory development of more inclusive identities* . . . I submit then, that Gandhi, in his immense intuition for historical actuality and his capacity to assume leadership in 'truth in action,' may have created a ritualization through which men, equipped with both realism and strength, can face each other with mutual confidence."

There is now more and more teaching of Erikson's concepts in psychiatry, psychology, education and social work in America and in other parts of the world. His description of the stages of the life cycle are summarized in major textbooks in all of these fields and clinicians are increasingly looking at their cases in Eriksonian terms.

Research investigators have, however, found Erikson's formulations somewhat difficult to test. This is not surprising, inasmuch as Erikson's conceptions, like Freud's, take into account the infinite complexity of the human personality. Current research methodologies are, by and large, still not able to deal with these complexities at their own level, and distortions are inevitable when such concepts as "identity" come to be defined in terms of responses to a questionnaire.

Likewise, although Erikson's life-stages have an intuitive "rightness" about them, not everyone agrees with his formulations. Douvan and Adelson in their book, "The Adolescent Experience," argue that while his identity theory may hold true for boys, it doesn't for girls. This argument is based on findings which suggest that girls postpone identity consolidation until after marriage (and intimacy) have been established. Such postponement occurs, says Douvan and Adelson, because a woman's identity is partially defined by the identity of the man whom she marries. This view does not really contradict Erikson's, since he recognizes that later events, such as marriage, can help to resolve both current and past developmental crises. For the woman, but not for the man, the problems of identity and intimacy may be solved concurrently.

Objections to Erikson's formulations have come from other directions as well. Robert W. White, Erikson's good friend and colleague at Harvard, has a long standing (and warmhearted) debate with Erikson over his life-stages. White believes that his own theory of "competence motivation," a theory which has received wide recognition, can account for the phenomena of ego development much more economically than can Erikson's stages. Erikson has, however, little interest in debating the validity of the stages he has described. As an artist he recognizes that there are many different ways to view one and the same phenomenon and that a perspective that is congenial to one person will be repugnant to another. He offers his stage-wise description of the life cycle for those who find such perspectives congenial and not as a world view that everyone should adopt.

It is this lack of dogmatism and sensitivity to the diversity and complexity of the human personality which help to account for the growing recognition of Erikson's contribution within as well as without the helping professions. Indeed, his psycho-historical investigations have originated a whole new field of study which has caught the interest of historians and political scientists alike. (It has also intrigued his wife, Joan, who has published pieces on Eleanor Roosevelt and who has a book on Saint Francis in press.) A recent issue of Daedalus, the journal for the American Academy of Arts and Sciences,

was entirely devoted to psycho-historical and psycho-political investigations of creative leaders by authors from diverse disciplines who have been stimulated by Erikson's work.

Now in his 68th year, Erikson maintains the pattern of multiple activities and appointments which has characterized his entire career. He spends the fall in Cambridge, Mass., where he teaches a large course on "the human life cycle" for Harvard seniors. The spring semester is spent at his home in Stockbridge, Mass., where he participates in case conferences and staff seminars at the Austen Riggs Center. His summers are spent on Cape Cod. Although Erikson's major commitment these days is to his psycho-historical investigation, he is embarking on a study of preschool children's play constructions in different settings and countries, a follow-up of some research he conducted with preadolescents more than a quarter-century ago. He is also planning to review other early observations in the light of contemporary change. In his approach to his work, Erikson appears neither drawn nor driven, but rather to be following an inner schedule as natural as the life cycle itself.

Although Erikson, during his decade of college teaching, has not seen any patients or taught at psychoanalytic institutes, he maintains his dedication to psychoanalysis and views his psycho-historical investigations as an applied branch of that discipline. While some older analysts continue to ignore Erikson's work, there is increasing evidence (including a recent poll of psychiatrists and psychoanalysts) that he is having a rejuvenating influence upon a discipline which many regard as dead or dying. Young analysts are today proclaiming a "new freedom" to see Freud in historical perspective—which reflects the Eriksonian view that one can recognize Freud's greatness without bowing to conceptual precedent.

Accordingly, the reports of the demise of psychoanalysis may have been somewhat premature. In the work of Erik Erikson, at any rate, psychoanalysis lives and continues to beget life.

Freud's "Ages of Man"

Erik Erikson's definition of the "eight ages of man" is a work of synthesis and insight by a psychoanalytically trained and worldly mind. Sigmund Freud's description of human phases stems from his epic psychological discoveries and centers almost exclusively on the early years of life. A brief summary of the phases posited by Freud:

Oral stage—roughly the first year of life, the period during which the mouth region provides the greatest sensual satisfaction. Some derivative behavioral traits which may be seen at this time are *incorporativeness* (first six months of life) and *aggressiveness* (second six months of life).

Anal stage—roughly the second and third years of life. During this period the site of greatest sensual pleasure shifts to the anal and urethral areas. Derivative behavioral traits are *retentiveness* and *expulsiveness*.

Phallic stage—roughly the third and fourth years of life. The site of

greatest sensual pleasure during this stage is the genital region. Behavior traits derived from this period include *intrusiveness* (male) and *receptiveness* (female).

Oedipal stage—roughly the fourth and fifth years of life. At this stage the young person takes the parent of the opposite sex as the object or provider of sensual satisfaction and regards the same-sexed parent as a rival. (The "family romance.") Behavior traits originating in this period are *seductiveness* and *competitiveness*.

Latency stage—roughly the years from age 6 to 11. The child resolves the Oedipus conflict by identifying with the parent of the opposite sex and by so doing satisfies sensual needs vicariously. Behavior traits developed during this period include *conscience* (or the internalization of parental moral and ethical demands).

Puberty stage—roughly 11 to 14. During this period there is an integration and subordination of oral, anal and phallic sensuality to an overriding and unitary genital *sexuality*. The genital sexuality of puberty has another young person of the opposite sex as its object, and discharge (at least for boys) as its aim. Derivative behavior traits (associated with the control and regulation of genital sexuality) are *intellectualization* and *estheticism*.

—D.E.

Television and the Young Viewer

Eli A. Rubinstein

Eli A. Rubinstein was, from 1966 to 1971, Assistant Director at the National Institute of Mental Health, where his last major responsibilities were as Vice Chairman of the Surgeon-General's Scientific Advisory Committee and co-editor of the five volumes of research reports which resulted from that program. He continued his research interest in television and social behavior while serving from 1971 to 1978 as Professor of Psychiatry and Psychology at the State University of New York at Stony Brook. In October 1978, he became Adjunct Research Professor of Psychology at the University of North Carolina, where he intends to pursue further the problem of relating television research to social policy. Address: Department of Psychology, University of North Carolina, Chapel Hill, NC 27514.

For *some* children, under *some* conditions, *some* television is harmful. For *other* children under the same conditions, or for the same children under *other* conditions, it may be beneficial. For *most* children, under *most* conditions, *most* television is probably neither particularly harmful nor particularly beneficial. [Schramm, Lyle, and Parker 1961, p. 1]

That assessment, made in 1961 by three leading Stanford researchers, was the general conclusion of one of the first major studies of television and children. Almost two decades and about two thousand studies later, their conclusion remains a reasonably accurate evaluation of the complex and differential impact of television on its millions of young viewers. The published research since 1961 has further confirmed the harmful effects to some children of some television under some conditions. At the same time, stronger evidence for the corollary has been found: for some children, under some conditions, some television is beneficial.

It is in the differentiation between *some* children and *most* children and in the distinction between *some* television and *most* television that the scientific findings are still not clear. As in so many other instances of exposure to persuasive messages, it is the cumulative impact over extended periods of time that should be the

crucial test of consequences. It seems reasonable to assume that when millions of young viewers each spend on average about a thousand hours per year watching hundreds of television programs, such time spent must have some significant effect on their social development. It is equally reasonable to assume that if the effect is so tangible there should be little difficulty in identifying its characteristics or assessing its strength. Here, however, the evidence is less than definitive—thus the continued applicability of the Schramm, Lyle, and Parker generalization.

While the total impact of television on the young viewer is still unclear, the pursuit of evidence has attracted increasing interest on the part of social scientists. In the appendix to the 1961 report by Schramm et al., 52 earlier publications dealing with television and children are annotated, and they make up a fairly complete list of relevant prior research. By 1970 (Atkin, Murray, and Nayman 1971) that list of publications had grown to a total of almost 500 citations. By 1974 a total of almost 2,400 publications were cited under the category of television and human behavior in a major review of the field by Comstock and Fisher (1975). Since 1974, research interest has continued unabated as new topics begin to be explored. The concern about televised violence has been augmented by a concern about sex on television, the persuasive power of television advertising on children, and, indeed, the effect of television on the entire socialization process of children.

Two events in the early 1970s provided the most compelling influence toward that growth of interest. One was the development of the program "Sesame Street," in which formative research was pursued in partnership with the production of the program itself. The other was the completion in 1972 of a major federally funded research program, now known as the

Surgeon-General's program, to evaluate the relationship between TV violence and aggressive behavior in children.

"Sesame Street"

"Sesame Street" provides the most extensive example of how television can be made beneficial for some children under some conditions. The story of its growth and development has been effectively told by its educational director (Lesser 1974). From the research perspective, "Sesame Street" marks a major innovation: it is the first intensive and continuing partnership between education specialists from academia and the creative and technical specialists responsible for putting television programs on the air. How that partnership evolved into not just constructive interchange but productive results is itself a lesson in formative research.

The educational goals of "Sesame Street" were developed over a series of working seminars in 1968, with participation by experts from all relevant specialties. The instructional goals were precisely formulated in a series of specific statements on five major topics: (1) social, moral, and affective development; (2) language and reading; (3) mathematical and numerical skills; (4) reasoning and problem-solving; (5) perception. The target audience was disadvantaged inner-city children.

Overall, the development of the total program toward the achievement of those goals was structured by the continuing interplay of production people and academic researchers in a feedback system involving observation of children viewing programs as they were produced. Happily, all the major participants in this innovative enterprise were completely dedicated to the larger task. Of equal good fortune was the initial allocation, from private and public sources, of $8 million for the start-up and produc-

From *American Scientist*, November 1978. Reprinted by permission, American Scientist, journal of Sigma Xi, The Scientific Research Society.

tion costs for the first eighteen months of "Sesame Street." While those three ingredients—dedicated talent, adequate start-up time, and ample funding—do not always produce success, they certainly represent a good beginning and were put to constructive use in the development of the program.

Some ten years after its introduction, "Sesame Street" has become not just a national but an international phenomenon. In addition to being the most widely viewed children's program in the United States, "Sesame Street," in both the original version and in foreign-language versions, is broadcast in more than 50 countries around the world. The Children's Television Workshop, the parent body for "Sesame Street" and all the other educational programs, cites more than 120 articles and books (Children's Television Workshop 1977) primarily on "Sesame Street" and "The Electric Company." Additional publications through early 1978 bring the total above 150 research reports. These range from studies of attention during the actual program viewing to major evaluations of both "Sesame Street" and "The Electric Company." The total literature provides an unprecedented body of research on how the entertainment appeal of television can be put to educational use.

Most, but not all, of the evaluations are positive. One major study suggests that "Sesame Street" has been less useful to disadvantaged children than advantaged children (Cook et al. 1975) because of differences in viewing interest. And, in England, for example, grave concern was initially raised that the very format of "Sesame Street" is inimical to the learning process because the program overemphasizes sheer attention-getting devices and because it links learning too closely to a commercial entertainment format. (Subsequently, "Sesame Street" was aired in Great Britain and achieved much viewer success.)

But these are issues for the educators. From the standpoint of research on television and the young viewer, the history of "Sesame Street" has been

of great significance. Formative research has achieved a new status through the ongoing efforts to evaluate the progress and achievements of what Joan Ganz Cooney, the director of the entire enterprise, has called "a perpetual television experiment." The program has clearly demonstrated that television can teach children while still holding their voluntary attention as well, if not better, than conventional television programming. It is the clearest example of the positive potential of television translated into performance.

Televised violence

At about the same time that "Sesame Street" was being prepared for broadcast in 1969, a major federal research program was initiated to assess the effects of televised violence on children. The history of that research enterprise has been thoroughly described and evaluated from a variety of perspectives (Bogart 1972; Cater and Strickland 1975; Rubinstein 1975). The belief is fairly widespread that the body of research, published in five volumes of technical reports, provided a major new set of findings.

There is much less agreement about the report and conclusions of the advisory committee itself, because of the cautious language used. Even now, years after the report was published, the conclusions are debated. The debate was sparked initially because of a misleading headline in a front-page story in the New York Times ("TV Violence Held Unharmful to Youth") when the report was first released. A careful analysis of the subsequent press coverage revealed how influential that headline was in further confusing the interpretation of the findings (Tankard and Showalter 1977). The committee had unanimously agreed that there was some evidence of a causal relationship between televised violence and later aggressive behavior. However, the conclusion was so moderated by qualifiers that it was, and still is, criticized and misinterpreted by industry spokesmen as being too strong and by researchers as being too weak.

The effect of televised violence has

been an issue of public concern almost from the inception of television in the early 1950s. Periodically, over the past 25 years, a variety of congressional inquiries as well as commissioned reports have drawn attention to the problem of televised violence. In almost every instance concern was raised about harmful effects. In all these reports, however, relatively little new research on the problem was produced. Even the prestigious Eisenhower Commission, which was asked by President Johnson in 1968 to explore the question within its total inquiry into violence in America, devoted its attention primarily to a synthesis of existing knowledge rather than to collecting new scientific information. Its conclusions—that violence on television encourages real violence—were seen as less than persuasive and were largely ignored, especially since attention was then focused on the new Surgeon-General's Committee.

The Surgeon-General's program provided the first major infusion of new monies into research on television violence, which in turn has stimulated a "second harvest," as Schramm (1976) calls it, of new work on television and social behavior. The debate on the evidence from the five volumes of research reports produced in 1972 by the Surgeon-General's program is also still lively. The essence of the debate emerges from two contrasting approaches to assessing the evidence. The Surgeon-General's advisory committee, while acknowledging flaws in many of the individual studies, held that the convergence of evidence was sufficient to permit a qualified conclusion indicating a causal relationship between extensive viewing of violence and later aggressive behavior. This conclusion, without the qualifications, is endorsed by a number of highly respected researchers, some of whom participated in the Surgeon-General's program and some who were not directly involved.

A different and seemingly more rigorous approach to the evidence is adopted by some other experts in the field. This contrasting view is epitomized by Kaplan and Singer (1976), who conclude that the total evidence does no more than support the null hypothesis.

A brief explanation is appropriate here about the theoretical formulations most common in the research underlying the whole question of television and aggressive behavior. Quite simply, three possibilities exist—and all have their proponents. (1) Television has no significant relationship to aggressive behavior. (2) Television reduces aggressive behavior. (3) Television causes aggressive behavior; a variant on this possibility is that both television viewing and aggressive behavior are related not to each other but to a "third variable" which mediates between the first two variables.

The Kaplan and Singer position, to give one recent example, is that the research so far has demonstrated no relationship between televised violence and later aggressive behavior. They characterize this as the "conservative" assessment of the evidence and come to that conclusion by finding no study persuasive enough in its own right to bear the burden of significant correlation, let alone causal relationship. They are not the only ones to conclude "no-effect": Singer (1971) came to the same conclusion, as did Howitt and Cumberbatch (1975).

The second point of view has been espoused primarily by Feshbach (1961). The catharsis hypothesis holds that vicarious experience of aggressive behavior, as occurs in viewing TV violence, may actually serve as a release of aggressive tensions and thereby reduce direct expression of aggressive behavior. This view has not been supported by research evidence, although it emerges time and again as a "common-sense" assessment of the relationship between vicarious viewing of violence and later behavior. Indeed, the thesis itself goes back to Aristotle, who considered dramatic presentations a vehicle for discharge of feelings by the audience. The Surgeon-General's committee, in considering this thesis, made one of their few unequivocal assessments—that there was "no evidence that would support a catharsis interpretation."

The third general conclusion, and the one now prevailing, is that there is a positive relationship between TV violence and later aggressive behavior. This facilitation of later aggression, explained primarily by social learning theory, is endorsed by a number of investigators. The basic theoretical formulation is generally credited to Bandura (Bandura and Walters 1963), who began his social learning studies in the early 1960s, when he and his students clearly demonstrated that children will imitate aggressive acts they witness in film presentations. These were the so-called "bobo doll" studies, in which children watching a bobo doll being attacked, either by a live model or a cartoon character, were more likely to imitate such behavior. These early studies were criticized both because bobo dolls, made for rough and tumble play, tend to provoke aggressive hitting and because the hostile play was only against inanimate play objects. Later studies have demonstrated that such aggression will also take place against people (Hanratty et al. 1972).

Variations on the basic social learning theory are rather numerous. Kaplan and Singer make a useful schema by incorporating three related theoretical branches under the general label of "activation hypotheses." Bandura and his students are included in the category of social learning and imitation. A second branch is represented by Berkowitz and his students, who follow a classical conditioning hypothesis, in which repeated viewing of aggressive behavior is presented to build up the probability of aggressive behavior as a conditioned response to the cues produced in the portrayal. A number of experiments by Berkowitz and his colleagues have shown that subjects viewing a violent film after being angered were more likely to show aggressive behavior than subjects, similarly angered beforehand, who saw nonaggressive films (Berkowitz 1965; Berkowitz and Geen 1966).

In still a third variation on the activation approach, Tannenbaum (1972) holds that a generalized emotional arousal is instigated by emotionally charged viewing material and that this level of arousal itself is the precursor of the subsequent behavior. Any exciting content, including erotic content, can induce this heightened arousal. The nature of response is then a function of the conditions that exist at the time the activation of behavior takes place. Thus, according to this theory, it is not so much the violent content per se that induces later aggressive behavior as it is the level of arousal evoked. Subsequent circumstances may channel the heightened arousal in the direction of aggressive behavior.

In an important examination of the utility of these various formulations, Watt and Krull (1977) reanalyzed data on 597 adolescents from three prior studies, involving both programming attributes (such as perceived violent content) and viewer attributes (such as viewing exposure and aggressive behavior) through a series of correlations. They contrasted three models, which they labeled catharsis model, arousal model, and facilitation model. The first two models are essentially as described above. The facilitation model is identified as a general social-learning model without regard to whether the process is primarily imitation, cueing, or legitimization of aggressive behavior. Thus, the Bandura and Berkowitz studies both fall into the facilitation model.

Through a series of partial correlations, Watt and Krull found (1) no support for the catharsis model; (2) support for a combination of the facilitation and arousal models; and (3) some differences due to age and/or sex, with the arousal model a somewhat better explanation for female adolescents, whereas the facilitation model better described the data for males. (Sex differences in results in many studies of television and behavior are quite common. One of the major studies in the field, by Lefkowitz et al., 1972, found significant correlations between TV violence and later aggressive behavior with boys but not with girls.)

What are the implications in this continuing controversy about the effects of television violence on aggressive behavior? As in so many other social science issues it depends on what you are looking for. The dilemma is neatly characterized in a legal case in Florida in October 1977, in which the defense argued that an adolescent boy, who admittedly killed an elderly woman, was suffering from "involuntary subliminal television intoxication." (This term, which appears nowhere in the scientific literature, was introduced by the defense attorney.) In trying to show that the scientific evidence on television's effects on behavior was not directly pertinent to this murder trial, the prosecuting attorney asked an expert witness if any scientific studies indicated that a viewer had ever been induced to commit a serious crime following the viewing of TV violence. The (correct) answer to that question was "no." The judge thereby ruled that expert testimony on the effects of televised violence would be inadmissible and brought back the jury, which had been sequestered during the interrogation of the expert witness. On the basis of the evidence presented to it, the jury found the defendant guilty of murder and rejected the plea of temporary insanity by virtue of "involuntary subliminal television intoxication."

While there is indeed no *scientific* evidence that excessive viewing of televised violence can or does provoke violent crime in any one individual, it is clear that the bulk of the studies show that if large groups of children watch a great deal of televised violence they will be more prone to behave aggressively than similar groups of children who do not watch such TV violence. The argument simply follows from the basic premise that children learn from all aspects of their environment. To the extent that one or another environmental agent occupies a significant proportion of a child's daily activity, that agent becomes a component of influence on his or her behavior. In a recent comprehensive review of all the evidence on the effects of television on children, Comstock et al. (1978) conclude that television should be considered a major agent of socialization in the lives of children.

An important confirmation of the more general influence of television on the young viewer derives from research on the so-called "prosocial" effects of television. Stimulated by the findings of the Surgeon-General's program, a number of researchers began in 1972 to explore the corollary question: If TV violence can induce aggressive behavior, can TV prosocial programming stimulate positive behavior? By 1975, this question was of highest interest to active researchers in the field, according to a national survey (Comstock and Lindsey 1975).

A significant body of literature has now been generated to confirm these prosocial effects (Rubinstein et al. 1974; Stein and Friedrich 1975). Research by network scientists (CBS Broadcast Group 1977) has confirmed that children learn from the prosocial messages included in programs designed to impart such messages. Because the effect of prosocial program content is so clearly similar in process to the effect of TV violence, confirmation of the former effect adds strength to the validity of the latter effect.

In all the intensive analysis of the effects of TV violence, perhaps the one scientific issue most strongly argued against by the network officials has been the definition and assessment of levels of violent content. The single continuing source of such definition and assessment has been the work of Gerbner and his associates (Gerbner 1972). Beginning in 1969 and continuing annually, Gerbner has been publishing a violence index which has charted the levels of violence among the three networks on prime time. The decline in violence over the entire decade had been negligible until the 1977–78 season (Gerbner et al. 1978), following an intensive public campaign against TV violence by both the American Medical Association and the Parent-Teacher Association.

Gerbner's definition of violence is specific and yet inclusive—"the overt expression of physical force against others or self, or compelling action against one's will on pain of being hurt or killed or actually hurting or killing." Despite criticism by the industry, the Gerbner index has been widely accepted by other researchers. An extensive effort by a Committee on Television and Social Behavior, organized by the Social Science Research Council to develop a more comprehensive violence index, ended up essentially endorsing Gerbner's approach (Social Science Research Council 1975).

Perhaps of more theoretical interest than his violence index is Gerbner's present thesis that television is a "cultural indicator." He argues that television content reinforces beliefs about various cultural themes—the social realities of life are modified in the mind of the viewer by the images portrayed on the television screen. To the extent that the television world differs from the real world, some portion of that difference influences the perception of the viewer about the world in which he or she lives. Thus, Gerbner has found that heavy viewers see the world in a much more sinister light than individuals who do not watch as much television. Gerbner argues that excessive portrayals of violence on television inculcate feelings of fear among heavy viewers, which may be as important an effect as the findings of increased aggressive behavior. Some confirmation of this feeling of fear was found in a national survey of children (Zill 1977): children who were heavy viewers were reported significantly more likely to be more fearful in general than children who watched less television.

TV advertising

An area of research that has been increasing in importance since the work of the Surgeon-General's program has been concerned with the effects of advertising on children. One of the technical reports in the Surgeon-General's program described a series of studies on this topic by Ward (1972), which was among the first major published studies in which children's reactions to television advertising were examined in their relationship to cognitive development. That report provided preliminary findings on (1) how children's responses to television advertising become increasingly differentiated and complex with age; (2) the development of cynicism and suspicion about television messages by the fourth grade; (3) mothers' perceptions about how television influences their children; and (4) how television advertising influences consumer socialization among adolescents.

The entire field of research on effects of television advertising—at least academic published research—has only begun to develop in the 1970s. A major review of the published literature in the field was sponsored and published by the National Science Foundation in 1977 (Adler 1977). It is noteworthy that only 21 studies, all published between 1971 and 1976, were considered significant enough to be singled out for inclusion in the review's annotated appendix. The total body of evidence is still so small that no major theoretical formulations have yet emerged. Instead, the research follows the general social-learning model inherent in the earlier research on televised violence.

Despite the lack of extensive research findings on the effects of television advertising on children, formal concern about possible effects began to emerge in the early 1960s. Self-regulatory guidelines were adopted by the National Association of Broadcasters in 1961 to define acceptable toy advertising practices to children. Subsequently, published NAB guidelines were expanded to include all advertising directed primarily to children. An entire mechanism has been established within the industry, under the responsibility of the NAB Television Code Authority, through which guidelines on children's advertising—as well as other broadcast standards—are enforced. In addition, in 1974 the National Advertising Division of the Council of Better Business Bureaus established a Children's Advertising Review Unit to help in the self-regulation of advertising directed to children aged eleven and under. That organization, with the assistance of a panel of social science advisors, developed and issued its own set of guidelines for children's advertising.

The role of research in helping to make those guidelines on children's advertising more meaningful is only now receiving some attention, thanks

in part to the NSF review cited above. Two recent events have highlighted both the paucity and the relevance of research in this field. In 1975, the Attorney General of Massachusetts, in collaboration with Attorneys General of other states, petitioned the Federal Communications Commission to ban all drug advertising between 9 A.M. and 9 P.M., on the ground that such advertising was harmful to children. After a series of hearings in May 1976, at which researchers and scientists testified, the petition was denied for lack of scientific evidence to support the claim.

In 1978, the Federal Trade Commission formally considered petitions requesting "the promulgation of a trade rule regulating television advertising of candy and other sugared products to children." A comprehensive staff report on television advertising to children (Ratner et al. 1978) made recommendations to the FTC, citing much of the relevant scientific literature on advertising to children as evidence supporting the need for such a trade rule. At the time of this writing, the entire matter was still under active consideration.

What does the existing research in this area demonstrate? It is clear that children are exposed to a large number of television commercials. The statistics themselves are significant. Annually, on average, children between two and eleven years of age are now exposed to more than 20,000 television commercials. Children in this age group watch an average of about 25 hours of television per week all through the year. The most clichéd statistic quoted is that, by the time a child graduates from high school today, he or she will have spent more time in front of a television set (17,000 hours) than in a formal classroom (11,000 hours). Indeed, all the statistics on television viewing from earliest childhood through age eighteen show that no other daily activity, with the exception of sleeping, is so clearly dominant.

Just as was shown in the earlier research examining the effects of programming content, even the limited research now available on television commercials documents that children

learn from watching these commercials. Whether it is the sheer recall of products and product attributes (Atkin 1975) or the singing of commercial jingles (Lyle and Hoffman 1972), the evidence is positive that children learn. More important, children and their parents are influenced by the intent of these commercials. One study (Lyle and Hoffman 1972) showed that nine out of ten preschool children asked for food items and toys they saw advertised on television.

A number of studies have also revealed various unintended effects of television advertising. While a vast majority of the advertisements adhere to the guidelines that attempt to protect children against exploitative practices, a number of studies have shown that, over time, children begin to distrust the accuracy of the commercial message. By the sixth grade, children are generally cynical about the truthfulness of the ads. A recent educational film by Consumers Union, on some of the excessive claims in TV advertising, highlights the problem of disbelief (Consumers Union 1976). There have also been a number of surveys in which parents have indicated negative reactions to children's commercials. In one study (Ward, Wackman, and Wartella 1975) 75% of the parents had such negative reactions.

In the survey of the literature evaluated in the 1977 NSF review, the evidence is examined against some of the major policy concerns that have emerged in the development of appropriate guidelines on children's advertising. These concerns can be grouped into four categories: (1) modes of advertising; (2) content of advertising; (3) products advertised; and (4) general effects of advertising.

Studies of "modes of advertising" show, for example, that separation of program and commercial is not well understood by children under eight years of age. While these younger children receive and retain the commercial messages, they are less able to discriminate the persuasive intent of the commercial and are more likely to perceive the message as truthful and to want to buy the product (Robertson and Rossiter 1974).

The format and the use of various audio-visual techniques also influence the children's perceptions of the message. This influence is clearly acknowledged by the advertisers and the broadcasters, who have included explicit instructions in the guidelines, especially for toy products, to ensure that audio and video production techniques do not misrepresent the product. What little research there is on this entire aspect of format is still far from definitive. What is clear is that attention, especially among young children, is increased by active movement, animation, lively music, and visual changes. (All of this, and more, is well understood by the advertising agencies and those who develop the ads, and they keep such knowledge confidential, much as a trade secret.)

One other relatively clear finding on audio-visual technique relates to the understanding of "disclaimers"—special statements about the product that may not be clear from the commercial itself, such as "batteries not included." A study of disclaimer wording and comprehension (Liebert et al. 1977) revealed that a standard disclaimer ("some assembly required") was less well understood by 6- and 8-year-olds than a modification ("You have to put it together"). The obvious conclusion—that wording should be appropriate to the child's ability to understand—is just one of the many ways in which this research can play a role in refining guidelines.

Studies on the content of advertising have shown that the appearance of a particular character with the product can modify the child's evaluation of the product, either positively or negatively, depending on the child's evaluation of the character. It is also clear that children are affected in a positive way by presenters of their own sex and race (Adler 1977). On a more general level, sexual stereotypes in advertising probably influence children in the same way they do in the program content.

Although there is relatively little significant research on the effects of classes of products, two such classes have been under intense public scrutiny in recent years: proprietary drug advertising and certain categories of food advertising. Governmental regulatory agencies are currently considering what kind of controls should be placed on such advertising to children.

Concerning the more general effects of advertising targeted to children, surveys suggest that parents have predominantly negative attitudes about such advertising because they believe it causes stress in the parent-child relationship. Studies on questions such as this, and on the larger issue of how such advertising leads to consumer socialization, are now being pursued. Ward and his associates (Ward, Wackman, and Wartella 1975) have been examining the entire question of how children learn to buy. The highly sophisticated techniques used by advertisers to give a 30-second or 60-second commercial strong impact on the child viewer make these commercials excellent study material for examining the entire process of consumer socialization. Much important research still remains to be done on this topic.

Sex on TV

Of the many public concerns about television and its potentially harmful effects on children, the issue of sex on television is at present among the most visible and the least understood. If research on the effects of advertising is still in its early development, research on sex on television has hardly begun.

It has been found that children who watch large amounts of television (25 hours or more per week) are more likely to reveal stereotypic sex role attitudes than children who watch 10 hours or less per week (Frueh and McGhee 1975). Research has documented the stereotyping on television of women as passive and rule-abiding, while men are shown as aggressive, powerful, and smarter than women. Also, youth and attractiveness are stressed more for females than males. This evidence of stereotyping was included as one part of an argument by the U.S. Commission on Civil

Rights that the Federal Communications Commission should conduct an inquiry into the portrayal of minorities and women in commercial and public television drama and should propose rules to correct the problem (U.S. Commission on Civil Rights 1977). Program content in 1977 and 1978 has given increased emphasis to so-called "sex on television," at the same time that violence on television is decreasing (Gerbner et al. 1978).

Despite all the public concern and attention, including cover stories in major newsweeklies, relatively little academic research has been done on sex on TV. Two studies reported in 1977 provided information on the level of physical intimacy portrayed on television (Franzblau et al. 1977 and Fernandez-Collado and Greenberg 1977). Franzblau, Sprafkin, and Rubinstein analyzed 61 prime-time programs shown on all three networks during a full week in early October 1975. Results showed that, while there was considerable casual intimacy such as kissing and embracing and much verbal innuendo on sexual activity, actual physical intimacy such as intercourse, rape, and homosexual behavior was absent in explicit form.

Fernandez-Collado and Greenberg examined 77 programs aired in prime time during the 1976–77 season and concluded that intimate sexual acts did occur on commercial television, with "the predominant act being sexual intercourse between heterosexuals unmarried to each other." An examination of the data, however, reveals that in this study, verbal statements—identified as verbal innuendo in the study by Franzblau et al.—served as the basis for the conclusion reached. In fact, explicit sexual acts such as identify an R- or an X-rated movie do not occur on prime-time network television.

Even though few published studies have so far examined the question of sex on television, at least two important issues have been highlighted by the two studies mentioned above. The most obvious point is the difference in interpretation of the data by the two reports—unfortunately not an uncommon occurrence in social science research. Labeling and defining the phenomena under examination, let alone drawing conclusions from results, show variations from investigator to investigator. While this kind of difference is not unique to the social sciences, the more complex the data and the less standard the measurement—qualities often inherent in social science studies—the more likely these individual differences of interpretation.

The second point illustrated by these two studies of sex on TV is more intrinsic to the subject matter itself. The public concern about sex on TV suggests that the general reaction is much in keeping with the substitution of behavior for verbal statements, as is found in the study by Fernandez-Collado and Greenberg. And, in fact, there are no scientific data to indicate that verbal innuendo may not affect the young viewer as much—or as little—as explicitly revealed behavior. What is important here is that we do not know the effects of either the verbal description or the explicit depiction on the young viewer. Research findings of the Commission on Obscenity and Pornography in 1970 suggest that exposure to explicit sexuality seems harmless. Nevertheless, public sensitivities are clearly high; whether those sensitivities are justified by the facts still remains an open question. At the very least, studies should be undertaken to give some objective answers to these questions.

One such effort is a recent content analysis by Rubinstein and his colleagues (Silverman et al. 1978), which confirms the absence of explicit sex in network programs aired in the 1977–78 season but documents a continued increase in sexual innuendos. Furthermore, sexual intercourse, which was never even contextually implied in the 1975–76 analysis by Franzblau et al. (1977), was so implied fifteen times during the week of programs analyzed in the 1977–78 report. Clearly the current decrease in violent content is partially offset by added emphasis on sexual content.

Issues of policy

What are the policy implications of research on television and social behavior? Perhaps the most fundamental point to be made is that even with fairly clear research findings, the policy to be followed rarely emerges as a direct result of the research.

The history of the Surgeon-General's program provides a useful case study of the complexities of this issue. When the Surgeon-General's program of research was initiated, the advisory committee was charged by the Secretary of HEW, Robert Finch, with the responsibility for answering the question originally raised by Senator John Pastore, Chairman of the Senate Subcommittee on Communications: Does the viewing of TV violence stimulate aggressive behavior on the part of young children? The committee was specifically enjoined from making policy recommendations, since the HEW has no regulatory responsibility in this area. Thus, when the committee report was issued in 1972, there was no discussion of direct policy implications, nor were there any specific policy recommendations in that final document.

Senator Pastore, on receiving the report in January 1972, was sufficiently concerned, both about the cautious wording of the conclusion and the absence of policy recommendations, to call another set of hearings in March 1972 to clarify the interpretation of the results and to ask the committee members for their policy recommendations now that they were no longer under official constraints. What Senator Pastore learned at those hearings is now a familiar characteristic of scientists speaking out on public policy: their scientific expertise affords them little advantage in the public policy arena. There were relatively few workable and concrete policy recommendations forthcoming. Indeed, the most specific recommendation came from the Senator himself: a request to the Secretary of HEW and the FCC that an annual violence index be published that would measure the amount of televised violence entering American homes. No such official index has ever emerged, although Gerbner has annually produced such a measure, as a continuation of his ongoing research program.

What is clear from an examination of the Surgeon-General's program in retrospect is that the advisory committee was correctly confined to the examination of the research question. But the next step was not taken—to set up a different committee, to develop policy recommendations on the basis of that research and in keeping with legal constraints and operational feasibility. Indeed, it might well have taken more time and care to examine the complexities of social policy in order to come to realistic and useful conclusions about a social course of action than it took to evaluate the research findings.

Attempts at policy formation concerning sexual content on TV will bring the complexities of social science research to public attention. For example, as Dienstbier (1977) has pointed out, the conclusions of the Surgeon-General's committee affirm the social learning model. The Commission on Obscenity and Pornography, on the other hand, concluded in 1970 that exposure to explicit sexuality seemed harmless. Aside from the fact that the differences in these two sets of conclusions may be partly a reflection of liberal versus conservative value judgments relating to aggression and sex (Berkowitz 1971), there are some intriguing implications for social policy in other differences between the portrayal on television of violence and physical intimacy. Dienstbier suggests that increased portrayal of sex on television may become an important substitute for extensive sex education programs. While such an assertion may provoke considerable debate among social scientists, let alone the public at large, it is worthy of further consideration, as still another pertinent research question.

Difficulties in arriving at policy guidelines for advertising to children are equally apparent. In connection with the current FTC examination of the merits of a trade rule to regulate television advertising of candy and other sugared products to children, the scientific evidence, primarily derived from the NSF report (Adler 1977) and from the interpretation of that evidence by the FTC (Ratner et al. 1978), is the source of much debate. Some of the scientists who contributed to the literature are publicly complaining that their findings are misinterpreted in the FTC staff report (Schaar 1978).

It is a minor irony that researchers are just as quick to take issue with interpretations—which they say go beyond the data—designed to support some change in policy on television advertising as their colleagues were in 1972 to take issue with interpretations by the Surgeon-General's committee which they felt did not go as far as their data indicated. The correct generalization may well be that social scientists find it difficult to accept someone else's interpretation of their findings regardless of the direction of the policy implications.

In all the present examination of research on television and social behavior and its implications for social policy there are a number of important issues to consider. One point that bears repeating is that the research does not by itself identify the policy direction. Nor, for that matter, does the research to date satisfactorily deal with the many research questions that are relevant to the policy directions. At a major conference on priorities for research on television and children held in Reston, Virginia, in 1975 (Ford Foundation 1976), an entire agenda for future research was developed. Topics and methodology recommended ranged from simple experiments to identify effects of disclaimers and warnings in television advertising to long-range studies, including cross-national studies, to study the effects of television on political and social beliefs.

However, except for the Surgeon-General's program of research, plus a new program supported by the NSF in 1976 following the 1975 Reston conference, no major federal program of research exists. Time and again over the past twenty years, following various congressional hearings dealing with the effects of television, recommendations have been made for a "television research center." In early 1978, Senator Wendell Anderson of Minnesota began exploring the feasibility of legislation to develop a "Television Impact Assessment Act,"

but to date no final draft bill has materialized.

The three major networks, primarily responding to the pressures from the Surgeon-General's program, have expended since 1970 approximately $3 million, primarily on the issue of televised violence. The American television industry seems much less willing to examine the need for a major program of research than does the British Broadcasting Corporation, which, in 1976, commissioned an eminent sociologist, Elihu Katz, to develop a comprehensive set of recommendations for a program of social research (Katz 1977). With the American television industry operating at about a $10 billion annual budget, even one-tenth of one percent devoted to social research would amount to $10 million a year. What Katz has recommended to the BBC would serve well both the American television industry and the public: a comprehensive program of research under the auspices of a new foundation funded by a variety of sources, including the broadcasting industry.

What is critical in such an endeavor is that it be seen as a long-term program. In an earlier paper (Rubinstein 1976) I proposed such a long-term instrumentality that would include studying ways of enhancing the value of television to the child viewer. It is likely that important findings still to be uncovered may provide guidelines for making television a more useful agent of socialization than it is at present.

A whole series of new populations of television viewers await the benefits of a constructive examination of the way television influences our lives. The evidence is already clear that older people watch increasing amounts of television. Organizations of older individuals have begun to criticize the televised stereotypes of the helpless and infirm elderly. Recent public broadcast programming such as "Over Easy," directed to an older audience, has shown how television can be of specific interest and benefit to this population.

Another group worthy of special at-

tention includes the institutionalized mental patients, who, in public mental hospitals, watch a large amount of commercial television in their day rooms (Rubinstein et al. 1977). Careful study may provide insights into how this leisure-time activity can be converted into a more meaningful part of the total therapeutic program of the institution. Rubinstein and his colleagues have been studying the effects of TV on institutionalized children (Kochnower et al. 1978).

A bridge between research and policy

What was initially a narrow focus on the presumed harmful effects of televised violence has begun to broaden into other areas that may have even more extensive and important policy implications. Social scientists can make important contributions to policy determinations, but there are important constraints that must be understood and accepted. In a persuasive argument, Bevan (1977) makes a case for the role of the scientist in contributing to the policy process. He stresses the need for scientists to "seek active roles in policy-making both in the public and in the private sectors." Fundamental to taking such a role is the need to recognize the difference between the world of the scientist and the world of the public official. There is a basic dichotomy between an emphasis on scientific inquiry and an emphasis on action and decision-making. That dichotomy is just as real between the social scientist looking at television and its effects on the viewer and the television officials who have the daily responsibility for deciding what does or does not go on the air.

All too often the social scientist venturing into television policy considerations makes naively sweeping recommendations with no understanding of the enormous complexity of responding to all the pressures and necessities of production. At the same time, some responsible members of the television industry take refuge in a defensive posture about the implications of the research findings. In this context, a variation on Bevan's recommendation that scientists engage in the policy process would be that the social scientists and the television industry officials engage in a continuing dialogue on how the research on television and children can be more effectively utilized.

Fortunately, some efforts in this direction are already under way. All three networks have a variety of activities in which outside research consultants meet with television personnel on programming for children. Special conferences and workshops on research have been sponsored in recent years by foundations, by the industry, by citizen action groups, and by professional organizations.

Perhaps the most compelling reason for more collaboration among all sectors—industry, researchers, the viewing public, foundations, and government agencies—is the common objectives held. Television is now a dominant voice in American life. It is a formidable teacher of children. Its healthy future should be the interest and responsibility of all of us.

References

Adler, R. 1977. *The Effects of Television Advertising on Children.* NSF.

Atkin, C. 1975. *Effects of Television Advertising on Children: First Year Experimental Evidence.* Report #1, Mich. State Univ.

Atkin, C. K., J. P. Murray, and O. B. Nayman, ed. 1971. *Television and Social Behavior. The Effects of Television on Children and Youth: An Annotated Bibliography of Research.* U. S. Government Printing Office.

Bandura, A., and R. H. Walters. 1963. *Social Learning and Personality Development.* Holt, Rinehart and Winston.

Berkowitz, L. 1965. Some aspects of observed aggression. *J. Pers. and Soc. Psych.* 2: 359–69.

———. 1971. Sex and violence: We can't have it both ways. *Psych. Today,* Dec. 1971.

Berkowitz, L., and R. Geen. 1966. Film violence and the cue properties of available targets. *J. Pers. and Soc. Psych.* 3:525–30.

Bevan, W. 1977. Science in the penultimate age. *Am. Sci.* 65:538–46.

Bogart, L. 1972. Warning, the Surgeon General has determined that TV violence is moderately dangerous to your child's mental health. *Pub. Opin. Quart.* 36:491–521.

Cater, D., and S. Strickland. 1975. *TV Violence and the Child: The Evolution and Fate of the Surgeon General's Report.* New York: Russell Sage Foundation.

CBS Broadcast Group. 1977. *Learning While They Laugh: Studies of Five Children's Programs on the CBS Television Network.* New York: CBS Broadcast Group.

Children's Television Workshop. 1977. *CTW Research Bibliography.* New York.

Comstock, G., S. Chaffee, N. Katzman, M. McCombs, and D. Roberts. 1978. *Television and Human Behavior.* Columbia University Press.

Comstock, G., and M. Fisher. 1975. *Television and Human Behavior: A Guide to the Pertinent Scientific Literature.* Santa Monica, CA: Rand Corporation.

Comstock, G., and G. Lindsey. 1975. *Television and Human Behavior: The Research Horizon, Future and Present.* Santa Monica, CA: Rand Corporation.

Consumers Union. 1976. *The Six Billion Dollar Sell.* Mount Vernon, NY.

Cook, T. D., H. Appleton, R. F. Conner, A. Shaffer, G. Tomkin, and S. J. Weber. 1975. *Sesame Street Revisited.* New York: Russell Sage Foundation.

Dienstbier, R. A. 1977. Sex and violence: Can research have it both ways? *J. Communication* 27:176–88.

Fernandez-Collado, C., and B. S. Greenberg. 1977. *Substance Use and Sexual Intimacy on Commercial Television.* Report #5, Mich. State Univ.

Feshbach, S. 1961. The stimulating versus cathartic effects of a vicarious aggressive activity. *J. Abnormal and Soc. Psych.* 63: 381–85.

Ford Foundation. 1976. *Television and Children: Priorities for Research.* New York.

Franzblau, S., J. N. Sprafkin, and E. A. Rubinstein. 1977. Sex on TV: A content analysis. *J. Communication* 27:164–70.

Frueh, T., and P. E. McGhee. 1975. Traditional sex-role development and amount of time spent watching television. *Devel. Psych.* 11:109.

Gerbner, G. 1972. Violence in television drama: Trends and symbolic functions. In *Television and Social Behavior,* vol. 1. *Media Content and Control,* ed. G. A. Comstock and E. A. Rubinstein. U. S. Government Printing Office.

Gerbner, G., L. Gross, M. Jackson-Beeck, A. Jeffries-Fox, and N. Signorielli. 1978. *Violence Profile No. 9.* Univ. of Pennsylvania Press.

Hanratty, M. A., E. O'Neal, and J. L. Sulzer. 1972. Effect of frustration upon imitation of aggression. *J. Pers. and Soc. Psych.* 21: 30–34.

Howitt, D., and G. Cumberbatch. 1975. *Mass Media Violence and Society.* Wiley.

Kaplan, R. M., and R. D. Singer. 1976. Television violence and viewer aggression: A reexamination of the evidence. *J. Soc. Issues* 32:35–70.

Katz, E. 1977. *Social Research on Broadcasting: Proposals for Further Development. A Report to the British Broadcasting Corporation.* British Broadcasting Corporation.

Kochnower, J. M., J. F. Fracchia, E. A. Rubinstein, and J. N. Sprafkin. 1978. *Television Viewing Behaviors of Emotionally Disturbed Children: An Interview Study.* New York: Brookdale International Institute.

Lefkowitz, M. M., L. D. Eron, L. O. Walder, and L. R. Huesmann. 1972. Television violence and child aggression: A follow-up study. In *Television and Social Behavior,* vol. 3. *Television and Adolescent Aggressiveness,* ed G. A. Comstock and E. A. Rubinstein. U. S. Gov. Printing Office.

Lesser, G. S. 1974. *Children and Television: Lessons from "Sesame Street."* Random House.

Liebert, D. E., R. M. Liebert, J. N. Sprafkin, and E. A. Rubinstein. 1977. Effects of television commercial disclaimers on the product expectations of children. *J. Communication* 27:118–24.

Lyle, J., and H. Hoffman. 1972. Children's use of television and other media. In *Television and Social Behavior,* vol. 5. *Television in Day-to-Day Life: Patterns of Use,* ed. E. A. Rubinstein, G. A. Comstock, and J. P. Murray. U. S. Government Printing Office.

Ratner, E. M., et al. 1978. *FTC Staff Report on Television Advertising to Children.* Washington, DC: Federal Trade Commission.

Robertson, T. S., and J. R. Rossiter. 1974. Children and commercial persuasion: An attribution theory analysis. *J. Consumer Research* 1:13–20.

Rubinstein, E. A. 1975. Social science and media policy. *J. Communication* 25:194–200.

———. 1976. Warning: The Surgeon General's research program may be dangerous to preconceived notions. *J. Soc. Issues* 32:18–34.

Rubinstein, E. A., J. F. Fracchia, J. M. Kochnower, and J. N. Sprafkin. 1977. *Television Viewing Behaviors of Mental Patients: A Survey of Psychiatric Centers in New York State.* New York: Brookdale International Institute.

Rubinstein, E. A., R. M. Liebert, J. M. Neale, and R. W. Poulos. 1974. *Assessing Television's Influence on Children's Prosocial Behavior.* New York: Brookdale International Institute.

Schaar, K. 1978. TV ad probe snags on Hill, researcher ire. *APA Monitor* vol. 9, no. 6, 1.

Schramm, W. 1976. The second harvest of two research-producing events: The Surgeon General's inquiry and "Sesame Street." *Proc. Nat. Acad. Educ.,* vol. 3.

Schramm, W., J. Lyle, and E. B. Parker. 1961. *Television in the Lives of our Children.* Stanford Univ. Press.

Silverman, L. T., J. N. Sprafkin, and E. A. Rubinstein. 1978. *Sex on Television: A Content Analysis of the 1977–78 Prime-Time Programs.* New York: Brookdale International Institute.

Singer, J. L., ed. 1971. *The Control of Aggression and Violence.* Academic Press.

Social Science Research Council. 1975. *A Profile of Televised Violence.* New York.

Stein, A. H., and L. K. Friedrich. 1975. *Impact of Television on Children and Youth.* Univ. of Chicago Press.

Surgeon-General's Scientific Advisory Committee on Television and Social Behavior. 1972. *Television and Growing Up: The Impact of Televised Violence.* U. S. Government Printing Office.

Tankard, J. W., and S. W. Showalter. 1977. Press coverage of the 1972 report on television and social behavior. *Journalism Quart.* 54:293–306.

Tannenbaum, P. H. 1972. Studies in film- and television-mediated arousal and aggression: A progress report. In *Television and Social Behavior,* vol. 5. *Television Effects: Further Explorations,* ed. G. A. Comstock, E. A. Rubinstein, and J. P. Murray. U. S. Government Printing Office.

U. S. Commission on Civil Rights. 1977. *Window Dressing on the Set: Women and Minorities in Television.* Washington, DC.

Ward, S. 1972. Effects of television advertising on children and adolescents. In *Television and Social Behavior,* vol. 5. *Television in Day-to-Day Life: Patterns of Use,* ed. E. A. Rubinstein, G. A. Comstock, and J. P. Murray. U. S. Government Printing Office.

Ward, S., D. B. Wackman, and E. Wartella. 1975. *Children Learning to Buy: The Development of Consumer Information Processing Skills.* Cambridge, MA: Marketing Science Institute.

Watt, J. H., and R. Krull. 1977. An examination of three models of television viewing and aggression. *Human Communications Research* 3:99–112.

Zill, N. 1977. *National Survey of Children: Preliminary Results.* New York: Foundation for Child Development.

MORAL THINKING
Can It Be Taught?

Howard Muson

As democracies go, this one is ragged, restless, and properly irreverent toward authority: 35 teenagers, black and white, street kids and middle class, with a half-dozen teachers and two consultants, all arranged in a rough circle, draped over desks, chairs, windowsills, at Cambridge High School in Massachusetts. They are called a Just Community, and they meet in a garishly orange schoolroom with graffiti on the back wall and paint peeling from the ceiling—hardly the setting, it would seem, for a revival of the Periclean ideal.

Their guiding light, watching from a lonely angle near a blackboard, attired in a drab gray wool shirt and blue trousers, is Professor Lawrence Kohlberg of Harvard University, the elite Ivy League institution down the street. The 51-year-old psychologist, who is best known for his six-stage theory of development in moral judgment, has invested much of his time for the past five years in the Cambridge Cluster School. The Cluster School operates as a separate enclave within the high school for half of every day and lets kids and teachers

settle their own problems and make their own rules on a one-person, one-vote basis.

The kids seem to have learned their lessons well. As soon as the meeting is called to order, a few of them propose to ask the two visitors to leave—an editor from *Psychology Today* and a man who runs homes for juvenile offenders in Massachusetts, whom Kohlberg has brought along to observe. One young woman complains that too often visitors to the community meetings are less interested in the students than in writing about Kohlberg's work (which they know just helps "Larry" get grant money, a teacher confides to me later). Another says the students resent being looked upon as "guinea pigs," but a third, a cool-looking blonde in the front of the room, quips, "We're all guinea pigs of nature!" Everyone breaks up, no one presses the issue, and the guests are allowed to stay, proving, perhaps, that democracy can be gracious as well as ornery.

Kohlberg's Just Community resembles a lively encounter group, but it is less concerned with emotional

catharsis than with the development of moral judgment toward issues of "justice and fairness." As such, it represents a small but significant experiment in what is called moral education, a relatively recent movement, a revival of interest, really, in the notion that moral issues are a proper part of the school curriculum.

Though moral instruction has always been regarded as the job of parents and churches, the schools have inevitably had a role in passing on the values of the larger culture. They strenuously pursued that mission in the 19th century when the *McGuffey's Readers* were teaching generations of school kids how to behave as well as how to read—or trying to teach them. But educators have been skeptical about all such lessons in virtue ever since a classic investigation was made by two psychologists, Harthorne and May, in the 1920s. Harthorne and May evaluated a variety of school programs designed to instill honesty, altruism, and self-control in the pupils through "moral urging" and rewards for desirable conduct. Their conclusion was that indoctrina-

From *Psychology Today*, February 1979. Copyright Ziff-Davis Publishing Company. Reprinted by permission of *Psychology Today* Magazine.

tive programs of this kind had little appreciable effect on the kids' subsequent behavior.

The reasons for the revival of interest in moral education are not hard to find. It began during the Vietnam war and the campus upheavals of the 1960s and gathered momentum during the 1970s, when many people saw a decline in standards of both public and personal conduct—from Watergate and other scandals in high public office and in American business to the breakdown of family loyalties, sexual experimentation, widespread drug use, and increasing youth crime, including the destruction of school property and assaults on teachers.

A Gallup poll in 1975 showed that 79 percent of the Americans queried were willing to turn over some of that responsibility for moral training to the schools. Hundreds of schools have thus experimented with some form of instruction in moral values, and a lively interest remains, despite the back-to-basics movement, and even though parents and educators are still suspicious of any teaching that smacks of religious indoctrination or, indeed, promotes political views that are not to their liking.

Kohlberg brought to the revival a theory, formulated in the late 1950s, which not only seemed to match, in its elegance, the real complexities of moral issues themselves, but also stressed the development of conscious processes of "moral reasoning," which could, presumably, be stimulated and advanced in the classroom. Moreover, since the aim of the method was to enhance the *capacity* for moral reasoning, it did not teach any particular set of values and was therefore not, Kohlberg emphasized, indoctrinative. Finally, Kohlberg conceived a series of hypothetical "moral dilemmas" that were clever and provocative, even if they sounded a little like fairy tales.

There was, for instance, the famous case of Heinz, whose wife is dying and can only be saved by a rare drug; the drug has been discovered by the local pharmacist, who is the sole owner and is charging an exorbitant price that Heinz cannot pay. Should Heinz steal the drug? Does the pharmacist have a right to charge so much for it? (There are no "right" answers, but for a few responses that are typical of dif-

ferent stages of moral reasoning, see box on page 164.)

Another popular Kohlberg story is the dilemma of Sharon, who goes shopping one day with her best friend, Jill. Jill tries on a sweater, and walks out of the store wearing it under her coat, leaving Sharon to face a security officer who demands that she tell him the name of the other girl. The owner of the store tells her she will be in serious trouble if she does not report her friend, who, he is sure, has been shoplifting. Should Sharon protect her friend and not reveal her name? Does she really owe anything to Jill, who has walked out and left her in this dilemma?

Kohlberg's hypothesis has inspired countless studies, doctoral theses, workshops, seminars, conference papers, and journal articles. It has also inspired a rather fierce controversy. Critics argue that, far from being value free, his work reflects a liberal, Ivy League emphasis on social conscience that has nothing whatsoever to do with the way most people view the world. In recent years, more empirically minded researchers have questioned whether there really are six distinct stages of development, whether the evidence is convincing, and whether children can actually be stimulated to climb the stage ladder by discussions of moral dilemmas in the classroom.

Such have been the methodological criticisms of the theory that some researchers are beginning to believe there is nothing much left of it. "I suspect the system is beginning to fall apart," said Joseph Adelson, an expert on adolescence, in a recent paper. Adelson, a clinician and professor of psychology at the University of Michigan, says of Kohlberg's cognitive theory: "Many of its early propositions are not easily replicable by others, producing, as it so often does, a sense of being beleaguered and an even greater insularity."

While his theory is under attack, however, Kohlberg himself has been moving in a much more pragmatic direction. Today, he speaks almost disparagingly of "science fiction" dilemmas that, he feels, have little to do with kids' real concerns. In the Just Community, he seeks to promote individual development through group action. Kohlberg thinks of himself as

more of an educator than a psychologist, believing that only by teaching others is he ethically justified in experimenting on them. (He is professor of education and social psychology in the Harvard Graduate School of Education.) He even admits that his approach is now "indoctrinative," by which he means that he is openly trying to instill an appreciation of democratic processes and a sense of community in the kids.

The Just Community is rooted in the idea, shared by many educators since John Dewey, that the most important values taught in school derive from the very way the schools are organized and governed. In this "hidden curriculum," the argument goes, the students learn not democracy but obedience to authority and to arbitrary rules made by adults. Kohlberg and his colleagues have introduced Just Communities at high schools in Pittsburgh, Pa., Brookline, Mass., and Scarsdale, N.Y., as well as in Cambridge; they have also tried establishing them in two prison programs at the Connecticut Correctional Institution in Niantic, and have taught the techniques to prison administrators from Iowa to Nevada.

But this, the most recent emphasis in Kohlberg's work, has already earned one devastating critique from a researcher named Roy Feldman, who was hired by the state of Connecticut in 1974—with Kohlberg's approval—to do a three-year evaluation of the Niantic programs. Feldman also interviewed senior school administrators in Cambridge about the high school project and concluded that the democracy in all three programs was a sham: "It appears that the pseudo-democratic means and procedures of Kohlberg's Just Communities are among the most important features of their operation to institutional administrators. This does not mean that social control is the only reason [they] have supported Just Communities. Some do believe that the program does or might produce more justice than prior alternatives. Nevertheless, virtually all the senior administrators interviewed by the author perceived that the Just Community . . . is a fundamental management technique of social control which utilized peer pressure to urge conformity to middle-class values."

Legend and Theory

The controversy over Kohlberg is likely to influence future research into moral development as well as the teaching about moral values in the schools. For his approach remains the most fully developed (over a period of 20 years) and sophisticated one around, and to understand the issues, it is essential to go back to the beginning of Kohlberg's odyssey.

As a doctoral candidate in clinical psychology at the University of Chicago, Kohlberg was fascinated by the work of Jean Piaget, particularly *The Moral Judgment of the Child* (1932), in which the Swiss psychologist described how children from the ages of about two to 12 grew in their reasoning about the rules of playing marbles. Kohlberg interviewed a group of 75 youths from 10 to 16, probing their responses to dilemmas drawn from old books of casuistry and from works like *Les Miserables* (*Psychology Today*, September 1968). From their responses and his own study of ideas about moral stages, from Plato to John Dewey, Kohlberg identified six types of moral reasoning, which he unveiled in his doctoral thesis in 1958.

Piaget believed that children progressed from a heteronomous stage of moral reasoning, in which their values were largely dictated by others, to an autonomous phase, when they began to make their own choices. Kohlberg came to believe that children moved to higher stages of moral judgment as their capacity for more sophisticated logical "operations" emerged and as their ability to empathize with others grew in their social interactions. He saw the stages as unfolding in an invariant sequence, in response to internal pressures and challenge from the environment.

At Stage One, the "punishment-and-obedience orientation," the child defers to the superior position and power of the parent. In Stage Two, the "instrumental-relativist orientation," he agrees to a rule or does a favor only if he conceives it will bring him some benefit in return. Stage Three is the "good boy–nice girl orientation," in which the child seeks the approval of others and conforms in order to please. Stage Four was originally defined as the "law-and-order orienta-

A MORAL DILEMMA: THE CASE OF HEINZ

Probably the most widely debated of Kohlberg's dilemmas is the story of Heinz. It is discussed in classrooms and in standard Kohlberg interviews that determine the stage level of moral reasoning achieved by people, according to his theory. The theory concerns the *ways* people think about moral values, not the actual choices they make. So, technically, there are no right or wrong answers to the question of whether Heinz should or should not steal in order to save his dying wife. However, Kohlberg hastens to add that in this particular case, all Stage Five people (the most principled stage, in Kohlberg's current schema) agree that the right to life takes priority over the right to property.

Here are the details of the dilemma, along with one young subject's responses in interviews over a period of several years:

In Europe, a woman was near death from a special kind of cancer. There was one drug that the doctors thought might save her. It was a form of radium that a druggist in the same town had recently discovered. The drug was expensive to make, but the druggist was charging 10 times what the drug cost him to make. He paid $200 for the radium and charged $2,000 for a small dose of the drug. The sick woman's husband, Heinz, went to everyone he knew to borrow the money, but he could only get together about $1,000, which is half of what it cost. He told the druggist that his wife was dying, and asked him to sell it cheaper or let him pay later. But the druggist said, "No, I discovered the drug and I'm going to make money from it." So Heinz gets desperate and considers breaking into the man's store to steal the drug for his wife.

Tommy at Age 10 (Stage One)

Heinz shouldn't steal; he should buy the drug. If he steals the drug, he might get put in jail and have to put the drug back anyway.

But maybe Heinz should steal the drug because his wife might be an important lady, like Betsy Ross; she made the flag.

Tommy at Age 13 (Stage Two)

Heinz should steal the drug to save his wife's life. He might get sent to jail, but he'd still have his wife.

(**Interviewer:** "Tommy, you said he should steal the drug for his wife. Should he steal it if it were a friend who was dying?")

That's going too far. He could be in jail while his friend is alive and free. I don't think a friend would do that for him.

Tommy at Age 16 (Stage Three)

If I was Heinz, I would have stolen the drug for my wife. You can't put a price on love, no amount of gifts make love. You can't put a price on life either.

Tommy at Age 21 (Stage Four)

When you get married, you take a vow to love and cherish your wife. Marriage is not only love, it's an obligation. Like a legal contract.

tion," characterized by adherence to rules for the sake of maintaining social order. (Kohlberg now sees it as being an enlargement of horizons away from one's narrow group and toward a concern for the wider community.) Stage Five was the "social-contract, legalistic orientation," in which justice flows from a contract between the governors and governed that assures equal rights for all.

At the summit of the hierarchy was the highly abstract Stage Six, in which the individual chooses according to ethical principles that, like Kant's categorical imperative, appeal to logical comprehensiveness, universality, and consistency. Borrowing from the philosophy of John Rawls, Kohlberg has said about this stage that "personally chosen moral principles are also principles of justice, the principles any member of society would choose for that society if he did not know what his position was to be in the society and in which he might be the least advantaged." What that means, to take a practical example, is that in deciding one's position on capital punishment, a person would have to view the issue from the standpoint of one sentenced to death as well as from that of the murder victim.

Everyone familiar with the Kohlberg legend knows what happened next. Along came Moshe Blatt, a graduate student of Kohlberg's at the University of Chicago, who in 1968 tried to raise stage levels of moral reasoning in a Jewish Sunday-school class by vigorous debate of hypothetical dilemmas. In his doctoral thesis, Blatt reported success: after a year, the pupils had advanced by an average of one-third of a stage.

Further studies by Kohlberg followers confirmed that it was possible: classroom discussions of moral dilemmas, guided by an active, probing teacher, brought the students into contact with higher stages of moral reasoning than their own, and, through the cognitive conflict that occurred, stimulated stage advances. The assessment of stage level was done in interviews that scored the subject on his or her responses to questions about standard dilemmas.

But in one large study of 957 individuals, more than 45 percent could not be placed in one stage or another; most of the group were in transition between two stages, but some gave

responses that straddled three stages. And how meaningful, after all, were the one-third or one-half stage advances the Kohlbergites were claiming, when dealing with such elusive categories?

In response, Kohlberg and his associates kept revising and redefining their stage criteria. But critics like William Kurtines of Florida International University and Esther Greif of Boston University, who did an extensive review of the research literature in 1974, concluded that the "scale" used to measure the stages lacked standardization in administration and scoring. Others complained about fudging in the scoring manual, arguing that the use of labels such as "transitional," or "ambiguous," or even "guess" to classify some responses revealed the shaky foundation of the whole edifice. To make matters worse, the manuals were not easy to get hold of, and researchers reported having to apply to Kohlberg personally to get one.

A fundamental reservation about the theory was that it concerned moral judgment, and was of little use in predicting behavior. Two people at the same level of reasoning might very well act quite differently under the pressure of circumstance. Or two people at different stages might make the same moral choice, as was demonstrated dramatically by a study at the University of California of students who participated in the Free Speech Movement in 1968: disproportionately large numbers of people at Kohlberg's highly principled Stages Five and Six took part in the sit-in; but so did a large percentage of students who were judged to be at the relatively primitive Stage Two.

Kohlberg himself stressed that the theory had to do with the form and not the substance of moral decision-making; the scoring manual, for instance, diligently describes possible reasons for which Heinz should and should *not* steal the drug, without endorsing either of the choices. On the other hand Kohlberg clearly believes that his higher stages lead to more principled behavior, and he often cites anecdotes of improvements in behavior by those who have been exposed to his method.

Another anomaly was discovered several years ago by Kohlberg and his associate Richard Kramer, when they

tested the stage levels of his original group of subjects. (Kohlberg has interviewed them every three years since he wrote his original thesis, and most are now in their 30s.) At the time, he and Kramer found that many who had been Stage Four in previous interviews had inexplicably regressed to Stage Two—a revelation that challenged the very assumption on which the theory was based: that stage change proceeds only upwards, to ever-higher levels.

Soon the Kohlberg camp came up with an intriguing explanation. They had been looking at their subjects during the 1960s, when many were college sophomores trying to make the difficult transition to the most principled levels of moral reasoning. In breaking out of the conventional mold of Stage Four, they were questioning every standard of morality and passing through a phase in which all values not based on instinct were distrusted. (Some people referred to the transition as Stage Four-and-a-half, but Kohlberg says it is not considered a stage.)

It was a theory that helped to explain what was going on at campuses like Harvard in those days; indeed, undergraduates showed up at Kohlberg lectures with buttons that read, "Stage Two— and Proud of It!" Looking back, Kohlberg says, "This transitional state led to a susceptibility to a variety of ideologies which mixed Stage Two instrumental hedonism with radical moral ideologies, as suggested by the famous [Stokely Carmichael] slogan that the proper revolutionary position for a woman was prone."

Patching a Leaky Boat

Today, to those critics like Kurtines and Greif who question his "scale," Kohlberg says that he never had one. He has had scoring systems that tried to describe the data adequately, he says, but he never claimed they were standardized enough to provide consistent measurements. Last year, however, Kohlberg and his colleagues completed a five-part manual that is based on interviews and testing with the original Ph.D. subjects. Kohlberg says the new manual, based on five years of "painfully boring work," can be considered a scale and will provide the consistency and reliability his critics have demanded.

Whether or not the manual will satisfy them remains to be seen. Even if it does not, Kohlberg's cognitive theory remains the most exciting one around. Many experts will agree with Piaget that moral judgment does seem to unfold in a developmental pattern, and Kohlberg's theory has provided the most comprehensive effort to describe it to date. Defending it before the American Psychological Association last summer, Kohlberg used an analogy from Charles Peirce, the noted empiricist philosopher. "Peirce compared scientific theory to a leaky boat: you patch in one place and then stand in another place while you patch or revise elsewhere," Kohlberg said. "Sometimes patching doesn't work and the boat sinks. But not, as Thomas Kuhn points out, until another boat comes along the scientist can move to. I'd be happy to stop patching up Piaget's assumptions if I could see another boat on the horizon."

Some of the "patching" Kohlberg has done turns out to be quite extensive. For one thing, Stage Six has been dropped from the manual entirely. It had always been criticized as elitist and culturally biased. Kohlberg estimated from field studies that only about 7 percent of 16-year-olds in America and Mexico used Stage Six reasoning; but less than 1 percent of that age group on Taiwan employed it, and none of those he studied in Turkey or Yucatan had even reached Stage Five.

Many who felt Kohlberg's theory was merely a scientific justification for libertarian values saw Stage Six as making moral heroes of people like Daniel Ellsberg whose consciences brought them into conflict with society. Kohlberg argues that, far from exalting the individual, Stage Six described individuals who appeal to a higher community. "Martin Luther King was trying to speak for an ideal community of some sort, one that would embody brotherhood, and so forth," he says. Pointing out that none of his longitudinal subjects had achieved Stage Six by 1976, Kohlberg lamented at a recent symposium: "Perhaps all the Sixth Stage persons of the 1960s had been wiped out, perhaps they had regressed, or maybe it was all my imagination in the first place."

A colleague named Carol Gilligan raised another argument that brought a significant revision in Kohlberg's stages. Gilligan discovered that, in a few studies of comparable groups of men and women, more women ended up in Stage Three and more men in Stage Four. She then pointed out that Stage Three qualities of pleasing others and mercy enabled women to play a useful social role in smoothing tensions and bringing people together. Why should that stage be regarded as inferior to Stage Four? (As Portia says to Shylock in *The Merchant of Venice*: ". . . though justice be thy plea, consider this, that in the course of justice none of us should see salvation. We do pray for mercy.")

But Kohlberg found the discrepancy between men and women was due to an error in his stage criteria—an initial tendency to put men with an Archie Bunker mentality in Stage Four, which had described a law-and-order mentality. Bunker belongs in Stage Three, Kohlberg now thinks, because he is not concerned with the larger society; rather, his reasoning is a "law-and-order within-our-group sort of thing." That would explain why in some studies more men than women have ended up in Stage Four, Kohlberg asserts; more recent work, he says, shows no significant sex differences. "Carol Gilligan would also make the claim that there's male bias built into our scale by the kind of moral dilemmas we choose to look at, which emphasize justice, property, and conflicts in rights," Kohlberg adds. "She would argue that some other kind of dilemmas, which involve issues of caring and responsibility toward the community—for example, how much you should sacrifice for the community—might show more women at the upper end of the scale. I would agree."

Moral Education in Prison

The language suggests the new emphasis in Kohlberg's thinking, which is on community rather than on abstract justice. In the symposium at the University of Illinois, he said: "Our Cluster approach is not merely Socratic and developmental, it is indoctrinative. Its goal is not attainment of the Fifth Stage, but a solid attainment of the Fourth Stage commitment to being a good member of a community or a good citizen."

In a prison setting, even that was an ambitious goal. Kohlberg and two doctoral candidates, Joseph Hickey and Peter Sharf, began working with about 20 male juveniles and 20 controls at the Cheshire reformatory in Connecticut in 1970. A few months later, after a riot at the state correctional institution for women in Niantic, they agreed to start a second project for about 20 inmates there. (A later group of the male offenders were moved from Cheshire to a more agreeable residence at the Niantic prison.)

Both programs were conceived as experiments in rehabilitating prisoners through discussions of moral dilemmas, which in the case of the women inmates were drawn from their lives in the prison. But after a couple of years, the consultants decided that individual progress depended on more basic changes in what they called the "moral atmosphere" of the prison. Thus was born the concept of the Just Community, in which guards and inmates were to settle, by democratic means, all major issues of rules and policy arising out of the group—within the limits of the law and state penal policy.

In their community meetings, the inmates were to discuss solutions based on fairness and morality; they were to be encouraged to engage in "role-taking"—putting themselves in the shoes of others in order to understand their thinking and feelings.

The kinds of issues that came before the two groups ranged from curfews and tampering with the prison security system to incidents of physical violence. In one videotape I saw, a small group sitting around a living room listened as one woman who was refusing to do her work assignment read a little essay she was required to write to explain her reasons. She said, in effect, that she simply did not feel like working. As the discussion went on, the other women gave her emotional support (tears were frequent at the women's meetings, evidently) and reminded her of what would happen if everyone in the cottage refused to work. Gradually, the woman revealed that she was resentful because her lover, another inmate, had been suspended by the group and forced to leave the cottage.

In his extremely critical report on the prison programs, Roy Feldman concedes that the meetings did encourage inmates and guards to speak openly with one another. Feldman, who taught political science at MIT for several years before becoming a research associate at Harvard, also grants that supervisors and staff were personally concerned with fairness.

But Feldman goes on to report that there was very little talk of concepts of fairness or justice at the meetings; the staff had difficulty introducing discussions of moral dilemmas; further, many decisions relating to the rules of the prison were made unilaterally by staff. When behavior was viewed as intolerable, administrators would, on occasion, suspend the workings of democracy, and might remove an inmate from the program—a decision that was supposed to be left to the community.

The only thing that seemed to unite the community, Feldman suggests, was a strong desire to keep it going. (The inmates certainly preferred it to the regular prison.) As a result, the guards seem to have used the meetings for investigating infractions that might have led to criticism of the program—for instance, when a hypodermic syringe or illicit drug had been found on the premises and the authorities wanted to find out who was responsible.

Feldman both examined the results of the moral-judgment interviews with the inmates undertaken by Kohlberg's associates and conducted interviews of his own. He concluded that the program did nothing to raise levels of moral reasoning or to lower the recidivism rate. He charges that those scorers who did report improvement often knew the dates of the interviews—which could bias them in judging stage changes over time—and that he was under pressure from one of the consultants to the program to produce positive results.

Kohlberg got into a hassle with Feldman over the renewal of his contract—the dispute concerned the adequacy of the first year's results—and has never seen the final report or the paper on it Feldman gave recently at Rutgers, though Kohlberg's office is on the third floor of Larson Hall at the Graduate School of Education and Feldman's is on the fourth. (Feldman's paper will be published this fall by Praeger in *Moral Development and Politics*, edited by Richard Wilson and Gordon Schochet.)

Reflecting on the prison experience, Kohlberg cites the difficult circumstances under which it was carried out. The majority of the inmates were at the lowest levels of moral reasoning, Stages One and Two. The early meetings at the Cheshire reformatory took place in a room filled with noise from the rest of the prison; on one occasion, Kohlberg mentioned, a guard was beating an inmate and the discussion of moral issues was punctuated with screams.

The Just Community for male inmates was shut down in 1977, when it was discovered that one of the night guards was being blackmailed by the men after he had made sexual propositions; he was smuggling dope into the prison for them. But the women's community continues. "I think the fact that it has stayed open is pretty impressive testimony," Kohlberg says. "I don't know if it's getting any stage change or if it's affecting recidivism—that would have required really heroic measures in terms of following those people when they got out and helping them adjust to their communities.

"But I know that some of those inmates were remarkably touched, as they might have been by any program that appealed to their better moral natures—the Black Muslims, Daytop, Synanon—but those are all indoctrinative and undemocratic. At least the Just Community idea had the virtue of fairness."

The Birth of the Cluster School

Although Kohlberg visited the prisons every few weeks, he says the program was really in the hands of two consultants. He has a larger stake in the Cluster School, which he believes has a much better chance of success, in part, because he is working with teachers who are more dedicated and intellectually sophisticated than prison guards.

The Cluster School grew out of an "alternative school" started at Cambridge High School in the 1960s, one of those experiments that enabled some students to develop their own ways of learning outside the impersonal curriculum of the larger school. The school couldn't handle all the students who wanted to get in, so another was set up in 1974, with Kohlberg's help, to govern itself as a Just Community.

The students were to be a cross-section of the high school, chosen from among volunteers, by neighborhood and race; they would spend half the day in a designated corridor of the building, where they would hold their community meetings and take English and social studies classes, in which discussions of moral issues would be encouraged, along with a few elective courses. The big question, of course, was whether the kids would govern themselves responsibly, or, intoxicated by their power, would make Stage Two decisions based on narrow self-interest.

The risks were soon evident. During the second week of school, while discussing a list of electives that were to be offered in the afternoons, a student said that he did not like any of them, would not vote for any, and proposed that students not have to attend classes. "Before the faculty quite knew what was happening, a vote was taken, compulsory afternoon school abolished, and the bell rang," Kohlberg recalls. "I yelled that it was only a straw vote, and the next day the teachers explained that the school could not vote to violate a state law."

By the second year, the community was wrestling with fundamental moral and social problems. Blacks in the group raised a fairness issue, and called for more equal representation in the community. There were 47 whites, 18 blacks, and six openings to be filled at the time. Only one of the six students on the waiting list was black. The blacks, explaining their feelings of isolation as a minority, proposed that all six places be given to blacks. One white student said he wanted more black kids in the community but confessed that he didn't know what the community was going to tell the whites on the waiting list.

Another student provided a justification: "All you have to do is explain to them that the community decided it was the best idea to take all blacks this time for the community's sake, and from now on, every June we're going to admit more kids, we'll admit half black, half white."

The community voted to admit six blacks. (The current group of 45 students is evenly divided racially.) But the vote raised an issue of reverse discrimination that, in turn, may illuminate Kohlberg's current priorities. In the winter issue of *The Public Interest*, William J. Bennett of the National Humanities Center and Edwin J. Delattre of the National Humanities Faculty argue that the discussion made a mockery of the notion that the students should develop "reasons" for their actions. Bennett and Delattre conclude: "At the end, the result is a pronunciamento of a 'general will of the democracy' class—a tyranny of a particular majority over students who ask questions (and over their rights) and over those on the waiting list who have a reasonable expectation to have themselves and their rights 'treated equally.'"

A Case of Theft

When I visited the Cluster School, the issue was stealing. "Due to a recent rash of thefts," announced the agenda for the community meeting on Friday, "it seems we're back to square one on theft." In the early months of the Cluster School, when a theft occurred on the premises, students tended to reason that anyone foolish enough to bring something valuable to school had to expect theft to occur. But in later incidents, the community assumed more responsibility and made a rule that if a member of the group was the culprit, he should come forward, make restitution, and apologize to the group.

In the spring, the community had gone on an outing to a camp in New Hampshire and some stereo equipment had been stolen from the grounds and put aboard the bus that took the group back to Cambridge. Now, a teacher named Diane Tabor is talking about money stolen from her handbag during a more recent community trip to a roller rink. The teacher has her suspicions about the identity of the thief or thieves. She suspects others in the group know who is responsible as well, but won't "squeal"; they had discussed it in their small-group meetings the previous day. "I don't want to be a bad guy any more than anyone else," Diane says. "Should I speak out?"

The issue is what everyone refers to as "community trust." A white girl asks how the members can trust one another if a member of their group is

ripping them off. Reluctantly, Diane, who is also white, reveals her suspicions. She names a black student, Keith (the students' names are changed), as possibly responsible in both cases. Keith is not present, but another black, Ray, reports that Keith told him he had taken the stereo on the bus because he thought it was Ray's (the equipment had been returned).

"I don't believe that!" says the pert, gum-chewing blonde in the front.

Then, when a black student remarks, "It's beginning to sound like only the black kids are thieves," the issue explodes into a discussion of racial stereotypes and prejudice that is rough-and-tumble but under control. Kohlberg and the teachers intervene only to focus the issue, which is whether the blacks, whose code calls on them to protect their own, will be more loyal to the thief or to the community. In Kohlberg's terms, it is a choice between Stage Three devotion to one's narrow group and a Stage Four commitment to the rules of the wider community.

"If someone was a friend of the thief's and a member of the community," says Kohlberg, "it seems to me—and maybe I am way out—that what is good for whoever stole is to return the money and be reinstated in the community. There's not going to be a drastic punishment. But that would be what is best for that person, and that is what a friend would help the person do."

"Do you think there's enough trust in this community so that you could be honest and not automatically protect another black kid?" asks Arthur Lipkin, an English teacher, addressing a tall black, Bobby, who happens to be a relative of the suspected thief and is a leader in the discussion.

"Let me tell you something, Arthur," he answers. "Personally, I would try to protect anyone in here that I didn't think did anything ridiculous. That is how I feel, that is what I think, that is what I was taught, that is what I believe."

What Kohlberg and the staff are suggesting is that the students bring "peer pressure" on the thief. Later on, Kohlberg's research associate Ann Higgins tells me that Bobby, after the meeting, has promised to produce the suspected boy, Keith, at the next session on Monday. Keith did show up, and denied everything, Ann Higgins

reported. But after further coaxing from his friends, who told him he was blowing his opportunity, he did admit stealing the stereo equipment and apologized for it at a third meeting on Tuesday.

Believing as they do in the worth of their community, Kohlberg and the teachers saw trust, which had taken so much effort to build in this heterogeneous group, as the important issue. Viewed through another lens, however, the heat on Keith could be interpreted as an insistence on group conformity that, under other circumstances, could turn ugly.

Was it really essential that he confess to the group and make a public apology? Couldn't a face-saving way be found for Keith to restore the stolen goods and be accepted back into the group's good graces? Perhaps a way could be found, Kohlberg and Ann Higgins agreed, but they did think that some sort of publicized apology was needed.

Asked if majority rule could turn into tyranny, Kohlberg replied: "In all the schools I've worked in, the first issue is whether the group has the right to make any rules at all. The issue doesn't come up in an authoritarian country. As soon as you have a democracy, particularly with the more sophisticated kids, you get the issue of whether it's desirable to make any rules that limit the rights of individuals. At the Just Community in Scarsdale, the majority voted a rule that the students couldn't come to class high. Some of the kids protested that this was a violation of their rights, that smoking pot was one of the Rights of Man, so to speak.

"If the majority could lawfully impose such a ban, one girl said, why could it not also make a rule against, say, picking one's nose? The kids' response was that, while picking one's nose might be offensive to some, coming to class high would be highly disruptive to learning, which was why they were all there. It is intrinsically disruptive, in that it prevents participation.

"Tyranny may occur when there is un-thought out conformity to the group rather than a highly rational dialogue on what are the limits of the group. Some of the things we do bear a resemblance to things I've seen on the kibbutz. I was heavily influenced by research some of my students and I did on the kibbutz. The kibbutz convinced me that the collectivist tradition could be combined with the democratic tradition."

From my brief visit to the Cluster School, I would say the discussions are open and surprisingly uninhibited. You can't tell kids they have a democracy and then urge them to keep their mouths shut. The students seemed to care for one another, to understand their differences, and to talk about them forcefully and honestly.

They are also weighing issues that are less academic than the normal social studies curricula and more momentous than those that have come before student governments in the past. (One teacher commented that in his own high school experience, the students usually had power to decide little more than the date of the senior prom.)

But do adults unfairly influence the dialogue, and do school administrators pull strings from behind the scenes? In other words, is there anything to Roy Feldman's charge that the Cluster School is a pseudodemocracy?

A Tender Experiment

As adults, Kohlberg and the teachers no doubt have a disproportionate influence. They do not see their role as being exclusively laid-back "facilitators" of discussion in the Rogersian mold; they believe in strong advocacy, when the issue warrants it.

It also appears that, on occasion, fearing their tender experiment might not survive, staff members have brought pressure on the kids to see things their way. Feldman, who is on the advisory commitee that oversees a Ford Foundation grant to study the Cluster School, says that one senior administrator used the term "blackmail" to describe how the staff had gotten the community to agree not to permit pot-smoking—a politically sensitive issue—at a school event.

William Lannon, superintendent of schools, who has a son in the program, and Elsa Wasserman, the school counselor who helped set up the school, strenuously disputed Feldman's judgment that senior administrators see it as a means of social control. Wasserman says the few instances when the staff tried to pressure the kids occurred in the first years. "In the beginning, we wanted to survive," Wasserman says. "But as the community grew, and we learned to care about each other, pressure was no longer necessary. . . . I know this program is good; it makes sense, and I've seen how it can change the kids' way of thinking about moral issues."

The students are given the moral-judgment interview when they first enter the school, each fall, and again when they graduate. Kohlberg has publicly stated that though most are at Stage Two when they enter, almost all are Stages Three and Four when they graduate. (Fifteen of 17 graduates went on to college last year.) But he admits that only a small portion of the three years' worth of data from the tests has actually been scored as yet.

"I don't think moral education ought to be based on Kohlberg's theory necessarily," Kohlberg says. "I would be happy for people to take an eclectic approach. I welcome working with a behavior modifier or anyone else." Nevertheless, theory may very well influence practice in one essential respect. If you believe, as Kohlberg does, that people like the students at the Cluster School start at a lower level of moral reasoning, and that a sense of community represents a higher stage, you might then believe that whatever serves the community is good and justifies any action, even if it ignores the rights of individuals. The argument resembles, in a way, Nixon's attempts to justify all manner of violations in the name of "national security."

Kohlberg still sees his Just Communities as stimulating individual stage development in the students, but he is increasingly concerned with how the progress of the group—the "moral atmosphere"—influences that development. Indeed, he now sees communities as evolving in stages that depend on how the members succeed in living up to their own "collective norms." He and his colleagues are studying the process, with Ford money, in both the Cambridge and Brookline Just Communities. "At the moment," he explains, "there's clearly a norm in the Cluster School of maintaining trust around property issues. But there's uncertainty about whether the norm has developed to the point, in terms of strength, where the kids are willing to force it on one another."

A great deal of loving attention has been lavished on the Cluster School, but can the experiment be duplicated elsewhere? Not easily. When I came across biographies of the teachers in the school, I was as dazzled by their qualifications as I was impressed, watching them in action, by their dedication: for example, Bill Ford, a black, has a B.A. from Columbia and an M.A. from the Harvard Graduate School of Education; Diane Tabor has a B.A. from Mount Holyoke, an M.A. in English literature from Middlebury, and a Ph.D. from the Harvard Graduate School of Education; Brian Mooney, a Vietnam veteran, has studied in Spain and Panama, spent a year in religious studies at a Catholic monastery, and is now a Ph.D. candidate at Boston University.

Guiding a Just Community seems to require teachers who are not only open-minded and caring, but have a real appreciation of the subtleties of participatory democracy and Kohlbergian dialectics. Educators will admit that not all teachers fit the description. "After five years of democracy at the Cluster School," Kohlberg says, "the staff still can't relax too much. That's probably why democracy doesn't spread more. You can make mistakes, as we do day after day, but you simply can't fall back on mechanical formulas."

The Just Community experiment provides a showcase for those who would try to keep democratic ideals alive in the post-Watergate generation. "Periodically," says Kohlberg, "someone comes along who rediscovers what John Dewey was trying to do in the schools or what Thomas Osborne was trying to do at Sing Sing in 1914. Somehow I'd like to keep those experiments in democracy alive and progressing, instead of having to rediscover them in each generation."

In adolescents who are leaving their families and who have a great deal of idealism, Kohlberg says, the desire for some kind of community is particularly strong—especially today. Kohlberg's work is, in part, a response to the loss of community trust he sees in the larger society, as he made plain in his paper at the University of Illinois:

"Today, participation represents an educational response to the growing privatism of youth. The opposite of

4. DEVELOPMENT

participation, the back-to-basics movement, is just the symptom of the current national disease of privatism which afflicts the youth even more than their elders.

"Behind the back-to-basics movement is the basic of California's Proposition 13, money. Behind money is the true basic expressed by the title of Robert Ringer's book at the top of the best-seller list, *Looking Out for No. 1*. In our stage system, by the way, if you look out for No. 1, you are probably

Stage Two. In terms of outcomes of education, the recent Gallup poll indicates that the most endorsed educational outcome is the ability to write a job application letter with correct grammar and spelling. In terms of educational input, the most endorsed input is not spending money.

"The new privatism unites the cynical or the disillusioned liberal with the cynical or the disillusioned conservative."

For further information, read:

Benson, George C. S. and Thomas S. Engeman. *Amoral America*, Hoover Institution Press, 1975, $8.95.

Hickey, Joseph and Peter Scharf. *Democratic Justice and Prison Reform*, Jossey-Bass, in press.

Hersh, Richard, Joseph Reimer, and Diana Pritchard Paolitto. *Promoting Moral Growth*, Longman, 1979, $12.50, paper, $6.95.

Kurtines, William and Esther Blank Greif. "The Development of Moral Thought: Review and Evaluation of Kohlberg's Approach," *Psychological Bulletin*, Vol. 81, No. 8, 1974.

Scharf, Peter, ed. *Readings in Moral Education*, Winston Press, 1978, $7.95.

Sprinthall, Norman A. and Ralph L. Mosher, eds. *Value Development As the Aim of Education*, Character Research Press, Union College, Schenectady, N.Y., 1978, $4.25.

We want your advice.

Any anthology can be improved. This one will be— annually. But we need your help.

Annual Editions revisions depend on two major opinion sources: one is the academic advisers who work with us in scanning the thousands of articles published in the public press each year; the other is you—the person actually using the book.

Please help us and the users of the next edition by completing the prepaid article rating form on the last page of this book and returning it to us. Thank you.

The Father of the Child

Fathers are taking a more active role in caring for their newborn babies

Ross D. Parke

Ross D. Parke is professor of psychology at the University of Illinois at Champaign-Urbana. He is the editor of Recent Trends in Social Learning Theory *(Academic Press, 1972),* Readings in Social Development *(Holt, Rinehart & Winston, 1969), and co-author with Mavis E. Hetherington, of* Child Psychology: A Contemporary Viewpoint *(McGraw-Hill, 1975, 1979).*

The days when fathers were only permitted a glance at their new offspring through the nursery window are past. Hospital practices are changing and many more fathers are now permitted to have direct contact with their babies in the hospital rather than waiting until they go home. Now that fathers and newborns are getting together more frequently, researchers are watching more often. The aim is to determine how fathers and mothers differ in their early interactions with young infants. Our own observations, which began in 1970, revealed that fathers were just as involved with their newborn infants as mothers. They looked at the infants, touched and rocked them and vocalized to them just as often as mothers. Fathers were just as active when they were alone with the babies as when their wives were present. Mothers surpassed fathers in only one way—smiling. However, the reason for the higher rate of mothers' smiling may be that females simply smile more than males—not just at babies, but at all kinds of people.

One of my students, David Phillips, has recently taken a closer look at one part of the early parent-infant exchange—the types of speech that mothers and fathers use in talking to their newborns. Fathers, as well as mothers, change their styles of speech when addressing their new offspring. They speak in shorter phrases—about half as long as the phrases used when speaking with adults. They repeat their messages much more often and slow their rate of talking. All of these changes in the style of speaking are likely to increase the extent to which the baby pays attention or looks at the parent. In turn, the changes may make it easier for the infant to learn to recognize his caregivers.

The social setting makes a difference in the behavior of fathers. When we observe fathers and mothers together, fathers smile and explore (count fingers and toes, check eyes and ears, etc.) more than when they are alone with the baby. Mothers show a similar pattern of increased interest when their husbands are present.

Fathers are active and involved, but are they involved in all aspects of early newborn care? Apparently not. Our studies indicate that fathers' involvement is selective even in the earliest interactions. Consistent with our cultural stereotypes, fathers are less likely than mothers to be actively involved in caretaking activities such as feeding or changing diapers. Fathers are more likely to play with a baby (vocalize, touch, imitate) than to feed it. These findings suggest that parental roles as caretaker or playmate begin to emerge even in the earliest days of the infant's life. This pattern may be part of a general shift toward a more traditional division of responsibilities that occurs in most families after the birth of a baby. Even in families where there is an egalitarian sharing of household tasks before a child arrives, this shift toward traditionally defined roles seems to occur, according to a recent study by Carolyn Cowan and her co-workers at Berkeley.

Are fathers less competent to care for infants? If so, this would easily explain their limited involvement in caretaking. This hypothesis, however, is wrong. Fathers are just as competent and capable of taking care of infants, according to our research. We define competence as the parent's ability to correctly "read," interpret and respond to the infant's cues or signals. To assess fathers' feeding skills, we determined how sensitively fathers reacted to infant distress signals, such as spitting up, sneezing and coughing. Fathers reacted just as quickly and appropriately as mothers did. Fathers, like mothers, adjusted their behavior by momentarily ceasing feeding the infant, looking more closely to check on the infant, and vocalizing to the infant. Moreover, babies drank about the same amount of milk from their fathers and mothers.

Play

Nearly all fathers play regularly with their infants and spend four to five times as much time playing as they spend in caretaking.

Fathers not only play more, they play differently than mothers. Based on home observations, fathers play more physically stimulating games, such as rough and tumble play and other types of unpredictable or idiosyncratic play. Mothers stimulate their infants verbally, rather than physically, use toys in their infant play, and choose conventional games such as peek-a-boo and pat-a-cake.

To examine fathers' play more closely, Harvard pediatricians Michael Yogman and T. Berry Brazelton and their colleagues videotaped playful interchanges between infants and their mother, father, and a strange adult in a laboratory setting. By slow motion analyses of the videotapes, Yogman found a number of differences in the patterns of infant play with different partners. Mothers spoke in a soft, repetitive and imitative fashion more often than fathers, while fathers did so more than strangers. Fathers poked and touched with rhythmic tapping patterns more often than mothers. The temporal pattern differed as well. Father-infant play shifted more rapidly from accentuated peaks of maximal infant visual attention and excitement to valleys of minimal attention. Mother-infant play had a less jagged and sawtooth quality; it was characterized by more gradual and modulated shifts.

Play patterns of fathers are, however, influenced by the amount of time that they spend with their infants. In a recent study, Tiffany Field of the University of Miami compared the play of fathers who served as primary caretakers for their infants to that of fathers who were secondary caretakers—the traditional father role. The primary caretaker fathers smiled more often, imitated their infants' facial expressions and their high-pitched vocalizations. These play patterns were similar to those of mothers who are primary caretakers. Probably mothers and fathers who spend a good deal of time with their infants recognize that infants of this age (four months) enjoy being imitated.

One important implication of the finding that primary caretakers—whether male or female—are similar, is that father-mother differences are not necessarily biologically fixed. Instead, these differences might be due to cultural factors such as the amount of experience males and females typically have with their infants. Biological sex of the caretaker may be a less important determinant of caretaker behavior than experience with infants.

Fathers and Sons
Although it is a common cultural stereotype that fathers want a boy, there is considerable truth to this view. Not only in our own culture, but in a wide variety of other cultures, fathers have a three-to-one preference for a boy over a girl—at least for their first-born. These preferences affect reproduction patterns. According to psychologist Lois Hoffman of Rutgers University: "Couples are more likely to continue to have children if they have only girls. They will have more children than they originally planned to try for a boy."

After the birth of their infant, parents, especially fathers, have clear stereotypes concerning the particular type of behavior that they expect of boy and girl babies. Even before the opportunity to hold their infants, fathers rated their sons as firmer, larger featured, better co-ordinated, more alert, and stronger, while they rated their daughters as softer, finer featured, weaker, and more delicate.

Not only do men prefer to have sons and expect them to be different, fathers treat them differently as well—even in the newborn period. In our own hospital-based observations of father-infant interaction, we found that fathers touched first-born boys more than either later-born boys or girls of either ordinal position. Fathers vocalize more to first-born boys than first-born girls. Nor are the differences in fathers' behavior with boy and girl infants restricted to the newborn period. Various investigators report that fathers look at their year-old male infants more, vocalize more to their sons, and play more with their sons than their daughters, particularly their first-born sons. Mothers, on the other hand, do not show as strong preferences, but if they do discriminate, they show heightened involvement with girls. Cross-cultural and comparative data tell a similar story. In studies of the Israeli kibbutzim, fathers were found to visit for longer periods in the children's house with their four-month-old sons than with their infant daughters. Even adult male rhesus monkeys play with male infants more than female infants while female adult monkeys interact more with female infants. Whether this pattern of heightened involvement of fathers with sons reflects what the sociobiologists, such as E.O. Wilson and Robert L. Trivers of Harvard University, call gene investment, or whether it is an outcome of cultural shaping, is still an open question.

Fathers' Effects on Infants and Mothers
Even though fathers spend less time with their infants than mothers, the quality rather than the quantity of parent-infant interaction is the important predictor of infant development. Not surprisingly, then, variations in father-infant interaction patterns do affect the infant's social and cognitive development. However, boys are generally affected more than girls.

The majority of infants develop a positive social relationship or "attachment" (a preference or desire to be close to a specific person) to both their fathers and their mothers by the end of the first year. This is an important finding which directly challenges the popular assumption of the influential British ethologist, John Bowlby, that infants should prefer or even be uniquely attached to their mothers. Clearly both fathers and mothers are important "attachment" objects for infants. As we have already seen, the roles that father and mother play in the infant's social world may be different. What behavior affects the strength of the father-infant relationship?

According to one study, the strength of the father-infant relationship—assessed by the infant's responsiveness to his father—is related to the degree of the father's involvement in routine caretaking and the stimulation level of paternal play. This relation was especially true for boys in this study of eight-month-old infants. Confirming this relationship are studies which show that social responsiveness of five-month-old male infants is lower where the father is absent than in homes where he is present. Not only is high involvement related to a stronger father-infant bond, but a high degree of father-infant interaction helps a child cope more adequately in other social situations as well. Children react to the stress of being left alone with a stranger better if their fathers are active and involved caretakers. Children who are not cared for by their fathers show extensive distress in the laboratory situation when left alone.

Cognitive progress is affected by the father-infant relationship as well. Scores on standard tests of infant mental development were positively related to the amount of contact with the father in five-to-six-month-old lower class black infants. However, variations in father interaction were unrelated to cognitive development of female infants. Similarly, infants from homes where fathers were absent performed less well on the tests of cognitive development. Other studies with older infants suggest that fathers and mothers contribute to their infants' cognitive development in different ways. While the quality of father-infant play patterns was related to higher cognitive progress, for mothers it was verbal stimulation that was the best predictor of infant cognitive status. In short, both parents may contribute, but in unique ways, to their developing infant.

The father's involvement, however, cannot be adequately understood independently of his role as part of the family. Fathers affect infants not only in the direct ways that we have described, but in a variety of indirect ways as well. For example, a father may affect his child by modifying his wife's attitudes and behaviors toward the child. Recent studies by Frank A. Pedersen and his colleagues at the National Institute of Child Health and Development in Washington, D.C. have shown that the adequacy of a mother's feeding skill was related to the degree of emotional support provided by her husband.

Cultural Supports for Father
Just as mothers can benefit from opportunities to learn and practice caretaking skills, in a time when fathers are increasingly being expected to share caretaking responsibilities, these learning opportunities need to be available for fathers as well.

Supportive intervention for fathers might assume a variety of forms. First, an increase in opportunities for learning caretaking skills is needed. Such opportunities might be provided through pre- and post-partum training programs for fathers. Second, fathers need increased opportunities to practice and implement these skills. Paternity leaves would help provide these opportunities. Opportunities for contact with the infant in the early post-partum period could alter subsequent parent-infant interaction patterns. Preliminary evidence from recent studies suggests that father-infant interaction patterns can be modified by hospital-based interventions. John Lind, a Swedish obstetrician, found that fathers who were provided the opportunity to learn and practice caretaking skills during the post-partum hospital period were more involved in the care of the infant three months later at home.

My colleagues Shelley Hymel, Thomas Power and Barbara Tinsley and I recently presented to American fathers a videotape of father-infant interaction during the early post-partum hospital period. The videotape provided information concerning the newborn infant's perceptual and social competence, play techniques and caretaking skills. Fathers were observed during feeding and play. Fathers who viewed the film were better able to maintain infant feeding and vocalized more to their infants—especially their first-born sons—during play. In addition, the fathers who saw the film in the hospital participated in feeding and diapering activities at home when their infants were three months old. However, the film increased the amount of caretaking only for fathers of boys; fathers of girls were unaffected by the film intervention. This selective effect of our intervention for boys is similar to earlier findings that fathers are more involved with sons than daughters.

Considerable care must be taken in the implementation of these support systems. One must consider parents' rights. The aim is not to impose on all families an implicit scenario of the liberated family and an endorsement of egalitarian family organization. Too often "more" is equated with "improvement." However, in many families, increased participation by the father may cause conflict and disruption as a result of the threat to well-established and satisfying role definitions. Intervention, therefore, should be sensitively geared to the needs of individual families, and the dynamics and beliefs of the couple should be recognized at the outset.

Fathers play a unique and important role in infancy. As social standards continue to change it is likely that fathers will be assuming an increasingly larger role in the care and feeding of infants and young children. Our evidence suggests that not only can they assume these responsibilities competently, but that the result is likely to be beneficial for all—infants, mothers and fathers.

MAKING IT TO MATURITY

David C. McClelland, Carol A.
Constantian, David Regalado,
and Carolyn Stone

A Harvard team sought to measure the maturity levels achieved by some young adults who had been raised by various methods. They found that what mattered was not technique but a few intangibles. Like love, and whether the home had been adult-centered.

ABOUT 25 YEARS AGO, three psychologists at Harvard carried out one of the most thorough studies of child-rearing ever done in the United States. Believing that the future of a society was more or less unconsciously shaped by the way it brought up its children, Robert Sears, Eleanor Maccoby, and Harry Levin felt it was vital to learn more about the impact of different parenting techniques on personality development. They were particularly interested in how a mother handled a range of developmental problems: Was she permissive or severe in dealing with sex play? Did she control the child by spanking? By withdrawing her love? By depriving him or her of privileges?

The Sears group interviewed 379 mothers of kindergartners in two towns near Boston in the early 50s. They rated each mother on about 150 different child-rearing practices. They compiled a complete record of the parenting methods typical of American mothers at that time and place, including variations of social class and sex and birth order of the child.

But they were less successful in demonstrating that one method or another had a significant effect on the child's personality, possibly because they did not study the children themselves but relied on the mothers' descriptions of them. Most important, they could not touch at all the key question that was the reason for much of the fuss over child-rearing in the first place: Did the way the mother treated the child really make a difference in adulthood? Did it really matter, years later, whether she had breast-fed the child, punished it, rejected it, or smothered it with love? Were the Freudians right in assuming that, for better or worse, what the parents did in the first five years was crucial?

Most of these questions remain unanswered today, despite all the attention given them in recent years. It is difficult to draw any clearly supported generalizations from the different kinds of studies that have been done, and this has led some psychologists—for example, Arlene Skolnick of the Institute of Human Development in Berkeley—to argue that parents have very little control over the formation of their child's personality and character (*Psychology Today*, February 1978).

We had an opportunity to seek some answers of our own last summer when we contacted many of the children of the mothers who had been interviewed by the Sears group 25 years ago. They were now 31 years old, and most of them were married and had children of their own. We were especially interested in determining how the different ways they had been brought up had helped or hindered them in achieving social and moral maturity. We based our measurements on Erikson's theory of stages of psychosocial development and the Piagetian theory of cognitive development. Under both theories, early stages are characterized by dependence on external authority, intermediate stages by greater self-reliance, and the highest stage by genuine concern for how others feel.

Through interviews and psychological tests, we concluded that most of what people do and think and believe as adults is not determined by specific techniques of child-rearing in the first five years. With Arlene Skolnick, we believe that parents should rest assured that what they *do* is not all that important in how their children turn out; many other influences in later life serve to shape what adults think and do.

But this hardly means that the way parents *feel* about their children cannot have a substantial impact. We found that when parents—particularly mothers—really loved their children, the sons and daughters were likely to achieve the highest levels of social and moral maturity. The only other dimension that had major importance for later maturity was how strictly the parents controlled their children's expressive behavior. A child was less apt to become socially and morally mature when his parents tolerated no noise, mess, or roughhousing in the home, when they reacted unkindly to the child's aggressiveness toward them, sex play, or expressions of dependency needs. In other words, when parents were concerned with using their power to maintain an adult-centered home, the child was not as likely to become a mature adult.

 From *Psychology Today*, June 1978. Copyright ®1978 Ziff-Davis Publishing Company. Reprinted by permission of *Psychology Today* Magazine.

The Interviews and Tests

When we approached the young men and women whose mothers had been part of the Sears study, we informed them that we wanted to compare their

> "Most of what people do and think as adults is not determined by how they were reared in the first five years."

views on child-rearing with those held by their mothers in the 1950s. It was thus easy to talk about moral values with them in the interviews, which were conducted by three graduate students in psychology who were about the same age as they.

Because of limits on time and money, we concentrated on the children of mothers who had been considered middle class by the Sears team. We succeeded in interviewing 78 of them. Of these, 49 had children of their own. About 35 percent were Jewish, 25 percent Catholic, and 18 percent Protestant. The sample was fairly representative of the original group of middle-class mothers. But we were able to persuade only 47 of the 78 children to come in after the interviews for psychological tests—and this smaller group was probably less representative.

For the most part, the informants were allowed to tell their stories freely. However, the interviewers made certain to elicit information from them on such things as friendships, work experiences, illnesses, what organizations they belonged to, whether they had ever been in trouble with the law.

When we asked them what things they thought were most important to teach children, they usually mentioned some general virtues, such as respect for the rights of others, confidence in themselves, knowing how to make their own decisions. The interviewer would then probe for concrete examples and explore them fully: what were the circumstances of the incident,

what were the people involved thinking, what did they eventually do? Finally, each person was also asked what kinds of problems they thought their children were likely to run into when they grew up. Many of them mentioned such things as the pressures to experiment with drugs, the problems of getting a job, the difficulties of getting along with people.

Later on, the interviewer rated each individual on 37 outcome variables, including the number of children, occupational achievement, participation in voluntary organizations. They also judged each on how important he or she considered a number of values, from 1 ("not very important") to 3 ("very important"). Among the things the interviewers tried to evaluate was how important the subjects considered other influences on their lives besides their parents. Most important, from all their material, the interviewers attempted to evaluate (on the 1 to 3 scale) how important each young adult considered the values in Erikson's stages of psychosocial development.*

Stage I (Receptivity). Showing respect for authority or tradition. Behaving properly, decently, or obediently.

Stage II (Autonomy). Self-reliance, ability to make up one's own mind about things, not always being dependent on others. Showing willpower, determination, or courage.

Stage III (Assertion). Doing well in school or on the job, developing skills, learning to appreciate music, nature, or art, speaking well, getting along with or influencing others.

Stage IV (Mutuality). Understanding other points of view, serving others or the common good (but not just following decent behavior, which is Stage I). We will refer to these characteristics as the "valuing" measure of maturity.

Those subjects who were willing to come in for further testing were first given a version of the Thematic Apperception Test (TAT). They were asked to write stories to go with six pictures, among them one showing two women scientists in a laboratory, another with a couple sitting on a bench by a river, and a third with a man and woman swinging on a trapeze. From their

---

* Two judges read all the interview summaries and independently rated each subject on the values in Erikson's stages. They agreed with the ratings made by the interviewers 80 percent of the time.

stories, we obtained further data on whether their thought patterns clustered around one or another of Erikson's stages by using an objective coding system empirically derived by Abigail Stewart of Boston University. We refer to this as the "thinking" measure of maturity.

Next, they took a multiple-choice version of Lawrence Kohlberg's well-known moral-dilemmas interview. James Rest of the University of Minnesota has developed a Defining Issues Test, which gives scores for each of the six stages of moral development spelled out by the Harvard psychologist. We evaluated our respondents on a summary score for the highest stages (5A, 5B, and 6), which Rest calls "principled thinking" (for example, "I will act morally because there are certain basic, universal principles that should govern my behavior"). There is considerable evidence that they represent a higher level of moral reasoning than Stage 4 reasoning ("I will be good because that's the law") or Stage 3 reasoning ("I will be good to please others"). We will call this measure of maturity "principled judging," to avoid confusion with our thinking measure of maturity, which derives from the TAT.

Of course, many psychologists would argue that there is no good evidence for a stage sequence of psychosocial maturity, but we have every reason to believe our three measures do represent actual stages in development (see box on page 178). We do not mean to imply, however, that maturity is the ultimate value that people must strive for at all costs. Moral maturity can conflict with survival needs, as Jesus and Socrates found out, and it may not be very functional for people who live under conditions of poverty and oppression. There is some truth in the old saw that only the rich can afford to be virtuous.

The Hypotheses

When we had finished testing, we had generated more than 4,000 correlations among a set of 35 child-rearing variables, 37 adult-outcome variables obtained in the interviews, and 85 other characteristics from the psychological test results. When we stripped down the list of variables to a few key ones, we found that the number of statistically significant relationships between child-rearing practices and adult outcomes only slightly exceeded what one would expect from chance.

The only conclusions to come from this first stage of analysis were that mother's affection relates to more adult outcomes than one would expect by chance, while physical punishment did not seem to be significantly related to any of the outcomes. Thus, how the parents had reared the children was not associated in any meaningful way with the number of children our subjects

---

"The parental policy we call strictness inhibited maturity later in life —unless there was also love in the home."

---

had, their occupational success, whether they married, how they felt about their parents, the importance they attached to such things as friends, sports, religion, or work.

To look at it another way, wide variations in the way parents reared their children didn't seem to matter much in the long run. Adult interests and beliefs were by and large not determined by the duration of breast-feeding, the age and severity of toilet-training, strictness about bedtimes, or indeed any of these things. Even the mother's anxiety about whether she was doing a good job didn't hurt (or help) her children.

We went on to check out specific hypotheses on how parenting practices might influence moral and social maturity. As already noted, we had developed three measures of maturity based on the Eriksonian and Kohlberg models. From the Erikson stages, we had a measure of the level of the subject's thinking maturity (stage stories from the TAT) and of his valuing maturity (based on values they said in the interviews they would teach their children). And from James Rest's multiple-choice version of the Kohlberg moral-dilemmas interview, we had a measure of the subject's capacity for principled judging.

Other researchers had studied the influence of child-rearing practices on so-

cial and moral maturity, and several years ago Martin Hoffman of the University of Michigan attempted to state a few propositions that appeared to be best supported by the findings from all sources. Hoffman concluded, in brief, that (1) power assertion by parents, as in heavy use of physical punishment, retards the development of both moral and social maturity; (2) "induction," or the use of reasoning to explain what the parents are doing and why, promotes it; and (3) parental affection also promotes it.

We tested each of Hoffman's three hypotheses. To measure the first, we made an index of punitiveness based on the average ratings of the Sears interviewers in 1951 on how often the children had been spanked by their fathers, how much they had been punished for aggressiveness toward their parents, how often they had been deprived of privileges as a punishment.

We found a slightly negative, insignificant correlation between punitiveness in childhood and adult functioning at the most mature level, by any of our three measures.

More inhibiting to adult maturity was the related parental practice called "strictness," because it defined the extent to which the parents suppress any tendency for the child to act out, be aggressive or noisy, or demand attention. Our data show that this type of parental policy strongly inhibits Stage IV maturity in thinking and judging in adulthood, as well as Stage III maturity in valuing—which may encompass the values most Americans associate with true maturity. (Further analyses showed that the impact of strictness depended very much on whether there was love in the home. If the mother really loved the child, how strict the parents were didn't seem to make much difference later on.)

Americans are strongly oriented toward self-reliance and doing well, which in the Eriksonian scheme are coded as Stage II and Stage III respectively. Thus, it is not surprising that in describing the values they want to teach their children, our sample scored higher in the average ratings in these two stages than for Stages I and IV.

But, theoretically, the highest stage of maturity—Stage IV—requires some loss of self-orientation in the interest of a higher good, as in parenting, mutual love, serving God and country. Our

data for Stage IV show an interesting difference between the thinking and valuing measures. Our sample was, on the average, strong on Stage IV for thinking and weak on Stage IV for valuing, meaning that people thought in terms of mutual give-and-take, but did not consciously stress service to others, tolerance, and understanding as the most important virtues to teach children. Instead, they valued self-reliance and self-actualization more. This strongly suggests that the two measures are getting at different aspects of maturity. It may be that the thinking measure reflects more how a person is actually functioning, while the valuing measure reflects cultural norms, which in America emphasize self-actualization. If we assume the thinking measure is less influenced by cultural values, this may indicate that our sample of adults is more mature—functions more at a Stage IV level—than their conscious stress on Stage II and III self-reliance and self-assertiveness suggests.

Our second hypothesis, much less strongly supported by previous research, is that reasoning with children or withdrawing love (Hoffman's "induction") promotes maturity. That is, parents who explain why they are doing things to their children develop an understanding that contributes to the child's maturation. We found no evidence of it in our sample. Those who were reasoned with more as children do not show signs of greater maturity as adults. Similarly, withdrawal of love has been associated with early development of conscience (if there is any love to begin with, according to Sears and his colleagues) and, consequently, adult maturity. Again, such is not the case in our sample.

Mother Love and Maturity

What is important for developing maturity is the amount of affection the mother shows for the child in the first place, just as our third hypothesis, based on previous research, predicts. Does a mother like her child and enjoy playing with him or her? Or does she consider the child a nuisance, with a lot of disagreeable characteristics? In the Sears study, the researchers rated mothers on the variable they called "mother's affectionate demonstrativeness toward the child." We called it "mother's warmth," and found that it is a key determinant of adult maturity, as measured by any of our three ways.

Father's affection for the child is also important for thinking maturity (based on the TAT), to a lesser extent for judging maturity (based on moral reasoning), but not at all for the Stage IV virtues of tolerance and service to others (based on the interviews). We are not sure why this is so, but can only speculate that the affectionate father provides a role model that is more associated with assertiveness (since he is the breadwinner) than with understanding and mutual love. Nevertheless, it is important to realize that children of affectionate fathers, whatever they may say they value, are, in fact, more apt to think and reason in ways that show tolerance and understanding. Perhaps it helps a child move beyond relying entirely on the self by providing an attractive authority figure, but does not promote valuing development to Erikson's Stages III and IV.

Many theorists, especially Urie Bronfenbrenner and Edward Devereux of Cornell, have argued that it is moderation in love and discipline that most promotes maturity. The clinical literature is full of examples of children who are crippled by too much love or too little discipline. As far as our measures of the conscious value placed on tolerance and service to others are concerned, the more mother love the better. But the seven mothers who were rated at the top of the mother's-warmth scale had children whose thinking showed fewer aspects of the kind of mutual give-and-take associated with Erikson's Stage IV maturity.

In other words, it looks as if strong mother love had given these children the conscious values of tolerance, sharing, and understanding, but had inhibited the development of actually thinking at this level. If the thought measure is tapping a deeper level, as it seems to be, one can infer that "smother love" can inhibit the development of the highest level of functioning. The same is not true of father love, which, even when it may seem excessive, promotes thinking or functioning at level IV—perhaps because fathers are home less often and therefore can't "smother" their children the way mothers might.

Was moderate strictness better than too easy or too strict discipline? We sorted parents into easy, moderate, and strict groups on the two disciplinary dimensions—punitiveness and strict-

ness—to see if moderate control fostered greater Stage IV thinking, valuing, or judging. The results do not conform to expectations. Moderately strict control by itself does not appear to favor the development of social and moral maturity by any of the three measures.

Only one other parental practice, not covered in our three hypotheses, came close to satisfying our criterion of being substantially related to at least two out of the three maturity measures. It was the habit some parents have of threatening punishment and not carrying out the threat. Not surprisingly, this kind of inconsistency inhibited the development of maturity, particularly as measured by the way people think about human relationships (the Stage IV scores from the TAT).

A Test of Moral Behavior

When psychologists first started studying morality, they concentrated on moral behavior, in line with the American belief that actions speak louder than words. One may now ask whether the measures of maturity included in this study are related to *acting* morally.

We estimated the deceitfulness of our subjects with a simple test. All were given a list of names of public figures, many of them very obscure, and asked if they knew who they were and the fields in which they were prominent. We measured the extent to which a subject misrepresented his knowledge by counting the number of times he said he knew the obscure figures but wrongly identified their fields. In addition, the subjects were asked to check how frequently they had performed a number of impulsive, aggressive, often antisocial acts, such as yelling at someone in traffic, not paying a bill because they were mad at someone, throwing things around a room, deliberately slamming a door, or taking a sign from a public place. The combined standard score on these two items represented a person's penchant for engaging in antisocial behavior.

At the same time, we tried to get a sense of their inclination to behave in a prosocial way. In one questionnaire item, we asked them to list several things they might do if they unexpectedly received $10,000: if they thought about giving some of it away, that was considered prosocial, as was willing-

ness to cooperate in our study. We found considerable variation in the extent to which they were willing to help us out—and contribute to science. The single most important measure was whether they came in to be tested when given several opportunities and offered pay for their time. But there were also differences in whether they refused at the outset, said they would

> "Parents can buy conformity in moral behavior from their children, but at the cost of true maturity."

come and didn't, or agreed willingly and came the first time—all of which were scaled on a dimension that might be called cooperativeness.

The results of these combined measures of moral behavior are a little surprising but also illuminating: people with high Stage I and Stage IV scores on the thinking measure (from the TAT) behave more morally than those with high Stage II and III scores, although none of the relationships is very strong (underlining the importance of situational factors in shaping moral actions).

Moral acts, as here defined, involve primarily relations with others, either helping them or at least not hurting them. Moral-maturity theory suggests that people may act morally for two different reasons—out of a relatively immature conformity to authoritative codes (Stage I) or out of a genuinely mature concern for others (Stage IV). People primarily concerned about the self (Stages II and III) will be more apt to behave antisocially because they are pursuing their own ends. For example, they exaggerate how many people they know in order to look good in the eyes of the experimenter or their own eyes. From the moral or social point of view, this is dishonesty.

The results obtained for the valuing and judging estimates of moral maturity fit in fairly well with this interpretation. They agree in showing that people at lower levels of maturity are more apt

WHAT ARE THE QUALITIES OF MATURITY?

Why do we believe that the measures in our study were really assessing maturity? One reason is that all ethical systems describe a similar hierarchal order of social and moral values: an unselfish person is better than a selfish one; one who freely chooses a moral act is better than one who is moral by compulsion. In our three measures of moral reasoning, the lowest stages reflect moral conformity based on external pressures; intermediate stages imply the capacity to incorporate the standards of one's teachers and make the free choices necessary for a moral act; and the highest stage represents some unselfish concern for others.

Another reason is that children go through the stages in this order as they mature cognitively. At the earliest stage, children act morally because they don't know any better; external forces shape their behavior. At the next stage of cognitive growth, they are able to think for themselves and make choices. Finally, at a still later stage, they are capable of taking the view of another, of seeing things through others' eyes; once they do that, they begin to act in ways that take others into account.

Still a third reason is empirical. Those who are more mature by our measures show other characteristics that ought to be related to maturity. For instance, education was significantly related to scoring higher on all three of our measures of maturity. Mothers with more education had children who as adults thought more maturely and chose more mature values to teach their children, according to the Eriksonian stages, and reasoned or judged more maturely about ethi-

cal dilemmas, according to the Kohlberg scheme. And if the children themselves had had more education, they also thought, valued, and judged more maturely. Since education should promote maturity, the fact that it correlates so consistently with our measures gives us more confidence in our method.

The same inference can be drawn from the fact that maturity was significantly correlated, by all three estimates, with a high score on a scale of "psychological mindedness." The scale measures the importance people give to dreams, fantasies, emotions, and self-knowledge, and whether they are inclined to interpret their dreams and try to understand why they do things. In short, these are individuals who observe their own psychological processes. They are more aware of what they are thinking, doing, and feeling. Thus, they believe in Socrates' motto, which has always been associated with maturity: "Know thyself."

Other characteristics of more mature individuals also give us confidence in our scales. By any measure, more mature people tended to report that they had remained closer to their parents after growing up. But this did not mean that they were not making their own decisions. The most mature individuals tended to report that they had grown away from their parents' views, and they were inclined to downplay the importance of tradition and authority.

The interviewers also tended to like them more. We had asked the graduate-student interviewers to state how much they enjoyed talking with each person. Plainly, they liked those indi-

viduals most who turned out to be more mature by later measures. Of course, this might mean the interviewers were biased, that they were giving higher maturity ratings to people they liked. But we emphasized to the interviewers the distinction between their report on their emotional reactions and their rational judgment of a person's stage of social maturity. The interviewers' subjective reaction was a potentially important datum, moreover, since Stage IV people, who are more service-oriented, were expected to be more interested in other people, easier to communicate with, and more likable.

We expected a Stage IV concern for other people to be linked with participation in voluntary organizations, in which people come together for the purpose of service. Indeed, we found that the higher the level of psychosocial maturity, either by the thinking or valuing measure, the more the individual took part in such organizations.

We also predicted from the theory of stages that occupational success or status would be most closely associated with Stage III, since a person at this level is most concerned with developing skills and impressing the world. If our measures reflected a true stage sequence, then occupational success would progress regularly up through Stage III and then fall off for those oriented toward Stage IV. Such was the case for both the thinking and valuing measures. And it was true for both men and women. On the whole, our measures of maturity corresponded with other things in a person's life that are related to maturity.

—D. McC. et al.

to be moral, or at least to avoid antisocial behavior. Those who stress the Stage I virtue of decency, or who reason at the level of law and order (Stage 4 in the Kohlberg scheme), lie less and are less aggressive. However, as we move up these scales of maturity, there is a tendency to engage in less moral behavior. How can we account for that?

Can we seriously contend that our measures reflect levels of maturity if people at the higher levels of maturity *behave* less morally?

The dilemma can be resolved, at least in part, if we assume that the conscious valuing and judging (or reasoning) measures are more influenced by cultural values and do not tap as high a

level of individual maturity as the thinking measure. In other words, the highest levels for valuing and judging still reflect a focus on the self, on self-actualization in line with American norms, rather than on the concerns and feelings of others. And focus on self-development, on being sure the individual knows his own mind and stands up for his rights and principles, does not particularly promote helping or not hurting others. Instead it may lead a person to violate codes of decent interpersonal behavior when he thinks a higher principle is involved.

Thus, as Kohlberg has insisted all along, moral maturity does not guarantee decent social behavior. Moral immaturity may be more effective for that—at least in preventing antisocial behavior. After all, Socrates, who scores high in moral reasoning by Kohlberg's theory, was notorious for neglecting his wife and children.

The Paradox of Maturity

How can parents do right by their children? If they are interested in promoting moral and social maturity in later life, the answer is simple: they should love them, enjoy them, want them around. They should not use their power to maintain a home that is only designed for the self-expression and pleasure of adults. They should not regard their children as disturbances to be controlled at all costs.

It was the easygoing, loving parents whose children turned out to be most mature. Is that a remarkable finding? Isn't it just common sense? The trouble with comon sense is that it is so uncommon.

But suppose the parents are interested, like most Americans, in moral *behavior*, in discouraging antisocial acts and encouraging social contributions. Herein lies a paradox. The mother who doesn't love her child much and insists on traditional Stage I decent behavior may produce an adult who conforms—but at the cost of his or her fuller development. To make the point more dramatically, mothers who didn't love their children much turned out adults who acted more morally: they did not misrepresent their knowledge as much on our tests. But strict parents also produced adults who were less inclined to engage in prosocial behavior. So parents can buy Stage I conformity in moral behavior, but at the cost of true maturity.

The paradox is that *promoting maturity leads first to a decrease in moral behavior*, as the person moves out of a Stage I reliance on external authority and becomes more oriented to making choices on his or her own. Only at the highest stage, when people become genuinely and emotionally aware of the feelings and viewpoints of others, do they again begin to behave less antisocially and more prosocially. This is not a new idea at all to moralists, who have always insisted there is a world of difference between being good out of custom or fear, and real goodness that comes from the heart. Jesus talked about "whited sepulchres"—those who slavishly followed Jewish law to the letter, but had no real charity in their hearts.

So parents also need faith—faith that loving and believing in their children will promote maturity in the long run, even though some of their offsprings' behavior seems outrageous in the short run as they learn to make their own decisions. There are no shortcuts to perfection. Children have to explore some detours if they are to reach the heights. The best we parents can do to help is to love them, and not stand in the way of their groping attempts to grow up or force them at all times to conform to adult-centered codes of moral behavior.

David McClelland, professor of psychology at Harvard University, is the author of both *The Achieving Society* (Halsted/Wiley, 1976) and also *Power: The Inner Experience* (Halsted /Wiley, 1975). He has had a lifelong interest in the study of human motivation and is now preparing a report by several contributors for The Cleveland Foundation on what behavioral scientists know about educating children for values. This article is based on research carried out for that report.

Carol A. Constantian is a doctoral candidate in the Department of Psychology and Social Relations at Harvard University. After receiving her B.A. in psychology in 1972 from Wellesley College, she worked in Los Angeles for four years, primarily in publishing. Her main interests in psychology include small-group behavior, human motivation, nonverbal sensitivity, and applications of social psychology within organizations.

David Regalado is a second-year graduate student in the Department of Psychology and Social Relations at Harvard University. After serving three years in the military, he received his B.A. *summa cum laude* from California State University, Long Beach, in 1976.

Carolyn Stone received her B.A. in psychology from Wellesley College in 1972. Currently she is a doctoral candidate at the Laboratory of Human Development of the Harvard Graduate School of Education. Her research interests include social cognitive development, peer relations in children, and the family's influence on development.

For further information, read:

Erikson, Erik H. *Childhood and Society*, 2nd ed., W. W. Norton, 1963, $10; paper, $3.45.

Kohlberg, Lawrence. "Stage and Sequence: The Cognitive-Developmental Approach to Socialization," in *Handbook of Socialization, Theory and Research*, David A. Goslin, ed., Rand McNally, 1969, $40.

McClelland, David C. *Power: The Inner Experience*, Halsted/Wiley, 1975, $16.95.

Rest, James R. "New Approaches in the Assessment of Moral Judgement," in *Moral Development and Behavior: Theory, Research, and Social Issues*, Thomas Lickona, ed., Holt, Rinehart and Winston, 1976, $15.95.

Sears, Robert, Eleanor Maccoby, and Harry Levin. *Patterns of Child Rearing*, Stanford University Press, 1957, $17.50; paper, $7.50.

Must Everything Be a Midlife Crisis?

The various stages in a person's life may well be normal turning points.

Bernice L. Neugarten

Bernice L. Neugarten, Ph.D., is a professor of human development at the University of Chicago. The above is adapted from an article published in the American Journal of Psychiatry.

The media have discovered adulthood. Gail Sheehy's *Passages*, Roger Gould's *Transformations*, and a dozen other popular books have all accorded adulthood the treatment of high drama, drawing from Erik Erikson's writings, George Vaillant's *Adaptation to Life*, Daniel Levinson's *The Seasons of a Man's Life* and other studies. Journalists and psychologists make news by describing a "midlife crisis" as if it were the critical turning point between joy and despair, enthusiasm and resignation, mental health and illness. People worry about their midlife crises, apologize if they don't seem to be handling them properly, and fret if they aren't having one.

From these books, one would predict the imminent arrival of Dr. Gesell or Dr. Spock guides for grown-ups: *The Adult from 40 to 45, The Parent from 55 to 60,* and the like. But the public should not be too quick to assume that adult life changes—whether mild "transitions," or dramatic "transformations," or full-fledged "crises"—define what is normal, or to think that the person who has *not* gone through such changes is somehow off the track. Many of my colleagues and I feel that media coverage of this subject has come too soon, is based on too little evidence, and generalizes too broadly from a highly select few to all of us. Levinson's study was based on only 40 men, for example, and Vaillant's on only 95 (Harvard graduates, at that).

Stage theories of adult development imply a fixed, one-way progression of issues and conflicts that occur at chronological intervals (such as Sheehy's "The Trying Twenties" and "Passage to the Thirties"). These notions appeal to us because they seem logical, and because they suggest a common pattern for the swirling, complex changes in our lives. But a Gesell for adults is unlikely to emerge—not because adults are changeless, but because adults change far more, and far less predictably, than the oversimplified stage theories suggest.

For many years, my students and I have studied what happens to people over the life cycle. The primary consistency we have found is a lack of consistency. We have had great trouble clustering people into age brackets that are characterized by particular conflicts; the conflicts won't stay put, and neither will the people. Choices and dilemmas do not sprout forth at ten-year intervals, and decisions are not made and then left behind as if they were merely beads on a chain.

It was reasonable to describe life as a set of discrete stages when most people followed the same rules, when major events occurred at predictable ages. People have long been able to tell the "right age" for marriage, the first child, the last child, career achievement, retirement, death. In the last two decades, however, chronological age has moved out of sync with these marking events. Our biological time clocks have changed: the onset of puberty for both sexes is earlier than it used to be just a generation ago; menopause comes later for women; most significantly, more people than ever now live into old age. And our social time clocks have

    "Must Everything Be a Midlife Crisis?" by Bernice L. Neugarten, *Prime Time*, February 1980. Reprinted by permission.

changed, too. New trends in work, family size, health, and education have produced phenomena that are unprecedented in our history: for example, a long "empty nest" period when the children have left home and the parents are together again. A growing prevalence of great-grandparenthood. An enormous number of people who are starting new families, new jobs, and new avocations when they are 40, 50, or 60 years old.

Old? Even that word has no chronological boundary anymore. Researchers now distinguish the young-old from the old-old, and it is not a given number of years that marks the dividing line. The young-old are a rapidly growing group of retired people who are physically and mentally vigor- the use of leisure time. They are healthy, financially comfortable, increasingly well-educated, politically active, and are eager consumers. They use their time productively, for self-fulfillment and community benefit. This sizable group of people is probably the first real leisure class America has ever had.

We are, in short, becoming an age-irrelevant society. We are already familiar with the 28-year-old mayor, the 30-year-old college president, the 35-year-old grandmother, the 50-year-old retiree, the 65-year-old father of a pre-schooler, the 55-year-old widow who starts a business, and the 70-year-old student. "Act your age" is an admonition that has little meaning for adults these days.

What gives people the feeling that they are going through "life crises" is not the events of adulthood themselves, but the fact that the events can no longer be keyed to our biological and social clocks. The stage theorists argue that crises occur at regular intervals, set off by natural changes in work, family, and personality.

I would argue precisely the opposite. Leaving the parents' home, marriage, parenthood, work, one's own children leaving home, menopause, grandparenthood, retirement—these are *normal* turning points, punctuation marks along the lifeline. They produce changes in self-concept and identity, of course, and people accept these events with various degrees of aplomb or difficulty; but whether or not they create *crises* usually depends on when they happen. For the majority of women in middle age, the departure of teenage children is not a crisis, but a pleasure. It is when the children do *not* leave home that a crisis occurs (for both parent and child). For the majority of older men, retirement is a normal event. It is when retirement occurs at 50 instead of 65 that it can become a crisis. Grandparenthood does not set off a "crisis" of worry about old age and death; it is more likely to be a problem when it comes too early, or simultaneously with a new, young family, or when it doesn't come at all.

The popular stage theories are inadvertently replacing one set of expectations about the life cycle with another, and that concerns me. Whether people think their lives consist of three, six, or ten stages, they develop a package of expectations about what will or should happen to them, and when. Men and women compare themselves constantly to their friends, siblings, colleagues, and parents to decide whether they are doing all right. They do not worry about being 40, 50, or 60, but about how they are doing for their age. They do not want to be young again, but they want to grow older in ways that are socially acceptable and, at the same time, personally satisfying.

Certainly there are some psychological preoccupations that are more powerful at one age than another. A study of reminiscence, for example, found that middle-aged people consciously select elements from their past to help them solve current problems; the very old put their store of memories in order, dramatizing some and rearranging others for consistency—creating a coherent life history. But most intrapsychic changes evolve very slowly, and they may or may not be linked with specific events. Divorce may provoke painful soul-searching for one woman, while another sails through the experience with a minimum of stress.

Most of the themes of adulthood appear and reappear in new forms over long periods of time. Issues of intimacy and freedom, for example, which are supposed to concern young adults just starting out in marriage and careers, are never settled once and for all. They haunt many couples continuously; compromises are found for a while, then renegotiated. Similarly, feeling the pressure of time, reformulating goals, coming to grips with success (and failure)—these are not the exclusive property of the 48-to-52-year-olds, by any means.

The new stage theories do not take into account the power of memory. Adults have a built-in dimension of thought that interprets the present relative to the past; the blending of past and present is our psychological reality. Our experiences with friends, lovers, children, parents, jobs become the fabric of our lives, and we are constantly reweaving these threads into new patterns. They are the stuff of which memories are made, the past reinvented, and the future planned. Whether we choose to celebrate our diversity and range, or confine ourselves to 10-year stages, is, of course, up to us.

'Old'
is not a four-letter word

A report on those who are euphemistically called "senior citizens." The topic is especially pertinent because of the aging of the American population and because of the extension of the mandatory retirement age from 65 to 70.

Alan Anderson, Jr.

Alan Anderson, Jr. is a writer living in Springfield, Illinois.

Meet Jim and Mary Johnson, Americans. Both are 65 years old, married to each other and about to embark on the perilous adventure of old age. This is a crucial year for them, and their success in getting through it—especially for Jim, who has just retired—will have a lot to do with how many more years they live, and how they feel about living. The year is crucial not because they are 65—a number more or less picked out of a hat by the Social Security Administration in the 1930s—but because the bureaucrats who set that benchmark had no idea how important it would become psychologically. Nor had they any idea how many people would be flooding past it today along the poorly marked paths of aging.

This country, with much the rest of the world soon to follow, is in the midst of a demographic upheaval unprecedented in history—a gray revolution, if you will. Today there are 21.8 million Americans 65 and older, nearly seven times as many as there were in 1900. Each day some 4,000 persons turn 65 and 3,000 in that category die, for a net gain of about 1,000 a day. By the year 2000 one out of five Americans will be over 65.

And we don't know what to do with them. They tend to be retired from work, ostracized socially, displaced from their traditional position as society's "elders." We don't yet understand them physically or psychologically, and we don't know how to make best use of their own desires and abilities to remain active. "The question of what to do with old people is a new one," says Chauncey Leake, a pharmacologist and student of aging at the University of California, San Francisco. "Over all the millennia of human existence, it could not have arisen until some 50 years ago. There simply weren't enough old people."

There are enough now, and modern America is baffled. A pension system carefully set up by Franklin Roosevelt is in trouble; within a few years, more people will be drawing from Social Security than are paying into it. We are trying (late, as usual) to stave off bankruptcy of the system. First, as everyone who works knows, Social Security taxes are zooming. Second, legislation has gone through Congress to extend the mandatory retirement age, generally 65, to 70; if the employee chooses to work until the age of 70, obviously there is no Social Security payout until that birthday. But there are more fundamental questions. How long *should* workers stay on the job—a particularly pertinent question in view of the change in mandatory retirement. What kind of job? Do they feel like working, and are they effective? Can families return to the custom of honoring the elderly? And what do Jim and Mary feel like, and how can they be most productive and happy?

The study of old people is a new pursuit—so much so that even the vocabulary is strange. Geriatrics, for example, is the study not of aging but of the aged and their diseases. The science of the processes of aging is gerontology; the first important work in this field was done as recently as the 1950s. There is also confusion between life expectancy (the expected length of a life) and life span (the theoretical limit of a lifetime). The

From *Across the Board*, May 1978. Reprinted by permission.

average human life expectancy has stretched from about 22 years in the time of ancient Greece to 47 years in turn-of-the-century America to 71 years now. The maximum life span, about 110 to 115 years, has not increased at all.

Another new vocabulary word is ageism—like "sexism," one of the uglier terms of tin-ear wordsmiths—the prejudice against the old that Jim and Mary have begun to encounter. Old people face a painful wall of discrimination that they are often too polite or too timid to attack. Elders are not hired for new jobs, and are eased out of old ones (they are considered rigid or feebleminded); they are shunned socially (they are thought "senile" or boring); they are edged out of family life (children often regard them as sickly or ugly or parasitic); they are equated with children (common adjectives are "cute" and "adorable"). In sum, elders are treated by many as though they were no longer people. A typical study at a California nursing home showed that staff members judged the residents less interested and able to take advantage of activities than did the residents themselves. Our humor about old people implies wickedness of sex in men (old goat, dirty old man) and ugliness in women (biddy, hag, crock). Women after menopause and men after retirement lose social status rapidly. They are considered incapable of thinking clearly, learning new things, enjoying sex, contributing to the community, holding responsible jobs; in short, incapable of living.

Can this be true? How, then, was it possible for Picasso to paint masterworks until a few months before his death at 91? Michelangelo was still sculpting a few weeks before he died at 90. Verdi wrote *Falstaff* at 80; Tolstoy wrote *What Is Art* at 88. Even Freud, who was pessimistic about the minds of old people, did not begin his best work until his forties and wrote *The Ego and the Id* at 67. Titian did his finest paintings just before he died at 100, Pablo Casals was still playing the cello in his nineties, Winston Churchill was Prime Minister at 81 and Georgia O'Keefe starred in her first television special at 90.

What, then, does life have in store for Jim and Mary Johnson? Though the science of gerontology is still in its adolescence, we can at least erase some old myths and make some predictions. In general, the needs of older persons are not much different from those of younger persons: They do best when they can enjoy friendships and social contacts, keep busy with work and leisure activities and maintain reasonably good health. True, they are more vulnerable to stresses. Physically they have less resistance to shock and disease; psychologically they are prone to loneliness, dependence, the effects of family conflicts, loss of status. But there is good evidence that failure is not inevitable. Instead it seems that the health and happiness of old people decline because we expect them to—and old people believe us.

As a married couple of 65, the Johnsons are typical in some ways and unusual in others. The marriage itself is unusual and important: Married elders live on the average five years longer than unmarrieds. Most older women (69 percent) are not married, most older men (79 percent) are. This is both because women live longer than men (75 versus 68 years) and because women tend to marry older men (by an average of three years). Although more boys are born than girls, women outnumber men by 130 to 100 in the 65–74 category; by 74+ they're ahead by 169 to 100, and by 85+ by two to one. The U.S. Bureau of the Census predicts 1,000 women to 675 men by the year 2000, with widows outnumbering widowers four to one. It's not only a gray revolution; it's a gray female revolution.

The Johnsons are typical in that they live in their community. Until a decade ago, it was widely assumed that most of our elders lived in nursing homes or other institutions. In fact, only about 5 percent do, though the number is rising. And though the Johnsons have a few chronic problems (Jim has arthritis and Mary has high blood pressure), they are freely mobile (as are about 81 percent of elders in the community). Both wear eyeglasses (90 percent do); have no hearing aids (about 5 percent do); will spend $791 each on health care this year (more than three times that spent by people under 65; about two-thirds of the bill will be paid by the government); will take in $3,540 in Social Security for the two of them; completed eight years of school each; are white (fewer blacks live to this age); and have no jobs (only 22 percent of men over 65 and 8 percent of women do). Oh, and they always vote: 51 percent of our elders do, and they are becoming an ever-stronger bloc.

Physically, Jim and Mary have aged in similar fashion. Both have slowed: Their base metabolic rate has dropped about 20 percent since they were 30. This means they need slightly less to eat and the effects of drugs and alcohol last longer. (Dr. Robert Butler, director of the two-year-old National Institute on Aging, recommends no more than one-and-a-half ounces of hard liquor a day or two six-ounce glasses of wine.) Their body temperature has declined to as low as 90°F.; the aging King David tried to prolong his life by lying against the bodies of warm young virgins.

Perhaps the most significant change is that the entire circulatory machinery is less efficient. There is less elastin, the molecules responsible for the elasticity of heart and blood vessels, and more collagen, the stiff protein that makes up about one-third of the body's protein. The heart rate does not rise as well in response to stress, the heart muscle cannot contract and relax as fast and the arteries are more resistant to the flow of blood. Heart output—about five quarts a minute at age 50—has been dropping at about 1 percent a year. With the heart muscle less efficient and the vessels more resistant, heart rate and blood pressure both rise—and are both related to heart disease. Jim's blood pressure was 100/75 when he was 25; now it is 160/90. His blood carries less oxygen to the brain and lungs. If he rises too suddenly from a chair he gets dizzy. Likewise, if Mary climbs the stairs too fast she must stop to catch her breath.

4. DEVELOPMENT

Both are slightly shorter than they used to be, and have a tendency to stoop. This is due both to muscle wastage (less skeletal muscle to hold the skeleton upright) and to loss of bone tissue. The individual vertebrae settle closer together as the discs that separate them flatten and collapse. Mary's bones began a steady loss when she was about 40; by the time she is 80 her skeleton will weigh 25 to 40 percent less. Jim's bone loss, unsuspected until two decades ago, began just a few years ago and will be less severe. Gerontologists do not understand the mechanism or cause of bone loss, though there is some evidence that a good diet (containing adequate calcium, in particular) and regular exercise can slow it.

Both Johnsons are in less direct communication with the world around them. Each is slightly nearsighted and slightly farsighted; to focus near or far the lens of the eye must flex, and their lenses are more rigid; the ciliary muscles that control the flexing are also weaker. But neither condition will get much worse and both can be corrected by bifocals. Eye pressure increases (which may lead to glaucoma) and the lens may become more opaque, leading to cataracts; the latter can now be corrected by surgery. The Johnsons cannot smell as well. Both optic and olfactory nerve fibers will eventually dwindle to about 25 percent of the number present at birth, and they are irreplaceable. Elsewhere in the body the sense of touch has begun to dull, faster in the feet than in the hands, and the pain threshold has risen, creating a greater danger from hot or sharp objects. The taste dims; the number of taste buds will have decreased by a third by age 75.

The nerve cells people worry about most are those of the central nervous system—principally the spinal cord and the brain. Studies as early as the 1920s indicated that brain cells begin to die off around age 30 and in 1958 one researcher estimated the loss rate at 100,000 a day. Unlike skin, blood, liver and other regenerative cells, neurons cannot be produced after maturity. It is now known that the brain of an aged person weighs about 7 percent less than it did at maturity. But there is no direct correlation between brain size and intelligence, and there is still no evidence that loss of brain cells means loss of intelligence.

There are, of course, other changes in the brain more worrisome—changes that seem to impair mental function. These changes are all microscopic, and involve the proliferation of abnormal blobs, tangles and intracellular "garbage." The blobs are plaques containing an abnormal protein called amyloid. By now both Jim and Mary are almost certain to have some plaques, but their role in the aging process is unknown. The tangles—called neurofibrillary—are inside nerve cells (and others) and just as poorly understood. They resemble old, snarled fishing line. The "garbage" is a mysterious brown pigment called lipofuscin, or age pigment. The accumulation of lipofuscin among cells is thought always to accompany aging, but it is not known whether the pigment is simply a by-product of cellular activity or is harmful. Pellets of lipo-fuscin form an outer coat by the same process oil-based paints harden, and are resistant to normal "garbage-removal" enzymes.

These mysterious blobs, tangles and pigments are linked to one of the least understood and most abused terms in the lexicon of aging: senility. The word is frequently used to apply to any act or gesture by an "old" person—forgetfulness, selfishness, a desire for a nap and so on. Health care professionals now seldom use it except to indicate senile brain disease, sometimes called chronic brain syndrome. Even these terms are vague; Robert Butler calls them "wastebasket diagnoses." Their greatest weakness is that they fail to separate those who are "senile" from those who are "normal." One expert, Adrian Ostfeld of the Yale University School of Medicine, decides it this way: "If a person knows when to get out of bed, wash, dress, eat and pay his bills, he is not a case."

Nor is there any certainty about whether dementia (the commonest designation is Alzheimer's disease) is really a disease or simply a normal part of the aging process. One reason for this confusion is that the primary indicators of dementia (plaques, tangles, lipofuscin) are also present in "normal" older people like Jim and Mary. Most cases of Alzheimer's disease show no simple pattern of inheritance, and no evidence that they are contagious. What is certain is that they are rare—more so than commonly supposed. Because diagnosis is so uncertain, the true incidence is not known. But it is known that only about 5 percent of elders live in institutions, and only a very small percentage of them can truly be called senile. In one study of 3,141 low-income persons between 65 and 74, only 12 could be identified as cases of senile brain disease. Most of the institutionalized elderly are victims of stroke, injury, arthritis, chronic respiratory diseases, alcoholism and other nonsenile conditions.

Physically, then, the elders have slowed somewhat, but they are by no means incapacitated. There is no physiological watershed at age 65 that should prevent people from working if they want to. Their strength is down slightly, their wind reduced; but neither condition is crippling and certainly not serious enough to disqualify them from most activities of "normal" life. But what of behavior? Is there something different about the workings of an older mind?

I have mentioned the irony of Sigmund Freud: At the same time he mistrusted elders (he seldom took them as patients), he himself did his best work after the age of 40. Freud referred to a "rigid ego" in old age and an "inverted Oedipal complex"—an exaggerated attachment to a child figure rather than a parent figure of the opposite sex. Jung, unlike Freud, refused to lump older people in such psychic ignominy, treating each as a unique individual.

In fact, there are signs of subtle, broad psychic changes in old age, but nothing to deserve Freud's prejudice. These are tough to test because old people are slightly less motivated than the young to take tests. A University of

Why do we have to die?

By nature's rules, death is as much a part of the game as life. Shortly after puberty (in humans as in other animals), the first signs of aging begin—a steady loss of irreplaceable cells, an accumulation of "wear-and-tear" mistakes, a slowing of metabolic rate. Eventually the accumulation of these changes and mistakes becomes fatal in one way or another.

But the death that comes to us all is not really so simple as this organic falling-apart. Otherwise we might be able to stave it off through care, just as we prolong the life of a well-loved automobile by proper maintenance and garaging. The hard truth is that humans and other animals have a maximum life expectancy that is rarely, if ever, exceeded. No matter how well sheltered from predation, disease and other "natural" causes of death, the Norway rat does not live past the age of four years, the gray squirrel past 15, the black bear past 35, the Asiatic elephant past 70 or *Homo sapiens* past 110. If death were the random result of accident and rusting away, we would expect to encounter wide variations in nature—the occasional octogenarian squirrel or, at the opposite extreme, the elephant that ages quickly and dies at 14. It is clear that a program for death is written in our genes.

The location and trigger of that program constitute the most hotly debated questions in gerontology today. By one theory, championed by Leonard Hayflick of Stanford, a clock of aging lies in each of our cells, where DNA molecules bear a gene or genes for their own destruction. Hayflick bases his thinking on his discovery less than two decades ago that even cells carefully nourished outside the body in tissue culture are programmed to die. Previous to that time, cells in tissue culture were thought to be immortal. But in the chick embryo cells he uses, Hayflick has shown that cell division ceases after about 50 generations—a seemingly clear case of genetic self-destruction. Similarly, he believes that cells in a whole-body context give orders, by some mysterious timing, for a progressive disruption of protein assembly lines and eventually their own death.

A more popular, though not incompatible, theory is that death is controlled by the endocrine system through some unidentified "death hormones." W. Donner Denckla of the Roche Institute of Molecular Biology in New Jersey is a leader in testing this hormonal clock theory. "I don't care what happens to cells in tissue culture," says Denckla. "What is important is what people die of." Denckla's clock, controlled by the brain and mediated by the thyroid gland, would, like Hayflick's, have genetic gearworks. The mechanism for either is not yet clear.

Why should we die at all? That is an evolutionary question, but one which gerontologists must consider. Presumably, the reasons humans live as long as they do is that the species is well served by a hierarchy of elders who are able to think, be wise and pass on their wisdom to younger generations. Why not let old humans do this to the age of 200, getting ever wiser? The most reasonable explanation is that more frequent death—and new life—among individuals is necessary to the survival of the species. Evolution by means of natural selection is based upon the selection of "favorable" genes and their passage to successive generations. This genetic turnover must be rapid if we are to keep up with environmental changes.

Ah, you say—but that's old-fashioned! We are seizing control of our evolution now; we'll soon be able to engineer our genes to fit the environment of our choice. That may indeed be true, and if it is we'll also be able to correct the genes that bring death. We might learn how to live in good health and sound mind to the age of 200 or 500; perhaps there will be no limit. But we can only begin to guess at the social tumult that would accompany this sudden excess of new old people. Many of us would probably prefer the stance of Lewis Thomas, president of Memorial Sloan-Kettering Cancer Center in New York and author of *The Lives of a Cell.* "At a certain age," says Thomas, "it is in our nature to wear out, to come unhinged and to die, and that is that."

—A.A. Jr.

Chicago report on interviews with schoolteachers indicates a general laying back with age: "One of the things they talked about is that they had come to deal with professional interests with less intensity in middle age. A high school principal said: 'When I started out, each disciplinary problem in the school was a special problem for me. I intervened; I went all out for it. Now I withdraw a little more and let the teacher handle it until I can see what is going on.' "

Jim and Mary find that they move more slowly now,

mentally as well as physically. Instead of making a quick response to a question, then tend to ponder it for a moment before answering. Their reaction time has slowed; in a simple response test requiring them to push a button as soon as a red light came on, both Jim and Mary took .212 seconds to react when they were in their fifties, .217 seconds now. In 10 years it will take them .245 seconds to push the button. To some people, this is evidence that older people should take driving tests periodically.

The breadth of their interests has narrowed a good deal; this seems to peak around the age of *nine,* when children respond to almost anything. They watch about the same amount of television they did when they were younger, though they prefer variety and talent shows to serious dramas or mysteries. They have adopted more solitary pursuits, especially reading, going to art galleries and spending evenings at home with each other. Both have less interest in driving automobiles, in sports and in exploring.

According to one psychologist, there is more concrete behavior after age 60, less conceptualizing. Jim and Mary are more likely to think there is only one answer to a question, or one meaning to a situation, than they used to. In one thinking test reported in the *Journal of Gerontology*, involving subjects aged 12 to 80, the older people tended to rely more on past experience for answers rather than on analytical thinking. Other intelligence tests indicate a decrease in short-term memory, more difficulty putting three random words in a sentence, poorer word association, less facile picture composition.

In other areas, the Johnsons have experienced no such decline. Their vocabulary, for example, has nearly doubled since their twenties. Definitions, verbal understanding, naming countries, counting pennies all stand up well with age. Worker studies have indicated that individual speed and efficiency do drop with age, but older people tend to take care of their age-associated handicaps better than young people take care of their deficiencies. "Considering total job behavior," writes Harold Geist, a clinical psychologist and professor at San Francisco State College, "the older worker is found to be more efficient than the younger—especially when considering accuracy, absenteeism and motivation." Other studies have revealed little or no truth in the myth that most jobs are too strenuous or dangerous for elders. The U.S. Department of Labor has found that only 14 percent of jobs in industry require much physical strength, and many surveys have shown that older workers have fewer accidents than younger workers.

Much of the pressure to retire, it seems, comes not from an inability to perform but from the negative attitude of younger people. The University of Maryland's Center on Aging has found that children typically view elderly people as "sick, sad, tired, dirty and ugly" and insist that they themselves would never be old. And the most damaging aspect of such attitudes is that old people themselves come to believe them. "They are being told it's all downhill financially, it's all downhill sexually, it's all downhill intellectually," says Edward Ansello of the Maryland group.

New research, however, is revealing no evidence that life has to be significantly downhill for the old. Duke University's Center for the Study of Aging and Human Development has been keeping tabs on more than 200 elders for the last 20 years, and the group's conclusion so far is that most old people remain sound of body and mind until the final weeks of life. "The characteristic they seem to suffer most from," says George Maddox, head of the

Duke Center, "is the tendency of society to treat them as though they are all alike."

Take sex, for example. NIA president Robert Butler has written a book called *Sex After Sixty* in which he says that this is one area where all people over a certain age are—wrongly—thought to be alike. "Many persons—not only the young and the middle-aged but older people themselves—simply assume that [sex] is over. This is nonsense. Our own clinical and research work, the work of other gerontologists, the research of Kinsey and the clinical discoveries of Masters and Johnson all demonstrate that relatively healthy older people who enjoy sex are capable of experiencing it often until very late in life."

Butler and other gerontologists argue that the myth of the sexless old is one of the most insidious symptoms of "ageism." He condemns the "aesthetic narrowness" by which we think of only the young as beautiful, and which makes it so difficult for grown children to deal with their parents' sexuality. Indeed, single or widowed parents who live with younger relatives are often made to feel guilty or indecent for wanting to date.

The field is riddled with additional myths. One of the most anxiety-producing is the fear of many men that they will have heart attacks during intercourse. It is, of course, possible, but fewer than 1 percent of all coronary deaths occur then, and 70 percent of those are during extramarital sex, which tends to feature nonphysical stresses like guilt or lack of time.

Another myth is the fear among women that a hysterectomy means the end of sex. In fact there is no evidence that removal of the womb produces any change in sexual desire or performance.

Then there are the false aphrodisiacs tried by many older people: alcohol (especially wine), Spanish fly, Cayenne pepper, black snakeroot, bloodroot, vitamin E, marijuana. Sometimes alcohol has benefit as a social icebreaker, but there the benefits end. Any stimulant works more on the mind than the body, and the effects lessen with use. The only true aphrodisiacs are good diet and good exercise.

Menopause in women, which typically occurs between 45 and 50, is a rich source of both myth and misunderstanding. Physiologically it is fairly straightforward, characterized by the ending of menstruation and a sharp decline in the output of hormones—chiefly the estrogen group. Some women, however, use menopause as an excuse, for themselves or others, to slow or even halt their sexual activity. Actually, about two-thirds of women experience no dramatic changes or discomfort with menopause. With a positive attitude, there is no reason that sex cannot remain a source of pleasure long after menopause. It is even common for sex to improve with the freedom from anxieties about becoming pregnant.

Jim, like Mary, can look forward to years of enjoyable sex. Both his fertility (the ability to have children) and potency (the ability to have intercourse) should last one or two decades, possibly even longer. Havelock Ellis, the renowned British psychologist and sexologist, overcame a lifetime of impotence when he reached old age. Jim will not have to go through the broad hormonal changes experienced by Mary; there is no menopause in men (though some experience a similar psychological shock) but rather a gradual decline in the output of testosterone, the male hormone.

If we make the assumption that old age is not a curse—and it now seems clear it should not be—can and should we prolong it? Here we come upon a stumbling block: It is assumed that aging is an inexorable part of life, programmed somehow in our genes, yet some scientists think that the wear-and-tear disease of aging might be "cured" by clever manipulation of body machinery. It seems, in any event, that for the foreseeable future our time on earth is limited to about 71 years. (See box on A/E page 185.)

Even the conquest of common diseases would not lead us to immortality. If all cardiovascular diseases—now causing more than half of all deaths—were eliminated, the average lifetime would increase only about ten years. If cancer were no longer a killer we would gain another two years. Wipe out all infectious and parasitic diseases and we'd last another year; hold all accidents, suicides and homicides and that's two more years—still far short of immortality. In fact, despite all the medical gains documented since 1900, most of which lessened the threats of infant death and childhood diseases, Jim and Mary at 65 stand to live only about two years longer than they might have in 1900.

Despite an immense amount of research, the only known ways to extend a human lifetime (not a human life span) are to have long-lived parents, to eat properly and to get regular exercise. The first possibility, of course, is beyond our control. The last two are matters of will. Most gerontologists agree that Americans are eating themselves into early graves. We eat too much fat, too much sugar, too much protein, too much refined carbohydrate and not enough fresh vegetables, whole grains or other roughage. Take calories alone: Male Americans aged 55–64 now get about 2,422 a day, and most nutritionists believe this is too much. The world's longest-lived people thrive on far less. The same age group of men in Hunza, in West Pakistan, get about 1,925 calories a day; the men of the Caucasus in southern Russia about 1,800. Life insurance actuaries judge that being overweight subtracts from three to 10 or more years from a lifetime. So does

Prejudiced Shakespeare?

The sixth age shifts
Into the lean and slipper'd pantaloon,
With spectacles on nose and pouch on side,
His youthful hose, well sav'd, a world too wide
For his shrunk shank; and his big manly voice,
Turning again toward childish treble, pipes
And whistles in his sound. Last scene of all,
That ends this strange eventful history,
Is second childishness, and mere oblivion,
Sans teeth, sans eyes, sans taste, sans everything.
As You Like It, Act II

cigarette smoking: for one pack a day figure seven years; for two packs, 12 years. High blood pressure, high cholesterol level, a tense disposition, and a high pulse all shorten the average lifetime as well.

Exercise is increasingly acknowledged to be an effective ingredient in building a long lifetime. But it is important that it be an endurance building kind—not intermittent bursts of youthful enthusiasm followed by weeks of spectatorship—and it must be continued into old age. The point of exercise is to strengthen the heart, and the best kinds for doing that are jogging, cross-country skiing, swimming, rowing, cycling, long walks—anything that gets the heart pumping and keeps it pumping for 20 minutes or more. It has even been demonstrated that the much-maligned weekend athlete, if he or she is vigorous enough, gains some protection against heart ailments. A recent study of 17,000 Harvard alumni has shown "strenuous leisure time exercise" to be valuable even if there are other negative factors, like cigarette smoking. And, of course, those long-lived folks from Hunza and the Caucasus get plenty of outdoor exercise all their lives.

Typically, we slow-to-arouse Americans do not yet realize the urgency of the gray revolution. Before 1950 little thought was given to systems for the elderly—easier-to-use mass transit, housing situated near vital services, a health system that has the patience to diagnose and cure old people's chronic diseases. Only now, with the emergency upon us, are we beginning to think about how to live with our elders. An important first step must be an attack on "ageism" and an acceptance of the old people who will be a larger and larger component of modern society. More and more it will have to be "in" to be old.

SOME OF US MAY NEVER DIE

There may be no biological limit to the human lifespan. In the near future a healthy 21 year old might live 200 years or more.

KATHLEEN STEIN

In October, 1976, Luna, the 16-year-old daughter of science writer Robert Anton Wilson, was brutally beaten and killed in a grocery store robbery. Helpless in the face of death, Wilson took the only action he could. He had the child's brain set immediately in cryonic suspension, frozen in liquid nitrogen at 320 degrees below zero (Fahrenheit). From this brain a part of Luna's identity may someday be reconstructed, or, from one of her stem cells, a new body cloned. Hers was the first brain to be frozen in this manner. Now, however, a special cryonic cylinder for the brain has been made available for the purpose of future cloning or identity reconstruction of some other kind.

Cryonic preservation is undertaken on the premise that the infinitely more advanced medical scientists of the future might be able to revive the dead and repair whatever killed them. It's a long shot, to say the least, but the odds are still better with freezing than they are with cremation or burial. Some cryobiologists estimate that certain bodies could be preserved for several hundred thousand years without any deterioration.

However desperate, bizarre, or macabre an effort it may seem, cryobiological interest is growing and profit-making organizations such as Trans Time in Berkeley, Bay Area Cryonics, and the Cryonics Society of Michigan are forming around the country. Adherents of the practice include people such as Woody Allen and Columbia University physicist Gerald Feinberg, who conceived the hypothetical faster-than-light particle, the tachyon. It is rumored, although without confirmation, that

Walt Disney is among those whose animation is cooling off until a better day.

Unlike Luna Wilson's body, most of the souls resting in cryonic suspension are intact. Immediately after death each body is packed in dry ice, drained of blood and filled with glycerol and DMSO (dimethyl-sulfoxide) an antifreezing agent, to prevent ice crystals from forming in the living tissue. The frozen body is then wrapped in aluminum foil and stored in a thermos-like insulated double-walled polished steel "cryonic storage capsule" until the millennium. The body is "buried" in a cryonic cemetary which uses auxiliary power sources to keep it frozen even in the event of a power shortage.

To keep the immortal fire burning, however, is no minor financial undertaking. For most people, the initial cost of interment amounts to about $15,000 with a maintenance charge of $1800 a year. At Bay Area Cryonics a $50,000 insurance policy is said to cover the whole thing. And you have to plan ahead!

DEATH VS. THE PEOPLE

The obvious drawback to cryonic suspension is that you have to die in order to enjoy an extended life. But movements such as cryobiology point to the growing rebellion against aging and death. People simply want to live longer, better, and are less and less willing to "go gentle into that good night." And the cryonic refrigeration revolution with its "freeze . . . wait . . . reanimate" is not the only front on which death and aging are being attacked.

In Robert Anton Wilson's *Cosmic Trigger,* Paul Segall, Ph.D., a researcher in the department of physiology at the University

of California, Berkeley, offers several approaches to longevity, which include:
- *Transplantation,* which might allow us to continue replacing organs "until the point where 'we' are still there, but our entire bodies are new."
- *Prosthetics* and *cyborgs,* machine-human combinations of which the Bionic Woman is a none-too-fanciful projection.
- *Identity reconstruction* through cloning.
- *Regeneration,* a process by which repressed genes are switched back on to renew cell tissue.

And at the heart of the matter is *gerontology.* This science investigates not only the chemical and biological processes of aging, but also the possibilities for extended healthy life. If gerontology research proves as promising as it looks, drastic measures such as freezing, cloning, and mechanizing humans in order to preserve your vital personality may not be necessary. Most efforts in the gerontological field are concerned with postponing senescence.

As early as 1962, Dr. Bernard Strehler, professor of biology at the University of Southern California, and one of the indefatigable warriors of the seige on death, announced that before long science will have understood aging's sources and that "toothless, wrinkled, mindless incontinent wrecks with Dorian Gray-like [sic] bodies—they will not exist!" In the absence of aging, Strehler said, the longevity of a healthy 21 year old could exceed 2000 years.

Following the startling hypothesis that aging could be curable, gerontologists have been piecing the puzzle together, moving closer to pinpointing the causes of aging, the sources of longevity.

Right now it seems quite possible that

From *OMNI,* October 1978. Copyright 1978 by OMNI International, Ltd. and reprinted with the permission of the copyright owner.

the underlying cause of aging may not be impossibly complex, but singular, primary. It may be that senescence is not a natural phenomenon, but a byproduct of social conditions. There may be, in fact, no biological limit to a healthy vigorous lifespan. To extend the accepted lifespan potential from 70—100 years to 120, 200, 400, 1000 and on up, may be part of *Homo sapiens* on-going evolutionary destiny.

With the tremendous explosion of knowledge of basic molecular biology and genetics, we are·learning the secrets of life and in doing so, we're learning how to control aging, to extend life.

Data now are beginning to indicate that life-extension is inevitable. We may have some way of lengthening our lives before the year 2000. Some of us may never die.

An array of potentially useful drugs are in various stages of testing, drugs which may not extend lifespan significantly, but which will stave off bodily wear and tear, perhaps rejuvenate the body and preserve energy and youthfulness past middle age. These drugs might contribute to a "synergistic effect" whereby one advance buys a person enough time to live well until the subsequent discovery prolongs his health even more.

Anti-aging therapies are being tested that combat free radicals, for example, those fragments of molecules which break off, careen about the body tissue wreaking havoc and contributing to the build-up of cellular garbage such as lipofuscins. Dr. Denham Harman, an internist-chemist at the University of Nebraska school of medicine is working on a series of antioxidants, which react with free radicals and minimize their effects.

Dr. Harman developed a number of compounds that increase life expectancy as much as 50 percent in mice. These include: Vitamin E; 2-MEA (mercaptoethylemine), a compound first used for radiation detection; BHT and Santoquin, commonly used as food preservatives; as well as sodium hypophosphite, an old drug used for the treatment of tuberculosis around 1900. These drugs all have extended life expectancy in mice, and Harman hopes this testing will now extend to larger mammals.

Another compound, DMAE (dimethylaminoethanol), is showing promising results, reports Albert Rosenfeld in his important book, *Pro-Longevity*. DMAE is a lysosome membrane stabilizer, and as such it strengthens cells against damage caused by lipofuscin accumulations. When lysosome membranes are damaged, harmful substances leak out and may be responsible for aging symptoms.

Dr. Richard Hochschild of the Microwave Instrument Company of Del Mar, California, found that by adding DMAE to the water of mice he increased their lifespans

significantly. Other investigators have successfully employed centrophenoxine, a synthetic compound derived in part from DMAE, to delay lipofuscion build-up in the brain of guinea pigs. Centrophenoxine, which has almost no toxic side effects, is already used experimentally with apparent success in France to improve the mental abilities of senile patients.

The first drug likely to pass through the FDA's interminable bureaucratic maze, however, is the well-publicized Gerovital, developed in 1945 by Dr. Ana Aslan of the Bucharest Geriatric Institute. In Romania it is possible to get "youth shots" of Gerovital's 2 percent procaine hydrochloride and haematoporphyrin solution from government doctors.

Over the last 25 years, Dr. Aslan has claimed to have cured people of everything from heart disease and athritis to impotence and gray hair. But few scientists are prepared to sing the drug's praises. Says Dr. Ruth Weg, of Andrus Gerontology Center of the University of Southern California: "We just don't know."

The list of potentially effective drugs, then, is growing geometrically, and the catalogue of agents that offer some chance of alleviating or postponing some debilitating symptoms are imminently testable. In the future, moreover, enzyme cocktails and genetic manipulation in pill form might be as commonplace as valium and birth control pills.

EAT LESS, LIVE LONGER

Since the 1930s, classic laboratory studies show that restricting an animal's diet in the first half of its life can double its lifespan—to the point where a 1000-day-old rat can be compared to a 90-year-old human with the body of John Travolta. These experiments have been conducted on everything from one-celled *Tokophrya*, to rotifers, worms, insects, mice, hamsters, and rats with similar results. This is a key concept in the theory of life-expansion. Restricting diet delays maturity and increases longevity.

Dr. Roy Walford, a pathologist at the UCLA school of medicine, a man with a reputation among his colleagues for meticulous research, recently has extended this nutritional study to include the testing of mental function. He will find out whether dietary restriction produces long-lived idiots or long-lived supermice. "It may well be the supermice," he says.

In a new development, Walford and his associate Dr. Richard Weindruck have discovered that when dietary restriction is begun in mid-life mice, the animals' immune systems seem to be rejuvenated. A chief researcher in immunological systems, and the author of the *The Immunologic Theory of Aging*, Walford has found that in aging

not only do the immune cells lose their ability to fight off the body's enemies, but they actually go berserk and turn against the very tissue they are supposed to protect. There is increasing evidence that this autoimmune response is a fundamental symptom of aging, which involves certain self-destructive acts: "like an art performance," Walford laughs.

Two years ago, Walford traveled extensively throughout India to measure body temperature regulation among the yogis. He found that through their yogic practices some could lower their body temperature one-half to one-degree Centigrade.

Why lower body temperature? Walford and others have found that reducing body temperature of humans a few degrees could greatly extend lifespan. "A very minor reduction, about three degrees Fahrenheit," says Bernard Strehler, "could well add as much as 30 years to human life."

Neither Walford nor anyone else, however, has succeeded in lowering temperature in "warm-blooded" (homeothermic) animals, although Walford has experiments with the diverse substances, including marijuana, to determine to what extent they could do the job. Marijuana is the best substance for lowering body temperature," he says. Yet his mice developed a tolerance to the drug, and, after a few weeks of injections it had no effect on their temperatures. "There might be an analogue or chemically similar substitute that could do it," he speculates.

Richard Cutler of the National Institute of Aging's Gerontology Research Center offers the bizarre, but workable, scheme of actually inserting a tiny ceramic device into the blood vessel preceding the hypothalamus (where temperature is controlled). A microwave unit also might be placed in the bedroom. At night during sleep, when the body's metabolic rate is slower, the microwave unit would beam on and the embedded device would, in turn, trick the hypothalamus into thinking the body was in a fever of one or two degrees. The hypothalamus consequently would lower the temperature a degree or so. In the early morning, before awaking, the microwave unit would switch off and the body temperature would be restored to 98.6°F. The user would not be bothered, but might live twice as long.

DEATH CLOCK?

As more is known about the genetic structure of life, biologists are coming to the conclusion that aging is not the result of slow "trashing" of all parts, but may be the result of a genetic program, coded along with the other instructions for the functioning of the cells in its DNA. The big question remains: Are we programmed to die? Is there a "death clock" that turns off the genes one by one? Or is nature simply indifferent to our fate after we've played our part in perpetuating the species? Or does the program for growth and sexual maturity contain within it what Dr. Richard Cutler of the National Institute on Aging calls "pleiotropic processes"—necessary functions which have by-products which in the long run are harmful to your health?

Many investigators on the case are now "pro-clock." Opinions vary drastically and vehemently, however, as to where the time-piece is located. One group theorizes that the aging mechanism occurs at the cellular level. Molecular biologist Dr. Leonard Hayflick discovered evidence that there are only so many times (± 50) a cell can divide in vitro before its descendants age and die. Thus, Hayflick concluded, the cell has a built-in genetic limit. And ever since the revolutionary "Hayflick Limit" was announced, it has been the target of continuous speculation. Critics scour the territory for evidence to refute it.

Dr. V.J. Cristofalo of Philadelphia's Wistar Institute, for instance, has prolonged cellular life by adding the hormones cortisone and hydrocortisone to culture solutions, thus suggesting that it is hormonal balance that signals the termination of cell division, not tiny clocks.

Dr. David Harrison of Jackson Laboratory, Bar Harbor, Maine, believes certain cells may indeed be immortal (as they were thought to be prior to Hayflick's results). When he transplanted stem cells, which have a large prolificacy capacity, from old animals into young, the old cells functioned as well as the young cells did when both were transplanted into young recipients.

Walford's rejuvenation of middle-aged mice's immunological response, as well as work he has done with congenic mice strains, leads him to believe that control of the entire immune system is located within a small region of genetic material—corresponding to the sixth chromosome in humans. He suspects that this control center is fundamentally involved in the aging process as a whole—that it may be "the man pulling the strings behind the scenes." These strings may involve only a few genes.

THE BRAIN, HORMONES & DECO

Many other scientists now think the program for aging is encoded in the hypothalamus-pituitary system. The hypothalamus, that tiny pea-sized node at the base of the brain, is the master regulator of hormone distribution, and, along with the pituitary and endocrine system, it comprises the regulation network affecting virtually all homeostatic systems as well as growth and sexual development.

The body flashes an uninterrupted series of response and feedback signals between the individual glands and the brain. Aging may disrupt the hypothalamus's ability to run the show. Years of evidence more than suggests that the hypothalamic control of hormonal release goes haywire with aging.

By stimulating the hypothalamus of aged female rats with electric impulses, Dr. Joseph Meites of Michigan State, has successfully reactivated their estrus cycles—put them back in heat. He also has reactivated the ovarian cycles of the old females by feeding them L-Dopa (a dopamine stimulator also used in the treatment of Parkinson's disease), and hormones such as progesterone, epinephrine, and iproniazid.

The exciting thing about this evidence is that the old ovaries still work and can be started up again when the "clock" in the hypothalamus is turned back. The implications for women past the menopause are astounding.

Dr. W. Donner Denckla, Associate Professor of Medicine at Harvard's Thorndike Laboratories, thinks he's close enough to hear the death clock ticking. An intense youngish man with collegiate horn rims and a wry sense of humor, Denckla explained recently to the large audience at a life-extension conference in St. Paul sponsored by the University of Minnesota, that he has "one very strong candidate for the demise of mammals."

Denckla's rather spectacular theory is based on the idea that humans have a built-in mechanism, not for aging, but for death itself. He believes the process of dying is built into our childhood; it starts around age ten.

Denckla proposes that at puberty the pituitary starts releasing an exceedingly powerful hormone, which he calls by the artful acronym DECO (for decreasing O_2 consumption). "This lovely little molecule," he says, "wanders out and progressively throws a block between the body's cells and its circulating thyroxin," the thyroid hormone vital to normal metabolism. Death comes as it does to the Pacific Salmon—by flooding the body with the "death hormone"—only more slowly; so insidiously as to seem not the cause.

In his super-realistic laboratories, Denckla removes the pituitaries (from whence, presumably, issues the DECO) of older rats. And, after adding hormone supplements to their diets, in a matter of months the old animals regain much of their pubescent glory.

One big hitch in the Denckla plan is that, although the pituitary-less rats are rejuvenated to adolescent physiological status, their lifespan does not seem to be prolonged. They die on schedule. It is possible, then, that DECO may serve an important life function.

THE LONGEVITY CLOCK

Richard Cutler is a man with a big plan, which, if it does not embrace all of the manifold theories of aging, is at least compatible with most of them. Cutler is looking, not so much for the causes of aging, as for reasons for the evolution of longevity. There is no genetic program for death, he thinks, but an open-ended potential for unlimited lifespan.

In charge of the Program on Comparative Biochemistry of Mammalian Aging, Cutler constructs his architectonic ideas from sources as eclectic as his background. Cutler personally evolved from a Colorado farmboy into a helicopter designer to a copter company owner at age 18. He discovered college a few years later and proceeded to get degrees in aeronautical and electrical engineering, in physics, and biophysics.

According to Cutler, the rate of aging might very well be regulated by relatively few genes, which we can discover and eventually control. He has reached this conclusion after carefully studying the evolution of long lifespan in humans. It seems that our lifespan increased so rapidly compared to our apelike ancestors that no more than a few genes could have changed during such a brief evolutionary period. Hence, Cutler concludes that only a few genes may control the rate of aging.

Slowing down the aging process doesn't have to be a formidable task. We already know much about what genetic controls are involved. The deceleration is likely to be achieved first by biochemical manipulation of the neuroendocrine system via the hypothalamus-pituitary controls and, later, when more is known, by genetic engineering. "The 'scenario', as they say," remarked Cutler, "is that you'd take a child when he's young, administer hormones to slow down his development and give him an analogue in his food to stimulate anti-aging processes." A person might become sexually mature by 28, full grown at 45, and middle aged by 120.

"I think within ten years, depending on how much we concentrate on learning to manipulate the controls of development, the slowdown might be accomplished," he predicts.

A trickier problem than slowing growth is maintaining the body's level of intrinsic wear and tear fighters, what Cutler calls "continuously acting antibiosenescent processes." These include free-radical scavengers, antioxidants, DNA repair and so forth. Genetic engineering of the regulatory genes is too complex at the present time, so Cutler found a short cut: trick the cells with an anti-aging vaccine. One could inject a bit of "fake aging" and the body would alter its level of protective enzymes to combat this fake aging antibody. It works on a similar principle as the smallpox vaccine.

One could pop a pill that would diffuse into the cells and fool them into thinking "Hey, we've got a lot of DNA damage." The cells, consequently, might raise the level of DNA repair enzyme to match the needs of a longer-lived organism. "We might be able to stimulate a whole battery of repair processes," Cutler speculates, "by inserting a highly damaged piece of DNA, with everything imaginable wrong with it. And all the repair mechanisms would be stimulated by the artifact. You don't even have to know how it works to use it."

LOOK OF THE FUTURE

Cutler, unlike many gerontologists, has been willing to speculate a bit on the nature of *Homo longevus*. He says: "My guess is that it would be best, not only to double man's maximum lifespan potential, but also to double his brain size. Although doubling size is not likely to improve the quality of the brain, it might provide a greater redundant capacity for neurons and their supporting cells, thereby, perhaps, delaying the onset of senility even further."

By reducing a person's growth rate by one-half and doubling the time for the brain's development and maturation (it's growth rate would remain the same as now, and only one extra division of cells is needed to double its size), one might grow up to be an adult who looked much like a 12-year-old of today in terms of body and brain-size proportion.

When will it happen? Science writer and author of the soon to be published *Life-Extension Handbook*, Saul Kent, believes predictions are irrelevant. "It's inevitable, but the timing depends completely on the effort. I could give you a sliding scale in years before the breakthrough, depending on the effort put into it."

"If life-extension becomes a national pri-

ority like the space program," says Paul Segall, "if the Americans, the Russians, and the Japanese join hands, if there were a $200 billion assault on aging and death, this could produce dramatic results in five years. Just $200 billion, involving tens of hundreds of scientists, hundreds of thousands of technicians—in five years we'd have a program that would put such a dent in death we might wipe it off the face of the earth. And a program such as this would cost no more than these countries are now spending on the maintenance of old age homes."

At present, however, there is no clear cut directive for life-extension research. The House Select Committee on Aging is holding hearings on the advisability of funding life-extension research. But as one committee member admitted privately, "we really don't know what we're doing. We don't know who to listen to."

Although NIA Director, Dr. Robert Butler, has officially stated that life-extension research is a "priority of the NIA," this priority is not reflected in the Gerontology Research Center's $7-million share of the total 1978 NIA budget of $37.3 million. And the entire NIA budget, moreover, pales beside the National Institute on Cancer's $872 million for 1978. The irony is profound, especially as evidence mounts that cancer is predominately an age-related disease. There may be no way to cure cancer without curing aging.

"A lot of resistance to life-extension comes in the form of questions about overcrowding the planet, population explosions, social security, jobs, etc.," explains F.M. Esfandiary, a normative philosopher who teaches courses at New York's New School For Social Research. "At its base the question is pathological. After eons of programming to accept death, we suddenly find we can conquer death. As we're getting closer to vanquishing it, people are getting up-tight—Elizabeth Kübler-Ross is a case in point. They are afraid to face the idea they can beat death. They are afraid to be disappointed. We still don't have the infrastructure for life, but in the demise of

religion, guilt-orientation, and orthodoxy, we're moving toward a life-orientation."

So prolonged lifespan is inevitable. But is it advisable? "It is impossible to foresee what it will do to society," says Roy Walford. "I think it will be highly destabilizing, and I'm in favor of that."

Lots of senile tricentenarians? Not so, says Rolf Martin, biochemist from the City University of New York. Martin designed a "survival curve" projecting that the proportion of nonproductive oldsters actually will be reduced by two-thirds if lifespan is doubled. People would die of other things before they got senile.

The biggest argument for life-extension, in some minds, is that the actual "advancement of civilization"—that sacred cow of the Western world—is imperiled by the exponential rise in knowledge.

The solution so far has been specialization. But as we become more and more specialized, our ability to communicate to people outside our field diminishes. Our awareness narrows. Fewer people are gifted with the ability to put it all together. We may simply require more time to learn.

"We need to investigate why man's lifespan evolved in the first place," Cutler says. "Because that is what made man what he is today. A longer lifespan allowed man to make use of a larger brain, become more self-conscious, see the world and learn. It is difficult for me to see why a continuation along the same lines wouldn't result in more of the benefits that accrued in the first place.

"In reality, the slowing down and cessation of the evolution of a longer lifespan might have been an artifact, a negative by-product of increasing civilization, and was, in a sense, *abnormal*. Continued self-evolution of extended lifespan and intelligence is getting back to the biological norm—getting back on the road again."

Says Cutler: "If you ask me about the ethics of extending our lifespan along evolutionary lines, I must say that, if we do not evolve a longer lifespan—that is unethical."

Individual Differences

5

What accounts for the diversity in the ways that people think, feel, and act? Psychologists have long been interested in both measuring and explaining individual differences. Through the years, a classic debate has taken shape about what accounts for individual differences: heredity (nature) or environment (nurture). Of course, both factors are important, and this section deals with the ways in which they interact to shape the individual.

"Attitudes, Interests, and IQ" reports on several studies to determine the influence of heredity on intelligence and behavior. Among other things, the authors present evidence that genetic factors exert a strong influence on IQ, vocational interests, and even attitudes like prejudice.

The question of genetics and IQ has some controversial racial and ethnic aspects. Psychological tests for individual differences often demonstrate tendencies for predictable group differences along ethnic or racial lines. As a consequence, these tests are sometimes used as or considered to be tools for perpetuating social injustices. "New Light on IQ" raises the issue of cultural bias in IQ testing.

Sexuality and sex roles are important aspects of the individual's social and psychological adjustment. "Sexuality and the Life Cycle" charts the presence of sexuality throughout the human life cycle, from embryo through old age, and points out some of the factors—physiological, emotional, social, and cultural—that affect sexual expression. "What We Know and Don't Know About Sex Differences" reviews extensive data compiled to determine sex differences in areas of motivation, social behavior and intellectual ability. Some sex stereotypes are upheld or qualified, others dismissed altogether.

The relationship of certain individual traits to problems of psychological and physical health has been traced by researchers working in several different areas. Longitudinal studies which follow a specific subject population over a period of time are useful in detecting cause-effect patterns. That certain personality traits such as fastidiousness and aggressiveness are linked with disease susceptibility is discussed in "Mental Patterns of Disease." "Cancer and the Mind: How Are They Connected?" reports on wide-ranging research regarding the psychosomatic aspects of cancer—research by biochemists, psychologists, and specialists in epidemiology, genetics, environmental carcinogens, and clinical oncology.

A review of this section will contribute to your understanding of the links between genetics and environment and how these factors affect and distinguish each individual. In addition you will learn about recent research into the relationships between certain personality types and disease susceptibility.

Looking Ahead: Challenge Questions

What are some of the practical applications of our growing understanding of the factors affecting individual differences?

In what ways might the cultural bias of intelligence tests be reduced or eliminated?

Certain character traits may correspond to certain forms of disease, but apparently not in every case. To what extent can the physician realistically use the available evidence linking personality type with disease susceptibility?

ATTITUDES, INTERESTS, AND IQ

When the environment is good, heredity exerts a strong
influence on IQ. Heredity also affects a
person's interests and attitudes toward authority.

SANDRA SCARR
AND
RICHARD A. WEINBERG

Sandra Scarr, *who received her Ph.D. from Harvard, is professor of psychology at Yale University. She was formerly on the faculty of the Institute of Child Development, University of Minnesota, and in 1976-1977 she was a fellow at the Center for Advanced Study in the Behavioral Sciences in Stanford, California. Scarr is a fellow of the American Association for the Advancement of Science and of the American Psychological Association, associate editor of the* American Psychologist, *and has finished a term on the APA's Board of Scientific Affairs. She is the author of many articles in the areas of human development and the genetics of behavior.*

Richard Weinberg *received his Ph.D. from the University of Minnesota, where he is professor of educational psychology and on the graduate faculties in psychology and child development. He is coordinator of the Psychology in the Schools Training Programs, associate director of the Center for Early Education and Development, and coauthor of* The Classroom Observer: A Guide for Developing Observation Skills. *Scarr and Weinberg have collaborated on their research since 1973, and are writing a child-development text, to be published by Harcourt Brace Jovanovich.* *The studies reported in their article were supported by the Grant Foundation, the National Institute of Child Health and Human Development, the graduate school of the University of Minnesota, and done in collaboration with the Minnesota State Department of Public Welfare, Adoption Unit.*

Each generation of scientists rediscovers the nature-nurture problem. In our day we were taught an environmentalism gone amok. Given the "right" experiences, we learned, any infant can become if not an Einstein at least a competent nuclear physicist.

Most parents (and many psychologists) probably had reservations about this view—in private—but the public stance dominated the Western philosophy of child rearing and social policy for many years. It was inevitable that the pendulum would swing far back toward biology, and now a spate of books has appeared arguing that genes, not cultures, control our fate and account for most of our social customs.

To write about the influence of heredity on intelligence and behavior is to court controversy, if not outrage. We are about to court both. Our data show the importance of experience on the development of human behavior, and dispel racist notions of genetic differences in the abilities of blacks and whites. But our studies also demonstrate the unmistakable contribution of genetic factors to individual differences in intellectual ability, interests, and even prejudices.

Let us get two facts straight. First, of course the environment has a strong effect on a person's development. We do not need sophisticated studies to prove that a child raised in a neglectful or abusive family will generally not turn out as well as a child raised in a warm, supportive one. Yet changes in environment cause changes in behavior, a process called malleability. Improvements in the former improve the latter.

Second, it is also true that human beings are not infinitely adjustable.

Malleability does not mean that given the same environment all individuals will end up alike. Common sense and a sheaf of studies indicate that people bring idiosyncratic responses to the same situations. Even in a perfect world, some people will be unhappier, more hyperactive, or less capable than others. The reason for these individual differences has much to do with genetic make-up.

Too many people believe the myth that if a characteristic is genetic, it cannot be changed. This is nonsense. Human behavior is much more complicated than a particular physical trait, such as blue eyes. Although genes may dictate the color of eyes or hair, they do not specify that Sally will have an IQ of 139 rather than 125 or 150. Genes do not fix behavior; rather, they establish a range of possible reactions to the range of possible experiences that the environment provides.

How people behave or what their measured IQs turn out to be depends on the quality of their environments and on the genetic endowments they have at birth. Some elements of the environment, such as having nurturing parents, are better for everyone, but some individuals respond better to one environment and others respond better to another. What occurs is an interaction between genes and environment, as the disease phenylketonuria (PKU) illustrates. Normal children need the amino acid phenylalanine in their diets to be

 From *Human Nature*, April 1978. Copyright © 1978 by Human Nature, Inc. Reprinted by permission of the publisher.

healthy; children with PKU are literally poisoned by it. The nutritional environment that allows normal children to flourish is deadly to children with this genetic deficiency. Similarly, many children thrive in a world that is rich and varied, whereas others react badly to overstimulation.

In these examples, a person's genetic make-up affects, or limits, the kind of environment he or she can tolerate. In other cases, genes and environment have reciprocal effects. Children who are skillful at sports spend more time on them than awkward children; adults who cannot carry a tune are embarrassed if they try out for a glee club; aggressive boys in elementary school are punished more often than docile ones. These predispositions affect what people do and do not enjoy and therefore the activities they continue to seek or avoid.

A child's particular genetic combination may cause him or her to develop in certain ways and to seek out some aspects of the environment but not others. The extreme examples are people—like Paul Gauguin, a financier who ran off to paint, and Elizabeth Blackwell, the first woman physician in America—who doggedly find ways to express their talents in spite of such huge environmental obstacles as parents who want them to run the family business or to produce babies, not to deliver them.

For too long we have assumed that people are passive lumps, to be molded into models of good or evil by surrounding influences. Some behavior is shaped by rewards and punishments, but just as often people actively select the environments that suit them and reject the aspects of those environments they dislike. Their choices are likely to be influenced by their genetic talents and interests. Some parents expect that their children can be molded into little replicas of themselves. They may be totally surprised when their children turn up with attitudes and ambitions that seem to spring from thin air: "No one in *our* family plays the piccolo" (or excels in geometry or runs the four-minute mile). Such is the nature of genetic sculpturing when parents and children

share only half their genes. But our work shows that members of biological families do resemble one another more than adoptive, genetically unrelated family members.

In 1973 we launched two large-scale studies of adoption in Minnesota, one of white adolescents, the other of black and interracial children adopted into white homes. The first study was designed to measure the cumulative impact of family environment (in contrast to biological heritage) at what should be its most discernible time, after some 15 to 20 years of living at home. The second study was expressly designed to see whether life in middle- and upper-middle-class families would significantly improve the IQ scores and school performance of black children.

We interviewed hundreds of children and their parents; we gave comparable tests for intelligence, interests, and attitudes to both generations; and our interviews and tests covered a great deal of information other than IQ. Most important, we were able to assess the relative effects of heredity and environment because we could compare biological and adopted children within the same family, compare adopted children with their biological and their adoptive parents, and explore the origins of differences between children who grow up in similar environments.

Some of our findings were expected. Others surprised us. In general, we found no evidence of genetic differences in IQ between blacks and whites: strong evidence of genetic origins of intellectual differences between individuals within each race; strong evidence of a genetic component in individual differences in some attitudes having to do with prejudice and authoritarianism; and good evidence of a genetic component in some vocational and personal interests.

Because these findings are, we have since discovered, controversial, we are presenting them here with considerable detail to support our conclusions.

For the white adoption study, we selected two groups of families that had at least two children in late adolescence: 122 "biological" families that had had children of their own and 115 "adoptive" families that had adopted children as in-

fants. The children in both sets of households were close in age, the average being 18½.

We found the adoptive families through the Minnesota Department of Public Welfare, which sent letters on our behalf to families who had adopted children between 1953 and 1959 (and who were thus at the ages we wanted for our study). To make sure our final sample of volunteers was representative of adoptive parents, we compared the participants with nonparticipants on critical characteristics. We found no differences between them in age, income, education, or occupational status at the time of adoption. Next we recruited a comparable sample of biological families through newspaper articles and advertisements, by word of mouth, and from the adoptive families themselves. The 122 families we eventually chose did indeed match the adoptive families in income (both groups averaged about $25,000 a year), education (generally at least two years of college for mothers and fathers), occupation (typically teacher and social worker), and IQ (an average of 117 for fathers and 113 for mothers). In short, both the biological and adoptive families were well above the national American average in socioeconomic status and intellectual ability. It is also significant that some families had incomes of $11,000; that some mothers and fathers were secretaries and electricians; that some parents had gone to work right after high school; and that some parents had IQs in the 90s—in other words, the sample was varied.

In contrast, the biological parents of the adopted children were of average intelligence, as we inferred from their educational levels. (In a large study we did recently, we found that education is an indirect but accurate index of intellectual ability.) Further, a survey of 3,600 unmarried mothers in Minnesota between 1948 and 1952, when IQ tests were required for all women who gave up children for adoption, found that their average IQ was right on the national mean: 100. Although our group of mothers had had their children between 1953 and 1959, there is no reason to think that they would differ from the in-

5. INDIVIDUAL DIFFERENCES

In biological families, IQ scores are significantly correlated between mother and child, father and child, and siblings. In adoptive families, adoptive children show a similarity to their parents and siblings only in vocabulary. (A correlation runs from 0 to 1 and is considered strong at about 0.3.)

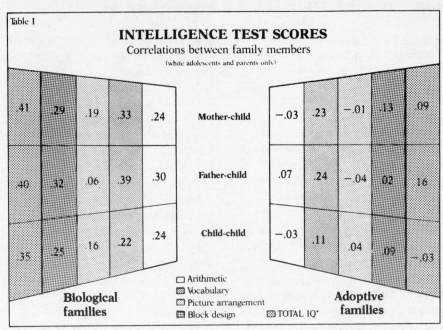

Table 1

INTELLIGENCE TEST SCORES
Correlations between family members
(white adolescents and parents only)

Biological families

						Adoptive families				
.41	.29	.19	.33	.24	**Mother-child**	−.03	.23	−.01	.13	.09
.40	.32	.06	.39	.30	**Father-child**	.07	.24	−.04	.02	.16
.35	.25	.16	.22	.24	**Child-child**	−.03	.11	.04	.09	−.03

☐ Arithmetic
▨ Vocabulary
▥ Picture arrangement
▦ Block design   ▧ TOTAL IQ*

*On Wechsler Adult Intelligence Scale

tellectually average generation that preceded them.

For the black adoption study, we recruited 101 families consisting of 176 adopted black children who had one or two black parents and 145 biological white children. Like our other sample of adoptive parents, these families were above average in income and education, stability and mental health, and interest in children. The biological parents of these adoptees were about average intellectually and educationally, as we determined from the adoption records.

The biological children in our two studies had the benefits of both genes and environment; the adopted children were born to intellectually average parents but raised in intellectually enriched homes. To make environmental conditions as similar as possible, we most often limited our analyses to the children who had been adopted in the first year of life—most during the first three months.

The benefit children derive from living in intellectually rich homes is astoundingly apparent. The IQs of the black adopted children averaged 110, which represents at least a 15-point jump over the scores of American black children reared by their own parents. The scores of the adoptees were higher than those estimated for their own biological parents, but not as high as those of their adoptive parents (about 119) or those of the biological children of the adoptive parents (116.7).

Next we looked at school achievement records—vocabulary, reading, mathematics, and overall aptitude (an IQ measure). The school tests are important because they come from many school districts and are unblemished by any biases that may have occurred in the testing situation in the children's homes. They are even more important as a measure of the children's daily intellectual performance on a range of tasks.

Again we found that the black children scored above the national norms on the standard achievement tests, as their above-average IQ levels would predict. Regardless of their age at adoption, the children averaged in the 55th percentile in reading and math, for example, whereas the average black child in Minneapolis scored in the 15th to 20th percentile. The biological children from these enriched homes, however, performed better than their adoptive siblings on the achievement tests (in the 70th percentile), also as their IQ scores would predict.

This pattern of results is exactly what we found in the study of adopted white adolescents. The IQs of the adopted children averaged 6½ points lower than those of the biological children but 6½ points higher than those of their own parents, whose scores were estimated to be average for the population.

Because the scores of the black children are exactly comparable to those of the white adopted children raised in similarly advantaged homes, it is unlikely that the heralded differences between blacks and whites are genetically based. Black children from families that teach them the culture, vocabulary, and skills that IQ and achievement tests reward perform well above the average.

Some people who believe in genetic differences between blacks and whites think that there is an easy way to prove their point: Blacks who have more European and less African ancestry should have higher IQs than blacks with less European and more African ancestry. Working with Andrew Pakstis, Solomon Katz, and William Barker, we tested this notion by giving several tests of intellectual skill to a sample of 350 blacks in the Philadelphia area. Instead of asking the participants directly what their heritage was, we could estimate each person's degree of African and European ancestry from blood samples, because Africans and Europeans differ in the average frequencies of certain types of blood groups and serum protein. If a person had a particular blood group or serum protein gene, the researchers could assign a probability that he got it from a European or African ancestor. The estimates were based on 12 genes. Though some error undoubtedly crept into the estimates, they were accurate enough, because they matched up with skin color and were similar for siblings.

The results were unequivocal. Blacks who had a large number of European ancestors did no better or worse on the tests than blacks of almost total African ancestry. These studies dispute the hypothesis that IQ differences between blacks and whites are in large part the result of genetic differences.

But this is not the same thing as saying that heredity is totally unrelated to an individual's performance. The origins of differences between groups are not necessarily the origins of differences between individuals. The question that remains is: Given similar home environments, why does one child turn out to be brighter than another, and why is one determined by the age of four to become a musician while another sets his or her young sights on science? We know that improving the intellectual environment of children raises their average IQs; this happened to the adopted children in both the black and white studies. But what accounts for the persistent differences between siblings, adopted or not?

Our two studies show that in advantaged environments, differences between children are largely due to differences in genetic programming. We reached this conclusion by using two statistical methods. First we put all the factors that might have something to do with intelligence (such as qualities of the parents and the children's home life) into a long equation that told us the relative importance of each factor in predicting a child's IQ.

In the first set of equations, we tried father's education and occupation, mother's education, and family income as predictors of the differences in the children's IQs. These factors had a mild impact on differences in the biological children's scores, but hardly any impact on the adoptees' scores. When we added parental IQ, however, we got an enormous effect in predicting the biological children's scores—but parents' IQs had virtually no effect on the scores of the adoptees. The power of adding parental IQ to the equation must reflect the genetic contribution of the biological parents to their children's intelligence.

In contrast, the best predictor of IQ differences in adopted children was the education of their biological mothers (and, when we had the information, of their biological fathers). The education of the biological mothers was more closely related to IQ differences in their children than the same information

AUTHORITARIAN ATTITUDES

Correlations between.

	Biological families	Adoptive families
Father-daughter	.34	.31
Father-son	.44	−.05
Mother-daughter	.40	.06
Mother-son	.41	−.06
Son-son	.46	*
Daughter-daughter	.36	*
Son-daughter	.41	.04
Mother-father	.43	.34

□ **Biological families**
▨ **Adoptive families**

*Too few cases

Attitudes toward authority appear to have a genetic component. In biological families, parents and children predictably shared the same level of authoritarianism. But adopted children were no more likely to share their parents' views than strangers,' with the exception of fathers and daughters.

about the adoptive parents—the adults with whom these children grew up. In both groups of adoptees, the black children and the white adolescents, the biological parents best accounted for the children's differences in IQ.

Our second method was to study the correlations of scores between related and unrelated family members. A correlation indicates the extent to which two items, such as events or attitudes or scores, are linked in predictable ways. A positive correlation may run from 0 (no relationship at all) to 1 (a perfect relationship, in which a high score on test X always means a high score on test Y). A negative correlation runs from 0 to −1 (a perfectly inverted relationship, in which a high score on test X means a low score on test Y). A correlation of about 0.3 is, in the case of our samples, unlikely to have occurred by chance.

More evidence of genetic effects came from the white study, when we correlated IQs for all pairs of adoptive and natural

relatives. Whether we used the overall IQs or the scores on the four subtests of the IQ tests (e.g., vocabulary, arithmetic), the correlations between biological family members were high and statistically significant, whereas the correlations between adopted children and their unrelated parents and siblings were weak or negligible. The only scores that were significant between adoptees and other family members were in vocabulary. This is not surprising, since people who live together tend to talk together. Vocabulary abilities are the most amenable to the influence of environment. But the lack of correlations between adopted children and their parents—with whom they have lived, remember, since infancy—must point to the influence of genetic factors on intellectual abilities. (See Table I.)

In our studies we expected that genetic background would be important in accounting for intelligence scores but that it would have nothing to do with political or social attitudes. To demonstrate our point, we included in the test battery a 20-item version of the California F-Scale, a set of 20 questions that measure a person's degree of authoritarianism, rigidity of belief, and prejudice. People taking the test indicate on a scale of 1 to 7 how much they agree or disagree with such statements as, "What youth needs most is strict discipline, rugged determination, and the will to work and fight for family and country," and "One of the most important things children should learn is when to disobey authorities."

Confident that our F-Scale would measure the effects of environment, we were utterly astonished by our findings. The attitudes captured by the authoritarianism test appear to be transmitted genetically from parents to children, just as verbal ability and intelligence are.

We make this remarkable statement because we found no correlation between the authoritarian attitudes of the adopted children and those of their parents or siblings, even though the adoptees had been exposed to their parents' attitudes since infancy. The parents' attitudes and those of the adopted children, in other words, were as different as if the adults and teenagers had been randomly paired on a street corner. But we found a highly significant correlation between the authoritarian attitudes of biological children and parents. Whether both were highly authoritarian or both were anti-authoritarian, their attitudes tended to be very similar.

All the strong correlations of attitudes toward authority occurred between biological relatives—fathers and children, mothers and children, brothers and sisters. Among adoptive relatives, the only significant correlation, the only predictably shared attitude, occurred between fathers and daughters. The reason for this exception we do not know.

One possible explanation for the similarities between biological relatives and the differences between adoptive relatives was that mothers and fathers of adopted children disagreed on their attitudes toward authority, whereas the parents of biological children shared similar attitudes. In that case, adopted children would have a choice of two opinions and values, one set being less authoritarian than the other. Not so. As the chart indicates, husbands and wives in both kinds of families tended to share their political and social attitudes.

We then looked at the comparable table of correlations of IQ scores. The patterns were amazingly similar to those for authoritarianism, including that baffling father-daughter resemblance in the adoptive families—which we are beginning facetiously to call the Electra phenomenon.

Another possibility for these results was that adoptive parents, knowing that their children were not "their own," somehow treated them differently from the way parents treat natural-born children. But if this were so, we would still expect to find the correlations between adoptive siblings to be similar to the correlations between biological siblings. They are not.

Perhaps, we thought, the finding reflected an artificial problem in the samples. For instance, more adoptive families than biological families came from small towns and rural areas. But then we would have been hard-pressed to explain why the authoritarianism patterns consistently distinguished adopted

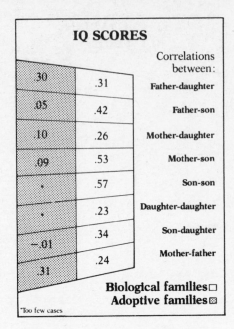

IQ SCORES		Correlations between:
.30	.31	Father-daughter
.05	.42	Father-son
.10	.26	Mother-daughter
.09	.53	Mother-son
*	.57	Son-son
	.23	Daughter-daughter
−.01	.34	Son-daughter
.31	.24	Mother-father

Biological families □
Adoptive families ⊠

*Too few cases

Biologically related parents and children were as similar in IQ as in authoritarianism, but among adoptive families, only fathers and daughters showed a similarity in IQ—as they had in authoritarianism (F-scale). The F-Scale apparently tests intellectual skills that are partly heritable.

children from biological ones, and other personality traits did not. On tests of introversion, neuroticism, and some forms of anxiety, parent-child correlations within adoptive and biological families were similar. Something unique about authoritarianism and IQ was afoot.

To track it down, we took a closer look at the relationship of intelligence to the F-Scale. One measure we used was the vocabulary subtest of the Wechsler Adult Intelligence Scale; the other was the Raven Standard Progressive Matrices, a nonverbal measure of intellectual ability. At this point the pieces of the puzzle began to fit.

Scores for authoritarianism turned out to be negatively correlated with verbal ability—the higher one's score on the WAIS vocabulary subtest, the lower the F-Scale score (the correlation for all participants in the study was −0.42, which is strong). In other words, the most articulate, verbal family members were the least authoritarian, and vice versa. But the relationship between the nonverbal IQ measure and authoritarianism was much weaker.

These results suggest to us that F-Scale scores are similar in biological but not in adoptive families because the F-Scale measures intellectual skills that are partly heritable. Many of those skills have to do with thinking and reasoning ability. The similarity of scores in biological families was remarkable and largely a result of the intellectual similarity of genetic relatives. Adopted children barely resembled their adoptive parents in F-Scale scores, and what little similarity there was could be ascribed to their similar vocabulary scores.

Previous studies had also found that authoritarianism was more characteristic of lower-class than of middle-class people, but psychologists assumed that this reflected the powerlessness and poorer circumstances of the working class. Our results require another interpretation. Differences in social class of the adoptive families were not related to the expected differences in authoritarianism and IQ: Although the adoptive parents varied in intelligence, education, occupation, and income (to be sure, none was truly poor), their adopted children were no more or less authoritarian because of their class backgrounds.

In our view, the only adequate explanation of the link between low IQ and high authoritarianism begins with a person's mental abilities. Scores on the F-Scale are the results of moral-reasoning ability that reflects the general level of verbal intelligence. We believe that moral decisions and authoritarian views are not learned by rote or by imitation of one's parents, teachers, and friends; instead, they represent conclusions that a person reaches by applying mental skills to social and political experiences, and through schooling that teaches abstract concepts that broaden perspective.

The F-Scale is a set of complex intellectual judgments about the world, examples of opinions that people have accepted or rejected about politics and values. IQ tests also contain items that tap everyday, commonsense judgments about social problems precisely to see how people use intellectual abilities to solve daily dilemmas. Consequently, in a way it is not surprising that the F-Scale should correlate with some of the broad

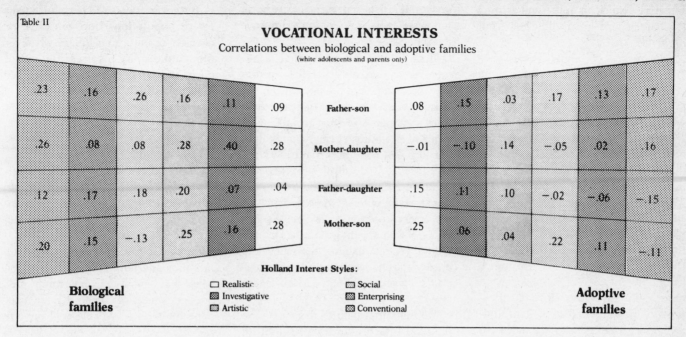

Table II

VOCATIONAL INTERESTS
Correlations between biological and adoptive families
(white adolescents and parents only)

Biological families — Adoptive families

Holland Interest Styles:
☐ Realistic ▨ Social
▨ Investigative ▨ Enterprising
▨ Artistic ▨ Conventional

measures of intellectual functioning that IQ tests represent.

Many developmental psychologists and parents believe that children acquire ambitions and interests by modeling themselves after their parents. Typically, boys model themselves after their fathers, girls after their mothers; some children, for unknown reasons, imitate their parents of the opposite sex. If the modeling theory were true, adoptive and biological children would be equally likely to resemble their parents.

But there is evidence for a genetic contribution to vocational interests. In 1934, for example, H. D. Carter reported a case study of a pair of identical twins who, having grown up together, had been separated for 20 years in adulthood. When they took a test of personal preferences and interests, their scores were so similar that it was as if, Carter observed, the same person had taken the test twice.

In association with Harold Grotevant, we gave our white adolescents and parents a reliable test on this question, the Strong-Campbell Interest Inventory. This inventory includes John L. Holland's model of vocational interests, which classifies people according to their scores on six "styles": (1) realistic (practical, aggressive persons who enjoy working outdoors and with their hands); (2) investigative (scientifically oriented persons); (3) artistic (self-expressive

On six measures of personal interests, biologically related family members resembled each other more closely than adopted children resembled their siblings or parents. In the biological family pairs, 15 correlations out of 24 were significant; only two such correlations held up in adoptive pairs.

and creative persons); (4) social (humanistic or religious persons who wish to help others); (5) enterprising (persons who like to sell, dominate, lead); and (6) conventional (persons who prefer highly ordered verbal or numerical work). People are scored on this test not only according to the style they most prefer but also according to how they score on each of the six types. The result is a profile of interests for each individual.

Once again our expectation, that children would model themselves after their parents, was not fulfilled. On the average, adoptive family members no more resembled one another in interests than parents and children paired randomly from the outside world. For all their similarity to their adoptive parents, the adopted children of teachers and engineers could have grown up with cattle ranchers or plumbers. (See Table II.)

We looked at the interest profiles of each family member in comparison with every other family member—mothers with sons and daughters, fathers with

sons and daughters, siblings with one another. Of the 24 possible correlations (each of the six interest scales by mother, father, daughter, son), only two were significant for the adoptive family pairs, and one of those would have been expected just by chance. In the biological family pairs, fully 15 correlations were significant. For example, biological fathers and sons resembled one another most on social interests; mothers and daughters, on investigative interests; fathers and daughters, on artistic interests; and mothers and sons, on realistic interests. Further, scores of biological siblings were strongly correlated on five of the six scales, but scores of adoptive siblings were correlated on only one scale.

The fact that biological parents and children shared the same specific interests and disinterests, whereas their adoptive counterparts did not, suggests that there is a small but reliable hereditary influence in people's professional ambitions. In most families, the interests of the parents were not alike, even after 20 years of marriage; but the biological siblings were the most alike—as a genetic explanation would predict. Also, siblings resembled one another more than they resembled their parents, because the children were raised in the same place and time. When Mozart composed his first minuets at the age of five, his precocious talent reflected his father's teaching, his opportunities to get to a harpsichord—and a little help from his genes.

Our review of family studies convinces us that the evidence for some genetic influence on intelligence, attitudes, and interests is simply overwhelming. How large is the component? It is impossible to put a precise number on the exact proportion of our behavior that is inherited, although many scientists are fighting over just this issue. One reason is that at different stages of a person's development, environment may play a greater or lesser role. Another is the problem of tests themselves. Different studies of different age groups using different tests—some of which are more culturally biased than others—produce inconsistent results. Some studies find a greater genetic role in certain behavior than do other studies; but no studies find that environment is everything.

Remember too that we are talking about genetic variability within a range of reasonably good environments. Few studies have dealt with children from abusive, hostile families. If one could include research on such children, environmental differences would undoubtedly show a greater impact on behavior and intelligence. When a child's environment is basically humane, we find that genetic background plays a larger part in accounting for individual differences.

We do not think that this conclusion is pessimistic in the slightest. Many people think that genetic studies automatically suggest conservative social policy; if everyone is born smart or stupid, there is no reason to change the educational system. If artists and scientists are born, not made, there is no reason to improve the schools.

It is true that some politicians and laymen use evidence of heritability to justify the status quo. It is no longer God, but "instincts" or "genes" that glue us to our roles and make sweeping social change impossible—human beings cannot fight the fact that they are "naturally" aggressive, or "naturally" stratified into dominance hierarchies. At the other extreme, some political systems (such as the Soviet Union and the People's Republic of China) deny genetic heritability altogether, maintaining that the state creates and changes human nature. Economics giveth, and economics taketh away.

We think that both of these extreme political interpretations of scientific research on heritability miss the point. Social policy should be determined by political and ethical values. Justice has nothing to do with genetics, and the latter cannot be summoned to excuse fascism or to deny a group fair play.

Once social policy has been determined, however, research can be useful. Governments can do a better job of designing effective intervention programs if people know which variations in the environment make a difference and which do not. The average level of a culture's environment determines the average level of individual achievement. By providing good schools, nutrition, health care, and psychological services a society can raise the overall level of health and attainment for the whole population. Resources spent in these areas should eliminate conditions that have definite deleterious effects on individual development.

But governments will never turn their entire populations into geniuses, or altruists, or entrepreneurs, or whatever their philosophy inspires. Biological diversity is a fact of life, and respect for individual differences derives from the genetic perspective. This research can spare us all a homogeneity of customs imposed on society by an omniscient professional or political class.

Three decades of naive environmentalism have locked most Westerners into wrong-headed assumptions about the limitless malleability of mankind, and programs based on this premise can lead a country into a thicket of unrealistic promises and hopes. The fallacy is the belief that equality of opportunity produces sameness of outcome. Equality of opportunity is a laudable goal for any society. Sameness of outcome is a biological impossibility.

For further information:

Grotevant, Harold, Sandra Scarr, and Richard Weinberg. "Patterns of Interest Similarity in Adoptive and Biological Families." *Journal of Personality and Social Psychology*, Vol. 35, 1977, pp. 667-676.

Jencks, Christopher. *Inequality: A Reassessment of the Effects of Family and Schooling in America.* Basic Books, 1972.

Loehlin, J., G. Lindzey, and J. N. Spuhler. *Race Differences in Intelligence.* W. H. Freeman, 1975.

Scarr, Sandra. "Genetics and the Development of Intelligence." *Review of Child Development Research*, Vol. 4, ed. by F. D. Horowitz. University of Chicago Press, 1975.

Scarr, Sandra, and Richard Weinberg. "IQ Test Performance of Black Children Adopted by White Families." *American Psychologist*, Vol. 31, 1976, pp. 726-739.

Scarr, Sandra, and Richard Weinberg. "Intellectual Similarities within Families of Both Adopted and Biological Children." *Intelligence*, Vol. 1, 1977, pp. 170-191.

New light on IQ

Thomas Sowell

Thomas Sowell is a fellow at the Center for Advanced Study in the Behavioral Sciences in Stanford, Calif.

Arthur Jensen was a little-known scholar at the University of California in Berkeley eight years ago when he reported on studies concluding that blacks have lower I.Q.'s than whites primarily because of their genetic heritage. His name became synonymous with racism in liberal circles. Last month, when Jensen was elected fellow of the American Association for the Advancement of Science, that normally sedate, scholarly group found itself embroiled in a bitter and embarrassing argument. Margaret Mead helped draw up a five-point resolution criticizing the psychologist's work, which she termed "unspeakable." William D. Wallace, director of Harvard University's health-career programs, called his election an "endorsement of racism" and "damaging to the credibility of the A.A.A.S. in its work with minority scientists." Wallace resigned from the association in protest.

The furor at the A.A.A.S. demonstrates that the issue of "Jensenism" has far from disappeared. It is hotly debated not only in academic and political circles, but in school districts which have increasingly questioned the worth of the tests and, in some places, even dropped them altogether. In the following pages, a black economist puts the controversy into a different historical perspective.

Despite the bitter controversies over how to explain low I.Q.'s among blacks, no one has asked whether there was really anything to explain. Is there anything peculiar about either the level or the pattern of black I.Q.'s?

Extensive I.Q. data are available on white ethnic minorities around the time of World War I and in the 1920's. The U.S. Army conducted massive mental tests during World War I and considerable I.Q. data were gathered by civilian researchers during the years of controversy preceding the passage of restrictive immigration laws in the mid-1920's. To fill in the picture since the 1920's a nationwide sample of more than 70,000 school records was collected by a project which I directed at the Urban Institute, with the assistance of Janella Moore. The various data sources all led to the same conclusion: The European immigrant I.Q.'s then were virtually identical to black I.Q.'s now. What is encouraging is that the low-I.Q. immigrant groups of the past now have I.Q.'s at or above U.S. average.

Surveys in the 1920's of mental-test studies of immigrants from southern and eastern Europe, such as Italians, Poles and Greeks, showed their average I.Q.'s to be in the 80's, occasionally in the 70's. Data on Jewish-Americans were harder to find, because the early researchers, during the controversies over immigration laws, focused on nationality groups. However, the U.S. Army tests showed soldiers of Polish and Russian ancestry scoring consistently at or near the bottom of the list of European ethnic groups, and it was known then that half or more of the Polish and Russian immigrants were Jews. This prompted a leading psychologist of that era, Carl Brigham (originator of the College Board Scholastic Aptitude Test), to declare that the Army tests tended to disprove the popular belief that the Jew is highly intelligent." His observation was at best premature. Over the years, more than a fourth of all American Nobel Prize winners have been Jewish, even though Jews make up only about 3 percent of the United States population.

The Germans, the Irish and other northern and western Europeans, who had immigrated generations earlier than the southern and eastern Europeans, had I.Q.'s around the American national average. The I.Q. differences between the older and the newer immigrant groups were widely noted at the time—and almost invariably attributed to genetic differences, rather than to the great difference in their number of years of exposure to American culture.

My surveys found that the I.Q.'s of later-arriving groups—Polish, Jewish and Italian—rose over the decades until today they equal or exceed the national average. This historical pattern is not confined to minorities of European ancestry. Chinese- and Japanese-Americans also had lower-than-average I.Q.'s in earlier surveys, but today both exceed the U.S. average in I.Q., as well as in other socioeconomic indicators.

By the same token, the I.Q. levels of certain groups with European ancestry have not risen because these groups have not experienced upward mobility. The I.Q.'s of Mexican-Americans and Puerto Ricans remain in the 80's, though both groups are predominantly white. Both Latin groups continue not only to suffer socioeconomic disadvantages, but, in addition, have a relatively slow assimilation of American culture. One indication of this is that most members of both groups report Spanish as the language spoken in the home— and those who do not have much higher incomes. Moreover, both groups have substantial movement

From *The New York Times*, March 27, 1977. Copyright © 1977 the The New York Times Company. Reprinted by permission.

back and forth between the United States and their Latin homelands. This also tends to retard assimilation of American culture.

Various other studies have shown I.Q.'s in the 80's for white groups in isolated communities in the United States, in socially isolated canal-boat communities in England, among inhabitants of the Hebrides Islands off Scotland.

In short, European ancestry has not meant high I.Q.'s, nor has non-European ancestry meant low I.Q.'s. The I.Q. average has varied widely with time, place and the circumstance of the groups tested. For groups with upward mobility, there has been a marked rise in I.Q.'s over time. The average I.Q.'s of Italian-Americans and Polish-Americans have risen by 20 to 25 points from the time of the surveys conducted around World War I to the surveys conducted in the 1970's. This rise is greater than the current I.Q. difference—about 15 points—between blacks and whites.

Comparison of any minority with the national average can be very misleading, unless one realizes that this "national average" is itself a product of widely varying averages for different groups, whether racial, regional, economic. Moreover, a group that has a rise in its absolute economic condition should not be expected to raise its I.Q., unless it has also risen *relative* to the position of the general population. Black and Hispanic minorities have had no substantial relative socio-economic rise before the present generation. It should be some time before dramatic I.Q. changes can be expected, but there are already some indications that this is likely. For example, black orphans raised in white families have an average I.Q. of 106, according to a recent study by Prof. Sandra Scarr of the University of Minnesota. In addition, several all-black schools I have studied have consistently equaled or exceeded national norms on mental tests. One such school in Washington, D.C., had an average I.Q. of 111 in 1939—15 years before the Supreme Court and the sociologists declared that separate schools are inherently inferior. That school happens to be within walking distance of the Supreme Court, which virtually declared its existence impossible.

□

Professor Arthur Jensen claims that what is peculiar about low black performance on mental tests is that it is lowest on *abstract* material—that is, material not dependent on specific cultural information, and therefore not explainable by "cultural deprivation." Powerful as this evidence might seem at first, a glance at the history of other low-I.Q. groups at various times and places shows a very similar pattern of poor performance on the abstract portions of mental tests.

In 1917, a study of various immigrant groups on Ellis Island found that they were particularly deficient on the abstract sections of mental tests. Four years earlier, the noted psychologist H. H. Goddard had summarized his

experience there by saying flatly: "These people cannot deal with abstractions." Similar results were found for white children in isolated mountain communities, among rural working-class children in England and even among Chinese-Americans during their early years in this country. The case of Chinese-Americans is striking because recent studies show them doing their best on the abstract portions of mental tests, and they are prominent among American scientists and mathematicians.

Another seemingly ominous pattern cited by Jensen and others is the tendency of black children's I.Q.'s to decline as they grow older. Again, it is necessary to determine whether there is in fact anything peculiar about the black pattern before trying to "explain" that pattern, either genetically or environmentally. The same pattern is common among low-I.Q. groups—it was observed in European immigrant children in the 20's and in native white American children in isolated mountain communities studied in the 1930's and 1940's. This pattern suggests nothing more than the continuing impact of early basics—including mental habits as well as basic knowledge.

Yet another way in which patterns found in black mental-test scores differ from the national average is that black females consistently score higher on mental tests than do black males. This has been true for decades and for a variety of mental tests. Among high-I.Q. individuals in the general population, the sexes are almost equally represented (with a slight male advantage), but the persistent female advantage among blacks becomes even more pronounced at the higher I.Q. levels. Studies of black children with I.Q.'s of 120 and above have found from three to five times as many girls as boys at these levels. Since blacks of both sexes have the same genetic background, there is obviously some unexplained influence here. But before trying to explain this apparent peculiarity, it should first be determined whether it really is a peculiarity of blacks.

There are few data available on differences in mental-test performance between the sexes during the immigrant era. But Jewish mental test scores during that period showed females generally scoring higher than males. In England, working-class girls score higher in mental tests than do working-class boys, even though there is no such difference among higher classes, which have higher I.Q.'s. My own data for Mexican-Americans and Puerto Ricans—whose I.Q.'s, still range in the 80's—show a small but persistent higher I.Q. among females.

There is considerable evidence of greater resistance to environmental influences among females from all races and classes. Infant mortality, for instance, is always higher among boys than girls, in every social class and in every culture. Epidemics kill a higher proportion of men than women. The death rate among survivors of the nuclear blasts at Hiroshima and

Nagasaki was higher among men than women. Indeed, this pattern extends not only across the human race but among mammals in general.

If differences in mental-test performance between the sexes are simply part of the general, biological pattern of greater female resistance to environmental forces, it has weighty implications. It is an important piece of evidence that a low I.Q. is an environmental phenomenon, which is why males are more affected by it. No alternative theory seems to explain why this difference should be peculiar to low-I.Q. groups. Among black orphans raised in white families, no such pattern was found, indicating that it is no more racial than the average I.Q. level of blacks.

□

Those who want quick and simple answers often act as if mental tests must either measure innate intelligence or else such tests are "irrelevant" or "biased" against the culturally deprived. But if tests are viewed, not as quasi-magic panaceas, but as limited tools for limited purposes, they can be judged by how well or how badly they serve various specific purposes, *compared to other ways of serving those same purposes.* In short, tests cannot be measured against perfection but only against alternative methods of detecting talent and predicting performance in an academic setting, on the job, or elsewhere.

Every school or college has its examples of students who scored low on mental tests but performed well in their academic work, as well as examples of high-scoring students who simply never produced up to expectations, or even up to prevailing norms. This merely establishes the imperfection of mental tests. The real issue revolves around the available alternatives.

There are instances where a shrewd and involved teacher can handpick a talented or hard-driving student who will succeed despite low mental test scores. This only shows that a sufficiently large input of human judgment, insight and intimate knowledge of the individual can substitute for test results and even do a better job. But the question is: How rare are such Solomon-like people, and can we confidently pick them out any better than we can sort out the students? In a similar way, there may also be shrewd and insightful people who could judge guilt and innocence better than our elaborate criminal justice system. But in both instances we rely on certain systematic processes instead because *in general* these processes produce better results than the arbitrary judgments of individuals. Moreover, in both instances the systematic procedures are supplemented by human judgments.

What about bias against the poor, the black or the "culturally deprived"? In one sense, that bias is admitted by virtually everyone, including Prof. Arthur Jensen, who has conducted research to document it. A detailed study of I.Q. test questions would also suggest cultural bias. Tests that ask, "Who wrote 'Faust'?" or use words like "hither" and "ingenuous" are clearly testing information more readily available to middle-class children than to lower-class children.

Some critics regard class bias as invalidating I.Q. and other mental tests for all selection or prediction purposes. But the hard evidence shows that mental tests *do* predict the future academic success of students from a lower-class background as accurately as they predict the success of students from middle- or upper-class backgrounds. Although this might seem, at first, to contradict the evidence on cultural bias, in reality two very different things are measured here. The evidence on cultural bias deals with some measure of mental capacity at a given time, but prediction involves future performance over some span of years, and performance in this sense involves much more than raw brainpower— it involves self-discipline, attitudes and a store of knowledge, among other things. To say that all measured differences in raw brainpower are "biases" is to ignore the important role of many other traits, which may not be randomly distributed across social or ethnic lines. As someone has said: "Tests are not unfair. Life is unfair, and tests measure the results."

Tests are not meant to predict what *would* happen in a vacuum, but what *will* happen in the real world. The tragedy is when test results are used by people who blindly regard them as measures of innate potential, and who use them to justify providing inferior education to children from disadvantaged backgrounds. If biased people use mental tests to discriminate, eliminating the test will not eliminate the bias. Objective tests at least put some limits on their bias. Tests can be used to open up opportunities as well as to close them. Historically, standardized tests first opened up many of the top colleges in America to bright youngsters from lower-class backgrounds who had previously been passed over by traditional methods of selection. Alfred Binet, the originator of intelligence tests, used them to rescue individuals incarcerated as mentally incompetent.

Tests for jobs often differ from academic tests in that there is usually little effort to relate test scores to subsequent work performance. Partly this is due to the greater complexity and subjectivity involved in measuring job performance over a career, as compared to measuring academic grades over a relatively short span of time. But partly also, it reflects the fact that sheer convenience in reducing the number of applicants and, in some cases, for the obvious purpose of eliminating those minority groups whose education has been lacking—even if not lacking in ways that would affect the particular job to be done. Again, tests are not immune to misuse any more than any of the other features or artifacts of human life. Tests do not need to be held in superstitious awe, but neither do they need to be banned in superstitious fear.

Sexuality and the Life Cycle

A Broad Concept of Sexuality

Lester A. Kirkendall, Ph.D. *and* **Isadore Rubin, Ph.D.** *A founder and member of the Board of SIECUS, Dr. Kirkendall is Professor of Family Life, Emeritus, Oregon State University. He is the author of the study* Premarital Intercourse and Interpersonal Relationships *and of other books and articles on family life education. The late Dr. Rubin was an officer and member of the Board of SIECUS, the editor of* Sexology *Magazine, coauthor with Dr. Kirkendall of* Sex in the Adolescent Years, *and author of* Sexual Life After Sixty.

Introduction

As the Group for the Advancement of Psychiatry noted, the concept of sexuality generally accepted today is that described by Anna Freud: "...The sexual instincts of man do not suddenly awaken between the thirteenth and fifteenth year, i.e. at puberty, but operate from the outset of the child's development, change gradually from one form to another, progress from one state to another, until at last adult sexual life is achieved as the final result from this long series of developments." Today we recognize that we must concern ourselves with sexual feelings and behavior throughout the life cycle.

Most people are accustomed to thinking of sex as something involving merely the genital organs or as simple physical expression. To avoid this narrow and limiting conception of sex, we prefer to use the term *sexuality* as a recognition that sex expression is a deep and pervasive aspect of one's total personality, the sum total of one's feelings and behavior not only as a sexual being, but as a male or a female.

Thus, expressions of sexuality go much beyond genital responses, and are constantly subject to modification as a consequence of sexual experience and learning. Throughout the life cycle, physiological, emotional, social, and cultural forces condition sexuality in intricate and important ways, most expecially during early and late childhood. As individuals age, these influences may result in a widening range of possible sexual attitudes and expressions.

Simple Definitions No Longer Suffice

With the development of sophisticated research into sex and gender roles it is clear that the old simple definitions of male and female no longer suffice. Individuals may be classified as male and female on the basis of a growing number of criteria. These have been identified as follows:

1. *Genetic or chromosomal sex, determined at the moment of conception.* The normal female has two X chromosomes, while the normal male has one X and one Y chromosome. Recent research has discovered many types of sex-chromosomal anomalies.
2. *Gonadal sex.* The male has testes, while the female has ovaries.
3. *Hormonal sex.* The actions of the so-called male and female hormones may have important effects in bringing about feminization and virilization during critical periods of fetal development and puberty.
4. *Internal accessory reproductive structures.* The female has a womb, fallopian tubes, ovaries, etc., while the male has a prostate gland, sperm ducts, seminal vesicles, etc.
5. *External genital structures.*
6. *Sex of assignment and rearing.*
7. *Gender role and sexual orientation established while growing up.*

These variables may be independent of each other, resulting in incongruity between gender identity and other variables and creating special developmental and educational problems.

Prenatal Development

Male and female individuals begin their early embryonic development as forms which cannot be differentiated. Some researchers suggest that all embryos begin as females. According to Mary Jane

204 "Sexuality and the Life Cycle" is reprinted by permission of Charles Scribner's Sons from SIECUS, Study Guide #8, from *Sexuality and Man.* Copyright © 1970 Sex Information and Education Council of the U.S., Inc.

Sherfey, "mammalian embryos, male and female, are anatomically female during the early stages of fetal life. In the human, the differentiation of the male from the female form by the action of fetal androgen (male sex hormone) begins about the sixth week of embryonic life and is completed by the end of the third month." So far as sexuality is concerned, more than the simple fact of differentiating male and female genitalia takes place during the prenatal period. Other organ systems and structures without which adult sexual responses would be impossible are developing also. The glandular system that will bring the childhood reproductive system into maturity during puberty is developing. The neural and muscular systems that make sexual responsiveness possible at various stages of life are also developing, as are the brain centers that later will send and receive sexual messages. As a consequence we can say that each human being is born with certain sexual capacities already present, and that these capacities looked at as a whole constitute a biological response system that can and does respond in an integrated and coordinated way to sexual stimuli.

Recent research with animals suggests the possibility that prenatal hormones affecting the nervous system may have important effects in making some individuals more or less ready than others to receive the definitions of masculinity and femininity from the parents. Freud proposed the theory of innate bisexuality; more recently a theory of psychosexual neutrality at birth has been put forward. On the basis of present knowledge, a more modest middle ground is indicated.

Sexuality in Infancy and Childhood

Prior to Freud, there was little understanding or acceptance of childhood sexuality. According to John Gagnon, "the shock for adults of Freud's discoveries was not that children might be involved in sexual activity, but that this activity was not confined to a few evil children and was, in fact, an essential precursor and component of the development of the character structure of the adult." Freud's theory of the stages of psychosexual development, which he called the oral, anal, and genital, has formed the basis of modern psychiatric thinking. These hypotheses, however, have never been subjected to sufficient scientific testing to be confirmed or disproven. Over the years this model of psychosexual development has been criticized on both empirical and theoretical grounds, primarily by learning theorists, who believe the whole theory is unnecessarily complex, and by anthropologists, who have attacked the idea that each of these stages, and particularly the stage of oedipal conflict, is necessary to normal personality development.

Carlfred B. Broderick, a leading researcher in preadolescent sexual behavior, has hypothesized that three primary conditions are necessary to normal heterosexual development: (1) the parent or parent substitute of the same sex must not be so punishing on the one hand or so weak on the other as to make it impossible for the child to identify with him; (2) the parent or substitute of the opposite sex must not be so seductive, so punishing, or so emotionally erratic as to make it impossible for the child to trust members of the opposite sex; (3) the parents must not systematically reject the child's biological sex and attempt to teach him cross-sex behavior. Thus, Freud's main contention, that normal heterosexual development is determined by a child's familial relationships and social experiences rather than by simple biological factors, seems to be borne out by the available data.

Children, even in infancy, clearly respond to stimuli which produce sexual reactions. Thus, infants of both sexes seem to experience pleasure from the stimulation of the genitals and other areas of the body which are commonly recognized as erogenous zones. Halverson demonstrated that male infants respond to certain internal or external stimuli with erections in the early weeks of life. There was a wide range in individual responsiveness—from 5 to as many as 40 erections daily. These were seemingly the consequence of body tensions rather than sexual reactions in the usual sense. The Kinsey studies showed that orgasmic experiences occurred in infants and children throughout the pre-adolescent period. Their data show an increase, with advancing age, in the percentage of children able to reach climax: 32% of the boys 2-12 months of age, 57% of the 2-5 year olds, and nearly 80% of the pre-adolescent boys between 10 and 13 years of age, reached climax. A recent study of 700 four-year-olds in an English urban community found that 17% of the children engaged in genital play at this age. Interestingly no class differences were found despite sharp differences in parental attitudes. Thus, punitive measures were apparently no more effective in discouraging such play than were either verbal discouragement or *laissez-faire* tactics.

The Learning of Gender Role

The establishment of gender role is of great importance to the developing child. John Money, who has made extensive studies of this aspect of sexuality, explains gender role as being "all those things that a person says or does to disclose himself or herself as having the status of boy or man, girl or woman, respectively. It includes but is not restricted to sexuality in the sense of eroticism. A gender role is not established at birth, but is built up cumulatively through experiences encountered and transacted — through casual and unplanned learning, through explicit instruction and inculcation. In brief, a gender role is established in much the same way as is a native language."

Money found it "definitely advantageous for a child to have been reared so that a gender role was clearly defined and consistently maintained from the beginning." Attempts to impose a change of gender role, in the case of hermaphrodites, after early infancy usually did not improve the child's life adjustment significantly. In fact it often made it worse. Money felt that the critical time for establishing a convincing awareness of gender on the part of the child was from around eighteen months until 3 or 4 years of age. It is important however, to recognize that role behavior is learned and that instruction in role behavior begins with birth.

In the process of establishing gender role or, to use another common term, of establishing a sexual identity, the parents and others around the child play an extremely important part. They convey to the child in both overt and covert ways what they consider appropriate role behavior. They do this through words they use, the name they give the child, the way they treat and dress the child, the kind of toys they buy, the games they encourage, the expectations they voice, the routines they establish, the kind of discipline exercised, and through their own examples. In this manner they give the child a concept of how he is to regard his own body, and how males and females relate themselves to each other.

"Big boys don't cry" and "little girls hug their daddies and mommies" are typical injunctions. They eventually result in the stereotyped and traditional American cultural pattern in which men deny their hurts and injuries and eschew crying as a sign of weakness, and women (who are commonly regarded as weaker than men to begin with) are encouraged to confirm this "weakness" by expressing tender and sentimental feelings. Men, to be "strong," renounce such expressions.

Patterns of individual interests are certain to be strongly influenced by gender, as is choice of leisure time activities, occupational choice, parental role, or mode of affectional expression (among many possible examples). These are, of course, mainly matters of cultural expectation and are learned reactions.

The child is aided in the development of gender role concepts by awareness and interpretation of responses which come from his own anatomy and physiology. Shuttleworth accounts for the greater male preoccupation with physical sex expression as compared to the female in this manner: Males, biologically, generally have more muscular power than females; they are better equipped for danger-

ous work or fighting. This physiological difference combined with social pressures which call for males to behave aggressively encourages them to be more active and forceful than females. This pattern of active, aggressive behavior logically carries over into their sexual behavior.

Differences in Male-Female Attitudes

Shuttleworth distinguished several factors which help to explain this difference in male-female attitudes toward sexual expression. The first is the male's greater awareness of genital responsiveness. Males from the very beginning and throughout their childhood years "…are more aware of their genitals and much more aware of the responsiveness of their genitals." Erections are an almost daily occurrence among all males. In his penis the male has an organ which can be seen, felt, named, and readily manipulated to bring about pleasure. Likewise his penis is the anatomical distinction which makes him clearly male. This greater awareness is intensified in adolescence with the production of semen in ejaculation. "Males behave as if they were under rather constant physiological pressures, strong in some individuals and weak in others, to obtain an orgasm which will release accumulated seminal fluids."

The development of an overt awareness of sexual feelings in the female is a more diffuse process, and generally comes at a later age. The learning is not so obviously associated with her physiology, but arises more clearly from her social and sexual contacts, particularly those with males. Nevertheless, a number of females do experience orgasm early in infancy or childhood. But the biological and social forces are intermingled in intricate ways and produce innumerable variations in behavior. Thus, one's role in the experience of intercourse and in the reproductive process is fixed in certain respects by one's biology, but even here learning and circumstance play an important part. Traditionally men have been the overt pursuers, women the coquettish, attracting, luring sex in the mating process. These roles almost surely are conditioned by both physical and cultural factors. The sexual double standard (a standard which implies a differential according to sex membership, in the privileges and penalties extended to men and women) is suggested by many to be a cultural hangover from the past. According to Reiss, man's physical abilities afforded him economic, political, and military advantages that made it possible for him to define woman as inferior. Since he was in power in other areas, it is easy to conceive of his usurping special sexual privileges in addition.

The degree of passivity or aggressiveness which a male or a female exhibits in intercourse is also to some extent a matter of custom and desire regardless of the fact that the act of intercourse requires, biologically, penetration of the vagina by the penis. Of course, the experience of maturing a fetus in one's own body, carrying it through the period of gestation and finally giving life to the child in birth, provides an experience for women which is unavailable to men. Whether the biological experience of childbearing has any deep-seated or pervasive psychological consequences for male/female roles is a matter about which there are differing opinions, but no certainty. Biological differences, however, clearly make for certain unchangeable and divergent experiences that both differentiate the sexes and provide for a fascinating attraction and for complications in understanding and communication.

Childhood Learning About Sexuality

Children learn about their sexuality in many ways. Curiosity leads them to engage in exploratory activities involving themselves and other male or female children. They learn about their own bodies, the bodies of others, and what physiological reactions can be expected. They learn whether it is "safe" to experiment with sensations which adults call sexual and what sensations may come from experimentation. Adults commonly frown severely upon such activities. From parental reactions to these experiences children quite frequently derive their first deep-seated feelings toward sex. The children may feel that adults cannot accept sexuality, or certain aspects of it, or, more likely, they develop a feeling that sex is threatening and that sexual expressions are to be regarded with guilt and shame.

Curiosity also prompts children to seek information about the reproductive processes, prenatal development and the roles of men and women in the sexual-procreative process. At this point more clearly than any other perhaps can be seen the divergence in the points of view of children and of adults concerning the children's intent. Many adults interpret the children's questions as "sex questions," but a more accurate interpretation is that they are questions designed to learn about life processes.

The Question of "Latency"

Traditionally, the years preceding puberty have been viewed as a period of "latency," as a phase of the child's psychosexual life when sexual development comes to a halt. However, this view is being increasingly challenged. Psychiatrist Harold I. Lief (in a private communication) has pointed out: "Latency does *not* involve an absolute decline of protosexual or sexual interests on the part of the post-Oedipal child, but a relative one at most. Between the ages of 5 and 11 (roughly) there is an enormous broadening of his range of interests as the child learns many things about the world in which he lives, and as he increases his contacts with his fellows. Curiosity about his family, including intense sexual curiosity, abates as he leaves the protective canopy of his family for the wider world. But his sexual interests are still there, somewhat masked by his involvement and commitment to the exploration of his milieu. If that environment is stagnant, or punitive, or otherwise inhibits his move outward to enlarge his horizons, the child's sexual curiosity and behavior may become active, even florid."

The research of Broderick and others has shown that, although there is a social segregation of the sexes in the middle grades which culminates at about age 12, there is *no* period in which the majority of boys and the great majority of girls are not interested in the opposite sex. This is shown by their conviction that they want to get married some day, by their reporting having a sweetheart, being in love (or having crushes), or liking love scenes in the movies. Only about 20% of the boys show the negative attitudes toward romance which are supposed to be typical of the latency period.

Is There a "Homosexual Stage?"

As youngsters move toward puberty, some go through a period (years 9—12 approximately) when their chief attachments are with members of their own sex. This has commonly been called the homosexual stage of development, but this concept, too, is questionable. There is no definite evidence that there is a homosexual stage during which all or most boys pass. During this period it is not uncommon, however, for exchanges of genital manipulation and exploration to occur. For most children probably the most traumatic part of such experiences is the horrified reaction of parents and/or other adults who may become aware of them, resulting in a conviction on the youngster's part that sex is dirty or evil. When they have an opportunity, children also engage in heterosexual play throughout prepuberty, but without the emotional commitment of love which comes later. The prepubertal age of "hating girls" is probably a period of consolidating masculinity more than of homosexual activity.

Puberty and Adolescence

A problem for children nearing the pubertal stage and those who have entered puberty is that they face physical and emotional changes and experiences for which they receive no explanation. Girls who are concerned about irregular menstruation or what they regard as atypical breast development, or boys who are concerned with masturbation or what they assume to be atypical penile size, experience difficulty in obtaining accurate and helpful information from parents, teachers or other adults. Most adults suppress or have forgotten their own childhood, or more often are too embarrassed to talk about it and consequently are neglectful of the extent to which worries and concerns about emerging sexuality trouble youth. Furthermore, many remain reticent about talking about these things.

Puberty arrives at different ages for different youth, ranging from ages 9–16 for girls and from 11–18 for boys. The average age is about two years earlier for girls than for boys. The available evidence suggests that the age of puberty has been lowering for both sexes over the past several decades. Ausubel notes a definite physical maturational sequence. "In girls the order is (1) initial enlargement of the breasts; (2) appearance of straight, pigmented pubic hair; (3) period of maximum growth; (4) kinky pubic hair; (5) the menarche; and (6) growth of axillary hair. In boys the corresponding order of pubescent phenomena is (1) beginning growth of the testes and penis; (2) appearance of straight, pigmented pubic hair; (3) early voice changes; (4) first ejaculation; (5) kinky pubic hair; (6) period of maximum growth; (7) axillary hair; (8) marked voice changes; and (9) development of the beard."

As the child enters adolescence he cannot be said to be fully mature sexually, yet he is reproductively and genitally mature and capable of reproduction. In our culture he now enters a period of stress. One source of stress is that he is physically ready for heterosexual genital expression, yet is denied it. In some other cultures this experience is more freely available to him than it has been in ours.

Masturbation becomes a central concern in early adolescence, particularly for the white middle class male, who almost universally engages in at least some masturbation during the teen years. Girls engage to a lesser extent. Although for a variety of reasons masturbation may become the focus of many anxieties and fears, the Committee on Adolescence of the Group for the Advancement of Psychiatry notes, it is essentially a "normal response to increased sexual development" which is "necessary to the control and integration of new urges and the working out of new relationships through trial acting and fantasy."

Their report on *Normal Adolescence* indicates how adolescent experiments with masturbation can serve normal development: "The adolescent learns that sexual excitement and engorgement and erection of the penis or the clitoris can be initiated at will, and that orgastic climax with the ensuing predictable subsidence of tension can be quickly brought about or repeatedly deferred by the manner of masturbation. This contributes to a developing sense of mastery over the sexual impulses and

the new sexual capacities and helps the adolescent prepare for heterosexual relationships."

The ages at which children reach puberty and the time immediately following are likely to see a good many youth (almost certainly more boys than girls) involved in erotic play, genital examination, and experimentation with members of their own sex. These experiences are ordinarily referred to as homosexual experiences, but when the typical cultural stereotypes about homosexuality are applied, undue significance is given them. In the majority of cases, such experiences are likely to be simply a part of the development process. Curious about his own growth patterns and physical reactions and those of other youth, and denied the desired information, the adolescent in his desire to know may turn to sexual experimentation with others of the same sex. In this manner he learns something of what may be expected in the way of sexual manifestations in himself and others.

Most adolescents in the American culture are moving into some kind of heterosexual expression by the early teens. Actually, the age for moving into heterosexual activities is probably lowering, as the studies of Broderick and others show. The pattern of heterosexual expression seems ordinarily to follow a definite sequence, moving through embracing and kissing, and light caressing, to the more involved stages with heavy petting to intercourse itself. Of course unmarried youth vary in the extent and rapidity to which they progress through this pattern. In our culture many of the unmarried (more males than females) go through the entire sequence, ultimately experiencing intercourse; a few never begin until marriage. The timing of marriage, social class, religious and moral factors may influence their premarital experience.

Sexuality in Adulthood
In adulthood a wide variety and many combinations of sexual behavior patterns exist. Some persons will achieve heterosexual adjustment; others will be relying on masturbation or homosexual activities. Some may have come close to a renunciation of overt sexual expression. Those who have moved into heterosexuality, whether married or unmarried, will have developed a variety of patterns also. Some will have an adequate and satisfying sex life; others will find limited satisfaction. Some will be plagued with frigidity or impotence, or will be uninterested in sexual expression. Some will find sexual expression imposing intolerable burdens, or creating serious difficulties in human relations. Still others may be obsessive or compulsive in their sexual behavior. Former experiences and attitudes which the individual has sought to deny or repress may now crop out to interfere with effectiveness in the spousal or parental role.

Desirable, or desired, patterns of male and female interaction (role behavior) are often the source of confusion and conflict. This is particularly true since various social changes and technological developments have called long-standing patterns and practices into question. Education for women has resulted in giving them a competence which enables them to be self-supporting, and has opened opportunities in the business and professional world which were not available to them fifty years ago. At the same time it often requires readjustments in other family and spousal roles.

The perfection of contraceptive methods has given women the ability to control reproduction. The separation of sexual functioning from reproductive outcomes, if the sexual partners wish it, is now an accomplishable fact. This has made it more possible for women to concentrate directly and exclusively on the pleasure-sensory aspects of sex without the fear of pregnancy than ever before. The result is a blurring of former sharply and easily distinguishable gender roles, or an intrusion of one sex into the role practices commonly considered the prerogative of the other sex. This phenomenon is likely to increase in importance rather than to diminish.

Parental roles are structured around both biological and cultural differences between the sexes. The fact that the woman carries the child and has the mammary equipment for nursing the child (even though less and less often utilized) has cast her in the nurturant role, the father in a protective, supporting role. The fact that today's father is still prone to see himself as the disciplinarian, as the one to handle the family finances and to feel that he should be the family bread winner is partially a reflection of the extent to which traditional patterns become imbedded in current cultural attitudes. But here, too, role patterns are changing.

In marriage and parenthood the effects of immature, self-defeating sexual attitudes and experiences are often compounded. Parents have difficulties in teaching children because of their own unresolved feelings concerning sex or earlier sexual experiences. They are anxious about the incompetencies which they recognize in themselves, but at the same time are threatened by their children. For parents who have prided themselves on either their masculine prowess or feminine sexual attractiveness, the prospect of diminution or a fading of these qualities may be frightening; thus personal anxieties may be aroused by the emergent virility and sexual attractiveness of their children.

Menopause and Aging

Menopause for women and late middle age for men were formerly considered to signal the end of sex life. New attitudes and better knowledge of physiology and sexuality have changed this concept and have at the same time brought about a much more positive attitude among women toward the menopause. While men do not go through a definite or pronounced "change of life" as the female does, they do experience, but at different ages, a gradually diminishing virility and a slackening in their capacity to perform sexually. This is disturbing to many men, particularly to those who may have depended upon sexual performance to sustain their sense of masculinity and youthfulness. Their disturbance is even greater if the potency of their wives remains undiminished. Sexual expression in old age is more possible and more common than has usually been considered the case. Rubin has assembled research evidence indicating that so far as age is concerned there is no automatic cut-off to sexual relations, and that some individuals may continue their sex lives into the 70's, 80's, and even 90's. The frequency with which the 250 subjects of one study, age 60 to 90 years, engaged in sexual relations "ranged from once every other month to three times weekly." For some individuals frequency of intercourse actually increases in in the very late years.

Lawrence K. Frank has suggested that continued sexual functioning can come to have a very important psychological meaning in the later stages of life. He writes, in *The Conduct of Sex*, "Sex relations can provide a much needed and highly effective resource in the later years of life when so often men face the loss of their customary prestige and self-confidence and begin to feel old, sometimes long before they have begun to age significantly. The premature cessation of sexual functioning may accelerate physiological and psychological aging since disuse of any function usually leads to concomitant changes in other capacities. After menopause, women may find that continuation of sexual relations provides a much needed psychological reinforcement, a feeling of being needed and of being capable of receiving love and affection and renewing the intimacy they earlier found desirable and reassuring."

For both men and women hormonal replacement therapy and a new psychological outlook have proven useful in the later years.

Sexuality in the Family Life Cycle

Just as there is a cycle of sexual growth, development, and decline which characterizes individuals, so is there a cycle of sexual interaction which characterizes most married couples and their families. This pattern has its inception, for any particular couple, before marriage. In the premarital period couples necessarily respond to each other as sexual beings. They may respond by pretending that no sexual feeling exists between them. They may express their sexual feelings in varying degrees of physical intimacy, ranging from kissing and embracing through various degrees of petting to complete intercourse. They are also developing varying kinds of verbal and non-verbal communication patterns. Some may find it so difficult to talk about sex that all verbal references are avoided. Other couples—probably in increasing numbers as our culture becomes more open—are achieving satisfying and meaningful verbal communication about sexual matters.

With marriage comes the need for developing satisfying patterns of marital sexual relationships. For many couples this requires a considerable period of time. For most couples the frequency of marital intercourse is usually higher in the early months of marriage than it will be thereafter. The need for or the interest in dealing with variety in sexual expression commonly arises at this time and for some spouses variations are intolerable. So does planning for the coming and spacing of children and decisions upon the use or non-use of contraceptives. Adjustments in sexual patterns will be necessitated when pregnancy occurs. With many couples, as the Kinsey data revealed, changes and divergencies in the degree of sexual interest on the part of the partners must be faced. A common family cycle pattern is for wives, as they lose their inhibitions and feel more secure, to show more interest in intercourse than do their husbands. The declining interest on the part of men in the later years may be due to their absorption in business or professional activities, a declining physical capacity, taking wives for granted, the routine quality that has been allowed to creep into their lives, or a possible need of change and variety in sexual stimuli if they are to remain responsive.

Parent-Child Relations

The presence of children may have considerable effect on the parents' sexual patterns. Parents must become concerned with the problems and techniques of sex education. They are often so miseducated themselves and so ill at ease with questions that some children, becoming aware of the disquiet of their parents, never ask. Other children learn after an experience or two with their parents' uneasiness that such questions are better unasked. And so may begin a process which creates a communication chasm between children or youth and their parents so far as sexual matters are concerned.

By the time their children have reached adolescence, American parents typically find themselves unable to discuss intimate aspects of sexual behavior with them. This holds true whether it is their own children's sexual problems or questions which need discussion. This may add significantly to the strained relations that are likely to occur between parents and adolescent children, and in turn be related to the push on the part of children for economic independence and the conflicting need they feel for continuing to belong to their families. Then, too, children may not be able to discuss freely all aspects of their sex lives with their parents. They need to develop their own separate sense of sex identity as growing persons who will leave their own family and found a new one. Consequently for many families this period is one of uneasiness and tension for all. The parents hope that their sons and daughters will go through their adolescence without "getting someone into trouble" or "getting into trouble." The parents breathe a secret but a very real sigh of relief when their children are safely married.

The gulf between parent and child is to a large extent probably inevitable, with its roots perhaps lying in the difficulty that children have in accepting their parents as sexual beings. At any rate, it points up the fact that adults outside of the family can often be useful to young people in sex education and counseling, largely because they are not personally involved with each other. Many adults need guidance from professional sources, since new questions about sexual needs and expression arise as individuals move from one stage of life to another. As spouses go on in their marriage, or as single persons age (our society has never displayed any real concern for the sexual needs or problems of the middle-aged or older single person), cultural inhibitions result in their sexual difficulties and needs becoming more and more exclusively their own private concern. They are seldom discussed even with physicians.

Conclusion

Certain developments seem to insure that our concepts concerning the nature and place of sex throughout the life cycle will continue to change. A feeling still exists among many that the only natural and proper use of sex requires its focus to be upon the reproductive process. The separation of reproductive outcomes from sexual functioning is certain to lay an increasing emphasis on the use of sex for communication, intimacy, and the enhancement of enjoyment. Over man's long history, his existence on the planet as a species was undoubtedly precarious and it is understandable that he should have been intensely preoccupied with the procreative aspects of sex. But today, the grave dangers reside in overpopulation. This, plus the fact that reproduction can now occur at will rather than by chance, necessitates a reassessment of the place of sex not only in the life cycle of individuals but in society as a whole.

Myth, Reality and Shades of Gray

WHAT WE KNOW AND DON'T KNOW ABOUT SEX DIFFERENCES

Eleanor Emmons Maccoby and Carol Nagy Jacklin

Eleanor Emmons Maccoby is professor of psychology and Chairman of the Department of Psychology at Stanford University. She is well-known for her work in many areas of developmental child psychology, including attachment in early childhood, and the development of sex differences. Maccoby has been a fellow at the Center for Advanced Study in the Behavioral Sciences, and is a past president of the American Psychological Association's Division of Developmental Psychology. Currently she is President of the Western Psychological Association, and was elected a Fellow of the American Academy of Arts and Sciences in 1974.

Carol Nagy Jacklin received her M.A. in psychology in 1961 from the University of Connecticut and her Ph.D. in 1972 from Brown University. In 1971-72 she worked with Professor Maccoby as an NIH postdoctoral fellow. Since 1972 she has been a research associate at Stanford University. Jacklin's interests are in the development of sex differences and infant learning and perception.

In a dispassionate look at all the evidence, two researchers lay the state of our psychological knowledge out flat. Yes, girls differ from boys, but…

THE PHYSICAL DIFFERENCES between men and women are obvious and universal. The psychological differences are not. Yet people hold strong beliefs about sex differences, even when those beliefs fail to find any scientific support.

Some popular views of sex differences are captured in a scene from the Rodgers and Hammerstein musical, *Carousel*. A young man discovers he is to be a father. He rhapsodizes about the kind of son he expects to have. The boy will be tall and tough as a tree, and no one will dare to boss him around. It will be all right for his mother to teach him manners, but she mustn't make a sissy out of him. The boy will be good at wrestling, and able to herd cattle, run a riverboat, drive spikes.

Then the prospective father realizes, with a start, that the child may be a girl. The music moves to a gentle theme. She will have ribbons in her hair. She will be sweet and petite, just like her mother, and suitors will flock around her. There's a comic relief from sentimentality, when the expectant father brags that she'll be half again as bright as girls are meant to be. But then he returns to the main theme: his daughter will need to be protected.

The lyrics in this scene reflect some common cultural stereotypes. There are also some less well-known stereotypes in the social science literature on sex differences. We believe there is a great deal of myth in both the popular and scientific views about male-female differences. There is also some substance.

In order to find out which generalizations are justified and which are not, we spent three years compiling, reviewing and interpreting a very large body of research—over 2,000 books and articles—on the sex differences in motivation, social behavior, and intellectual ability. We examined negative as well as positive evidence. At the end of our exhaustive and exhausting search, we were able to determine which beliefs about sex differences are supported by evidence, which beliefs have no support, and which are still in-slightly discordant note, introduced for adequately tested.

First, the myths:

MYTH ONE:
Girls are more "social" than boys.

There is no evidence that girls are more likely than boys to be concerned with people, as opposed to impersonal objects or abstract ideas. The two sexes are equally interested in social stimuli (e.g., human faces and voices), and are equally proficient at learning by imitating models. They are equally responsive to social rewards, such as praise from others, and neither sex consistently learns better for this form of reward than for other forms.

In childhood, girls are no more dependent than boys on their caretakers, and boys are no more willing than girls to re-

Adapted and Reprinted from *The Psychology of Sex Differences* by Eleanor Emmons Maccoby and Carol Nagy Jacklin with the permission of the publishers, Stanford University Press. Copyright © 1974 by the Board of Trustees of the Leland Stanford Junior University.

5. INDIVIDUAL DIFFERENCES

From preschool to early adolescence, the sexes are very similar in their verbal abilities. But at about age 11, they begin to diverge.

main alone. Girls do not spend more time with playmates; the opposite is true, at least at certain ages. The two sexes appear to be equally adept at understanding the emotional reactions and needs of others, although measures of this ability have been narrow.

Any differences that do exist in the sociability of the two sexes are more of kind than of degree. Boys are highly oriented toward a peer group and congregate in larger groups; girls associate in pairs or small groups of children their own age, and may be somewhat more oriented toward adults, although the evidence on this is weak.

MYTH TWO:
Girls are more suggestible than boys.

Boys are as likely as girls to imitate other people spontaneously. The two sexes are equally susceptible to persuasive communications, and in face-to-face situations where there is social pressure to conform to a group judgment about an ambiguous situation, there are usually no sex differences in susceptibility. When there are, girls are somewhat more likely to adapt their own judgments to those of the group, although some studies find the reverse. Boys, on the other hand, appear to be more likely to accept peer group values when these conflict with their own.

MYTH THREE:
Girls have lower self-esteem than boys.

Boys and girls are very similar in overall self-satisfaction and self-confidence throughout childhood and adolescence. (The information on childhood is meager, but what there is indicates no sex difference.) The sexes do differ in the areas in which they report greatest self-confidence. Girls rate themselves higher in the area of social competence, while boys more often see themselves as strong, powerful, dominant, potent.

Through most of the school years, boys and girls are equally likely to believe they

can influence their own fate, as opposed to falling victim to chance. During the college years (not earlier or later), men have a greater sense of control over their destiny, and are more optimistic in predicting their own performance on a variety of school-related tasks. However, this does not imply a generally lower level of self-esteem among women of this age.

MYTH FOUR:
Girls lack motivation to achieve.

In the pioneering studies of achievement motivation, girls were more likely to report imagery about achievement when asked to make up stories to describe ambiguous pictures, as long as the instructions did not stress either competition or social comparison. Boys need to be challenged by appeals to their ego or competitive feelings, for their achievement imagery to reach the level of girls'. Although boys' achievement motivation does appear to be more responsive to competitive arousal, that does not imply that they have a higher level of achievement motivation in general. In fact, when researchers observe behavior that denotes a motive to achieve, they find no sex differences or find girls to be superior.

MYTH FIVE:
Girls are better at rote learning and simple repetitive tasks. Boys are better at high-level tasks that require them to inhibit previously learned responses.

Neither sex is more susceptible to simple conditioning, in which stimuli become connected with responses in what is assumed to be a rather automatic process. Neither sex excels in rote-learning tasks,

such as learning to associate one word with another. Boys and girls are equally proficient at tasks that call on them to inhibit various responses, e.g., discrimination of certain items from others, a task requiring the subject to avoid attending or responding to irrelevant cues.

Boys are somewhat more impulsive during the preschool years, but after that the sexes do not differ in ability to wait for a delayed reward or inhibit early, incorrect responses, or on other measures of impulsivity.

MYTH SIX:
Boys are more "analytic" than girls.

The sexes do not differ on tests of cognitive style that measure one's ability to analyze, i.e., the ability to respond to a particular aspect of a situation without being influenced by the context, or restructure the elements of a problem in order to achieve a solution. Boys and girls are equally likely to respond to contextual aspects of a situation that are irrelevant to the task at hand. Boys are superior only on problems that require visual discrimination or manipulation of objects set in a larger context; this superiority seems to be accounted for by spatial ability, which we discuss below, and does not imply a general analytic superiority.

MYTH SEVEN:
Girls are more affected by heredity, boys by environment.

Male identical twins are intellectually more alike than female identical twins, but the two sexes resemble their parents to the same degree. Boys are more vulnerable to damage by a variety of harmful agents in the environment both before and after birth, but this does not mean that they are more affected by environmental influences in general.

The two sexes learn with equal facility

Male superiority on visual-spatial tasks is not found in childhood, but appears fairly consistently in adolescence and adulthood.

in a wide variety of situations. If learning is the primary means by which the environment affects us, then the two sexes are equivalent in this regard.

MYTH EIGHT:
Girls are "auditory," boys "visual."

Male and female infants do not seem to respond differently to sounds. At most ages, boys and girls are equally adept at discriminating speech sounds. There is no sex difference in memory for sounds previously heard.

No study shows a sex difference among newborns in time spent looking at visual stimuli. During the first year of life, neither sex emerges clearly as more responsive to what they see. From infancy to adulthood, the sexes exhibit a similar degree of interest in visual stimuli. They also seem to be alike in ability to discriminate among objects, identify shapes, estimate distances, and perform on a variety of other tests of visual perception.

Our examination of the social science literature also revealed some sex differences that are fairly well-established:

DIFFERENCE ONE:
Males are more aggressive than females.

A sex difference in aggression has been observed in all cultures in which aggressive behavior has been observed. Boys are more aggressive physically and verbally. They engage in mock-fighting and aggressive fantasies as well as direct forms of aggression more frequently than girls. The sex difference manifests itself as soon as social play begins, at age two or two and a half. From an early age, the primary victims of male aggression are other males, not females.

Although both sexes become less aggressive with age, boys and men remain more aggressive through the college years. Little information is available for older adults.

DIFFERENCE TWO:
Girls have greater verbal ability than boys.

Girls' verbal abilities probably mature somewhat more rapidly in early life, although a number of recent studies find no sex differences. During the period from preschool to early adolescence, the sexes are very similar in their verbal abilities. But at about age 11, they begin to diverge; female superiority increases through high school, and possibly beyond. Girls score higher on tasks that involve understanding and producing language, and on "high-level" verbal tasks (analogies, comprehension of difficult written material, creative writing) as well as "lower-level" measures (such as fluency and spelling).

DIFFERENCE THREE:
Boys excel in visual-spatial ability.

Visual-spatial ability involves the visual perception of figures or objects in space and how they are related to each other. One visual-spatial test has the subject inspect a three-dimensional pile of blocks, and estimate the number of surfaces visible from a perspective different than his own. Another has him look at a figure, then select one from a set of four that matches the original if rotated in a plane. Male superiority on visual-spatial tasks is not found in childhood, but appears fairly consistently in adolescence and adulthood, and increases through the high-school years. The sex differences are approximately equal on analytic tasks (those that require separation of an element from its background) and nonanalytic ones.

DIFFERENCE FOUR:
Boys excel in mathematical ability.

The two sexes are similar in their early acquisition of quantitative concepts and their mastery of arithmetic in grade school. Beginning at about age 12 or 13, however, boys' mathematical skills increase faster than girls'. The greater rate of improvement does not seem to be entirely due to the fact that boys take more math courses, although the question has not been extensively studied.

The magnitude of the sex difference varies depending on the study, and is probably not as great as the difference in spatial ability. Both visual-spatial and verbal processes are sometimes involved in solving math problems; some problems can be solved in either way, while others cannot, a fact that may help to explain why the size of the sex difference varies from one study to another.

On some questions, we found ambiguous findings or too little evidence on which to base conclusions. These questions are still open to further research.

QUESTION ONE:
Are there differences in tactile sensitivity?

Most studies of tactile sensitivity in infancy or ability to perceive by touch at later ages do not show sex differences. When differences are found, girls are more sensitive, but since this finding is rare, we cannot be confident that it is meaningful. Most studies in which the results are analyzed by sex deal with newborns; more work is needed with other ages.

QUESTION TWO:
Are there differences in fear, timidity and anxiety?

Studies that involve direct observation of fearful behavior usually do not find sex differences. But teacher ratings and self-reports usually reveal girls as more timid or more anxious. The problem with self-reports is that we do not know whether

5. INDIVIDUAL DIFFERENCES

It is true that boys and men are more aggressive, but this does not mean that females are the passive victims of aggression.

the results reflect real differences, or only differences in people's willingness to report anxiety.

Since the very willingness to assert that one is afraid may lead to fearful behavior, the problem may turn out to be unimportant. But it would be desirable to have measures other than self-reports, which now contribute most of the data from early school age on.

QUESTION THREE:
Is one sex more active than the other?

Sex differences in activity level do not appear in infancy. They begin to show up when children reach the age of social play. Some studies find that during the preschool years, boys tend to be more active, but many studies do not find a sex difference. This discrepancy may be partially traceable to the kind of situation in which measurements are made. Boys appear to be especially stimulated to bursts of high activity when other boys are present. But the exact way in which the situation controls activity level remains to be established.

Activity level is also affected by motivational states—fear, anger, curiosity—and therefore is of limited usefulness in identifying stable individual or group differences. We need more detailed observations of the vigor and quality of children's play.

QUESTION FOUR:
Is one sex more competitive than the other?

Some studies find boys to be more competitive than girls, but many find the sexes to be similar in this regard. Almost all the research on competition has involved situations in which competition is maladaptive. For example, two people might be asked to play the prisoner's dilemma game, in which they have to choose between competitive strategies that are attractive to the individual in the short run, and co-operative strategies that maximize both players' gains in the long run. In such situations, the sexes are equally cooperative.

In settings where competitiveness produces greater individual rewards, males might be more competitive than females, but this is a guess based on common-sense considerations, such as the male interest in competitive sports, and not on research in controlled settings. The age of the subject and the identity of the opponent no doubt make a difference too; there is evidence that young women hesitate to compete against their boyfriends.

QUESTION FIVE:
Is one sex more dominant than the other?

Dominance appears to be more of an issue in boys' groups than in girls' groups. Boys make more attempts to dominate each other than do girls. They also more often attempt to dominate adults.

But the dominance relations between the sexes are complex. In childhood, the segregation of play groups by sex means that neither sex frequently tries to dominate the other; there is little opportunity. When experimental situations bring the two sexes together, it is not clear whether one sex is more successful in influencing the behavior of the other. In mixed adult groups or pairs, formal leadership tends to go to the males in the early stages of an interaction, but the longer the relationship lasts, the more equal influence becomes.

QUESTION SIX:
Is one sex more compliant than the other?

During childhood, girls tend to be more obedient to the commands and directions of adults. But this compliance does not carry over into relationships with peers. Boys are especially concerned with maintaining their status in their peer group, and therefore are probably more vulnerable than girls to pressures and challenges from that group, although this has not been well-established. It is not clear that

in adult interactions, one sex is consistently more willing to comply with the wishes of the other.

QUESTION SEVEN:
Are nurturance and "maternal" behavior more typical of one sex?

There is very little information about the tendencies of boys and girls to be nurturant or helpful toward younger children or animals. Cross-cultural work does indicate that girls between six and 10 are more often seen behaving nurturantly. In our own society, the rare studies that report nurturant behavior involve observation of free play among nursery-school children. These studies do not find sex differences, but the setting usually does not include children who are much younger than the subjects being observed. It may be that the presence of younger children would elicit sex differences in nurturant behavior.

Very little information exists on how adult men respond to infants and children, so we can't say whether adult females are more disposed to behave maternally than adult males are to behave paternally. But if there is a sex difference, it does not generalize to a greater female tendency to behave altruistically. Studies of people's willingness to help others in distress have sometimes found men to be more helpful, sometimes women, depending on the identity of the person needing help and the kind of help that is required. Overall, the sexes seem similar in degree of altruism.

QUESTION EIGHT:
Are females more passive than males?

The answer is complex, but for the most part negative. The two sexes are highly alike in their willingness to explore a novel environment, when they both have freedom to do so. Both sexes are highly responsive to social situations of all kinds, and although some individuals tend to withdraw from social interaction and simply watch from the sidelines, they are as likely to be male as female.

We said earlier that girls are more likely to comply with adult demands, but compliance can take an active form; running errands and performing services for others are active processes. Young boys seem more prone than girls to put out energy in bursts of strenuous physical activity, but the girls are not sitting idly by while the boys act; they are simply playing more quietly. Their play is fully as organized and planned, possibly more so. When girls play, they actively impose their own design upon their surroundings as much as boys do.

It is true that boys and men are more aggressive, but this does not mean that females are the passive victims of aggression—they do not yield or withdraw in the face of aggression any more frequently than males do, at least during the phases of childhood that have been observed. We have already noted the curious fact that while males are more dominant, females are not especially submissive, at least not to boys and girls their own age. In sum, the term "passive" does not accurately describe the most common female personality attributes.

We must conclude from our survey of all the data that many popular beliefs about the psychological characteristics of the two sexes have little or no basis in fact. Yet people continue to believe, for example, that girls are more "social" than boys, or are more suggestible than boys, ignoring the fact that careful observation and measurement show no sex differences.

The explanation may be that people's attention is selective. It is well-documented that whenever a member of a group behaves the way an observer expects him to, the observer notes the fact, and his prior belief is confirmed and strengthened. But when a member of the group behaves in a way that is not consistent with the observer's expectations, the behavior is likely to go unnoticed, so the observer's prior belief remains intact.

This probably happens continually when those with entrenched ideas about sex differences observe male and female behavior. As a result, myths live on that would otherwise rightfully die out under the impact of negative evidence.

Mental Patterns of Disease

JOAN AREHART-TREICHEL

The type of person you are may tell you more than just how you handle your social relationships. Some medical researchers are now finding evidence that, for some of us, it can predict what kind of disease we're likely to get. Small comfort unless we can find out early enough to change our ways.

Joan Arehart-Treichel is medical editor of *Science News* in Washington, D.C.

There is increasing evidence that certain personality types are prone to specific physical diseases or impairments—heart attacks, cancer, arthritis, ulcers, asthma and others. The personalities of three real people are described below. Try to predict the health risks inherent in each of their personalities.

Melinda B of San Diego, California, has been secretary to a bank vice-president for 14 years. The vice-president has keen admiration for her quiet efficiency, willingness to work overtime and dedication to the job even when she is sick. He is concerned, however, that Melinda is a loner who keeps her emotions bottled up inside her. He's right. Melinda has feelings of isolation and tendencies toward emotional repression that go back to her childhood. Her parents died when she was five, and she was raised by a possessive uncle who refused to let her marry the one man she loved.

Wally R of Nashville, Tennessee, is a devoted husband, father and a hard-working gas station manager. He dotes on activity and adventure. When he's not scrubbing the station driveway or fixing the roof of his house, he's off bass fishing or quail hunting. Wally's family and friends think of him as a happy, bustling fellow who also has a tendency to be clumsy. Wally is forever falling off a ladder, hitting his thumb with a hammer or tripping over a hose.

Robert G is one of the busiest gynecologists in Scarsdale, New York. Before he gets out of bed in the morning, he dictates patient histories and correspondence. He often reads his medical journals while shaving or eating breakfast. He regularly puts in a 15-hour day and boasts to both colleagues and friends that he has the largest gynecologic caseload on the East Coast. Much of his limited time away from the office is also taken up with professional matters—running the county medical society and building a new medical arts building. Both his colleagues and his family describe him as aggressive, time urgent, competitive and, of course, eminently successful.

Doctors who have studied the link between personality traits and susceptibility to certain diseases or physical impairments would predict cancer for Melinda, a fatal accident for Wally and a heart attack for Robert.

In fact, Melinda did die from pancreatic cancer two years ago. And Wally did die 11 months ago on a fishing trip. His motorboat hit a submerged root and tossed him out of the boat. He was knocked unconscious and, not having a lifejacket on, he drowned. Fortunately, Robert is not dead yet, and if he's smart, he'll set about immediately altering his heart attack-prone behavior.

The link between personality and disease susceptibility is nothing new; it goes back centuries. Hippocrates, the father of Western medicine, was interested in the link between psyche and soma. However, modern medicine dating from the 17th century on has given psychosomatic medicine short shrift, paying more attention to how the mind or body works independently than to how they hook up and function as a unit. Psychiatrists think "it's all in the mind"; nephrologists, that "it's all in the kidneys"; proctologists, that "it's all up the rectum." Or as Philip Pinkerton, M.D., of Liverpool, England, puts it more politely in the *British Medical Journal:* "The psychosomatic approach is by no means universally endorsed by the medical profession. The conservative doctor views it with mistrust, believing that psychology bears little relevance to 'real disease.'" John W. Mason, M.D., a psychoendocrinologist with the Walter Reed Army Medical Center in Washington, D.C., agrees: "We must face the fact that the psychosomatic approach has not yet had the sweeping revolutionary impact on medicine of which it appears capable."

During the past several decades, however, some intrepid doctors have been trying to put Humpty Dumpty back together again. And one of the most striking findings to emerge from their research is that certain personality traits can predispose people to certain physical illnesses.

Probably the toughest evidence to date indicating that personality can do a person in concerns the link between so-called Type A personality and heart attacks. The bulk of the research in this area has been conducted by two San Francisco cardiologists, Meyer Friedman, M.D., and Ray H. Rosenman, M.D. These two physicians have spent 15 years associating the aggressive, time urgent, competitive, highly successful person (Type A) with the occurence of heart attacks; and his or her counterpart, the more relaxed, easygoing Type B person with the lack of them. Friedman and Rosenman's evidence is impressive not only because they have spent a long time collecting it, but because it consists of both retrospective and prospective studies. In other words, they first spent time looking back into the personalities of men who had already had heart attacks.

From *Human Behavior*, January 1976. Copyright © 1976 Human Behavior Magazine. Reprinted by permission.

And when they found striking similarities in their personalities, they then studied the personalities of men who had not yet had heart attacks—and successfully predicted which men would.

One of the most noticeable characteristics of the Type A personality, the San Francisco cardiologists have found, is the inability to derive real satisfaction from achievements. That type of person is more interested in the number of achievements he racks up (seeing 160 patients a day, playing eight sets of tennis or selling 60 insurance policies).

Another interesting aspect they've found is that women as well as men span Type A and B personalities. Historically, men have been far more susceptible to heart attacks than have women, at least up until the onset of menopause. So many physicians assumed that sex hormones offer women protection against heart attacks. During the past couple of years, however, heart attacks among younger women have soured at an alarming rate. Some investigators attribute this rise to an increase of smoking among women. But some others concede that the rise might also be due to women competing more in the marketplace. As more and more women assume professional responsibilities, it will be interesting to see whether female heart attacks increase commensurately.

Still another link between personality and disease susceptibility that has been building during the past few years concerns the lonely, emotionally repressed individual and a vulnerability to cancer. An outstanding researcher in this area is Caroline Thomas, M.D., of the Johns Hopkins University School of Medicine. And Thomas's study is especially impressive because it is exclusively prospective.

From 1947 to 1964, Thomas studied 17 successive classes of students at the Johns Hopkins Medical School. The students were checked out for heartbeat rate, cholesterol level in the blood and reactions to cold, exercise and other stresses. If they had diseases, the diseases were noted. The causes of death for their parents, grandparents, uncles and aunts were recorded. The students filled in detailed questionnaires about their early childhood, schooling, family life, diet, medication, hobbies, emotional outlook, aims, as well as habits such as smoking or drinking. They were given Rorschach and figure-drawing tests to reveal such characteristics as aggression, passivity, anxiety, hostility and depressive trends.

By the middle of the 1960s, then, Thomas had exhaustive prospective data on 1,337 subjects, and all but six of the subjects have kept in touch with her as they have moved from early adulthood into middle age. So far, 15 of the subjects have suffered heart attacks, 46 have gotten cancer and 16 have committed suicide. Thomas has looked back on the personality information that she had for these victims to see whether certain traits might have predicted the causes of death and found that indeed they might have.

She found, as had Friedman and Rosenman, that the attack victims had been high-gear persons. She found that the suicide victims had not been close to their parents in childhood, and even as young people had been especially sensitive to stress, reacting to it with irritability and an urge to get away from it all. And the cancer victims were low-gear persons, seldom prey to outbursts of emotions. They had had feelings of isolation and unhappiness dating back to childhood.

"We did not make up any hypotheses beforehand about cancer patients," Thomas explains. "I had selected them as a comparison group for the suicides, thinking that the cancer victims have solid, demonstrable physical illnesses." When the different personality types were analyzed, Dr. Thomas says, "it turned out, however, that cancer victims were much more like the suicide victims than they were like the heart attack victims."

Claus and Marjorie Bahnson, a husband and wife psychology team at the Eastern Pennsylvania Psychiatric Institute in Philadelphia, have described both the heart attack personality and the cancer personality with their own retrospective studies. Says Claus Bahnson: "The heart attack personality vents his frustrations, irritations, anxieties and other negative emotions outwardly by bellowing, cursing or what have you. The cancer personality takes the same negative emotions out inwardly, that is, he internalizes them."

Another striking aspect of the cancer personality, the Bahnsons have found, is that he believes his mental and bodily strength to be greater than that of other people. Says Claus Bahnson: "They are master builders and independent people who operate on their own motivations." Or as Marjorie Bahnson puts it: "The heart attack personality feels that he is under greater stress than are other people, even when this is not true. The cancer personality may be under greater stress than other people, but he will say, 'Everything is fine.'"

The ego strength of the cancer personality, in fact, is further buttressd by the Bahnsons' findings that cancer personalities tend to have fewer psychiatric disturbances than do the mentally ill. "The cancer personality," Claus Bahnson declares, "has accepted social restrictions more than has the heart attack personality. He is religious, committed, good—perhaps too good for his own health."

The heart attack personality, on the other hand, seems to be without religious beliefs. Or as Friedman and Rosenman report: "We cannot say positively that the increase in the Type A behavior pattern has been directly influenced by the continuing loss of religious faith and other sustaining myths and rituals. We can declare, however, with considerable certainty, that we have rarely encountered this behavior pattern in any person whose religious and patriotic beliefs take precedence over his preoccupation with the accumulation of 'numbers' or the acquisition of personal power."

The Bahnsons have asked cancer patients to describe their childhoods, and they sound similar to those of Thomas's cancer victims—lonely, unhappy, lacking in communication with their parents. If there were any two adjectives the patients had for their parents, they were "unloving" and "cold." If the absence of parental warmth leaves a child susceptible to cancer, then perhaps the loss of one's parents has the same effect. The Bahnsons are now undertaking an epidemiological study with the Western German Research Institute in Heidelberg to find out. They want to determine whether the 1.8 million German children who lost their parents during World War II are now experiencing, as 40 and 50 year-olds, more incidences of cancer than Germans of comparable age who did not lose their parents during the war.

Sarah J of Cleveland, Ohio, was brought up in a well-to-do family. Her mother was warm and loving, but her father was cold and strict. He made it clear that he believed women to be inferior to men. He sent Sarah's brother to the university, but not Sarah. Then the depression hit. Sarah was on her own in the world, resentful that she had been denied the education that her brother had frittered away. Some years later Sarah married, had her own family and threw herself into her roles with zest. She was a super wife, mother and housekeeper but made it apparent to her husband and children that she would much rather be out of the house holding down a professionally challenging position. When her family encouraged her to seek a position, however, she said, "Oh, who would want to hire me? My education is limited; I have no skills." Then came the time for her children to go away to college; Sarah no longer had a challenge. Just about that time, she had to undergo a serious operation that left her physically exhausted and depressed. Shortly thereafter, she came down with the rheumatoid arthritis that she has to this day. It causes her intense pain and some crippling.

Sarah, by all accounts, is a rheumatoid arthritis personality, according to various studies that have been conducted in recent years. Four out of five rheumatoid arthritis victims are women, and for good reason—the disease appears to arise in those frustrated by the traditional female sex role. The evidence that has accumulated shows that rheumatoid arthritis victims tend to be frustrated over unfulfilled ambitions primarily because they have feelings of inadequacy harking back to their childhood. Their feelings of inadequacy have arisen because they had strict parents who did not encourage them to strike out on their own and achieve. Because of these frustrations, rheumatoid arthritis victims often funnel their need for recognition outside the home into being exceptional housekeepers and mothers. They are self-sacrificing, orderly, punctual, tidy perfectionists.

One of the best studies underscoring the rheumatoid arthritis personality as a stifled, frustrated woman was undertaken several years ago by Dr. Franz Alexander and his colleagues. Nine psychoanalyst judges reviewed personality information on 83 patients with rheumatoid arthritis, asthma, ulcers, hypertension or other disease. The judges were significantly more successful in picking out the rheumatoid arthritis victims on the basis of their personalities than they were with the other disease victims. They correctly picked the rheumatoid arthritis patients two out of three times. It will be interesting to see, as more and more women seek professional fulfillment, whether the incidences of rheumatoid arthritis among women drop.

Gastrointestinal ulcers is still another physical illness that seems to occur in persons with a particular personality. Evidence for this personality basis, as for rheumatoid arthritis, has been accumulating from numerous studies for some years now. Back in 1957, for instance, Herbert Weiner, M.D., of the Albert Einstein College of Medicine in New York City did a fascinating study on the personality underlying ulcer susceptibility. He evaluated 2,073 army inductees for psychological characteristics and measured the levels of pepsinogen in their blood. (Pepsinogen is secreted by the stomach lining and oversecretion of it has been strongly linked with peptic ulcers.) He found a strong correlation between high levels of pepsinogen in the blood and certain psychological characteristics. He then predicted which of the men would get peptic ulcers during basic training on the basis of both pepsinogen levels and the corresponding psychological profile. Nine men developed ulcers. Weiner had predicted seven of the nine.

The major characteristics that Dr. Weiner found in the ulcer personality are intense needs that are principally "oral" in nature and that are exhibited in terms of wishing to be fed, to lean on others, to seek close bodily contact with others. When attempts to fulfill these needs fail, the victim becomes angry, but he does not express his anger because he is afraid he will lose further that which he desires. The nonulcer personalities, Dr. Weiner found, were, in contrast, less dependent, more narcissistic and freer in expressing their anger.

Weiner's findings are similar to those of William J. Grace, M.D., Stewart Wolf, M.D., and Harold G. Wolff, M.D., who analyzed 19 patients who had been plagued by ulcerative colitis for six months to 24 years. Psychiatric interviews exposed these characteristics: overdependence on parents, which reflected itself in a need to please other people. One patient said, "I can't stand having anybody mad at me."

Other characteristics of the ulcer personality that have emerged from these and other studies are tendencies to be tidy, prim, mild, mannerly, conscientious, punctual and inhibited. People with such personalities are also thin-skinned, alert to real or imagined assaults from the world. They fear rejection and thus make few advances to other people; however, they form strong attachments, usually toward older persons, whom they often end up marrying. The male ulcer patients tend to marry wives who are mother substitutes.

Still another illness that seems to arise from parental interactions in early childhood is asthma. But unlike cancer, which seems to stem from a lonely, unhappy childhood; rheumatoid arthritis, which seems to strike persons having overly strict parents; and unlike ulcers, which seem to develop in individuals who are overly dependent on Mother; asthma's origin is not so clear-cut. Some evidence suggests that it too strikes those who are overly dependent on their parents. Other evidence, however, suggests that it assails those whose parents are not concerned enough about them. Two case histories cited by Pinkerton in the *British Medical Journal* illustrate both theories.

James, age 10, is a mild asthmatic whose breathing is virtually unimpaired; yet he goes to the doctor often and frequently misses school. He is an only child, born after three abortions, and is said to have been a weakling as a baby. When he first developed asthma at age four, both parents became acutely concerned and stayed up nights with him.

John, age nine, on the other hand, has been asthmatic since infancy and still spends a lot of time in the hospital. John's father was away from home for long periods when the boy was younger. The father is as intolerant of illness in others as he is in himself and constantly exorts the boy to do away with his medicine. John's mother has a better understanding of the problem but is unable to influence her husband. There is now a two-year-old sister who is asthma-free and clearly the father's favorite. As a result, John resents his asthma and tries to suppress symptoms and medication when he really needs it.

James, Pinkerton concludes, illustrates the asthma personality that arises from having overly protective parents. John, he says, illustrates the asthma personality caused by parents who don't evidence enough concern.

If the asthma personality is hard to pin down, the migraine personality is even more diffuse. Wolff studied 46 migraine sufferers and found that nine-tenths of them were "unusually ambitious and preoccupied with achievement and success." But this was an Anglo-American study. German studies show a link between hysteria, depression and migraines. For example, Gerhard S. Barolin, M.D., of the University Nerve Clinic in Vienna studied 450 migraine sufferers over a decade and found that many of them were prone to hysteria and depression. But then some French studies depict the migraine victim as a bon vivant— a happy-go-lucky type who likes to dine and make love.

Are there national differences among migraine victims? "I doubt it," Barolin replies. "More likely these are different interpretations of very 'soft' data."

Soft data, yes, that is the weak link in all the studies tying certain personalities with certain diseases. Thoughts, emotions and behavior are incredibly complex and even tougher to link up with specific physiological events in the body. "There is no shortage of data relating disease to psychosocial factors," Walter Reed's Mason admits. "The shortage is in the mediating mechanisms."

Still, investigators are making progress in this direction. Friedman and Rosenman, for example, have hard-core evidence that Type A behavior leads to a marked rise of cholesterol in the blood—a major risk factor in heart disease. In a pilot study, the Bahnsons have found a strong correlation between depression in psychiatric patients and lowered immune competence. Since the immune system is known to play a major role in warding off cancer, this finding could help explain why people with lonely, unhappy childhoods might be more prone to cancer.

Emotions have also been found to act on the brain's hypothalamus, and the hypothalamus links directly with the autonomic nervous system that controls chemical secretions in the gastrointestinal tract. So it is quite possible that if an ulcer personality is upset, an emotional disturbance will signal the hypothalamus, the autonomic nervous system and, in turn, gastric secretions in the stomach; and too much gastric secretion will set an ulcer into motion. Neal E. Miller, M.D., of Rockefeller University has also found that chronic fear increases gastric secretions in the stomachs of rats and gives them ulcers.

Numerous questions, of course, remain to be answered. How might the same personality trait, say fastidiousness, lead to ulcers in some people, yet to rheumatoid arthritis in others? Why don't all people with the same personality traits end up with the same diseases? Surely other factors must also enter the picture—such as sex, age, weight, certain stressful events—that trigger the disease or genetic predisposition to it. The cancer personality, for example, might not get a tumor unless he has also inherited a defective immune system. The rheumatoid arthritis personality would probably not develop that disease unless some event in her life deprived her of her usual outlets for personal fulfillment. Perhaps the ulcer personality would not develop an ulcer unless he had also inherited an overly active stomach.

Even with this constellation of factors to be considered, though, the link between personality and disease susceptibility is becoming even more compelling. This is the admission of physicians who are in the vanguard, and they are attempting to impress this fact on their less astute (or less open-minded) colleagues. For instance, Irvine H. Page, M.D., editor of the medical publication with the world's largest circulation, *Modern Medicine*, recently admonished his physician readers: "The sensible physician will recognize and evaluate personality types in relation to other risk factors."

Cancer and the Mind:
How Are They Connected?

The notion that the emotions are related to the onset and course of cancer is an ancient one. The 2nd-century physician Galen is said to have observed that women with melancholic dispositions seemed more inclined to breast cancer than those of a sanguine bent.

Scientists nowadays put little stock in such an idea. Nonetheless there is a modest body of research that tentatively links psychological stress and certain emotional characteristics to cancer.

Growing interest in the psychosomatic aspects of cancer is reflected in the publicity spurred by an epidemiological study of medical students begun in 1946 by Caroline Bedell Thomas of Johns Hopkins Medical School. Thomas used psychological tests given the students in medical school, plus yearly questionnaires about their health and living habits, to discover the precursors of five conditions: coronary heart disease, hypertension, mental disorders, malignant tumors, and suicide. She used cancer as a disorder that was presumably not related to psychological factors; but a "striking and unexpected" finding was that the psychological profiles of those who have developed cancer (48 as of last year) bore strong similarities to those who committed suicide. They were generally "low-gear" people, little given to expressions of emotion, whose relationships with their parents had been much more cold and remote than those of individuals who developed other kinds of diseases.

Other preliminary findings have recently been reported by Nicholas Rogentine, immunologist at the National Cancer Institute (NCI) who has found that among patients successfully operated on for malignant melanoma in stages I and II, patients who relapsed had tended to minimize the significance of their illness. This supports the theory that repression and denial is related to poor prognosis.

Interest in studies relating psychological factors and stress to cancer is growing apace. The NCI, for example, has recently funded several large epidemiological studies that are attempting to see whether psychological factors are pre-

dictive of the disease. A number of factors are contributing to this phenomenon. According to NCI's Bernard Fox new information on the immune system—particularly evidence that the hypothalamus has a major effect on its functioning—is opening the way for research that could link specific emotions to specific biochemical events. And the fast-blooming area of behavioral medicine provides a favorable context for these initiatives to flourish. Also, evidence supplied by research with biofeedback and behavior modification has demonstrated the extent to which the mind can influence physiological processes hitherto thought to be inaccessible to voluntary control.

Theories about psychological precursors of cancer cluster around several related notions—about "helplessness and hopelessness"; denial and repression of negative emotions, particularly anger; and inability to cope successfully with a severe emotional loss. Some of these ideas were explored in the years surrounding World War II when psychosomatic medicine was developing and psychoanalysis was enjoying its heyday in America. Rapid advances in biomedical research shifted interest away from these concerns.

Some Americans are now taking a new look at some studies that were conducted after the war in England and America. One of the best known researchers was internist D. M. Kissen of the University of Glasgow who did psychological studies of industrial workers (all of them smokers), comparing those with various lung ailments, primarily tuberculosis, with those whose diagnoses were subsequently found to be cancer. He found that cancer victims suffered particularly from denial and repression of their emotions—they had "poor outlet for emotional discharge," as measured by personality tests used to gauge "neuroticism." Cancer victims scored very low, which Kissen took to indicate low emotional lability. He believed that smokers who got cancer had different personalities from the general population

of smokers, who tend to score high on neuroticism. He concluded that the more repressed the individual, the fewer cigarettes it took to induce cancer.

Cancers of breast and reproductive organs in women have also come under considerable scrutiny. Arthur Schmale of the University of Rochester 10 years ago set up a project to see if he could predict cancer through psychological means. With women who had suspicious cell changes in the cervix, he conducted interviews and administered the Minnesota Multiphasic Personality Inventory (MMPI). Looking for "hopelessness" and recent emotional losses, he predicted correctly in 36 cases out of 51 which women would turn out on further examination to have cancer.

A more recent study (1975) by S. Greer and T. Morris at Kings College Hospital in London found that inappropriate coping with anger—usually suppression, but sometimes extreme expression—was correlated with discovery of breast malignancy in women coming for examination of lumps.

Another oft-cited researcher whose work was done in the 1950's is William Greene, internist and professor of psychiatry at the University of Rochester. He tested patients with leukemia and Hodgkin's disease and found that "the manifest development of the disease occurred in a setting of emotional distress." In nine out of ten cases, he says, the time the disease develops is when a person feels alone, helpless, and hopeless.

A recent study has added to the sparse existing data on whether emotional states affect the prognosis once patients are diagnosed with cancer. At Johns Hopkins Medical School Leonard Derogatis, a psychologist, and oncologist Martin Abeloff surveyed 35 women with breast cancer. They found that the women who expressed a high degree of anger toward not only their disease but their doctors lived longer than those who were pliant and cooperative. Arbitrarily setting 1 year as the dividing line for survival, the doctors found that the women who were good at "externalizing nega-

 From *Science*, Vol. 200 p. 1363, 23 June 1978. Copyright 1978 by the American Association for the Advancement of Science.

tive affects" did better even though that group, had, if anything, a poorer prognosis than those who succumbed quickly. "I was cynical about there being any difference," says Derogatis, but it did appear that the fighters had a better chance.

A pioneer in the field of cancer and personality is New York psychologist Lawrence LeShan. LeShan is pretty much a lone wolf, and is regarded as something of an extremist even by those who respect his ideas. Nonetheless he is perhaps unique in the degree to which he has been involved with the emotional lives of cancer patients. LeShan conducted a study lasting from 1952 to 1964 of more than 400 cancer patients (the only major types of cancer he did not encounter were those of blood and lymph, he says), using various psychological tests and interviews. In addition, he did more than 100 hours of psychotherapy apiece with 71 of the patients. He found that 72 percent of the patients had suffered the loss of a central relationship in the period ranging from 8 years to a few months prior to the onset of the disease—compared to 10 percent in a control group of people in psychotherapy for other reasons. And, unlike the controls, most of the cancer patients evinced a profound sense of "despair"—feelings of futility and isolation that were beyond emotion—that he claims they had lived with for many years before they got ill.

Currently, Klaus Bahnson, a psychologist and psychoanalyst at Eastern Pennsylvania Psychiatric Institute, is one of few researchers to be studying cancer from a predominantly psychoanalytic viewpoint. He has proposed a theory of "complementarity" between somatic and emotional disorders: in some people, he believes, irresolvable conflicts may build to the extent that the only way out is psychosis, while in others, cancer is the ultimate route. In a test in which cancer victims and others were asked to assign adjectives to various neutral sounds (a sort of auditory Rorschach test), he found that cancer patients used more benign and positive adjectives than did others. This was construed as evidence that cancer victims are more likely to repress negative emotions.

The kinds of investigations cited above hold considerable attraction for psychologists and psychiatrists but they do not even begin to take into account the differing etiologies of different kinds of cancers, or the vast range of genetic,

environmental, viral, age-related, and other factors that have been identified with cancer. Omitted from any of these studies is an attempt to identify mediating mechanisms—immunological or endocrinological—that might translate emotions into neoplasms. And as Fox pointedly remarks, in a lengthy paper discussing the problems of research in the field, psychological examination of people who already have cancer (whether or not the diagnosis is known at the time) is almost tautological. "To the researchers who claim to have shown differences between cancer and well patients, I say that you are all probably right." Says Fox, "Cancer patients *are* different." But the psychological differences may be ascribable to hormonal changes associated with the disease.

Therefore, what is needed, on the one hand, are biochemical studies linking immunological and hormonal events to particular emotions; on the other hand is a requirement for data that can only be gained through long-term prospective studies of large populations.

The NCI in 1975 issued a request for proposals on projects related to personality, stress, and cancer. Two studies were funded as a result.

One, conducted by Ralph Paffenbarger of Stanford University, is looking for occurrence of cancer and heart attacks among two groups of male college graduates—36,000 who entered Harvard between 1916 and 1950, and 14,000 who entered the University of Pennsylvania between 1931 and 1940. All the men had psychological tests in college and have been filling out periodic questionnaires about health, jobs, habits, and so forth. Paffenbarger hasn't completed analysis of his data, but he says "My guess is there is no relationship between psychosocial factors and the risk of getting cancer."

The other study is headed by Richard B. Shekelle, epidemiologist at Rush Presbyterian–St. Luke's Medical Center in Chicago, who is looking at psychological data obtained from 2107 workers at a Western Electric Company plant who were tested several times between 1958 and 1962. Eighty-two of the men, who are now between 60 and 75, had died of cancer by 1975. Shekelle expects the final tally to be about 300. Relying mostly on the MMPI, he is looking for correlations between cancer and two psychological states: depression, and denial and repression.

The only other related extramural NCI grant that *Science* learned of was to Frances Cohen of Langley Porter Neuropsychiatric Institute, who is looking at the role of early childhood factors in cancer and heart disease. She is using data from two detailed longitudinal studies—the Berkeley Guidance Study and the Oakland Growth Study—begun when the subjects were children. They are now middle-aged and haven't developed many diseases yet. Cohen is skeptical about the theories on loss, repression, and denial. Her hypothesis is geared to uncovering the relation of life stresses to the availability of emotional supports.

So far, the evidence linking emotional states with specific hormonal states, and the hormonal activity with specific immune functions or with direct action on tumors, is sparse indeed. The study of malignant melanoma patients by Rogentine of NCI includes the collection of immunological and endocrinological data for an integrated psychological-physiological profile of those patients in whom the disease recurs, but he doesn't have any results yet.

Several studies have been cited that contribute little fragments to the biochemical picture. John Mason, neuroendocrinologist at Yale, found that levels of a certain adrenocortical hormone (17-hydroxy-corticosteroid) were raised in the mothers of leukemic children. He has also found it raised in the urine of Army recruits who had lost their mothers, although it was lowered among those who lost their fathers. He concluded there was an interaction between parental loss, one's psychologic defenses, and one's hormone level—although the complexity of the matter is obvious from the fact that different kinds of loss were associated with different hormonal reactions.

Another researcher is Vernon Riley of Pacific Northwest Research Foundation, who has conducted two novel studies with mice. In one, he concluded that high levels of corticosteroids lower immune function, because, when he injected the animals with a corticosteroid antagonist, immune function was restored. In the other study he found that mice injected with mammary tumor virus developed tumors much more quickly in a stressful atmosphere (where adrenal output increased) than in a protected environment.

In a unique study with humans, J. W. Bartrop of the University of New South

5. INDIVIDUAL DIFFERENCES

Wales in Australia found function of T cells (part of the immune system) significantly depressed in 26 people, aged 20 to 65, who were grieving over the loss of a spouse.

Clearly, it's going to be a while before biochemical research establishes the role of the mind in precipitating cancer, or of that ill-defined but potent factor—"the will to live"—in mobilizing physical defenses once the disease has set in.

Nonetheless, for a growing cadre of people involved in the psychological treatment of cancer victims, the evidence, while not definitive, is enough. "The [psychological] treatment should be based on good solid research, but we are doing it anyway because we don't want to condemn a lot of people to death," says psychologist Charles Bustya of the Morton Prince Clinic for Hypnosis in New York. Bustya considers himself one of the "second generation" of therapists spawned by Carl Simonton, a radiation oncologist in Fort Worth, Texas, and his wife, Stephanie, a psychologist. Many hospitals are now offering psychological support programs to help patients and their families cope with the disease, but the Simontons go beyond that. Their aim is not only to help patients improve the quality of their lives, but to prolong their survival. Influenced by the growing evidence of links between psychological stress and various illness—particularly the plethora of cardiovascular and gastrointestinal disorders—as well as by theories associating particular emotional configurations with diseases as varied as diabetes and arthritis, Simonton and others think it very likely that cancer belongs on the list of stress-related disorders.

And if that is the case, they believe that people may be able to influence the course of their disease by reversing the psychological processes that precipitated it. After all, people have learned through biofeedback, hypnosis, and even simple relaxation techniques to regulate the muscles under the control of the autonomic nervous system so they can reduce hypertension and migraines, for example. People have also learned to control their perception of pain by altering their focus of attention; similarly they have learned to stave off epileptic attacks by slowing down activity in the abnormal brain foci where the attacks are triggered. If all this is possible, it seems reasonable to some people that cancer patients can also gain control over endocrine functions that affect the immune system, or whatever other physiological processes that govern the course of the disease.

It is on premises such as these that the Simontons have founded the Cancer Counseling and Research Center, a private outfit that in the minds of some people is merely a successor to Laetrile, and to others is the generative force in a new and effective approach to helping cancer victims battle their disease. The Simontons are particularly interested in imagery, a technique associated with such practices as biofeedback and hypnosis. In the treatment, used in conjunction with medical therapy, patients are encouraged to visualize and draw pictures of their cancers and what they think—or hope—is happening in their bodies. They depict their cancer cells and, in often highly symbolic images, show how they think radiation and drugs are affecting the tumor. They are encouraged to see their white blood cells charging in, swarming over the cancer cells, and demolishing them. In conjunction with relaxation and visualization exercises, patients are invited to examine how they may have participated in bringing on the disease and to learn ways of overcoming old angers and resentment and to confront their fears about death. The basic idea is to help people gain a sense that they have control over what's happening to them. The imagery is thought to be a very sensitive reflection of a patient's emotional state and therefore his prospects for improvement. People who can't envisage their white cells in an aggressive role, for example, are thought to have difficulty expressing anger.

Jeanne Achterberg, a psychologist at the University of Texas Health Science Center, has found imagery a useful tool in predicting the course of a number of diseases including cancer. She and Frank Lawlis of North Texas State University surveyed 126 patients who had elected to follow the Simonton treatment, 90 percent of whom had widely metastasized cancers. They found that results of psychological tests, particularly imagery, were more predictive of length of survival than the status of the disease as determined through a battery of blood chemistry tests. "Blood chemistries," they wrote, "are merely reflective of the body's current status. . . . Psychological factors, on the other hand, seem to foretell or precede certain physical response patterns."

The Simontons claim in a book published this year* that after 4 years they had treated 159 patients with "medically incurable" malignancies and average life expectancies of a year. They claim that of those who died the average survival time was 20.3 months. Of the 63 surviving, 22.2 percent then had "no evidence of disease," and tumors were regressing in 19 percent. (This result is similar to that claimed by LeShan. He has had about 40 allegedly incurable patients in therapy over the last dozen years and he says half of them are now "well.")

There are those who wish the Simontons would talk less (they are currently engaged in a book-publicizing tour) and publish more. So far, they have only contributed two articles to the scientific literature; the latest is a comparison between two very small patient populations who are defined only by their diseases (multiple and metastasized) and their psychological states. Those whose survival exceeds their doctors' expectations are described as professionally successful, aggressive, verbal, scrappy, and generally active.

Among groups who have taken their cues from the Simontons is the Newton Center for Clinical Hypnosis in Los Angeles. Psychologist Bernauer Newton says they use a Simonton-type approach augmented by hypnosis, which is useful in alleviating nausea, pain, insomnia, and other side effects of treatment as well as in enhancing the effectiveness of visualization exercises. "We believe that psychological factors in many cases influence the onset and the progression of the disease," says Newton. "Over and over and over" he sees individuals who have difficulty expressing strong emotions, who feel unwanted, who have few satisfactions in life—a state that appears to have existed for a long time prior to the onset of the disease.

Psychologist Bustya, who is in New York on leave from the Newton Center, also claims to see a preponderance of characteristics among patients that—according to testimony from spouses and friends—long predated the disease. Many, he says, have a lifelong history of unsuccessful coping mechanisms; an inability to express strong emotions, particularly anger; inhibition, self-con-

*Getting Well Again (J. P. Tarcher, Inc., Los Angeles, 1978), a book written for patients and their families.

sciousness, conformity to the expectations of others, strong "giving-up feelings," and "an awful lot of self-sacrifice."

Those involved in this treatment movement readily acknowledge that their patient population is self-selected (those whose relatives shove them into it rarely do well, says Bustya); furthermore, the Simontons are reluctant to accept patients who they feel have such negative attitudes that they don't stand to profit. Both agree that a patient's acceptance of the basic premises—that their attitudes can affect the course of their disease—and a willingness to work are crucial to positive outcomes.

The Simontons and others emphasize that their program is complementary to, and not a substitute for, orthodox medical therapy. Physicians are described as sympathetic to the treatment so long as no one holds out promises of miracle cures. Nonetheless, there are those who believe the movement could get out of hand, offering false hope in lieu of proven medical therapies.

Jimmie Holland, chief of Sloan-Kettering's psychiatry service and a woman who knows about research in the psychology-cancer area, thinks things have already gotten out of hand. She says there are no scientific data linking psychological factors to cancer, either in predisposing a person to the disease or in determining how well a cancer patient will respond to treatment. She believes that the Simontons, therefore, are perpetrating a "cruel hoax—worse than Laetrile."

The Simontons, however, are trying to directly evoke, through imagery and suggestion, the same activity that Laetrile occasionally appears to evoke through its placebo effect. Elmer Green of the Menninger Foundation, a leading biofeedback researcher, says "the placebo effect is where it's at." Says Green, "Everybody knows there is such a thing as a placebo effect but they don't think about what it is."

Obviously, says Green, it is an activation of the body's self-regulatory mechanisms produced by the individual's expectation. The most startling example of this effect is manifested in the rare cases of sudden remission from cancer. No one knows what causes them, but according to NCI's Fox, investigators have found that "very powerful belief" is the common factor in such cases.†

Potential research has been greatly impeded by the fact that biochemists don't know about psychology and psychologists don't know about biochemistry. Thus we have psychotherapists at one end of the spectrum and mouse researchers at the other and no communication between them. These types, in addition to specialists in epidemiology, genetics, environmental carcinogens, and clinical oncology, will have to be brought together in team efforts if scattered hints are ever going to become merged in a fuller picture. As Bernard Fox wrote in his paper (which, as published in the first issue of the *Journal of Behavioral Medicine*, has 417 references): "It is, truly, a most difficult type of research."

—CONSTANCE HOLDEN

---

†One thought-provoking case history, reported by Bruno Klopfer in *Psychological Variables in Human Cancer*: A man with advanced lymphosarcoma was included in an experimental study of the since-discredited drug Krebiozen. After one administration, his tumors disappeared. When reports came out that the drug was ineffective he again became bedridden. His physician, in a last-ditch attempt to save him, told him not to believe what he read and treated him with "double strength" Krebiozen—actually an injection of water. The man again experienced rapid remission. Then the AMA and FDA pronounced the drug worthless. The man died within a few days.

Disorders and Therapy

One aspect of psychology, that of diagnosing and treating disorders, is widely recognized. But a major issue within the field of clinical psychology today is whether or not psychological disorders should be thought of in terms of "mental illness." Many people take for granted (and are satisfied with) the historical change from regarding the disordered as possessed by demons to regarding them as suffering from a sickness comparable to a physical illness. In recent years, however, a number of psychologists have begun to contest the "illness" point of view.

Psychiatric labeling may have seriously detrimental effects on mental patients, their families, and the psychiatric community itself. "On Being Sane in Insane Places" challenges basic psychiatric concepts and practices, charging that psychiatric diagnosis is often a self-fulfilling prophecy. "More on Pseudoscience in Science and the Case for Psychiatric Diagnosis" takes up the challenge, discussing the central issues involved in psychiatric diagnosis.

Another approach to mental illness—using pharmacological treatment—is covered in "Medical Treatment of Mental Illness" and "The Second Death of Sigmund Freud," in which organic therapy is compared to classic psychoanalysis. "New Light on Schizophrenia" investigates the origins and development of this disorder.

Not all disorders are considered "illnesses" or insanity. Some, like boredom and depression, are occasionally experienced by most of us. It is when these disorders become chronic that they are serious problems. Depression—its causes, symptoms, and treatment—is the subject of two articles, "A Darkness at Noon" and "The Age of Melancholy."

A number of different kinds of psychotherapy and chemical therapies are used in treating mental disorders. It is important that the patient be familiar with the alternative therapies that are available. Morris Parloff provides an overview of the field in "Shopping for the Right Therapy," outlining the basics of analysis, behavior, humanistic and transpersonal therapies, and others.

A review of this section will provide some insight into the central issues of mental disorder. The most common forms of mental disorder—schizophrenia, depression, phobia—are discussed, as well as the variety and forms of therapy currently available.

Looking Ahead: Challenge Questions

How can psychiatric diagnosis serve to perpetuate mental disorder?

What are some potential roles of nonprofessionals in the field of psychotherapy?

On Being Sane in Insane Places

D. L. Rosenhan

The author is professor of psychology and law at Stanford University, Stanford, California 94305. Portions of these data were presented to colloquiums of the psychology departments at the University of California at Berkeley and at Santa Barbara; University of Arizona, Tucson; and Harvard University, Cambridge, Massachusetts.

If sanity and insanity exist, how shall we know them?

The question is neither capricious nor itself insane. However much we may be personally convinced that we can tell the normal from the abnormal, the evidence is simply not compelling. It is commonplace, for example, to read about murder trials wherein eminent psychiatrists for the defense are contradicted by equally eminent psychiatrists for the prosecution on the matter of the defendant's sanity. More generally, there are a great deal of conflicting data on the reliability, utility, and meaning of such terms as "sanity," "insanity," "mental illness," and "schizophrenia" (1). Finally, as early as 1934, Benedict suggested that normality and abnormality are not universal (2). What is viewed as normal in one culture may be seen as quite aberrant in another. Thus, notions of normality and abnormality may not be quite as accurate as people believe they are.

To raise questions regarding normality and abnormality is in no way to question the fact that some behaviors are deviant or odd. Murder is deviant. So, too, are hallucinations. Nor does raising such questions deny the existence of the personal anguish that is often associated with "mental illness." Anxiety and depression exist. Psychological suffering exists. But normality and abnormality, sanity and insanity, and the diagnoses that flow from them may be less substantive than many believe them to be.

At its heart, the question of whether the sane can be distinguished from the insane (and whether degrees of insanity can be distinguished from each other) is a simple matter: do the salient characteristics that lead to diagnoses reside in the patients themselves or in the environments and contexts in which observers find them? From Bleuler, through Kretchmer, through the formulators of the recently revised *Diagnostic and Statistical Manual* of the American Psychiatric Association, the belief has been strong that patients present symptoms, that those symptoms can be categorized, and, implicitly, that the sane are distinguishable from the insane. More recently, however, this belief has been questioned. Based in part on theoretical and anthropological considerations, but also on philosophical, legal, and therapeutic ones, the view has grown that psychological categorization of mental illness is useless at best and downright harmful, misleading, and pejorative at worst. Psychiatric diagnoses, in this view, are in the minds of the observers and are not valid summaries of characteristics displayed by the observed (3–5).

Gains can be made in deciding which of these is more nearly accurate by getting normal people (that is, people who do not have, and have never suffered, symptoms of serious psychiatric disorders) admitted to psychiatric hospitals and then determining whether they were discovered to be sane and, if so, how. If the sanity of such pseudopatients were always detected, there would be prima facie evidence that a sane individual can be distinguished from the insane context in which he is found. Normality (and presumably abnormality) is distinct enough that it can be recognized wherever it occurs, for it is carried within the person. If, on the other hand, the sanity of the pseudopatients were never discovered, serious difficulties would arise for those who support traditional modes of psychiatric diagnosis. Given that the hospital staff was not incompetent, that the pseudopatient had been behaving as sanely as he had been outside of the hospital, and that it had never been previously suggested that he belonged in a psychiatric hospital, such an unlikely outcome would support the view that psychiatric diagnosis betrays little about the patient but much about the environment in which an observer finds him.

This article describes such an experiment. Eight sane people gained secret admission to 12 different hospitals (6). Their diagnostic experiences constitute the data of the first part of this article; the remainder is devoted to a description of their experiences in psychiatric institutions. Too few psychiatrists and psychologists, even those who have worked in such hospitals, know what the experience is like. They rarely talk about it with former patients, perhaps because they distrust information coming from the previously insane. Those who have worked in psychiatric hospitals are likely to have adapted so thoroughly to the settings that they are insensitive to the impact of that experience. And while there have been occasional reports of researchers who submitted themselves to psychiatric hospitalization (7), these researchers have commonly remained in the hospitals for short periods of time, often with the knowledge of the hospital staff. It is difficult to know the extent to which they were treated like patients or like research colleagues. Nevertheless, their reports about the inside of the psychiatric hospital have been valuable. This article extends those efforts.

Pseudopatients and Their Settings

The eight pseudopatients were a

From *Science*, January 19, 1973, by D. L. Rosenhan, Vol. 179, pp. 250-258. Copyright © 1973 by the American Association for the Advancement of Science.

varied group. One was a psychology graduate student in his 20's. The remaining seven were older and "established." Among them were three psychologists, a pediatrician, a psychiatrist, a painter, and a housewife. Three pseudopatients were women, five were men. All of them employed pseudonyms, lest their alleged diagnoses embarrass them later. Those who were in mental health professions alleged another occupation in order to avoid the special attentions that might be accorded by staff, as a matter of courtesy or caution, to ailing colleagues (8). With the exception of myself (I was the first pseudopatient and my presence was known to the hospital administrator and chief psychologist and, so far as I can tell, to them alone), the presence of pseudopatients and the nature of the research program was not known to the hospital staffs (9).

The settings were similarly varied. In order to generalize the findings, admission into a variety of hospitals was sought. The 12 hospitals in the sample were located in five different states on the East and West coasts. Some were old and shabby, some were quite new. Some were research-oriented, others not. Some had good staff-patient ratios, others were quite understaffed. Only one was a strictly private hospital. All of the others were supported by state or federal funds or, in one instance, by university funds.

After calling the hospital for an appointment, the pseudopatient arrived at the admissions office complaining that he had been hearing voices. Asked what the voices said, he replied that they were often unclear, but as far as he could tell they said "empty," "hollow," and "thud." The voices were unfamiliar and were of the same sex as the pseudopatient. The choice of these symptoms was occasioned by their apparent similarity to existential symptoms. Such symptoms are alleged to arise from painful concerns about the perceived meaninglessness of one's life. It is as if the hallucinating person were saying, "My life is empty and hollow." The choice of these symptoms was also determined by the *absence* of a single report of existential psychoses in the literature.

Beyond alleging the symptoms and falsifying name, vocation, and employment, no further alterations of person,

history, or circumstances were made. The significant events of the pseudopatient's life history were presented as they had actually occurred. Relationships with parents and siblings, with spouse and children, with people at work and in school, consistent with the aforementioned exceptions, were described as they were or had been. Frustrations and upsets were described along with joys and satisfactions. These facts are important to remember. If anything, they strongly biased the subsequent results in favor of detecting sanity, since none of their histories or current behaviors were seriously pathological in any way.

Immediately upon admission to the psychiatric ward, the pseudopatient ceased simulating *any* symptoms of abnormality. In some cases, there was a brief period of mild nervousness and anxiety, since none of the pseudopatients really believed that they would be admitted so easily. Indeed, their shared fear was that they would be immediately exposed as frauds and greatly embarrassed. Moreover, many of them had never visited a psychiatric ward; even those who had, nevertheless had some genuine fears about what might happen to them. Their nervousness, then, was quite appropriate to the novelty of the hospital setting, and it abated rapidly.

Apart from that short-lived nervousness, the pseudopatient behaved on the ward as he "normally" behaved. The pseudopatient spoke to patients and staff as he might ordinarily. Because there is uncommonly little to do on a psychiatric ward, he attempted to engage others in conversation. When asked by staff how he was feeling, he indicated that he was fine, that he no longer experienced symptoms. He responded to instructions from attendants, to calls for medication (which was not swallowed), and to dining-hall instructions. Beyond such activities as were available to him on the admissions ward, he spent his time writing down his observations about the ward, its patients, and the staff. Initially these notes were written "secretly," but as it soon became clear that no one much cared, they were subsequently written on standard tablets of paper in such public places as the dayroom. No secret was made of these activities.

The pseudopatient, very much as a

true psychiatric patient, entered a hospital with no foreknowledge of when he would be discharged. Each was told that he would have to get out by his own devices, essentially by convincing the staff that he was sane. The psychological stresses associated with hospitalization were considerable, and all but one of the pseudopatients desired to be discharged almost immediately after being admitted. They were, therefore, motivated not only to behave sanely, but to be paragons of cooperation. That their behavior was in no way disruptive is confirmed by nursing reports, which have been obtained on most of the patients. These reports uniformly indicate that the patients were "friendly," "cooperative," and "exhibited no abnormal indications."

The Normal Are Not Detectably Sane

Despite their public "show" of sanity, the pseudopatients were never detected. Admitted, except in one case, with a diagnosis of schizophrenia (10), each was discharged with a diagnosis of schizophrenia "in remission." The label "in remission" should in no way be dismissed as a formality, for at no time during any hospitalization had any question been raised about any pseudopatient's simulation. Nor are there any indications in the hospital records that the pseudopatient's status was suspect. Rather, the evidence is strong that, once labeled schizophrenic, the pseudopatient was stuck with that label. If the pseudopatient was to be discharged, he must naturally be "in remission"; but he was not sane, nor, in the institution's view, had he ever been sane.

The uniform failure to recognize sanity cannot be attributed to the quality of the hospitals, for, although there were considerable variations among them, several are considered excellent. Nor can it be alleged that there was simply not enough time to observe the pseudopatients. Length of hospitalization ranged from 7 to 52 days, with an average of 19 days. The pseudopatients were not, in fact, carefully observed, but this failure clearly speaks more to traditions within psychiatric hospitals than to lack of opportunity.

Finally, it cannot be said that the failure to recognize the pseudopatients' sanity was due to the fact that they were not behaving sanely. While there was clearly some tension present in all of them, their daily visitors could detect no serious behavioral consequences—nor, indeed, could other patients. It was quite common for the patients to "detect" the pseudopatients' sanity. During the first three hospitalizations, when accurate counts were kept, 35 of a total of 118 patients on the admissions ward voiced their suspicions, some vigorously. "You're not crazy. You're a journalist, or a professor [referring to the continual note-taking]. You're checking up on the hospital." While most of the patients were reassured by the pseudopatient's insistence that he had been sick before he came in but was fine now, some continued to believe that the pseudopatient was sane throughout his hospitalization (11). The fact that the patients often recognized normality when staff did not raises important questions.

Failure to detect sanity during the course of hospitalization may be due to the fact that physicians operate with a strong bias toward what statisticians call the type 2 error (5). This is to say that physicians are more inclined to call a healthy person sick (a false positive, type 2) than a sick person healthy (a false negative, type 1). The reasons for this are not hard to find: it is clearly more dangerous to misdiagnose illness than health. Better to err on the side of caution, to suspect illness even among the healthy.

But what holds for medicine does not hold equally well for psychiatry. Medical illnesses, while unfortunate, are not commonly pejorative. Psychiatric diagnoses, on the contrary, carry with them personal, legal, and social stigmas (12). It was therefore important to see whether the tendency toward diagnosing the sane insane could be reversed. The following experiment was arranged at a research and teaching hospital whose staff had heard these findings but doubted that such an error could occur in their hospital. The staff was informed that at some time during the following 3 months, one or more pseudopatients would attempt to be admitted into the psychiatric hospital. Each staff member was asked to rate each patient who presented himself at admissions or on the ward according to the likelihood that the patient was a pseudopatient. A 10-point scale was used, with a 1 and 2 reflecting high confidence that the pa-

tient was a pseudopatient.

Judgments were obtained on 193 patients who were admitted for psychiatric treatment. All staff who had had sustained contact with or primary responsibility for the patient—attendants, nurses, psychiatrists, physicians, and psychologists—were asked to make judgments. Forty-one patients were alleged, with high confidence, to be pseudopatients by at least one member of the staff. Twenty-three were considered suspect by at least one psychiatrist. Nineteen were suspected by one psychiatrist *and* one other staff member. Actually, no genuine pseudopatient (at least from my group) presented himself during this period.

The experiment is instructive. It indicates that the tendency to designate sane people as insane can be reversed when the stakes (in this case, prestige and diagnostic acumen) are high. But what can be said of the 19 people who were suspected of being "sane" by one psychiatrist and another staff member? Were these people truly "sane," or was it rather the case that in the course of avoiding the type 2 error the staff tended to make more errors of the first sort—calling the crazy "sane"? There is no way of knowing. But one thing is certain: any diagnostic process that lends itself so readily to massive errors of this sort cannot be a very reliable one.

The Stickiness of
Psychodiagnostic Labels

Beyond the tendency to call the healthy sick—a tendency that accounts better for diagnostic behavior on admission than it does for such behavior after a lengthy period of exposure—the data speak to the massive role of labeling in psychiatric assessment. Having once been labeled schizophrenic, there is nothing the pseudopatient can do to overcome the tag. The tag profoundly colors others' perceptions of him and his behavior.

From one viewpoint, these data are hardly surprising, for it has long been known that elements are given meaning by the context in which they occur. Gestalt psychology made this point vigorously, and Asch (13) demonstrated that there are "central" personality traits (such as "warm" versus

"cold") which are so powerful that they markedly color the meaning of other information in forming an impression of a given personality (14). "Insane," "schizophrenic," "manic-depressive," and "crazy" are probably among the most powerful of such central traits. Once a person is designated abnormal, all of his other behaviors and characteristics are colored by that label. Indeed, that label is so powerful that many of the pseudopatients' normal behaviors were overlooked entirely or profoundly misinterpreted. Some examples may clarify this issue.

Earlier I indicated that there were no changes in the pseudopatient's personal history and current status beyond those of name, employment, and, where necessary, vocation. Otherwise, a veridical description of personal history and circumstances was offered. Those circumstances were not psychotic. How were they made consonant with the diagnosis of psychosis? Or were those diagnoses modified in such a way as to bring them into accord with the circumstances of the pseudopatient's life, as described by him?

As far as I can determine, diagnoses were in no way affected by the relative health of the circumstances of a pseudopatient's life. Rather, the reverse occurred: the perception of his circumstances was shaped entirely by the diagnosis. A clear example of such translation is found in the case of a pseudopatient who had had a close relationship with his mother but was rather remote from his father during his early childhool. During adolescence and beyond, however, his father became a close friend, while his relationship with his mother cooled. His present relationship with his wife was characteristically close and warm. Apart from occasional angry exchanges, friction was minimal. The children had rarely been spanked. Surely there is nothing especially pathological about such a history. Indeed, many readers may see a similar pattern in their own experiences, with no markedly deleterious consequences. Observe, however, how such a history was translated in the psychopathological context, this from the case summary prepared after the patient was discharged.

This white 39-year-old male . . . manifests a long history of considerable ambivalence in close relationships, which begins in early childhood. A warm relationship with his mother cools during his adolescence. A distant relationship to his father is described as becoming very intense. Affective stability is absent. His attempts to control emotionality with his wife and children are punctuated by angry outbursts and, in the case of the children, spankings. And while he says that he has several good friends, one senses considerable ambivalence embedded in those relationships also. . . .

The facts of the case were unintentionally distorted by the staff to achieve consistency with a popular theory of the dynamics of a schizophrenic reaction (15). Nothing of an ambivalent nature had been described in relations with parents, spouse, or friends. To the extent that ambivalence could be inferred, it was probably not greater than is found in all human relationships. It is true the pseudopatient's relationships with his parents changed over time, but in the ordinary context that would hardly be remarkable—indeed, it might very well be expected. Clearly, the meaning ascribed to his verbalizations (that is, ambivalence, affective instability) was determined by the diagnosis: schizophrenia. An entirely different meaning would have been ascribed if it were known that the man was "normal."

All pseudopatients took extensive notes publicly. Under ordinary circumstances, such behavior would have raised questions in the minds of observers, as, in fact, it did among patients. Indeed, it seemed so certain that the notes would elicit suspicion that elaborate precautions were taken to remove them from the ward each day. But the precautions proved needless. The closest any staff member came to questioning these notes occurred when one pseudopatient asked his physician what kind of medication he was receiving and began to write down the response. "You needn't write it," he was told gently. "If you have trouble remembering, just ask me again."

If no questions were asked of the pseudopatients, how was their writing interpreted? Nursing records for three patients indicate that the writing was seen as an aspect of their pathological behavior. "Patient engages in writing behavior" was the daily nursing comment on one of the pseudopatients who was never questioned about his writing. Given that the patient is in the hospital, he must be psychologically disturbed.

And given that he is disturbed, continuous writing must be a behavioral manifestation of that disturbance, perhaps a subset of the compulsive behaviors that are sometimes correlated with schizophrenia.

One tacit characteristic of psychiatric diagnosis is that it locates the sources of aberration within the individual and only rarely within the complex of stimuli that surrounds him. Consequently, behaviors that are stimulated by the environment are commonly misattributed to the patient's disorder. For example, one kindly nurse found a pseudopatient pacing the long hospital corridors. "Nervous, Mr. X?" she asked. "No, bored," he said.

The notes kept by pseudopatients are full of patient behaviors that were misinterpreted by well-intentioned staff. Often enough, a patient would go "berserk" because he had, wittingly or unwittingly, been mistreated by, say, an attendant. A nurse coming upon the scene would rarely inquire even cursorily into the environmental stimuli of the patient's behavior. Rather, she assumed that his upset derived from his pathology, not from his present interactions with other staff members. Occasionally, the staff might assume that the patient's family (especially when they had recently visited) or other patients had stimulated the outburst. But never were the staff found to assume that one of themselves or the structure of the hospital had anything to do with a patient's behavior. One psychiatrist pointed to a group of patients who were sitting outside the cafeteria entrance half an hour before lunchtime. To a group of young residents he indicated that such behavior was characteristic of the oral-acquisitive nature of the syndrome. It seemed not to occur to him that there were very few things to anticipate in a psychiatric hospital besides eating.

A psychiatric label has a life and an influence of its own. Once the impression has been formed that the patient is schizophrenic, the expectation is that he will continue to be schizophrenic. When a sufficient amount of time has passed, during which the patient has done nothing bizarre, he is considered to be in remission and available for discharge. But the label endures beyond discharge, with the unconfirmed expectation that he will behave as a schizo-

phrenic again. Such labels, conferred by mental health professionals, are as influential on the patient as they are on his relatives and friends, and it should not surprise anyone that the diagnosis acts on all of them as a self-fulfilling prophecy. Eventually, the patient himself accepts the diagnosis, with all of its surplus meanings and expectations, and behaves accordingly (5).

The inferences to be made from these matters are quite simple. Much as Zigler and Phillips have demonstrated that there is enormous overlap in the symptoms presented by patients who have been variously diagnosed (16), so there is enormous overlap in the behaviors of the sane and the insane. The sane are not "sane" all of the time. We lose our tempers "for no good reason." We are occasionally depressed or anxious, again for no good reason. And we may find it difficult to get along with one or another person—again for no reason that we can specify. Similarly, the insane are not always insane. Indeed, it was the impression of the pseudopatients while living with them that they were sane for long periods of time—that the bizarre behaviors upon which their diagnoses were allegedly predicated constituted only a small fraction of their total behavior. If it makes no sense to label ourselves permanently depressed on the basis of an occasional depression, then it takes better evidence than is presently available to label all patients insane or schizophrenic on the basis of bizarre behaviors or cognitions. It seems more useful, as Mischel (17) has pointed out, to limit our discussions to *behaviors*, the stimuli that provoke them, and their correlates.

It is not known why powerful impressions of personality traits, such as "crazy" or "insane," arise. Conceivably, when the origins of and stimuli that give rise to a behavior are remote or unknown, or when the behavior strikes us as immutable, trait labels regarding the *behaver* arise. When, on the other hand, the origins and stimuli are known and available, discourse is limited to the behavior itself. Thus, I may hallucinate because I am sleeping, or I may hallucinate because I have ingested a peculiar drug. These are termed sleep-induced hallucinations, or dreams, and drug-induced hallucinations, respectively. But when the stimuli to my hallucinations are unknown, that is called craziness, or schizophrenia—as if that inference were somehow as illuminating as the others.

The Experience of
Psychiatric Hospitalization

The term "mental illness" is of recent origin. It was coined by people who were humane in their inclinations and who wanted very much to raise the station of (and the public's sympathies toward) the psychologically disturbed from that of witches and "crazies" to one that was akin to the physically ill. And they were at least partially successful, for the treatment of the mentally ill *has* improved considerably over the years. But while treatment has improved, it is doubtful that people really regard the mentally ill in the same way that they view the physically ill. A broken leg is something one recovers from, but mental illness allegedly endures forever (18). A broken leg does not threaten the observer, but a crazy schizophrenic? There is by now a host of evidence that attitudes toward the mentally ill are characterized by fear, hostility, aloofness, suspicion, and dread (19). The mentally ill are society's lepers.

That such attitudes infect the general population is perhaps not surprising, only upsetting. But that they affect the professionals—attendants, nurses, physicians, psychologists, and social workers—who treat and deal with the mentally ill is more disconcerting, both because such attitudes are self-evidently pernicious and because they are unwitting. Most mental health professionals would insist that they are sympathetic toward the mentally ill, that they are neither avoidant nor hostile. But it is more likely that an exquisite ambivalence characterizes their relations with psychiatric patients, such that their avowed impulses are only part of their entire attitude. Negative attitudes are there too and can easily be detected. Such attitudes should not surprise us. They are the natural offspring of the labels patients wear and the places in which they are found.

Consider the structure of the typical psychiatric hospital. Staff and patients are strictly segregated. Staff have their own living space, including their dining facilities, bathrooms, and assembly places. The glassed quarters that contain the professional staff, which the pseudopatients came to call "the cage," sit out on every dayroom. The staff emerge primarily for caretaking purposes—to give medication, to conduct a therapy or group meeting, to instruct or reprimand a patient. Otherwise, staff keep to themselves, almost as if the disorder that afflicts their charges is somehow catching.

So much is patient-staff segregation the rule that, for four public hospitals in which an attempt was made to measure the degree to which staff and patients mingle, it was necessary to use "time out of the staff cage" as the operational measure. While it was not the case that all time spent out of the cage was spent mingling with patients (attendants, for example, would occasionally emerge to watch television in the dayroom), it was the only way in which one could gather reliable data on time for measuring.

The average amount of time spent by attendants outside of the cage was 11.3 percent (range, 3 to 52 percent). This figure does not represent only time spent mingling with patients, but also includes time spent on such chores as folding laundry, supervising patients while they shave, directing ward clean-up, and sending patients to off-ward activities. It was the relatively rare attendant who spent time talking with patients or playing games with them. It proved impossible to obtain a "percent mingling time" for nurses, since the amount of time they spent out of the cage was too brief. Rather, we counted instances of emergence from the cage. On the average, daytime nurses emerged from the cage 11.5 times per shift, including instances when they left the ward entirely (range, 4 to 39 times). Late afternoon and night nurses were even less available, emerging on the average 9.4 times per shift (range, 4 to 41 times). Data on early morning nurses, who arrived usually after midnight and departed at 8 a.m., are not available because patients were asleep during most of this period.

Physicians, especially psychiatrists, were even less available. They were rarely seen on the wards. Quite commonly, they would be seen only when they arrived and departed, with the remaining time being spent in their offices or in the cage. On the average, physi-cians emerged on the ward 6.7 times per day (range, 1 to 17 times). It proved difficult to make an accurate estimate in this regard, since physicians often maintained hours that allowed them to come and go at different times.

The hierarchical organization of the psychiatric hospital has been commented on before (20), but the latent meaning of that kind of organization is worth noting again. Those with the most power have least to do with patients, and those with the least power are most involved with them. Recall, however, that the acquisition of role-appropriate behaviors occurs mainly through the observation of others, with the most powerful having the most influence. Consequently, it is understandable that attendants not only spend more time with patients than do any other members of the staff—that is required by their station in the hierarchy—but also, insofar as they learn from their superiors' behavior, spend as little time with patients as they can. Attendants are seen mainly in the cage, which is where the models, the action, and the power are.

I turn now to a different set of studies, these dealing with staff response to patient-initiated contact. It has long been known that the amount of time a person spends with you can be an index of your significance to him. If he initiates and maintains eye contact, there is reason to believe that he is considering your requests and needs. If he pauses to chat or actually stops and talks, there is added reason to infer that he is individuating you. In four hospitals, the pseudopatient approached the staff member with a request which took the following form: "Pardon me, Mr. [or Dr. or Mrs.] X, could you tell me when I will be eligible for grounds privileges?" (or " . . . when I will be presented at the staff meeting?" or ". . . when I am likely to be discharged?"). While the content of the question varied according to the appropriateness of the target and the pseudopatient's (apparent) current needs the form was always a courteous and relevant request for information. Care was taken never to approach a particular member of the staff more than once a day, lest the staff member become suspicious or irritated. In examining these data, remember that the behavior of the pseudopatients was neither bizarre nor

Table 1. Self-initiated contact by pseudopatients with psychiatrists and nurses and attendants, compared to contact with other groups.

| Contact | Psychiatric hospitals | | University campus (nonmedical) | University medical center | | |
| | | | | Physicians | | |
	(1) Psychiatrists	(2) Nurses and attendants	(3) Faculty	(4) "Looking for a psychiatrist"	(5) "Looking for an internist"	(6) No additional comment
Responses						
Moves on, head averted (%)	71	88	0	0	0	0
Makes eye contact (%)	23	10	0	11	0	0
Pauses and chats (%)	2	2	0	11	0	10
Stops and talks (%)	4	0.5	100	78	100	90
Mean number of questions answered (out of 6)	*	*	6	3.8	4.8	4.5
Respondents (No.)	13	47	14	18	15	10
Attempts (No.)	185	1283	14	18	15	10

* Not applicable.

disruptive. One could indeed engage in good conversation with them.

The data for these experiments are shown in Table 1, separately for physicians (column 1) and for nurses and attendants (column 2). Minor differences between these four institutions were overwhelmed by the degree to which staff avoided continuing contacts that patients had initiated. By far, their most common response consisted of either a brief response to the question, offered while they were "on the move" and with head averted, or no response at all.

The encounter frequently took the following bizarre form: (pseudopatient) "Pardon me, Dr. X. Could you tell me when I am eligible for grounds privileges?" (physician) "Good morning, Dave. How are you today?" (Moves off without waiting for a response.)

It is instructive to compare these data with data recently obtained at Stanford University. It has been alleged that large and eminent universities are characterized by faculty who are so busy that they have no time for students. For this comparison, a young lady approached individual faculty members who seemed to be walking purposefully to some meeting or teaching engagement and asked them the following six questions.

1) "Pardon me, could you direct me to Encina Hall?" (at the medical school: ". . . to the Clinical Research Center?").

2) "Do you know where Fish Annex is?" (there is no Fish Annex at Stanford).

3) "Do you teach here?"

4) "How does one apply for admission to the college?" (at the medical school: ". . . to the medical school?").

5) "Is it difficult to get in?"

6) "Is there financial aid?"

Without exception, as can be seen in Table 1 (column 3), all of the questions were answered. No matter how rushed they were, all respondents not only maintained eye contact, but stopped to talk. Indeed, many of the respondents went out of their way to direct or take the questioner to the office she was seeking, to try to locate "Fish Annex," or to discuss with her the possibilities of being admitted to the university.

Similar data, also shown in Table 1 (columns 4, 5, and 6), were obtained in the hospital. Here too, the young lady came prepared with six questions. After the first question, however, she remarked to 18 of her respondents (column 4), "I'm looking for a psychiatrist," and to 15 others (column 5), "I'm looking for an internist." Ten other respondents received no inserted comment (column 6). The general degree of cooperative responses is considerably higher for these university groups than it was for pseudopatients in psychiatric hospitals. Even so, differences are apparent within the medical school setting. Once having indicated that she was looking for a psychiatrist, the degree of cooperation elicited was less than when she sought an internist.

Powerlessness and Depersonalization

Eye contact and verbal contact reflect concern and individuation; their absence, avoidance and depersonalization. The data I have presented do not do justice to the rich daily encounters that grew up around matters of depersonalization and avoidance. I have records of patients who were beaten by staff for the sin of having initiated verbal contact. During my own experience, for example, one patient was beaten in the presence of other patients for having approached an attendant and told him, "I like you." Occasionally, punishment meted out to patients for misdemeanors seemed so excessive that it could not be justified by the most radical interpretations of psychiatric canon. Nevertheless, they appeared to go unquestioned. Tempers were often short. A patient who had not heard a call for medication would be roundly excoriated, and the morning attendants would often wake patients with, "Come on, you m-----f-----s, out of bed!"

Neither anecdotal nor "hard" data can convey the overwhelming sense of powerlessness which invades the individual as he is continually exposed to the depersonalization of the psychiatric hospital. It hardly matters *which* psychiatric hospital—the excellent public ones and the very plush private hospital were better than the rural and shabby ones in this regard, but, again, the features that psychiatric hospitals had in common overwhelmed by far their apparent differences.

Powerlessness was evident everywhere. The patient is deprived of many of his legal rights by dint of his psychiatric commitment (21). He is shorn of credibility by virtue of his psychiatric label. His freedom of movement is restricted. He cannot initiate contact with the staff, but may only respond to such overtures as they make. Personal privacy is minimal. Patient quarters and possessions can be entered and examined by any staff member, for whatever reason. His personal history and anguish is available to any staff member (often including the "grey lady" and "candy striper" volunteer) who chooses to read his folder, regardless of their therapeutic relationship to him. His personal hygiene and waste evacuation are often monitored. The water closets may have no doors.

At times, depersonalization reached such proportions that pseudopatients had the sense that they were invisible, or at least unworthy of account. Upon being admitted, I and other pseudopatients took the initial physical examinations in a semipublic room, where staff members went about their own business as if we were not there.

On the ward, attendants delivered verbal and occasionally serious physical abuse to patients in the presence of other observing patients, some of whom (the pseudopatients) were writing it all down. Abusive behavior, on the other hand, terminated quite abruptly when other staff members were known to be coming. Staff are credible witnesses. Patients are not.

A nurse unbuttoned her uniform to adjust her brassiere in the presence of an entire ward of viewing men. One did not have the sense that she was being seductive. Rather, she didn't notice us. A group of staff persons might point to a patient in the dayroom and discuss him animatedly, as if he were not there.

One illuminating instance of depersonalization and invisibility occurred with regard to medications. All told, the pseudopatients were administered nearly 2100 pills, including Elavil, Stelazine, Compazine, and Thorazine, to name but a few. (That such a variety of medications should have been administered to patients presenting identical symptoms is itself worthy of note.) Only two were swallowed. The rest were either pocketed or deposited in the toilet. The pseudopatients were not alone in this. Although I have no precise records on how many patients rejected their medications, the pseudopatients frequently found the medications of other patients in the toilet before they deposited their own. As long as they were cooperative, their behavior and the pseudopatients' own in this matter, as in other important matters, went unnoticed throughout.

Reactions to such depersonalization among pseudopatients were intense. Al-

though they had come to the hospital as participant observers and were fully aware that they did not "belong," they nevertheless found themselves caught up in and fighting the process of depersonalization. Some examples: a graduate student in psychology asked his wife to bring his textbooks to the hospital so he could "catch up on his homework"—this despite the elaborate precautions taken to conceal his professional association. The same student, who had trained for quite some time to get into the hospital, and who had looked forward to the experience, "remembered" some drag races that he had wanted to see on the weekend and insisted that he be discharged by that time. Another pseudopatient attempted a romance with a nurse. Subsequently, he informed the staff that he was applying for admission to graduate school in psychology and was very likely to be admitted, since a graduate professor was one of his regular hospital visitors. The same person began to engage in psychotherapy with other patients—all of this as a way of becoming a person in an impersonal environment.

The Sources of Depersonalization

What are the origins of depersonalization? I have already mentioned two. First are attitudes held by all of us toward the mentally ill—including those who treat them—attitudes characterized by fear, distrust, and horrible expectations on the one hand, and benevolent intentions on the other. Our ambivalence leads, in this instance as in others, to avoidance.

Second, and not entirely separate, the hierarchical structure of the psychiatric hospital facilitates depersonalization. Those who are at the top have least to do with patients, and their behavior inspires the rest of the staff. Average daily contact with psychiatrists, psychologists, residents, and physicians combined ranged from 3.9 to 25.1 minutes, with an overall mean of 6.8 (six pseudopatients over a total of 129 days of hospitalization). Included in this average are time spent in the admissions interview, ward meetings in the presence of a senior staff member, group and individual psychotherapy contacts, case presentation conferences, and discharge meetings.

Clearly, patients do not spend much time in interpersonal contact with doctoral staff. And doctoral staff serve as models for nurses and attendants.

There are probably other sources. Psychiatric installations are presently in serious financial straits. Staff shortages are pervasive, staff time at a premium. Something has to give, and that something is patient contact. Yet, while financial stresses are realities, too much can be made of them. I have the impression that the psychological forces that result in depersonalization are much stronger than the fiscal ones and that the addition of more staff would not correspondingly improve patient care in this regard. The incidence of staff meetings and the enormous amount of record-keeping on patients, for example, have not been as substantially reduced as has patient contact. Priorities exist, even during hard times. Patient contact is not a significant priority in the traditional psychiatric hospital, and fiscal pressures do not account for this. Avoidance and depersonalization may.

Heavy reliance upon psychotropic medication tacitly contributes to depersonalization by convincing staff that treatment is indeed being conducted and that further patient contact may not be necessary. Even here, however, caution needs to be exercised in understanding the role of psychotropic drugs. If patients were powerful rather than powerless, if they were viewed as interesting individuals rather than diagnostic entities, if they were socially significant rather than social lepers, if their anguish truly and wholly compelled our sympathies and concerns, would we not *seek* contact with them, despite the availability of medications? Perhaps for the pleasure of it all?

The Consequences of Labeling and Depersonalization

Whenever the ratio of what is known to what needs to be known approaches zero, we tend to invent "knowledge" and assume that we understand more than we actually do. We seem unable to acknowledge that we simply don't know. The needs for diagnosis and remediation of behavioral and emotional problems are enormous. But rather than acknowledge that we are just embarking on understanding, we continue to label patients "schizophrenic," "manic-depressive," and "insane," as if in those words we had captured the essence of understanding. The facts of the matter are that we have known for a long time that diagnoses are often not useful or reliable, but we have nevertheless continued to use them. We now know that we cannot distinguish insanity from sanity. It is depressing to consider how that information will be used.

Not merely depressing, but frightening. How many people, one wonders, are sane but not recognized as such in our psychiatric institutions? How many have been needlessly stripped of their privileges of citizenship, from the right to vote and drive to that of handling their own accounts? How many have feigned insanity in order to avoid the criminal consequences of their behavior, and, conversely, how many would rather stand trial than live interminably in a psychiatric hospital—but are wrongly thought to be mentally ill? How many have been stigmatized by well-intentioned, but nevertheless erroneous, diagnoses? On the last point, recall again that a "type 2 error" in psychiatric diagnosis does not have the same consequences it does in medical diagnosis. A diagnosis of cancer that has been found to be in error is cause for celebration. But psychiatric diagnoses are rarely found to be in error. The label sticks, a mark of inadequacy forever.

Finally, how many patients might be "sane" outside the psychiatric hospital but seem insane in it—not because craziness resides in them, as it were, but because they are responding to a bizarre setting, one that may be unique to institutions which harbor nether people? Goffman (4) calls the process of socialization to such institutions "mortification"—an apt metaphor that includes the processes of depersonalization that have been described here. And while it is impossible to know whether the pseudopatients' responses to these processes are characteristic of all inmates—they were, after all, not real patients—it is difficult to believe that these processes of socialization to a psychiatric hospital provide useful attitudes or habits of response for living in the "real world."

Summary and Conclusions

It is clear that we cannot distinguish the sane from the insane in psychiatric hospitals. The hospital itself imposes a special environment in which the meanings of behavior can easily be misunderstood. The consequences to patients hospitalized in such an environment—the powerlessness, depersonalization, segregation, mortification, and self-labeling—seem undoubtedly countertherapeutic.

I do not, even now, understand this problem well enough to perceive solutions. But two matters seem to have some promise. The first concerns the proliferation of community mental health facilities, of crisis intervention centers, of the human potential movement, and of behavior therapies that, for all of their own problems, tend to avoid psychiatric labels, to focus on specific problems and behaviors, and to retain the individual in a relatively nonpejorative environment. Clearly, to the extent that we refrain from sending the distressed to insane places, our impressions of them are less likely to be distorted. (The risk of distorted perceptions, it seems to me, is always present, since we are much more sensitive to an individual's behaviors and verbalizations than we are to the subtle contextual stimuli that often promote them. At issue here is a matter of magnitude. And, as I have shown, the magnitude of distortion is exceedingly high in the extreme context that is a psychiatric hospital.)

The second matter that might prove promising speaks to the need to increase the sensitivity of mental health workers and researchers to the *Catch 22* position of psychiatric patients. Simply reading materials in this area will be of help to some such workers and researchers. For others, directly experiencing the impact of psychiatric hospitalization will be of enormous use. Clearly, further research into the social psychology of such total institutions will both facilitate treatment and deepen understanding.

I and the other pseudopatients in the psychiatric setting had distinctly negative reactions. We do not pretend to describe the subjective experiences of true patients. Theirs may be different from ours, particularly with the passage of time and the necessary process of adaptation to one's environment. But we can and do speak to the relatively more objective indices of treatment within the hospital. It could be a mistake, and a very unfortunate one, to consider that what happened to us derived from malice or stupidity on the part of the staff. Quite the contrary, our overwhelming impression of them was of people who really cared, who were committed and who were uncommonly intelligent. Where they failed, as they sometimes did painfully, it would be more accurate to attribute those failures to the environment in which they, too, found themselves than to personal callousness. Their perceptions and behavior were controlled by the situation, rather than being motivated by a malicious disposition. In a more benign environment, one that was less attached to global diagnosis, their behaviors and judgments might have been more benign and effective.

6. DISORDERS AND THERAPY

References and Notes

1. P. Ash, *J. Abnorm. Soc. Psychol.* **44**, 272 (1949); A. T. Beck, *Amer. J. Psychiat.* **119**, 210 (1962); A. T. Boisen, *Psychiatry* **2**, 233 (1938); N. Kreitman, *J. Ment. Sci.* **107**, 876 (1961); N. Kreitman, P. Sainsbury, J. Morrisey, J. Towers, J. Scrivener, *ibid.*, p. 887; H. O. Schmitt and C. P. Fonda, *J. Abnorm. Soc. Psychol.* **52**, 262 (1956); W. Seeman, *J. Nerv. Ment. Dis.* **118**, 541 (1953). For an analysis of these artifacts and summaries of the disputes, see J. Zubin, *Annu. Rev. Psychol.* **18**, 373 (1967); L. Phillips and J. G. Draguns, *ibid.* **22**, 447 (1971).
2. R. Benedict, *J. Gen. Psychol.* **10**, 59 (1934).
3. See in this regard H. Becker, *Outsiders: Studies in the Sociology of Deviance* (Free Press. New York, 1963); B. M. Braginsky, D. D. Braginsky, K. Ring, *Methods of Madness: The Mental Hospital as a Last Resort* (Holt, Rinehart & Winston, New York, 1969); G. M. Crocetti and P. V. Lemkau, *Amer. Sociol. Rev.* **30**, 577 (1965); E. Goffman, *Behavior in Public Places* (Free Press, New York, 1964); R. D. Laing, *The Divided Self: A Study of Sanity and Madness* (Quadrangle, Chicago, 1960); D. L. Phillips, *Amer. Sociol. Rev.* **28**, 963 (1963); T. R. Sarbin, *Psychol. Today* **6**, 18 (1972); E. Schur, *Amer. J. Sociol.* **75**, 309 (1969); T. Szasz, *Law, Liberty and Psychiatry* (Macmillan, New York, 1963); *The Myth of Mental Illness: Foundations of a Theory of Mental Illness* (Hoeber-Harper, New York, 1963). For a critique of some of these views, see W. R. Gove, *Amer. Sociol. Rev.* **35**, 873 (1970).
4. E. Goffman, *Asylums* (Doubleday, Garden City, N.Y., 1961).
5. T. J. Scheff, *Being Mentally Ill: A Sociological Theory* (Aldine, Chicago, 1966).
6. Data from a ninth pseudopatient are not incorporated in this report because, although his sanity went undetected, he falsified aspects of his personal history, including his marital status and parental relationships. His experimental behaviors therefore were not identical to those of the other pseudopatients.
7. A. Barry, *Bellevue Is a State of Mind* (Harcourt Brace Jovanovich. New York, 1971); I. Belknap, *Human Problems of a State Mental Hospital* (McGraw-Hill, New York, 1956); W. Caudill, F. C. Redlich, H. R. Gilmore, E. B. Brody, *Amer. J. Orthopsychiat.* **22**, 314 (1952); A. R. Goldman, R. H. Bohr, T. A. Steinberg, *Prof. Psychol.* **1**, 427 (1970); unauthored, *Roche Report* **1** (No. 13), 8 (1971).
8. Beyond the personal difficulties that the pseudopatient is likely to experience in the hospital, there are legal and social ones that, combined, require considerable attention before entry. For example, once admitted to a psychiatric institution, it is difficult, if not impossible, to be discharged on short notice, state law to the contrary notwithstanding. I was not sensitive to these difficulties at the outset of the project, nor to the personal and situational emergencies that can arise, but later a writ of habeas corpus was prepared for each of the entering pseudopatients and an attorney was kept "on call" during every hospitalization. I am grateful to John Kaplan and Robert Bartels for legal advice and assistance in these matters.
9. However distasteful such concealment is, it was a necessary first step to examining these questions. Without concealment, there would have been no way to know how valid these experiences were; nor was there any way of knowing whether whatever detections occurred were a tribute to the diagnostic acumen of the staff or to the hospital's rumor network. Obviously, since my concerns are general ones that cut across individual hospitals and staffs, I have respected their anonymity and have eliminated clues that might lead to their identification.
10. Interestingly, of the 12 admissions, 11 were diagnosed as schizophrenic and one, with the identical symptomatology, as manic-depressive psychosis. This diagnosis has a more favorable prognosis, and it was given by the only private hospital in our sample. On the relations between social class and psychiatric diagnosis, see A. deB. Hollingshead and F. C. Redlich, *Social Class and Mental Illness: A Community Study* (Wiley, New York, 1958).
11. It is possible, of course, that patients have quite broad latitudes in diagnosis and therefore are inclined to call many people sane, even those whose behavior is patently aberrant. However, although we have no hard data on this matter, it was our distinct impression that this was not the case. In many instances, patients not only singled us out for attention, but came to imitate our behaviors and styles.
12. J. Cumming and E. Cumming, *Community Ment. Health* **1**, 135 (1965); A. Farina and K. Ring, *J. Abnorm. Psychol.* **70**, 47 (1965); H. E. Freeman and O. G. Simmons, *The Mental Patient Comes Home* (Wiley, New York, 1963); W J. Johannsen, *Ment. Hygiene* **53**, 218 (1969); A. S. Linsky, *Soc. Psychiat.* **5**, 166 (1970).
13. S. E. Asch, *J. Abnorm. Soc. Psychol.* **41**, 258 (1946); *Social Psychology* (Prentice-Hall, New York, 1952).
14. See also I. N. Mensh and J. Wishner, *J. Personality* **16**, 188 (1947); J. Wishner, *Psychol. Rev.* **67**, 96 (1960); J. S. Bruner and R. Tagiuri, in *Handbook of Social Psychology*, G. Lindzey, Ed. (Addison-Wesley, Cambridge, Mass., 1954), vol. 2, pp. 634–654; J. S. Bruner, D. Shapiro, R. Tagiuri, in *Person Perception and Interpersonal Behavior*, R. Tagiuri and L. Petrullo, Eds. (Stanford Univ. Press, Stanford, Calif., 1958), pp. 277–288.
15. For an example of a similar self fulfilling prophecy, in this instance dealing with the "central" trait of intelligence, see R. Rosenthal and L. Jacobson, *Pygmalion in the Classroom* (Holt, Rinehart & Winston, New York, 1968).
16. E. Zigler and L. Phillips, *J. Abnorm. Soc. Psychol.* **63**, 69 (1961). See also R. K. Freudenberg and J. P. Robertson, *A.M.A. Arch. Neurol. Psychiatr.* **76**, 14 (1956).
17. W. Mischel, *Personality and Assessment* (Wiley, New York, 1968).
18. The most recent and unfortunate instance of this tenet is that of Senator Thomas Eagleton.
19. T. R. Sarbin and J. C. Mancuso, *J. Clin. Consult. Psychol.* **35**, 159 (1970); T. R. Sarbin, *ibid.* **31**, 447 (1967); J. C. Nunnally, Jr., *Popular Conceptions of Mental Health* (Holt, Rinehart & Winston, New York, 1961).
20. A. H. Stanton and M. S. Schwartz, *The Mental Hospital: A Study of Institutional Participation in Psychiatric Illness and Treatment* (Basic, New York, 1954).
21. D. B. Wexler and S. E. Scoville, *Ariz. Law Rev.* **13**, 1 (1971).
22. I thank W. Mischel, E. Orne, and M. S. Rosenhan for comments on an earlier draft of this manuscript.

More on Pseudoscience in Science and the Case for Psychiatric Diagnosis

A Critique of D. L. Rosenhan's "On Being Sane in Insane Places" and "The Contextual Nature of Psychiatric Diagnosis"

Robert L. Spitzer, MD

● **Rosenhan's 1973 article,[1] "On Being Sane in Insane Places,"* was pseudoscience presented as science. Just as his pseudopatients were diagnosed at discharge as having "schizophrenia in remission," so a careful examination of this study's methods, results, and conclusions leads to a diagnosis of "logic in remission." Rosenhan's study proves that pseudopatients are not detected by psychiatrists as having simulated signs of mental illness and that the implementation of certain invalid research designs can make psychiatrists appear foolish. These rather unremarkable findings are irrelevant to the real problems of the reliability and validity of psychiatric diagnosis and only serve to obscure them. A correct interpretation of his own data contradicts his conclusions. There are purposes to psychiatric diagnosis that Rosenhan's article ignores. His more recent suggestion that certain requirements be met prior to the adoption of a new psychiatric classification system is unrealistic.**

(Arch Gen Psychiatry 33:459-470, 1976)

In January 1973, *Science*, the official journal of the Association for the Advancement of Science, reported a small study with a catchy title—"On Being Sane in Insane Places.[1]" This was no ordinary study that merely added further knowledge to our understanding of psychiatric disorders; this study challenged basic psychiatric concepts and practices. If the author, D. L. Rosenhan, a professor of psychology and law, is correct, the results clearly show that psychiatrists are unable to distinguish the "sane" from the "insane" in psychiatric hospitals, and that the traditional psychiatric classification of mental disorders is unreliable, invalid, and harmful to the welfare of patients.

Partly because of the prestige of the journal in which it first appeared, and more importantly, because it said something that many were delighted to hear, the study was widely acclaimed in the popular news media (*New York Times*, Jan 20, 1974; *Saturday Review of Science*, March 1, 1973, pp 55-56; *Newsweek*, Jan 29, 1973, p 46). As a consequence, this single study is probably better known to the lay public than any other study in the area of

psychiatry in the last decade.

Although the study has been attacked by many mental health professionals,[2-9] most articles that refer to the study have accepted its conclusions and implications.[10-24] Furthermore, two editorials in *The Journal of the American Medical Association* were devoted to an endorsement of the study's findings. [13, 14]

The study has probably had its greatest impact in the field of psychology. Of 31 recently published psychology textbooks, 15 cite Rosenhan's article. Fully 12 of these texts [25-36] present the results uncritically with only five [27,35,37-39] even acknowledging controversy over the study's conclusions. Only three [37-39] question its results. The implication is clear: large numbers of undergraduate and graduate psychology students are being taught to accept the conclusions of this study.

Although there have been references to Rosenhan's study in articles appearing in well-known psychiatric journals, none has presented a thorough critique of this study. Such a critique would be useful, not only for what it tells us about Rosenhan's remarkable study, but also for clarifying some of the fundamental issues regarding psychiatric diagnosis. This article is such an attempt, and presents an elaboration of my contribution to a symposium that appeared in *The Journal of Abnormal Psychology,* [40-45] which was devoted to exploring the strengths and weaknesses of the Rosenhan study. In addition, this article includes a critique of Rosenhan's contribution to the symposium, an article entitled, "The Contextual Nature of Psychiatric Diagnosis,[43]" in which he responded to the critiques provided by the participants in the symposium.

Rosenhan stated the basic issue in his original article as follows:

Do the salient characteristics that lead to diagnoses reside in the patients themselves or in the environments and contexts in which observers find them? From Bleuler, through Kretchmer, through the formulators of the recently revised *Diagnostic and Statistical*

*A/E Editor's note: See article 47 p. 226.

"More on Pseudoscience in Science and the Case for Psychiatric Diagnosis," by Robert L. Spitzer, M.D., *Archives of General Psychiatry*, April 1976, Volume 33. Reprinted by permission.

235

Manual of the American Psychiatric Association, the belief has been strong that patients present symptoms, that those symptoms can be categorized, and, implicitly, that the sane are distinguishable from the insane. More recently, however, this belief has been questioned. Based in part on theoretical and anthropological considerations, but also on philosophical, legal and therapeutic ones, the view has grown that psychological categorization of mental illness is useless at best and downright harmful, misleading, and pejorative at worst. Psychiatric diagnoses, in this view, are in the minds of the observers and are not valid summaries of characteristics displayed by the observed. [1(p 251)]

Rosenhan proposed that an adequate method to study this question was for normal people who had never had symptoms of serious psychiatric disorders to be admitted to psychiatric hospitals "and then determining whether they were discovered to be sane." Therefore, eight "sane" people, or "pseudopatients," gained admission to 12 different hospitals, each with a single complaint of hearing voices. On admission to the psychiatric ward, each pseudopatient ceased simulating any symptoms of abnormality.

The diagnostic results were as follows:

Admitted, except in one case, with a diagnosis of schizophrenia, each was discharged with a diagnosis of schizophrenia "in remission." The label "in remission" should in no way be dismissed as a formality, for at no time during any hospitalization had any question been raised about any pseudopatient's simulation. [1 (p 252)]

(It should be noted that while preparing my original critique, personal communication with Rosenhan indicated that "in remission" referred to use of that term or one of its equivalents, such as "recovered" or "no longer ill," and that it also applied to the one patient who was given the diagnosis of manic-depressive psychosis. Thus, *all* of the patients were apparently discharged "in remission." However, in his 1975 article,[43] he notes that only eight of the patients were discharged "in remission" and that one was noted as "asymptomatic" and three as "improved." The discrepancy between the 1973 and 1975 articles is puzzling but does not substantially alter my interpretation of the results.)

Rosenhan concluded, "It is clear that we cannot distinguish the sane from the insane in psychiatric hospitals."[1(p 257)] According to him, what is needed is the avoidance of "global diagnosis" as exemplified by such diagnoses as schizophrenia or manic-depressive psychosis, and attention should be directed instead to "behaviors, the stimuli that provoke them, and their correlates."

THE CENTRAL QUESTION

One hardly knows where to begin. Let us first acknowledge the potential importance of the study's central research question. Surely, if psychiatric diagnoses are, to quote Rosenhan, "only in the minds of the observers," and do not reflect any characteristics inherent in the patient, then they obviously can be of no use in helping patients. (It is remarkable that the original article, which was concerned with the validity of psychiatric diagnosis, did not contain a single sentence about the intended purposes of psychiatric diagnosis—more of this later.) However, the study immediately becomes hopelessly confused when Rosenhan suggests that his research question can be answered by studying whether or not the "sanity" of pseudopatients in a mental hospital can be discovered. Rosenhan, a professor of law and psychology, knows that

the terms "sane" and "insane" are legal, not psychiatric, concepts. He knows that no psychiatrist makes a *diagnosis* of "sanity" or "insanity," and that the true meaning of these terms, which varies from state to state, involves the inability to distinguish right from wrong—an issue that is totally irrelevant to this study.

DETECTING THE SANITY OF A PSEUDOPATIENT

However, if we are forced to use the terms "insane" (to mean showing signs of serious mental disturbance) and "sane" (the absence of such signs), then clearly there are three possible meanings to the concept of "detecting the sanity" of a pseudopatient who feigns mental illness on entry to a hospital but then acts "normal" throughout his hospital stay. The first is the recognition, *when he is first seen*, that the pseudopatient is feigning insanity as he attempts to gain admission to the hospital. This would be detecting sanity in a sane person simulating insanity. The second would be the recognition, *after* having observed him acting normally during his hospitalization, that the pseudopatient was initially feigning insanity. This would be detecting that the currently sane person never was insane. Finally, the third possible meaning would be the recognition, *during hospitalization*, that the pseudopatient, though initially appearing to be "insane," was no longer showing signs of psychiatric disturbance.

These elementary distinctions of "detecting sanity in the insane" are crucial to properly interpreting the results of Rosenhan's study. The reader is misled by Rosenhan's implication that the first two meanings of detecting the sanity of the pseudopatients, which involve determining the pseudopatient to be a fraud, are at all relevant to the central research question. Further, the true results of his study are obscured because they fail to support the conclusion when the third meaning of detecting sanity is considered, that is, a recognition that after their admission as "insane," the pseudopatients were not psychiatrically disturbed while in the hospital.

Let us examine these three possible meanings of detecting the sanity of the pseudopatient, their logical relation to the central question of the study, the actual results obtained, and the validity of Rosenhan's conclusions.

THE PATIENT IS NO LONGER "INSANE"

We begin with the third meaning of detecting sanity. It is obvious that if the psychiatrists judged the pseudopatients as seriously disturbed while they acted "normal" in the hospital, this would be strong evidence that their assessments were being influenced by the context in which they were making their examination rather than the actual behavior of the patient. This, after all, is the central research question. (I suspect that many readers will agree with Hunter, who, in a letter to *Science*, pointed out:

The pseudopatients did *not* behave normally in the hospital. Had their behavior been normal, they would have walked to the nurses' station and said, "Look, I am a normal person who tried to see if I could get into the hospital by behaving in a crazy way or saying crazy things. It worked and I was admitted to the hospital, but now I would like to be discharged from the hospital.[46])

What were the results? According to Rosenhan, all of the patients were diagnosed at discharge as being "in remission." The meaning of "in remission" is obvious: it means without signs of illness. Thus, the psychiatrists apparently recognized that the pseudopatients were, to use Rosenhan's term, "sane." (This would apply to all of the 12 pseudopatients according to the 1973 article and to eight of them according to the 1975 article.) However, lest the reader appreciate the significance of these findings, Rosenhan gives a completely incorrect interpretation: "If the pseudopatient was to be discharged, he must naturally be 'in remission'; but he was not sane, nor, in the institution's view, had he ever been sane."[1(p 252)] Rosenhan's implication is clear—the patient was diagnosed "in remission" not because the psychiatrist correctly assessed the patient's hospital behavior, but only because the patient had to be discharged. Is this interpretation warranted?

I am sure that most readers who are not familiar with the details of psychiatric diagnostic practice assume from Rosenhan's account that it is common for schizophrenic patients to be diagnosed "in remission" when discharged from a hospital; as a matter of fact, this is extremely unusual. The reason is two-fold. First of all, patients with a diagnosis of schizophrenia are rarely completely asymptomatic at discharge. Second, the discharge diagnosis frequently records the diagnostic conditions associated with the *admission* to the hospital without any reference to the condition of the patient at discharge.

Rosenhan does not report any data concerning the discharge diagnoses of the real schizophrenic patients in the 12 hospitals used in his study. However, I can report on the frequency of a discharge diagnosis of schizophrenia "in remission" at my hospital, the New York State Psychiatric Institute, a research, teaching, and community hospital where diagnoses are made in a routine fashion, undoubtedly no differently from the 12 hospitals of Rosenhan's study. I examined the official book that the record room uses to record discharge diagnoses and their statistical codes for all patients. Of more than 300 patients discharged in the year prior to September 1974 with a diagnosis of schizophrenia, not one was diagnosed "in remission." It is only possible to *code* a diagnosis of "in remission" by adding a fifth digit (5) to the four-digit code number for the subtype of schizophrenia (eg, paranoid schizophrenia is coded as 295.3, but paranoid schizophrenia "in remission" is coded as 295.35). I realize, however, that a psychiatrist might *intend* to make a discharge diagnosis of "in remission" but fail to use the fifth digit, so that the official recording of the diagnosis would not reflect his full assessment. I therefore had research assistants read the discharge summaries of the last 100 patients whose discharge was schizophrenia to see how often the terms "in remission," "recovered," "no longer ill," or "asymptomatic" were used, even if not recorded with the fifth digit in the code number. The result was that only one patient, who was diagnosed paranoid schizophrenia, was described in the summary as being "in remission" at discharge. The fifth digit code was not used.

To substantiate my view that the practice at my hospital of rarely giving a discharge diagnosis of schizophrenia "in remission" is not unique, I had a research assistant call the record room librarians of 12 psychiatric hospitals, chosen "catch-as-catch-can." (Rosenhan explains his refusal to identify the 12 hospitals used in his study on the basis of his concern with issues of confidentiality and the potential

for ad hominem attack. However, this makes it impossible for anyone at those hospitals or elsewhere to corroborate or challenge his account of how the pseudopatients acted and how they were perceived.) The 12 hospitals used in my ministudy were the following: Long Island Jewish-Hillside Medical Center, New York; Massachusetts General Hospital, Massachusetts; St. Elizabeth's Hospital, Washington, DC; McLean Hospital, Massachusetts; UCLA, Neuropsychiatric Institute, California; Meyer-Manhattan Hospital (Manhattan State), New York; Vermont State Hospital; Medical College of Virginia; Emory University Hospital, Georgia; High Point Hospital, New York; Hudson River State Hospital, New York; and New York Hospital-Cornell Medical Center, Westchester Division. The record room librarians were told that we were interested in knowing their estimate of how often, at their hospitals, schizophrenics were discharged "in remission" (or "no longer ill" or "asymptomatic"). The results were that 11 of the 12 hospitals indicated that the term was either never used or, at most, was used for only a handful of patients in a year. The remaining hospital (a private one) estimated that the term was used in roughly 7% of the discharge diagnoses.

This leaves us with the conclusion that the pseudopatients were given a discharge diagnosis (All 12 of them? Eight of them?) that is rarely given to real patients with an admission diagnosis of schizophrenia. Therefore, the diagnoses given to the pseudopatients *were* a function of the patients' behaviors and not of the setting (psychiatric hospital) in which the diagnoses were made. In fact, a moment's reflection may cause many a reader familiar with usual diagnostic practice to marvel that so many psychiatrists acted so rationally as to use at discharge precisely the same diagnostic category, "in remission," that is rarely used with real patients. In any case, the data as reported by Rosenhan contradict his conclusions.

It is not only in his discharge diagnosis that the psychiatrist had an opportunity to assess the patient's true condition incorrectly. In the admission mental status examination, during a progress note or in his discharge note, that psychiatrist could have described any of the pseudopatients as "still psychotic," "probably still hallucinating but denies it now," "loose associations," or "inappropriate affect." Because Rosenhan had access to all of this material, his failure to report such judgments of continuing serious psychopathology, either in the original study or in his 1975 symposium article,[43] strongly suggests that they were never made.

All pseudopatients took extensive notes publicly to record data on staff and patient behavior. Rosenhan claimed that the nursing records indicated that "the writing was seen as an aspect of their pathological behavior."[1(p 253)] The only datum presented to support this claim is that the daily nursing comment on one of the pseudopatients was "patient engages in writing behavior." Because nursing notes frequently and intentionally comment on nonpathological activities that a patient engages in so that other staff members have some knowledge of how the patient spends his time, this particular nursing note in no way supports Rosenhan's thesis. Once again, the *failure* to provide data regarding instances where normal hospital behavior was categorized as pathological is remarkable. The closest that Rosenhan comes to providing such data is his report of an instance where a kindly nurse asked if a pseudopatient, who was pacing the long hospital corridors because of boredom, was "nervous." It was, after all, a question and not a final judgment.

Let us now examine the other two meanings of detecting sanity in the pseudopatients, that is, the recognition that the pseudopatient was a fraud either when he sought admission to the hospital or during his hospital stay, and the relationship of those meanings to the central research question.

DETECTING "SANITY" BEFORE ADMISSION

Whether or not psychiatrists are able to detect individuals who feign psychiatric symptoms is an interesting question, but it is clearly of no relevance to the issue of whether or not the salient characteristics that lead to diagnoses reside in the patient's behavior or in the minds of the observers. After all, a psychiatrist who believes a pseudopatient who feigns a symptom *is* responding to the pseudopatient's *behavior*. Rosenhan does not blame the psychiatrist for believing the pseudopatient's fake symptom of hallucinations. He blames him for making the diagnosis of schizophrenia. He states:

The issue is not . . . that the psychiatrist believed him. . . . Neither is it whether the pseudopatient should have been admitted to the psychiatric hospital in the first place. . . . The issue is the diagnostic leap that was made between the single presenting symptom, hallucinations, and the diagnosis, schizophrenia (or, in one case, manic-depressive psychosis). . . . Had the pseudopatients been diagnosed "hallucinating" there would have been no further need to examine the diagnostic issue. The diagnosis of hallucinations implies only that: no more. The presence of hallucinations does not itself define the presence of "schizophrenia." And schizophrenia may or may not include hallucinations. [47 (pp 366, 367)]

Let us see. Unfortunately, as judged by many of the letters to *Science* commenting on the study," many readers, including psychiatrists, accepted Rosenhan's thesis that it was irrational for the psychiatrists to have made an initial diagnosis of schizophrenia *as the most likely condition* on the basis of a single symptom. In my judgment, these readers were wrong. Their acceptance of Rosenhan's thesis was aided by the content of the pseudopatients' auditory hallucinations, which were voices that said "empty," "hollow," and "thud." According to Rosenhan, these symptoms were chosen because of "their apparent similarity to existential symptoms [and] the *absence* of a single report of existential psychoses in the literature." [1(p 251)] The implication is that if the *content* of specific symptoms has never been reported in the literature, then a psychiatrist should somehow know that the *symptom* has no diagnostic significance. This is absurd. Recently I saw a patient who kept hearing a voice that said. "It's OK. It's OK." I know of no such report in the literature. So what? I agree with Rosenhan that there has never been a report of an "existential psychosis." However, the diagnoses made were schizophrenia and manic-depressive psychosis, not existential psychosis. (I am reminded of a game that was played when I was a kid. "I can prove that you are not here." "How?" "Are you in Chicago?" "No." "Then you must be in some other place. If you are in some other place then you can't be here.")

DIFFERENTIAL DIAGNOSIS OF AUDITORY HALLUCINATIONS

Rosenhan is entitled to believe that pschiatric diagnoses are of no use and therefore should not have been given to the pseudopatients. However, it makes no sense for him to claim that *within* a diagnostic framework it was irrational to consider schizophrenia seriously as the most likely condition *without* his presenting a consideration of the differential diagnosis. Let me briefly give what I think is a reasonable differential diagnosis, based on the initial clinical picture of the pseudopatient when he applied for admission to the hospital.

Rosenhan says that "beyond alleging the symptoms and falsifying name, vocation, and employment, no further alterations of person, history, or cirumstances were made." [1 (p 251)] However, the clinical picture clearly includes not only the symptom (auditory hallucinations) but also the desire to enter a psychiatric hospital, from which it is reasonable to conclude that the symptom is a source of significant distress. (In fact, in his 1975 symposium article Rosenhan acknowledges that the pseudopatients reported that "the hallucinations troubled them greatly at the outset." [43(p 471)] This, plus the knowledge that the auditory hallucinations were reported to be of three weeks' duration (D. L. Rosenhan, oral communication), establishes the hallucinations as significant symptoms of psychopathology as distinguished from so-called "pseudohallucination" (hallucinations while falling asleep or awakening from sleep, or intense imagination with the voices heard from inside of the head).

Auditory hallucinations can occur in several kinds of mental disorders. The absence of a history of alcohol, drug abuse, or some other toxin, the absence of any signs of physical illness (such as high fever), the absence of evidence of distractibility, impairment in concentration, memory or orientation, and negative results from a neurological examination all make an organic psychosis extremely unlikely. The absence of a recent precipitating stress rules out a transient situational disturbance of psychotic intensity or (to use a nonofficial category) hysterical psychosis. The absence of a profound disturbance in mood rules out an affective psychosis (we are not given the mental status findings for the patient who was diagnosed manic-depressive psychosis).

What about simulating mental illness? Psychiatrists know that occasionally an individual who has something to gain from being admitted to a psychiatric hospital will exaggerate or even feign psychiatric symptoms. This is a genuine diagnostic problem that psychiatrists and other physicians occasionally confront and is called "malingering." However, there was certainly no reason to believe that any of the pseudopatients had anything to gain from being admitted to a psychiatric hospital except relief from their alleged complaint, and therefore there was no reason to suspect that the illness was feigned. What possible diagnoses are left in the classification of mental disorders now used in this country for a patient with a presenting symptom of hallucinations, with the previously considered conditions having been ruled out? There is only one— schizophrenia!

Admittedly, there is a hitch to a definitive diagnosis of schizophrenia. Almost invariably there *are* other signs of the disorder present, such as poor premorbid adjustment, affective blunting, delusions, or signs of thought disorder. I would hope that if I had been one of the 12 psychiatrists presented with such a patient, I would have been struck by the lack of other signs of the disorder, but I am rather sure that having no reason to doubt the authenticity of the patient's claim of auditory hallucinations, I also would have beel fooled into noting schizophrenia as *the most likely* diagnosis.

What does Rosenhan really mean when he objects to the diagnosis of schizophrenia because it was based on a "single symptom"? Does he believe that there are real patients with the single symptoms of auditory hallucinations who are misdiagnosed as schizophrenic when they actually have some other condition? If so, what is the nature of that condition? Is Rosenhan's point that the psychiatrists should have used "diagnosis deferred," a category that is available but rarely used? I would have no argument with this conclusion. Furthermore, if he had presented data from real patients indicating how often patients are erroneously diagnosed on the basis of inadequate information and what the consequences are, it would have been a real contribution.

Until now, I have assumed that the pseudopatients presented only one symptom of psychiatric disorder. Actually, we know very little about how the pseudopatients presented themselves. What did the pseudopatients say when asked, as most must have been, what effect the hallucinations were having on their lives? Did any of the pseudopatients depart from the protocol (which called for describing only one symptom), perhaps in an effort to justify admission to the hospital? (It occurred to me that the best way to shed light on this question would be to read the original admission notes to determine just how the psychiatrist described the present illnesses of pseudopatients. Communication with Rosenhan indicated that he has this material. I have made several requests for him to send me copies, with deletion of all information that could possibly identify the particular hospitals that were involved. To summarize a lengthy correspondence, he has indicated that editing this material is more difficult than I would judge and that he would be glad to supply the material after he has completed analyzing it for a book he is preparing.)

DETECTING SANITY AFTER ADMISSION

Let us now examine the relationship to the central research question of the last meaning of detecting sanity in the pseudopatients, namely, the psychiatrist's recognition, *after* observing the pseudopatient act normally during his hospitalization, that he was initially feigning insanity. If a diagnostic condition were known to be always chronic and unremitting, it would be irrational not to question the original diagnosis if a patient were later found to be asymptomatic. As applied to this study, if the concept of schizophrenia did not admit the possibility of recovery, then failure to question the original diagnosis when the pseudopatients were no longer overtly ill would be relevant to the central research question. It would be an example of the context of the hospital environment influencing the psychiatrist's diagnostic decision. How-

ever, neither any psychiatric textbook nor the American Psychiatric Association's *Diagnostic and Statistical Manual of Mental Disorders*[48] suggests that mental illnesses endure forever. Oddly enough, it is Rosenhan who, without any reference to the psychiatric literature, says, "A broken leg is something one recovers from, but mental illness allegedly endures forever."[1(p254)] Who, other than Rosenhan, alleges it?

Rosenhan should know that although some American psychiatrist restrict the label of schizophrenia to mean chronic or process schizophrenia, most American psychiatrists include an acute subtype from which there is often remission. The *Diagnostic and Statistical Manual* in describing the subtype, "acute schizophrenic episode," states that "in many cases the patient recovers within weeks."[48]

A similar straw man is created when Rosenhan says:

The insane are not always insane...the bizarre behaviors upon which their [the pseudopatients'] diagnoses were allegedly predicated constituted only a small fraction of their total behavior. If it makes no sense to label ourselves permanently depressed on the basis of an occasional depression, then it takes better evidence than is presently available to label all patients insane or schizophrenic on the basis of bizarre behaviors or cognitions.[1(p254)]

Who ever said that the behaviors that indicate schizophrenia or any other diagnostic category comprise the totality of a patient's behavior? A diagnosis of schizophrenia does not mean that *all* of the patient's behavior is schizophrenic, any more than a diagnosis of carcinoma of the liver means that all of the patient's body is diseased. (While discussing the pitfalls of generalizing, how about Rosenhan's conclusion that "It is clear that we cannot distinguish the sane from the insane in psychiatric hospitals,"[1(p257)] which is based on a sample size of eight pseudopatients admitted to 12 hospitals!)

Does Rosenhan at least score a point by demonstrating that, although the professional staff never considered the possibility that the pseudopatient was a fraud, this possibility was often considered by other patients? Perhaps, but I am not so sure. Let us not forget that all of the pseudopatients "took extensive notes publicly." Obviously, this was highly unusual patient behavior and Rosenhan's quote from a suspicious patient suggests the importance it had in focusing the other patients' attention on the pseudopatients: "You're not crazy. You're a journalist, or a professor [referring to the continual note-taking]. You're checking up on the hospital."[1(p252)]

Rosenhan presents ample evidence, which I find no reason to dispute, that the professional staff spent little time actually with the pseudopatients. The note-taking may easily have been overlooked, and therefore the staff developed no suspicion that the pseudopatients had simulated illness to gain entry into the hospital. The note-taking, in which all of the pseudopatients engaged, may well have been *the* cue that alerted the patients to the possibility that the pseudopatients were there under false pretenses. However, I would predict that a pseudopatient on a ward of patients with mixed diagnostic conditions would have no difficulty in masquerading convincingly as a true patient to both staff and patients if he did nothing unusual to draw attention to himself.

Rosenhan presents one way in which the diagnosis did affect the psychiatrist's preception of the patient's circumstances—historical facts of the case were often distorted by the staff to achieve consistency with psychodynamic theories. Here, for the first time, I believe Rosenhan has hit the mark. What he described happens all the time and often makes attendance at clinical case conferences extremely painful, especially for those with logical minds and research orientations. Although his observation is correct, it would seem to be more a consequence of individuals attempting to rearrange facts to comply with an unproven etiological theory than a consequence of diagnostic labeling. One could easily imagine a similar process occurring when a weak-minded, behaviorally oriented clinician attempts to rewrite the patient's history to account for "hallucinations reinforced by attention paid to patient by family members when patient complains of hearing voices." Such is the human condition.

One final finding requires comment. In order to determine whether "the tendency toward diagnosing the sane insane could be reversed," the staff of a research and teaching hospital was informed that at some time during the following three months, one or more pseudopatients would attempt to be admitted. No such attempt was actually made. Yet approximately 10% of 193 real patients were suspected by two or more staff members (we are not told how many made judgments) to be pseudopatients. Rosenhan concluded, "Any diagnostic process that lends itself so readily to massive errors of this sort cannot be a very reliable one."[1(p 252)] My conclusion is that this experimental design practically assures only one outcome. (Did the hospital director, or whoever it was that agreed to participate in this ministudy, really believe that the design was relevant to some serious research question?)

ELEMENTARY PRINCIPLES OF RELIABILITY OF CLASSIFICATION

Some very important principles that are relevant to the design of Rosenhan's study are taught in elementary psychology courses and should not be forgotten. One of them is that a measurement or classification procedure is not reliable or unreliable *in itself* but only in its application to a specific population. There *are* serious problems with the reliabiltiy of psychiatric diagnoses as they are applied to the population to which psychiatric diagnoses are *ordinarily* given. However, I fail to see, and Rosenhan does not even attempt to show, how the reliability of psychiatric diagnoses applied to a population of individuals seeking help is at all relevant to the reliability of psychiatric diagnoses applied to a population of pseudopatients (or one including the threat of pseudopatients). The two populations are just not the same. Kety has expressed it dramatically:

If I were to drink a quart of blood and, concealing what I had done, come to the emergency room of any hospital vomiting blood, the behavior of the staff would be quite predictable. If they labeled and treated me as having a bleeding peptic ulcer, I doubt that I could argue convincingly that medical science does not know how to diagnose that condition.[3(p 959)]

(I have no doubt that if the condition known as "pseudopatient" ever assumed epidemic proportions among admissions to psychiatric hospitals, psychiatrists would in time become adept at identifying them, though at what risk to real patients I do not know.)

ATTITUDES TOWARD THE "INSANE"

The latter part of Rosenhan's study[1] deals with the experience of psychiatric hospitalization. The staff and the patients were strictly segregated. The professional staff, especially the psychiatrists, were not available and were rarely seen. When the staff was asked for information "their most common response consisted of either a brief response to the question, offered while they were 'on the move' and with head averted, or no response at all."[1(p 255)] "Attendants delivered verbal and occasionally serious physical abuse to patients in the presence of other observing patients."[1(p 256)] One attendant awakened patients with "Come on you m-----f-----s, out of bed!"[1(p 256)] "One patient was beaten in the presence of other patients for having approached an attendant and told him, 'I like you.'"[1(p 256)]

Because some of the hospitals participated in residency training programs and are described as "research oriented," I do find it hard to believe that the conditions were quite as bad as depicted. Perhaps they were. But how are we then to understand Rosenhan when in the summary to his original article he says:

It could be a mistake, and a very unfortunate one, to consider that what happened to us derived from malice or stupidity on the part of the staff. Quite the contrary, our overwhelming impression of them was of people who really cared, who were committed and who were uncommonly intelligent.[1(p 257)]

Surely what he described, including the verbal and physical abuse given to patients, is hardly what most people would regard as the behavior of people who "really cared" and were "uncommonly intelligent."

There is an obvious reason for the discrepancy between the actual behavior of the staff that Rosenhan describes and his exoneration of them for any responsibility for "malice" or "stupidity." To direct attention to any shortcomings on the part of the staff would detract attention from the real culprit, namely, diagnostic labels. Thus, Rosenhan asserts, without a shred of evidence from his study, that "Negative attitudes [toward psychiatric patients]...are the natural offspring of the labels patients wear and the places in which they are found."[1(p 254)] Nonsense! This makes as much sense as asserting that the attitude of the public toward cancer is the natural offspring of the label "cancer" without considering the attitude of the public to any of the *features* of neoplastic disease.

In recent years, large numbers of chronic psychiatric patients, many of them chronic schizophrenic and geriatric patients with organic brain syndromes, have been discharged from state hospitals and placed in communities that have no facilities to deal with them. The affected communities are up in arms not primarily because they are mental patients labeled with psychiatric diagnoses (because the majority are not recognized as expatients) but because the *behavior* of some of them is sometimes imcomprehensible, deviant, strange, and annoying. In a similar fashion, in a study of psychiatric labeling and the rehabilitation of former psychiatric inpatients, Schwartz and colleagues[49] found that an expatient's level of impairment (his behavior) was far more important in determining whether or not he was rejected by the community than knowledge that the individual was receiving psychiatric treatment (and therefore was labeled mentally ill).

Rosenhan never considers the possibility that the negative attitude toward patients with psychiatric diagnostic labels might at least have *something* to do with the attitude of people toward the very behaviors that might be the basis for the diagnostic labels. For example, he says:

The stigmatizing effects of psychiatric labels are so well known empirically and experientially (how might you feel if your colleagues believed you were a paranoid schizophrenic?) that it is hard to understand how or why those effects could be denied. [50(p 1647)]

Does Rosenhan think the answer to his hypothetical question would be any different if put solely in behavioral terms without a diagnostic label—"how might you feel if your colleagues believed that you had an unshakeable but utterly false conviction that everybody was out to harm you"?

It is informative to consult the references [51-53] that Rosenhan[1] cited as offering data that "a psychiatric diagnosis is harmful." My interpretation of these data is that they merely show that the general public in a variety of ways ascribes a negative valuation to behavior that has been identified as mental illness. It is hard to see how the public would have a more positive attitude toward individuals with behavioral diagnoses unless you could convince the public that what was wrong with these individuals had nothing to do with mental illness. Merely changing the name of the type of mental illness will not eliminate the negative attitude. That is why the attempt every few decades to change the name of the condition given to individuals whose behavior is negatively evaluated by the public, with the hope of thereby changing the attitude towards such individuals, is largely doomed to fail. Recall how "psychopath" became "sociopath" and more recently "antisocial personality." Recall how the "sexual perversions" became "sexual deviations," which might become (according to a recommendation of the Task Force on Nomenclature and Statistics, Subcommittee on Sexual Disorders) "sexual object and situation disorders." As soon as everyone finds out what the new terms really mean, the basic attitude toward individuals with these conditions reappears.

Rosenhan does not propose the "mental illness as myth" notion, although why he does not is a mystery, since it clearly is consistent with his basic hypothesis that diagnoses are in the minds of the observers and not the behavior of the patients. Furthermore, the only way to avoid the stigma of the mental illness diagnoses that Rosenhan decries would be to do away with the concept of mental illness itself. Can this be done? In a fascinating study of psychiatric labeling among Eskimos, Jorubas, and other divergent groups, J. M. Murphy, PhD (unpublished data), noted the following:

Explicit labels for insanity appear to exist in most groups. The labels refer to beliefs, feelings, and actions which are thought to emanate from the mind or inner state of an individual; they cause such persons to seek the aid of healers; and they bear strong resemblance to what we call schizophrenia. Of signal importance is the fact that the labels for insanity do not refer to one specific attribute but to a pattern of several interlinked phenomena. Despite wide variation in culture, a pattern composed of halluci-

nations, delusions, disorientations, and behavioral aberrations appears to identify the idea of "losing one's mind" almost everywhere even though the content of these behaviors is colored by cultural beliefs.

The implication is clear—mental illness is a label for phenomena that apparently exist in all cultures. Efforts to avoid the negative attitudes toward the phenomena by eliminating the label are misdirected. The most effective way of improving attitudes toward mental illness (as toward "cancer" or any other frightening illness) is to develop treatments that work and then convey this information to the public.

THE USES OF DIAGNOSIS

Rosenhan believes that the pseudopatients should have been diagnosed as having hallucinations of unknown origin. It is not clear what he thinks the diagnosis should have been if the pseudopatients had been sufficiently trained to talk, at times, incoherently, and had complained of difficulty in thinking clearly, lack of emotion, and that their thoughts were being broadcast so that strangers knew what they were thinking. Is Rosenhan perhaps suggesting multiple diagnoses of hallucinations, difficulty in thinking clearly, lack of emotion, and incoherent speech, all of unknown origin?

It is no secret that we lack a full understanding of such conditions as schizophrenia and manic-depressive illness, but are we quite as ignorant as Rosenhan would have us believe? Do we not know, for example, that hallucinations, in the context just described, are symptomatic of a different condition than are hallucinations of voices accusing the patient of sin, when associated with depressed affect, diurnal mood variation, loss of appetite, and insomnia? What about hallucinations of God's voice issuing commandments, associated with euphoric affect, psychomotor excitement, and accelerated and disconnected speech? Is this not also an entirely different condition?

There is a *purpose* to psychiatric diagnosis.[54] It enables mental health professionals to *communicate* with each other about the subject matter of their concern, *comprehend* the pathological processes involved in psychiatric illness, and *control* psychiatric disorders. Control consists of the ability to predict outcome, prevent the disorder from developing, and treat it once it has developed. Any serious discussion of the validity of psychiatric diagnosis or suggestions for alternative systems of classifying psychological disturbance must address itself to these purposes of psychiatric diagnosis.

In terms of its ability to accomplish these purposes, I would say that psychiatric diagnosis is moderately effective as a shorthand way of communicating the presence of constellations of signs and symptoms that tend to cluster together and is woefully inadequate in helping us understand the pathological processes of psychiatric disorders; however, it does offer considerable help in the control of many mental disorders. Control is possible because psychiatric diagnosis often yields information of value in predicting the likely course of illness (eg, an early recovery, chronicity, or recurrent episodes) and because for many mental disorders (particularly the severe ones), it is useful in suggesting the best available treatment.

Let us return to the three different clinical conditions that I described, each of which had auditory hallucinations as one of its manifestations. The reader with any familiarity with psychopathology will have no difficulty in identifying the three hypothetical conditions as schizophrenia, psychotic depression, and mania. Anyone familiar with the literature on psychiatric treatment will know that there are numerous well-controlled studies[55] indicating the superiority of the major tranquilizers for the treatment of schizophrenia, electroconvulsive therapy for the treatment of recurrent unipolar depression and, more recently, lithium carbonate for the treatment of mania. Furthermore, there is convincing evidence that these three conditions, each of which is often accompanied by hallucinations, are influenced by separate genetic factors. As Kety[3] said, "If schizophrenia is a myth, it is a myth with a strong genetic component."

Should psychiatric diagnosis be abandoned for a purely descriptive system that focuses on simple phenotypic behaviors *before* it has been demonstrated that such an approach is more useful as a guide to successful treatment or for understanding the role of genetic factors? I think not. It is of interest that examination of the behavior therapy literature, which is full of theoretical attacks on the usefulness of psychiatric diagnosis, does not indicate that it has been abandoned in actual practice by behaviorally oriented therapists. The traditional diagnostic categories of anxiety neurosis, phobia, anorexia nervosa, obsessive-compulsive disorder, schizophrenia, and depression and sexual dysfunction, to name but a few, are apparently alive and well, and presumably responding to specific behaviorally oriented therapies. (I have a vision. Traditional psychiatric diagnosis *has* long been forgotten. At a conference on behavioral classification, a keen research investigator proposes that the category "hallucinations of unknown cause" be subdivided into three different groups based on associated symptoms. The first group is characterized by depressed affect, diurnal mood variation, and so on, the second group by euphoric mood, psychomotor excitement, etc.

If psychiatric diagnosis is not quite as bad as Rosenhan would have us believe, that does not mean that it is all that good. What *is* the reliability of psychiatric diagnosis? A review of the major studies of the reliability of psychiatric diagnosis prior to 1972, revealed:

Reliability appears to be only satisfactory for three categories: mental deficiency, organic brain syndrome . . . and alcoholism. The level of reliability is no better than fair for psychosis and schizophrenia and is poor for the remaining categories.[56]

So be it. But where did Rosenhan get the idea that psychiatry is the only medical specialty that is plagued by inaccurate diagnosis? Studies have shown serious unreliability in the diagnosis of pulmonary disorders,[57] in the interpretation of electrocardiograms,[58] in the interpretation of roentgenograms,[59,60] and in the certification of causes of death.[61] A review of diagnostic unreliability in other branches of physical medicine is given by Garland [62] and the problem of the vagueness of medical criteria for diagnosis is thoroughly discussed by Feinstein.[63] The poor reliability of medical diagnosis, even when assisted by objective laboratory tests, does not mean that medical diagnosis is of no value. So it is with psychiatric diagnosis.

Recognition of the serious problems of the reliability of psychiatric diagnosis has resulted in a new approach to psychiatric diagnosis—the use of specific inclusion and exclusion criteria, as in contrast to the usually vague and ill-defined general descriptions found in the psychiatric literature and in the standard psychiatric glossary of the American Psychiatric Association. This approach was started by the St Louis group associated with the Department of Psychiatry of Washington University[64] and has been further developed by my co-workers and myself[65] as a set of criteria for a selected group of functional psychiatric disorders, called the Research Diagnostic Criteria (RDC). The Table shows the specific criteria for a diagnosis of schizophrenia from the latest version of the RDC.

Reliability studies utilizing the RDC with case record material (from which all cues as to diagnosis and treatment were removed), as well as with live patients, indicate high reliability for all of the major categories and reliability coefficients generally higher than have ever been reported.[66] It is therefore clear that the reliability of psychiatric diagnosis can be greatly increased by the use of specific criteria. (The interjudge reliability [chance corrected agreement, kappa] for the diagnosis of schizophrenia, using an earlier version of the RDC criteria with 68 psychiatric inpatients at the New York State

---

Diagnostic Criteria for Schizophrenia From the Research Diagnostic Criteria*

A. At least two of the following are required for definite and one for probable diagnosis:
1. thought broadcasting, insertion, or withdrawal (as defined in this manual)
2. delusions of control, other bizarre delusions, or multiple delusions (as defined in this manual), of any duration as long as definitely present
3. delusions other than presecutory or jealousy, lasting at least one week
4. delusions of any type if accompanied by hallucinations of any type for at least one week
5. auditory hallucinations in which either a voice keeps up a running commentary on the patient's behavior or thoughts as they occur, or two or more voices converse with each other
6. nonaffective verbal hallucinations spoken to the subject (as defined in this manual)
7. hallucinations of any type throughout the day for several days or intermittently for at least one month
8. definite instances of formal thought disorder (as defined in this manual)

B. A period of illness lasting at least two weeks

C. At no time during the active period of illness being considered did the patient meet the criteria for either probable or definite manic or depressive syndrome (criteria A and B under Major Depressive or Manic Disorders) to such a degree that it was a prominent part of the illness

*For what it is worth, the pseudopatient would have been diagnosed as "probable" schizophrenia using these criteria because of A6. In an oral communication, Rosenhan said that when the pseudopatients were asked how frequently the hallucinations occurred, they said "I don't know." Therefore, criterion A7 is not met.

Psychiatric Institute, was .88, which is a thoroughly respectable level of reliability.) It is very likely that the next edition of the American Psychiatric Association's *Diagnostic and Statistical Manual* will contain similar specific criteria.

There are other problems with current psychiatric diagnosis. The recent controversy over whether or not homosexuality per se should be considered a mental disorder highlighted the lack of agreement within the psychiatric profession as to the definition of a mental disorder. (It is difficult to determine at twilight whether it is day or night, but we have no such difficulty at midnight or noon. So too, our difficulty in defining the precise border of mental disorder and nonmental disorder in no way indicates the lack of utility of the concepts involved.) To the extent that our profession defines mental disorder as any significant deviation from the "good life" or "optimal human functioning," we will needlessly label many individuals as ill who are in no distress, function reasonably well, and hurt no one. This is a utopian conception of mental health that subjects the profession to the accusation that the sole function of the concept of mental disorder is social control and the pejorative labeling of all forms of social deviance. It is for this reason that we have proposed a more circumscribed definition,[54] but the criteria for this definition now appear to me to have incorrectly omitted certain, but by no means all, forms of antisocial behavior.

There are serious problems of validity. Many of the traditional diagnostic categories, such as some of the subtypes of schizophrenia and of major affective illness, and several of the personality disorders, have not been demonstrated to be distinct conditions or to be useful for prognosis or treatment assignment. In addition, despite considerable evidence supporting the distinctness of such conditions as schizophrenia and manic-depressive illness, the boundaries separating these conditions from other conditions are certainly not clear. Finally, the categories of the traditional psychiatric nomenclature are of least value when applied to the large numbers of outpatients who are not seriously ill. This may be a result of our greater ease in classifying conditions, such as the organic mental disorders and the psychoses, where the manifestations of the illness are qualitatively different from normal functioning. (For example, hallucinations are not part of normal functioning.) In contrast, with the personality disorders, we are dealing with quantitative variations in the intensity and pervasiveness of ubiquitous traits. (For example, some degree of suspiciousness or histrionic behavior is part of normal functioning.)

ROSENHAN'S RESPONSE TO CRITIQUES OF HIS STUDY

In his recent symposium article, "The Contextual Nature of Psychiatric Diagnosis," Rosenhan[43] responded to the critiques offered by me and by the other participants. My impending exhaustion, and I suspect, that of most readers who have gotten this far with my article, suggests the need for a *limited* critique of Rosenhan's article, which is as fascinating for what it omits as for what it says.

Let us start with the former. The interested reader can decide for himself which of the specific critiques of Rosenhan's original study that I presented in the earlier part of this article are telling and therefore worthy of a response

from Rosenhan, and which his article neglected to discuss. I believe they are numerous.

What is most significant is his omission of any discussion of the crucial issue of how diagnostic labels given to pseudopatients with unusual complaints are at all relevant to the problems of the psychiatric diagnosis of real patients. There is also no discussion of the criticism that the concept of schizophrenia does not exclude the possibility of recovery, so there was no reason why the admission diagnosis of schizophrenia should have been revised merely because of normal behavior while in the hospital.

There is a most remarkable response to my demonstration that the pseudopatients were given an unusual diagnosis at discharge, "in remission," thus proving that the diagnoses given to the pseudopatients were a function of their behavior and not of the setting. Rosenhan states:

Spitzer (1975) points out that the designation "in remission" is exceedingly rare. It occurs in only a handful of cases in the hospitals he surveyed, and my own cursory investigations that were stimulated by his confirm these observations. His data are intrinsically interesting, as well as interesting for the meaning they have for this particular study. How shall they be understood?

Once again we return to the influence of context on psychiatric perception. Consider two people who show no evidence of psychopathology. One is called sane and the other is called paranoid schizophrenic, in remission. Are both characterizations synonymous? Of course not. Would it matter to you if on one occasion you were designated normal, and on the other you were call psychotic, in remission, with both designations arising from the identical behavior? Of course it would matter. The perception of an asymptomatic status implies little by itself. It is the context in which that perception is embedded that tells the significant story.[43(p 468)]

Amazing! Of course "in remission" is not the same as "normal," but neither are the behaviors that are the basis for such categorization. The individual labeled "in remission" has the same behavior as the individual labeled "normal" only for one period of observation (current examination). He has a different history. The individual who has recovered (partially or completely) from an episode of schizophrenia has a probability of recurrence that far exceeds the probability for individuals who have never had such an episode of illness.[67] There is also evidence that maintenance phenothiazine treatment is effective in decreasing the probability of recurrence of a schizophrenic episode.[55] Therefore, if I, or a member of my family, had in fact recently recovered from an episode of schizophrenic illness and were currently asymptomatic, I would *prefer* a diagnosis of schizophrenia in remission to a diagnosis of "normal," since it would suggest that a particular kind of treatment might well be indicated. That, after all, is one of the purposes of diagnosis. The same argument would apply with even greater force to the justification of the category "in remission" for individuals who have had recurrent episodes of depressive or manic illness or both and who at a particular examination are asymptomatic. Without the concept of affective disorder in remission, how could one justify the use of lithium carbonate as a prophylactic agent?

The justification of the category "in remission" for certain psychiatric disorders that tend to be chronic and recurrent in no way minimizes the difficulty in providing specific guidelines as to when use of this category is appropriate. Just as it would make no sense to use this category after all episodes of psychiatric illness regardless of type or duration of asymptomatic status, so it makes no sense to argue on logical grounds that it should never be used.

Rosenhan apparently believes he has discovered a scandal regarding the process by which the official nomenclature of the American Psychiatric Association is developed and adopted. He states:

Unlike most medical diagnoses, which can be validated in numerous ways, psychiatric diagnoses are maintained by consensus alone. This is not commonly known to either the consumer or the mental health profession. Spitzer and Wilson [54] clarify the matter:

In 1965 the American Psychiatric Association ... assigned its Committee on Nomenclature and Statistics ... the task of preparing for the APA a new diagnostic manual of disorders ... A draft of the new manual, DSM II, was circulated in 1967 to 120 psychiatrists known to have special interests in the area of diagnosis and was revised on the basis of their criticisms and suggestions. After further study it was adopted by the APA in 1967, and published and officially accepted throughout the country in 1968. [43(p 464)]

Does Rosenhan believe that it is only the psychiatric portion of the medical nomenclature that is decided on by a committee? (I am haunted by visions. The scene is Geneva, Switzerland, the offices of the World Health Organization. A senior official is overheard talking to a new employee who has recently joined his unit. "In order to keep on schedule, this would be a good time for you to go up to the mountain and bring down the stones that have the latest revision of the ICD [International Classification of Diseases] for the ninth edition. I wonder if He will make many changes?" The junior official, demonstrating his ignorance, asks, "Does He give us the entire medical classification that way?" The senior official replies: "Of course not. We only get the nonpsychiatric part that way. In order for us to get the psychiatric classification we have to have a committee that gets together and votes on the changes. It's all very messy and thank God it's only a small part of the entire medical classification.")

Classifications are all man-made, and either some single person or a group of individuals decides what they shall be. When a committee to develop a psychiatric classification functions, it can act, like any committee, wisely or foolishly. A committee acts foolishly if it has no clear understanding of the purposes of the classification it is developing and if it merely perpetuated traditional nosologic distinctions that are based on theoretical assumptions not supported by data. A committee acts wisely if it understands the multiple purposes of psychiatric classification, if it makes a serious effort to consider the data that have accumulated regarding such issues as the internal consistency of the phenomenology, differential response to treatment, outcome, familial pattern and genetic loading, and the understanding of basic psychopathological and physiological processes. A committee acts wisely if it consults with experts in the various areas under consideration and if draft proposals of the classification are subjected to public scrutiny.

Let us return again to Rosenhan's statement that "Unlike most medical diagnoses, which can be validated in numerous ways, psychiatric diagnoses are maintained by consensus alone."[43(p 464)] Here Rosenhan is confusing the validation of the medical examination with the validation of a medical diagnosis. The distinction is subtle but important for understanding the true differences between psychiatric and nonpsychiatric medical diagnoses.

The validity of a procedure or concept is determined by how useful it is for the particular purposes for which it is intended. Consider the medical examination. The purpose is to make a correct diagnosis. Let us assume that a physician, during the course of a medical examination, determines on the basis of the patterning and course of symptoms and the physical examination that the most likely diagnosis is diabetes. The use of a laboratory procedure such as a glucose tolerance test can then validate the *examination* that led to the diagnosis of diabetes. The laboratory procedure, however, does not in any way validate the diagnostic category of diabetes. The validity of diabetes as a diagnosis is a function of the ability of physicians to understand and treat patients who have medical problems that are categorized as either diabetes or not diabetes. This is a function of our understanding of the illness, its course and associated features, and the availability of specific treatments. As greater understanding of the pathophysiology of diabetes and as more effective methods for treating diabetes are developed, the validity of the diagnostic category of diabetes increases.

Now let us consider the psychiatric examination. Its purpose is to make the correct psychiatric diagnosis. It is true that except for the organic brain disorders, we have no laboratory procedures that can be used to validate the psychiatric *examination*. That does not mean, as Rosenhan suggests, that we have no procedures for validating psychiatric diagnoses other than consensus. The procedures for validating psychiatric diagnoses do not differ in principle from those used to validate nonpsychiatric medical diagnoses. They consist of studies that indicate the extent to which knowledge of *membership* in a given diagnostic category provides useful information, not already contained in the defining characteristics of the diagnostic category. Reference has already been made to studies indicating the specificity of various forms of somatic treatment and separate genetic factors for several of the major psychiatric diagnostic categories. These studies, as well as other studies dealing with some of the other purposes of psychiatric diagnosis, *are* the procedures by which psychiatric diagnoses are validated.

ROSENHAN'S SUGGESTIONS FOR THE FUTURE

Rosenhan[13] concludes his response to the critiques of his study with a section entitled "The Future." It begins as follows: "It is natural to infer that what I have written here argues against categorization of all kinds. But that is not the case. I have been careful to direct attention to the present system of diagnosis, the DSM-II [*Diagnostic and Statistical Manual of Mental* Disorders[48]]."[43(p 472)] Only DSM II and not the general utility of psychiatric diagnosis? What about the following statements in the original article[1]?

Psychiatric diagnoses, in this view, are in the minds of the observers and are not valid summaries of characteristics displayed by the observed ... It seems more useful ... to limit our discussions to behaviors, the stimuli that provoke them, and their correlates ... Rather than acknowledge that we are just embarking on understanding, we continue to label patients "schizophrenic," "manic-depressive," and "insane," as if in those words we had captured the essence of understanding. [43(pp 251, 254, 257)]

What about the following statement in the same article, in which Rosenhan claims to be discussing the DSM II only?

Indeed, at present, my own preference runs to omitting diagnoses entirely, for it is far better from a scientific and treatment point of view to acknowledge ignorance than to mystify it with diagnoses that are unreliable, overly broad, and pejoratively connotative. [43(p 467)]

Rosenhan continues:

Nothing that is said here is intended to deprive the researchers of his classificatory system. He cannot proceed without it, but as long as his diagnostic data remain in his file until they are fully validated, they can do patients and treatment no harm. [43(p 473)]

What in the world is a "fully validated" diagnostic system? What is the clinician, who has to do the best he can with what information is currently available, to do as he waits for the appearance of the "fully validated" classification? Rosenhan ignores the historical fact that classification in medicine has always been preceded by clinicians using *imperfect* systems that have been improved on the basis of clinical and research experience.

(Hang on reader. We are almost finished.) Rosenhan again states:

What might we require of new diagnostic systems before they are published and officially accepted?... We should ask that coefficients of agreements between diagnosticians in a variety of settings *commonly* reach or exceed .90. That figure, which is associated with a bit more than 80% of the variance in diagnosis, is a liberal one in terms of the possible consequences of misdiagnosis and the reversibility of the diagnoses. The full reasoning behind that figure takes us away from the central thrust of this paper, but interested readers can confirm it for themselves in Cronbach, Gleser, Harinder, and Nageswari [68], and Cronbach and Gleser [69]. [43(p 473)]

First of all, the coefficients of agreement, such as the kappa index to which Rosenhan previously referred, unlike product moment correlations, are already in units of the proportion of subject variance and do not need to be squared. [70, 71] Thus, a kappa of .8 means that 80% of the variance is associated with true subject variability.

The more important error is Rosenhan's justification of an entirely arbitrary requirement of a given level of interrater agreement by citing a tradition in psychometrics, which makes an assumption that cannot be made in psychiatric diagnosis. Rosenhan's reference to the two excellent psychometric textbooks discusses the desirability of avoiding decisions when the likelihood of an error exceeds .05 or .10. What about situations when a decision cannot be avoided, which is the general rule when a patient is examined psychiatrically? Let us take the example of a decision regarding suicidal behavior (which admittedly is not a diagnosis but illustrates the issues well). Interrater agreement regarding suicidal potential is undoubtedly much below .8. Does that mean that a clinician should never make a management decision based on his best judgment? Obviously, he must—to avoid making a decision is itself a decision. The facts are that despite our difficulty in reliably making medical judgments regarding diagnostic categories in psychiatry and the rest of medicine, patients must be treated and that treatment must follow from the decision of the clinician as to what he thinks is wrong with the patient. And that is what a diagnosis is.

Finally, Rosenhan concludes:

We should require that the proven untility of such a system exceed its liabilities for patients. Understand the issue. Syphilis and cancer both have negative social and emotional overtones. But the treatments that exist for them presumably exceed the personal liabilities associated with the diagnosis. [43(p 472)]

The implications of this are staggering! Is Rosenhan suggesting that prior to the development of effective treatments for syphilis and cancer, he would have decried the use of these diagnostic labels? Should we eliminate the diagnoses of antisocial personality, drug abuse, and alcoholism until we have treatments for these conditions whose benefits exceed the potential liabilities associated with the diagnosis? How do we study the effectiveness of treatments for these conditions if we are enjoined from using the diagnostic categories until we have effective treatments for them?

I have not dealt at all with the myriad ways in which psychiatric diagnostic labels can be and are misused and hurt patients rather than help them. This is a problem requiring serious research that Rosenhan unfortunately does not help illuminate. However, whatever the solutions to that problem, the available evidence that psychiatric diagnostic labels are *inherently* harmful to patients is scant indeed. Their misuse is not sufficient reason to abandon their use; when properly used, they have been shown to be of considerable value.

This article is a revision of that which appeared in the 1975 volumes of The Journal of Abnormal Psychology. *The need for serious consideration of issues that can so mischievously mislead the serious agenda of a field is well met therein; Professor Rosenhan also there amplifies his view of both the data and the controversy. The space and attention given the original article, in part because of its sponsorship, evoked concern among those researchers and clinicians working seriously in the range of issues relevant to general psychiatry. Rather than launch more attention to the* Science *article and deprive our contributors of* ARCHIVES *space for original research and scholarly communications (that are scrutinized by stiff peer review), we have awaited an article suitable to the issue of science and sanity. We recommend most highly* The Journal of Abnormal Psychology's *symposium and especially the masterful analysis of philosophy of science issues by I. E. Farber (J Abnorm Psychol 84:442-452, 589-620, 1975)—ED.*

Jean Endicott, PhD, Joseph Fleiss, PhD, Joseph Zubin, PhD, Janet Forman, MSW, Karen Greene, MA, and Rose Bender assisted with the preparation of this article.

This article is a revision of one that appeared in *The Journal of Abnormal Psychology* (84:442-452, 1975).

Nonproprietary Name and Trademarks of Drug

Lithium carbonate—*Eskalith, Lithane, Lithotabs.*

References

1. Rosenhan DL: On being sane in insane places. *Science* 179:250-258, 1973.

2. Dimond RE: Popular opinion is not empirical data. *Clin Soc Work J* 2:264:270, 1974.

3. Kety SS: From rationalization to reason. *Am J Psychiatry* 131:957-963, 1974.

4. Rifkin A, Klein DF, Quitkin F, et al: Sane: Insane. *JAMA* 224:1646-1647, 1973.

6. DISORDERS AND THERAPY

5. Klein DF, Rifkin A, Quitkin FM: Sane: Insane. *JAMA* 226:1569, 1973.

6. Fleischman PR, Israel JV, Burr WA, et al: Psychiatric Diagnosis. *Science* 180:356-365, 1973.

7. Pattison EM: Social criticism and scientific responsibility. *J Am Sci Affil* 26:110-114, 1974.

8. Rabichow HG, Pharis ME: Rosenhan was wrong: The staff was lousy. *Clin Soc Work J* 2:271-278, 1974.

9. Shectman F: On being misinformed by misleading arguments. *Bull Menninger Clin* 37:523-525, 1973.

10. Abrahamson D: Procedure re-examined. *Lancet* 1:1153-1155, 1974.

11. Arthur RJ: Social psychiatry: An overview. *Am J Psychiatry* 130:841-849, 1973.

12. Burdsal C, Greenberg G, Timpe R: The relationship of marihuana usage to personality and motivational factors. *J Psychol* 85:45-51, 1973.

13. Sane: Insane, editorial. *JAMA* 223:1272, 1973.

14. Insane: Sane, editorial. *JAMA* 223:1381, 1973.

15. Glaser FB: Medical ethnocentrism and the treatment of addiction. *Int J Offender Ther Comp Crimino* 18:13-27, 1974.

16. Hoekstra A: Concerning science and society. *Clin Soc Work J* 2:299-306, 1974.

17. Kane RA: Look to the record. *Soc Work* 19:412-419, 1974.

18. Levy CS: On sane social workers in insane places. *Clin Soc Work J* 2:257-263, 1974.

19. Mark VH: A psychosurgeon's case *for* psychosurgery. *Psychol Today* 8:28ff, 1974.

20. Morse N: Some problems with insane institutions. *Clin Soc Work J* 2:291-298, 1974.

21. Oran D: Judges and psychiatrists lock up too many people. *Psychol Today* 7:20ff, 1973.

22. Perry TL, Hansen S, Tischler B, et al: Unrecognized adult phenylketonuria. *N Engl J Med* 289:395-398, 1973.

23. Scheff TJ: The labelling theory of mental illness. *Am Sociol Rev* 39:444-452, 1974.

24. Walden T, Singer G, Thomet W: Students as clients: The other side of the desk. *Clin Soc Work J* 2:279-290, 1974.

25. Daves WF: *Textbook of General Psychology*. New York, Thomas Y Crowell Co, 1975.

26. Davison G, Neale JM: *Abnormal Psychology—An Experimental Clinical Approach*. New York, John Wiley & Sons Inc, 1974.

27. Haber R, Fried A: *An Introduction to Psychology*. New York, Holt Rinehart & Winston Inc, 1975.

28. Hilgard E, Atkinson R, Atkinson R: *Introduction to Psychology*, ed 6. New York, Harcourt Brace Jovanovich Inc, 1975.

29. Kleinmuntz B: *Essentials of Abnormal Psychology*. New York, Harper & Row Publishers Inc, 1974.

30. Krech D, Crutchfield R, Livson N: *Elements of Psychology*, ed 3. New York, Alfred A Knopf Inc, 1974.

31. London P: *Beginning Psychology*. Homewood, Ill, Dorsey Press Inc. 1975.

32. McMahon FB: *Psychology: The Hybrid Science*, ed 2. Englewood Cliffs, NJ, Prentice-Hall Inc, 1974.

33. Rubinstein J: *The Study of Psychology*. Guilford, Conn, Dushkin Publishing Group Inc, 1975.

34. Ullman L, Krasner L: *A Psychological Approach to Abnormal Behavior*, ed 2. Englewood Cliffs, NJ, Prentice-Hall Inc, 1975.

35. Wrightsman L, Sanford F: *Psychology: A Scientific Study of Human Behavior*, ed 4. Monterey, Cal, Brooks/Cole Publishing Co, 1975.

36. Zimbardo P, Ruch F: *Psychology and Life*, ed 9. Glenview, Ill, Scott Foresman & Co, 1975.

37. Brown R, Herrnstein R: *Psychology*. Boston, Little Brown & Co, 1975.

38. Kimble G, Garmezy N, Zigler E: *Principles of General Psychology*, ed 4. New York, Ronald Press Co, 1974.

39. Lindzey G, Hall C, Thompson R: *Psychology*. New York, Worth Publishers Inc, 1975.

40. Crown S: On being sane in insane places: A comment from England. *J Abnorm Psychol* 84:453-455, 1975.

41. Farber IE: Sane and insane: Constructions and misconstructions. *J Abnorm Psychol* 84:589-620, 1975.

42. Millon T: Reflections on Rosenhan's "On being sane in insane places." *J Abnorm Psychol* 84:456-461, 1975.

43. Rosenhan DL: The contextual nature of psychiatric diagnosis. *J Abnorm Psychol* 84:462-474, 1975.

44. Spitzer RL: On pseudoscience in science, logic in remission, and psychiatric diagnosis: A critique of Rosenhan's "On being sane in insane places." *J Abnorm Psychol* 84:442-452, 1975.

45. Weiner B: On being sane in insane places: A process (attributional) analysis and critique. *J Abnorm Psychol* 84:433-441, 1975.

46. Hunter FM: Psychiatric diagnosis. *Science* 180:361, 1973.

47. Rosenhan DL: Psychiatric diagnosis. *Science* 180:365-369, 1973.

48. *Diagnostic and Statistical Manual of Mental Disorders*, ed 2. Washington DC, American Psychiatric Association, 1968.

49. Schwartz CC, Myers JK, Astrachan BM: Psychiatric labeling and the rehabilitation of the mental patient: Implications of research findings for mental health policy. *Arch Gen Psychiatry* 31:329-334, 1974.

50. Rosenhan DL: *Sane: Insane. JAMA* 224:1646-1647, 1973.

51. Nunnally JC Jr: *Popular Conceptions of Mental Health*. New York, Holt Rinehart & Winston Inc, 1961.

52. Sarbin TR: On the futility of the proposition that some people be labelled "mentally ill." *J Consult Clin Psychol* 31:447, 1967.

53. Sarbin TR, Mancuso JC: Failure of a moral enterprise: Attitudes of the public toward mental illness. *J Consult Clin Psychol* 35:159-173, 1970.

54. Spitzer RL, Wilson PT: Nosology and the official psychiatric nomenclature, in Freedman A, Kaplan H, Sadock B (eds): *Comprehensive Textbook of Psychiatry*. Baltimore, Williams & Wilkins Co, pp 826-845.

55. Klein D, Davis J: *Diagnosis and Drug Treatment of Psychiatric Disorders*. Baltimore, Williams & Wilkins Co, 1969.

56. Spitzer RL, Fleiss JL: A reanalysis of the reliability of psychiatric diagnosis. *Br J Psychiatry* 125:341-347, 1974.

57. Fletcher A: Clinical judgment of pulmonary emphysema-an experimental study. *Proc R Soc Med* 45:577-584, 1952.

58. Davies LG: Observer variation in reports on electrocardiograms. *Br Heart J* 20:153-161, 1958.

59. Cochrane AL, Garland LH: Observer error in interpretation of chest films: International investigation. *Lancet* 2:505-509, 1952.

60. Yerushalmy J: Statistical problems in assessing methods of medical diagnosis, with special reference to x-ray techniques. *Public Health Rep* 62:1432-1449, 1947.

61. Markush RE, Schaaf WE, Seigel DG: The influence of the death certifier on the results of epidemiologic studies. *J Natl Med Assoc* 59:105-113, 1967.

62. Garland LH: The problem of observer error. *Bull NY Acad Med* 36:570-584, 1960.

63. Feinstein A: *Clinical Judgment*. Baltimore, Williams & Wilkins Co, 1967.

64. Feighner JP, Robins E, Guze SB, et al: Diagnostic criteria for use in psychiatric research. *Arch Gen Psychiatry* 26:57-63, 1972.

65. Spitzer RL, Endicott J, Robins E: *Research Diagnostic Criteria (RDC)*. New York, Biometrics Research, New York State Department of Mental Hygiene, 1974.

66. Spitzer RL, Endicott J, Robins E, et al: Preliminary report of the reliability of Research Diagnostic Criteria applied to psychiatric case records, in Sudilofsky A, Beer B, Gershon S (eds): *Prediction in Psychopharmacology*. New York, Raven Press, 1975, pp 1-47.

67. Gunderson JG, Autry JH, Mosher LR, et al: Special report: Schizophrenia, 1974. *Schizophrenia Bull* 9:15-54, 1974.

68. Cronbach LJ, Gleser GC, Harinder N, et al: *The Dependability of Behavioral Measurements: Theory of Generalizability for Scores and Profiles*. New York, John Wiley & Sons Inc, 1972.

69. Cronbach LJ, Gleser GC: Interpretation of reliability and validity coefficients: Remarks on a paper by Lord. *J Educ Psychol* 50:230-237, 1959.

70. Fleiss JL, Cohen J: The equivalence of weighted kappa and the intraclass correlation coefficient as measures of reliability. *Educ Psychol Meas* 33:613-619, 1973.

71. Fleiss JL: Measuring agreement between two judges on the presence or absence of a trait. *Biometrics* 31:651-659, 1975.

Medical Treatment of Mental Illness

Pharmacotherapies revolutionize psychiatric care and
present scientific and ethical challenges to society.

Summary. Psychotherapeutic drugs have dramatically improved the prognosis for patients with severe mental illness. The drug treatments are not a panacea. The medications sometimes cause irreversible side effects, and they are not helpful for all patients. They allow large numbers of individuals to leave the hospital, but to return to communities that are often poorly prepared to provide continuing care. Despite their limitations, psychotherapeutic drugs relieve a great deal of human suffering. They also involve psychiatry in modern biological science. This has led to the continuing search for more effective medications based on the study of possible biochemical substrates of psychiatric disorders.

Philip A. Berger

The author is an assistant professor in the Department of Psychiatry and Behavioral Sciences, Stanford University School of Medicine, Stanford, California 94305, and director of the Stanford Psychiatric Clinical Research Center, Palo Alto Veterans Administration Hospital, Palo Alto, California 94304.

Effective pharmacological treatments for mental illness have existed only during the last quarter-century. This period has also witnessed a revolution in the care of patients with psychiatric disorders, and the number of patients in state and county mental hospitals has sharply declined. The introduction and evaluation of drug treatments required the development of more accurate methods of classification and of assessment of severity, and better criteria of improvement in mental patients. These more accurate methods could then be applied to nondrug treatments that were introduced in the optimistic period that followed the first successful drug trials. The resulting combination of drug therapy and psychological or socioenvironmental treatment is responsible for the vastly improved prognosis for patients with mental illness today (*1*).

Psychotherapeutic drugs have also helped wed some aspects of psychiatry with biological science, a source of significant therapeutic advances in the other medical specialities. Biological psychiatrists attempting to explain pharmacotherapies have also begun to investigate possible biochemical causes of mental illness.

The use of drug treatments for mental illness is not all positive: problems have arisen for patients, physicians, and society. The drugs are not ideal. Not all patients are helped, and many are only partially improved. Like other useful medications, the pharmacological agents used in mental illness can cause severe adverse reactions; some of these side effects are irreversible. Certain classes of drugs for psychiatric patients are toxic when taken in an overdose and thus can be used in suicide attempts. The use of psychotherapeutic drugs poses ethical questions for physicians and society. The symptoms of some mental disorders make it difficult for patients to understand their pharmacological treatments, and therefore they cannot base their decision on whether to take medications on a true understanding of the potential benefits and risks. Whether involuntary treatment of psychiatric patients is ever justified is the appropriate subject of vigorous debate. The factors that must be weighed include the patients' rights, the duties and responsibilities that a physician feels towards the patients, and the right of society to be protected from dangerous behaviors (*1*).

In this article I will discuss some of the practical, scientific, and ethical aspects of the medical treatment of mental illness. A description of the predrug era is followed by a discussion of the impact of recent therapeutic innovations. Three major psychiatric disorders are described: schizophrenia, depression, and mania. The important current drug treatments for these disorders are the antipsychotics for schizophrenia, tricyclic antidepressants or monoamine oxidase inhibitors for depression, and lithium salts for mania. Evidence for their efficacy, practical aspects of treatment, and critical evaluations of their hypothesized biochemical mechanisms of action are described. Finally, the ethical problems created by the drug treatments of mental disorders are outlined.

The Revolution in Psychiatric Care

Firsthand descriptions by physicians who worked with the mentally ill before the introduction of effective pharmacotherapies paint a dismal picture of the predrug era. There were few outpatient psychiatric clinics, and general medical hospitals rarely admitted patients with severe mental illness. Most patients were sent quickly to state mental hospitals, which were more like custodial facilities than medical treatment centers. Pessimism about psychiatric disorders was widespread, admissions increased, and discharges remained low.

Living areas in public mental hospitals were poorly furnished and crowded. Hallucinating patients paced the floor, or rocked in chairs, and talked to their "voices"; paranoid patients scanned the rooms, ever vigilant and ever fearful. Catatonic patients remained in fixed positions for days at a time, developing swollen limbs and pressure sores; withdrawn patients sat on wooden benches, year after year, doing nothing, while their physical health deteriorated. Manic patients joked, laughed, and moved about rapidly for days at a time until they collapsed, exhausted. Violent or agitated patients attacked other patients or staff members in response to idiosyncratic beliefs. Such patients were often kept in nearly empty "seclusion rooms," strapped to beds that were bolted to the floor or placed in warm baths or wrapped in wet sheets in an attempt to calm them (*1, 2*).

6. DISORDERS AND THERAPY

The physicians responsible for the treatment of patients in public mental hospitals were poorly equipped for the task. Before World War II, many of these physicians were trained in general medicine or neurology; during the postwar period some had also studied psychoanalytic psychotherapy. However, neither neurological diagnosis nor psychoanalysis had much to offer patients in public mental institutions. Thus, physicians acted mainly as custodians and administrators. Many of the people who worked in public mental hospitals were courageous and caring, but they faced an impossible task, not only because of the social stigma of mental illness, public apathy, and lack of adequate funds for patient facilities and staff, but also because there simply were few effective treatments for severe psychiatric disease (1, 2).

A dramatic change in the treatment of patients with mental illness began in the 1950's. For nearly 100 years, the number of patients in public mental institutions in the United States had increased by about 2 percent per year, reaching a peak of 559,000 in 1955 (Fig. 1) (3). Then in 1956, for the first time in history, more of these patients were discharged than admitted, a trend that continues despite a steady increase in both the admission rate and the national population. Today there are less than 200,000 patients in these institutions (3, 4). However, not even the majority of the individuals who leave public mental hospitals are free of psychiatric symptoms, and many continue to receive treatment in transitional facilities or outpatient clinics. Still, most are able to reestablish family relationships, find employment, and participate in community life (1, 4).

Conditions have also improved for patients in the hospitals. Very few patients require seclusion rooms and physical restraints; those who do usually respond rapidly to treatment. Most hospital wards are unlocked. Many are set up as "therapeutic communities," where patients and staff meet regularly to discuss all aspects of life in the hospital. Patients are treated with respect and encouraged to determine many of the conditions of their hospitalization. Increased patient government improves the hospital environment and also helps patients in the transition from hospitalization to home by making the hospital more like a family or a community. Other improvements in modern mental hospitals increase the similarities between the hospital and the rest of society. Plays, concerts, movies, sports equipment, and arts and crafts are available to most patients. Some psychiatric hospitals have small companies that contract to do piecework for local industries, so that patients can be economically productive even during their hospital stay (1).

These dramatic changes in the treatment of psychiatric patients are the result of many interrelated factors. Much of the momentum, however, came from the development and use of psychotherapeutic drugs. Use of these drugs led to a climate that favored innovation and encouraged the development and evaluation of other new therapeutic approaches. As with all important social changes, there have been some negative results from the discharge of large numbers of patients from public mental hospitals. In some areas, planning was inadequate for the return of psychiatric patients to the community (4, 5). Reich (6) reports that many patients discharged from New York State mental hospitals are living in cheap hotels, where they are robbed and abused by people who take advantage of their relative helplessness. Arnhoff (7) suggests that the impact of community treatment on the families of mental patients has not been carefully studied. He finds no convincing evidence that home or community treatment is better than hospital treatment in either its short- or its long-term effects (7).

The location of psychiatric treatment is certainly less important than its quality. While much remains to be done, it is clear that the quality of treatment for patients with severe mental illness has vastly improved since the introduction of psychotherapeutic drugs.

Schizophrenia

The schizophrenic syndrome usually begins in young adulthood. Symptoms include altered motor behavior, perceptual distortions, disturbed thinking, altered mood, and unusual interpersonal behavior. Occasionally, a schizophrenic syndrome appears suddenly; more commonly the symptoms have an insidious onset. In many cases the patient has a history of being somewhat withdrawn and introverted since childhood. In the prodromal phase of schizophrenia, commonplace reality may begin to seem strange. Patients often withdraw into

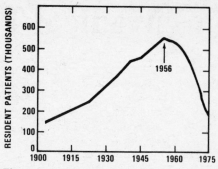

Fig. 1. Patient population in public mental institutions, 1900 through 1975 (3).

themselves to focus on internal experiences. Commonly they feel depersonalized, as if their identity were being dissolved or lost. Those close to these individuals often have increasing difficulty empathizing with and understanding their unusual feelings, thoughts, and experiences. Normal diurnal rhythms of sleep, appetite, and sexual interest may be disrupted. Gradually, full-blown schizophrenic syndromes develop. Although symptoms vary from patient to patient, they usually make normal functioning difficult or impossible.

The motor behavior of schizophrenics ranges from total immobilization, called catatonia, to frenetic and purposeless activity often accompanied by peculiar mannerisms. Perceptual distortions include hallucinations, which can arise in any sensory modality, although auditory hallucinations ("hearing voices") are the most common. Frequently, the voices are threatening or obscene and may instruct the patient to perform specific acts. Sometimes patients hear their own thoughts out loud. Disturbances in thinking in schizophrenic patients lead to distorted concept formation, bizarre speech, and illogical thought patterns. The illogical thought patterns are often expressed as delusions, ideas that are false or improbable but that cannot be modified by persuasion or contradictory evidence. Common paranoid delusions lead schizophrenic patients to believe that they have been chosen for special missions or that they are the object of persecution by a group with complex plots against them. Some schizophrenics have the delusions that unseen forces are controlling their thoughts or behavior or "reading their minds." Delusions are reinforced by misinterpretations of reality. Thus schizophrenics often believe that items on television or in newspapers are cryptic messages confirming their beliefs.

Schizophrenic patients also have disorders of the thought process. This causes the speech pattern to wander and fail to lead to its apparent goal, a process called looseness of associations. Expressions of emotion in schizophrenic patients are often absent, blunted, or inappropriate to the content of the conversation. Sometimes schizophrenics are overwhelmed with intense anxiety or deep rage, unrelated to any obvious environmental stimuli.

In schizophrenic patients these profound disturbances in motor behavior, perceptions, thinking, and mood cause severe difficulties in everyday tasks and interpersonal relationships. Patients often behave in an impulsive, disorganized, or unusual manner. Schizophrenic patients are rarely dangerous, but they are unpredictable and may occasionally act violently if directed by "a voice," if they feel they must defend themselves against an imaginary enemy, or if they are overactive and severely disorganized (1, 8).

What is the incidence of schizophrenia? At present about 180,000 patients are hospitalized in the United States with the diagnosis of schizophrenia; another 800,000 are being treated as outpatients or have active symptoms but are not being treated. The number of individuals who develop schizophrenic symptoms each year is approximately 150 per 100,000. The chances that a person will be treated for schizophrenia in his lifetime have been estimated to be about 1 percent. About half of the available beds for the mentally ill and the mentally retarded, or about one-quarter of all available beds in hospitals, are occupied by patients with the diagnosis of schizophrenia. Despite the widely held belief that schizophrenia is more common in complex modern societies, the incidence of schizophrenia has been relatively constant for the last 100 years in the United States. In addition, preliminary results of recent international collaborative studies show a similar incidence in all nations that have been studied (9).

Depression

The term depression is used to describe both a normal mood and a serious mental disorder. As a normal mood, depression refers to the transitory feelings of sadness, grief, disappointment, loneliness, or discouragement that everyone feels during the difficult times of life. As a mental disorder, depression is an illness with many symptoms, only one of which is sadness. Those with depression have changes in mood, thinking patterns, motor activity, and behavior. They also have somatic or physical symptoms and frequently have suicidal ideas that can lead to self-destructive behavior.

The mood of depressed individuals is variable but includes profound sadness and often a loss of the ability to feel pleasure. The ideas, activities, and relationships that usually bring pleasure can seem empty or hollow. The changes in thinking patterns lead to pessimism about the future and low self-esteem. Depressed people often deny their past accomplishments or feel unworthy of current achievements. Feelings of low self-esteem or worthlessness combine with pessimism to rob them of their motivation, making it difficult to maintain either jobs or interpersonal relationships. Often they feel guilty about not living up to the expectations of others. Guilt can be even more generalized, so that some depressed people may feel they have committed a sin or a crime and fear discovery or think they deserve punishment. Some severely depressed patients develop psychosis. A psychotic patient distorts or perceives reality incorrectly. This can lead to unusual beliefs or behaviors. For example, some depressed patients may feel they have actually become hollow inside, that their internal organs have "turned to dust." To give another example, a psychotically depressed individual may blame himself for a tragic world event such as a war or a flood. Many depressed people are fearful or anxious. They may be agitated and quite physically active but unable to concentrate on any task; or they may move very slowly, feel extremely weak, tired, and helpless, and have slow and labored thoughts that make it difficult to concentrate, to read, or even to form sentences for conversation.

Physical symptoms are often a prominent part of the depression syndrome. Those with severe depression often have no appetite and lose weight. Sleep disturbance is another common symptom, causing insomnia, restless nights, and early morning awakening. In severe depression a patient often wakes at 3 or 4 a.m. and is unable to get back to sleep. Some depressed patients also experience constipation, dry mouth, tight feelings in the chest, and aches and pains, particularly headaches and backaches. Many depressed people lose interest in sexual activity, and depressed women often have changes in their menstrual cycle.

Thoughts of death and suicide are the most dangerous symptom of severe depression. The hopelessness, guilt feelings, and low self-esteem can all contribute to suicidal thinking. Some patients see suicide as an escape from their psychic pain. Others feel there is no reason to go on living since things will never get better. Some believe that their death would relieve their family of the burden of caring for them; others feel that death is the appropriate punishment for their imagined sin or crime. Whatever the cognitive origin, suicide must be considered a possibility in anyone with depression.

Most depressed patients do not have a history of any other psychiatric illness. About one-fifth of depressed patients have episodes of both depression and mania and are called bipolar patients. Unipolar patients are those who suffer only recurrent depressive episodes. This distinction between bipolar and unipolar depression is increasingly important in both research and pharmacotherapy (9).

Mania

Mania is a severe emotional disorder that superficially appears to be the opposite of depression. Symptoms can be divided into changes in mood, thought, motor activity, and behavior. The mood is elated—sometimes euphoric, overconfident, or carefree. A manic individual is optimistic and may feel attractive, desirable, efficient, and alert. However, this mood often is brittle, and these individuals become irritable if frustrated. The thought patterns of manics are disturbed, with one thought rapidly following another in what is called flight of ideas. Ideas of potency, knowledge, and special abilities occur in severe mania. The motor activity of manics is also accelerated; they are restless and may work energetically, but may move from project to project, unable to complete any. Manic individuals may sleep little and eat less; like patients with severe depression, they tend to lose weight. Mild forms of mania, called hypomania, may serve a person well, since our society is more appreciative of, and even selects for success, people with some manic traits in preference to more depressive or contemplative individuals. In contrast, severe mania causes significant life disruptions and can be devastating to personal relationships and careers.

Some bipolar patients alternate between depression and mania. However, many have long periods of normal functioning in between episodes. In general, manic episodes are more common when bipolar patients are younger, while depression is more frequent with age. The duration of the episodes of bipolar illness varies. One common pattern is for depressive episodes to last about 6 months and manic episodes about 3 months. However, a few patients have been known to cycle from mania to depression in periods as short as 24 hours, while others have manic and depressed episodes that seem to last for years (10).

How common are depression and mania? The major problem in determining the incidence is the lack of a universal definition of depression or mania. The incidence of bipolar illness is about 300 per 100,000 or 0.3 percent. Perhaps 600,000 bipolar patients are identified and treated each year in the United States. The number of patients with severe unipolar depression is certainly much larger. According to the National Institute of Mental Health (NIMH) and other sources, some 1.5 million people are being treated for depression today. But perhaps three or even five times that number may actually need such treatment. Thus, there may be from 4.5 to 7.5 million individuals in the United States who are suffering the psychic pain, life disruptions, and risk of suicide associated with depression and who could benefit from treatment. The results from an NIMH and a British study suggest that perhaps as many as 15 percent of the population will have at least one depressive episode during their lifetime. There are at least 26,000 reported deaths by suicide each year, making it the tenth leading cause of death. Thus, depression and suicide are major public health concerns that require vigorous medical treatment (10, 11).

Antipsychotic Medications

The drug treatments of schizophrenia include substances from at least eight different chemical classes. The drugs are remarkable in their ability to counteract hallucinations, delusional thinking, assaultiveness, severe excitement or withdrawal, and unusual behavior and to fa-

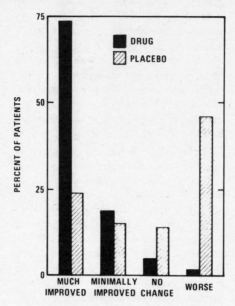

Fig. 2. Physicians' global ratings of patients' responses to treatment with antipsychotics or placebo (13).

cilitate the social adjustment of schizophrenic patients. Unfortunately, they are not effective in all patients and are only partially effective in others. They can also have troublesome and sometimes irreversible side effects (12).

Several important questions can be asked about the antipsychotics: Are they effective when compared to a placebo? Are they useful as maintenance treatments to prevent a return of schizophrenic symptoms? Do they produce serious or irreversible side effects? How do they work; what is the biochemical mechanism of their action on the brain?

The efficacy of the antipsychotic drugs in the treatment of schizophrenia has been established in numerous clinical trials. The drugs are effective in all subtypes of schizophrenia, at all stages of the illness, at all ages, and in every country where they have been studied (12). In the studies that established this efficacy the quantitative, double-blind, controlled research method was used. In this design, symptoms are quantitated by having one or more psychiatrists rate a patient's symptoms on standardized rating scales after a daily interview. The studies are double-blind in that both the investigator and the patient are unaware of what the patient is receiving, and they are controlled because one or more drugs are compared to a medically inert placebo or to a drug with known efficacy.

Figure 2 summarizes some of the results of an NIMH collaborative study of the efficacy of the treatment of acute

schizophrenia with antipsychotics (13). Approximately three-fourths of patients were "much improved" by antipsychotics during the 6-week study, while nearly half of the placebo group were "worse." Double-blind, controlled studies have also been used to determine the efficacy of maintenance antipsychotic drugs in preventing the return of schizophrenic symptoms after an initial response to treatment.

A recent review summarized the 24 studies that met criteria for appropriate design (14). It was reported in this review that 698 of 1068 patients (65 percent) who received a placebo relapsed, compared to 639 of 2127 (30 percent) receiving maintenance antipsychotics; thus, the relapse rate in the drug-treated group was less than half that in the placebo group. Two conclusions can be drawn from this review of maintenance treatment. First, maintenance antipsychotics can prevent relapse in many but not all patients with schizophrenia. Second, since some patients do not relapse on placebo, these patients do not require maintenance treatment. Unfortunately, although some progress has been made, it is still not possible to predict with certainty which patients will relapse. The urgency of such a prediction is increased by several reversible but troublesome side effects, and by the one potentially irreversible side effect, caused by antipsychotics.

Antipsychotics are relatively safe, but they occasionally do produce troublesome side effects. Extrapyramidal motor reactions is the general term given to a wide variety of muscle or movement side effects sometimes caused by these medications. Some patients experience uncontrollable restlessness or muscle spasms in the neck, trunk, or eyes. Others develop muscle side effects that resemble the symptoms of Parkinson's disease, such as muscle rigidity, tremors, altered posture, and shuffling gait. Most of these extrapyramidal muscle reactions occur soon after antipsychotics are started and usually disappear spontaneously. They can also be controlled by the anticholinergic drugs that are used to treat Parkinson's disease (12).

Tardive dyskinesia is a movement disorder that is distinct from the early extrapyramidal reactions in several ways. It usually occurs only after prolonged treatment with antipsychotics. It does not usually respond to anticholinergic medications, and it is sometimes irre-

Table 1. Dopamine pathways.

Pathway	Anatomic location	Hypothesized roles
Nigrostriatal	Substantia nigra (A9) to caudate-putamen (striatum)	Muscle and movement coordination Parkinson's disease Extrapyramidal symptoms of antipsychotics Animal stereotypy(?) Tardive dyskinesia(?)
Mesolimbic-mesocortical	Substantia nigra and area medial to substantia nigra (A9, A10) to limbic nucleii and cortical regions	Emotional tone(?) Antipsychotic action of neuroleptics(?) Amphetamine and L-dopa psychosis(?) Schizophrenia(?)
Tuberoinfundibular	Arcuate nucleus to median eminence	Modulation of some endocrine functions Antipsychotic drug action on prolactin

versible. Tardive dyskinesia consists of frequent, repetitive, involuntary movements of the lips, tongue, jaw, face, and sometimes of the trunk or limbs. These movements can be socially embarrassing and can make speech, eating, and sometimes even breathing difficult (15). The reported prevalence of tardive dyskinesia in hospitalized patients with mental illness varies between 0.5 and 40 percent, with a mean of about 15 percent (16). Differences in methods of case finding and definitions of the disorder make it difficult to accurately determine prevalence. However, the possibility that a patient will develop tardive dyskinesia makes the decision to place him on maintenance antipsychotics extremely difficult. The risk of and potential for life disruptions from a relapse of schizophrenic symptoms must be weighed against the risk of tardive dyskinesia.

Some patients probably should not be placed on maintenance antipsychotics. Patients with good social adjustment who develop schizophrenic symptoms suddenly in response to stress usually respond rapidly to antipsychotics and may never develop symptoms again. Hospitalized patients with chronic schizophrenic symptoms that respond only minimally to antipsychotics may not require drug maintenance. The gains from drug therapy in such patients are small. Relapse is not as much of a life problem as it would be for an employed outpatient, and the risk of tardive dyskinesia is great. However, for many patients the return of schizophrenic symptoms can cause severe life disruptions, and the benefits of maintenance antipsychotics would seem to outweigh the risk of tardive dyskinesia.

Antipsychotics and Brain Chemistry

A considerable body of evidence has accumulated showing that antipsychotic medications act by blocking the receptors of brain neurons that are stimulated by the neurotransmitter dopamine (17). Such chemical neurotransmitters are released by a small electrical potential in a neuron. The chemical diffuses across the microscopic gap, the synaptic cleft, that separates one neuron from another. The neurotransmitter then stimulates a receptor in the second neuron, causing it to increase its electrical activity.

Dopamine is presumed to serve as the neurotransmitter in at least three specific pathways in the brain: the nigrostriatal,

the mesolimbic-mesocortical, and the tuberoinfundibular pathways (17, 18). The anatomic localization and some proposed functions for these pathways are listed in Table 1. Antipsychotic medications block dopamine receptors in all three; nigrostriatal blockade causes the extrapyramidal reactions, tuberoinfundibular blockade causes endocrine changes, and mesolimbic-mesocortical blockade is presumed to yield the antipsychotic activity of the medications (17). Seven separate types of evidence support the concept that antipsychotics block dopamine receptors.

1) Antipsychotics increase the turnover (synthesis and breakdown) of dopamine, as demonstrated first by Carlsson and Lindqvist in 1963 (19). These investigators suggested that the increased turnover results from a feedback mechanism attempting to overcome dopamine receptor blockade. Increased turnover has also been shown in humans. However, one antipsychotic, clozapine, fails to have the expected effect on dopamine turnover in humans (20).

2) All antipsychotics except clozapine cause extrapyramidal reactions that sometimes mimic the symptoms of Parkinson's disease (21). Parkinson's disease results from degeneration of the nigrostriatal dopamine pathway, leading to a predominance of cholinergic over dopamine activity in this region (22). The similarity of antipsychotic-induced extrapyramidal reactions to the symptoms of Parkinson's disease suggests that antipsychotics inhibit dopamine activity in this nigrostriatal pathway. The improvement of both Parkinson's disease and extrapyramidal symptoms by anticholinergic drugs is further evidence of their similar biochemical mechanisms. The failure of clozapine to produce extrapyramidal reactions may be due to its potent anticholinergic activity (17).

3) Antipsychotics counteract the electrical response of neurons to the application of microscopic amounts of dopamine (23). The effects of amphetamine on neuronal activity are similar to the effects of dopamine. Antipsychotics also reverse the effects of amphetamine on the electrical activity of neurons (23).

4) In animals, antipsychotics reverse the behavioral effects of drugs that alter central dopamine activity. Amphetamine and apomorphine both cause altered behaviors in animals that are thought to be due to increased activity in brain dopamine pathways. These animal behaviors are reversed, blocked, or normalized by antipsychotics (17, 24).

5) Antipsychotics inhibit the activity of the enzyme dopamine-sensitive adenylate cyclase. Kebabian et al. (25) have suggested that this enzyme may be involved in the mechanism of dopamine receptors. Activity of this enzyme is increased in the presence of dopamine and decreased in the presence of antipsychotics. However, some antipsychotics, particularly butyrophenones, are less active against this enzyme than would be predicted from their clinical potency (17, 25).

6) Antipsychotics are found to inhibit the binding of dopamine to nerve cell membranes in laboratory preparations made from animal brain homogenates. Studies by Snyder (26) and Seeman et al. (27) suggest that the neurotransmitter may bind to the dopamine receptor in these preparations. The relative potency of antipsychotics in this system closely parallels both their clinical potency and their ability to inhibit dopamine-sensitive adenylate cyclase. Again, the butyrophenones inhibit dopamine binding less well than is predicted from clinical potency. However, all antipsychotics inhibit the binding of the butyrophenone haloperidol to nerve cell membranes, with a po-

tency that parallels their clinical potency (26). Snyder (26) suggests that dopamine and haloperidol bind to discrete agonist and antagonist states of the dopamine receptor and that displacement of antagonist or haloperidol binding may be a better test of antipsychotic activity.

7) Antipsychotics stimulate the release of the hormone prolactin from the pituitary gland, and the tuberoinfundibular pathway plays a major inhibitory role in the regulation of prolactin release (17, 28). Sachar and his associates (28) report a close correlation between the prolactin response and the antipsychotic potency of the various chemical classes of antipsychotics.

Thus, there is considerable evidence that antipsychotics block brain dopamine receptors. This evidence led to the hypothesis that dopamine neuronal activity is excessive in schizophrenic patients, possibly in the mesolimbic-mesocortical pathway (17). This hypothesis of schizophrenia is supported by other indirect pharmacological evidence, but there is not yet any consistent direct evidence of altered brain dopamine metabolism or activity in schizophrenics (29).

Tardive dyskinesia is also thought to result from dopamine hyperactivity, but in the nigrostriatal pathway. The prolonged dopamine receptor blockade could lead to supersensitive receptors causing a relative predominance of dopamine over acetylcholine activity in this region (30). This imbalance in tardive dyskinesia would be the opposite of the imbalance in extrapyramidal reactions to antipsychotics and in Parkinson's disease, where acetylcholine is predominant. Since Parkinson's disease and extrapyramidal reactions respond to anticholinergics, tardive dyskinesia might reasonably respond to increasing acetylcholine activity. In preliminary studies the acetylcholine precursor choline chloride has been found to improve the movements of some patients with tardive dyskinesia (31). This finding supports the imbalance hypothesis of tardive dyskinesia and offers a potential treatment strategy for the disorder.

Antidepressant Medications

The two major types of drugs used to treat depression are the tricyclic antidepressants (tricyclics) and the monoamine oxidase inhibitors. Drugs from both pharmacological classes were first introduced in 1957, but monoamine oxidase inhibitors are used much less commonly than are tricyclics—they are generally thought to be less effective and more toxic. Tricyclics take 2 to 4 weeks to alter the symptoms of severe depression, but they are effective in about 70 percent of patients. In most cases tricyclics cause a complete remission of depressive symptoms; they improve mood, restore confidence, relieve the numerous physical symptoms, and eliminate suicidal thinking. Some patients may fail to respond to one tricyclic but will respond to another. In patients who remain depressed after a trial of two tricyclics, the monoamine oxidase inhibitors sometimes reverse depressive symptoms (32).

The same questions that were asked about the antipsychotics can be asked about the tricyclics: Are they effective in acute depressions or useful as maintenance treatments when compared to a placebo? Do they have dangerous or irreversible side effects? What is the biochemical mechanism of tricyclic action?

The efficacy of tricyclics in the treatment of depression has been established in numerous clinical trials. In one recent literature review, which summarized only double-blind, placebo-controlled studies, tricyclics were found to be more effective than a placebo in 61 of 93 studies (33). The fact that 32 studies did not find tricyclics superior to a placebo may seem surprising. However, this is probably due to the high spontaneous remission rate in depression and the slow action of tricyclics. Mild depressions are more likely to remit spontaneously than severe depressions, but it has been estimated that about 30 percent of patients with severe depression recover without drug treatment. Studies that include patients with mild depression may have a placebo group with a remission rate nearly as high as that of the tricyclic group. Thus, tricyclics are more appropriately used to treat severe depression. Even though some of these patients would recover without drug treatment, the danger of suicide in severe depression makes tricyclic treatment not only important in relieving suffering, but also potentially lifesaving (32).

Three major collaborative studies, two in the United States and one in England, have found that tricyclics significantly reduced the relapse rate in patients who were initially treated with them (34). Since tricyclics have several potentially troublesome side effects, they probably should not be used as a maintenance treatment after recovery for a patient with a single depressive episode. However, for patients with repeated episodes of severe depression the side effects of tricyclic maintenance seem to be a small risk compared to the suffering and potential for suicide associated with multiple depressive episodes (32).

Tricyclics can be fatal when a large overdose is taken. This is an unfortunate characteristic for a drug used for the treatment of illness that can lead to suicide. Standard doses of tricyclics also cause several troublesome side effects, but they are usually not dangerous, except in patients with heart disease. Rarely, tricyclics can precipitate mania or schizophrenia in patients with a history of these illnesses. Tricyclics do not seem to cause the extrapyramidal motor reactions seen with the antipsychotics. Perhaps most importantly, tricyclics do not seem to cause tardive dyskinesia. Thus, the decision to place a patient on a maintenance drug is less complicated with tricyclics than with antipsychotics, except in patients with concurrent heart disease (32).

Despite an impressive quantity of data accumulated over the last 20 years, the exact mechanism of action of tricyclics is unknown (32). The most important hypothesis is that tricyclics increase the functional activity of the brain neurotransmitters norepinephrine and serotonin. Tricyclics are thought to potentiate norepinephrine and serotonin by preventing their uptake by the neuron that released them into the synaptic cleft. Their reuptake prevents these chemicals from continuing to act on the receptor on the second neuron and thus is one physiological mechanism for deactivating them. Reuptake blockade therefore should increase the concentration of norepinephrine and serotonin at the receptor (35). Reuptake blockade as a mode of action of tricyclics is suggested by numerous studies which show that these drugs inhibit the uptake of norepinephrine or serotonin injected into the rat brain (35).

The reuptake blockade of tricyclics forms part of the basis of the norepinephrine and serotonin hypothesis of affective disorders. This hypothesis, which is supported by several pharmacological and physiological findings, states that depression is due to a functional underactivity or deficiency of these neurotransmitters, while mania is associated with their functional hyperactivity (35). The other major class of antidepressants inhibits the action of the enzyme monoamine oxidase, which breaks down norepinephrine and serotonin, and thus monoamine oxidase inhibitors should also increase the concentration of the neurotransmitters (36). Reserpine is used to treat hypertension; it depletes brain norepinephrine and serotonin and causes a "depressionlike" syndrome in some patients. Some depressed patients seem to excrete lower amounts of 3-methyoxy-4-hydroxyphenylglycol, the most important breakdown product of norepinephrine. [Others have low spinal fluid concentrations of 5-hydroxyindoleacetic acid, the major metabolite of serotonin (35)]. Some depressed patients also have specific abnormalities in endocrine systems that are controlled by the hypothalamus and the pituitary gland (37). Hypothalamic-pituitary function also seems to be influenced by serotonin and norepinephrine activity (38).

Thus, there is some evidence that decreased norepinephrine or serotonin is associated with depression, but the hypothesis cannot be considered to be established. Much of the evidence is controversial. The true mechanism of action of either the monoamine oxidase inhibitors or the tricyclics is not known. Reserpine does not cause a depressionlike syndrome in everyone, and the similarity between this syndrome and clinical depression is the subject of debate. Not every depressed patient has low excretion of 3-methoxy-4-hydroxyphenylglycol, low concentrations of 5-hydroxyindoleacetic acid in the spinal fluid, or specific endocrine abnormalities (37).

A major problem for the norepinephrine-serotonin hypothesis of depression comes from the actions of tricyclics themselves. These medications immediately cause neurotransmitter reuptake blockade in animal studies, but they take 2 to 4 weeks to have antidepressant action in patients. The long-term effects of tricyclics on norepinephrine and serotonin are difficult to study and may not be the same as short-term ones. In addition, iprindole is an effective tricyclic that has been used in Europe and that does not seem to inhibit reuptake of norepinephrine or serotonin (37, 39). Thus, neither the biochemical basis of depression nor the mechanisms of action of antidepressants are known with certainty. The reuptake blockade of norepinephrine and serotonin by tricyclics and the norepinephrine-serotonin hypothesis of depression may be oversimplifications, but both hypotheses have helped

organize important research on the biochemistry of the brain. More recent hypotheses of depression and of the biochemical mechanisms of tricyclics suggest an altered balance between the functional activities of two or more neurotransmitters, the possible involvement of acetylcholine in depression, and the hypothesis that depression and the action of tricyclics are the result of alterations in neurotransmitter receptors rather than the neurotransmitters themselves (37).

Lithium Carbonate

The discovery by John Cade in Australia in 1949 that lithium salts are effective antimanic agents marked the advent of modern psychopharmacology. Curiously, the drug was not introduced into the United States until 1969. Lithium is a unique drug for several reasons. It is highly specific in relieving manic symptoms—normalizing mood and slowing down thinking, motor activity, and other behaviors—all without causing oversedation. In addition, lithium seems to prevent or decrease the severity of both manic and depressive episodes in some bipolar patients. Finally, the lithium compounds used are simple inorganic salts that have no known function in normal physiology (40).

The efficacy of lithium in treating acute mania has been established in at least ten controlled studies (41). In general, these studies showed that lithium has more specific or unique effects in manic patients than do antipsychotics. However, lithium takes 4 to 10 days to begin to reduce manic symptoms. Thus, for some severely hyperactive and agitated patients with mania, the sedative and tranquilizing effects of the antipsychotics are necessary for 1 or 2 weeks (41).

Eight controlled, blind studies have shown that maintenance lithium either prevents or decreases the number of manic episodes in bipolar patients (42). Lithium also seems to prevent or decrease the number of depressive episodes in bipolar patients, and may prevent depressive episodes in some patients with severe recurrent unipolar depression (34). Since tricyclics also prevent depressive episodes in unipolar depressed patients and are the current treatment, controlled trials comparing lithium and tricyclics as maintenance

treatments in unipolar depressed patients are urgently needed.

Unlike the antipsychotics and tricyclics, lithium seems to have a narrow range of effective concentrations in blood. Therefore, blood levels of lithium are measured frequently at first, but as the dose is established the interval between measurements can be extended to weeks or even months. Lithium can have numerous troublesome side effects on many organ systems, but most of these occur early in treatment, and no long-term or permanent side effects have been reported (40).

The biochemical mechanism of action of lithium on the brain is unknown. Lithium is distributed throughout the body and interacts with numerous biological systems, including the brain neurotransmitters norepinephrine and serotonin. The norepinephrine hypothesis of affective disorders proposes a norepinephrine overactivity in mania. Lithium decreases the electrically stimulated release of norepinephrine and seems to enhance its reuptake from the synaptic cleft (37, 43). This action is opposite to that of the tricyclics, and could explain the effect of lithium on mania. However, any biochemical hypothesis of the action of lithium must also explain its positive effect in some depressed patients (37). Thus, further studies of both the short- and long-term effects of lithium are needed to help clarify its mode of action.

Ethics and Psychopharmacology

Among the many ethical issues surrounding the use of psychotherapeutic agents, involuntary treatment is a particular subject of debate both within and outside the psychiatric profession. Should patients ever be given drug treatments without their consent? The exact legal mechanism varies, but severely disturbed patients often do receive such treatment. In California, patients must be a danger to themselves, a danger to others, or gravely disabled as a result of mental illness (44). Those who meet these criteria are often depressed patients with suicidal intentions or schizophrenic patients who are violent or unable to care for their basic needs.

Some argue that this involuntary treatment, although well intentioned, alters behavior by external means and that patients should have a right to refuse such treatment even when they are mentally ill (45). Szasz (46), an articulate spokesman for this viewpoint, believes that the government and the mental health profession have joined together, as did the state and the church in the past, to force people to conform to certain behaviors and beliefs (45). Szasz believes that individuals should be free to determine their own behavior, their own beliefs, and their own future, even if this behavior is potentially dangerous to the individual or to society. The logical consequence of this belief is that mental patients have the same rights and responsibilities as other members of the community. A psychiatric patient who harms someone should be tried and held responsible even if the action was due to a mental illness. Szasz's viewpoint has other logical consequences that are difficult for many people to accept. For instance, it suggests that a depressed patient should be allowed to commit suicide and a schizophrenic patient should be allowed to die from dehydration if he feels that fluids are poisoned (1).

In practice, many people feel that it is more humane to treat some patients without their consent. Suicidal feelings and delusional beliefs usually are temporary and respond to drug treatment. Patients are often grateful that their transient self-destructive or dangerous behavior was stopped. Suicidal thoughts and delusions are powerful controls over a person's behavior. Involuntarily treatment can remove these emotions and thus can be seen as liberating rather than restricting, since they can allow patients to return rapidly to their former lives, free of dangerous behaviors and self-destructive impulses (1).

There is no simple solution to the ethical dilemma of involuntary treatment. When used inappropriately, involuntary treatment can become one of the instruments a totalitarian state uses to control deviant behavior. When used in a humane manner, it can be lifesaving. Clearly, ethical inquiry must play a larger role in psychiatric treatment than it has in the past.

Conclusion

Remarkable progress has been made in the drug treatment of psychiatric disorders. Psychopharmacological agents are the cornerstone of the vastly improved mental health treatment structure for patients with schizophrenia, depres-

sion, and mania. The medications have also prompted psychiatrists to become more rigorous and quantitative in the diagnosis and longitudinal assessment of mental disorders. Perhaps most importantly, psychopharmacological agents have provided an interface between psychiatry and modern biological sciences. This has led to laboratory and clinical research that has improved our understanding of the human brain and of behavior and that offers hope for understanding the biochemical substrates of mental illness.

The pharmacotherapies themselves are far from ideal. Antipsychotics improve schizophrenic symptoms, but do not often "cure" the disease. Maintenance antipsychotics reduce the likelihood of a return of schizophrenic symptoms but add the risk of the sometimes irreversible movement disorder, tardive dyskinesia. Tricyclics do not seem to cause irreversible side effects and often reverse depressive symptoms, but they work slowly and are ineffective in 20 to 30 percent of patients. Tricyclics also can be fatal if taken in sufficiently large doses. Lithium salts can markedly improve the life of a manic-depressive patient, but they have troublesome side effects and do not help all patients. Thus, more effective and less toxic medications are an important goal of research in psychiatry. The combination of basic laboratory studies and carefully designed clinical evaluations is urgently needed to develop and test new medical treatments for mental illness.

Psychotherapeutic drugs are not a panacea. They allow a large number of psychiatric patients to be discharged, sometimes to communities that are poorly prepared to receive them and to provide the continuing care that many patients require. Further efforts are needed to determine the best ways to care for formerly hospitalized individuals and to help them become happy and productive members of society. Too often physicians rely solely on medications when psychological and socioenvironmental treatments are needed. Finally, the existence of potent psychotherapeutic drugs will continue to present ethical challenges to society.

References and Notes

1. P. A. Berger, B. Hamburg, D. A. Hamburg, *Daedalus* **106**, 261 (1977); J. Barchas, P. Berger, R. Ciaranello, G. Elliott, in *Psychopharmacology: From Theory to Practice*, J. D. Barchas, P. A. Berger, R. D. Ciaranello, G. R. Elliott, Eds. (Oxford, New York, 1977), p. 527.
2. F. J. Ayd, Jr., *Discoveries in Biological Psychiatry* (Lippincott, Philadelphia, 1970), p. 230.
3. E. L. Bassuk and S. Gerson, *Sci. Am.* **238**, 46 (February 1978).
4. M. Greenblatt, in *Psychopharmacology: A Generation of Progress*, M. A. Lipton, A. DiMascio, K. F. Killam, Eds. (Raven, New York, 1978), p. 1179.
5. M. Greenblatt, *N. Engl. J. Med.* **296**, 246 (1975).
6. R. Reich, *Bull. N.Y. State Dist. Branches Am. Psychiatr. Assoc.* **15**, 6 (1972).
7. F. N. Arnhoff, *Science* **188**, 1277 (1975).
8. L. C. Wynne and M. T. Singer, *Arch. Gen. Psychiatry* **9**, 191 (1963); S. Arieti, in *Psychopathology of Schizophrenia*, P. H. Hoch and J. Zubin, Eds. (Grune & Stratton, New York, 1966), p. 37; R. Cancro, *Dis. Nerv. Syst.* **29**, 846 (1968); W. T. Carpenter, J. Strauss, S. Maleh, *Arch. Gen. Psychiatry* **28**, 847 (1973); H. E. Lehmann, in *Comprehensive Textbook of Psychiatry*, A. M. Freedman, H. I. Kaplan, B. J. Sadock, Eds. (Williams & Wilkins, Baltimore, ed. 2, 1975), p. 890.
9. H. M. Babigian, in *Comprehensive Textbook of Psychiatry*, A. M. Freedman, H. I. Kaplan, B. J. Sadock, Eds. (Williams & Wilkins, Baltimore, ed. 2, 1975), p. 860; H. E. Lehmann, in *ibid.*, p. 851.
10. J. M. Mendels, *Concepts of Depression* (Wiley, New York, 1970); G. R. Klerman, in *Comprehensive Textbook of Psychiatry*, A. M. Freedman, H. I. Kaplan, B. J. Sadock, Eds. (Williams & Wilkins, Baltimore, ed. 2, 1975), p. 1003; F. F. Flach and S. C. Draghi, *The Nature and Treatment of Depression* (Wiley, New York, 1975); G. Usdin, *Depression: Clinical Biological and Psychological Perspectives* (Brunner/Mazel, New York, 1977); W. E. Fann, I. Karacan, A. D. Pokorny, R. L. Williams, Eds., *Phenomenology and Treatment of Depression* (Spectrum, New York, 1977).
11. N. Kline, *Dis. Nerv. Syst.* **37**, 10 (1976).
12. R. I. Shader and A. H. Jackson, in *Manual of Psychiatric Therapeutics*, R. Shader, Ed. (Little, Brown, Boston, 1975); p. 63; J. O. Cole, in *Drug Treatment of Mental Disorders*, L. Simpson, Ed. (Raven, New York, 1976), p. 13; L. E. Hollister, in *Psychopharmacology: From Theory to Practice*, J. D. Barchas, P. A. Berger, R. D. Ciaranello, G. R. Elliott, Eds. (Oxford, New York, 1977), p. 121.
13. J. Cole, S. Goldberg, G. Klerman, *Arch. Gen. Psychiatry* **10**, 246 (1964); R. F. Prien and J. Cole, *ibid.* **18**, 482 (1968); J. M. Davis, *Am. J. Psychiatry* **133**, 208 (1976).
14. J. M. Davis, *Am. J. Psychiatry* **132**, 1237 (1975).
15. E. G. DeFraites, K. L. Davis, P. A. Berger, *Biol. Psychiatry* **12**, 267 (1977); R. J. Balderessarini and D. Tarsy, in *Psychopharmacology: A Generation of Progress*, M. A. Lipton, A. DiMascio, K. F. Killam, Eds. (Raven, New York, 1978), p. 993.
16. W. E. Fann, J. M. Davis, D. S. Janowsky, *Dis. Nerv. Syst.* **33**, 182 (1972); R. J. Baldessarini, *Can. Psychiatr. Assoc. J.* **19**, 551 (1974).
17. P. A. Berger, G. R. Elliott, J. D. Barchas, in *Psychopharmacology: A Generation of Progress*, M. A. Lipton, A. DiMascio, K. F. Killam, Eds. (Raven, New York, 1978), p. 1071; A. Carlsson, *Am. J. Psychiatry* **135**, 164 (1978).
18. U. Ungerstedt, *Acta Physiol. Scand. Suppl. 367* (1971), pp. 1-48.
19. A. Carlsson and M. Lindqvist, *Acta Pharmacol. Toxicol.* **20**, 140 (1963).
20. J. Gerlach, K. Thorsen, R. Fog, *Psychopharmacologia* **40**, 341 (1975).
21. H. R. Bürki, E. Eichenberger, A. C. Sayers, T. C. White, *Pharmakopsychiatr. Neuro Psychopharmakol.* **8**, 115 (1975).
22. O. Hornykiewicz, *Klin. Wochenschr.* **75**, 309 (1963).
23. B. S. Bunney and G. K. Aghajanian, in *Predictability in Psychopharmacology: Preclinical and Clinical Correlations*, A. Sudilovsky, S. Gershon, B. Beer, Eds. (Raven, New York, 1975), p. 225.
24. J. D. Barchas, P. A. Berger, S. Matthysse, R. J. Wyatt, in *Principles of Psychopharmacology*, W. G. Clark and J. del Guidice, Eds. (Academic Press, New York, in press).
25. J. W. Kebabian, G. L. Petzgold, D. Greengard, *Proc. Natl. Acad. Sci. U.S.A.* **69**, 2145 (1972).
26. S. H. Snyder, *Am. J. Psychiatry* **133**, 197 (1976).
27. P. Seeman, M. Chou-Wong, J. Tadesco, K. Wong, *Proc. Natl. Acad. Sci. U.S.A.* **72**, 4376 (1975).

28. E. J. Sachar, P. H. Gruen, N. Altman, G. Langer, F. S. Halpern, M. Liefer, in *Neuroregulators and Psychiatric Disorders*, E. Usdin, D. A. Hamburg, J. D. Barchas, Eds. (Oxford, New York, 1977), p. 242.

29. J. D. Barchas, P. A. Berger, G. R. Elliott, E. Erdelyi, R. J. Wyatt, in *Biochemistry and Function of Monoamine Enzymes*, E. Usdin, N. Weiner, M. B. H. Youdin, Eds. (Dekker, New York, 1977), p. 863.

30. H. L. Klawans, Jr., *Am. J. Psychiatry* **130**, 82 (1973); K. L. Davis, L. E. Hollister, P. A. Berger, J. D. Barchas, *Psychopharmacol. Commun.* **1**, 533 (1975).

31. K. L. Davis, L. E. Hollister, P. A. Berger, *N. Engl. J. Med.* **293**, 152 (1975); K. L. Davis, L. E. Hollister, J. D. Barchas, P. A. Berger, *Life Sci.* **19**, 1507 (1976); J. H. Growdon, M. J. Hirsch, R. J. Wurtman, W. Wiener, *N. Engl. J. Med.* **297**, 524 (1977); K. L. Davis and P. A. Berger, *Biol. Psychiatry* **13**, 23 (1978).

32. J. J. Schildkraut and D. F. Klein, in *Manual of Psychiatric Therapeutics*, R. I. Shader, Ed. (Little, Brown, Boston, 1975), p. 39; J. M. Davis, in *Drug Treatment of Mental Disorders*, L. Simpson, Ed. (Raven, New York, 1976), p. 127; P. A. Berger, in *Psychopharmacology: From Theory to Practice*, J. D. Barchas, P. A. Berger, R. D. Ciaranello, G. R. Elliott, Eds. (Oxford, New York, 1977), p. 174.

33. J. B. Morris and A. T. Beck, *Arch Gen. Psychiatry* **30**, 667 (1974).

34. J. M. Davis, *Am. J. Psychiatry* **133**, 1 (1976).

35. J. J. Schildkraut, *ibid.* **122**, 509 (1965); W. E. Bunney and J. M. Davis, *Arch. Gen. Psychiatry* **13**, 483 (1965); P. A. Berger, in *Neurotransmitter Function*, W. S. Fields, Ed. (Grune & Stratton, New York, 1977), p. 305.

36. P. A. Berger and J. D. Barchas, in *Psychotherapeutic Drugs*, E. Usdin and I. S. Forrest, Eds. (Dekker, New York, 1977), p. 1173.

37. ———, in *Psychopharmacology: From Theory to Practice*, J. D. Barchas, P. A. Berger, R. D. Ciaranello, G. R. Elliott, Eds. (Oxford, New York, 1977), p. 151.

38. P. A. Berger, J. D. Barchas, J. Vernikos-Danellis, *Nature (London)* **248**, 424 (1974); B. S. Carroll and J. Mendels, in *Hormones, Behavior and Psychopathology*, E. J. Sachar, Ed. (Raven, New York, 1976), p. 193.

39. S. B. Ross, A. L. Renyi, S. O. Ogren, *Life Sci.* **10**, 1267 (1971); M. H. Bickel, in *Psychotherapeutic Drugs*, E. Usdin and I. S. Forrest, Eds. (Dekker, New York, 1977), p. 1131.

40. R. R. Fieve, in *Drug Treatment of Mental Disorders*, L. Simpson, Ed. (Raven, New York, 1976), p. 193; R. L. Sack and E. DeFraites, in *Psychopharmacology: From Theory to Practice*, J. D. Barchas, P. A. Berger, R. D. Ciaranello, G. R. Elliott, Eds. (Oxford, New York, 1977), p. 208.

41. S. Gershon, in *Psychotherapeutic Drugs*, E. Usdin and I. S. Forrest, Eds. (Dekker, New York, 1977), p. 1377.

42. F. Quitkin, A. Rifkin, D. Klein, *Arch. Gen. Psychiatry* **33**, 337 (1976).

43. S. M. Schanberg, J. J. Schildkraut, I. J. Kopin, *Biochem. Pharmacol.* **16**, 393 (1967); R. I. Katz, T. N. Chase, I. J. Kopin, *Science* **162**, 466 (1968).

44. The California Community Mental Health Services Act (Lantermann-Petris-Short Act), division 5, part I, chaps. 1, 2, and 3.

45. T. A. Gonda and M. B. Waitzkin, *Curr. Concepts Psychiatry* **1**, 5 (1976).

46. T. Szasz, *Law, Liberty, Psychiatry* (Macmillan, New York, 1963).

47. I thank J. D. Barchas, G. R. Elliott, and S. I. Watson for helpful discussions and J. S. Magliozzi for manuscript preparation. Supported by National Institute of Mental Health Specialized Research Center grant MH-30854 and the Medical Research Service of the Veterans Administration.

The second death of Sigmund Freud

*Why the emergence of the new neurochemists could
mean the decline and fall of psychoanalysis*

Jo Durden-Smith

Once upon a time Sigmund Freud belonged to the psychoanalysts. A grave, grey priesthood, only they had been initiated into his mysteries. And only they could see lurking behind every neurosis, every bit of aberrant behavior, its symbolic and historical causes, its underlying meaning. They had seen inside themselves, and they had acquired, by the laying on of other initiates' hands, the power to see inside others. It was something like the Roman Catholic Church. The mantle of succession passed from St. Sigmund to his popes, and from them to every cardinal, bishop and priest. All the superstitious congregation had to offer, in the rites of psychiatric celebration, was the small change of their pain.

In the 1950s and '60s, though, the notions of Freud spread, and more and more power was passed to the lay officers of his church. This was boom-time North America, where people were being introduced by the advertising industry to the idea of their general inadequacy; where they were being taught to hand over to experts, from Dr. Spock on up, the care of their children and themselves. And in this Freud played an essential part. For, with only a few of his words and his concepts, the teacher and the social worker, the artist and the advertising executive, could sound adept and knowing. Today North America is the bastion of Freudian psychology. There are two significant parts to Freud's work. There is the therapy for neurotic and psychotic patients, and there is the general theory of human behavior. And, though the therapy is still off-limits, the theory is splendidly accessible. Never mind that it

is involuted, contradictory and often extremely vague. That only makes it all the more attractive to North Americans. For its involution makes it both difficult and authoritative: "*scientific*." Its contradictoriness makes it impossible to disprove. And its vagueness makes it fit virtually any ideas at all about the way human beings behave. Small wonder, then, that its language is the language par excellence of the educators and counselors, the helpers and the sellers. It confirms them in their positions. It is the mark of their professionalism. The congregation doesn't have the expertise to understand its own ailments of the spirit; only the church-wardens, sextons and vergers, the sidemen of the helping professions, do.

All this, naturally, makes lay people uneasy and insecure. (It is in the interests of the sidemen to harp on their needs and sicknesses rather than their strengths.) And when the '60s and the postwar boom came to an end and the laymen's confidence in their ability to intervene in the outside world began to ebb, too, they went through a peculiar crisis. They retreated into themselves. The family could no longer take up the slack of meaning left by the dwindling of opportunity. Nor could such public space as had been left by the inroads of television and the dying of cities. Nor could the saving intimacy of close relationships. Each had been made a source of anxiety by the sidemen. Each had been successfully psychologized. So where else could people now look for their sense of themselves, the answer to the enigma of who they were, but the holy of holies of the self itself? Where else could the individualism that had been the legacy of continuous expansion go but inside? There, where a man was alone with his feelings, there was an unshifting truth, the truth of feeling. There, where a man was his own expert, his own do-it-your-

selfer, the ideals of radical change, self-improvement and the pursuit of happiness still made sense. There, where he was actor, producer and critic of his own theatre, a man could be *his own* man.

The congregation, in other words, did the only thing it could under the circumstances. It took over the church. In an atmosphere that had been subtly psychologized over the years, North American individualism (you are what you make of yourself) met Freudian individualism (you are everything that has happened to you).

The result of this takeover was a creeping self-absorption, the public and private effects of which touch us all, whether we are directly involved or not. The language of feeling has little by little replaced the language of thought. Personal salvation threatens shared commitments. Taste lords it over value. And a narcissistic theatre has invaded our living rooms, our bedrooms, our friendships and our cafés. Over all of this presides the enigmatic figure of Freud. For at the root of it all is a sort of demotic 20th-century distortion of his hieratic Victorian ideas.

Freud's theory that feeling is the language of the unconscious has led us to the bastard belief that what we *feel* is all-important. His concept of repression has spawned the convictions that we *must act out* our feelings: that our behavior, however bad, is acceptable so long as it is "authentic"; and that, of our fantasies, the only ones not worth having are the unenacted ones. And his materialism and his concentration on sexuality have persuaded us, in the translation, that hedonism and indiscriminate sexuality are signs of health.

What, then, of the Freud of the people's church? What of this psychologist of the self-made man in this North America of men and women still making

From *Toronto Life*, June 1978. Reprinted by permission.

themselves? Now that he has been internalized and has become the presiding genius of our age of anxiety, where does he stand? Under ordinary circumstances, perhaps, this would be a question for academics to haggle over in fusty common rooms. But these are not ordinary circumstances. These are not ordinary times. Reports show that 85% of all patients now visiting doctors have physical problems that are to some extent created by psychological disorders. Billions of dollars are being poured every year into mental health and the self-improvement industry. In the United States centres are now being set up for the study of narcissism, as being the quintessential 20th-century disease.

And from the University of Houston comes a report, based on the predictive and suggestive powers of mass advertising, that in the society of the 1980s concern for others will disappear, leisure will become a solo activity and one-person households will become the norm. These things are the legacy of a *selfishness* that is spreading and pathological. And that selfishness is underwritten by the belief that there is a science of the self, that the self is private, diseased and curable. But the fact is, all this is legitimated, in the end, by Freud. The question "What of Freud?", then, is not only not academic, it is of vital importance to everyone. For if Freud was wrong, then this society is on a road going nowhere. Freud's work is, as I have said, divided into two parts: the theory and the therapy. And Freudians insist on two things: that the theory is a *scientific* one and that the therapy *works*. These propositions are the pillars on which the house of Freud rests. And even Freudians agree that if one comes down, so does the other. If the theory is not a scientific theory, then the therapy can have little value. If the therapy doesn't work, then the theory can't have much interest.

Is Freud's theory of human behavior a scientific theory? Most of the great modern philosophers of science are at one that it is not. In order for a theory to be scientific, you have to be able to find out whether it is right. You have to be able to make deductions from it that can be tested. You have to be able to predict, on the basis of the theory, that this will happen and that will not. And the problem with Freud's theory is that it is too complex, rambling and plain contradictory for either side in the argument to be able to do this to the other's satisfaction. Every time a Freudian stands back from an experi-

ment and cries "Aha!", an antiFreudian rushes in and shouts: "Your deduction doesn't follow from the theory," or else: "I've just demonstrated that the opposite is true. The theory can't have it both ways." And every time an antiFreudian claims to have found a Freudian prediction that is false, a Freudian appears to exclaim: "You're just testing your own fantasies. The theory doesn't predict what you say it does," or else: "Yes, but the theory predicts *your* results, too."

An example: Freud's theory holds that there are four stages of development in human beings: oral, anal, genital and latent. People who are dependent are stuck at the oral stage, when sucking at the mother's breast is normal behavior. On the basis of this, Alvin Scodel made the prediction (commonly accepted by Freudians) that dependent men would prefer big-breasted women. He tested this in an ingenious experiment, and concluded in his paper, published by Ohio State University in 1957, that, in fact, the opposite was true. Dependent men, in reality, tended to prefer *small*-breasted women. The theory was wrong. Enter, however, a determined defender of the Freudian faith, Dr. Paul Kline, a British professor and author of *Fact and Fantasy in Freudian Theory*, to immediately invoke the Freudian notion of "reaction formation." "Reaction formation" is a real track-coverer of a concept. It holds that an unconscious drive may show up in consciousness as its own antithesis. Thus unconscious hatred may show up as excessive tenderness. And fixation with big breasts may show up as an obsession with small ones. What Dr. Kline was saying, in other words, was that Alvin Scodel, while believing that he had shown the theory to be false, had in fact demonstrated that it was true. For with the help of "reaction formation," truth is truth to Freudians. But so is its opposite. The theory, that is to say, is not at all good at *predicting* things (black *or* white) with any certainty. But it's very good at *explaining* everything (black *and* white) after the event.

There are lots of transforming mechanisms like "reaction formation" in the theory, little conceptual plugs that hold inside them every conceivable kind of human behavior and stop the whole thing from leaking. Together with the theory's sprawling vagueness, they make it virtually impossible to show conclusively what is a true deduction and what is an unequivocal result from its testing. The only thing that *is* demonstrable is the endless theological bickering of Freudian and antiFreudian on the point. We're on safer ground, then,

if we turn from vexed interpretations of the Word to the Word of the theory itself. And here we're in luck. For right at the heart of Freud's theory is a prediction that can be shown to be quite straightforwardly false.

Freud was essentially a Victorian. And one of the linchpins of his theory seems to have been drawn from 19th-century hydraulics. All neuroses are deep-seated and give rise to various symptoms; if you treat the symptoms and not the neurosis that causes them, the neurosis will reassert itself later with the same or different symptoms. If you plug up a leak in the basement, in other words, and don't redesign the water system, sooner or later water will come spewing out in the attic or elsewhere. Now this flies in the face of all the successes of a discipline called behavior therapy. For behavior therapy holds that neuroses aren't deep-seated at all. They are simply conditioned reactions, like the salivation of Pavlov's dogs at the sound of a bell, or the head-banging of a child who, in the absence of shown affection, knows that he will get attention and comfort if he appears to be punishing himself. The symptoms, for behavior therapists, *are* the disease. *De*condition them (punish the child for banging his head and reward him with attention for other things) and they will disappear, be cured. No recurrence, no symptom-substitution, no new leaks, as Freud clearly predicted there would be.

An example: Six years apart, several Americans—Freudian Bruno Bettelheim and behavior therapists Montrose Wolf and Todd Risley—treated similar cases. Bettelheim's patient was a 4-year-old girl, diagnosed as psychotic, who was always trying to smash other people's eyeglasses and who went wild when stopped. The patient that Wolf and Risley treated was a 3½-year-old boy, diagnosed as schizophrenic, who had had cataracts at 9 months, wouldn't wear the glasses required and went into violent rages, hurting himself, when near them. Bettelheim put up with his patient's behavior for three years until she was able to yield up to him the "psychological meaning" of her behavior. (Her mother was a chronic schizophrenic who wore glasses. When the child tried on her glasses she could not see any better because her eyesight was normal. She became infuriated at the injustice of this. Others who wore glasses could see better. But when she tried to see—i.e. understand her mother—better, she couldn't.) The behavior therapists took another tack with their child. The boy was punished for his tantrums by being sent to his room. He was rewarded, first for touching, and finally for wearing, his glasses. At no time did the therapists deal with the underlying meaning or the historical or symbolic causes of the boy's destructive behavior. And yet he was "cured," as the girl was, though in a much shorter time.

The point here is that Freud predicted, quite simply, that the method used by Wolf and Risley would not work. The underlying pathology would break out in a new form, he insisted. And there is now enough evidence to show that this is untrue. Behavior therapy often works, it has permanent effects and it takes a great deal less time than the required four years or so of psychoanalysis. There is no need, then, to delve into the unscientific mumbo jumbo of the Blackie test (reactions to pictures of a dog doing unsavory things psychoanalytically interpreted) or the famous Rorschach ink-blot test (seeing the written associations blind, analysts are majestically unable to sort those of the well from those of the seriously ill). It is enough to say that Freud's theory of human behavior, inasmuch as it is not testable, is not scientific. Where it is testable, and therefore scientific, it is wrong.

Does psychoanalysis work? There is no evidence, beyond the circumstantial and the subjective, that it does. Indeed there is no evidence that there *is* such a thing as a consistent program of treatment that we can call psychoanalysis. Dr. Hans Eysenck, a British author and professor of psychology at the University of London, in the January 1978 *Encounter* magazine article *How Scientific Is Freudianism?* describes an interesting experiment: As early as 1941, two years after Freud's death, Dr. G.A. Oberndorf wrote to 24 analysts with more than 20 years' experience each and asked them to answer questions about their methods and approaches. Eighteen replied and, rather to Oberndorf's surprise, agreed on *nothing:* neither on the kind of people who would benefit from analysis, nor on methods, nor on results, nor on the number of people who had actually been helped. They had nothing in common, it seemed, beyond their professional titles. Modern researchers have borne out this observation. They have been unable to find a common ground of practise and conclusion that would give uniformity to what analysts do in the confines ·of their consulting rooms.

If this is so, though, why does the laity persist in believing that psychoanalysis is a scientific technique and that it works? It's partly due to the astonishing ease with which Freudian terms have passed into the language, complete with "scientific" aura. (People have a vested interest in thinking they refer to a scientific process.) It's partly due to the massive interpretational industry the theory has spawned in education, literature, Academe and the social sciences. (The theory has the merit of being able to explain *everything*, so it has given the industry—which has its vested interests, too—its common language.) But most importantly, perhaps, it's due to the fact that the neuroses the various forms of Freudian therapy are designed to cure are *self-terminating disorders*. Neurotics get better and often completely recover whether they go through the rites of psychoanalysis or not. Analysts, then, are in much the same position as manufacturers of cold medicines. They get the credit for a return to health that would have happened in any case. They reinforce a far from disinterested attitude to sickness. (This cold/perceived unhappiness can only be cured by pills/treatment.) And they end up by making proselytes of their patients. This is particularly true of psychoanalytic patients. With a dollar a minute on the line, they are inclined, of course, to be true believers. What little doubt they may have is soon exorcised by the confessional atmosphere of the sessions, the induced dependence of "transference," and the gratification of being able to talk about themselves to the exclusion of all else. Knowing nothing about spontaneous remission, then (largely because Freud said it was impossible), they go forth, at the end of their treatment, as missionaries to spread the Word.

The house of Freud, then, rests on two pillars made of plasterboard. The theory is a closed system of interlocking axioms: too perfect to be scientific, and not perfect enough to be true. The analytic session is an exercise in the manipulation of faith. The house should be in ruins. But it's not. The irony is that Freud's work is now at its most insidiously influential at precisely the time it is most universally under attack, from philosophers of science, psychologists and the new neurochemists. Many things have played a part in this: the marketing of need by advertising and the peddling of inadequacy by the helping professions; the undermining of traditional ties, the encroachment of central government and the erosion of a sense of community; the failure of expansion and the dwindling of individual power and opportunity; the retreat of religion and the rise of science-worship. And there is also the delayed action of time. For the generation that grew up in the Freudian heyday of the late '50s and the '60s, in permissive home and school environments (only in easy atmospheres could deep-rooted "emotional disturbances" and "underlying mental conflicts" be spotted), has now come of age. And it has transported into its maturity the same concern for selfhood and psychic ailment that marked its upbringing. Now it is passing this on to its children, denying them authority figures and bequeathing them a sickness that is less obvious and more profound than any caused by Victorian harshness. In defiance of the facts, it is polluting the wells of public discourse with self-fulfilling prophecies of anxiety and distress.

The irony is, in fact, a double one. For we now have available to us models of the workings of the brain and the human organism which, if we made use of them, would help us reduce the level of self-serving mumbo jumbo in the way we talk about ourselves and one another. The revelations of the chemical brain are already making it clear that serious mental disorders are organic diseases. They are promising to bring back those we call "dangerously crazy" from generations of superstition and neglect. At the same time, the successes of behavior therapy are negating the idea that our more everyday disorders of the self are buried deep in a private world within us. They are reminding us that we are *public* creatures, that our neuroses are events that happen *between* us, that we *are* what we *do*.

If we were to incorporate the language of these disciplines as we have incorporated the language of Freud, then our attitude to the pining self would change and the slide toward narcissism would be halted. The self-termination of neuroses would encourage us toward the British cure-all: "If you don't think about it, it will go away." Behavior therapy would encourage us to stop treating our children as if they were fragile psyches on the hoof, potential basket cases, and start dealing with their behavior, *on which we, their parents, are the greatest experts*. In our own lives, we would stop thinking of our disorders as if they were on the same sliding scale as paranoia and schizophrenia. We would pay less attention to how we feel and more attention to what we do. We would abandon the idea of the static private self to which we alone have access. And we would learn again to intervene in our own lives, without the help of a priesthood. Freud gave us the 50-minute session and the psychiatric couch. But he also gave us a disease for which we should now find a cure.

"There's still this superstition, this primitive mystique about mental disorders." The speaker is Terry Christian, a Birmingham, Alabama, neurochemist who is working on the presence in the brain of a substance called dimethyltryptamine (DMT). DMT was a hallucinogen you could buy on street corners in the 1960s. It was called "the businessman's trip." Now it's been found in the brain. "I mean, people are still saying: 'This guy is crazy. Stay away from him. Lock him up. It's not an organic disease. He's just crazy.' But the fact is, it is organic. It has to be organic. There's nothing up there but organic matter. Even Freud, who did a terrible disservice to chemistry, said as much."

Last November, 4,000 neuroscientists committed to this proposition met in a Neuroscience Society conference at Anaheim, near Disneyland, California. It was the largest gathering of brain specialists ever held. And it served to emphasize that neuroscientists are now at work in one of the hottest of scientific fields. Using new techniques, they are making maps of the activities central to the brain's functioning. They are opening the way to a whole new family of drugs. And they are suggesting radically new approaches to addiction and insanity.

When the U.S. government, in the 1960s, poured money into drug and addiction programs, one of the questions it wanted answered was: What happens when such drugs as heroin and LSD enter the brain and the neuronic pathways to it? By the beginning of the '70s, thanks to its large investment, the government had an answer. The drugs appeared to home in on the synapses, the points where nerve cells make junctions with one another and communicate via messenger chemicals called neurotransmitters. And they seemed to bind there to what are called receptor sites, receiving stations for the chemical instructions the neurotransmitters carry. What the drugs were doing, in other words, was breaking into the nerve cells' lines of communication and interrupting their normal signaling processes.

Later it was found that the receptor sites for the morphinelike drugs did not match any of the sites known to be involved in routine cell interaction. And this raised an enormously important question. For man wasn't born with morphine inside him. Nor heroin, nor LSD. (Morphine, for example, wasn't discovered until 1803.) Why, then, should they fit so perfectly onto receptor sites that stretched back, unchanged, through evolution? Did it mean that they were displacing in the body chemicals almost exactly like them: *natural* opiates and *natural* hallucinogens?

The answer was yes. The first natural opiate was discovered by John Hughes and Hans Kosterlitz at the University of Aberdeen in 1975, following a clue provided by Dr. Lars Terenius of Sweden. They called it enkephalin (Greek: "in the brain"). Almost immediately Dr. C.H. Li, a researcher at the University of California, found a similar substance in camel pituitaries and discovered that it was about 30 times more powerful than morphine when injected into the brain of mice and rats. He called his substance beta-endorphin (for endogenous morphine). Later, beta-endorphin was found in pigs, and later still two other chemicals, alpha-endorphin and gamma-endorphin, were discovered. Both had behavioral effects.

At the same time, huge strides were being made in the work on neurotransmitters, which operate in different parts of the brain's "wiring" and seem to play different roles in the body's most intimate functionings: sleep, memory, pleasure, pain, perception, and so on. The number of known transmitters rose from a single figure to a current 25 or so. And a good deal was learned about their mechanisms. Connections were found, for example, between serotonin and sleep, DMT and stress, dopamine and alcoholism, and epinephrine and dreaming. Dopamine, DMT and gamma aminobutyric acid have all been implicated in schizophrenia.

The work still has a long way to go. But, under-financed as a field though it is, it is moving forward at enormous speed. Already, an explanation for acupuncture's pain-killing ability has been found. (It is seen as stimulating the production of the body's natural opiates.) Some of the mysteries of addiction have been elucidated. (The pain of "cold turkey," for example, seems to have to do with the same opiate-making machinery; prolonged use of narcotics depresses it, and the addict then becomes abnormally sensitive when he withdraws.) Dreaming, natural analgesia, sexual pleasure and hallucinatory disorders are within range of being accounted for chemically. And an Israeli scientist has demonstrated just how delicate and far-reaching the brain's chemical communication will be found to be. At just over normal levels, he has shown that a brain protein can produce epileptic convulsions; just below, it produces feelings of pleasure and gratification.

At the centre of this exciting new field are three Canadian scientists. Recently, Dr. Philip Seeman's group at the University of Toronto studied material from autopsies of the brains of schizophrenic patients and found an abnormally high number of dopamine receptors in it. He suggests that certain kinds of schizophrenia may be due to overproduction of, and acute sensitivity to, dopamine. In related work, Dr. Steve Garnett and his nuclear-medicine team at McMaster University Medical Centre in Hamilton have found a way of measuring and tracking dopamine in an intact, living brain: one possible step toward the purely chemical diagnosis and treatment of schizophrenia. And Dr. Heinz Lehmann of McGill University has shown that beta-endorphin, the body's own opiate, is extraordinarily effective in the treatment of schizophrenia and severe neurosis. When injected with beta-endorphin rather than their usual medication, schizophrenics with auditory hallucinations stopped hearing voices, and neurotics were returned to their pre-illness personalities.

What effect this work, when it becomes public knowledge, will have on the current general acceptance of Freudian categories, Freudian language and Freudian explanations for mental disorders remains to be seen. But if the neurochemists have their way when it comes to treatment, chemistry "will rescue the mad, the stressed, the deranged and the disordered from the dark ages of Victorian Vienna," as one neurochemist puts it. But the real question now is, will Freud survive this vital new force?

NEW LIGHT ON SCHIZOPHRENIA

THE GENETIC LINK

Strong evidence
that this debilitating mental disease
can be inherited
is emerging from studies of the family.
Despite problems of identifying schizophrenia
its shadowy borders are being defined.

Ben Rose

Current research in many fields on schizophrenia has fostered a mood of optimism among scientists. The shrouds around the disease appear to be lifting, and on CBC radio last February, Dr. David Suzuki foresaw a test as simple as blood typing to detect a potential schizophrenic.

At a recent conference of psychopathologists, Dr. Seymour S. Kety, professor of psychiatry, Harvard Medical School, stated: "I have the feeling, which I have never had before, that we are beginning to see the light at the end of the tunnel. Never has the time been more propitious or progress more promising."

About 250 000 Canadians now suffer from schizophrenia; that is one in every 100, and they fill about half the mental hospital beds in the country.

The word itself is enough to start the old "nature or nurture" debate again. Is it a result of heredity, environment or a combination of both? Or is this disease with its shadowy borders really only a myth as some investigators have suggested?

"If schizophrenia is a myth, it is a myth with a substantial genetic component," responds Dr. Kety.

As Kety infers, geneticists in recent years have piled up impressive evidence that schizophrenia is heritable and to some extent they have mollified critics who charged bias in some of the earlier studies.

Even so, as the mode of inheritance transmission slowly becomes clearer, research on the biochemical side is sharpening the focus on how closely environmental factors are also linked to its development.

The disease itself is so hard to define that terms such as "schizophrenia spectrum" and "schizoid personalities" pop up in the literature to describe patients without true schizophrenia, but with symptoms that resemble it. The oft-heard description, "He's a schiz!" is about as revealing as "He's a cancer!" would be, according to Dr. W.O. McCormick, associate professor of psychiatry at the University of Toronto.

What is true schizophrenia then? Is it a case of two minds in one body, a split personality, as so many people believe? No, say scientists, it is a condition in which the patient loses touch with reality, hears voices, suffers delusions, and suffers a loss of the ability to relate the right emotion to the right action. In the movie, The Three Faces of Eve, the title chararter was *not* a schizophrenic, but a woman suffering from hysteria.

"Only a small minority of schizophrenics are ever violent and even these will respond to treatment," says Dr. McCormick. "They come quickly under control, and at our hospital no mechanical restraints are needed."

Some famous figures in history are thought to have been schizophrenic: Joan of Arc, with her voices and visions, is one, while Louis Riel has been so described by Dr. S.K. Littman of the Clarke Institute, Toronto.

Among the most persuasive genetic studies in the field are five dealing with twins, and in all of them concordance of schizophrenia was higher in identical twins than in the fraternal (non-identical) twins. For example, in one study where one of the identical twins developed the disease, it also developed in the other twin in about 45 percent of cases, while in non-identical twins the rate of concordance was only that of siblings in the general population — about 8 percent. (Incidentally, there is no higher incidence of schizophrenia in twins than in the general population.)

Strong evidence of hereditary factors comes from a study of 47 children of schizophrenic mothers, all of whom were placed in foster or adoptive homes at an early age. As they grew up, five of these children developed schizophrenia. But among· 50 children of normal parents also adopted or fostered at an early age and matched with the others for sex, age and race, no cases of schizophrenia occurred. This research, directed by Dr. Leonard L. Heston, professor of psychiatry, University of Minnesota Medical School, also revealed that the group with schizophrenic mothers scored higher on every index of mental disorder. For example, 11 of this group eventually spent more than one year in a penal or psychiatric hospital, compared with only two in the control group.

Another pioneering study was that directed by Dr. Laurette Bender, onetime professor of psychiatry at Columbia University, New York. It compared the family history of 59 schizophrenic children observed at Bellevue Hospital from 1935 to 1952 with that of 50 nonschizophrenic children observed for other problems at the same time. The first group had 39 schizophrenic relatives, while the control

 Reprinted from *SCIENCE FORUM Magazine*, May/June 1978, pp. 11-13 with the permission of the publisher.

group had none, and there were no correlations with socio-economic groups.

DANISH STUDY OF ADOPTED CHILDREN REVEALS TREND

One method of trying to separate hereditary and environmental factors is to study adopted children and their natural and adoptive families. This is the object of a remarkable continuing cross-Atlantic project and its reports have stimulated wide discussion. The team is headed by Dr. Kety and includes Dr. David Rosenthal and Dr. Paul H. Wender of the U.S. National Institute of Mental Health, and Dr. Fini Schulsinger and Dr. Bjorn Jacobsen of the Psychological Institute, Kommunehospitalet, Copenhagen.

Its aim is to compare mental illness in the natural and adoptive families of adopted children who are schizophrenic with that of relatives of a control group of adopted non-schizophrenic children.

Denmark was chosen because of the compactness of its population, its excellent adoption records and its Folkeregister, which permits one to trace a person's address, household, family and children.

The team took elaborate precautions to eliminate bias of any kind. Any reference that might indicate whether the relative was a natural or adoptive kin, or related to an index or control case was edited out of the transcripts. Each of the team worked "blind", unaware of the diagnosis of others.

The records of 5481 children adopted between 1924 and 1947 were examined and revealed that 507 of them were at one time or another admitted to a mental institution. Of this group, 33 who were diagnosed as schizophrenic were chosen as the "index" cases. A control group of 34 nonschizophrenic children was selected by matching the index cases for age, sex, length of time with the natural family and so on.

After two years and amazing patience, Dr. Jacobsen traced and interviewed 341 relatives (parents, siblings and half-siblings) from the natural and adoptive families of these children. He found them in Denmark, Norway and Sweden and they represented 94 per cent of the relatives who were alive, had not disappeared or become institutionalized and had not emigrated beyond Scandinavia. He encountered the usual number of uncooperative people but this tactful and persuasive Dane did not give up easily. In the end, only 23 refused to supply enough information, and they were randomly distributed.

Dr. Jacobsen's interviews with the relatives were exhaustive and included a 35-page questionnaire, check lists, narrative material, and covered the major aspects of the life experience: sociological, educational, marital, occupational and peer relationship history from birth, medical background, and a careful mental status examination.

In their desire to keep the research "clean," the team even asked Jacobsen to list the hunches he had about whether the person being interviewed was a relative of an index or control case. Even when these "hunch" cases were eliminated, the results stayed the same.

A diagnosis of schizophrenia was made in 13.9 percent of the natural relatives of the index cases, and only in 3.4 percent of the natural relatives of the controls, the non-schizophrenic children. A similar low percentage was found in both groups of adoptive relatives.

In a previous report based only on institutional records, they found 21 people in the schizophrenia spectrum, while in the larger study they found 67, a threefold increase. This confirmed a previous indication that there is considerably more schizophrenia-related illness in the population than reaches the doors of psychiatric hospitals.

EVIDENCE OF ENVIRONMENTAL FACTORS

The actual mode of inheritance of the disease is not yet well established. Rather than being passed on by a single recessive or dominant gene, investigators believe there may be several genes involved. Says one geneticist of this "polygenic model": "It's a complicated picture, something like diabetes."

The spurt in genetic research has served to increase interest in environmental factors, as the best studies in twins and adoptees show that the disease needs a trigger of some kind, one that is thought to be rooted in the environment (which, of course, includes the schizophrenic's family).

One indication in this environmental research is that poverty very likely does not produce the disease. After a series of studies in downtown and suburban areas of Detroit, one team reported that it is schizophrenia that results in an individual's social class rather than the other way around. "Environmental influences are nothing so simple and obvious as membership in a particular culture, subculture, or social class," reported Dr. E. Warren Dunham, professor of psychiatry at State University of New York in Stony Brook, N.Y.

The family of the schizophrenic continues to be the key area of research into the disease, both for its effect on the patient, and vice versa. One recent study proposes that the way to prevent relapse is to keep the patient on maintenance doses of phenothiazines while at the same time drastically reducing the face-to-face contact between the patient and relative, if the relative interacts with a high degree of expressed emotion.

The nine-month relapse rate in a group of 125 patients was only 12 percent if the patient stayed on drugs and had contact with a relative who interacted with little overt emotion. On the other hand, it rose to 55 percent if the drugs continued, but the patient had more than 35 hours a week contact with a highly emotional relative. In this last group, when the patients were not on drugs, the relapse rate zoomed to 92 percent.

The new genetic studies have built a stronger base on which to counsel couples on the possibility of their children being affected by the disease.

"It's very rare for a couple to come to a genetic counsellor about schizophrenia, but we should give the facts to anyone who asks," says Dr. McCormick, who is also director of psychiatric education at the Queen St. Mental Health Centre in Toronto.

According to Dr. Heston, physicians who are confronted with the question, explicit or implicit, from the family of a schizophrenic patient, "What did we do wrong?" should answer "Nothing that medical science can yet identify."

A normal individual with a schizophrenic parent or sibling, married to a normal person with a nonschizophrenic pedigree will almost certainly produce a normal child, says University of Minnesota's Leonard Heston, the risk not being significantly greater than in the normal population. But for two people with schizophrenic pedigrees, the risk is significantly greater, he added.

CHEMICAL ROOTS OF THE DISEASE

Research on the disease has now moved into an unexpected and exciting phase, with significant potential benefits to the public. Some of the excitement flows from the recent discovery that an excess of the chemical dopamine in the brain produces schizophrenic-like actions. A clue to this finding came from studies of amphetamine overdoses, which stimulate dopamine production and result in bizarre behavior.

If the genetic mechanism can be traced, it may be possible to identify persons with genetic predisposition to schizophrenia, affirming David Suzuki's prediction about a simple diagnostic test.

So, willy nilly, the geneticists and environmentalists are coming to sup at the same table, as guests of the biochemists. This could be a harbinger of more effective treatments for this crippling disease.

THE BIOCHEMICAL BLUEPRINT

**Perception and behavior
are ultimately rooted in nerve cell chemistry
and biochemists are now discovering the nature
of the underlying chemical disorders
in mental disease.**

Joan Hollobon

Is the schizophrenic mind the result of disordered chemistry or of faulty emotional development early in life?

Abnormal brain chemistry does not in itself prove anything: brain chemistry could become abnormal *in reponse* to emotional stress. Emotions indeed express themselves biochemically: adrenalin secretion in response to anger, fear or other strong emotion is a well-documented stress response.

Until the new and exciting discoveries of the past three years, the search for abnormalities in brain structure or chemistry affecting perception and behavior were disappointing. Researchers reported pink spots and mauve spots in urine and abnormal chemicals in the blood of schizophrenic patients, only to have later researchers report that they were unable to duplicate the findings or show them to be a product of the research method.

Over the years there have been many theories advanced on the cause of schizophrenia: vitamin deficiency, slow viruses, allergies, autoimmune reactions, gluten in wheat, the hormone serotonin and a host of chemicals. All remained just that: theories. It was never possible to go that essential next step to show how these agents caused the brains of schizophrenic patients to see, hear and feel so realistically the unrealities of their delusions and hallucinations.

Despite disappointments, three research areas have kept scientists plowing on: genetic studies, transmission of nerve impulses, and psychoactive drugs. All have to do with biochemistry.

Genes write their blueprints of heredity in chemicals, so evidence of a genetic component is a strong indication of altered biochemistry. As to impulses carried from one nerve cell to another, recent research has shown this to be largely through chemicals. Finally there is the demonstrable effect of psychoactive drugs in allaying psychotic behavior.

DRUGS THAT MODIFY THE MIND

If chemicals in drugs can affect behavior, they must do it by some effect on the brain cells that control emotions, perception, moods. That was the starting point for Dr. Philip Seeman of Toronto: how do the major tranquilizers affect the mind?

His research showed for the first time that they work by quite specifically inactivating what are called dopamine receptors. Dopamine, with other brain amines, had been suspect for some time, partly because certain patients given L-dopa to treat their Parkinson's disease developed psychotic symptoms similar to those of schizophrenia. And L-dopa is the substance from which the brain manufactures dopamine.

But while scientists had suspected dopamine metabolism might play some role, they did not know what that role was: Dr. Seeman's work was the first indication of a mechanism of action for psychoactive drugs.

Dopamine is one of several chemicals the brain uses to transmit "on-off" messages from cell to cell. One cell releases dopamine which the next cell "catches" in receptors specifically designed to recognize and bind dopamine molecules.

Dr. Seeman, in collaboration with U.S., Britist and Austrian scientists, subsequently showed that the brains of people who had suffered from schizophrenia contained too many dopamine receptors, particularly in regions governing emotional expression and modulating body motion.

Seeman postulated that too many receptors would make schizophrenics super-sensitive to their own dopamine, causing the flooding of hallucinations, delusions and tangential ideas so typical of the condition, as well as the clumsy physical movements often also seen.

This was the first hard, consistently reproducible evidence for an organic abnormality that could have a bearing on the development of this tragic disorder. Much work remains to be done, but it opens the way to possible chemical intervention based on understanding of the chemical processes involved, instead of relying on cook-book empirical observations that some drugs simply "work".

CHEMICAL TOXINS AND MENTAL DISEASE

In mulling over the results of a Danish study on adopted children, Dr. James Cade, a University of Florida kidney specialist, wondered if the chemical abnormality in schizophrenia might be a missing enzyme that allows a build-up of a toxic chemical.

Many well-known inherited diseases, such as phenylketonuria, are caused by the lack of a catalyst that helps convert body chemicals to substances the body can eliminate.

Both Dr. Cade and Dr. Herbert Wagemaker of the University of Louisville found that putting schizophrenic patients on artificial kidney machines improved their mental states, the implication being that the machine cleared some harmful substance(s) from the body. But the treatments met skepticism and criticism. Harvard University's Dr. Seymour Kety was quoted by *Medical World News* as expressing doubt because no hard evidence exists of any circulating poison. More pilot studies are needed "to relieve Dr. Cade and Dr. Wagemaker of the criticism they may be victims of their own enthusiasm." Critics also noted that the experiment had not been double-blind (where doctors and patients do not know who is getting the real treatment and who is getting a similar sham treatment, thus eliminating the possible effect of expectations).

Discovery of endorphin and its breakdown products (enkephalins) within the past three years marks a dramatic advance in brain research, providing the most powerful clues yet to the physiological mechanisms of the emotions, pain and pleasure perception, drug addiction and, possibly, mental illness.

NARCOTICS RESEARCH PRODUCES SURPRISES

In other work involving the action of narcotic drugs, addiction researchers deduced the existence of specific opiate receptor sites in the brain, and more particularly, from the ability of narcotic antagonists to "switch off" the effects of narcotics. (A dose of the drug naloxone can rapidly reverse the effects of a narcotic, such as heroin or morphine).

As one scientist said, human beings are not born containing morphine, so the only explanation is that the brain contains its own opiate-like substances. The first clues from a California group that this might be so were followed up by scientists at the University of Aberdeen, Scotland, who identified just such a substance in December 1975. They called it "enkephalin" from the Greek, meaning "in the head".

Enkephalin is a short-chain peptide containing five amino acids. Subsequently, U.S. scientists found a longer chain peptide with morphine-like activity from which enkephalin is very likely derived. They called it "endorphin", meaning "morphine within".

These materials have powerful pain-relieving properties, and are short-lived due to rapid enzyme degradation. Those in the brain are found particularly in the area that regulates the emotions. Enkephalins also exist in the small intestine. Scientists do not know the exact function of endorphin (more specifically, beta-endorphin), produced by the pituitary gland, but they think it may play a role in regulating hormone secretion (morphine is known to affect the secretion of hormones).

Two well-known psychiatrists reported at an international symposium on endorphins last December in San Juan, Puerto Rico, that some of the depressed and schizophrenic patients to whom they administered beta-endorphin showed dramatic improvement. Patients whose major symptoms were anger or hostility failed to respond, however. The one normal control, Dr. Edward Laski, a psychiatrist at Albert Einstein School of Medicine, New York City, said he experienced a "spaced out, floating feeling," which went away after five hours as suddenly as "flipping an on-off switch".

The psychiatrists, Dr Nathan Kline of the Rockland Research Institute, Orange-

burg, N.Y., and Dr Heinz Lehmann, professor and former head of psychiatry at McGill University, were criticized for raising public hopes without sound evidence. The experiment was uncontrolled, leading one critic to suggest the patients who did well may have simply responded to their own expectations. Negativistic, hostile people invariably resist this "placebo effect," the critics noted.

Indeed, these particular experiments prove little, but discovery of the new chemicals and their complex inter-relationships with hormones and other chemicals offers real hope for the future. Clarification of the chemical picture may even tie together many of the past theories that died aborning for lack of sufficient basic knowledge. For instance, a biochemist at the U.S. National Institute of Mental Health has detected a peptide in wheat gluten "that proves to be an enkephalin-like opioid."

Medical World News reported that Dr. Candace Pert, of the National Institute of Mental Health, "a founding mother of endorphin-enkephalin science," predicted that within 10 years there will be "at least one fantastic new drug for mental health acting by a totally new mechanism".

A DARKNESS AT NOON

Carl Edgar Law

"I have of late, — but wherefore I know not — lost all my mirth, forgone all custom of exercises; and — indeed — it goes so heavily with my disposition that this goodly frame, the earth, seems to me a sterile promontory."

That's how Hamlet saw things in Act II, Scene II; and, say Canadian psychiatrists, that's how 15 to 20 per cent of Canadians see things at some time in their lives — seriously enough to require at least one contact with a hospital.

In fact, 50 per cent or more of Canadians may experience depression at least once in their lives. While many will simply not contact professional help despite the severity, others will find the episode sufficiently mild or short in duration to cope using their own mental resources.

Fortunately, says Dr. Sarwer-Foner, director of psychiatry for the Ottawa General Hospital and the elder statesman of psychiatry in Canada, most depression is self-limiting, with almost 90 per cent of depressions remitting within 30 days to six months. Some cases may persist up to two years and about 15 per cent tend to become resistant to treatment. The pattern may continue throughout life but even stubbornly-resistant depressions tend to mitigate with advancing age unless there are underlying organic problems.

Patients whose depressions are punctuated by periods of euphoria, often leading to extreme feelings of energy and omnipotence, as well as loss of judgment and hyper-sensitivity to criticism, are characterized as "manic-depressives" and form a relatively small subgroup.

To the layman — aided by the popular press — depression is often seen as a byproduct of an industrial, rootless age in which the increasing stress of burgeoning technology and possible breakdowns in the social and moral order constitute insidious assaults on sanity. History, however, does not bear this thesis out.

The Babylonian King Nebuchadnezzar is reputed to have suffered intensely from insomnia, with wildly erratic mood swings, corresponding to a possible diagnosis of manic depression (it is rarer in men than in women). Chroniclers also describe the biblical Kings Saul and Herod as less-than-happy men.

Homer and Plutarch made *their* contributions to the literature on depression, joining a trend that has continued among philosophers and writers to the present day. The evidence is convincing then, that depression has been an unrelenting feature of human existence throughout Mankind's history.

Throughout history, the major technique for treating depression has remained largely the same.

"Psychotherapy continues as the treatment of choice for depression," Dr. Sarwer-Foner says, although he includes a number of important qualifications.

Psychotherapy, which has become very sophisticated in recent times, had its beginnings in the practices of witch-doctors, magicians, elders of the tribe, even family members; in fact, therapeutic help could be provided by anyone whom the depressive trusted and respected. And, if one word is vital in treating depression, it is "hope". The loss of hope (a state of despair) is a prominent feature in depression. The glimmerings of renewed hope are important indicators in the cure.

EVENT-RELATED DEPRESSION

In the vast majority of cases depression is a response to a real or perceived object loss: the loss of a wife, husband, lover, mother, father, a cherished pet — in fact, any object or relationship the subject holds dearly as central to his or her happiness.

What happens frequently in the beginnings of depression is the onset of a sense of inferiority, says Dr. Sarwer-Foner who also teaches at the Ottawa University

Faculty of Medicine, acts as a consultant, and has contributed prolifically to the literature since the 1950's.

"There is a shattering of the concept of the person, a sense of not being good enough. Depressed people haven't got the strength to live and they may exhibit passive dependency."

What they need is to be valued as a person, to have a place in life, to have people care for them, to be respected and to feel that they can get what they deserve from life without superhuman or abnormal effort — such as that exhibited by the "workaholic" who withdraws from social contact because he is "too busy". ("Normal" people believe that they are deserving just by virtue of existing, without having to solicit outside approval excessively, or do anything specifically "good" to feel whole and well.).

These depressions are known as "reactive" depressions because they involve a reaction to a tangible loss. They are "event-related", and range from the normal grief reaction to an extreme withdrawal syndrome that precludes the maintaining of normal responsibilities and behavior.

The clinical signs psychiatrists and physicians look for in depression include: mood change; psychomotor retardation and anxiety; loss of self-esteem; delusions and hallucinations, sleep disturbance; loss of energy; change in appetite and change in sexual drive. But not all signs and symptoms will be present in individual cases. Mood changes may include an active descent into gloom and misery, or a less-pronounced loss of well-being. Psychomotor retardation means a slowing down of the mental and physical faculties. In many cases the subject's life simply grinds to a halt.

"A depression starts with a feeling of general tiredness which does not respond

 Reprinted from SCIENCE FORUM magazine, July/August 1978, pp. 32-38, with the permission of the publisher.

favorably to resting or sleeping," recounts one patient.

"Within a few days a bitter taste develops in my mouth and I lose my appetite. At night I have difficulty in sleeping.

"Within a week to 10 days an intense feeling of depression sets in, creating the impression that I am quite incapable of doing my job; unable to drive my car and, in fact, afraid to do anything involving any skill or responsibility.

"This deepens my feeling of depression and soon brings me to contemplating suicide."

Not all depressives contemplate suicide, but when depressions are put together with other mental illnesses predisposing to suicide, the figures become startling. Suicide is the leading cause of death in certain young age groups and a major cause of death in most others, tapering off at the extreme ends of the scale (childhood and old age).

Surprisingly, many elderly patients develop a condition known as organic brain syndrome, which often makes them too confused to commit suicide even when they contemplate the act. Thus, lowered suicide deaths in the elderly may indicate a lack of skill at consummating the act rather than a diminished incidence of suicidally-depressive thinking.

DEPRESSION FROM WITHIN

The second major group of depressions is classified as "endogenous" (coming from within). In these cases there is no obvious precipitating event.

In fact, though, says Dr. Sarwer-Foner, "good clinical studies show that there usually is a precipitating factor, but the patient can't talk about it while still ill."

The psychiatrist can usually distinguish between these two types of depressions by symptoms. Both types share many common symptoms, but in endogenous depression symptoms may be more severe and greater in number. Delusions and visual or auditory hallucinations are more common in this group.

For Dr. Sarwer-Foner, a primary question to ask is: "Can the patient relate — that is, communicate with — the psychiatrist or therapist?"

If the patient can communicate it is important to establish at the outset whether suicidal or homicidal tendencies are present. These questions can be answered from the patient's history and from the comments of family and friends or whoever accompanies the patient to treatment.

Such questions are vital because these tendencies suggest a crisis that must be treated immediately, in a hospital setting. The patient may be quieted with drugs. A violent episode may be halted by the use

of ECT — electro-convulsive therapy — which Dr. Sarwer-Foner calls "life-saving", even though it fell into some disrepute in the late sixties and early seventies.

"When the patient is severely disturbed and pre-disposed to violence against himself and others this treatment can be life-saving," says Dr. Sarwer-Foner. It is not a punishment — although public critics may sometimes term it that — and it has few if any lasting side effects.

It is also safe. The primary side effect is short-term memory loss. The patient may not remember what happened during the day or two preceding treatment and for a time may have marked memory loss of past events, but these memories usually return over a period of days or weeks.

Six to eight shock treatments are commonly given in depression and they may be combined with antidepressant drugs. ECT has proved particularly useful in the "endogenous" depressions. If the patient does not appear suicidal or homicidal but cannot communicate, hospitalization is still generally necessary. Either ECT, anti-depressant drug therapy, or a combination of the two will frequently alleviate the worst symptoms within a period of weeks. Only then can meaningful psychotherapy begin. Neither drugs nor ECT are panaceas, but they can help restore contact with reality.

Thus, drugs and ECT are common treatments in the primary or crisis stage. In the secondary stage when psychotherapy has begun, drugs are frequently valuable adjuncts. Should the depression prove refractory (that is, long-term or chronic) drug treatment may continue for many years.

DRUGS, DRUGS... AND DRUGS

The hierarchy of drugs is fairly straightforward in psychiatry and although new derivatives of old drugs are being synthesized, the classic preparations have been used for two decades or more. While this suggests no great improvements in drug therapy, clinicians have nonetheless built up vast experience in their use. To the patient that means more likelihood of getting the "right" drug first time round, and less likelihood of severe side effects from the "wrong" prescription.

The heavyweight drugs in depression are the "neuroleptics". The most popular of these is chlorpromazine, marketed under such names as Largactil (Canada) and Thorizaine (United States). Neuroleptics may also be called "major tranquilizers" or, simply, antipsychotic drugs. In the psychotic depressions (and in schizophrenia) they reduce hallucinations, delusions, combativeness, tension, restlessness and social withdrawal. Over-all there is an emotional quieting effect.

Some of these drugs have sedative effects, useful in the therapy of some patients, but considered an undesirable side effect in others.

A major feature of neuroleptics is that, though they are antipsychotic in appropriate dosage, they can be used to treat lesser disorders simply by reducing the amount administered.

"They are very effective in the treatment of anxiety in all psychiatric disorders," say Drs. E.L. Bassuk and S.C. Schoonover, in their book, The Practicioner's Guide to Psychoactive Drugs.

Patients who are not severely disturbed may often be prescribed anti-depressants. The two major families are known as "tricyclics" (because of their molecular structure) and "monoamine oxidase inhibitors' or MAOIs, (because they inhibit the destruction of certain nerve transmission substances (neurotransmitters). Both of these drugs affect neurotransmitters without specifically sedating the patient or producing unmanageable side effects.

To understand what a neurotransmitter substance is, one needs an idea of how nerve transmission works. Nerve cells or neurons in the body and brain never quite meet. There is a narrow gap between each neuron. When a single nerve fires, a current sweeps along the neuron to its end, where it stimulates the production of neurotransmitter chemicals which cross the narrow gap to receptor sites on the surface of the next nerve cell; this causes it to fire in turn. Thus, these substances are vital to the healthy operation of the nervous system.

When the nerve transmission is finished, the neurotransmitter is destroyed by other chemicals and recycled metabolically to be stored and re-used for future nerve transmissions.

Some anti-depressants simply block the chemicals that destroy these neurotransmitters, causing a higher rate of nervous activity, while others increase the overall availability of neurotransmitters in the brain. In either case, the heightened nerve activity seems to improve mood and make the patient feel more energetic and motivated.

The patient who is depressed will often be started on a tricyclic. It takes two to four weeks for such drugs to exert their full effect, at which point the physician may try another tricyclic if the first hasn't produced good results, or vary the dose according to the side effects.

When tricyclics don't work, monoamine oxidase inhibitors or MAOIs are often prescribed, but because of their potentially severe side effects (including coma and death), they are generally given in hospital where the patient can be monitored closely. These drugs produce the well-known "cheese" effect. Certain cheeses, (as well as Chianti wine and other foods), contain byproducts of fermentation called "tyramines", which can react violently with monoamine oxidase inhibitors; the effect can often be reversed however by the neuroleptic chlorpromazine.

That's why out-patients taking MAOIs are sometimes prescribed a neuroleptic drug to carry as an emergency kit in case they inadvertently (or intentionally in the case of wine and beer lovers) eat or drink anything that causes a violent reaction.

If anti-depressant effects are not produced in the patient even with MAOIs, the physician or psychiatrist may prescribe a combination of tricyclics and MAOIs, but this requires in-depth clinical experience. Each drug is administered in half its usual dose (if used alone) and the diet is carefully controlled to avoid the adverse reactions previously noted.

In depressions with anxiety as an important component, "anxiolytics" may be prescribed. The trade names Librium and Valium are virtually household words in North America and may be the most widely-prescribed drugs in the western world. Their chemical names are, respectively, chlordiazepoxide and diazepam.

These anxiolytics are widely abused by large numbers of people to relieve normal day-to-day stress. However, the word "abused" in a clinical sense does not necessarily imply over-dosing or extremely irresponsible use; rather it refers to their use for purposes other than that indicated by strict medical considerations — as a crutch to "get through a rough day at the office", for example. Fortunately, anxiolytic drugs have few side effects and even massive over-doses generally produce few, if any, long-term side-effects. Thus, unlike neuroleptics, tricyclics and MAOIs, they are relatively safe for the user who may be a potential suicide risk.

While anti-anxiety drugs may be safe in moderation, the dangers doctors watch for are gradual increase in dose by the patient, or steady long-term use for frivolous or less-than-medical reasons. With burgeoning research, more cases of long-term side-effects are being noted in users.

For example, certain patients will experience "paradoxical reactions" on anti-anxiety drugs. That is, they may become restless, agitated, aggressive, even violent — just the opposite of the drug's intended effect. It may be that anxiety is an external manifestation of bottled-up rage, anger, or frustration in such patients, the anxiety keeping a lid on "acting-out" this rage in terms of verbal and physical violence. If this theory holds, remove the anxiety and the anger surges to the surface. As one Ottawa psychiatrist put it, tongue-in-cheek, "the chap may take a swing at you but he certainly won't feel anxious about it."

Since alcohol may increase the effects of anti-anxiety drugs (as well as other psychiatric drugs) it is especially undesirable in these "paradoxical" patients. A binge on Valium and scotch, for instance, can produce a very dangerous individual. On the other hand, patients who are quieted by anti-anxiety preparations may find that mixing them with alcohol makes them drowsy or produces varying degrees of euphoria. The medical opinion on this combination: generally risky.

RARE TREATMENTS AND BREAKTHROUGHS

Four types of treatment are of special interest, and point out some directions in current research and the prospects of better cures in the future.

Insulin sub-coma treatment is not well-known but as Dr. Sarwer-Foner points out, "it is useful in patients with passive dependency needs." These are patients who feel so low that they really require "lots of tender loving care". In such cases closely-monitored doses of insulin can be extremely useful.

Too much insulin produces classic "insulin coma" because the hormone depletes the blood sugar, thereby starving the brain of this vital nutrient. This is not a desirable goal, although it was a popular treatment some years ago with certain psychiatrists. Insulin sub-coma (that is, sugar depletion, but not enough to knock the patient out) is induced in closely-monitored treatment units that feature highly-trained nurses and individualized care. This provides the patient with tangible evidence of caring people. It may also have a quieting effect, making the patient drowsy and helping him sleep when insomnia is a problem. It also increases appetite, an important feature in patients whose depression includes loss of interest in eating.

Megavitamin therapy is widely-touted by believers, but very few of these are physicians. That's why the medical literature generally dismisses megavitamin therapy in a few terse paragraphs. High doses of many vitamins, particularly B and C, have been recommended in many psychiatric illnesses by theorists who believe that some patients have physiological systems that prevent them from absorbing, storing or using these vitamins properly.

A feature of megavitamin therapy is that there is relatively little evidence of any toxicity in large doses of vitamins B, C or E. (The evidence to the contrary is generally based on extremely high doses). Vitamins A and D are very toxic in over-doses, but are not a primary focus of interest in psychiatry.

Lithium carbonate (a salt of the metal lithium) is used to treat the manic stage of manic-depression. This phase of manic-depression may begin with increased energy on the part of the victim. He may hatch grandiose plans and become impatient of criticism. This is the "workaholic" syndrome taken to extremes. His agitation may become so intense that he will go long periods without sleep and make errors in judgment, perhaps indulging in spending sprees or unwise investments that he would not normally contemplate.

Then comes the crash into depression and withdrawal, perhaps with an interim — a period of normality. In certain cases, depression is the first clinical sign, with the mania coming later. Some patients may only experience one such cycle during their lives and thus may not be considered "classical" manic-depressives, while others become chronic with the cycle repeating itself.

Lithium carbonate has been found very effective in controlling and limiting the "manic" phase of the illness, its effect in many patients also being beneficial during the depressive phase, when anti-depressants are normally prescribed. There is some evidence that lithium carbonate may be effective in illnesses involving depression alone, but it is not strong. There is also suggestive evidence that the drug can be extremely useful in the "pre-menstrual" syndrome in women. That would be good news for certain women who experience pre-menstrual distress as a real and powerful illness.

Dr. Brent Waters, a Royal Ottawa Hospital psychiatrist with experience in manic depression, says that while lithium carbonate has been considered a relatively "safe" drug, recent evidence shows that "it has to be watched for toxic effects. Lithium carbonate should be treated as conservatively as many other psychotropic (mood-altering) drugs and this finding is relatively new."

Dr. Waters' comment illustrates a central issue in psychiatry. While many promising drugs appear periodically in the field, it is only after years of follow-up that long-term effects become matters of record. The other point to be made about drug therapy is that the psychiatrist does not want simply to remove all pain and anxiety from the patient in psychotherapy. An important treatment goal is to bring the patient face to face with grief, pain and anxiety and focus on mechanisms for coping with it. In fact, many psychiatrists believe much depression is a mental "reorganizing and strengthening" process that provides important experiences in growing and maturing.

Nietzsche stated, bluntly, that everything that doesn't destroy one makes one stronger and, further, there is no sun without shadow; it is essential to know the night. It is easy to see why librarians used to classify philosophy and psychotherapy under the same catalogue numbers. Both the philosopher and the psychotherapist are intimately involved with "the dark night of the soul". It can be debated, constructively, that the psychotherapist includes the role of "philosopher-mentor" among his many treatment strategies.

THE FUTURE:

The newest frontiers of psychiatry are often anything but philosophic — they are biochemical; the primary focus is on chemicals produced by the body itself, particularly the brain. Of course, there are philosophic frontiers, too, as new schools of psychotherapy evolve and older ones are refined and synthesized with others. But biochemistry and molecular biology are in the forefront of psychiatric research more intensively than ever before. While not all this research is aimed strictly at depression (schizophrenia and major psychoses are prime targets) it should have important benefits for depressive illness too.

A key area of the brain involved in the body's "chemical control" system is the hypothalamus. It produces many "releasing factors" that stimulate the nearby pituitary gland to produce a range of hormones, many of which affect mood. But there is a heated controversy between theorists who believe that hormones affect mood in complex ways. This area of study is called psychoendocrinology (endocrinology is the medical term for the study of the hormonal system).

Psychoendocrinology has addressed itself to depression more than to other psychiatric illnesses because there are sexual differences in the incidence of depression (women are more prone than men to many types) and hormones have a direct effect on sexual psychology and physiology. Indeed, some theorists see the menstrual cycle as a model-in-miniature of clinical depression because the changing hormonal balances during this cycle are closely mirrored by mood swings. This should not be interpreted as sexism since theorists suggest that men may have analogous hormonal cycles too, albeit less evident and harder to study. By comparison, menstrual mood swings in women have been recorded for thousands of years.

The "biogenic amine" theory of psychoendocrinology may not be a household word, but is one of the new buzzwords in the psychiatric lexicon. Biogenic amines (literally, body-produced amine compounds) are organic substances like adrenalin, noradrenalin, dopamine, tryptophan and serotonin that can act as neurotransmitters. Adrenalin is contained in a major, well-known drug used for asthma and other allergy treatments (generally in spray form) because it dilates the airway (bronchodilation) permitting easier breathing. It is also used in emergency treatment of allergy shock (such as that caused by bee stings) and is a powerful stimulant to the heart in emergency treatment of cardiac arrest.

The biogenic amine theory states that these substances, when acting as neurotransmitters, have important effects on emotion, states of consciousness, responses to stress and related behaviors. But they may act abnormally in certain psychiatric illnesses. In particular, the increased activity of noradrenalin in the brain has been suggested as a cause for mania while decreased activity of this neurotransmitter has been suggested as a cause of endogenous depression. Overactivity of dopamine has been suggested as contributing to schizophrenia and hyperactivity in children.

According to the biogenic amine theory, the activity of anti-depressant and anti-psychotic drugs seems best explained by their ability to increase, or to block, the actions of these amines in the brain.

But one should not be overly seduced by biological theories of depression as the prime hope for the future. For the moderately-depressed and anxious patient, such simple treatments as change to a pleasanter environment, contact with loving, caring people, social counselling leading to better management of personal affairs and involvement in new and rewarding activities, work wonders. Team counselling including psychiatrists, nurses, social workers and other professionals is expanding and changing. Preventive psychiatry in the form of social facilities, sports activities, better working environments and "amateur" or "volunteer" crisis centres also have an ever-growing role, providing a less obvious but very real hope for the future.

In 1973, depression accounted for six per cent of patient hospital days in Canada, making it the fifth largest reason for hospital admission (the third largest in the 15-65 year group). Many other depressions go unrecognized because the patient does not seek help — often because of innate societal prejudice, oftimes manifest in the phrase "lack of moral fibre".

Depression is a real illness and it is pandemic. The direct cost to the health care system, as well as the immense social cost, make it a major focus for research. The director of the United States National Institute of Mental Health, Dr. Bertram S. Brown, says three million Americans will seek help from a mental health professional annually to the end of the decade — assuming current episode rates remain constant. United Kingdom and Western European figures emphasize the point, although there are differences between the various countries.

Although biochemical and biomolecular research are exciting leads for the future, there still is a major role to be played by families and communities and by mental health workers other than physicians and psychiatrists. Depression will always be with us, but in future more cures will be effected in severe depressions, while many other types will be shortened due to newer treatments. The majority of sufferers — those with self-limiting reactive depressions — probably have the least to gain from chemical research, but new programs of short-term psychotherapy are helping them, too, to adjust more quickly and effectively to these painful episodes.

THE AGE OF MELANCHOLY

There are growing signs that melancholy—ranging from ordinary
sadness to severe depression—is the most common psychological complaint
of our times. On the following pages, the nation's highest-ranking
mental-health officer ponders the evidence, while other
authorities explore social and biological forces contributing to the
malaise, the roots of the depressive personality, and the startling
numbers that show women are much more likely to suffer than men.

Gerald L. Klerman

Gerald L. Klerman, M.D., is administrator of
the federal Alcohol, Drug Abuse, and Mental
Health Administration. This article has been
adapted from a paper presented at the conference "Vulnerable Youth: Hope, Despair,
and Renewal," sponsored by the University
of Chicago's Student Mental Health Clinic
and Department of Psychiatry in April of
1978. The conference papers, edited by
Miriam Elson and John F. Kramer, will be
published by University of Chicago Press.

It is the pastime of some writers, historians, and psychiatrists to divide life into various "Ages." One very successful instance of this labeling was the 1947 poem by W. H. Auden, "The Age of Anxiety," which seemed to capture a syndrome that was widespread in the population. Many people, particularly psychiatrist Robert Lifton, related that anxiety to man's awareness of the power to destroy our entire species by nuclear means.

Auden's poem has had tremendous intellectual and even clinical impact. It inspired a symphony by Leonard Bernstein and a ballet by Jerome Robbins, both called "The Age of Anxiety." By focusing public attention on anxiety, it may have also contributed to the development of new drugs (like tranquilizers) and new psychothera-

peutic techniques (like biofeedback and desensitization) for coping with the symptoms.

In the mid-60s, a series of papers began to speculate that anxiety was giving way to depression and despair as dominant moods in modern man. Whereas the middle decades of this century were labeled an Age of Anxiety, there are indications that the later decades will be considered an Age of Melancholy.

How good is the evidence indicating an actual increase in epidemiologic rates of depression? Some is valid and some is not. For instance, more articles about depression are written now than ever before. There is an increase in the prescription of antidepressant drugs, yet there is also an increase in use of antianxiety drugs. A slight increase in the diagnosis of depression is seen in nationwide data. But the fact that more people are being diagnosed as depressed—in general hospitals, community mental-health centers, and clinic settings—may be an artifact of the greater attention given to the problem and of extensions in insurance coverage. For the record, it is nicer to call someone depressed than schizophrenic or paranoid.

Excellent data worldwide indicate a rise in suicide attempts, although

not necessarily deaths. In the United States, the suicide-attempt rate has increased dramatically, almost tenfold, and mostly among young adults. Women have higher rates than men do, with the highest prevalence under age 30. The most common technique is pill ingestion, perhaps a tribute to our new technology.

Other findings, less well documented, also show that the median age of depressed patients is dropping. The textbooks written before World War I concentrated, in their discussion of depressions, on "involutional melancholia" (a disorder of the middle years), and found the median age to be in the 40s and 50s. A study examining the discharge records at the Massachusetts Mental Health Center found that immediately after World War II the median age of patients was in the 40s, and the most common diagnosis was involutional melancholia. But in three recent studies in the United States, the median age of patients admitted to depression research studies was in the early 30s.

The depressive phenomenon is well known throughout the history of Western civilization. There are excellent descriptions in the Bible, particularly of Saul's depression, which was

From *Psychology Today,* April 1979. Reprinted by permission of the author.

treated by David with some success. Clinical descriptions also appear in Egyptian, Greek, and Roman literature, in which a modern clinician has no difficulty in recognizing the symptoms of depression. It is hard to find an equally good description of schizophrenia in ancient literature, although many hallucinatory states are described.

Writers in at least two periods of Western European literature paid increased attention to depression. Most notable was the interest in depression of Elizabethan writers in the 16th century; later came the emotional outpourings of the Romantics, particularly the German, French, and Russian writers. More recently, a number of influential literary figures—Samuel Beckett, Walker Percy, A. Alvarez, Sylvia Plath—have portrayed themes of alienation, despair, and depression.

To what extent literature reflects epidemiologic trends, nobody knows. It is easy to believe that we have moved into an Age of Melancholy, preceded by an Age of Anxiety. The Age of Melancholy is a period when rising expectations, generated after World War II, have come up against the harsh realities of population explosion and doomsday prophecies—such as those of the Club of Rome and other seers of the future. A situation that may psychologically predispose individuals to depression is a gap between expectations and actuality. We experience feelings of despair perhaps not so much when a situation is bad, but when we have given up hope.

In addition to looking at depression clinically and developmentally, it is useful to step back a bit and consider depression as an evolutionary phenomenon for our species, and for most mammalian species. Emotional states like depression, anxiety, fear, and anger have a function in the lives of organisms, including human organisms, in that they promote adaptation of the organism to the environment. That idea was first enunciated by Darwin in his book *The Expression of the Emotions in Man and Animals*: not only are morphologic structures adapted by natural selection, he proposed, but there is also an evolutionary selective sequence to emotional states, which he called "mental and expressive capacities."

Darwin described in great detail his observations of emotional expression in lower animals, as well as in primates and humans, and showed by drawings that in monkeys and humans, the same facial muscles are involved in the expression of anger, fear, and sadness. Many of Darwin's ideas and observations lay dormant until after World War II, when a remarkable upsurge of interest and study in the biology of behavior occurred. For example, the field popularly known as ethology has emerged, in which zoologists like Konrad Lorenz and Niko Tinbergen observe animal behavior under natural conditions.

Harry F. Harlow, William T. McKinney, and their colleagues have gone one step further from natural observations and experimentally induced various emotional states. By separating rhesus monkey offspring from their mothers or from their peers, the researchers induced certain psychopathologic states—most prominently depression—in the babies. The baby monkey is first separated from the mother. The two can see each other through a cage, but they cannot touch each other. That may seem like a cruel thing to do, but human beings sometimes do the equivalent inadvertently.

In Harlow's model, there is a two-stage sequence to the emotional response of the monkeys. The first stage of behavioral response, as described by the authors, is that of protest. An increase in motor activity occurs, as well as an increase in vocalization, and the animals run around the cage and pound on the window separating them from their mothers, as though they are seeking to reestablish contact. If there were close-up films of the monkeys' faces, we would see expressions that we would register empathically as anguish and fearfulness, maybe even anxiety. In the second stage—which the investigators call the despair stage—the parties give up, the infant huddles in the corner, the mother turns away and her face begins to droop. All motor activity is reduced. Again, the facial expressions are empathically identifiable as despair to most human observers. Jane Goodall reports similar observations in chimpanzees separated from one another. There are even death reactions among some chimps she has studied in the African setting.

In a series of studies based upon dogs, psychologists John Paul Scott and John L. Fuller showed that the most reliable index of a dog's reaction to separation was the high-pitched wail. They studied the various effects of drugs on that form of vocalization, and the only drugs they found that reduced the dog's wail were the imipramine medications, which are used for their antidepressant effect upon human beings. Such drugs as the barbiturates and thorazine had no effect on the high-pitched wail, until the drugs actually put the animal to sleep. The vocalization of the dog is related to the degree of separation, as anyone who has left a dog in an automobile while shopping knows. The vocalization is an indirect form of evidence that there are biochemical and physiologic mechanisms built into mammals that react to the disruption of the attachment bonds.

Though the capacity to become depressed seems not to be an exclusively human one, it has been part of our evolutionary heritage and has played a biologically adaptive function. It performs what psychiatrist George L. Engel called a "signal" function, by alerting the social group, particularly the parental or mothering group, that one of its precious offspring is in some danger. That function is based in part on two facts

"Attachment bonds have been essential to the survival and development of our species."

about mammalian species in general, and primates in particular: first, we produce very few offspring compared with fish or insects; and, second, our offspring are born biologically immature and truly helpless.

Many of us as adults may feel, at times, that we are helpless and we need to be taken care of, but we are for the most part capable of biological survival. That assurance is not true of human infants or other mammalian infants. In order for the species to have survived as long as we have, mechanisms had to develop to nurture and protect helpless offspring.

One general thesis that can be drawn from these data is that the affective state of depression is a specific response to the disruption of attachment bonds. Attachment bonds have been useful, even essential, to the survival and development of our species. They are served by a psychobiological apparatus developed through the centuries that we have inherited from our mammalian ancestors, particularly the primates. One interesting aspect of the apparatus is that we resist with great biological force any disruption of attachments. We do not give up our bonding without great psychological and physiological anguish. One index of the strength of our attachments is the effect of bereavement on our physical and emotional health.

Data from a study in England and Wales of more than 4,000 widowed men indicate that widowers have mortality rates over and above age-matched male peers for the first year of being widowed. During the first four to six months, a widower's death rate increases by more than 140 percent, compared with men of the same age and social class. After that period, the ratio returns to some degree of normality, but it does not become totally normal for one year. There are other indices that the loss of a mate, or other bereavement, has a powerful impact. People with previous histories of alcoholism increase their drinking. There is a general increase in ingestive behaviors, in pill-taking of various sorts, and in cigarette smoking. Humans react vigorously, with the total body, to the disruption of attachment bonding.

Now, what is the clinical significance? How do those manifestations of separation relate to the phenomena that may be seen in clinical work? In a large project in New Haven, Connecticut, we attempted to investigate some of the effects of disruptions of attachment bonding on human beings by looking at 185 clinically depressed individuals who met certain research criteria. We had the good fortune of being able to compare the patients with 185 normals selected in a household survey and matched for age, sex, and social class.

Both samples were interviewed for the presence or absence of various types of life stress—in the six to 12 months prior to the onset of symptoms in the case of patients and, in the case of the normals, the six to 12 months prior to the actual interviews. We used a modification of a common technique involving a checklist of various kinds of life events that are considered to be stressful, such as death, separation, and divorce. Supposedly positive events, such as Christmas and taking a vacation, were also included. From that list of over 60 items, we extracted several events and grouped them according to a rather simple distinction between "exits and entrances." Some events represent the exits or disappearances of people from the social field, such as death, separation, divorce, or a son going into the army, whereas others represent entrances of people into the life space, or interpersonal space, of the individual.

When patients and controls were compared, there was no statistically significant difference between them regarding entrances, but there was a very dramatic difference with regard to exits. The depressives had experienced far more episodes of loss and separation, in one form or another.

How does the evidence on the effects of life stresses relate to the kinds of phenomena that we deal with clinically in the cases of young adults? Eriksonian concepts of developmental stages are pertinent here. Young individuals in our society, in particular, are involved in a number of developmental tasks, the most important of which includes leaving the parental home and establishing independence. As part of modern life, we place a high value on independence. This goes against a certain amount of our biological heritage. As I have already indicated, we do not give up our attachment bonds easily; we do so at an emotional and physiologic cost. Yet, in a modern industrial society such as ours, we move from one place to another—for school, for a job, and from that job to another. We send our children to summer camp, to pajama parties, on weekend trips.

In other words, we purposely train our children to anticipate the disruption of attachment bonding and to be

able to cope with the uncomfortable sense of separation and anxiety it brings. Anybody who has worked at a summer camp has seen the frequent mood of anxiety among the children or even the counselors. I have read accounts of the military during the Civil War, and the most common neurological diagnosis in the Union camps was something called nostalgia. There is a brilliant set of descriptions of the emotional reactions, particularly in periods of nostalgia, in young enlisted men entering the camps. From those accounts came physician George Beard's 1880 description of "neurasthenia," with its fatigue, weakness, and sense of despair—symptoms that we would see now as a reaction to separation.

"Compared to others, depressives experience far more episodes of loss or separation—of exits over entrances."

We expect our young today to move out, to leave the attachment of the primary family. In fact, if they stay too long with the primary family, we consider them dependent and as not moving along properly in the developmental cycle. More important, we see separation as an opportunity for growth and development. In the Eriksonian scheme, the outcome is the achievement of the capacity for intimacy, in order to create new forms of attachment bonding, especially with members of the opposite sex. With new attachments come a commitment to some sense of enduring responsibility and a capacity to share in emotional give-and-take.

I would propose that the sharp separation of old and new attachment bonding is a relatively new experience in the history of our species. Most of the social support systems on which our forebears relied until recently have emphasized some degree of stability and continuity.

The three most common social support systems have been the family, the church, and the immediate neighborhood. Ever since the introduction of urban life, we have relied upon those three social support systems as buttresses against disruptive emotional states, including depression, fear, and anger. It is a characteristic of the present time that all three of those social support systems are in various degrees of disarray.

Many people talk about the changes in the family, the extent to which the family seems to exist only at Thanksgiving, funerals, or other ritualistic occasions. The nuclear family is the subject of a good deal of criticism. People even claim that it is about to be done away with, given the high divorce rate. I do not hold with the conventional wisdom. If divorce is an actual illness, its cure seems to be the remarriage of the partners. People may not like marriage, but they seem to seek it out with a certain repetitive compulsion.

The church—organized religion—has played two important roles as a social support system. It attempted to provide cognitive meaning to life, and consolation during periods of despair, particularly those associated with death and other mysteries of existence. Second, the church was until recently the main system for the delivery of social services. We have now secularized the process with social-service agencies, child-guidance clinics, family services, and so on.

For most Americans, the church no longer provides cognitive meaning or a support system. However, the fact that many of today's youths are seeking alternative religious groups indicates that there are limits to which people in general, and the young in particular, can exist without some kind of a social support system. As for continuity and support from a community of neighbors, in an era marked by personal mobility and urban change, the neighborhood that has remained intact for 25 years is considered so rare as to merit a news story.

The theory that all or most depression can be explained as a reaction to loss or separation is a tempting one. Many theorists and textbook writers have emphasized one aspect or another of those phenomena as a necessary condition to understanding depression, whether as a normal mood, as a symptom, or as a syndrome. However, I think it is more important

to recognize that there are limits to that theory of depression.

First of all, loss and separation are not the antecedent events in all clinical depressions. In the group of depressives from the New Haven study mentioned previously, we could find a history of discernible loss or separation only in about 25 percent of the patients who were clinically depressed, although there was a predominance of exits or entrances with the group. Of course, 25 percent is far higher than the 5 to 10 percent incidence found for normal controls. From the point of view of causation, loss and separation are important factors; they increase the relative risk of certain populations to depression, but they cannot be regarded as universal. Some people have attempted to extend the point and talk about unconscious loss or symbolic loss. While that approach has some utility, I think it blurs what is an important fact: only in about a quarter of adult cases do we find a clear precipitating event that falls in the category of loss or separation. Second, not all individuals who are exposed to loss, separation, or disruption of attachment bonds become depressed. Most individuals do cope with things like going to college, being drafted, or going to summer camp. Most even cope with so profound a disruption as the death of a parent or a child. There have been some very good studies of individuals in the bereavement situation. Evidence from those studies indicates that the majority of individuals who are widowed and bereaved do go through a period of emotional distress, with increased susceptibility to physical illness and increased use of the health-care system. However, by the end of one year, about 85 percent of them are back to normal.

In the third place, loss, separation, and disruption are not specific to depression. By that I mean that they have been described as the precipitating events for a wide variety of clinical conditions, not only psychiatric but also medical, such as coronary artery disease, peptic ulcer, rheumatoid arthritis, and automobile accidents.

Loss, separation, and disruption of attachment bonding thus seem to result in a general propensity for illness, perhaps more so for depression; but on the evidence, their influence is not

conclusive. I believe that environmental stress, particularly loss or separation or disruption of bonding, cannot explain the clinical phenomena by itself. One must look to other aspects of the life of the individual or the social support systems available to give an explanation, let alone a prediction, of the individuals who adapt and the others who do not. Some of those factors may be genetic; others may be early life experiences in which the individual became sensitive to loss, a major theme in clinical theory. Another possible factor is any circumstance that lowers the self-esteem of the individual. Still other factors mentioned in the literature are changes in the social support system, the absence of the extended family, and the inability to make friends or develop group supports.

Peter M. Lewinsohn, a behaviorist, defines one of the propensities to depression as the absence of a social repertoire: one of the things that characterizes normal people, he says, is the capacity to elicit from those around us the positive social reinforcements that are necessary for building self-esteem. He speculates that the depressed individual is lacking in that set of social skills—per-

---

> ## "In modern life, the main forces that initiate depression are threats to the sense of self."

---

haps because of some failure in early development or social learning.

While the accelerated pace of loss and separation in modern life may not alone explain the seeming surge in depressive disorders, it seems to provide a climate in which such disorders are likely to proliferate. As we mature from the state of actual biological helplessness of our infancy, we become less dependent for biological survival upon our attachments, particularly those to parents. Attachments to human beings acquire a new function in our adaptation. They are not as important as they have been in the biological past of our species for survival, but they become important for our sense of self-worth, for our identity, and for the meaning and value we give to ourselves.

It is a thesis of many who have studied those phenomena that the biological function of depressive feelings changes as the maturity of the organism unfolds. Yet the psychophysiological and biological apparatus that we have inherited through the millennia has not been modified. We still resist with great protest any disruption of our attachment bonding. What has changed are the stimuli, the environmental circumstances that initiate or terminate those profound reactions. In modern life, the main forces that initiate depressive responses are more often threats to the psychosocial integrity of the individual—to the sense of self, which is enhanced by our attachment to work, family, friends, and community— than to our physical well-being and survival.

For further information, read:

Klerman, G. L. and J. E. Izen. "The Effects of Bereavement and Grief on Physical Health and General Well-Being," Advances in Psychosomatic Medicine, Vol. 9, 1977.

Goodall, Jane. In the Shadow of Man, Houghton Mifflin, 1971, out of print.

Lorenz, K. and P. Leyhausen. Motivation of Human and Animal Behavior: An Ethological View, Van Nostrand Reinhold, 1973, $18.95, paper, $7.95.

Scott, J. P., J. M. Stewart, and V. J. De Ghett. In Separation and Depression: Clinical and Research Aspects, J. P. Scott and E. C. Senay, eds., American Association for the Advancement of Science, 1973, $19.95.

We want your advice.

Any anthology can be improved. This one will be— annually. But we need your help.

Annual Editions revisions depend on two major opinion sources: one is the academic advisers who work with us in scanning the thousands of articles published in the public press each year; the other is you—the person actually using the book.

Please help us and the users of the next edition by completing the prepaid article rating form on the last page of this book and returning it to us. Thank you.

Shopping for the Right Therapy

The four main schools of psychotherapy are split into more than 130 sub-schools. Choosing the "best" one can be tricky.

Morris B. Parloff

Morris B. Parloff, a clinical psychologist, is chief of the Psychotherapy and Behavioral Intervention Section, Clinical Research Branch, National Institute of Mental Health.

There is nothing absolute about the aims of psychotherapy. They are, rather, tied closely to current standards of well-being and social effectiveness. In the past, these social standards have seemed relatively fixed and stable. Today, however, our society changes its standards with ever-increasing speed, while the sciences keep fashioning new mirrors to reflect the new images of man. As a result, innumerable images are now simultaneously extant; which image we see depends on where we look.

At the same time, we make increasing demands on psychotherapy. In the past, religion and science were the main ways of achieving our aspirations. More recently, to the consternation of some and the satisfaction of others, the license for ensuring our well-being has apparently been transferred to psychotherapy! The boundaries of the treatment, never firm, have become increasingly

ambiguous and provisional; in fact, they now seem to be infinitely expansible. Within the past decade the role of the psychotherapist has been greatly extended. Not only is he expected to help the patient achieve relief from psychologically induced discomfort and social ineffectuality—that is, to treat "mental disorders"; he is also expected to help the client achieve positive mental health, a state presumably defined by the extent to which the patient experiences "self-actualization," growth, even spiritual oneness with the universe. Thus, some therapists have moved away from the earlier aim of "head-shrinking" to the loftier goal of "mind-expanding."

The range of problems brought to the psychotherapist has broadened to include not only the major mental disorders—the psychoses and neuroses—but also the celebrated problems of aliena-

tion and the meaninglessness of life. The conception of "pathology"—that is, what needs changing—has been modified. Where formerly the internal and unconscious conflicts of the *individual* were treated, the targets of change now encompass the interpersonal relationship, the family system, and, more recently, even society and its institutions.

CREDENTIALS for practicing psychotherapy have been broadened and, by some standards, lowered. What was initially almost the exclusive domain of the medical profession—of the psychoanalyst and psychiatrist—has slowly been opened up to include the related professions of clinical psychology, psychiatric social work, and psychiatric nursing. Among those more recently invited to provide some psychiatric services are the "paraprofessional," the nonprofessional, and even the former patient. The belief that "it takes [a former] one to treat one" has gained popularity, particularly in the treatment of drug abusers, alcoholics, criminals, and delinquents.

The number of "therapeutic techniques" also continues to grow. More than 130 different approaches are now being purveyed in the marketplace of psychosocial therapies.

New schools emerge constantly, heralded by claims that they provide better treatment, amelioration, or management of the problems and neuroses of the day. No school has ever withdrawn from the field for failure to live up to its claims, and as a consequence all continue to co-exist. This remarkable state of affairs is explained in part by the fact that each school seems to be striving for different goals—goals reflecting different views of the "nature of man" and his potential. All approaches to treatment are sustained by their appeals to different constituencies in our pluralistic society.

BY WAY OF general introduction, I shall briefly review the four self-proclaimed major schools of psychotherapy. Then I'll describe several other forms of treatment that are difficult to categorize but that currently also enjoy special popularity.

The four major schools of therapy are (1) analytically oriented therapy, (2) behavior therapy, (3) humanistic therapy, and (4) transpersonal therapy.

Analytically Oriented Therapy

The analytic (or psychodynamic, or depth) forms of therapy have evolved in a more or less direct line from classical psychoanalysis. While still flourishing, and perhaps the most frequently encountered form of treatment, this school appears—like unemployment and inflation—to be growing at a declining rate.

These psychodynamic therapies assume that people have innate and acquired drives which conflict with both the "external" requirements of society and the "internal" needs and "internalized" standards of the individual. Unacceptable drives are forced out of the conscious awareness—that is, repressed—but they continue, unconsciously or subconsciously, to press for expression.

A person's normal development may be interrupted by early-life experiences that either do not satisfy innate drives sufficiently or gratify them excessively.

In either event, the child's development may be blocked. The emotions and fantasies derived from these unacceptable drives may be allowed partial expression in a disguised and compromised form. In some instances these emotions are "sublimated" into creative, socially beneficial channels. In other cases they "surface" as undesirable physical symptoms, or as socially unacceptable character traits and behavior patterns. The psychodynamic approach postulates that socialization is required in order for the person to become human.

Psychoanalytic treatment tries to unravel internal problems by bringing the unconscious neurotic conflicts into the patient's consciousness. The direct target of treatment is not the patient's *symptoms*, but rather the forces that are believed to generate these symptoms.

The formula for bringing this repressed material squarely into the patient's awareness is: clarify, confront, interpret. Understanding and insight of this kind are presumed to be in themselves "curative," provided that they evoke emotional experiences of a compelling nature.

Typically, psychoanalytic approaches involve analysis of the relationship that the patient attempts to establish with the therapist. This relationship is presumed to mirror the patient's unresolved pathological childhood conflicts.

More recently, the analytically oriented therapist has begun taking into account the social and cultural context in which the patient lives. The classical patient-therapist pairing has been widened to permit treatment in groups as well. Some psychodynamic therapies

ity development, or internal underlying conflict. The problem is defined in terms of specific behavior that the patient or society considers to be maladaptive. The aim of treatment is to change behavior—to change, specifically, its frequency, intensity, and appropriateness.

The behavior therapist does not consider maladaptive forms of behavior as evidence of "pathology" but rather as ways in which people have learned to interact with their environment. He believes that behavior disorders develop according to the same principles of learning evident in so-called normal learning.

"Behavioral" treatment begins with detailed study of the events that precede and follow occurrences of a particular behavior problem—phobic avoidances, compulsions, temper tantrums, sexual dysfunctions, and so on.

One major form of behavior therapy consists in changing environmental conditions that stimulate or maintain the unwanted behavior; this therapeutic technique is known as "operant conditioning." Behavior therapy now includes a broad spectrum of techniques, known by such names as systematic desensitization, assertiveness training, aversive conditioning, token economy, and modeling. These procedures are offered by psychologists, psychiatrists, educators, social workers, speech therapists, and others concerned with modifying behavior.

The procedure popularly labeled as *biofeedback* is used as a potential treatment for a variety of psychosomatic disorders, such as headaches, insomnia, high blood pressure, asthma, circulatory problems, and backache. The primary principle in biofeedback* is that if some-

---

"The psychotherapist's role has been greatly extended. Some therapists have moved away from 'head-shrinking' to the loftier goal of 'mind-expanding.'"

---

have moved from long-term to brief, time-limited courses of treatment. Though many of the classic procedures have been revised and relaxed, the basic assumption that dynamic forces underlie symptomatic behavior remains unchanged.

Behavior Therapy

Most behavior therapy derives from laboratory studies of learning processes. The therapist does not postulate the existence of any disease, aberrant personal-

one is provided with information about certain changes occurring in his body, that person can "learn" to: (1) increase awareness of his or her bodily processes, and (2) bring these processes under conscious control. This control should then permit the patient to change the autonomic processes in a more benign or healthful direction. Awareness of events within the body is achieved by

*See "Biofeedback: An Exercise in 'Self-Control'" by Barbara Brown, *SR*, Feb. 22, 1975.

means of monitoring instruments, which detect the relevant internal physiological change, amplify it, and translate it into a visual or auditory display.

Humanistic Therapy

This umbrella term shelters a wide range of therapies and techniques. Perhaps the most important factor uniting them is their strong reaction against what they view as limited conceptions of human nature offered by the analytic and behavioristic therapies.

Humanists postulate that man is driven by an overarching need for self-actualization. Man's needs are, they assert, "higher" than simply mindless pleasure-seeking or avoidance of pain. Goodness, truth, beauty, justice, and order are not to be explained away as byproducts of man's efforts to sublimate, divert, or block the direct expression of the baser drives that lurk within—an explanation sometimes attributed to analytically oriented therapy. Humanists believe that the failure to express and to realize the potential of higher human needs, motives, and capacities is the cause of emotional distress.

The goals of humanistic therapy are self-actualization and the enrichment and fuller enjoyment of life, not the cure of "disease" or "disorders." To realize your potential, you must develop increasing sensitivity to your own—and others'—feelings. Such heightened awareness will help establish warm relationships and improve your ability to perceive, intuit, sense, create, fantasize, and imagine.

The humanists stress that the only reality that merits concern is one's own emotional experience—in contrast to what they view as the unwarranted faith that other therapists have placed in thought, insight, and understanding.

The analytic view holds that man's impulses must be frustrated and redirected in order that he be more fully human. But humanists argue that direct gratification of needs is ennobling and good.

Humanists such as the late Abraham Maslow hold that each individual has a biological essence, or self, that he must discover and develop, but that external influences are more powerful than biologically given characteristics and may distort or block our personal awareness and development.

The panoply of self-actualizing techniques ranges from nondirective counseling and gestalt therapy to the multiple and ever-evolving variants of "growth" groups: the encounter group, the T-group, sensory-awareness training, and so on.

Transpersonal Therapy

Unlike the humanists, the transpersonalists are not content with the aim of integrating one's energies and expanding the awareness of oneself as an entity separate from the rest of the universe. Instead, the transpersonalists' goal is to help the individual transcend the limits of ordinary waking consciousness and to become at one with the universe. The various levels and dimensions of awareness are as follows: "intuitive" states, in which vague, fleeting experiences of trans-sensory perception begin to enter waking awareness; the "psychical," in which the individual transcends sensory awareness and experiences integration with humanity; and the "mystical," representing a union of enlightenment in which the self transcends duality and merges with "all there is." Finally, there may be yet a further level of potential development—personal/transpersonal integrative—in which all dimensions are experienced simultaneously.

Transpersonalists do not share an organized theory or a clearly defined set of concepts, but, like the humanists, they assume that we all have large pools of untapped abilities, along with a drive toward spiritual growth.

One may achieve these levels by means of various techniques, including Arica training, the Gurdjieff method, Zen, psychosynthesis, yoga, Sufism, Buddhism, and transcendental meditation.

THREE TRANSPERSONAL approaches have achieved considerable popularity: psychosynthesis, Arica training, and transcendental meditation.

Psychosynthesis was developed by a Florentine psychiatrist, Roberto Assagioli. As a form of therapy, it tries to help people develop "the will" as a constructive force guiding all psychological functions—emotion-feeling, imagination, impulse-desire, thought, and intuition. Treatment aims at enabling the patient to achieve harmony within himself and with the world as a path to attaining the higher self. It consists of techniques for training the will in order that one can master life and merge with "the universal will."

Arica training is an eclectic system, devised by Oscar Ichazo in Chile. It has incorporated many of the teachings of the Middle East and the Orient, including yoga, Zen, Sufism, Kabbala, and the martial arts. The branches of the Arica Institute now established in some major American cities stress these features: special diet, sensory awareness, energy-generating exercises, techniques for analysis in personality, interpersonal and group exercises, and various forms of meditation.

Transcendental meditation (TM), a variant of Raja yoga, has become extraordinarily popular in the United States and Europe. This form of meditation has been adapted to the habits of Westerners and does not require special postures, forced concentration, lengthy or arduous training, or religious belief. Each person is assigned a mantra—a special incantatory catch-phrase—which he is to keep secret and meditate on twice a day for about 20 minutes. This meditation helps people attain deep states of relaxation that are said to release creative energies. The advocates of TM hold that if 1 percent of the population in a given area meditate properly, the energies generated will benefit the rest of the population.

Special Treatment Forms

Most techniques of psychotherapy can be included under one or another of these four rubrics—analytic, behavioral, humanistic, and transpersonal—but there remain a number of approaches that do not claim allegiance to any school and are not claimed by any. Some of these special approaches may be termed "pan-theoretical"; others have evolved self-consciously "novel" techniques and procedures. The broad class of group psychotherapies and the many community-oriented therapies illustrate "pan-theoretical" approaches; the "novel" therapies will be illustrated here by perhaps the best known—primal therapy.

"Group psychotherapy" does not represent any particular set of techniques or common philosophy of treatment. It refers to the *setting* in which the particular views and techniques of the analytic, behavioral, humanistic, and transpersonal schools have been implemented. In addition to having a knowledge of his own school, the practitioner of group psychotherapy must understand the dynamics and processes of small groups.

Of the many forms of group therapy, one of the best known is *transactional analysis* (TA), of *I'm OK, You're OK* fame. TA was developed by Eric Berne and represents an adaptation and extension of the psychodynamic orientation. The treatment attempts to identify covert gratifications—the "payoffs" of the "games" that people play with one another. The tasks of both the therapists and the group patients include identifying the moment-to-moment ego states (parent, child, adult) that characterize each participant's interactions. A further step is to name the "game" that the individual is playing and, finally, to identify the "unconscious" life plan that the patient appears to have selected for himself during early childhood. The life plan involves the relatively enduring position of whether the self and others are "okay" or "not okay." The dynamics of change are believed to consist in the patient's learning to shift his "real self" from one ego state to another by an act of will.

Family therapy involves the collective treatment of members of the same family in a group by one or more psychotherapists. This approach treats not merely the individual but the family unit. The individual "patient" is viewed as but a symptom of a dysfunctional family system—a system that has produced and now maintains the problems manifested in a given family member.

The pan-theoretical approaches include those therapies which extend the therapeutic focus to the community and society. The premise that environmental influences may interfere with a person's development has been taken up by a variety of therapists loosely associated with humanistic psychology. Perhaps the most extreme position is that taken by the group espousing *radical therapy*, which holds that society is responsible for most mental and emotional ills, and that, therefore, society rather than the patient is sick. People in psychological distress are considered oppressed rather than ill, and traditional psychotherapy is "part of the problem rather than part of the solution to human misery." The therapist attempts to help the patient recognize not merely his own problems but also the realities of his life situation and the role played by society in generating and perpetuating emotional problems.

Like radical therapy, *feminist therapy* believes that the root of emotional problems may be found in society rather than in the individual. Feminist therapy emphasizes that all psychotherapy must be freed of its traditional sex-role biases. Sexism is viewed as a major force impeding the "growth" of both men and women. This approach is not characterized by any particular techniques, but rather by a shared ideology. Consciousness-raising groups, too, which were initially politically motivated, have recently become oriented toward providing women with help for their personal problems.

Primal therapy is viewed by its inventor, Arthur Janov, as unique in both its effects and its techniques, and as the "only cure of the neuroses." According to Janov, a neurosis occurs when the unexpressed physical and psychological pains experienced in childhood accumulate to the point where they are unbearable and can no longer be simply suppressed. The awareness of these feelings and needs is then "split off" when the child interprets the parents' behavior as meaning that they hate him. This formulation may occur at about the age of five or six and represents to Janov the "primal scene" that precipitates the neurosis.

In Janov's theory the pain of unmet needs is stored away somewhere in the brain and produces tension, which the patient may deal with by developing a variety of tension-relieving symptoms. Treatment requires the release and full expression of the underlying pain, by restoring physical access to the stored memories. Cure occurs only when each old painful feeling is linked to its origins. The living and reliving of the primal scene is accompanied by a "tower of terror" usually associated with screaming, violent thrashing about, pounding, and even convulsions. The screaming may go on for hours and may be repeated periodically over a period of many months as one event after another is recalled.

According to Janov, the cured individual should ideally have no psychological defenses, nor need any, since all pain and its associated tensions have been dispelled. The recovered patient thus becomes a "natural man," who is "non-industrial, non-compulsive, and non-driving," and finds much less need for sex; women experience sexual interest no more than twice a month.

therapies. Clearly, the basic conceptions differ as to who and what needs treating. It is not easy to prove that changes observed in patients and clients are due to the specific techniques and interventions. The therapist may wittingly or unwittingly provide the patient with experiences other than those assumed to be critical. It cannot be assumed that the same therapist will behave similarly with each of his patients—much less that different therapists espousing the same theory will behave similarly with all patients. The problems of research on the outcome of psychotherapy are further compounded by the concurrent impact of other events in the patient's life.

In terms of consumer guidance, then, I shall report only the most consistent trends that emerge from a review of a large number of studies:

• Most forms of psychotherapy are effective with about two-thirds of their non-psychotic patients.

• Treated patients show significantly more improvement in thought, mood, personality, and behavior than do comparable samples of untreated patients.

• Behavior modification appears to be particularly useful in some specific classes of phobias, some forms of compulsive or ritual behavior, and some sexual dysfunctions. Although behavior-therapy techniques appear to produce rapid improvement in the addictive disorders, such as alcoholism, drug abuse, obesity, and smoking, these changes are usually not maintained and relapse occurs in most cases.

• Biofeedback has been applied to tension headaches, migraine, hypertension, epilepsy, some irregularities of heartbeat. The evidence, while encouraging, has not yet established such treatment as being clinically significant.

• Meditation techniques of a wide variety all produce comparable degrees of relaxation, with associated physiological and metabolic changes. Currently, "non-cultist" adaptations of meditative procedures are being applied with some

---

"It is wise for the patient to select carefully from among an array of qualified therapists the one whose style of relating is acceptable to him."

Even this truncated review of the major schools and techniques indicates the enormous complexity of any serious research effort that undertakes to compare the relative effectiveness of available

success in the treatment of anxiety, hypertension, and cardiac arrythmias. Again, findings must be viewed as tentative pending further research.

• The criteria of "growth," "self-actualization," and the attainment of transpersonal levels of consciousness remain ambiguous, and it is therefore difficult to measure them objectively.

• Apparent differences in the relative effectiveness of different psychotherapies gradually disappear with time.

• Although most studies report that similar proportions of patients benefit from all tested forms of therapy, the possibility remains open that different therapies may effect different kinds of change.

All forms of psychotherapy tend to be reasonably useful for patients who are highly motivated, experience acute discomfort, show a high degree of personality organization, are reasonably well educated, have had some history of social success and recognition, are reflective, and can experience and express emotion.

Jerome D. Frank has proposed that all therapies may incorporate the same common (non-specific) elements, although in differing degrees: an emotionally charged relationship with a helping person; a plausible explanation of the causes of distress; provision of some experiences of success; and use of the therapist's personal qualities to strengthen the patient's expectation of help.

This statement in no way endorses tactlessness, insensitivity, or psychological assault. The therapist has no license to humiliate—or to thrill. A large-scale, careful study of participants who suffered psychological injury during encounter groups (led by acknowledged experts) revealed that the incidence of such casualties was disproportionately high among clients of so-called charismatic therapists, with their often aggressive, impatient, and challenging confrontation techniques.

No matter how specific the theory, no matter how clearly prescribed the techniques for a given therapy, treatment is far from standardized. Psychotherapy is mediated by the individual therapist and further modified by the nature of the interaction with the particular patient.

When the patient is "therapist-shopping," it is wise for him to select carefully from among an array of qualified therapists the one whose style of relating is acceptable to him—and preferably from a school whose philosophy, values, and goals are most congenial to his own.

Social Behavior

A well-known psychologist asked, half jokingly, what would have happened if behaviorist B.F. Skinner had put two pigeons in the Skinner box instead of one. The social psychology of pigeons would have emerged because, characteristically, social psychologists have been interested in what happens between organisms. This section sketches several important themes of recent work in the field of social psychology.

Individual behavior is often based not so much on established personality traits, character, and will power as it is on social forces and situational controls. That we actually have less control of our behavior than we think is the subject of two articles. "If Hitler Asked You to Electrocute a Stranger, Would You?" describes Stanley Milgram's now-famous experiment designed to test his subject's willingness to obey authority without question. He found them disturbingly obedient, willing to inflict, as ordered, increasingly greater shocks to perfect strangers, as long as they were released from responsibility for the consequences of their actions. "Pathology of Imprisonment" reviews Philip Zimbardo's experiment to determine the psychological effects of imprisonment on both guards and prisoners. His subjects, bright, middle-class students, were paid to act out roles of "guards" and "prisoners" in a laboratory "prison." In very little time both groups had succumbed to the social psychological forces of the "prison," exhibiting pathological behavior characteristic of the real thing.

Zimbardo concludes that the prison situation in and of itself generates pathological behavior.

Another study of imprisonment—self-imprisonment—is reported in "The Social Disease Called Shyness." This article shows the role of social programming in the development of shyness.

"How Groups Intensify Opinions" demonstrates that not only do like-minded people tend to attract one another, but their discussions tend to strengthen their commonly held opinions. This article cites research on the subject of group polarization.

Finally, one of the most interesting areas of social behavior is reviewed in "The American Way of Mating." Angus Campbell uses information gathered in a survey to make some generalizations about how men and women view marriage and children in evaluating their own happiness and satisfaction.

A review of this section will familiarize you with some of the factors affecting, as well as some manifestations of, social behavior.

Looking Ahead: Challenge Questions

Under what circumstances is civil disobedience a positive social phenomenon?

What means are available to help the individual resist unwanted social pressures?

How might living and working spaces be designed to enhance the individual's self-concept?

279

If Hitler Asked You to Electrocute a Stranger, Would You?

Probably

Philip Meyer

In the beginning, Stanley Milgram was worried about the Nazi problem. He doesn't worry much about the Nazis anymore. He worries about you and me, and, perhaps, himself a little bit too.

Stanley Milgram is a social psychologist, and when he began his career at Yale University in 1960 he had a plan to prove, scientifically, that Germans are different. The Germans-are-different hypothesis has been used by historians, such as William L. Shirer, to explain the systematic destruction of the Jews by the Third Reich. One madman could decide to destroy the Jews and even create a master plan for getting it done. But to implement it on the scale that Hitler did meant that thousands of other people had to go along with the scheme and help to do the work. The Shirer thesis, which Milgram set out to test, is that Germans have a basic character flaw which explains the whole thing, and this flaw is a readiness to obey authority without question, no matter what outrageous acts the authority commands.

The appealing thing about this theory is that it makes those of us who are not Germans feel better about the whole business. Obviously, you and I are not Hitler, and it seems equally obvious that we would never do Hitler's dirty work for him. But now, because of Stanley Milgram, we are compelled to wonder. Milgram developed a laboratory experiment which provided a systematic way to measure obedience. His plan was to try it out in New Haven on Americans and then go to Germany and try it out on Germans. He was strongly motivated by scientific curiosity, but there was also some moral content in his decision to pursue this line of research, which was, in turn, colored by his own Jewish background. If he could show that Germans are more obedient than Americans, he could then vary the conditions of the experiment and try to find out just what it is that makes some people more obedient than others. With this understanding, the world might, conceivably, be just a little bit better.

But he never took his experiment to Germany. He never took it any farther than Bridgeport. The first finding, also the most unexpected and disturbing finding, was that we Americans are an obedient people: not blindly obedient, and not blissfully obedient, just obedient. "I found so much obedience," says Milgram softly, a little sadly, "I hardly saw the need for taking the experiment to Germany."

There is something of the theatre director in Milgram, and his technique, which he learned from one of the old masters in experimental psychology, Solomon Asch, is to stage a play with every line rehearsed, every prop carefully selected, and everybody an actor except one person. That one person is the subject of the experiment. The subject, of course, does not know he is in a play. He thinks he is in real life. The value of this technique is that the experimenter, as though he were God, can change a prop here, vary a line there, and see how the subject responds. Milgram eventually had to change a lot of the script just to get people to stop obeying. They were obeying so much, the experiment wasn't working—it was like trying to measure oven temperature with a freezer thermometer.

The experiment worked like this: If you were an innocent subject in Milgram's melodrama, you read an ad in the newspaper or received one in the mail asking for volunteers for an educational experiment. The job would take about an hour and pay $4.50. So you make an appointment and go to an old Romanesque stone structure on High Street with the imposing name of The Yale Interaction Laboratory. It looks something like a broadcasting studio. Inside, you meet a young, crew-cut man in a laboratory coat who says he is Jack Williams, the experimenter. There is another citizen, fiftyish,

"If Hitler Asked You to Electrocute a Stranger, Would You?" by Philip Meyer, from *Esquire* (February, 1970). Reprinted by permission of Esquire Magazine Inc. Copyright © 1970 Esquire, Inc.

Irish face, an accountant, a little overweight, and very mild and harmless-looking. This other citizen seems nervous and plays with his hat while the two of you sit in chairs side by side and are told that the $4.50 checks are yours no matter what happens. Then you listen to Jack Williams explain the experiment.

It is about learning, says Jack Williams in a quiet, knowledgeable way. Science does not know much about the conditions under which people learn and this experiment is to find out about negative reinforcement. Negative reinforcement is getting punished when you do something wrong, as opposed to positive reinforcement which is getting rewarded when you do something right. The negative reinforcement in this case is electric shock. You notice a book on the table, titled, *The Teaching-Learning Process,* and you assume that this has something to do with the experiment.

Then Jack Williams takes two pieces of paper, puts them in a hat, and shakes them up. One piece of paper is supposed to say, "Teacher" and the other, "Learner." Draw one and you will see which you will be. The mild-looking accountant draws one, holds it close to his vest like a poker player, looks at it, and says, "Learner." You look at yours. It says "Teacher." You do not know that the drawing is rigged, and both slips say "Teacher." The experimenter beckons to the mild-mannered "learner."

"Want to step right in here and have a seat, please?" he says. "You can leave your coat on the back of that chair . . . roll up your right sleeve, please. Now what I want to do is strap down your arms to avoid excessive movement on your part during the experiment. This electrode is connected to the shock generator in the next room.

"And this electrode paste," he says, squeezing some stuff out of a plastic bottle and putting it on the man's arm, "is to provide a good contact and to avoid a blister or burn. Are there any questions now before we go into the next room?"

You don't have any, but the strapped-in "learner" does.

"I do think I should say this," says the learner. "About two years ago, I was at the veterans' hospital . . . they detected a heart condition. Nothing serious, but as long as I'm having these shocks, how strong are they—how dangerous are they?"

Williams, the experimenter, shakes his head casually. "Oh, no," he says. "Although they may be painful, they're not dangerous. Anything else?"

Nothing else. And so you play the game. The game is for you to read a series of word pairs: for example, blue-girl, nice-day, fat-neck. When you finish the list, you read just the first word in each pair and then a multiple-choice list of four other words, including the second word of the pair. The learner, from his remote, strapped-in position, pushes one of four switches to indicate which of the four answers he thinks is the right

one. If he gets it right, nothing happens and you go on to the next one.

If he gets it wrong, you push a switch that buzzes and gives him an electric shock. And then you go to the next word. You start with 15 volts and increase the number of volts by 15 for each wrong answer. The control board goes from 15 volts on one end to 450 volts on the other. So that you know what you are doing, you get a test shock yourself, at 45 volts. It hurts. To further keep you aware of what you are doing to that man in there, the board has verbal descriptions of the shock levels, ranging from "Slight Shock" at the left-hand side, through "Intense Shock" in the middle, to "Danger: Severe Shock" toward the far right. Finally, at the very end, under 435- and 450-volt switches, there are three ambiguous X's. If, at any point, you hesitate, Mr. Williams calmly tells you to go on. If you still hesitate, he tells you again.

Except for some terrifying details, which will be explained in a moment, this is the experiment. The object is to find the shock level at which you disobey the experimenter and refuse to pull the switch.

When Stanley Milgram first wrote this script, he took it to fourteen Yale psychology majors and asked them what they thought would happen. He put it this way: Out of one hundred persons in the teacher's predicament, how would their break-off points be distributed along the 15-to-450-volt scale? They thought a few would break off very early, most would quit someplace in the middle and a few would go all the way to the end. The highest estimate of the number out of one hundred who would go all the way to the end was three. Milgram then informally polled some of his fellow scholars in the psychology department. They agreed that very few would go to the end. Milgram thought so too.

"I'll tell you quite frankly," he says, "before I began this experiment, before any shock generator was built, I thought that most people would break off at 'Strong Shock' or 'Very Strong Shock.' You would get only a very, very small proportion of people going out to the end of the shock generator, and they would constitute a pathological fringe."

In his pilot experiments, Milgram used Yale students as subjects. Each of them pushed the shock switches, one by one, all the way to the end of the board.

So he rewrote the script to include some protests from the learner. At first, they were mild, gentlemanly, Yalie protests, but, "it didn't seem to have as much effect as I thought it would or should," Milgram recalls. "So we had more violent protestation on the part of the person getting the shock. All of the time, of course, what we were trying to do was not to create a macabre situation, but simply to generate disobedience. And that was one of the first findings. This was not only a technical deficiency of the experiment, that we didn't get disobedience. It really was the first finding: that obedience would be much greater than we had assumed it would be and disobedience would be much more difficult than we had assumed."

As it turned out, the situation did become rather macabre. The only meaningful way to generate disobedience was to have the victim protest with great anguish, noise, and vehemence. The protests were tape-recorded so that all the teachers ordinarily would hear the same sounds and nuances, and they started with a grunt at 75 volts, proceeded through a "Hey, that really hurts," at 125 volts, got desperate with, "I can't stand the pain, don't do that," at 180 volts, reached complaints of heart trouble at 195, an agonized scream at 285, a refusal to answer at 315, and only heart-rending, ominous silence after that.

Still, sixty-five percent of the subjects, twenty- to fifty-year-old American males, everyday, ordinary people, like you and me, obediently kept pushing those levers in the belief that they were shocking the mild-mannered learner, whose name was Mr. Wallace, and who was chosen for the role because of his innocent appearance, all the way up to 450 volts.

Milgram was now getting enough disobedience so that he had something he could measure. The next step was to vary the circumstances to see what would encourage or discourage obedience. There seemed very little left in the way of discouragement. The victim was already screaming at the top of his lungs and feigning a heart attack. So whatever new impediment to obedience reached the brain of the subject had to travel by some route other than the ear. Milgram thought of one.

He put the learner in the same room with the teacher. He stopped strapping the learner's hand down. He rewrote the script so that at 150 volts the learner took his hand off the shock plate and declared that he wanted out of the experiment. He rewrote the script some more so that the experimenter then told the teacher to grasp the learner's hand and physically force it down on the plate to give Mr. Wallace his unwanted electric shock.

"I had the feeling that very few people would go on at that point, if any," Milgram says. "I thought that would be the limit of obedience that you would find in the laboratory."

It wasn't.

Although seven years have now gone by, Milgram still remembers the first person to walk into the laboratory in the newly rewritten script. He was a construction worker, a very short man. "He was so small," says Milgram, "that when he sat on the chair in front of the shock generator, his feet didn't reach the floor. When the experimenter told him to push the victim's hand down and give the shock, he turned to the experimenter, and he turned to the victim, his elbow went up, he fell down on the hand of the victim, his feet kind of tugged to one side, and he said, 'Like this, boss?' ZZUMPH!"

The experiment was played out to its bitter end. Milgram tried it with forty different subjects. And thirty percent of them obeyed the experimenter and kept on obeying.

"The protests of the victim were strong and vehement, he was screaming his guts out, he refused to participate, and you had to physically struggle with him in order to get his hand down on the shock generator," Milgram remembers. But twelve out of forty did it.

Milgram took his experiment out of New Haven. Not to Germany, just twenty miles down the road to Bridgeport. Maybe, he reasoned, the people obeyed because of the prestigious setting of Yale University. If they couldn't trust a center of learning that had been there for two centuries, whom could they trust? So he moved the experiment to an untrustworthy setting.

The new setting was a suite of three rooms in a run-down office building in Bridgeport. The only identification was a sign with a fictitious name: "Research Associates of Bridgeport." Questions about professional connections got only vague answers about "research for industry."

Obedience was less in Bridgeport. Forty-eight percent of the subjects stayed for the maximum shock, compared to sixty-five percent at Yale. But this was enough to prove that far more than Yale's prestige was behind the obedient behavior.

For more than seven years now, Stanley Milgram has been trying to figure out what makes ordinary American citizens so obedient. The most obvious answer—that people are mean, nasty, brutish and sadistic—won't do. The subjects who gave the shocks to Mr. Wallace to the end of the board did not enjoy it. They groaned, protested, fidgeted, argued, and in some cases, were seized by fits of nervous, agitated giggling.

"They even try to get out of it," says Milgram, "but they are somehow engaged in something from which they cannot liberate themselves. They are locked into a structure, and they do not have the skills or inner resources to disengage themselves."

Milgram, because he mistakenly had assumed that he would have trouble getting people to obey the orders to shock Mr. Wallace, went to a lot of trouble to create a realistic situation.

There was crew-cut Jack Williams and his grey laboratory coat. Not white, which might denote a medical technician, but ambiguously authoritative grey. Then there was the book on the table, and the other appurtenances of the laboratory which emitted the silent message that things were being performed here in the name of science, and were therefore great and good.

But the nicest touch of all was the shock generator. When Milgram started out, he had only a $300 grant from the Higgins Fund of Yale University. Later he got more ample support from the National Science Foundation, but in the beginning he had to create this authentic-looking machine with very scarce resources except for his own imagination. So he went to New York and roamed around the electronic shops until he found some little black switches at Lafayette Radio for a dollar apiece. He bought thirty of them. The generator was a metal box, about the size of a small footlocker, and he drilled the thirty holes for the thirty switches himself in a Yale machine shop. But the fine detail was left to professional industrial engravers. So he ended up with a splendid-looking control panel dominated by the row of switches, each labeled with its voltage, and each having its own red light that flashed on when the switch was pulled. Other things happened when a switch was pushed. Besides the ZZUMPHing noise, a blue light labeled "voltage energizer" went on, and a needle on a dial labeled "voltage" flicked from left to right. Relays inside the box clicked. Finally, in the upper left-hand corner of the control panel was this inscription, engraved in precise block letters:

SHOCK GENERATOR TYPE ZLB
DYSON INSTRUMENT COMPANY
WALTHAM, MASS.
OUTPUT: 15 VOLTS—450 VOLTS

One day a man from the Lehigh Valley Electronics Company of Pennsylvania was passing through the laboratory, and he stopped to admire the shock generator.

"This is a very fine shock generator," he said. "But who is this Dyson Instrument Company?" Milgram felt proud at that, since Dyson Instrument Company existed only in the recesses of his imagination.

When you consider the seeming authenticity of the situation, you can appreciate the agony some of the subjects went through. It was pure conflict. As Milgram explains to his students, "When a parent says, 'Don't strike old ladies,' you are learning two things: the content, and, also, to obey authority. This experiment creates conflicts between the two elements."

Here is a partial transcription from one of the experiments. The naive "teacher" is a heavy set, worried-looking man with prematurely grey hair. He is wearing a polo shirt. He is very polite. He has just pushed the 180-volt lever. A hidden camera is recording the performance.

LEARNER (who, from the teacher's point of view is heard but not seen, an offstage voice): Ow, I can't stand the pain. Don't do that. . . .

TEACHER (pivoting around in his chair and shaking his head): I can't stand it. I'm not going to kill that man in there. You hear him hollering?

EXPERIMENTER: As I told you before, the shocks may be painful, but—

TEACHER: But he's hollering. He can't stand it. What's going to happen to him?

EXPERIMENTER: (his voice is patient, matter-of-fact): The experiment requires that you continue, Teacher.

TEACHER: Aaah, but, unh, I'm not going to get that man sick in there . . . know what I mean?

EXPERIMENTER: Whether the learner likes it or not, we must go on, through all the word pairs.

TEACHER: I refuse to take the responsibility. He's in there hollering!

EXPERIMENTER: It's absolutely essential that you continue, Teacher.

TEACHER (indicating the unused questions): There's too many left here, I mean, Geez, if he gets them wrong, there's too many of them left. I mean who's going to take the responsibility if anything happens to that gentleman?

EXPERIMENTER: I'm responsible for anything that happens to him. Continue please.

TEACHER: All right. (Consults list of words.) The next one's "Slow—walk, truck, dance, music." Answer, please. (A buzzing sound indicates the learner has signaled his answer.) Wrong. A hundred and ninety-five volts. "Dance." (Zzumph!)

LEARNER: Let me out of here. My heart's bothering me! (Teacher looks at experimenter.)

EXPERIMENTER: Continue please.

LEARNER (screaming): Let me out of here, you have no right to keep me here. Let me out of here, let me out, my heart's bothering me, let me out! (Teacher shakes head, pats the table nervously.)

TEACHER: You see, he's hollering. Hear that? Gee, I don't know.

EXPERIMENTER: The experiment requires. . . .

TEACHER (interrupting): I know it does, sir, but I mean—hunh! He don't know what he's getting in for. He's up to 195 volts! (Experiment continues, through 210 volts, 225 volts, 240 volts, 255 volts, 270 volts, delivered to the man in the electric chair, at which point the teacher, with evident relief, runs out of word-pair questions.)

EXPERIMENTER: You'll have to go back to the beginning of that page and go through them again until he's learned them all correctly.

TEACHER: Aw, no. I'm not going to kill that man. You mean I've got to keep going up with the scale. No sir. He's hollering in there. I'm not going to give him 450 volts.

EXPERIMENTER: The experiment requires that you go on.

TEACHER: I know it does, but that man is hollering in there, sir.

EXPERIMENTER (same matter-of-fact tone): As I said before, although the shocks may be painful. . . .

TEACHER (interrupting): Awwww. He—he—he's yelling in there.

EXPERIMENTER: Start with "Blue," please, at the top of the page. Continue, please, Teacher. Just go ahead.

TEACHER (concentrating intently on list of words in front of him, as if to shut everything else out): "Blue—boy, girl, grass, hat." (Buzz indicates answer.) Correct. "Night—day, sky, job, chair. (Buzz) Wrong. The answer is "day." Two hundred and eighty-five volts. (Zzumph!)

LEARNER: Ohhhuhhoohhh!

EXPERIMENTER: Continue please.

TEACHER: "Fat—man, lady, tub, neck." Answer, please. *(Buzz)* Wrong. The answer is "neck." Three hundred volts. *(Zzumph!)*

LEARNER: Ohhh. I absolutely refuse to answer any more. *(Shouting urgently, now)* Let me out of here. You can't hold me here. Get me out. Get—me—out—of—here.

EXPERIMENTER: Continue. The next word is "Green," please.

TEACHER: "Green—grass, hat, ink, apple." *(Nothing happens. No answering buzz. Just gloomy silence.)*

TEACHER: I don't think he is going to answer.

EXPERIMENTER: If the learner doesn't answer in a reasonable time, about four or five seconds, consider the answer wrong. And follow the same procedures you have been doing for wrong answers. Say "Wrong," tell him the number of volts, give him the punishment, read him the correct answer. Continue, please.

TEACHER: "Green—grass, hat, ink, apple." Answer, please. *(More silence. Teacher just sits there.)*

EXPERIMENTER: Go on with the procedure, please, Teacher.

TEACHER: Three hundred and fifteen volts. The answer is "ink." *(Zzumph!)*

LEARNER: Ohh. Ooohh.

TEACHER *(relieved to hear response)*: Next one. . . .

LEARNER: I absolutely refuse to answer.

TEACHER: You got to. You get a shock if you don't answer. *(Experiment continues with learner refusing to answer, and, finally, failing even to grunt or groan. At 375 volts, the teacher stands up. Has he had enough? Will he break off the experiment? Will he disobey?)*

TEACHER: I think something's happened to that fellow in there. I don't get no answer. He was hollering at less voltage. Can't you check in and see if he's all right, please?

EXPERIMENTER *(same detached calm)*: Not once we've started. Please continue, Teacher.

TEACHER *(sits down, sighs deeply)*: "Cool—day, shade, water, paint." Answer, please. Are you all right in there? Are you all right?

EXPERIMENTER: Please continue, Teacher. Continue, please. *(Teacher pushes lever. Zzumph!)*

TEACHER *(swiveling around in his chair)*: Something's happened to that man in there. *(Swiveling back)* Next one. "Low—dollar, necklace, moon, paint." *(Turning around again)* Something's happened to that man in there. You better check in on him, sir. He won't answer or nothing.

EXPERIMENTER: Continue. Go on, please.

TEACHER: You accept all responsibility.

EXPERIMENTER: The responsibility is mine. Correct. Please go on. *(Teacher returns to his list, starts running through words as rapidly as he can read them, works through to 450 volts.)*

TEACHER: That's that.

EXPERIMENTER: Continue using the last switch on the board, please. The four-fifty switch for each wrong answer. Continue, please.

TEACHER: But I don't get no anything!

EXPERIMENTER: Please continue. The next word is "White."

TEACHER: Don't you think you should look in on him, please.

EXPERIMENTER: Not once we've started the experiment.

TEACHER: But what if something has happened to the man?

EXPERIMENTER: The experiment requires that you continue. Go on, please.

TEACHER: Don't the man's health mean anything?

EXPERIMENTER: Whether the learner likes it or not. . . .

TEACHER: What if he's dead in there? *(Gestures toward the room with the electric chair.)* I mean, he told me he can't stand the shock, sir. I don't mean to be rude, but I think you should look in on him. All you have to do is look in the door. I don't get no answer, no noise. Something might have happened to the gentleman in there, sir.

EXPERIMENTER: We must continue. Go on, please.

TEACHER: You mean keep giving him what? Four hundred fifty volts, what he's got now?

EXPERIMENTER: That's correct. Continue. The next word is "White."

TEACHER *(now at a furious pace)*: "White—cloud, horse, rock, house." Answer, please. The answer is "horse." Four hundred and fifty volts. *(Zzumph!)* Next word, "Bag—paint, music, clown, girl." The answer is "paint." Four hundred and fifty volts. *(Zzumph!)* Next word is "Short—sentence, movie. . . ."

EXPERIMENTER: Excuse me, Teacher. We'll have to discontinue the experiment.

(Enter Milgram from camera's left. He has been watching from behind one-way glass.)

MILGRAM: I'd like to ask you a few questions. *(Slowly, patiently, he dehoaxes the teacher, telling him that the shocks and screams were not real.)*

TEACHER: You mean he wasn't getting nothing? Well, I'm glad to hear that. I was getting upset there. I was getting ready to walk out.

(Finally, to make sure there are no hard feelings, friendly, harmless Mr. Wallace comes out in coat and tie. Gives jovial greeting. Friendly reconciliation takes place. Experiment ends.)

©Stanley Milgram 1965.

Subjects in the experiment were not asked to give the 450-volt shock more than three times. By that time, it seemed evident that they would go on indefinitely. "No one," says Milgram, "who got within five shocks of the end ever broke off. By that point, he had resolved the conflict."

Why do so many people resolve the conflict in favor of obedience?

Milgram's theory assumes that people behave in two different operating modes as different as ice and water. He does not rely on Freud or sex or toilet-training hang-ups for this theory. All he says is that ordinarily we operate in a state of autonomy, which means we pretty much have and assert control over what we do. But in certain circumstances, we operate under what Milgram calls a state of agency (after agent, n . . . one who acts for or in the place of another by authority from him; a substitute; a deputy. —*Webster's Collegiate Dictionary*). A state of agency, to Milgram, is nothing more than a frame of mind.

"There's nothing bad about it, there's nothing good about it," he says. "It's a natural circumstance of living with other people . . . . I think of a state of agency as a real transformation of a person; if a person has different properties when he's in that state, just as water can turn to ice under certain conditions of temperature, a person can move to the state of mind that I call agency . . . the critical thing is that you see yourself as the instrument of the execution of another person's wishes. You do not see yourself as acting on your own. And there's a real transformation, a real change of properties of the person."

To achieve this change, you have to be in a situation where there seems to be a ruling authority whose commands are relevant to some legitimate purpose; the authority's power is not unlimited.

But situations can be and have been structured to make people do unusual things, and not just in Milgram's laboratory. The reason, says Milgram, is that no action, in and of itself, contains meaning.

"The meaning always depends on your definition of the situation. Take an action like killing another person. It sounds bad.

"But then we say the other person was about to destroy a hundred children, and the only way to stop him was to kill him. Well, that sounds good.

"Or, you take destroying your own life. It sounds very bad. Yet, in the Second World War, thousands of persons thought it was a good thing to destroy your own life. It was set in the proper context. You sipped some saki from a whistling cup, recited a few haiku. You said, 'May my death be as clean and as quick as the shattering of crystal.' And it almost seemed like a good, noble thing to do, to crash your kamikaze plane into an aircraft carrier. But the main thing was, the definition of what a kamikaze pilot was doing had been determined by the relevant authority. Now, once you are in a state of agency, you allow the authority to determine, to define what the situation is. The meaning of your action is altered."

So, for most subjects in Milgram's laboratory experiments, the act of giving Mr. Wallace his painful shock was necessary, even though unpleasant, and besides they were doing it on behalf of somebody else and it was for science. There was still strain and conflict, of course.

Most people resolved it by grimly sticking to their task and obeying. But some broke out. Milgram tried varying the conditions of the experiment to see what would help break people out of their state of agency.

"The results, as seen and felt in the laboratory," he has written, "are disturbing. They raise the possibility that human nature, or more specifically the kind of character produced in American democratic society, cannot be counted on to insulate its citizens from brutality and inhumane treatment at the direction of malevolent authority. A substantial proportion of people do what they are told to do, irrespective of the content of the act and without limitations of conscience, so long as they perceive that the command comes from a legitimate authority. If, in this study, an anonymous experimenter can successfully command adults to subdue a fifty-year-old man and force on him painful electric shocks against his protest, one can only wonder what government, with its vastly greater authority and prestige, can command of its subjects."

This is a nice statement, but it falls short of summing up the full meaning of Milgram's work. It leaves some questions still unanswered.

The first question is this: Should we really be surprised and alarmed that people obey? Wouldn't it be even more alarming if they all refused to obey? Without obedience to a relevant ruling authority there could not be a civil society. And without a civil socity, as Thomas Hobbs pointed out in the seventeenth century, we would live in a condition of war, "of every man against every other man," and life would be "solitary, poor, nasty, brutish and short."

In the middle of one of Stanley Milgram's lectures at C.U.N.Y. recently, some mini-skirted undergraduates started whispering and giggling in the back of the room. He told them to cut it out. Since he was the relevant authority in that time and that place, they obeyed, and most people in the room were glad that they obeyed.

This was not, of course, a conflict situation. Nothing in the coeds' social upbringing made it a matter of conscience for them to whisper and giggle. But a case can be made that in a conflict situation it is all the more important to obey. Take the case of war, for example. Would we really want a situation in which every participant in a war, direct or indirect—from front-line soldiers to the people who sell coffee and cigarettes to employees at the Concertina barbed-wire factory in Kansas—stops and consults his conscience before each action. It is asking for an awful lot of mental strain and anguish from an awful lot of people. The value of having civil order is that one can do his duty, or whatever interests him, or whatever seems to benefit him at the moment, and leave the agonizing to others. When Francis Gary Powers was being tried by a Soviet military tribunal after his U-2 spy plane was shot down, the presiding judge asked if he had thought about the possibility that his flight might have provoked a war. Powers replied with Hobbesian clarity: "The people who sent me should think of these things. My job was to carry out orders. I do not think it was my responsibility to make such decisions."

It was not his responsibility. And it is quite possible that if everyone felt responsible for each of the ultimate consequences of his own tiny contributions to complex chains of events, then society simply would not work. Milgram, fully conscious of the moral and social implications of his research, believes that people should feel responsible for their actions. If someone else had invented the experiment, and if he had been the naive subject, he feels certain that he would have been among the disobedient minority.

"There is no very good solution to this," he admits, thoughtfully. "To simply and categorically say that you won't obey authority may resolve your personal conflict, but it creates more problems for society which may be more serious in the long run. But I have no doubt that to disobey is the proper thing to do in this [the laboratory] situation. It is the only reasonable value judgment to make."

The conflict between the need to obey the relevant ruling authority and the need to follow your conscience becomes sharpest if you insist on living by an ethical system based on a rigid code—a code that seeks to answer all questions in advance of their being raised. Code ethics cannot solve the obedience problem. Stanley Milgram seems to be a situation ethicist and situation ethics does offer a way out: When you feel conflict, you examine the situation and then make a choice among the competing evils. You may act with a presumption in favor of obedience, but reserve the possibility that you will disobey whenever obedience demands a flagrant and outrageous affront to conscience. This, by the way, is the philosophical position of many who resist the draft. In World War II, they would have fought. Vietnam is a different, an outrageously different, situation.

Life can be difficult for the situation ethicist, because he does not see the world in straight lines, while the social system too often assumes such a God-given, squared-off structure. If your moral code includes an injunction against all war, you may be deferred as a conscientious objector. If you merely oppose this particular war, you may not be deferred.

Stanley Milgram has his problems, too. He believes that in the laboratory situation, he would not have shocked Mr. Wallace. His professional critics reply that in his real-life situation he has done the equivalent. He has placed innocent and naive subjects under great emotional strain and pressure in selfish obedience to his quest for knowledge. When you raise this issue with Milgram, he has an answer ready. There is, he explains patiently, a critical difference between his naive subjects and the man in the electric chair. The man in the electric chair (in the mind of the naive subject) is helpless, strapped in. But the naive subject is free to go at any time.

Immediately after he offers this distinction, Milgram anticipates the objection.

"It's quite true," he says, "that this is almost a philosophic position, because we have learned that some people are psychologically incapable of disengaging themselves. But that doesn't relieve them of the moral responsibility."

The parallel is exquisite. "The tension problem was unexpected," says Milgram in his defense. But he went on anyway. The naive subjects didn't expect the screaming protests from the strapped-in learner. But they went on.

"I had to make a judgment," says Milgram. "I had to ask myself, was this harming the person or not? My judgment is that it was not. Even in the extreme cases, I wouldn't say that permanent damage results."

Sound familiar? "The shocks may be painful," the experimenter kept saying, "but they're not dangerous."

After the series of experiments was completed, Milgram sent a report of the results to his subjects and a questionnaire, asking whether they were glad or sorry to have been in the experiment. Eighty-three and seven-tenths percent said they were glad and only 1.3 percent were sorry; 15 percent were neither sorry nor glad. However, Milgram could not be sure at the time of the experiment that only 1.3 percent would be sorry.

Pathology of Imprisonment

Philip G. Zimbardo

*Philip G. Zimbardo is professor
of social psychology
at Stanford University.*

I was recently released from solitary confinement after being held therein for 37 months [months!]. A silent system was imposed upon me and to even whisper to the man in the next cell resulted in being beaten by guards, sprayed with chemical mace, blackjacked, stomped and thrown into a strip-cell naked to sleep on a concrete floor without bedding, covering, wash basin or even a toilet. The floor served as toilet and bed, and even there the silent system was enforced. To let a moan escape your lips because of the pain and discomfort . . . resulted in another beating. I spent not days, but months there during my 37 months in solitary. . . . I have filed every writ possible against the administrative acts of brutality. The state courts have all denied the petitions. Because of my refusal to let the things die down and forget all that happened during my 37 months in solitary . . . I am the most hated prisoner in [this] penitentiary, and called a "hard-core incorrigible."

Maybe I am an incorrigible, but if true, it's because I would rather die than to accept being treated as less than a human being. I have never complained of my prison sentence as being unjustified except through legal means of appeals. I have never put a knife on a guard's throat and demanded my release. I know that thieves must be punished and I don't justify stealing, even though I am a thief myself. But now I don't think I will be a thief when I am released. No, I'm not rehabilitated. It's just that I no longer think of becoming wealthy by stealing. I now only think of killing—killing those who have beaten me and treated me as if I were a dog. I hope and pray for the sake of my own soul and future life of freedom that I am able to overcome the bitterness and hatred which eats daily at my soul, but I know to overcome it will not be easy.

This eloquent plea for prison reform—for humane treatment of human beings, for the basic dignity that is the right of every American—came to me secretly in a letter from a prisoner who cannot be identified because he is still in a state correctional institution. He sent it to me because he read of an experiment I recently conducted at Stanford University. In an attempt to understand just what it means psychologically to be a prisoner or a prison guard, Craig Haney, Curt Banks, Dave Jaffe and I created our own prison. We carefully screened over 70 volunteers who answered an ad in a Palo Alto city newspaper and ended up with about two dozen young men who were selected to be part of this study. They were mature, emotionally stable, normal, intelligent college students from middle-class homes throughout the United States and Canada. They appeared to represent the cream of the crop of this generation. None had any criminal record and all were relatively homogeneous on many dimensions initially.

Half were arbitrarily designated as prisoners by a flip of a coin, the others as guards. These were the roles they were to play in our simulated prison.

The guards were made aware of the potential seriousness and danger of the situation and their own vulnerability. They made up their own formal rules for maintaining law, order and respect, and were generally free to improvise new ones during their eight-hour, three-man shifts. The prisoners were unexpectedly picked up at their homes by a city policeman in a squad car, searched, handcuffed, fingerprinted, booked at the Palo Alto station house and taken blindfolded to our jail. There they were stripped, deloused, put into a uniform, given a number and put into a cell with two other prisoners where they expected to live for the next two weeks. The pay was good ($15 a day) and their motivation was to make money.

We observed and recorded on videotape the events that occurred in the prison, and we interviewed and tested the prisoners and guards at various points throughout the study. Some of the videotapes of the actual encounters between the prisoners and guards were seen on the NBC News feature "Chronolog" on November 26, 1971.

At the end of only six days we had to close down our mock prison because what we saw was frightening. It was no longer apparent to most of the subjects (or to us) where reality ended and their roles began. The majority had indeed become prisoners or guards, no longer able to clearly differentiate between role playing and self. There were dramatic changes in virtually every aspect of their behavior, thinking and feeling. In less than a week the experience of imprisonment undid (temporarily) a lifetime of learning; human values were suspended, self-concepts were challenged and the ugliest, most base, pathological side of human nature surfaced. We were horrified because we saw some boys (guards) treat others as if they were despicable animals, taking pleasure in cruelty, while other boys

Published by permission of Transaction, from *Society*, April 1972. Copyright ©1972 by Transaction, Inc.

(prisoners) became servile, dehumanized robots who thought only of escape, of their own individual survival and of their mounting hatred for the guards.

We had to release three prisoners in the first four days because they had such acute situational traumatic reactions as hysterical crying, confusion in thinking and severe depression. Others begged to be paroled, and all but three were willing to forfeit all the money they had earned if they could be paroled. By then (the fifth day) they had been so programmed to think of themselves as prisoners that when their request for parole was denied, they returned docilely to their cells. Now, had they been thinking as college students acting in an oppressive experiment, they would have quit once they no longer wanted the $15 a day we used as our only incentive. However, the reality was not quitting an experiment but "being paroled by the parole board from the Stanford County Jail." By the last days, the earlier solidarity among the prisoners (systematically broken by the guards) dissolved into "each man for himself." Finally, when one of their fellows was put in solitary confinement (a small closet) for refusing to eat, the prisoners were given a choice by one of the guards: give up their blankets and the incorrigible prisoner would be let out, or keep their blankets and he would be kept in all night. They voted to keep their blankets and to abandon their brother.

About a third of the guards became tyrannical in their arbitrary use of power, in enjoying their control over other people. They were corrupted by the power of their roles and became quite inventive in their techniques of breaking the spirit of the prisoners and making them feel they were worthless. Some of the guards merely did their jobs as tough but fair correctional officers, and several were good guards from the prisoners' point of view since they did them small favors and were friendly. However, no good guard ever interfered with a command by any of the bad guards; they never intervened on the side of the prisoners, they never told the others to ease off because it was only an experiment, and they never even came to me as prison

superintendent or experimenter in charge to complain. In part, they were good because the others were bad; they needed the others to help establish their own egos in a positive light. In a sense, the good guards perpetuated the prison more than the other guards because their own needs to be liked prevented them from disobeying or violating the implicit guards' code. At the same time, the act of befriending the prisoners created a social reality which made the prisoners less likely to rebel.

By the end of the week the experiment had become a reality, as if it were a Pirandello play directed by Kafka that just keeps going after the audience has left. The consultant for our prison, Carlo Prescott, an ex-convict with 16 years of imprisonment in California's jails, would get so depressed and furious each time he visited our prison, because of its psychological similarity to his experiences, that he would have to leave. A Catholic priest who was a former prison chaplain in Washington, D. C. talked to our prisoners after four days and said they were just like the other first-timers he had seen.

But in the end, I called off the experiment not because of the horror I saw out there in the prison yard, but because of the horror of realizing that I could have easily traded places with the most brutal guard or become the weakest prisoner full of hatred at being so powerless that I could not eat, sleep or go to the toilet without permission of the authorities. I could have become Calley at My Lai, George Jackson at San Quentin, one of the men at Attica or the prisoner quoted at the beginning of this article.

Individual behavior is largely under the control of social forces and environmental contingencies rather than personality traits, character, will power or other empirically unvalidated constructs. Thus we create an illusion of freedom by attributing more internal control to ourselves, to the individual, than actually exists. We thus underestimate the power and pervasiveness of situational controls over behavior because: a) they are often non-obvious and subtle, b) we can often avoid entering situations where we might be so controlled,

c) we label as "weak" or "deviant" people in those situations who do behave differently from how we believe we would.

Each of us carries around in our heads a favorable self-image in which we are essentially just, fair, humane and understanding. For example, we could not imagine inflicting pain on others without much provocation or hurting people who had done nothing to us, who in fact were even liked by us. However, there is a growing body of social psychological research which underscores the conclusion derived from this prison study. Many people, perhaps the majority, can be made to do almost anything when put into psychologically compelling situations—regardless of their morals, ethics, values, attitudes, beliefs or personal convictions. My colleague, Stanley Milgram, has shown that more than 60 percent of the population will deliver what they think is a series of painful electric shocks to another person even after the victim cries for mercy, begs them to stop and then apparently passes out. The subjects complained that they did not want to inflict more pain but blindly obeyed the command of the authority figure (the experimenter) who said that they must go on. In my own research on violence, I have seen mild-mannered co-eds repeatedly give shocks (which they thought were causing pain) to another girl, a stranger whom they had rated very favorably, simply by being made to feel anonymous and put in a situation where they were expected to engage in this activity.

Observers of these and similar experimental situations never predict their outcomes and estimate that it is unlikely that they themselves would behave similarly. They can be so confident only when they were outside the situation. However, since the majority of people in these studies do act in non-rational, non-obvious ways, it follows that the majority of observers would also succumb to the social psychological forces in the situation.

With regard to prisons, we can state that the mere act of assigning labels to people and putting them into a situation where those labels acquire validity and meaning is sufficient to elicit pathological behavior. This pathology is not predictable from any available diagnostic indicators we have in the social sciences, and is extreme enough to modify in very significant ways fundamental attitudes and behavior. The prison situation, as presently arranged, is guaranteed to generate severe enough pathological reactions in both guards and prisoners as to debase their humanity, lower their feelings of self-worth and make it difficult for them to be part of a society outside of their prison.

For years our national leaders have been pointing to the enemies of freedom, to the fascist or communist threat to the American way of life. In so doing they have overlooked the threat of social anarchy that is building within our own country without any outside agitation. As soon as a person comes to the realization that he is being imprisoned by his society or individuals in it, then, in the best American tradition, he demands liberty and rebels, accepting death as an alternative. The third alternative, however, is to allow oneself to become a good prisoner—docile, cooperative, uncomplaining, conforming in thought and complying in deed.

Our prison authorities now point to the militant agitators who are still vaguely referred to as part of some communist plot, as the irresponsible, incorrigible troublemakers. They imply that there would be no trouble, riots, hostages or deaths if it weren't for this small band of bad prisoners. In other words, then, everything would return to "normal" again in the life of our nation's prisons if they could break these men.

The riots in prison are coming from within—from within every man and woman who refuses to let the system turn them into an object, a number, a thing or a no-thing. It is not communist inspired, but inspired by the spirit of American freedom. No man wants to be enslaved. To be powerless, to be subject to the arbitrary exercise of power, to not be recognized as a human being is to be a slave.

To be a militant prisoner is to become aware that the physical jails are but more blatant extensions of the forms of social and psychological op-pression experienced daily in the nation's ghettos. They are trying to awaken the conscience of the nation to the ways in which the American ideals are being perverted, apparently in the name of justice but actually under the banner of apathy, fear and hatred. If we do not listen to the pleas of the prisoners at Attica to be treated like human beings, then we have all become brutalized by our priorities for property rights over human rights. The consequence will not only be more prison riots but a loss of all those ideals on which this country was founded.

The public should be aware that they own the prisons and that their business is failing. The 70 percent recidivism rate and the escalation in severity of crimes committed by graduates of our prisons are evidence that current prisons fail to rehabilitate the inmates in any positive way. Rather, they are breeding grounds for hatred of the establishment, a hatred that makes every citizen a target of violent assault. Prisons are a bad investment for us taxpayers. Until now we have not cared, we have turned over to wardens and prison authorities the unpleasant job of keeping people who threaten us out of our sight. Now we are shocked to learn that their management practices have failed to improve the product and instead turn petty thieves into murderers. We must insist upon new management or improved operating procedures.

The cloak of secrecy should be removed from the prisons. Prisoners claim they are brutalized by the guards, guards say it is a lie. Where is the impartial test of the truth in such a situation? Prison officials have forgotten that they work for us, that they are only public servants whose salaries are paid by our taxes. They act as if it is their prison, like a child with a toy he won't share. Neither lawyers, judges, the legislature nor the public is allowed into prisons to ascertain the truth unless the visit is sanctioned by authorities and until all is prepared for their visit. I was shocked to learn that my request to join a congressional investigating committee's tour of San Quentin and Soledad was refused, as was that of the news media.

There should be an ombudsman in every prison, not under the pay or control of the prison authority, and responsible only to the courts, state legislature and the public. Such a person could report on violations of constitutional and human rights.

Guards must be given better training than they now receive for the difficult job society imposes upon them. To be a prison guard as now constituted is to be put in a situation of constant threat from within the prison, with no social recognition from the society at large. As was shown graphically at Attica, prison guards are also prisoners of the system who can be sacrificed to the demands of the public to be punitive and the needs of politicians to preserve an image. Social scientists and business administrators should be called upon to design and help carry out this training.

The relationship between the individual (who is sentenced by the courts to a prison term) and his community must be maintained. How can a prisoner return to a dynamically changing society that most of us cannot cope with after being out of it for a number of years? There should be more community involvement in these rehabilitation centers, more ties encouraged and promoted between the trainees and family and friends, more educational opportunities to prepare them for returning to their communities as more valuable members of it than they were before they left.

Finally, the main ingredient necessary to effect any change at all in prison reform, in the rehabilitation of a single prisoner or even in the optimal development of a child is caring. Reform must start with people—especially people with power—caring about the well-being of others. Underneath the toughest, society-hating convict, rebel or anarchist is a human being who wants his existence to be recognized by his fellows and who wants someone else to care about whether he lives or dies and to grieve if he lives imprisoned rather than lives free.

HOW GROUPS INTENSIFY OPINIONS

Associating with like-minded people may help you lose weight
or stop smoking, but it can also increase your prejudices.

DAVID G. MYERS

David G. Myers *is professor of psychology at Hope College in Holland, Michigan. A longer version of this article recently won the Gordon Allport Prize, awarded for the best paper of the year on intergroup relations. Myers' book* The Human Puzzle *was published by Harper & Row in 1978.*

We live our lives within small groups. From infancy through old age we move in congenial groups whose attitudes and interests we generally share. Their influence is powerful. Several years ago Yale psychologist William McGuire concluded that the mass media have less impact on opinion than do informal conversations with family, friends, neighbors, and co-workers.

Recently, the inclination toward forming small groups has become less casual. The act of people coming together to discuss issues and solve problems seems increasingly integral to our existence. Alcoholics, dieters, and edu-

cators draw on the presumed power of mutual assistance typical of a small group, and individual psychotherapy moves more and more in the direction of various group therapies. Group-oriented management methods are displacing authoritarian control.

It is no secret that people associate with others whose attitudes and values are similar to their own. Most of us need only look at our circle of friends to illustrate this point. When people come together in a group, whether it be to combat a drinking problem, to lose weight, or to make a decision regarding management policy, members are apt to carry certain shared inclinations. In the case of losing weight, they have a mutual desire to stop their excessive eating.

When group members share common attitudes, does discussion do anything more than converge their opinions? Social psychologists have found that it does. As members of diet groups discuss their mutual problem, their shared desire to cut their food consumption may strengthen. In commu-

nity controversies, according to sociologist James Coleman, like-minded people increasingly associate with one another as a conflict evolves, amplifying their shared tendencies. The President's Commission on Campus Unrest noted the same dynamic at work during the evolution of the radical student movement in the 1960s. Similarly, investigators of gang delinquency have observed a process of mutual reinforcement within neighborhood gangs whose members have a common socioeconomic and ethnic background. Shakespeare portrayed the polarizing power of the like-minded group when he described Julius Caesar's followers:
Antony: Kind souls, what weep you when you but behold
Our Caesar's vesture wounded? Look you here,
Here is himself, marr'd, as you see, with traitors.
First Citizen: O piteous spectacle!
Second Citizen: O noble Caesar!
Third Citizen: O woeful day!
Fourth Citizen: O traitors, villains!
First Citizen: O most bloody sight!

From *Human Nature,* January 1978. Copyright © 1978 by Human Nature, Inc. Reprinted by permission of the publisher.

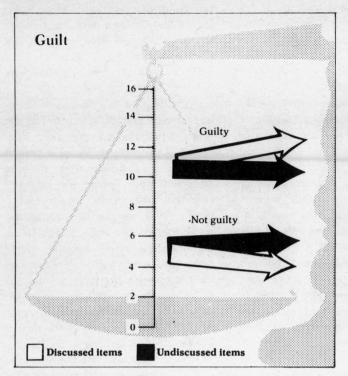

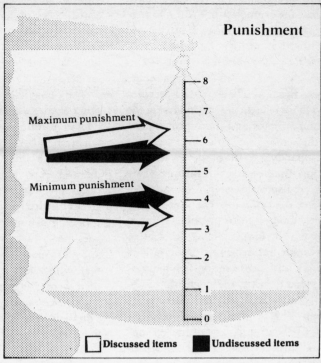

Second Citizen: We will be revenged!
All: Revenge! About! Seek! Burn! Fire! Kill!
Slay! Let not a traitor live!

Observations of small groups, together with recent experiments in social psychology, have provided insights concerning the effects of talking in small groups. Researchers now realize that discussion generally strengthens the average inclination held by group members before the discussion. To test this theory of group polarization, researchers have asked individuals to discuss statements that most people like themselves either favor or oppose.

In France, Serge Moscovici and Marisa Zavalloni observed that discussion enhanced French students' initially positive attitude toward de Gaulle and negative attitude toward Americans. Likewise, Willem Doise found that discussion magnified negative attitudes that some French architectural students had toward their school. Martin Kaplan and I studied the effect of simulated jury deliberations in an attempt to find out whether decisions following jury deliberations differed in any predictable way from the average initial opinions of individual jury members. We asked people to discuss traffic cases in which the defendant obviously appeared either guilty or innocent. In cases where the defendant appeared not guilty, the "jurors," after deliberation, became even more definite in their judgments of innocence and more lenient in their recommended punishments. In cases where the defendant seemed guilty, deliberation moved the jurors toward harsher judgments.

Another research strategy has been to pick issues where opinion is mixed and then isolate those who share attitudes in common. Once each person's opinion is established, he or she is assigned to a group of like-minded people, where the statement is discussed. The purpose is to see whether discussion with similarly minded people polarizes the attitude gap between the two groups.

In one of my own experiments studying polarization, I separated college students into "chauvinist" and "feminist" groups. I then introduced topics on the role of women and asked each group to discuss them—for instance, the argument that women with children should not work outside the home if they are not required to for financial reasons. After each group discussed such topics, their attitudes on them were even further apart than they were before. Apparently the discussion among the liberal, feminist-oriented groups served as a consciousness-raising session.

George Bishop and I set up groups of relatively prejudiced and unprejudiced high-school students and asked them to respond—both before and after discussion—to issues involving racial attitudes, such as property rights versus open housing. We found that discussion among like-minded students increased the initial gap between the two groups.

The reliability of these experiments established, we were prompted to examine group polarization outside the laboratory. It is difficult to disentangle cause and effect when observing natural occurrences, but I believe there are many parallels between the laboratory situation and everyday life. Kenneth Feldman and Theodore Newcomb have found, for example, that initial differences among students in attitudes and intellectual ability become accentuated as they progress through college. Likewise, attitude differences between those who belong to a fraternity and those who do not are modest at the freshman level and more pronounced in the senior year. This effect seems at least partly a result of the tendency of group members to reinforce their shared dispositions.

One discouraging example of the power implicit in group polarization is its potential for producing destructive governmental decisions. In situations fraught with possible conflict, individuals tend to justify their behavior, especially after discussion within their group. The resulting group-enhanced self-justification is part of the "groupthink" process that Irving Janis proposed could help explain the failure of certain political and military decisions, namely the escalation of the Vietnam War.

Robert Riley and Thomas Pettigrew have observed that dramatic events can polarize attitudes also. Surveys of white Texans—before and after the 1957 desegregation of the Little Rock, Arkansas, schools, the assassination of Martin Luther King, Jr., and the subsequent civil disorders in 1968—revealed that the opinions of various groups tended to polarize following the dramatic events. When measuring attitudes before the events, for instance, Riley and Pettigrew found that lower-class groups tended to be more segregationist than middle-class ones, and that East Texans favored segregation more than West Texans. After the assassination and the civil disorders, these group differences became even greater as each group became more convinced of what it believed before the events.

Riley and Pettigrew also found that the forms of racial contact most acceptable prior to these events, such as riding the same bus, were even more acceptable after the turmoil and that the least acceptable realms of contact, such as rooming together in college, became even less so. Dramatic events apparently stimulate discussions that intensify the locally dominant point of view. In the absence of dramatic events and the accompanying group discussion, influences common to all groups, such as television or economic and international events, may reduce polarization at a local level.

Religious fellowship provides another example of group polarization; it heightens religious identity, especially when members of a religious body concentrate their interaction among themselves. A chief feature of many religious movements is the mutual strengthening provided by small, interacting groups. An example of this goes back to early Christianity. The apostles Peter and Paul, freed from jail, met with their fellow believers and then went out to proclaim their message with even greater boldness. Whether the religious group consists of born-again Christians or members of a Catholic religious order, the ardor and devoutness of the group often enhances that of its individual members.

Why polarization takes place at all has become a tantalizing puzzle for a number of social psychologists. Why do groups of people seem to adopt stances more exaggerated than those held by their average individual members? The answer might provide new insights into how people influence one another.

It has been suggested that the role of the strong leader is the source of group polarization. The reasoning is that one person in a group probably emerges as the most forceful member and sways the others. Although it is indeed true that some members of a group are more verbal and assertive than others, this argument assumes that those who emerge as leaders express the exaggerated view that the group will later reach. Yet we have found that leaders are not always extreme in their views.

Among several other possible explanations, two have survived critical scrutiny. One of these has to do with the arguments presented during a discussion, the other with how members of a group view themselves vis-à-vis other members during a discussion. In the former, group discussion permits a pooling of ideas, most of which favor the dominant viewpoint. These arguments may include persuasive points that some group members had not previously considered.

To examine this theory, researchers have tried to discover what importance arguments play in a discussion. They have done this both by controlling the introduction of arguments and by analyzing their content. When a person says "I feel so-and-so about this," the statement typically combines information about the person's arguments regarding the issue with information about the person's position on the issue. Disentangling these two factors, it has been found that when people hear relevant arguments but gain no information about the stands that other people assume, they still shift their positions. Arguments are apparently the principal factor in polarizing attitudes.

Researchers have also examined the content of the arguments. Studies by Amiram Vinokur, Eugene Burnstein, and our own laboratory confirm that the arguments presented in a group mostly favor the group's initial preference. The amount of shift can be predicted by mathematical models that combine the direction, cogency, and novelty of the expressed arguments. New arguments, for example, tend to have more influence over a group than typical ones.

The models also explain why a group that is already quite extreme in its views before discussion will often not show as much polarization as a less extreme group. A well-polarized group has less to learn because members already share the most persuasive arguments. On the other hand, less polarized groups have more to learn from exchanging arguments.

Researchers have also found that active participation in discussion elicits more attitude change than does passive eavesdropping. Both participants and observers hear the same ideas, but when participants must put them into their own words, the resulting verbal commitment seems to magnify the impact of the discussion. This finding parallels attitude research done by Anthony Greenwald showing that people who actively reformulate a persuasive message in their own words are most influenced by it.

In the second explanation of polarization, social comparison plays an important role. People want to be perceived favorably and will modify their expressed opinions to this end, especially if they discover that other people share their inclinations. In several experiments, we have shown people either the true average response or the distribution of others' responses, sometimes providing them with a peek at "early returns" from a survey. This simple exposure to others' positions stimulates a small polarization. Instead of simply joining the crowd, as many conformity experiments have found, the people in our experiments responded with statements slightly more extreme than the average.

Perhaps this dynamic has contributed to the tax revolt that has gained momentum in recent months. As a result of California's Proposition 13, many people have found that their antitax sentiments are shared more widely than they previously imagined. This new information about others' attitudes seems to have magnified antitaxation opinions and emboldened people to express them more openly.

The tendency to "one-up" the observed norm may reflect the fact that people want to view and present themselves as better than the average person. National surveys show that most

business people perceive the average business person as less ethical than themselves. Most community residents see their friends and neighbors as more racially prejudiced than themselves. These beliefs are, of course, distorted—the average person is not better than the average person. In a group situation, the same thing may be true. After sensing the predominant inclination of a group, a member may attempt to get away from the average inclination but still be looked upon favorably by espousing an opinion a bit more extreme than the consensus.

This shift allows people to differentiate themselves within a group, but only to a small extent—and in the approved direction. As experiments by Howard Fromkin have shown, people feel better when they see themselves as being unique, and they will act in ways that create a sense of individuality.

Researchers have obtained interesting results from several discussion experiments that show an accentuation of the average response is not inevitable. When people are given a choice between behaving selfishly and altruistically, group interaction often brings out their selfish inclinations, even if these have not surfaced before the discussion. But most of these results are consistent with the explanation of group polarization; even if social inhi-

bitions cause people to conceal their private leanings, discussion may accentuate such inclinations.

Social comparison and information processing can explain group polarization and its variants. Group interaction affects responses when people want to act in a given way but are restrained from doing so by their perception of a social norm. When several such people find themselves in a group, they soon learn that they are not alone in their feelings, and as they express their shared inclinations in discussion, arguments become polarized. As a result, discussion with similarly inclined people generally magnifies the internal preferences of people who feel a conflict between what they ought to do and what they want to do.

For further information:

Burnstein, Eugene, and Amiram Vinokur. "Persuasive Argumentation and Social Comparison as Determinants of Attitude Polarization." *Journal of Experimental Social Psychology*, Vol. 13, 1977, pp. 315-332.

Lamm, Helmut, and David G. Myers. "Group-Induced Polarization of Attitudes and Behavior." *Advances in Experimental Social Psychology, Vol. II*, ed. by Leonard Berkowitz. Academic Press, 1978.

Moscovici, Serge, and Marisa Zavalloni. "The Group as a Polarizer of Attitudes." *Journal of Personality and Social Psychology*, Vol. 12, 1969, pp. 125-135.

Myers, David G., and Helmut Lamm. "The Polarizing Effect of Group Discussion." *American Scientist*, Vol. 63, 1975, pp. 297-303.

A Shrinking Violet Overreacts

THE SOCIAL DISEASE CALLED SHYNESS

Silent, eyes down-
cast, heart pounding,
40% of these
students live in
a cultural prison
of their own making.

by Philip G. Zimbardo,
Paul A. Pilkonis,
and Robert M. Norwood

Philip G. Zimbardo has taught psychology at Stanford since 1968. His present research grew out of a shyness seminar for undergraduates that was encouraged by studies of imprisonment and self imprisonment, of which shyness is only one form. Zimbardo was born and raised in New York City. He earned his doctorate at Yale and later taught at both Yale and New York University.

Robert M. Norwood, after spending several years in military service and in business, received his B.A. from Stanford. Somewhat older than the average college student, Norwood was the dynamic force that helped recruit other shy undergraduates into Zimbardo's seminar on shyness; it was probably the first such course on a college campus.

Paul A. Pilkonis is a graduate student in social psychology at Stanford. He has been active from the start in the shyness project.

"THERE I WAS," reports a shy high-school girl, "sitting all alone on the side while everyone else was having a good time dancing together. I just knew they were all noticing me and feeling sorry for me. I kept looking down at my shoes the whole evening until the awful dance ended."

This must be one of the oldest stories ever told. Certainly it's common enough in the U.S. According to a survey of more than 800 students that we conducted recently at two major universities and one high school, over 40 percent of the respondents currently considered themselves shy people. This is an amazing proportion when we consider that the reputation of American college students is one of brashness and boldness, of protest and publicity.

This figure suggests that shyness, however painful it may be, is part of a normal person's life. Awareness of this fact alone, we hope, will take some of the pressure off millions of shy people who tend to think of themselves as odd.

Among those who are presently shy, three fourths of our respondents told us they didn't like being shy; the proportion rose to 90 percent among those who had once been shy but had gotten over it by the time we got in touch with them. It seems that people look back on the shyness of their youth with about the same tenderness that they recall adolescent pimples.

Most people think of shyness as a definite personal problem. And when they break down the consequences of shyness, they report the following:

1 SOCIAL PROBLEMS in meeting new people, making new friends, or enjoying potentially good experiences.

2 NEGATIVE EMOTIONAL CORRELATES, such as depression, isolation and loneliness.

3 Difficulty in being APPROPRIATELY ASSERTIVE or expressing opinions and values.

4 CONFUSING OTHERS. Shyness makes it harder for other people to perceive the shy person's real assets.

5 POOR SELF-PROJECTION allows others to make totally incorrect evaluations. For instance, a shy person may strike others as snobbish, bored, unfriendly or weak.

6 DEFICIENCY IN THINKING CLEARLY and communicating effectively in the presence of others.

From *Psychology Today*, May 1975. Copyright © 1975 Ziff-Davis Publishing Company. Reprinted by permission of *Psychology Today* Magazine.

Under some conditions what was originally just gauche behavior may develop into a pathology of total withdrawal and a life of excruciating loneliness.

7 SELF-CONSCIOUSNESS and an excessive preoccupation with one's own reactions.

These seven painful consequences are so extreme that in one of our early surveys more than half of the shy respondents declared they could use therapeutic help for their problem and would go to a "shyness clinic" if one existed. Findings like these suggest that most psychologists haven't taken shyness seriously enough.

We have been studying the mysteries of shyness for several years, and our early data have convinced us that shyness is just as prevalent as the U.S. Navy and other organizations that deal with large numbers of young people have always recognized. In fact, the Group Effectiveness Program of the Office of Naval Research, together with the Boys Town Center for the Study of Youth Development, have helped support our work.

In Front of the Klieg Lights. Our highly competitive, individualistic, egocentric culture puts a person on the spot dozens of times each day. Most of us (although not a huge majority) react appropriately and without shyness to the demands of the social environment. The shy person, however, overindulges his normal feedback processes of self-monitoring and social evaluation; he becomes a super-sensitive individual and overreacts. The presence of other people doesn't just place him in the sunlight of publicity; it shoves him out in front of the klieg lights.

We all live in both public and private worlds. Sometimes the two are compatible, as when we say what we mean, mean what we say, do what we want, follow the dictates of conscience, and so forth. Not so, however, for the shy individual. The public behavior of a shy person is best characterized as a kind of nonbehavior. The shy person's private world, meanwhile, may be seething with intense thoughts, feelings, and physiological reactions.

Our data suggest the following public portrait of the shy person. He or she is almost always silent, especially in the company of strangers, members of the opposite sex, and other threats. He frequently avoids eye contact and often tries to avoid other people completely, taking refuge, perhaps, in books, nature or some other private project. He avoids taking action and he speaks in a quiet voice when he speaks at all.

While this sort of nonbehavior is going on externally, the inner world of shyness is filled with self-consciousness; concern for what other people think, and plans for managing their impressions; negative self-evaluation; thoughts about the unpleasantness of the situation; and various other thoughts and distractions aimed at averting all of the above. The dominant physiological reactions reported are increased pulse, blushing, perspiration, butterflies in the stomach, and a pounding heart. Motionless on the outside, a chaos within. It's easy to understand why shyness can be so painful.

Remarkably enough, the feelings and thoughts associated with shyness are very similar among people who consider themselves shy by temperament and those who have simply experienced a few shy moments, or anxiety in coping with certain stressful situations.. People who describe themselves as shy do, of course, think and worry about their shyness more frequently, and they avoid the company of others more regularly; but these are small differences.

The only crucial difference between the shy personality and the nonshy personality is a difference of self-evaluation. The shy person labels himself or herself shy and therefore reacts much more sensitively to the kinds of situations that elicit shyness in everyone.

The worlds of shy and nonshy people are fairly similar, in other words, in terms of what triggers shyness and in the public behaviors and private events that follow. And the real distinction lies not in any objective experience but rather in what a person *believes* is the cause of shyness. The cause of shyness in the minds of dispositionally shy people is nothing other than themselves. It is a trait, an element of personality. In contrast, the nonshy person believes that external events cause shyness, that particular people and situations trigger anxiety and "stage fright" in them—and probably in most others.

Thus shyness is either viewed as something personal, abnormal and painful; or else it is viewed as something impersonal, normal and not very serious. The view makes all the difference, as in the case of any other self-fulfilling prophecy.

Types of Shyness. Despite the fact that nearly everybody agrees about what it feels like to feel shy, there are still varieties of shy experience. For some it is the reserved manner of the introvert; for others, a kind of modesty or diffidence. It can shade from bashfulness through timidity to a chronic fear of people. Shyness is an attribute that spans a wide behavioral-emotional continuum.

At one end of the scale are those people who choose a shy demeanor because they feel more comfortable with things, ideas or their work than they do with other people. They are not particularly apprehensive about being with people or about joining the crowd when necessary; they would simply rather be alone.

The middle ground of shyness consists of those people whose lack of self-confidence, inadequate social skills, and easily triggered embarrassment produce a reluctance to approach people. This form of shyness is typified by the socially inept adolescent who can't ask for a date, a favor, or better service.

But at the other extreme, shyness becomes a form of imprisonment in which the person plays both the role of guard, who constantly enforces restrictive rules, and the role of prisoner, who sheepishly follows them and thus earns the contempt of the guard. The guard knows that the prisoner wants to engage in the given behavior and usually knows how to do so; consequently, his shyness is obviously not a question of lack of motivation or lack of ability. The issue is one of imposing rules that limit the prisoner's freedom to act spontaneously.

Under some conditions what was originally just gauche behavior may develop into a pathology of total withdrawal and a life of excruciating loneliness. Isolation from people is both a significant contributor to, and a consequence of, many forms of psychopathology.

"I remember as far back as four years old," a 17-year-old high-school student told us, "and some of the stuff I used to do to avoid seeing people that came to visit

Shyness in America is a consequence of cultural norms that overemphasize competition, individual success, and personal responsibility for failure.

us. They were people I knew, like cousins, aunts, uncles, friends of the family, and even my brothers and sister. I hid in clothes baskets, hampers, closets, in sleeping bags, under beds; and there's probably an endless list, all because I was scared of people.

"As I grew up, things got worse . . ."

Shyness quietly intrudes upon the lives of many people who can't stand up and be counted, who don't speak up for their rights, and who never become leaders even when they might be the most qualified to do so. Students have told us that shyness can become so incapacitating that because of it they have lost not only dates, but jobs and awards they had earned.

The multidimensional nature of shyness can also lead to confusion. Several shy students we talked with—bright young people who were quite attractive physically—appeared to others as condescending, aloof, bored or hostile. It was obvious that "they had everything going for them" and could make positive contact if they chose to. Similarly, the shy person is also sometimes misjudged as being unmotivated, ignorant, and emotionally cold.

On the other hand, shyness can serve as a convenient excuse for avoiding challenges, unpredictable situations or people, and the possibility of rejection. It may be more tolerable to call oneself "shy" than to acknowledge feelings of being unwanted, unloved, ugly, different, uninteresting, lonely or neurotic. It is also possible to imagine shyness as a kind of ingratiation tactic or a strategy for facing the world. By asserting "I am shy," a person may be passively acknowledging social uneasiness, attempting to disarm potentially negative evaluations, avoiding personal responsibility for failure in social encounters, and forcing others to take the initiative.

Don't Take It Personally. Eventually, though, most shy people turn out to be unhappy with what seems to be a chronic and unchangeable personal problem.

We doubt that shyness is incurable. Various kinds of guidance, modeling, practice in social skills and assertiveness training (maybe even Dale Carnegie courses) seem to bolster the morale and self-confidence of people who think of

themselves as shy. It also seems likely that the mere knowledge of how widespread shyness is might help people feel less isolated and embarrassed. This was certainly true of our shy college students, many of whom seemed relieved to hear how widespread shyness was. Perhaps a kind of Shy Persons' Anonymous might be useful.

Whatever sort of therapy turns out to be most effective, we feel strongly that the problem of shyness is not essentially a *personal* problem. It is really a social problem. Certain kinds of social and cultural values lead people to imprison themselves within the egocentric predicament of shyness, and to torture themselves with that culturally determined sensitivity we referred to earlier.

And yet these social values differ from age to age and place to place. Young women, for instance, were once supposed to be very shy. "Be conspicuous by being inconspicuous," advised the headmistress of a proper school for girls. And, if we are to take European and American literature at face value, a great many young women actually were very shy. Times have certainly changed. Our shyness survey indicates that females aren't any shier than males—at least at Stanford and Berkeley, and at Palo Alto High School in California.

Moreover, the incidence of shyness among Jewish students was considerably lower than among Protestants and Catholics. Only 24 percent of our 121 Jewish students described themselves as shy, a proportion about half that of most other subgroups.

We hope to explore the basis for this cultural-religious difference more fully in the future. Meanwhile, we're convinced of its importance. Crosscultural comparisons of self-reported shyness among Orientals in our California sample, a University of Hawaii sample, and a University of Tokyo sample reveal a much higher incidence of shyness among traditional Orientals than among Americans from the mainland. As in our California sample, the Japanese students did not like being shy; and yet, unlike the Americans, they spontaneously mentioned various positive consequences of shyness. Shyness for the Japanese may create a modest, appealing impression. It can make one appear discreet and introspective, and it can encourage friendships by not

intimidating other people. The shy person may also be a good listener.

Cultural Values, Personal Prisons. This comparison of Japanese and American attitudes makes it clear how important a particular culture and its values can be to the prevalence and even the private experience of shyness. Shyness in America, we suspect, like the even greater shyness of Japan, is a consequence of cultural norms that overemphasize competition, individual success, and personal responsibility for failure. Parents, as the agents of socialization, encourage shyness in their children by adhering to the traditional values of individual achievement, aspiration and social approval as the primary measures of self-worth. The most effective therapy for shyness, therefore, may be to understand and change cultural values rather than individuals.

It is at least possible that the Chinese in recent years, among other mind-boggling transformations, have eliminated shyness. After a recent visit to the People's Republic of China by a delegation of American developmental psychologists, Eleanor Maccoby of Stanford and Urie Bronfenbrenner of Cornell independently reported to us not remembering having seen a single shy child among the thousands they observed. Yale's William Kessen, chairman of the delegation, recently described how the Communist ideology and needs of the state have produced a theory of the child as docile, perfectible, and similar to all other children. Across a wide variety of educational settings, psychologists observed "quiet orderliness," the "absence of disruptive, hyperactive, noisy children," intense "concentration on tasks," and "rapt attention to work." And significantly, Kessen goes on to note, "the docility did not seem to us to be the docility of surrender and apathy; the Chinese children we saw were socially gracious and adept."

We don't want to recommend a major revolution just to overthrow the rule of shyness in America. We bring up the Chinese example to show again that shyness stems from social programing. To understand that is to know something basic about shyness, about self-confidence, and about how cultural values may create personal prisons.

The American Way of Mating

MARRIAGE SÍ, CHILDREN ONLY MAYBE

A survey of 2,164 adults shows:

- Marrieds Are Happier Than Singles
- The Patter of Little Feet Makes the Temples Pound
- Women Get Along Without Men Better Than Men Get Along Without Women
- After Marriage Women Report Less Stress and Men Report More
- Couples Snuggle Comfortably in the Empty Nest

by Angus Campbell

Angus Campbell won the American Psychological Association's Distinguished Scientific Contribution Award for his varied research in social psychology. Campbell pioneered in studies of political attitudes and actions, codirected a national study of race problems in 15 cities, and most recently began work to pinpoint the subjective quality of life in America. He took his Ph.D. at Stanford, taught at Northwestern, and in 1946 went to the University of Michigan's Institute for Social Research, where he has been ever since. For 23 years he was director of its Survey Research Center, and is now director of the institute.

ND SO THEY MARRIED, and lived happily ever after." This classic fairy-tale ending, which has raised the eyebrows and occasionally the hackles of many adult readers, may not be as far off the mark as skeptics suppose. We find that married Americans are far happier and more satisfied with their lives than singles are, in spite of national mumblings and grumblings about the tired institution of matrimony.

However, most marriages are followed by children, and having children, it turns out, is a mixed experience. The patter of little feet aggravates as well as delights. The positive effect of marriage and the stress-producing impact of children on the quality of life in America are two striking results from our recent national survey. Philip Converse,

From *Psychology Today,* May 1975. Copyright © 1975 Ziff-Davis Publishing Company. Reprinted by permission of *Psychology Today* Magazine.

7. SOCIAL BEHAVIOR

William Rodgers, and I studied a random sample of 2,164 adults in order to get a sense of how people feel subjectively about the quality of their lives, and how their feelings change with experiences over the life cycle. Previous quality-of-life studies have concentrated on objective indicators—the money a person earns, health statistics, education, the amount of pollution one has to endure, and so on. We were less interested in how people's lives look from the outside than in how they *feel* to those who are living them.

We asked our interviewees, first, to give us a judgment of their satisfaction with their lives in general. Then we tapped more emotional dimensions, to find out whether they were in high spirits, jolly and optimistic, or discouraged, lonely, or bored. We gave them eight pairs of adjectives (such as "interesting/boring") and asked them to check, on each pair, the point that best represented their current mood about their lives. And finally, as a third measure of the emotional quality of life, we developed a scale of six questions that probed their feelings of pressure or stress.

Overall, men and women evaluate their lives in very similar terms; we did not find, as some might have expected, that more women than men are unhappy or dissatisfied. On the contrary, Americans of both sexes seem to be a contented crowd, in spite of their various problems. Fewer than 10 percent described their lives in sour terms—boring, miserable, lonely, empty, useless—and far more than half think their lives are worthwhile, full, hopeful, interesting, and other happy positives. They admit to some stress—about one fourth feel rushed all the time and often worry about bills—but overall they are stubbornly cheerful. (See chart, page 299.)

Dissatisfactions and sex differences show up, however, when we compare people at nine various phases of the life cycle. Six of these categories represent the typical life-patterns, from young adulthood before marriage, through marriage and parenthood, to the death of one's spouse. The last three categories cover people who diverge from the typical pattern: the four percent who never marry, the five percent who are married but never have children, and the 10 percent who, at any moment in time, are divorced.

"The world has grown suspicious of anything that looks like a happy married life," wrote Oscar Wilde, but if marriages aren't happy today, at least married people are. All of the married groups—men and women, over 30 and under, with children and without—reported higher feelings of satisfaction and general good feelings about their lives than all of the unmarried groups—the single, divorced, or widowed. (Remember, though, that I am talking about group averages—there are plenty of miserable married people and satisfied singles.) The link between marriage and satisfaction is striking and consistent, whichever the cause or effect: marriage may make people happy, or perhaps happy people are more likely to marry.

Good feelings about the emotional quality of one's life, oddly enough, are not necessarily related to the absence of stress. A person who feels many pressures may be less satisfied with his or her life overall; but a person under little stress is not automatically more satisfied with life. Widowed men and women, whose feelings about their lives are generally depressed, nonetheless report the lowest amount of stress and pressure. And married couples with small children, who are happier than singles, report the greatest amount of stress.

Carefree Spinsters, Anxious Bachelors. Unmarried women are healthier, physically and psychologically, than married women, according to many studies; but they aren't happier. Apparently most young women in America still believe that marriage is essential for fulfillment, for they consider their lives less worthwhile without it.

For women, age 30 is still the Great Divide. Most under 30 will eventually marry; those over 30 are much less likely to. Whether she doesn't marry by choice or circumstance, the older single woman is not as negative in her feelings about life and does not feel nearly as much stress as her younger counterpart. Perhaps this is because the longer a woman remains single, the more she likes it, or at least adjusts to it; and because she is more likely to hold a satisfying, better-paying job, and to have a well-defined career.

Women get along without men better than men get along without women, contrary to what John Wayne and Sam Peckinpah would have us believe. Single women of all ages are happier and more satisfied with their lives than single men. So much for the stereotype of the carefree bachelor and the anxious spinster; the truth is that there are more carefree spinsters and anxious bachelors.

Euphoric Brides, Nervous Grooms. The best of all possible worlds, for most Americans, is to be newly married and not have children. If single people in their 20s feel that something is lacking in their lives, married couples of that age are the happiest of all groups—especially young wives, who are more satisfied than anyone else, anywhere, any age. They are positively euphoric; they are the most likely group to enjoy doing housework, which single women consider drudgery. It appears that marriage is still considered a woman's greatest achievement, and when she marries, the sigh of relief is almost audible.

Young men get happier with their lives when they marry too—though they don't reach the glowing level of their wives—but the two sexes' feelings of pressure change in opposite ways. The women report much *less* stress after marriage than before, but their husbands now feel *more* stress. This cannot be explained by any storybook scenario that pictures the carefree young wife spending her day getting ready to welcome her husband home from the office. Three out of four of these young wives are themselves employed, almost as high a proportion as that of their husbands. Despite whatever trends there may be toward equal roles among young married couples these days, the man still appears to feel more burdened by the responsibilities of marriage than the woman. In our study, only 20 percent of the young wives said that they worry at least some of the time about paying the household bills, but twice as many of their husbands (38 percent) do. Eighteen percent of these wives describe their lives as "hard" rather than "easy"; 34 percent of the husbands see their lives as hard. These differences disappear, however, when the first child arrives and this phase of the life cycle ends.

The Stress of Parenthood. "Familiarity breeds contempt," wrote Mark Twain, "and children." Almost as soon as a couple has kids, their happy bubble bursts. For both men and women, reports of happiness and satisfaction drop to average, not to rise again significantly until their children are grown and about to leave the nest (age 18).

Couples with young children also report feeling more stress and pressure than any other group. The mothers, most of whom are between the ages of 25 and 34, carry the burden of childrearing, and the pressures are most acute for them. They are the most likely of any other group of wives or husbands to describe themselves as feeling tied down, to express doubts about their marriages and to wish occasionally to be free of the responsibilities of parenthood. The husbands feel less satisfied with children too; but they don't show the great swing that their wives do, partly because they were less euphoric

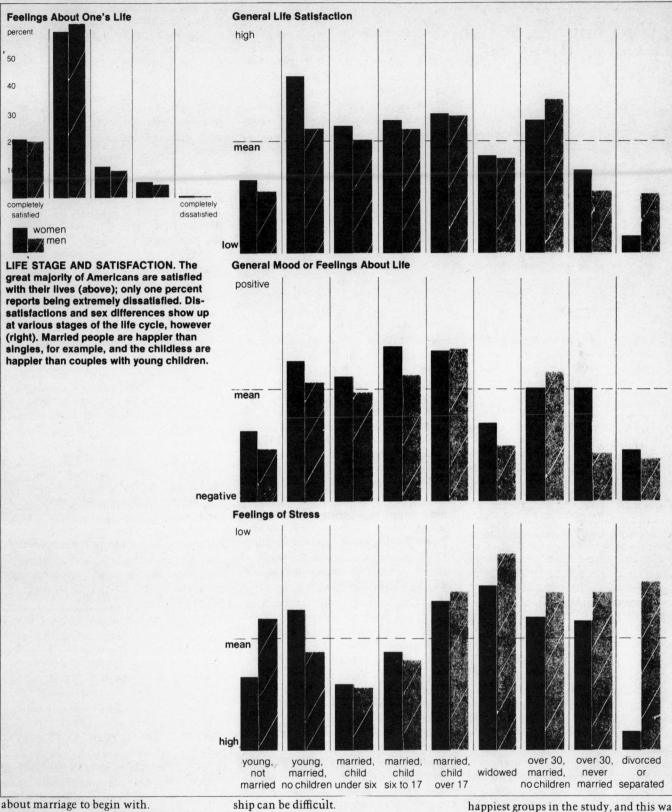

Feelings About One's Life

percent

50

40

30

2

1

completely
satisfied

completely
dissatisfied

■ women
■ men

LIFE STAGE AND SATISFACTION. The great majority of Americans are satisfied with their lives (above); only one percent reports being extremely dissatisfied. Dissatisfactions and sex differences show up at various stages of the life cycle, however (right). Married people are happier than singles, for example, and the childless are happier than couples with young children.

General Life Satisfaction

high

mean

low

General Mood or Feelings About Life

positive

mean

negative

Feelings of Stress

low

mean

high

young,
not
married

young,
married,
no children

married,
child
under six

married,
child
six to 17

married,
child
over 17

widowed

over 30,
married,
no children

over 30,
never
married

divorced
or
separated

about marriage to begin with.

For most couples, the arrival of a child is a happy event, but one that puts unanticipated strains on the marriage. Part of the strain is economic, part is psychological; inevitably, husbands and wives have less time for each other after a baby is born, and adjusting to the loss of companion-ship can be difficult.

There is hope for the disgruntled or disappointed parent, however. Wait 17 years or so until you are alone with your spouse again. Your satisfaction with life and your all-around good mood will return to where it was before you had kids. Indeed, parents of older children were among the

happiest groups in the study, and this was true for both sexes. Couples settled back in the "empty nest" reported feelings of companionship and mutual understanding even higher than they felt as newlyweds. Raising a family seems to be one of those tasks, like losing weight or waxing the car, that is less fun to be doing than to have done.

Runaway Wives
"HUSBANDS DON'T PICK UP THE DANGER SIGNALS THEIR WIVES SEND OUT."

Angus Campbell's research defines the dissatisfaction and alienation of young American housewives with small children. This discontent is a major concern of the women's movement, and feminists encourage young wives to do something to get out of the kiddie corner. One clear result has been a sharp rise in the number of runaway wives.

Betty Friedan, in *The Feminine Mystique,* first described these grievances. She called the distress "the problem that has no name." Since then we have learned a lot more about trapped housewives, and Hollywood has made a movie about one. *Diary of a Mad Housewife* accurately reflects the feelings of many young women. To them the American dream is a nightmare. They feel unwanted, unneeded, unappreciated, and most of all, unfulfilled. They are out there in suburbia slowly going bananas. And so, some of them are running.

Ed. Goldfader owns and operates Tracers Company of America, Inc., a New York agency that specializes in finding lost persons. He says more wives than ever are running away, not because they have found new lovers, but because they are bored and feel there must be more to life than playing handmaiden to unappreciative husbands and children.

"Ten years ago," says Goldfader, "we were looking for 300 runaway husbands for every wife who fled. By 1973 the number of women caught up to the number of men, and last year we were searching for 147 more missing wives than husbands."

Goldfader's profile of a typical runaway wife jibes with Campbell's description of the unhappy young married mother. She is a 34-year-old middle- or upper-middle-class woman who married young, had a child less than two years after she married and another a year or two later. She is intelligent, mature, responsible, a car-

ing person. Her husband is a successful executive who lives on the company cuff; he lunches at "21," attends conventions in Nassau. The most exciting part of her life is checking out at the supermarket. The marriage is intellectually unfair.

"The amazing thing," says Goldfader, "is that these husbands don't pick up the danger signals their wives send out. They don't listen to their spouses, or if they do, they don't take them seriously. When these women finally run off, their husbands are flummoxed."

When a man comes to Tracers for help, Goldfader interviews him and asks questions about his wife's personal history and physical appearance. During the interview a distraught husband often realizes that he knows very little about his wife. He may not be able to remember the color of her eyes. This realization usually is his first sight of the reason she left him.

While he is suffering from guilt and worry, his runaway wife is suffering too. She knows that home is hell, but life on the outside is worse. After a few days in a sleazy motel, she wants to come home, but is too embarrassed. Instead, she leaves clues to her whereabouts. She calls a relative collect, knowing the number will show up on the next bill; uses credit cards so the bill will reach her husband; or turns herself into the police feigning amnesia, hoping the officers will match her up to the correct missing-persons report.

If the wife does not turn up within a few days, Tracers goes to work. Goldfader says the agency locates about three out of four missing wives. The Agency informs a husband of his wife's whereabouts and of her present living conditions. He usually goes after her, and usually she is relieved to be found and returns home. "But," says Goldfader, "the pain both have suffered, and his increased awareness of her dissatisfaction, makes the marriage a whole new ball game."

Although most women want to be found and eventually get home, some do not. They disappear abruptly, leaving no clues. One particularly confounding case involved a couple who were driving back

to New York from a visit to Washington, D.C. "They came through the Lincoln Tunnel, and were heading east on 44th St. in the dusk of a Sunday evening," says Goldfader, "when they were stopped by a traffic light turning red. The car windows were covered with late winter slush, so the husband got out to wipe off the front windshield before the light turned green.

"His wife got out on the other side, saying, 'I'll get the back window.' The light changed, the husband got back in the car; his wife wasn't in yet. He glanced in the rear-view mirror at the back window still covered with slush, then he jumped out to look for her. She was gone...She has never been found."

Bruce Woodson of Woodson Enterprises, Inc., in San Diego and Stan Comstock of West Coast Detectives and Special Police Patrol in Los Angeles both report an increased number of cases of runaway wives. But on the West Coast, the ratio of fleeing wives to husbands is just reaching 50–50. And many California cases involve love triangles. But Comstock says that the 15 percent of wives who go off alone do so to escape stifling marriages. "They want to do their own thing," says the investigator. "They're tired of the married lifestyle, hope something better will come along, and they're not at all interested in remarriage."

He describes one woman as typical of this breed: "She left three or four years ago. She has a job and her own apartment. She sees her lover two or three times a week, and reports she has never been so happy."

Freedom and self-determination are important to these women. Comstock believes the phenomenon definitely is a sign of the times. "Women have more freedom today," he says, "with changing morals, the Pill, and better job opportunities."

Woodson, who is an ex-Pinkerton investigator, puts it simply, "Women with children are getting fed up." Comstock adds, "It seems that today, a large majority of runaway women feel that 10 years is long enough to spend with any man."

—Margie Casady

Children and marriage still go together and always will, but children are becoming less popular. The continuing, substantial decline in the birth rate in this country indicates that many people no longer regard having children as an inevitable process. The childfree marriage, once pitied or

disparaged, is now increasingly recognized as a fulfilling lifestyle and many young couples simply admit, without embarrassment or apology, that they do not intend to have children. Sociologist Jessie Bernard marshalls evidence that they may have happier marriages as a result.

The decision not to have children does not doom a couple to loneliness, despair, and misery as the prochildren forces have assumed for years. Childless husbands over 30 reported the highest satisfaction with life, and they feel less pressure than most men. Altogether, the quality of their

What Mother Knows Best
IF ONE BABY'S NICE, WHAT'S WRONG WITH TWO?

Some of the simplest questions are the hardest to answer. For example, do American women like the idea of being mothers? If you look at what they *do*, the answer is yes because 84 percent of those who marry have children. If you listen to what they *say*, the answer is yesnomaybe because they keep changing their minds.

Kenneth W. Terhune, a psychologist at SUNY at Buffalo, asked 600 women how many children they wanted. The 600 replies gave him no clear answers, but the reasons they gave to explain their desired family size showed a discomfort more chronic than postpartum blues.

Regardless of how many children they wanted, women without children and women with only one child talked about family size in positive terms. They spoke of watching children develop, continuing the family line, or simply the pleasures of caring for children.

As soon as more than two little feet were thumping around the house, the reasons changed. Mothers began to talk about why they didn't want to have many more children—or any more. They spoke of family expenses, squabbling children, lack of privacy and overpopulation.

Now Terhune is trying to find out why the emphasis so predictably shifts from positive to negative with the arrival of a second baby. Perhaps women in the early stages of marriage and motherhood view children through a rosy glow. Perhaps it's a case of grass is greener on the other side. Perhaps experience teaches women the financial and emotional costs of children.

But women with more than one child also tend to be older. It may be that age alone alters the picture of mother's joy. Terhune expects to have an answer before too long. Until then, each of us can argue for the explanation that appeals to us the most.

—Joyce Dudney Fleming

---

lives is higher than that of any other group of males, with the possible exception of fathers of children over 17 (which makes them childfree too, in a sense). Freedom from the economic worries that parents have is part of the reason. Childfree couples over 30 do not have particularly high incomes, but they are the most likely group to be satisfied with their savings and the least likely to worry about bills.

Childless wives over 30 also describe their lives in generally positive terms. They aren't quite as rosy about life as their husbands, but they aren't *less* satisfied than women their age who do have children. Childlessness offers women a different but not unsatisfying life—much less stress, somewhat fewer emotional rewards, but overall the same level of satisfaction. In view of the strong cultural pressures for women to have children, we were surprised that childfree wives find the grass on their own side of the fence green enough. Perhaps having children is no longer as essential to woman's role as it once was.

Possibly these couples will feel different about not having children when they are old, or when one spouse dies. When wife or husband is left alone, without the psychological support that the other provided, she or he may feel more keenly the absence of children. Still, grown children do not always pay much attention to their aging and sometimes lonely parents; perhaps a widowed person is better off with no expectations about children than with shattered ones.

Stress Dies With the Spouse. We tend to think that the quality of life for most widowed people is bleak, but this perception misses the mark. In terms of general life satisfaction, widows and widowers dip to slightly below average; even so, they are quite a bit more content than single or divorced people of any age. And they report the least amount of stress and pressure of any other group, even though their family incomes are the lowest. They don't, after all, have to worry about work—the great majority are of retirement age—or young children, and many feel free of the pressures to marry that the single and divorced experience. On the other hand, widows and widowers did describe the emotional quality of their lives in negative terms, about as negatively as single and divorced people. The difference between the two groups is that the widowed are more satisfied with their lives than singles are, which may simply reflect the willingness or resignation of older people to accept the conditions of their lives.

Divorce: Anxious Women, Carefree Men. In spite of all the cheerful books on creative divorce, no-fault divorce, and better living through divorce, people whose marriages fail are miserable. Most of them, men more than women, marry again, but while divorced they face problems that their single and married friends do not.

Divorce hits women hardest. Most of them have to work (71 percent) and care for children (84 percent), without moral, economic, or psychological support from a husband or partner. They earn less than single women their age, certainly less than divorced men, and less than married women who can rely on family incomes. Only four percent of all divorced women can afford to hire someone to help with the housework, so they have that to do too. And they lack the opportunities that divorced men have to date and remarry. For all these reasons, divorced women feel the greatest pressure and stress of any group, report the greatest dissatisfaction with their lives, and describe the emotional quality of their lives in gloomy terms. Indeed, one fourth of these women admit to worrying that they might have a nervous breakdown, compared to only eight percent of the divorced men.

Divorced men aren't so happy with their lives either, but they feel less pressure than almost any other group of males. It is as if divorce was an instant relief; over half, 58 percent, say they never worry about meeting their bills, compared to 30 percent of the divorced women who report being that confident. Only 12 percent of the divorced men say they always feel rushed, but nearly three times as many divorced women (34 percent) see themselves as always rushed. Twenty-five percent of these men, but 42 percent of the women, describe their lives as difficult.

Then too, divorced men who find their new-found single status intolerable remarry more easily than their former wives, while those who enjoy the single life may choose to keep it. Divorced women have less freedom of choice, economically or socially, which contributes to their dissatisfactions. Of course, we do not know how the attitudes or feelings of divorced people change in the years after the marriage ends; we have only the sketch they paint as a group.

Life Stages and Satisfaction. When we compared all of the women in our study with all of the men, we found few differences. There were some reasons to expect, overall, that women would be more dissatisfied than men, but it turned out that it was necessary to specify *which* women and *which* men. There are some groups of women, such as those divorced, who describe their lives as more frustrating and less rewarding than men do. But there are also some groups of males who are less happy than their female peers, such as unmarried men. To understand how people feel about their lives, it is less important to know whether a person is a woman than to know whether she is a young, childless wife or a single career woman or married with grown children. We can't assume that all men view their lives as rich and fulfilling, either; we must know first whether the man is an aging bachelor or an empty-nest father.

Several recent reviews of community-mental-health surveys found that women are in worse shape than men. Women consistently have higher rates of mental illness—both psychosis and neurosis, including depression, anxiety, suicidal tendencies—regardless of whether they come voluntarily for treatment, are committed, or take part in a random survey. Such symptoms of pathology would suggest that women's lives are less satisfying than men's, but women overall did not report this.

The reason may be that a person's evaluation of her life is based partly on the fit, or lack of it, between her objective circumstances, and her hopes and expectations. The black community in this country has raised its sights dramatically in the last 10 years, and women are beginning to do so also. The dissatisfactions reported by college-educated and divorced women in our study, for example, indicate that changes are occurring in the traditional values and roles for women. More women are going to college, working, and having fewer children. That's bound to make some changes eventually in the institution of marriage, which is currently the rock on which both sexes base much of their happiness and satisfaction with life. We can be sure that pressures for change will be met by resistance to change, and whether the irresistible force or the immovable object gives way, we'll be part of an interesting transition.

ANNUAL EDITIONS

We want your advice

Any anthology can be improved. This one will be—annually. But we need your help.

Annual Editions revisions depend on two major opinion sources: one is the academic advisers who work with us in scanning the thousands of articles published in the public press each year; the other is you—the person actually using the book.

Please help us and the users of the next edition by completing the prepaid article rating form on the last page of this book and returning it to us.

Thank you.

WHO'S WRITING AND WRITTEN ABOUT

INDEX

Credits/Acknowledgments

Cover design by Charles Vitelli
1. The Science of Psychology
Facing overview—Freelance Photographers Guild/Dennis R. Campagnone.

2. The Biological Bases of Behavior
Facing overview—Freelance Phsotographers Guild/Dwight Ellefsen. 52—Alan E. Cober. 61—The Dushkin Publishing Group, Inc. *The Study of Psychology.* 67—Danilo Nardi/Freelance Photographers Guild.

3. Processes Underlying Behavior
Facing overview—David Attie © 1978. 92—Drawings by Art Sudduth/Newsday.

4. Development
Facing overview—David Attie © 1975. 151—Clemens Kalischer/Image Photo.

5. Individual Differences
Facing overview—Freelance Photographers Guild/Robert J. Bennett.

6. Disorders and Therapy
Facing overview—David Attie © 1978.

7. Social Behavior
Facing overview—Ewing Galloway.